William Youatt, H. S Randall, W. C Spooner

Youatt on the Structure and the Diseases of the Horse

with Their Remedies - Also Practical Rules to Buyers, Breeders, Breakers, Smith etc.

William Youatt, H. S Randall, W. C Spooner

Youatt on the Structure and the Diseases of the Horse
with *Their Remedies - Also Practical Rules to Buyers, Breeders, Breakers, Smith etc.*

ISBN/EAN: 9783337143800

Printed in Europe, USA, Canada, Australia, Japan

Cover: Foto ©Andreas Hilbeck / pixelio.de

More available books at www.hansebooks.com

YOUATT

ON

THE STRUCTURE

AND THE

DISEASES OF THE HORSE,

WITH THEIR REMEDIES.

ALSO,

PRACTICAL RULES TO BUYERS, BREEDERS, BREAKERS, SMITHS, ETC.

BEING

THE MOST IMPORTANT PARTS OF THE ENGLISH EDITION OF "YOUATT ON THE HORSE," SOMEWHAT SIMPLIFIED.

BROUGHT DOWN

BY W. C. SPOONER, M. R. C. V. S.,

AUTHOR OF SEVERAL VETERINARIAN WORKS,

TO WHICH IS PREFIXED,

AN ACCOUNT OF THE BREEDS IN THE UNITED STATES,

COMPILED BY

HENRY S. RANDALL.

WITH NUMEROUS ILLUSTRATIONS.

NEW YORK:
C. M. SAXTON, BARKER & CO.,
25 PARK ROW.
1860.

INTRODUCTORY.

THE universal popularity and pre-eminence in the public favor, both in this country and England, of Mr Youatt's work on the Horse, is well known. It has had a far wider circulation in the United States than any other veterinary work, and but for one or two circumstances, it is believed, had prevented it from attaining a still vastly wider circulation,—from becoming the common hand-book of nearly every farmer in the land who breeds or owns horses, who is willing to *read anything* on a subject in which he is so much interested.

The first of these circumstances is the *size* of Mr. Youatt's entire work. This renders it too expensive for general circulation. And it is too minute and voluminous in its details for ordinary readers. This elaborateness, so far from aiding, confuses the common reader; the precise facts which he seeks—the symptoms and remedies of diseases, &c.,—are too often so scattered through the glowing amplifications of the accomplished author, that it is difficult to clearly distinguish, collect, and apply them. And many are repelled not only from the work itself, but from reading the author's discussion of a disease, a point in breeding, or the like, from impatience of its *mere* length. In a work of this kind, more perhaps than anywhere else, applies the often quoted remark of Dr. Johnson: "*Books that you may carry to the fire, and hold reading in your hand, are most useful after all A man will often look at them, and be tempted to go on, when he would have been frightened at books of a larger size, and of a more erudite appearance.*"

The following abridgment is intended to obviate the above objections. While it is believed, that every thought or fact in the original, of any importance to the general reader, is preserved *entire*, much that tended to swell unnecessarily the limits of the work for such a reader, has been omitted. The omissions have been merely anecdotes, historical narrations, accounts of particular cases, and, in some instances, the less necessary parts of those long anatomical descriptions which could be understood only by the surgeon. The *symptoms* and *remedies* of diseases—all that tends to the full understanding of the horse and his ailments, is given entire, and almost invariably *in the precise language of Mr. Youatt*. The aim of this work has not been to re-write Youatt,—but simply to strike out what is superfluous in him.

The second circumstance prejudicial to a wide, popular circulation of Mr. Youatt's work, has been, according to the common phrase, the "learnedness of its language." The work, as again and again avowed in it, was *not* so much written to instruct the horse-owner or breeder, as the veterinary surgeon—at least in relation to important diseases, operations, &c. Mr. Youatt is therefore often at little pains to make himself intelligible to uninstructed readers. His language is always learned—frequently highly technical. So far as it could be conveniently and properly done, an attempt has been made in the following pages, to translate his language into that better adapted to ordinary comprehension. A common word is often substituted for the more learned one of Mr. Youatt, or an explanatory one put after it in brackets. The former is all the liberty taken in this way with the text,—and this is only done where the meaning could be accurately preserved.

But every thinking man will readily see from the very nature of the subject, that the improvement to be made on the text in the above particulars is limited. When speaking of anatomical details, diseases, particular processes, &c., *no language is fixed and definite but that of science*. And it frequently obviates the necessity of very tedious and often repeated circumlocution. Take for example the word "*auscultation*," which signifies disti" guishing disease by observing the sounds in the part, by means of the ear, with or without a tube, applied to the surface. Is it necessary to repeat all this every time this process is adverted to? Clearly not. The word "*Thorax*" signifies the cavity of the body above or forward of the diaphragm or midriff,—the word "*Abdomen*" the cavity of the body below or behind the diaphragm. Can any common words—any of the terms of vulgar quackery—be given which will definitely express the above ideas, and *which can be any way more easily remembered than these?* There cannot. In all such cases, therefore, no change of language is attempted. And Webster's Dictionary will help the reader out of every difficulty of this kind.

We have here a remark to submit to all readers, and especially the *young* reader, in relation to the PROPER MANNER OF READING YOUATT—where the aim is to *fully understand* him, or the subject which he treats. This never can be done by dipping into the book here and there, in search of information now on one topic, and now on another, as the occasion seems to demand it. The work should be read *consecutively* and carefully from beginning to end. If this is done, and the reader *fixes in his mind anatomical names and details*, as he advances, he will have no difficulty in fully understanding every part, and he will be infinitely better prepared to form a correct judgment in any case where he is called upon to make a practical application of his knowledge. The horse-owner who takes this course will find Youatt's work an invaluable advantage to him—worth a thousand of the common empirical recipe books on farriery. The one who does not, will find it, or *any other work*, of little avail.

W. C. Spooner, Esq., one of the most distinguished veterinary writers and practitioners of England, wrote, in 1849, a Supplement to Mr. Youatt's work, designed to "advance it to the present state of veterinary science." All that is of any importance in this supplement—in fact, most of Mr. Spooner's additional remarks entire, have been added to the present work in the convenient form of notes. Several of them will be found valuable. And we conceive this gives the work a decided advantage over any previous American edition.

We are enabled to point with much pleasure to the illustrations in our volume. They are much more complete in execution than those of any other similar American publications, and are decidedly superior to those of the late English editions of Youatt. They are fully equal to the *original* English cuts.

The present abridgment has been carefully prepared by a distinguished and well-known American agriculturist, whose writings have been extensively read throughout the United States, for years. The peliminary chapter in relation to the breeds now in the United States, was complied by Henry S. Randall, Esq., it being thought that this would be much more valuable to the American reader, than Mr. Youatt's first chapter. We believe that the author has been fortunate in the execution of his task, and we present the work to the public in the confident belief that we are rendering a valuable service to an important department of American Agriculture.

THE PUBLISHERS.

CONTENTS

INTRODUCTION BY THE PUBLISHERS.

CHAPTER I.

	PAGE
BREEDS OF HORSES IN THE UNITED STATES	17
The English Race Horse	17
The Arabian	25
The Canadian	29
The Norman	29
The Morgan	36
The Cleveland Bay	38
The Dray	39
The Trotting Horse	40

CHAPTER II.

THE ZOOLOGICAL CLASSIFICATION OF THE HORSE	44
The Sensorial Function	46

CHAPTER III.

INJURIES AND DISEASES OF THE SKULL—THE BRAIN—THE EARS—AND THE EYES	68
Fracture	68
Exostosis	68
Caries	68
Compression of the Brain	69
Pressure on the Brain	69
Megrims	69
Apoplexy	70
Phrenitis	74
Rabies, or Madness	76
Tetanus, or Locked Jaw	79
Cramp	82
Stringhalt	83
Chorea	83
Fits, or Epilepsy	84

Palsy	84
Rheumatism	85
Neurotomy	86
Insanity	90
Diseases of the Eye	91
Common Inflammation of the Eye	93
Specific Ophthalmia, or Moon-Blindness	94
Gutta Serena	97
Diseases of the Ear	98
Deafness	98

CHAPTER IV.

THE ANATOMY AND DISEASES OF THE NOSE AND MOUTH	99
Nasal Polypus	104
Nasal Gleet, or Discharge from the Nose	104
Ozena	105
Glanders	107
Farcy	114
The Lips	117
The Bones of the Mouth	118
The Palate	118
Lampas	119
The Lower Jaw	120
Diseases of the Teeth	130
The Tongue	131
Diseases of the Tongue	132
The Salivary Glands	132
Strangles	133
The Pharynx	135

CHAPTER V.

THE ANATOMY AND DISEASES OF THE NECK AND NEIGHBORING PARTS	136
Poll-Evil	136
The Muscles and proper form of the Neck	138
The Blood-Vessels of the Neck	140
The Veins of the Neck	140
Inflammation of the Vein	141
The Palate	142
The Larynx	142
The Trachea or Windpipe	143
Tracheotomy	143
The Bronchial Tubes	144

CHAPTER VI.

THE CHEST	145
The Spine and Back	149
The Loins	150

	PAGE
The Withers	150
Fistulous Withers	151
Warbles, Sitfasts, and Saddle Galls	151
Chest-Founder	152

CHAPTER VII.

THE CONTENTS OF THE CHEST	153
The Thymus Gland	153
The Diaphragm	153
Rupture of the Diaphragm	154
The Pleura	154
The Lungs	155
The Heart	155
Diseases of the Heart	156
The Arteries	158
The Pulse	158
Inflammation	160
Fever	163
The Veins	164
Bog and Blood Spavin	164
Bleeding	166

CHAPTER VIII.

THE MEMBRANE OF THE NOSE	169
Catarrh, or Cold	169
Inflammation of the Larynx	170
Inflammation of the Trachea	172
Roaring	172
Bronchocele	174
Epidemic Catarrh	176
The Malignant Epidemic	181
Bronchitis	184
Pneumonia—Inflammation of the Lungs	186
Chronic Cough	193
Thick Wind	194
Broken Wind	196
Phthisis Pulmonalis, or Consumption	199
Pleurisy	200

CHAPTER IX.

THE ABDOMEN AND ITS CONTENTS	206
The Stomach	206
Bots	208
The Intestines	210
The Liver	213
The Pancreas	213
The Spleen	213
The Omentum	213

CHAPTER X.

	PAGE
THE DISEASES OF THE INTESTINES	215
The Duodenum	215
Spasmodic Colic	215
Flatulent Colic	218
Inflammation of the Bowels	220
Enteritis	220
Physicking	224
Calculi, or Stones, in the Intestines	226
Introsusception of the Intestines	226
Entanglement of the Bowels	226
Worms	227
Hernia, or Rupture	227
Diseases of the Liver	228
Jaundice	229
The Kidneys	230
Inflammation of the Kidneys	231
Diabetes, or Profuse Staling	233
Bloody Urine—Hæmaturia	233
Albuminous Urine	234
The Bladder	234
Inflammation of the Bladder	234
Stone in the Bladder	235

CHAPTER XI.

BREEDING, CASTRATION, &c.	237
Castration	244

CHAPTER XII.

THE FORE LEGS	247
Sprain of the Shoulder	246
Slanting direction of the Shoulder	247
The Humerus, or Lower Bone of the Shoulder	252
The Arm	252
The Knee	253
Broken Knees	254
The Leg	256
Splint	256
Sprain of the Back-Sinews	258
Wind-Galls	261
The Pasterns	263
Injuries to the Suspensory Ligament	265
The Fetlock	265
Grogginess	265
Cutting	266
Sprain of the Coffin-Joint	269
Ringbone	268

CHAPTER XIII.

	PAGE
THE HIND LEGS	271
The Haunch	271
The Thigh	272
The Stifle	275
Thorough-Pin	277
The Hock	277
Enlargement of the Hock	279
Curb	280
Bog Spavin	281
Bone Spavin	283
Capped Hock	285
Mallenders and Sallenders	286
Swelled Legs	287
Grease	288

CHAPTER XIV.

THE FOOT	293
The Crust or Wall of the Hoof	294
The Coronary Ring	296
The Bars	296
The Horny Laminæ	297
The Sole	297
The Frog	298
The Coffin-Bone	299
The Sensible Sole	300
The Sensible Frog	300
The Navicular Bone	300
The Cartilages of the Foot	301

CHAPTER XV.

THE DISEASES OF THE FOOT	302
Inflammation of the Foot, or Acute Founder	302
Chronic Founder	305
Pumiced Feet	305
Contraction	307
The Navicular-Joint Disease	311
Sand-Crack	317
Tread and Over-reach	319
False Quarter	320
Quittor	321
Prick or Wound in the Sole or Crust	324
Corns	326
Thrush	328
Canker	330
Ossification of the Cartilages	331
Weakness of the Foot	331

CHAPTER XVI.

Fractures 333

CHAPTER XVII.

On Shoeing.. 343
    The putting on the Shoe................................. 345
    Calkins 346
    Clips 346
    The hinder Shoe.. 347
    Different kinds of Shoes............................... 347
    The Concave-seated Shoe................................ 348
    The Unilateral, or one side nailed Shoe................ 349
    The Hunting Shoe....................................... 351
    The Bar Shoe... 352
    Tips... 352
    The Expanding Shoe..................................... 353
    Felt or Leather Soles.................................. 353
    Stopping the Feet...................................... 355
    The Sandal... 556
    To Manage a Fallen Horse............................... 358

CHAPTER XVIII.

Operations.. 359
    Bleeding 361
    Blistering 362
    Firing 364
    Setons 366
    Docking.. 367
    Nicking 368

CHAPTER XIX.

The Vices and Disagreeable or Dangerous Habits of the Horse 370
    Restiveness.. 370
    Backing or Gibbing..................................... 370
    Biting 372
    Getting the Cheek of the Bit into the Mouth............ 372
    Kicking.. 373
    Unsteadiness while being Mounted....................... 374
    Rearing.. 374
    Running Away... 375
    Vicious to Clean....................................... 375
    Vicious to Shoe.. 376
    Swallowing without Grinding............................ 377
    Crib-Biting.. 378

Wind-Sucking.. ... 379
Cutting ... 379
Not Lying Down ... 380
Overreach ... 380
Pawing ... 380
Quidding ... 381
Rolling ... 381
Shying ... 381
Slipping the Collar ... 383
Tripping ... 384
Weaving ... 384

CHAPTER XX.

THE GENERAL MANAGEMENT OF THE HORSE ... 385
Air ... 385
Litter ... 387
Light ... 388
Grooming ... 389
Exercise ... 391
Food ... 392

CHAPTER XXI.

THE SKIN AND ITS DISEASES ... 405
Hide-bound ... 407
Pores of the Skin ... 409
Moulting ... 410
Color ... 411
Surfeit ... 415
Mange ... 416
Warts ... 419
Vermin ... 419

CHAPTER XXII.

ON SOUNDNESS, AND THE PURCHASE AND SALE OF HORSES ... 420

CHAPTER XXIII.

A LIST OF THE MEDICINES USED IN THE TREATMENT OF THE DISEASES OF THE HORSE ... 435

LIST OF ILLUSTRATIONS.

PORTRAIT OF CONSTERNATION, ... FRONTISPIECE
PORTRAIT OF FLYING CHILDERS, ... 18
PORTRAIT OF LOUIS PHILIPPE (NORMAN), ... 30
PORTRAIT OF GENERAL GIFFORD (MORGAN), ... 35
PORTRAIT OF LADY SUFFOLK (TROTTER), ... 41
FIG. 1. SKELETON OF THE HORSE, ... 45
" 2. BONES OF THE HORSE'S HEAD, ... 47
" 3. SECTION OF THE HORSE'S HEAD, ... 49
" 4. DIAGRAM OF THE SKULL, ... 53
" 5. OCCIPITAL BONE OF THE HORSE, ... 54
" 6. SPINAL CHORD, WITH BRANCHING NERVES, . . 57
" 7. SECTION OF THE EYE, ... 62
" 8. MUSCLES OF THE EYE, ... 66
" 9. HORSE WITH LOCKJAW, ... 79
" 10. ANATOMY OF THE LEG AND FOOT, . . . 87
" 11. SECTION OF UPPER JAW BONE, ... 101
" 12. MUSCLES, NERVES, AND BLOOD-VESSELS OF THE HEAD
AND UPPER PART OF NECK, ... 102
" 13. THE PALATE, ... 118
" 14. TEETH OF A FOAL A FEW DAYS AFTER BIRTH, . 121
" 15. TEETH OF A FOAL AT TWO MONTHS, . . . 121
" 16. TEETH OF A FOAL AT TWELVE MONTHS, . . 122
" 17. TRANSVERSE SECTION OF A GRINDER, . . . 123
" 18. TEETH OF A YEAR AND A HALF, . . . 123
" 19. TEETH OF THREE YEARS, ... 124
" 20. TEETH AT THREE YEARS AND A HALF, . . 126
" 21. TEETH AT FIVE YEARS, ... 126
" 22. TEETH AT SIX YEARS, ... 127
" 23. TEETH AT SEVEN YEARS, ... 128
" 24. TEETH AT EIGHT OR NINE YEARS, . . . 128
" 25. FINEST SHAPE OF HEAD AND NECK, . . 138

		PAGE
FIG. 26. THE RIBS AND VERTEBRÆ,		145
" 27. THE STOMACH,		206
" 28. THE BOT FLY IN ITS VARIOUS STAGES,		208
" 29. THE INTESTINES,		210
" 30. SECTION OF THE BLIND GUT,		212
" 31. ENTANGLEMENT OF THE INTESTINES,		226
" 32. CURVED AND STRAIGHT CATHETER,		336
" 33. BONES OF THE LEGS,		247
" 34. SIMPLE LEVER,		248
" 35. MUSCLES OF OUTSIDE OF THE SHOULDER,		250
" 36. MUSCLES OF INSIDE OF SHOULDER AND FOREARM,		251
" 37. SECTION OF THE PASTERN,		263
" 38. INSIDE VIEW OF BONES OF PASTERN,		267
" 39. OUTSIDE VIEW OF BONES OF PASTERN,		267
" 40. ATTACHMENTS OF THE MUSCLES OF PASTERN,		267
" 41. DISEASES OF THE FORE LEG,		269
" 42. INSIDE MUSCLES OF HIND LEG,		273
" 43. OUTSIDE MUSCLES OF HIND LEG,		274
" 44. THE HAUNCH AND HIND LEGS,		276
" 45. THE HOCK JOINT,		278
" 46. ANATOMY OF THE FOOT,		293
" 47. ANATOMY OF THE BASE OF THE FOOT,		293
" 48. THE CORONARY RING,		296
" 49. PERCEVALL'S SUSPENSORY APPARATUS,		334
" 50. THE CONCAVE SEATED SHOE,		348
" 51. THE UNILATERAL SHOE,		350
" 52. OPERATION FOR CORNS,		351
" 53. PERCEVALL'S SANDAL,		356
" 54. PERCEVALL'S SANDAL FASTENED TO THE FOOT,		357

THE HORSE.

CHAPTER I.

PRINCIPAL BREEDS AND VARIETIES OF HORSES IN THE UNITED STATES.

The horse was not known on any part of the American Continent, until introduced by Europeans.

The principal breeds and varieties which now prevail in the United States, are the common horse, descended from the horses originally introduced by the English colonists, and mixed, more or less, with varieties of later introduction: the thorough-bred or Race-horse; the Arabian; the Canadian; the Norman; the Morgan; the Cleveland Bay; the Dray; and the American Trotting-horse.

The mongrel known as the "common horse," is too various in blood, and too multiform in his characteristics, to admit of any particular description.

THE RACE-HORSE.

Mr. Youatt says: "There is much dispute with regard to the origin of the *thorough-bred horse*. By some he is traced through both sire and dam to Eastern parentage; others believe him to be the native horse, improved and perfected by judicious crossing with the Barb, the Turk, or the Arabian. The Stud Book, which is an authority acknowledged by every English breeder, traces all the old racers to some Eastern origin; or it traces them until the pedigree is lost in the uncertainty of an early period of breeding. If the pedigree of a racer of the present day be required, it is traced back to a certain extent, and ends with a well-known racer; or, if an earlier derivation be required, that ends with an Eastern horse, or in obscurity.

It must on the whole, be allowed, that the present English

FLYING CHILDERS.

thorough-bred horse is of foreign extraction, improved and perfected by the influence of the climate, and by diligent cultivation. There are some exceptions, as in the case of Sampson and Bay-Malton, in each of whom, although the best horses of their day, there was a cross of vulgar blood; but they are only exceptions to a general rule. In our best racing stables, and, particularly in the studs of the Earls of Grosvenor and Egremont, this is an acknowledged principle; and it is not, when properly considered, a principle at all derogatory to the credit of the country. The British climate, and British skill, made the thorough-bred horse what he is.

The beautiful tales of Eastern countries, and somewhat remoter days, may lead us to imagine that the Arabian horse possesses marvellous powers; but it cannot admit of a doubt, that the English trained horse is more beautiful, and far swifter and stouter than the justly-famed coursers of the desert. In the burning plains of the East, and the frozen climate of Russia, he has invariably beaten every antagonist on his native ground. A few years ago RECRUIT, an English horse of moderate reputation, easily beat PYRAMUS, the best Arabian on the Bengal side of India.

It must not be objected, that the number of Eastern horses imported is far too small to produce so numerous a progeny. It will be recollected, that the thousands of wild horses on the plains of South America descended from only two stallions and four mares, which the early Spanish adventurers left there.

Whatever may be the truth as to the origin of the race-horse, the strictest attention has for the last fifty years been paid to pedigree. In the descent of almost every modern racer, not the slightest flaw can be discovered : or when, with the splendid exception of Sampson and Bay-Malton, one drop of common blood has mingled with the pure stream, it has been immediately detected in the inferiority of form, and deficiency of bottom, and it has required two or three generations to wipe away the stain, and get rid of its consequences.

The racer is generally distinguished by his beautiful Arabian head; his fine and finely-set-on neck; his oblique, lengthened shoulders; well-bent hinder legs; his ample, muscular quarters; his flat legs, rather short from the knee downward, although not always so deep as they should be; and his long and elastic pastern. These are separately considered where the structure of the horse is treated of.

The racer, however, with the most beautiful form, is occasionally a sorry animal. There is sometimes a want of energy in an apparently faultless shape, for which there is no accounting; but there are two points among those just enumerated, which will rarely or never deceive, a well-placed shoulder and a well-bent hinder leg.

The Darley Arabian was the parent of our best racing stock He was purchased by Mr. Darley's brother, at Aleppo, and was bred in the neighboring desert of Palmyra.

The immediate descendants of this invaluable horse, were the Devonshire or Flying Childers; the Bleeding or Bartlett's Childers, who was never trained; Almanzor, and others.

The two Childers were the means through which the blood and fame of their sire were widely circulated, and from them descended another Childers, Blaze, Snap, Sampson, Eclipse, and a host of excellent horses.

The DEVONSHIRE or FLYING CHILDERS, so called from the name of his breeder, Mr. Childers, of Carr-House, and the sale of him to the Duke of Devonshire, was the fleetest horse of his day. He was at first trained as a hunter, but the superior speed and courage which he discovered caused him to be soon transferred to the turf. Common report affirms, that he could run a mile in a minute, but there is no authentic record of this. Childers ran over the round course at Newmarket (three miles six furlongs and ninety-three yards) in six minutes and forty seconds; and the Beacon course (four miles one furlong and one hundred and thirty-eight yards) in seven minutes and thirty seconds. In 1772 a mile was run by Firetail, in one minute and four seconds

In October, 174_, at the Curragh meeting in Ireland, Mr. Wilde engaged to ride one hundred and twenty-seven miles in nine hours. He performed it in six hours and tewnty-one minutes. He employed ten horses, and, allowing for mounting and dismounting, and a moment for refreshment, he rode for six hours at the rate of twenty miles an hour.

Mr Thornhill, in 1745, exceeded this, for he rode from Stilton to London and back, and again to Stilton, being two hundred and thirteen miles, in eleven hours and thirty-four minutes, which is, after allowing the least possible time for changing horses, twenty miles an hour for eleven hours, and on the turnpike road and uneven ground.

Mr. Shaftoe, in 1762, with ten horses, and five of them ridden twice, accomplished fifty miles and a quarter, in one hour and forty-nine minutes. In 1763, Mr. Shaftoe won a more extraordinary match. He was to procure a person to ride one hundred miles a day, on any one horse each day, for twenty-nine days together, and to have any number of horses not exceeding twenty-nine. He accomplished it on fourteen horses; and on one day he rode one hundred and sixty miles, on account of the tiring of his first horse.

Mr. Hull's Quibbler, however, afforded the most extraordinary instance on record, of the stoutness as well as speed of the racehorse. In December, 1786, he ran twenty-three miles round the flat at Newmarket, in fifty-seven minutes and ten seconds.

ECLIPSE was got by Marsk, a grandson of Bartlett's Childers.

Of the beauty, yet peculiarity of his form, much has been said The very great size, obliquity, and lowness of his shoulders were the objects of general remark—with the shortness of his forequarters, his ample and finely proportioned quarters, and the swelling muscles of his fore-arm and thigh. Of his speed, no correct estimate can be formed, for he never met with an opponent sufficiently fleet to put it to the test.

He was bred by the Duke of Cumberland, and sold at his death to Mr. Wildman, a sheep salesman, for seventy-five guineas. Col. O'Kelly purchased a share of him from Wildman. In the spring of the following year, when the reputation of this wonderful animal was at its height, O'Kelly wished to become sole owner of him, and bought the remaining share for one thousand pounds.

Eclipse was what is termed a thick-winded horse, and puffed and roared so as to be heard at a considerable distance. For this or some other cause, he was not brought on the turf until he was five years old.

O'Kelly, aware of his horse's powers, had backed him freely on his first race, in May, 1769. The first heat was easily won, when O'Kelly, observing that the rider had been pulling at Eclipse during the whole of the race, offered a wager that he placed the horses in the next heat. This seemed a thing so highly improbable, that he immediately had bets to a large amount. Being called on to declare, he replied, "Eclipse first, and the rest nowhere!" The event justified his prediction: all the others were distanced by Eclipse with the greatest ease; or, in the language of the turf, they had no place.

In the spring of the following year, he beat Mr. Wentworth's Bucephalus, who had never before been conquered. Two days afterwards he distanced Mr. Strode's Pensioner, a very good horse; and, in the August of the same year, he won the great subscription at York. No horse daring to enter against him, he closed his short career of seventeen months, by walking over the Newmarket course for the king's plate, on October the 18th, 1770. He was never beaten, nor ever paid forfeit, and won for his owner more than twenty-five thousand pounds.

Eclipse was afterwards employed as a stallion, and produced the extraordinary number of three hundred and thirty-four winners, and these netted to their owners more than a hundred and sixty thousand pounds exclusive of plates and cups. This fine animal died in 1789, at the age of twenty-five years.*

More than twenty years after the Darley Arabian, and when the value of the Arabian blood was fully established, Lord Godolphin possessed a beautiful, but singularly-shaped horse, which he called an Arabian, but which was really a Barb. His crest, lofty and arched almost to a fault, will distinguish him from every other horse.

He had a sinking behind his shoulders, almost as peculiar, and a corresponding elevation of the spine towards the loins. His muzzle was uncommonly fine, his head beautifully set on, his shoulders capacious, and his quarters well spread out. He was picked up in France, where he was actually employed in drawing a cart; and when he was afterwards presented to Lord Godolphin, he was in that nobleman's stud a considerable time before his value was discovered. It was not until the birth of Lath, one of the first horses of that period, that his excellence began to be appreciated. He was then styled an Arabian, and became, in even a greater degree than the Darley, the founder of the modern thorough-bred horses. He died in 1753, at the age of twenty-nine.

An intimate friendship subsisted between him and a cat, which either sat on his back when he was in the stable, or nestled as closely to him as she could. At his death, the cat refused her

* The produce of King Herod, a descendant of Flying Childers, was even more numerous. He got no less than four hundred and ninety-seven winners, who gained for their proprietors upwards of two hundred thousand pounds. Highflyer was a son of King Herod.

food, and pined away, and soon died.—Mr. Holcroft gives a similar relation of the attachment between a race-horse and a cat, which the courser would take in his mouth and place in his manger and upon his back without hurting her. Chillaby, called from his great ferocity the Mad Arabian, whom one only of the grooms dared to approach, and who savagely tore to pieces the image of a man that was purposely placed in his way, had his peculiar attachment to a lamb, who used to employ himself for many an hour, in butting away the flies from him.

It has been imagined that the breed of racing horses has lately very considerably degenerated. This is not the case. Thoroughbred horses were formerly fewer in number, and their performances created greater wonder. The breed has now increased twenty-fold, and superiority is not so easily obtained among so many competitors. If one circumstance could, more than any other, produce this degeneracy, it would be our absurd and cruel habit of bringing out horses too soon, and the frequent failure of their legs before they have come to their full power. Childers and Eclipse did not appear until they were five years old; but many of our best horses, and those, perhaps, who would have shown equal excellence with the most celebrated racers, are foundered and destroyed before that period.

Whether the introduction of short races, and so young horses, be advantageous, and whether stoutness and usefulness may not thus be somewhat too much sacrificed to speed : whether there may be danger that an animal designed for service may, in process of time, be frittered away almost to a shadow of what he was, in order that at two years old, over the one-mile-course, he may astonish the crowd by his fleetness,—are questions that more concern the sporting man than the agriculturist ; and yet they concern the agriculturist too, for racing is principally valuable as connected with breeding, and as the test of breeding.

The horse is as susceptible of pleasure and pain as ourselves. He was committed to us for our protection and our use ; he is a willing, devoted servant. Whence did we derive the right to abuse him ? Interest speaks the same language : many a race has been lost by the infliction of wanton cruelty."

CONSTERNATION, whose portrait fronts the title-page, is the property of John B. Burnett, Esq., Syracuse, N. Y. He was bred by Matthew Hornsey, Esq., Sittenham, near York, Yorkshire, England, in 1841. He was sold by that gentleman to C. T. Albot, Esq., who imported him into the United States in 1846, and introduced him into Stokes, Oneida Co., N. Y. He is a brown horse, dappled with bay—an unusual, but a rich and pleasing color. He is fully fifteen hands and three inches high, without his shoes, and weighs between eleven and twelve hundred pounds He is

PEDIGREE OF CONSTERNATION

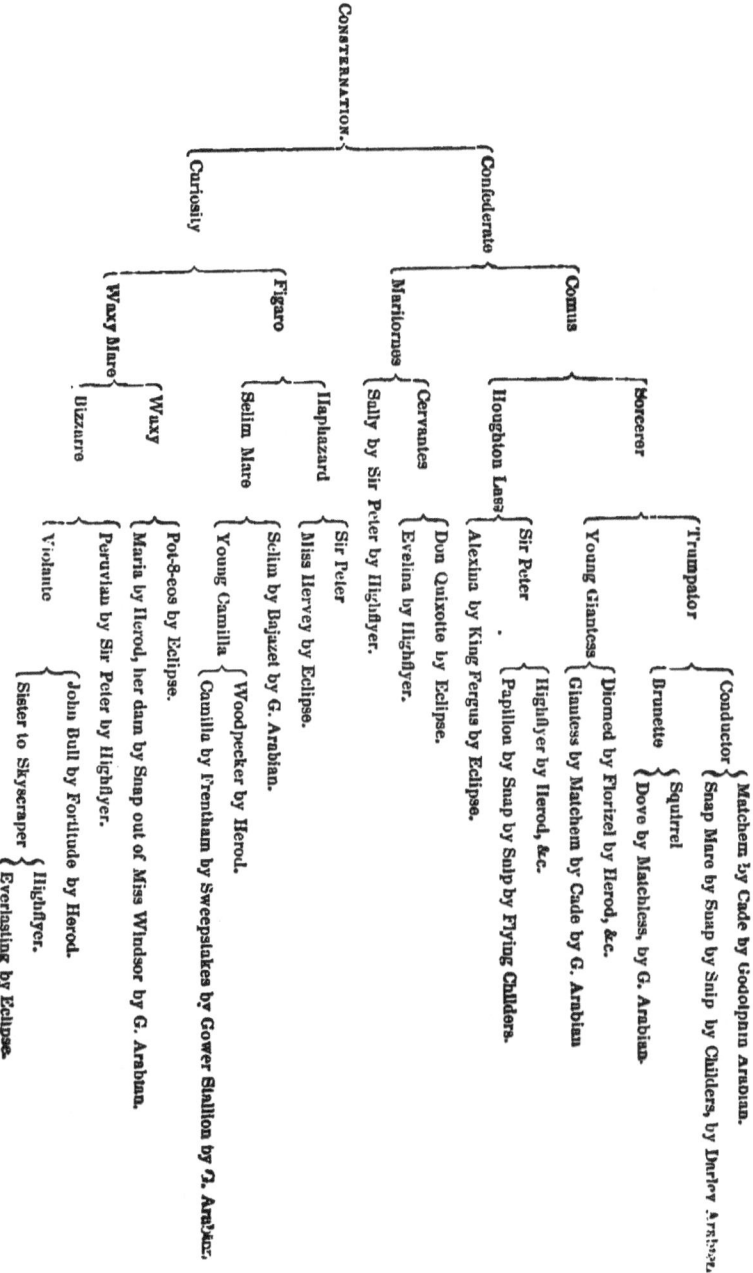

a compact, and, for a thorough-bred, very bony horse, like his immediate ancestors, Confederate, Curiosity, Figaro, &c. Indeed, his sire, Confederate, after being withdrawn from the turf, was kept by his breeder, Earl Fitzwilliam, to breed hunters and carriage-horses from, owing to his size, bone, and symmetry,— properties which eminently marked his progeny. His dam, Curiosity, was a large, strong mare; and her sire, Figaro, possessed the same characteristics. The size and bone of Consternation are not, therefore, accidental, or merely individual traits; they belong to his family, and are, consequently, far more likely to be transmitted to his descendants; and experience *has* shown, that he almost invariably transmits these properties to his descendants.*

Consternation is beautifully symmetrical in all his proportions, with a plumpness and roundness of outline unusual in the thorough-bred; more like a perfect hunter, or exceedingly stylish carriage-horse, but without a particle of coarseness, cloddiness, or deviation from a true blood-like look.

He is a horse of extraordinary mettle and activity, rapid in all his paces, singularly elastic and graceful in his movements. He walks nearly five miles an hour, and is a beautiful and rapid trotter. We believe he might be made a fleet, if not a "crack" trotter, under the training of Woodruff or Wheelan. He ran but one race in England, beating Phœnician, at York. (See Johnson's Racing Calendar, 1845.) He was entered for the St. Leger, but, owing to an accident, which injured his off fore-leg, he was disqualified temporarily, and perhaps permanently, from running. Before this point was decided, Mr. Albot purchased and imported him to America for a breeding stallion. He was selected with more especial reference to the improvement of our common stock of horses.

Consternation arrived in the United States in the latter part of June, 1845, and was shown in the September following, while still suffering from the effects of his voyage, at the N. Y. State Fair at Utica. He received the first premium in the class of blood horses, beating Mr. Hungerford's Sir Henry, Mr. Crosby's Florizelle, Mr. Thompson's Sir Charles—the viewing committee consisting of Col. J. M. Sherwood, Hon. John A. King, and Col. Edward Long. He was not again shown at a State Fair until 1849, at Syracuse. He here received the certificate of superior-

---

* The writer of this has seen perhaps fifty colts, from one to three years old, the get of Consternation, from common dams, and those possessing different proportions of blood. Every one of these has shown good size, and quite as much bone as it is common to see in the get of the common coarse stallions of the country.

ity,* beating Lance, Waxy Pope (imported), Young Alexander Sir Henry (by the horse of the same name, exhibited at Utica) Waxy (by Waxy Pope), and several others.

We have been thus full in speaking of Consternation, because we believe that it is by a *judicious* cross with the *thorough-bred* horse, that the greatest improvement is to be made with *a class* of our common mares, in breeding animals with style, speed, and, above all, *bottom*, for the carriage, the buggy, and the saddle; and because we believe on the principle that *like produces like*, Consternation *promises* better for such a cross than any other blood stallion of which we have any knowledge.

His pedigree includes a host of winners, and the most celebrated horses of England. It is given on the preceding page.

It may interest some who wish to breed common mares to Consternation, and who, very properly, consider *color* an important consideration in carriage and saddle horses, to know that of his ancestors above given *thirty-five* were bay—*twelve*, brown—*ten*, chestnut—and *two*, black.

THE ARABIAN HORSE.

Mr. Youatt says:—"Although in the seventh century the Arabs had no horses of value, yet the Cappadocian and other horses which they had derived from their neighbors, were preserved with so much care, and propagated so uniformly and strictly from the finest of the breed, that in the 13th century the Arabian horse began to assume a just and unrivalled celebrity.

There are said to be three breeds or varieties of Arabian horses: the *Attechi*, or inferior breed, on which they set little value, and which are found wild on some parts of the deserts; the *Kadischi*, literally horses of an unknown race, answering to our half-bred horses—a mixed breed; and the *Kochlani*, horses whose genealogy, according to the Arab account, is known for two thousand years. Many of them have written and attested pedigrees extending more than four hundred years, and, with true Eastern exaggeration, traced by oral tradition from the stud of Solomon. A more careful account is kept of these genealogies than belongs to the most ancient family of the proudest Arab chief, and very singular precautions are taken to

---

* His having once drawn the first premium in the same class, by the regulations of the Society, disqualified him from again receiving it. But in such cases, the former winner, if adjudged best, receives a certificate to that effect.

prevent the possibility of fraud, so far as the written pedigree extends.

The *Kochlani* are principally reared by the Bedouin Arabs, in the remoter deserts. A stallion may be procured without much difficulty, although at a great price. A mare is rarely to be obtained, except by fraud and excessive bribery. The Arabs have found out that which the English breeder should never forget, that the female is more concerned than the male in the excellence and value of the produce; and the genealogies of their horses are always reckoned from the mothers.

The Arabian horse would not be acknowledged by every judge to possess a perfect form: his head, however, is inimitable. The broadness and squareness of the forehead, the shortness and fineness of the muzzle, the prominence and brilliancy of the eye, the smallness of the ears, and the beautiful course of the veins, will always characterize the head of the Arabian horse.

His body may be considered as too light, and his chest as too narrow; but behind the arms the barrel generally swells out, and leaves sufficient room for the play of the lungs.

In the formation of the shoulder, next to that of the head, the Arab is superior to any other breed. The withers are high, and the shoulder-blade inclined backward, and so nicely adjusted, that in descending a hill the point or edge of the ham never ruffles the skin. He may not be thought sufficiently high; he seldom stands more than fourteen hands two inches.

The fineness of his legs, and the oblique position of his pasterns, may be supposed to lessen his apparent strength; but the leg, although small, is flat and wiry; anatomists know that the bone has no common density, and the startling muscles of the fore-arm and the thigh indicate that he is fully capable of accomplishing many of the feats which are recorded of him.

The Barb alone excels him in noble and spirited action; and if there be defects about him, he is perfect for that for which he was designed. He presents the true combination of speed and bottom—strength enough to carry more than a light weight, and courage that would cause him to die rather than to give up.

We may not, perhaps, believe all that is told us of the Arabian. It has been remarked, that there are on the deserts which this horse traverses no mile-stones to mark the distance, or watches to calculate the time; and the Bedouin is naturally given to exaggeration, and, most of all, when relating the prowess of the animal, which he loves as dearly as his children: yet it cannot be denied that, at the introduction of the Arabian into the European stables, there was no other horse comparable to him.

The Arab horse is as celebrated for his docility and good

temper as for his speed and courage. In that delightful book, 'Bishop Heber's Narrative of a Journey through the Upper Provinces of India,' the following interesting character is given of him. "My morning rides are very pleasant. My horse is a nice, quiet, good-tempered little Arab, who is so fearless, that he goes without starting close to an elephant, and so gentle and docile that he eats bread out of my hand, and has almost as much attachment and coaxing ways as a dog. This seems the general character of the Arab horses, to judge from what I have seen in this country. It is not the fiery dashing animal I had supposed, but with more rationality about him, and more apparent confidence in his rider, than the majority of English horses."

The kindness with which he is treated from a foal, gives him an affection for his master, a wish to please, a pride in exerting every energy in obedience to his commands, and, consequently, an apparent sagacity which is seldom seen in other breeds. The mare and her foal inhabit the same tent with the Bedouin and his children. The neck of the mare is often the pillow of the rider, and, more frequently, of the children, who are rolling about upon her and the foal: yet no accident ever occurs, and the animal acquires that friendship and love for man which occasional ill-treatment will not cause him for a moment to forget.

When the Arab falls from his mare, and is unable to rise, she will immediately stand still, and neigh until assistance arrives. If he lies down to sleep, as fatigue sometimes compels him, in the midst of the desert, she stands watchful over him, and neighs and rouses him if either man or beast approaches. An old Arab had a valuable mare that had carried him for fifteen years in many a hard-fought battle, and many a rapid weary march; at length, eighty years old, and unable longer to ride her, he gave her, and a scimiter that had been his father's, to his eldest son and told him to appreciate their value, and never lie down to rest until he had rubbed them both as bright as a looking-glass. In the first skirmish in which the young man was engaged he was killed, and the mare fell into the hands of the enemy. When the news reached the old man, he exclaimed that "life was no longer worth preserving, for he had lost both his son and his mare and he grieved for one as much as the other;" and he immediately sickened and died.

Man, however, is an inconsistent being. The Arab who thus lives with and loves his horses, regarding them as his most valuable treasure, sometimes treats them with a cruelty scarcely to be believed, and not at all to be justified. The severest treatment which the English race-horse endures is gentleness compared with the trial of the young Arabian. Probably the filly has never before been mounted; she is led out; her owner springs on her back, and goads her over the sand and rocks of the desert at full speed for fifty or sixty miles without one moment's respite. She is then forced, steaming and panting, into water deep enough for her to swim. If, immediately after this, she will eat as if nothing had occurred, her character is established, and she is acknowledged to be a genuine descendant of the *Kochlani* breed. The Arab is not conscious of the cruelty which he thus inflicts. It is an invariable custom, and custom will induce us to inflict many a pang on those whom, after all, we love.

The following anecdote of the attachment of an Arab to his mare has often been told, but it comes home to the bosom of every one possessed of common feeling. "The whole stock of an Arab of the desert consisted of a mare. The French consul offered to purchase her in order to send her to his sovereign, Louis XIV. The Arab would have rejected the proposal at once with indignation and scorn; but he was miserably poor. He had no means of supplying his most urgent wants, or procuring the barest necessaries of life. Still he hesitated;—he had scarcely a rag to cover him—and his wife and children were starving. The sum offered was great,—it would provide him and his family with food for life. At length, and reluctantly, he consented. He brought the mare to the dwelling of the consul,— he dismounted,—he stood leaning upon her;—he looked now at the gold, and then at his favorite; he sighed—he wept. 'To whom is it,' said he, 'I am going to yield thee up? To Europeans, who will tie thee close,—who will beat thee,—who will render thee miserable. Return with me, my beauty, my jewel, and rejoice the hearts of my children.' As he pronounced the last words, he sprung upon her back, and was out of sight in a moment."

Our horses would fare badly on the scanty nourishment afforded the Arabian. The mare usually has but one or two meals in twenty-four hours. During the day she is tied to the door of the tent, ready for the Bedouin to spring, at a moment's warning, into the saddle; or she is turned out before the tent ready saddled, the bridle merely taken off, and so trained that she gallops up immediately at her master's call. At night she receives a little water; and with her scanty provender of five or six pounds of barley or beans, and sometimes a little straw, she lies down content, in the midst of her master's family. She can, however, endure great fatigue; she will travel fifty miles without stopping; she has been pushed, on emergency, one hundred and twenty miles, and occasionally, neither she nor her rider has tasted food for three whole days.

To the Arabian, principally, England is indebted for her improved and now unrivalled breed of horses for the turf, the field, and the road."

As already said, when speaking of the English race-horse, the Arabian is not equal to his English descendant. This has also been incontestably proved in the United States. Pure blood Arabians of the highest pretensions have at various times been imported into our country; but they have never compared in either speed or bottom, with the English race-horse and his descendants.

THE CANADIAN HORSE,

Found in the Canadian Provinces, and somewhat in the Northern United States, is too well known to require any particular description. He is mainly of French descent—though many so called, and doubtless some of the fleetest ones, are the produce of a cross between the Canadian and the English thorough-bred stallion. They are a long-lived, easily kept, and exceedingly hardy race, making good farm and draft horses, when sufficiently large. In form, many of them display in a marked manner the characteristics of the Norman—so too in their general qualities—but they are usually considerably smaller. Stallions of this breed have in various instances, of late, been introduced into New York and other northern States, to cross with our common mares. The result has been decidedly satisfactory, particularly in giving compactness and vigor of constitution, where the dam does not excel in those particulars.

A black stallion imported from Canada, a few years since, by Mr. John Legg, of Skaneateles, N. Y., has got several hundred colts, which, when broken, have averaged about one hundred dollars a piece in value; a sum considerably above the average prices of horses in the country. They are almost invariably fair roadsters, and excellent farm-horses. This cross is more and more finding favor among our farmers.

THE NORMAN HORSE.

In connection with the Canadian—though not so old a variety in the United States, as some of which we have presently to speak—we will advert to the French or Norman horse, from which the Canadian is descended. We cannot do this more satisfactorily to ourselves, or more usefully to the reader, than to publish entire the following interesting and admirably candid 'etter from Edward Harris, Esq., of Moorestown, Burlington Co., New Jersey, who introduced this breed into the United States.

LOUIS PHILLIPE.*

Moorestown, April 6, 1850.

My dear Sir:—Your kind favor of the last of March has been duly received. I regret that, in consequence of the decease of a near relative, it has been out of my power to prepare my answer as soon as you desired.

I thank you, my dear sir, for the order you have suggested to be observed in my communication. You will soon perceive that I am by no means a practised writer, therefore your suggestions are the more acceptable in aiding me to draw up my " plain, unvarnished tale."

These horses first came under my observation on a journey through France in the year 1831. I was struck with the immense power displayed by them in drawing the heavy diligences of that country, at a pace which, although not as rapid as the stage-coach travelling of England, yet such a pace, say from five to nine miles per hour, the lowest rate of which I do not hesitate to say, would, in a short time, kill the English horse if placed before the same load. In confirmation of this opinion I will give you an extract from an article on the Norman horse in the British Quarterly Journal of Agriculture, which I quoted in my communication to the Farmer's Cabinet of Philadelphia, in 1842, as follows:—

---

* Bred by Edward Harris, Esq., of Moorestown, New Jersey (in 1843), from his pure imported Norman stock. (See Mr. Harris's letter which follows.) Louis Phillipe is an excellent characteristic specimen of the Norman horse, is a dapple gray, fifteen hands one and one half inches high and weighs twelve hundred pounds, in good condition. He is owned by R B. Howland, Esq., of Union Springs, Cayuga County, N. Y.

"The writer, in giving an account of the origin of the horse, which agrees in tracing it to the Spanish horse (of Arabian ancestry), with the account which I have given above, which I procured from French sources, says, 'The horses of Normandy are a capital race for *hard work and scanty fare*. I have *never seen* such horses at the collar, under the diligence, the post-carriage, the cumbrous and heavy voiture or cabriolet for one or two horses, or the farm-cart. They are *enduring and energetic beyond description*; with their necks cut to the bone, they flinch not; they put forth all their efforts at the voice of the brutal driver, or at the dreaded sound of his never-ceasing whip; *they keep their condition when other horses would die of neglect and hard treatment*. A better cross for some of our horses can not be imagined than those of Normandy, provided they have not the ordinary failing, of too much length from the hock downwards, and a heavy head.' I think that all who have paid attention to this particular breed of Norman horses (the Percheron, which stands A No. 1), will bear me out in the assertion that the latter part of this quotation will not apply to them, and that, on the contrary, they are short from the hock downwards; that their heads are short, with the true Arabian face, and not thicker than they should be to correspond with the stoutness of their bodies. At all events you can witness that *Diligence* has not these failings, which, when absent, an Englishman (evidently, from his article a good horseman) thinks, constitutes the Norman horse the best imaginable horse for a cross upon the English horse of a certain description. Again he says, 'They are very gentle and docile; a kicking or vicious horse is almost unknown there; any person may pass in security at a fair at the heels of hundreds.'"

My own impressions being fortified by such authority from such a source (where we look for little praise of anything French), and numerous others, verbal and written, I made up my mind to return to France at an early day and select a stallion at least, as an experiment in crossing upon the light mares of New Jersey. My intention was unavoidably delayed until the year 1839, when I went seriously to work to purchase two stallions and two mares with the aid of a veterinary surgeon of Havre, Monsieur St. Marc, to whose knowledge of the various distinct breeds which exist in France, and his untiring zeal in aiding my enterprise, I take great pleasure in making acknowledgments. The animals in due time were procured, but the last which was brought for my decision, although a fine stallion, showed such evident signs of a cross of the English blood (afterwards acknowledged by the owner), that I rejected him, and the packet being about to sail, and preparations being made for the shipment, I was obliged to put the stallion and two mares on board, no time being left to look up another stallion. Here another difficulty arose—I could find no competent groom in Havre to take charge of them on the voyage, and deliver them in New York. I was obliged to make an arrangement with one of the steerage passengers, a German, who had never been to sea before, to attend to them to the best of his ability. As you may suppose, I did not feel very well satisfied with this arrangement. I therefore wrote to M. Meurice of Paris, to take charge of my baggage which I had left at his hotel, and the next morning I was on my way to New York on the packet ship Iowa, Captain Peck, where I lived in the round-house on deck, with himself and officers. It was the Iowa's first voyage, and her cabin had not been finished, so great was the fear of the owners, at that time, that their "occupation was gone" of carrying cabin passengers, in consequence of the recent success of the English sea-steamers. We had three hundred steerage, and I was the only *cabin* passenger. The horses were also on deck. The first night, so great was the change in the temperature, on the occurrence of a slight storm, that all the horses took violent colds, and, unfortunately, with the best use

I could make of M. St. Marc's medicine-chest, and his very judicious directions for the treatment of the horses under this anticipated state of affairs, I could not prevent the death of the stallion from inflammation of the lungs, before reaching New York. The mares were landed safely, but too much stiffened by the voyage and their sickness, to make the journey at once across the Jerseys on foot. I procured a trusty man to accompany them, and sent them by railroad for Burlington. The next morning I had the mortification to see my man returned with the sad news that the finest mare had broken through the bottom of the car, and fractured one of her hind legs Thus left with one horse out of four selected, the only alternative was to give up, or go back for more. I did not hesitate about the latter, and in three weeks I was steaming it on board the Great Western. My next purchase was "Diligence," another stallion, and two mares. This time I was more fortunate, and procured an excellent groom to accompany them, who succeeded in getting them safely to New York and to Moorestown, *carefully shunning the railroad.* I have, since that time, lost one of the mares, and the other stallion went blind after making one season. Not wishing to run the risk of perpetuating a race of horses with weak eyes, I have not since permitted him to cover mares; though I must say for him that his colts have all good eyes, and stand high in public favor.

Those who are acquainted with the thorough-bred Canadian horse, will see in him a perfect model, on a small scale, of the PERCHERON horse. This is the peculiar breed of Normandy which are used so extensively throughout the northern half of France for diligence and post-horses, and from the best French authorities I could command (I cannot now quote the precise authorities), I learned that they were produced by the cross of the Andalusian horse upon the old heavy Norman horse, whose portrait may still be seen as a war-horse on the painted windows of the cathedral of Rouen, several centuries old. At the time of the occupation of the Netherlands by the Spaniards, the Andalusian was the favorite stallion of the north of Europe, and thus a stamp of the true Barb was implanted, which remains to the present day. If you will allow me to digress a moment, I will give you a short description of the old Norman draught-horse on which the cross was made. They average full sixteen hands in height, with head short, thick, wide and hollow between the eyes; jaws heavy; ears short and pointed well forwards; neck very short and thick; mane heavy; shoulder well inclined backwards; back extremely short; rump steep; quarters very broad; chest deep and wide; tendons large; muscles excessively developed; legs very short, particularly from the knee and hock to the fetlock, and thence to the coronet, which is covered with long hair, hiding half the hoof; much hair on the legs.

The bone and muscle, and much of the form of the Percheron is derived from this horse, and he gets his spirit and action from the Andalusian. Docility comes from both sides. On the expulsion of the Spaniards from the north, the supply of Andalusian stallions was cut off, and since that time in the Perche district in Normandy, their progeny has doubtless been bred in-and-in; hence the remarkable uniformity of the breed, and the disposition to impart their form to their progeny beyond any breed of domestic animals within my knowledge. Another circumstance which I think has tended to perpetuate the good qualities of these horses, is the fact of all their males being kept entire; a gelding is, I believe, unknown among the rural horses of France. You may be startled at this notion of mine, but if you reflect a moment, you must perceive that in such a state of things (so contrary to our practice and that of the English) the farmer will always breed from the best horse, and he will have an opportunity of judging, because the horse has been broken to harness and his qualities known before he could command business as a stallion. Hence, too, their indifference to pedigree.

If the success of Diligence as a stallion is any evidence of the value of the breed, I can state, that he has averaged eighty mares per season for the ten seasons he has made in this country, and as he is a very sure foal getter, he must have produced at least four hundred colts; and as I have never yet heard of a colt of his that would not readily bring one hundred dollars, and many of them much higher prices, you can judge of the benefit which has accrued from his services. I have yet to learn that he has produced one worthless colt, nor have I heard of one that is spavined, curbed, ringboned, or has any of those defects which render utterly useless so large a number of the fine-bred colts of the present day. The opinion of good judges here is, that we have never had, in this part of the country at least, so valuable a stock of horses for farming purposes; and further, that no horse that ever stood in this section of the country has produced the same number of colts whose aggregate value has been equal to that of the colts of Diligence; for the reason that, although there may have been individuals among them which would command a much higher price than any of those of Diligence, yet the number of blemished and indifferent colts has been so great, as quite to turn the scale in his favor.

In reply to your queries, I would say to the first, that Diligence has not been crossed at all with thorough-bred mares—such a thing is almost unknown here at the present day; but those mares the nearest approaching to it have produced the cleanest, neatest, and handsomest colts, though hardly large enough to command the best prices. Those I know of that cross are excellent performers.

2. The style of mares with which Diligence breeds best, appears to me to be the mare which you would choose to breed carriage-horses from, with a good length of neck, and tail coming out on a line with the back, to correct the two prominent faults in form of the breed, the short neck and steep rump.

3. What is the result of the cross with different styles (as regards size and shape)? This may be answered in a general way by stating, the size will depend somewhat upon the size of the mare, with due allowance for casting after back stock, which will be well understood by breeders. As regards shape, you may depend upon the predominance of the form of the horse in nine cases out of ten; indeed, I have only seen one of his colts that I could not instantly recognize from the form. The reason will occur to you from what I have said of the extreme purity of the breed: such as they are they have been for centuries; and could you find another race of horses of entirely different form in the same category as regards their pedigree, my belief is, that when you should see the first colt from them, you would see the model of all that were to follow.

4. Can you breed carriage-horses sufficiently fashionable for the city markets? I do not hesitate to say that it cannot be done with the first cross. There is too much coarseness about them, which must be worn down by judicious crossing; and I think a stallion got by Diligence upon a large-sized thorough-bred mare, would go very far towards producing the desired result. Should this fail, I feel very confident that another cross from these colts on the thorough-bred mare, will give you the *Morgan-horse on a larger scale.* I still hold to the opinion I expressed to you years ago, that the action of our common horses would be improved by this cross. His colts have higher action than their dams, and generally keep their feet better under them; in other words, they pick them up quicker, not suffering them to rest so long upon the ground.

THE COLTS OF DILIGENCE.

Your fifth and sixth questions will be answered by what I have further to say in regard to the progeny of Diligence.

I may safely say they are universally docile and kind, at the same time spirited and lively. They break-in without any difficulty. As regards their speed, I do not know of any that can be called fast horses, though many smart ones among ordinary road horses. Diligence, as I have said elsewhere, was chosen (for obvious reasons) as a full-sized specimen of the breed. As for speed in trotting, we cannot doubt its being in the breed, when we look at the instances among the thorough-bred Canadian ponies. Could I have made my selection from the stallions which I rode behind in the diligences, I could have satisfied the most fastidious on this point, but, unfortunately, these horses all belonged to the government, and are never sold until past service. My main object was to produce a valuable farm horse. The chance of fast colts is not very great; because those persons having fast mares to breed from, naturally look for a fast stallion, and failing to find him, take one of the best English blood they can find; and should they occur, they will be mares, or, ten to one, horses, gelded before their good qualities are discovered. Perhaps some part of what I say above will be more clear to you if I say, that I hold to the opinion that the Percheron blood still exists in Canada in all its purity.

You will think, perhaps, that I have said quite enough about my humble hobby, and you will have found out too, that I have no idea, contrary to your good-natured warning, of making "swans of my geese." What I should like to see would be further importations of these horses, thereby multiplying the chances for a happy hit in crossing, and to draw public attention to them, which would do more for them than writing till doomsday. So far from considering these horses as capable by any crossing of producing the very best of horses for all purposes, that is to say, the best horse-of-all-work, I believe that if I had my time to live over again, had a very large landed estate, an unlimited supply of "*the dust*," I could produce that horse by breeding from the thorough-bred English racer. It would not be difficult now to select, to start from, stallions and mares possessing all the requisites of size, form, temper, &c.; but each of these individuals is such a compound of all kinds of ancestors, good, bad, and indifferent, that you would be obliged from their progeny to select and reject so often, for faults of size and form, and for blemishes and vices, that your allotted days would be near a close before you produced anything like uniformity in the breed. Still, we see what has been done by Bakewell and others in breeding stock, therefore I contend, à la Sam Patch, that what has been done may be done again.

I therefore am decidedly of opinion, that we cannot do better, if we wish to produce in any reasonable time a most invaluable race of horses for the farm and the road, than to breed form the full-sized Norman or Percheron horse.

Mr. Howland's horse (the portrait of which is given at the beginning of this article) is of the true breed, having been raised by me from one of my imported mares, put to Diligence, and I consider him a remarkably fine specimen of the breed.

I remain, yours very sincerely,
EDWARD HARRIS.

Mr Youatt in speaking of the French horses, says: "The best French horses are bred in Limousin and Normandy. From the former district come excellent saddle-horses and hunters; and from the latter a stronger species for the road, the cavalry, or the carriage. The Norman horses are now much crossed by our hunters, and occasionally by the thorough-bred; and the English roadster and light draft horse has not suffered by a mixture with the Norman." In his remarks on the Coach Horse, Mr. Y. says:—" The Normandy carriers travel with a team of four horses, and from fourteen to twenty-two miles in a day, with a load of *ninety hundred* weight."

THE MORGAN HORSE.

GENERAL GIFFORD.*

Of this celebrated American variety or family of horses, the writer of this possesses little knowledge derived from personal experience. That they have obtained much celebrity as light buggy and saddle horses,—attracted much notice and admiration at the New York State Fairs from their remarkably spirited action and evident docility—sold for high prices not only for the

* "General Gifford" was got by Gifford Morgan, he by Burbank, he by the original "Morgan Horse." The dam of General Gifford was got by Sherman Morgan. He is 15½ hands high, of a dark chestnut color, exceedingly compact; remarkable for his muscular development, and is said by a correspondent in the Genessee Farmer, in "only decent working condition" to have weighed 1040 pounds. The same correspondent states on the authority of Mr. Mason (who has owned the horse), that he has trotted a mile inside of three minutes. He is a horse of great action, and is considered a very characteristic and favorable specimen of the breed in all particulars He is now owned by Charles W Ingersoll Esq., of Lodi. Seneca Co., N. Y

saddle and buggy, but as stallions to extend the breed,—is cei
tain. They have many warm admirers, and find ready purchasers. Others, on the contrary, are disposed to concede to
them no uncommon value as a family, as will be seen by some
quotations which we shall presently make.

The origin of the Morgans is thus stated in a letter to us from
a highly intelligent and, as we believe, perfectly responsible
source:—

Burlington, March 8th, 1850.

MY DEAR SIR,—The conflicting reports concerning the origin of the
"Morgan" horse are so numerous, and come in "such questionable shapes,"
that no one can be *satisfied beyond a doubt* of the truth of any one story.

The pedigree given by the descendants of Mr. Justin Morgan, is, in my
estimation, the one entitled to the most credit. They have made oath to
certain statements in regard to the pedigree of the "Morgan" horse. But
these statements, so far as I can learn, depend upon the reminiscences of
early childhood, and consequently are not entitled to *implicit* confidence.
Adopting the pedigree, as given by a son of Mr. Justin Morgan, as the
most reliable pedigree, I will proceed. The original "Morgan" horse, the
founder of the family of horses known by that name, was brought, at two
years old, in 1795, from Springfield, Mass., to Randolph, Vt., by Justin
Morgan, of the latter place. He was got by "True Britton," he by More-
ton's "Traveller" (imported), among whose ancestors are found "English
Eclipse," "Childers," and the "Godolphin Arabian." "True Britton" (not
the horse of same name mentioned in the Stud Book, and got by imported
"Othello"), was stolen from Gen. Delancey, of New York, while with a
band of refugee troops on Long Island. Gen. Delancey was the importer
of the horses "Wild-air" and "Lath," both thorough-bred horses—the former of such superiority that he was sent back to England, in 1772.
Judging from Gen. Delancey's *taste* in horses, it is but right to infer
that "True Britton" was thorough-bred. Thus much for the sire of the
"Morgan" horse. Concerning his dam, Mr. F. A. Weir, of Walpole, N.
H., writes as follows (Cultivator, January, 1840, p. 19.): "The dam is
described by Mr. John Morgan, who knew her, as of the 'Wild-air' breed,
of middling size, with a heavy chest, of a very light bay color, with a
bushy mane and tail, the hair on the legs rather long, and a smooth, handsome traveller. She was got by 'Diamond,' a thick heavy horse, of about
the middling size, with a thick heavy mane and tail, hairy legs, and a smooth
traveller." "Diamond," Mr. Weir further says, was got by "Wild-air," out
of the "noted imported *mare* 'Wild-air.'" I can find no account of any
such importation, and deem it improbable that a mare and horse should
have been imported about the same time, and allowed to retain one and
the same name. However, I may be wrong, and Mr. Weir right. "Wild-
air," sire of "Diamond," was got by imported "Wild-air."

The reasonable conclusion from this statement is, that the dam of the
old "Morgan" had some good blood in her veins, but was *not thorough-
bred.* This, it is believed, is as correct and reliable an account of the pedigree of the "Morgan" horse as can be obtained. From the appearance of
those horses now living, nearest related to the original "Morgan," it is evident
that the old horse was possessed of no small share of *pure blood.* There
can be no good reason to doubt the above pedigree, if we judge from the
character of the *immediate* descendants of the old horse.

There were but four colts of the original "Morgan" kept as stallions,
and concerning the blood of their dams nothing is known.

I. "Revenge" was foaled in Claremont, N. H., out of a "middle-sized white mare, of no particular blood."

II. "Sherman Morgan," raised in Lyndon, Vt., was from a "chestnut colored mare, of rather light bone, and *said* to be of English blood."

III. "Bulrush," bred by Mr. Gifford, of Tunbridge, Vt., was out of a "thick, heavy, dark bay and rather lazy mare."

IV. "Woodbury," or "Burbank," was also foaled in Tunbridge, Vt., and was out of a "bay mare, said to weigh about 1000 pounds, a smart, good lriver."

"Burbank" was doubtless the best colt from the loins of the old horse, kept as a stallion. He was the sire of the "Gifford Morgan, now owned by F. A. Weir, of Walpole, N. H.," [and grandsire of "General Gifford," given in our cut.—*Ed.*]

The Committee of the N. Y. State Agricultural Society, "on stock owned out of the State," at the State Fair at Auburn, in 1846, thus spoke of the Morgans, and of the horse (General Gifford) represented in the cut, and of his sire Gifford Morgan:—

"Gifford Morgan, a dark chestnut stallion, fourteen hands and three inches high, aged twenty years, was exhibited by F. A. Weir, of Walpole, N. H. It is claimed on the part of his owner, that this horse possesses the celebrated "Morgan" blood in greater purity than any other now living. "General Gifford," got by the above-named horse, was exhibited by Mr. C. Blodget, of Chelsea, Vt. In his size, figure, action, and color, he closely resembles his sire. Both are exceedingly compact horses, deep-chested, strong-backed, with fore-legs set wide apart, and carrying their heads (which are small, with fine, well set eyes) high and gracefully, without a bearing-rein. Their action attracted the marked admiration of all. This breed are reputed to possess great bottom and hardiness, and everything about the two presented, goes to prove that their reputation, in this particular, is well founded. For light carriage or buggy horses, it would be difficult to equal them, and if by crossing with prime large mares, of any breed, size could be obtained in the progeny, without losing the fire and action of the Morgan, the result of the cross would be a carriage of very superior quality. Your committee are not aware of the extent or result of such crosses, in the region where the Morgans originated. Unless experience has already demonstrated their inutility, we could recommend to our horse-breeders, some well-considered experiments, limited at first, to test the feasibility of engrafting the Morgan characteristics on a larger horse."

A distinguished judge of horses in Vermont, writes us:—

" The original Morgan ought not to be pronounced a *thorough-bred* horse, not having been bred from a full blood mare. Yet it is evident that the rich, high blood from which he sprung, though slightly diluted, is the cause of the reputation to which his stock has attained. But when we trace down his stock, we find, in the very first generation, an admixture of cold, worthless blood, to the full measure of one half. The result, usual in similar cases, is found here. Many of the colts related more or less nearly to the old horse, exhibit the characteristics of the "Morgan" *form*, but lack compactness—not of general form, *but of muscle*, and they lack bottom. The general characteristics of the Morgan family, are small size, weighing from seven hundred to one thousand pounds—a long but strong back—plump ness of general contour, like a Berkshire pig—short, strong, hairy legs—a *brusque* air—a bustling gait, with more pucker and gather than freedom and elasticity of step—long, coarse hair—heavy mane and tail—and a surprising predisposition to accumulate fat, instead of muscle—and a remarkably docile and tractable temper. As a general thing, the "Morgans" have not length of stride enough to be *good* roadsters. They take too many steps in a mile. It is but very rarely one can be found that proves to be a good "all-day horse." It often occurs that one can be driven ten miles within the hour, and perhaps at the same rate for the second hour, without apparent distress or injury. But for a high rate of speed *throughout the day*, search must be made among other families than the "Morgan." There is a place for them, however. They are good for an hour's drive—for short stages. They are good to run around town with. They are good in the light pleasure-wagon—prompt, lively (not spirited) and "trappy." There is no question among those who have had fair opportunities of comparing the "Morgans" with horses of purer blood, and descended from different stocks, in regard to the relative position of the "Morgan." He is, as he exists at the present day, inferior in size, speed, and bottom, in fact, in all those qualities necessary for the performance of "great deeds" on the road or the farm, to the descendants of Messenger, Duroc, imp. Magnum Bonum, and of many other horses of deserved celebrity. The Gifford Morgan embodies the characteristics of the "Morgan" form, or *did* embody them, better, and in more prominent and pleasant relief than any other horse I am acquainted with, of this family." * * *

The above is *not*, as already stated, the *popular* estimate of this family. Having stated both sides of the question, we leave it to the judgment of the public.

THE CLEVELAND BAY.

According to Mr. Youatt, the *true* Cleveland Bay is nearly extinct in England. They were formerly employed as a heavy, slow coach-horse. Mr. Y. says: "The origin of the better kind of coach-horse is the Cleveland Bay, confined principally to Yorkshire and Durham, with, perhaps, Lincolnshire on one side, and Northumberland on the other, but difficult to meet with pure in either county. The Cleveland mare is crossed by a three-fourths, or thorough-bred horse of sufficient substance and height, and the produce is the coach-horse most in repute, with his arched crest and high action. From the thorough-bred of sufficient height, but not of so much substance, we obtain the four-in-hand, and superior curricle-horse.

From less height and more substance we have the hunter and better sort of hackney; and, from the half-bred, we derive the machineer, the poster, and the common carriage-horse: indeed, Cleveland, and the Vale of Pickering, in the East Riding of Yorkshire, may be considered as the most decided breeding country in England for coach-horses, hunters, and hackneys."

Again, in his article on the Farmer's Horse, Mr. Y. says: "If he (the farmer) has a superior mare, one of the old Cleveland breed, and puts her to a bony, three-fourths-bred horse, or, if he can find one stout and compact enough, a seven-eighths, or a thorough-bred one. he will have a fair chance to rear a colt that will amply repay him as a hunter or carriage-horse."

In his article on Heavy Draught Horses, Mr. Y. says: "The Cleveland horses have been known to *carry* more than seven hundred pounds sixty miles in twenty-four hours, and to perform this journey four times in a week."

Cleveland Bays were imported into western New York, a few years since, where they have spread considerably. They have often been exhibited at our State Fairs. They are monstrously large, and, for their size, are symmetrical horses, and possess very respectable action. Whether they would endure on the road, at any but a moderate pace, we are not informed, and have some doubts. Whether they spring from the genuine and unmixed Cleveland stock, now so scarce in England, we have no means of knowing. The half-bloods, the produce of a cross with our common mares, are liked by many of our farmers. They are said to make strong, serviceable farm beasts—though rather prone to sullenness of temper.

THE DRAY HORSE.

Of the Heavy Black Dray Horses, but few have been imported into this country, and they do not seem likely to become favorites here. Mr. Youatt says of them:

"The Heavy Black Horse is the last variety it may be necessary to notice. It is bred chiefly in the midland counties from Lincolnshire to Staffordshire. Many are bought up by the Surrey and Berkshire farmers at two years old,—and being worked moderately until they are four, earning their keep all the while, they are then sent to the London market, and sold at a profit of ten or twelve per cent.

It would not answer the *breeder's* purpose to keep them until they are fit for town-work. He has plenty of fillies and mares on his farm for every purpose that he can require; he therefore sells them to a person nearer the metropolis, by whom they are gradually trained and prepared. The traveller has probably wondered to see four of these enormous animals in a line before a plough, on no very heavy soil, and where two lighter horses would have been quite sufficient. The farmer is training them for their future destiny; and he does right in not requiring the exertion of all their strength, for their bones are not yet perfectly formed, nor their joints knit; and were he to urge them too severely, he would probably injure and deform them. By the gen tle and constant exercise of the plough, he is preparing them for that *continued and equable* pull at the collar, which is afterwards so necessary. These horses are adapted more for parade and show, and to gratify the ambition which one brewer has to outvie his neighbor, than for any peculiar utility. They are certainly noble-looking animals, with their round fat carcases, and their sleek coats, and the evident pride which they take in themselves; but they eat a great deal of hay and corn, and at hard and long-continued work they would be completely beaten by a team of active muscular horses an inch and a half lower.

The only plea which can be urged in their favor, beside their fine appearance, is, that as shaft-horses over the badly-paved streets of the metropolis, and with the immense loads they often have behind them, great bulk and weight are necessary to stand the unavoidable shaking and battering. Weight must be opposed to weight, or the horse would sometimes be quite thrown off his legs. A large heavy horse must be in the shafts, and then little ones before him would not look well.

Certainly no one has walked the streets of London without pitying the poor thill-horse, jolted from side to side, and exposed to many a bruise, unless, with admirable cleverness, he accommodates himself to every motion; but, at the same time, it must be evident, that bulk and fat do not always constitute strength, and that a compact muscular horse, approaching to sixteen hands high, would acquit himself far better in such a situation. The dray-horse, in the mere act of ascending from the wharf, may display a powerful effort, but he afterwards makes little exertion, much of his force being expended in transporting his own overgrown mass."

THE AMERICAN TROTTING-HORSE.

Before leaving the consideration of our present topic—the consideration of the principal breeds and varieties of horses now in the United States—we cannot refrain from calling attention to our trotting-horses, though in reality they do not, at least as a whole, constitute a breed, or even a distinct variety or family. There *is* a family of superior trotters, including several the best our country has ever produced, the descendants of Abdallah and Messenger, and running back through their sire Mambrino, to the thorough-bred horse, old Messenger. But many of our best trotters, including the extraordinary animal of which we have given a cut, have no known pedigrees, and some of them, without doubt, are entirely destitute of the blood of the race-horse. Lady Suffolk is by Engineer, but the blood of Engineer is unknown (she is a gray mare, fifteen hands and two inches high). Dutch

SUPERIORITY OF AMERICAN TROTTERS. 41

LADY SUFFOLK.

man has no known pedigree. Other celebrated trotters stand in the same category,—though we are inclined to think that a decided majority of the best, especially at long distances, have a greater or less infusion of the blood of the race-horse.

The United States has undoubtedly produced more superior trotters than any other country in the world, and in no other country has the speed of the best American trotters been equalled. The New York "Spirit of the Times"—the best authority in our country on this and all kindred topics—thus compares the English and American trotters:—

> "Nimrod, in admitting the superiority of our trotting-horses to the 'English,' claims that the English 'approach *very near* to the Americans, even in this breed of cattle. Possibly the characteristic national vanity would not allow him to make a further concession. But there is no comparison whatever between the trotting-horses of the two countries. Mr Wheelan, who took RATTLER to England last season, and doubly distanced with ease every horse that ventured to start against him, as the *record shows*, informs us that there are twenty or more roadsters in common use in this city, that could compete successfully with the fastest trotters on the English turf. They neither understand the art of training, driving, or riding, there. For example: some few years since, ALEXANDER was purchased by Messrs. C. and B. of this city, for a friend or acquaintance, in England. Alexander was a well-known roadster here, and was purchased to order at a low rate. The horse was sent out and trials made of him; but so unsuc

cessful were they, that the English importers considered him an imposition. Thus the matter stood for a year or more. When Wheelan arrived in England, he recognized the horse, and learned the particulars of his purchase and subsequent trials there. By his advice the horse was nominated in a stake at Manchester (we believe) with four or five of the best trotters in England, he (Wheelan) engaging to train and ride him. When the horses came upon the ground, the odds were 4 and 5 to 1 against Alexander, who won by nearly a *quarter of a mile!* Wheelan says he took the track at starting, and widened the gap at his ease—that near the finish, being surprised that no horse was anywhere near him, as his own had not yet made a stroke, he got frightened, thinking some one might outbrush him—that he put Alexander up to his work, and finally won by an immense way, no horse, literally, getting to the head of the quarter stretch, as he came out at the winning stand! The importers of Alexander, at any rate, were so surprised and delighted at his performance, that they presented Wheelan with a magnificent gold timing-watch, and other valuable presents, and sent Messrs. C. and B. a superb service of plate, which may be seen at any time at their establishment in Maiden Lane."

From whence does this superiority of the American trotters spring? Is it from *blood?* This would seem to be disproved from the facts already shown. The American trotter belongs to no particular breed or blood. Many of our celebrated trotters have partaken more or less deeply of the blood of the *English* race-horse. The Abdallah and Messenger family are considerably more than half-bloods—the dams of these horses being also of Messenger blood. Unless it is shown that the unknown or common blood which they possess, has been the *source of their superiority* as trotters, then it is certain that England possesses as good materials as ourselves, so far as blood is concerned, for breeding trotters. The former has never, so far as we are aware, been claimed, and there is not a reasonable doubt that England does possess all the requisite materials to equal us. The difference has been occasioned by management, training, and *attention to this definite object.* On this subject, we quote the following just and highly spirited remarks from a dissertation on American Trotting Horses[*] by that talented but *ill-rewarded* veteran agricultural writer, Hon. J. S. Skinner:—

"According to the theory here maintained, the great number of trotters in America that can go, as before said, their mile under three minutes, and there are many who do it under 2m. 40s., and even in some cases under 2m. 30s.,—as for instance in the case of Ripton and Confidence, whose performances have given so much gratification to sportsmen, is to be explained in the same way that we account for the *great number of superb hunters* that are admitted to abound in England above all countries, not excepting our own. There, in every county in the Kingdom, there are organized "*Hunts*," with their whippers-in, and huntsmen, and earth-stoppers, and

---

[*] See prefatory chapter to the American edition of Youatt on the Horse. Lea & Blanchard: Philadelphia, 1849.

costly appointments of every kind to accommodate some fifty or an hundred couple of high-bred hounds, whose pedigrees are as well preserved as those of Priam or Longwaist; and a wide district of country is reserved and assigned exclusively to each hunt. Fox-hunting is there termed *par excellence*, a princely amusement, and gentlemen of the most exalted rank and largest fortune, take pride in the office of "*Master of the hounds*," and assuredly in all the wide field of manly exercises, none can compare with an English fox or steeple-chase, for union of athletic vigor and daring skill, and magnificence of equitation; unless perhaps it were some splendid *charge de cavalrie*, like those we used to read of, made by the gallant Murat at a critical moment of the battle, when he was wont, in his gorgeous uniform and towering plumes, to fall with his cavalry like an avalanche upon his adversary, confounding and crushing him at a blow! Truly, it would well be worth a trip across the Atlantic, to see a single "turn out" of an English hunt, all in their fair tops, buckskin smalls, and scarlet coats, mounted on hunters that under Tattersall's hammer would command from one to two hundred guineas! Imagine such a field with thirty couple of staunch hounds, heads up and sterns down, all in full cry, and well away with their fox!!

"——————— Now, my brave youths,
Flourish the whip, nor spare the galling spur;
But in the madness of delight, forget
Your fears. Far o'er the rocky hills we range,
And dangerous our course; but in the brave
True courage never fails."

To indicate more strongly the prevalence of this partiality for trotting-horses, and emulation to own the fastest goer, and the number and extent of associations and arrangements for this sort of trial and amusement, it need only be mentioned that the "Spirit of the Times," published in New York, contains lists of matches and purses, and of thousands on thousands of dollars in small purses, won and lost on these performances on *trotting courses!* These performances show that the excellence which is conceded to American trotters, is not founded on a solitary achievement or very rare cases, nor to be ascribed to the possession of any distinct and peculiar breed of horses; but is the natural and common fruit of that union of blood and bone, which forms proverbially the *desideratum* in a good hunter, with the superaddition of *skilful training, much practice*, and *artful jockeying*, for the trotting course. Who can doubt that if Hiram Woodruff were to go to England, having the run of their hunting-stables, he might select nags enough which could soon be made, under his training and consummate jockeyship, to go along with Edwin Forrest and Lady Suffolk, Ripton, Rattler, Confidence, and the Dutchman?"

CHAPTER II.

THE ZOOLOGICAL CLASSIFICATION OF THE HORSE.

[Before commencing the perusal of the following chapters, the reader, and particularly the young reader, is earnestly requested to turn back and read the INTRODUCTION. It is believed that he will there find some highly useful and important hints in regard to the manner of acquiring a full knowledge of the contents of the work,—much of which, comparatively speaking, will be but imperfectly understood by him, without attention to the rules there laid down.—*Am. Ed.*]*

In his zoological classification, the Horse ranks under the division vertebrata—the class mammalia—the tribe ungulata—the order pachydermata—and the family solipeda.

The solipeda consist of several *species*, as the horse, the ass, the mule, and the quagga.

First stands the EQUUS CABALLUS, or COMMON HORSE.

The horse has six *incisors* or *cutting* teeth in the front of each jaw; and one *canine* tooth or *tusk*.

On each side, above and below—at some distance from the incisors, and behind the canines, and with some intervening space—are six *molar* teeth, or grinders; and these molar teeth have flat crowns, with ridges of enamel, and that enamel penetrating into the substance of the tooth.

The whole is thus represented by natural historians:—

HORSE.—Incisors $\frac{6}{6}$, canines $\frac{1-1}{1-1}$, molar $\frac{6-6}{6-6}$. Total, forty teeth.

---

* The work should be read through *in course*, ealier being frequently necessary to explain later portions of it; and he who would derive the full advantage of it, should never pass over a word without understanding its signification. Many of the scientific terms admit of no substitutes—at least without much and frequently recurring circumlocution—and their definitions will usually be found in Webster's dictionary. These should be committed to memory; and especially the *names* of the different parts and tissues. Much less trouble of this kind is necessary, than would be supposed, to r full understanding of the work.

SKELETON OF THE HORSE.

Fig. 1.

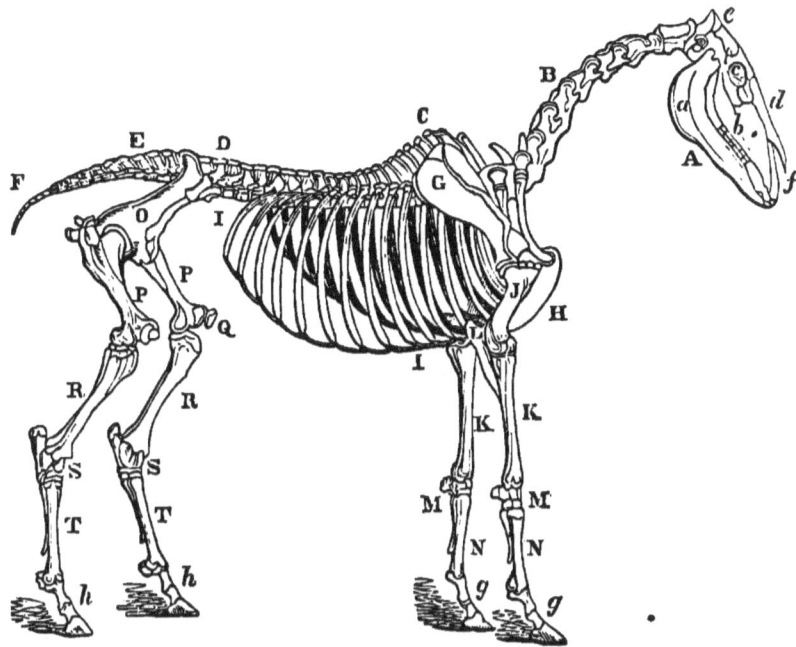

A   The Head.
a   The posterior maxillary or under jaw.
b   The superior maxillary or upper jaw. A little lower down than the letter is a foramen, through which pass the nerves and blood vessels which chiefly supply the lower part of the face.
c   The orbit, or cavity containing the eye.
d   The nasal bones, or bones of the nose.
e   The suture dividing the parietal bones below from the occipital bones above.
f   The inferior maxillary bone, containing the upper incisor teeth.
B   The Seven Cervical Vertebræ, or bones of the neck.
C   The Eighteen Dorsal Vertebræ, or bones of the back.
D   The Six Lumbar Vertebræ, or bones of the loins.
E   The Five Sacral Vertebræ, or bones of the haunch.
F   The Caudal Vertebræ, or bones of the tail, generally about fifteen.
G   The Scapula, or shoulder-blade.
H   The Sternum, or fore-part of the chest.
I   The Costæ, or ribs, seven or eight articulating with the sternum, and called the *true ribs*, and ten or eleven united together by cartilage, called the *false ribs*.
J   The Humerus, or upper bone of the arm.
K   The Radius, or upper bone of the arm.
L   The Ulna, or elbow. The point of the elbow is called the Olecranon.
M   The Carpus, or knee, consisting of seven bones.
N   The Metacarpal bones. The larger metacarpal or cannon or shank in front, and the smaller metacarpal or splint bone behind.

g The fore pastern and foot, consisting of the Os Suffraginis, or the upper and larger pastern bone, with the sesamoid bones behind, articulating with the cannon and greater pastern; the Os Coronæ, or lesser pastern; the Os Pedis, or coffin bone; and the Os Naviculare, or navicular, or shuttle-bone, not seen, and articulating with the smaller pastern and coffin bones.
h The corresponding bones of the hind-feet.
O The Haunch, consisting of three portions, the Ilium, the Ischium, and the Pubis.
P The Femur, or thigh.
Q The stifle joint with the Patella.
R The Tibia, or proper leg bone—behind is a small bone called the fibula.
S The Tarsus, or hock, composed of six bones. The prominent part is the Os Calcis, or point of the hock.
T The Metatarsals of the hind leg.

THE SENSORIAL FUNCTION

An accurate knowledge of what constitutes the just structure of the horse—the form and connection of parts on which strength, or fleetness, or stoutness, must necessarily depend, is claimed by nearly all who have had anything to do with this noble animal; but in reality it is possessed by very few.

In speaking of the structure of this animal, and the points which guide the opinion of real judges of him, we shall, as briefly and as simply as we are able, explain those fundamental principles on which his usefulness and beauty must depend. We require one kind of horse for slow and heavy draught, and another for lighter and quicker work; one as a pleasant and safe roadster—another, with more speed and equal continuance, as a hunter—and another still is wanted for the race-course. What is the peculiarity of structure—what are the particular points that will fit each for his proper business, and, to a certain degree, unfit him for everything else? The farmer will require a horse of *all-work*, that can carry him to market and take him round his farm—on which he can occasionally ride for pleasure, and which he must sometimes degrade to the dung-cart or the harrow. What combination of powers will enable the animal to discharge most of these duties well, and all of them to a certain extent profitably?

Much time spent among horses, an acquired love of them, and a little, sometimes possibly too dearly-bought experience, may give the agriculturist some insight into these matters. And we shall try to render him some useful assistance in this affair—to teach him why certain points must be good or bad—and to induce him to discard many common but dangerous errors and prejudices. It is only by being well acquainted with the structure and anatomy of the horse, that we can appreciate his shape and uses, or understand the different diseases to which he is liable.

The nervous system will first pass in review, for it is the moving power of the whole machine. It consists of the *brain*, to which all sensation is referred or carried, and from which all voluntary motion is derived—the spinal cord, a prolongation of the brain, and thus connected with sensation and voluntary motion, governing all the involuntary motions of the frame, and by power from which the heart beats, and the lungs heave, and the stomach digests; and one other system of nerves—the ganglionic —presiding over the functions of secretion and of nutrition, and the repair and the welfare of the frame generally.

THE HEAD.—The following cut represents the head of the horse divided into the numerous bones of which it is composed, and the boundaries of each bone clearly marked by the sutures which connect it with those around. It is composed of nine bones.

Fig. 2.

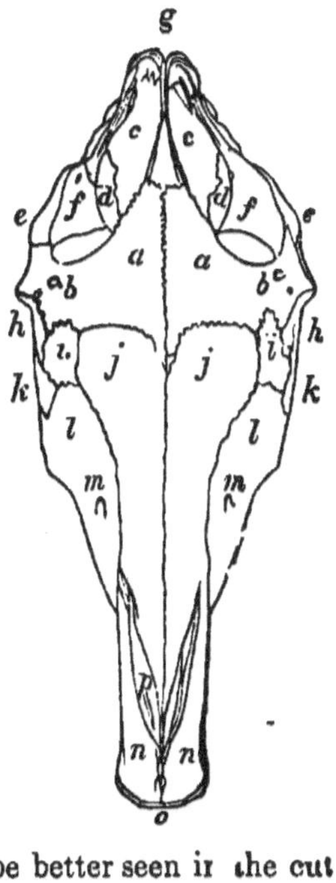

a a The frontal bones, or bones of the forehead.
b b The supra-orbital foramina or holes above the orbit, through which the nerves and blood-vessels supplying the forehead pass out. The small hole beneath receives the vessels which dip into and supply the bone.
c c The parietal bones, or walls of the skull.
d d The temporal bones, or bones of the temples.
e e The zygomatic, or yoke-shaped arch.
f f The temporal fossa, or pit above the eye.
g g The occipital bone, or bone of the hinder part of the head.
h h The orbits containing and defending the eye.
i i The lachrymal bones belonging to the conveyance of the tears from the eyes.
j j The nasal bones, or bones of the nose.
k k The malar, or cheek-bones.
l l The superior maxillary, or that portion of the upper jaw containing the molar teeth or grinders.
m m The infra-orbital foramen—a hole below the orbit, through which pass branches of nerves and blood-vessels to supply the lower part of the face.
n n The inferior maxillary, the lower part of the upper jaw-bone—a separate bone in quadrupeds, containing the incisor or cutting teeth, and the upper tushes at the point of union between the superior and inferior maxillaries.
o The upper incisor or cutting teeth.
p The openings into the nose, with the bones forming the palate.

The ethmoid and sphenoid bones will be better seen in the cut Fig. 3.

There is an evident intention in this division of the head into so many bones. When the fœtus—the unborn foal—first begins to have life, that which afterwards becomes bone, is a mere jelly-like substance. This is gradually changed into a harder material —cartilage; and, before the birth of the animal, much of the cartilage is taken away by vessels called absorbents, and bone deposited in its stead. In flat bones, like those of the head, this deposit takes place in the centre, and rays or radiations of bone extend thence in every direction. Then, by having so many bones, there are so many centres of radiation; and, consequently, the formation of bone is carried on so much the more rapidly, and perfected at the time when the necessities of the animal require it. At the period of birth, however, this process is not completed, out the edges of the bones remain somewhat soft and pliant, and therefore, in parturition, they yield a little and overlap each other, and thus, by rendering the birth more easy, they save the mother much pain, and contribute to the safety of the foal.

The frontal bones are united by a curious and intricate dovetailing to defend from injury the brain which lies beneath the upper part of them. Lower down, and where the cavity of the nose is only to be defended, their union is sufficient, but far less complicated. Here we have a proof of wise design.

Few things more clearly indicate the breed or blood of the horse than the form of the frontal bones. Who has not remarked the broad angular forehead of the blood horse, giving him a beautiful expression of intelligence and fire, and the face gradually tapering from the forehead to the muzzle, contrasted with the large face of the cart or dray-horse, and the forehead scarcely wider than the face?

At f, between the frontal bones, is the pit or cavity above the eye, and by the depth of which we form some idea of the age of the horse. There is placed at the back of the eye, a considerable quantity of fatty substance, on which it may revolve easily and without friction. In aged horses, and in diseases attended with general loss of condition, much of this disappears; the eye becomes sunken, and the pit above it deepens.

The sinuses on the different sides of the forehead do not communicate with each other, but with other sinuses in the ethmoid, and sphenoid, and upper jaw-bones, and also with the cavities of the nose on their respective sides. These sinuses afford a somewhat increased protection to the brain beneath; and by the continuous and slightly projecting line which they form, they give beauty to the forehead; but their principal use probably is, like the windings of the French horn, to increase the clearness and loudness of the neighing. It will be remarked that they are very irregular in depth, which at one place is an inch or more.

In the sheep, and occasionally in the ox—rarely in the horse — the larvæ of maggots, produced by certain species of flies, crawl up the nose, lodge themselves in these sinuses, and produce intolerable pain.

Veterinary surgeons have availed themselves of these sinuses to detect the existence of glanders in doubtful cases. If the horse is glandered, there will probably be a considerable ulceration in the upper part of the cavity of the nose, and a collection of matter there. This is ascertained by making an opening into the sinuses, which may be done with perfect safety. [See Glanders.]

Section of the Head.

Fig. 3.

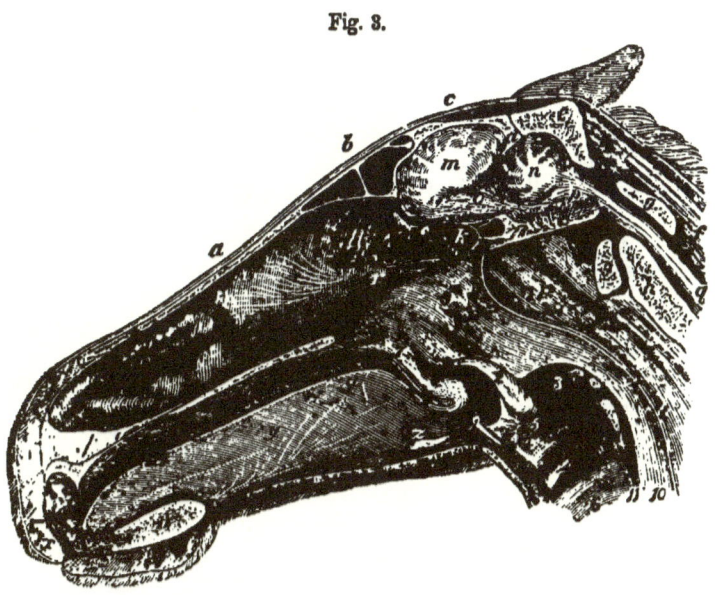

a The nasal bone, or bone of the nose.
b The frontal bone. The cavities or cells beneath are called the frontal sinuses
c The crest or ridge of the parietal bones.
d The tentorium or bony separation between the cerebrum and cerebellum.
e The occipital bone.
f The ligament of the neck, or *pack-wax*, by which the head is chiefly supported
g The atlas, *sustaining* or *carrying:* the first bone of the neck.
h The dentata, *tooth-like*, or second bone of the neck.
i The cuneiform, or *wedge-shaped* process, or base of the occipital bone. Between it and the other portion of the occipital bone, e, lies the great foramen or aperture through which the prolongation of the brain—the spinal marrow—issues from the skull.
k The sphenoid, *wedge-like*, bone, with its cavities.
l The ethmoid, *sieve-like*, bone, with its cells.
m The cerebrum, or brain, with the appearance of its cortical and medullary substance.
n The cerebellum, or little brain, with its beautiful arborescent appearance.
o A portion of the central medullary, *marrow-like*, substance of the brain, and the prolongation of it under the name of the crus cerebri, *leg of the brain*, and from which many of the nerves take their origin.
p The medulla oblongata—the prolongation of the brain after the medullary substance of the cerebrum and cerebellum have united, and forming the commencement of the spinal marrow. The columnar appearance

of this portion of the brain is represented, and the origins of the respiratory nerves.
q The spinal marrow extending through a canal in the centre of the bones of the neck, back, and loins, to the extremities of the tail, and from which the nerves of feeling and of motion, that supply every part of the frame except the head, arise.
r The septum narium, or cartilaginous division between the nostrils.
s The same cut off at the lower part, to show the spongy turbinated, *turban shaped*, bones, filling the cavity of the nostril.
t The palate.
u The molar-teeth, or grinders.
v The inferior maxillary bone, containing the incisor teeth, or nippers. The canine tooth, or tush, is concealed by the tongue.
w The posterior maxillary, or lower jaw with its incisors.
x The lips.
y The tongue.
z A portion of the os hyoides, or bone of the tongue, *like a Greek u, v.*
1 The thyroid, *helmet-shaped*, cartilage, enclosing and shielding the neighboring parts.
2 The epiglottis, or *covering of the glottis*, or aperture of the wind-pipe.
3 The artyenoid, *funnel-shaped*, cartilages, having between them the aperture leading into the trachea or wind-pipe.
4 One of the chordæ vocales, *cords* or ligaments concerned in the formation *of the voice.*
5 The sacculus laryngis, sac or *ventricle* of the larynx, (*throat*, to modulate the voice.
6 The trachea, or wind-pipe, with its different rings.
7 The soft palate at the back of the mouth, so constru ted as almost to prevent the possibility of vomiting.
8 The opening from the back part of the mouth into the nostril.
9 The cartilage covering the entrance into the eustachia tube, or communication between the mouth and internal part of the ear.
10 The œsophagus, or gullet.
11 The cricoid, *ring-like*, cartilage, below and behind th thyroid.
12 Muscle of the neck, covered by the membrane of the back part of the mouth.

As the frontal sinuses are lined by a continuation of the membrane of the nose, they will sympathize with many of the affections of that cavity; but the membrane of the sinuses is susceptible of an inflammation peculiar to itself. The disease is rare, and the cause of it has not been fully ascertained. It is oftenest metastasis of inflammation of the brain,—shifting of inflammation from the brain to the membrane of the sinus, or communication of inflammation from the brain by proximity of situation.

INFLAMMATION OF THE MEMBRANE OF THE FRONTAL SINUSES. —The attack is usually sudden—the horse is dull, lethargic, and almost as comatose as in stomach-staggers. The first thing that excites suspicion of the actual character of the disease, is heat in the situation of the frontal sinus, when the hand is placed on the forehead. The lethargy soon passes over, and a state of the highest excitation succeeds. The conjunctiva and the membrane of the nose are injected—the pulse is quick and hard—the horse becomes violent and dangerous; he kicks, plunges, and, half conscious and half unconscious, he endeavors to do all the mischief that he can. The disease is now evidently combined with, or is essentially, inflammation of the brain. It is distinguished from madness by this half-consciousness, and also by his being more disposed to bite than he is in pure phrenitis.

The disease is usually fatal. It rarely lasts more than eight-and-forty hours.

The *post-mortem* appearances are, great inflammation of the brain, with frequent effusions of blood. The sinuses are sometimes filled with coagulated blood. The brain seems to be affected just in proportion to the violence which the animal has exhibited.

The treatment should consist of copious bleeding, application of ice to the head, blistering the head, and physic. The trephine is scarcely admissible, from the danger of producing greater irritation.

Sometimes the disease assumes a more chronic form. There is ulceration of the membrane, but not cerebral affection. A purulent discharge then appears from the nose, evidently not of a glanderous character, and none of the submaxillary glands are enlarged. In both the acute and chronic form, it is usually confined to one sinus.

The inner plate of the frontal bone covers a considerable portion of the anterior part of the brain, and it is studded with depressions corresponding with irregularities on the surface of the brain.

Immediately above the frontal, and extending from the frontal to the poll, are the *parietal* bones. They are two, united together by a suture when the animal is young, but that suture soon becoming obliterated. They are of a closer and harder texture than the frontals, because they are more exposed to injury, and more concerned in defending the brain.

A very small portion only of the *parietals* is naked, and that is composed of bone even harder than the other part, and with an additional layer of bone rising in the form of a crest or ridge externally. Every other part of these bones is covered by a thick mass of muscle, the *temporal* muscle, which is principally concerned in chewing the food, but which, likewise, by its yielding resistance, speedily and effectually breaks the force of the most violent blow.

On the side of the head, and under the parietals ($d\ d$, Fig. 3), are the *temporal bones*, one on each side, ff. These again are divided into two parts, or consist of two distinct bones; the *petrous* portion, so called from its great or *stony* hardness, and containing the wonderful mechanism of the ear, and the *squamous* portion, from the appearance of its union with the parietal, overlapping it like a great *scale*.

From the latter there projects a portion of bone, *e* which

unites with the frontal, and forms a strong arch—the zygomatic—distinctly to be felt at the side of the head, immediately above the eye. This arch is designed to protect the upper part of the lower jaw, the motion of which may very plainly be seen beneath it when the horse is feeding.

At the base of the arch is an important cavity not visible in the cut, receiving into it, and forming a joint with, the head of the lower jaw—it will be presently described.

Having reached the base of the temporal bone, it is found united to the parietal, not by a simple suture, as the lower part of the frontals, or the bones of the nose (see fig. a and j, Fig. 2), nor by a dove-tailed suture, as the upper part of the frontals (see the same cut), but it is spread over the parietal in the form of a large scale, and hence, as before observed, called the *squamous* portion of the temporal bone. In fact, there are two plates of bone instead of one. Was there design in this? Yes, evidently so. In the first place, to increase the strength of the base of the *zygomatic* arch. This extensive union between the temporal and parietal bones, resembles the buttress or mass of masonry attached to the base of every arch, in order to counteract its lateral pressure. The concussion, likewise, which might be communicated by a blow on the top of the arch, is thus spread over a large surface, and consequently weakened and rendered comparatively harmless; and that surface is composed of the union of two bones of dissimilar construction. The hard *stony* structure of the parietal is very different from the tougher material of the temporal; and thus, as a finger acts on a sounding-glass, the vibration communicated to the temporal is at once stopped, and the brain receives no injury.

There is another proof of admirable design. Where is this *squamous* portion of the temporal bone situated? On the side of the head. And what is the figure of the cranium or skull, and principally that part of it which contains the cerebrum or brain? It is an elliptical or oval arch (see fig. m, n, o, Fig. 3). If pressure is made on the crown of that arch—if a blow is received on the suture between the parietals sufficient to cause the elastic materials of which the skull is composed to yield—the seat of danger and injury is at the side. If a man receives a violent blow on the crown or back part of the head, the fracture, if there is any, is generally about the temple, and the extravasation of blood is oftenest found there. The following figure will explain this:—

Let the line A B C represent an elliptical arch, composed of elastic materials. Some force shall be applied at B, sufficient to cause it to yield. We cannot compress it into smaller compass; but just in proportion as it yields at B, will it spur or bulge out at

D, and give way sometimes as represented at E. In a dome the weight of the materials constantly acting may be considered as representing the force applied at B; and so great is the lateral pressure, or tendency to bulge out (*vide* D and E), that it is necessary either to dove-tail the materials into one another, or to pass strong iron chains round them. For want of sufficient attention to this, "the dome of St. Sophia in Constantinople, built in the time of the emperor Justinian, fell three times during its erection; and the dome of the cathedral of Florence stood unfinished an hundred and twenty years, for want of an architect."

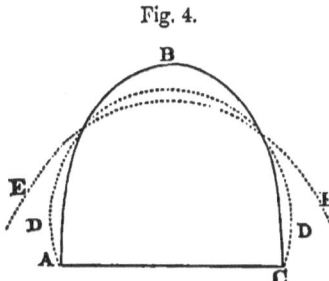

Fig. 4.

Nature, in the construction of the horse's head, has taken away the pressure, or removed the probability of injury, by giving an additional layer of bone, or a mass of muscle, where alone there was danger, and has dove-tailed all the materials. Farther than this, in order to make assurance doubly sure, she has placed this effectual girder at the base, in the overlapping of the squamous portion of the temporal bone.

Above the *parietals*, and separated from them by a suture (fig. g, Fig. 2, and fig. e, Fig. 3), is the *occipital* bone. Superiorly it covers and protects the smaller portion of the brain, the cerebellum; and as it there constitutes the summit or crest of the head, and is particularly exposed to danger, and not protected by muscles, it is. interesting to see what thickness it assumes. The head of the horse does not, like that of the human being, ride upright on the neck, with all its weight supported by the spinal column; but it hangs in a slanting position from the extremity of the neck, and the neck itself projects a considerable distance from the chest. and thus the whole weight of the head and neck is suspended from the chest, and require very great power in order to support them.

How is this weight to be supported?

From the back of the occipital bone (fig. *f*, Fig. 3), and immediately below the crest, proceeds a round cord of considerable bulk, and composed of a ligamentous substance, which reaches down and is securely attached to the spines of the vertebræ, or bones of the back; and by this ligament—the *ligamentum colli*, ligament of the neck—the head is supported.

There are, however, some admirable contrivances connected with this ligament. As it proceeds from the head, it is in the form of a round cord.. It passes over the *atlas*, or first bone of the neck, without touching it, and then, attaching itself strongly to the second bone, principally supports the head by its union with this bone. The mechanical disadvantage is increased; but the head is turned more freely on the first and second bones The principal stress is on the *dentata* or second bone, so much so, that in poll-evil, this ligament may be divided without serious inconvenience to the horse. It then suddenly sinks deeper, and communicates with all the other vertebræ. Each of these communications becomes a separate point of support, and as they approach nearer to the base, the mechanical disadvantage, or the force with which the weight of the head and neck presses and acts, is materially lessened.

The head, then, while the animal is in a state of rest, is supported by this ligament, without any aid from muscular energy. It differs from the other ligaments of the body, in the fact that it is *elastic*. It stretches full two inches longer when the horse is browsing, and resumes its natural dimensions when the head is held erect.

The ligament of the neck is inserted into the centre of the back part of the occipital bone, and immediately below the vertex or crest of that bone; and therefore the bone is so thick at this part (see fig. *e*, Fig 3).

Many large and powerful muscles are necessary to turn the head in various directions, as well as to assist in raising it when depressed. The occipital bone, as will be seen in the cut, presents a spine running down the centre, B, and a large roughened surface for the attachment of these muscles, C C.

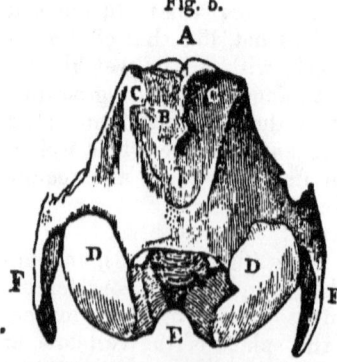

Fig. 5.

Lower down, and still at the back of the occipital bone, are two rounded protuberances D D, by which the head is connected with the *atlas*, or upper or first vertebra, or bone of the neck; and these are called the *condyloid*, cup-shaped, processes of the occipital bone. All the motions of the head are partly, and many of them wholly, performed by this joint.

Between them is a large hole, the *foramen magnum*, or great aperture, E, through which the continuation of the brain, termed the spinal cord or marrow, passes out of the skull.

As an additional contrivance to support the enormous weight of the head, are two other projections of the occipital bone, peculiar to animals whose heads are set on in a slanting direction, and into which powerful muscles are inserted. They are called the *coracoid*, beak-like, processes or prolongations, F F, of the occipital bone.

Running forward, and forming outwardly a part of the base, and inwardly a portion of the floor of the skull, is what, from its wedge-like shape, is called the *cuneiform* process of the occipital bone (fig. *i*, Fig. 3). It is thick, strong, and solid, and placed at the bottom of the skull, not only to be a proper foundation for, and to give additional strength to, the arch on either side, but speedily to stop all vibration and concussion.

At the base of the skull, and anterior to or below the *occipital*, lies the *sphenoid*, wedge-like bone (fig. *k*, Fig. 3). Its body, likewise called the *cuneiform* or wedge-shaped process, is a continuation of the same process of the occipital, and, like it, is thick and solid, and for the same important purpose. This bone branches out into four irregular bodies or plates, two of which are called the *wings*, and two running to the palate, the legs. They could not be represented in the cut, and there is nothing important belonging to them, so far as this work is concerned. Internally (fig. *k*), the sphenoid forms a portion of the cavity of the skull.

Of the *ethmoid*, sieve-like, bone, little can be seen outwardly. A small portion is found in the back part of the orbit, and in the cavity of the cranium; but the most important part of it is that which is composed of a great number of thin plates, forming numerous cavities or cells (fig. *l*, Fig. 3), lined with the membrane of the nose, and entering into its cavity. The upper portion is called the cribriform or sieve-shaped plate, from its being perforated by a multitude of little holes, through which the nerve connected with smelling passes and spreads over the nose.

Altogether these bones form a cavity of an irregular oval shape, but the tentorium penetrating into it, gives it the appearance of being divided into two (*d*, Fig. 3).

The cavity of the skull may be said to be arched all round. The builder knows the strength which is connected with the form of an arch. If properly constructed, it is equal to a solid mass of masonry. The arch of a horse's skull has not much weight to support, but it is exposed to many injuries from the brutality of those by whom he should be protected, and from accidental causes.

On raising any part of the skull of the horse, the dense and strong membrane which is at once the lining of the cranium and the covering of the brain—the *dura mater*—presents itself. It is united to the membranes below by numerous little cords or prolongations of its substance, conveying blood and communicating strength to the parts beneath. Between this membrane common to the cranium and the brain, and the proper investing tunic of that organ, is found that delicate gossamer's web, appropriately called the *arachnoid*—the spider's membrane—and which is seen in other animals, designed either to secrete the fluid which is interposed, for the purpose of obviating injurious concussion, or perhaps, to prevent the brain from readily sympathizing with any inflammatory action produced by injury of the skull.

Beneath is the proper investing membrane of the brain—the *pia mater*—which not only covers the external surface of the brain, but penetrates into every depression, lines every ventricle, and clothes every irregularity and part and portion of the brain.

THE BRAIN.—We now arrive at the brain itself. The brain of the horse corresponds with the cavity in which it is placed (*m*, Fig. 3). It is a flattened oval. It is divided into two parts, one much larger than the other—the *cerebrum* or brain, and the *cerebellum* or little brain (*n*, Fig. 3). The brain of a horse is only about half the size and weight of that of a man.

When the brain is cut, it is found to be composed of two substances very unlike in appearance (*m*, Fig. 3); one, principally on the outside, gray, or ash-colored, and therefore called the *cortical* (*bark-like*) from its situation, and *cineritious* (*ashen*) from its color; and the other, lying deeper in the brain, and from its pulpy nature called the *medullary* substance. Although placed in apposition with each other, and seemingly mingling, they never run into the same mass, or change by degrees into one another, but are essentially distinct in construction as well as in function.

The *medullary* portion is connected with the nervous system. The nerves are prolongations of it, and are concerned in the discharge of all the offices of life. They give motion and energy to the limbs, the heart, the lungs, the stomach, and every part connected with life. They are the medium through which sensation is conveyed; and they supply the mind with materials to think and work upon.

The *cineritious* part has a different appearance, and is differently constituted. Some have supposed, and with much appearance of truth, that it is the residence of the mind—receiving the impressions that are conveyed to the brain by the sensitive nerves, and directing the operation and action of those which give motion to the limbs.

From the medullary substance—as already stated—proceed certain cords or prolongations, termed *nerves*, by which the animal is enabled to receive impressions from surrounding objects, and to connect himself with them; and also to possess many pleasurable or painful sensations. One of them is spread over the membrane of the nose, and gives the sense of smell; another expands on the back of the eye, and the faculty of sight is gained; and a third goes to the internal structure of the ear, and the animal is conscious of sound. Other nerves, proceeding to different parts, give the faculty of motion, while an equally important one bestows the power of feeling.

One division of nerves (h, Fig. 3), springing from a prolongation of the brain, and yet within the skull, wanders to different parts of the frame, for important purposes connected with respiration or breathing. The act of breathing is essential to life, and were it to cease, the animal would die. These are nerves of *involuntary* motion; so that, whether he is awake or asleep, conscious of it or not, the lungs heave and life is supported. Lastly, from the spinal cord q—a farther prolongation of the brain, and running through a cavity in the bones of the neck, back, and loins, and extending to the very tip of the tail—other nerves are given off at certain intervals. The cut below delineates a pair of them. The spinal cord a, is combined of six distinct columns

Fig. 6.

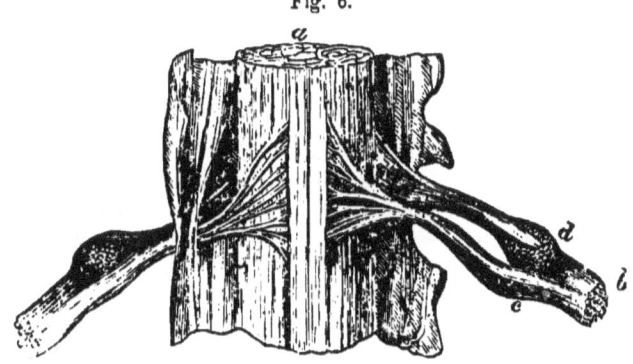

or rods, running through its whole length—three on either side The two upper columns—the portion of spinal marrow represented in our cut, is supposed to be placed with its inner or lower surface towards us—proceed from those tracks of the brain devoted to sensation. Numerous distinct fibres spring abruptly from the column, and which collect together, and, passing through a little ganglion or enlargement, d—an enlargement of a nervous cord is called a ganglion—become a nerve of sensation. From the lower or inner side,—a prolongation of the track devoted to motion,—proceed other fibres, which also collect gradually together, and form a nervous cord, c, giving the power of motion. Beyond the ganglion the two unite, and form a perfect spinal nerve, *b*, possessing the power both of sensation and motion; and the fibres of the two columns proceed to their destination, enveloped in the same sheath, and apparently one nerve. Our cut, closely examined, will give at *b* some idea of the manner in which these distinct fibres are continued;—each covered by its own membrane, but all enveloped in a common envelope.

All these nerves are organs of sensation and motion alone; but there are others whose origin seems to be outside of and below the brain. These are the *sympathetic*, so called from their union and sympathy with all the others, and identified with life itself. They proceed from a small ganglion or enlargement in the upper part of the neck, or from a collection of little ganglia in the abdomen. They go to the heart, and it beats, and to the stomach, and it digests. They form a net-work round each blood-vessel, and the current flows on. They surround the very minutest vessels, and the frame is nourished and built up. They are destitute of sensation, and they are perfectly beyond the control of the will.

The reader, we trust, will now comprehend this wonderful, yet simple machinery, and be able, by and by, to refer to it the explanation of several diseases, and particularly of the operation to which we have referred.

Two of the senses have their residence in the cavity of the cranium—those of hearing and sight.

THE EAR.—They who know anything of the horse, pay much attention to the size, setting on, and motion of the ear. Ears rather small than large—placed not too far apart—erect and quick in motion, indicate both breeding and spirit; and if a horse is frequently in the habit of carrying one ear forward, and the other backward, and especially if he does so on a journey, he will generally possess both spirit and continuance.

The ear of the horse is more intelligible even than the eye, in indicating his temper and intentions. His hearing is remarkably acute. The cartilage of the ear is attached to the head by ligaments and sustained by muscles, on which its action depends. The ear is covered by skin thinner than in most other parts of the body, and is destitute of other tissues unnecessarily increasing its bulk and weight. Under the skin are glands that secrete and throw out a white greasy matter, destined to keep the parts supple and smooth. Below this are other glands which deposit *the wax*, which is supposed to be necessary to deter insects from crawling into the ear, by its offensiveness to them, or by mechanically arresting their progress. Long hair standing across the inner passage of the ear in every direction, keeps out insects, cold, and properly breaks sounds striking on the membrane covering the drum of the ear. It should not therefore be cut out, as is sometimes customary.

The sound, collected by the outer ear, is conveyed through the external auditory passage to the *membrana tympani*—the membrane of the drum, stretching across and closing the external passage. Between this and another membrane still deeper in the ear, are four little bones, highly elastic, and covered with a highly elastic cartilage, by means of which the vibrations of sound are conveyed more perfectly than they would be through the mere air of the cavity.

It is conveyed to a strangely irregular cavity, filled with an aqueous fluid, and the substance or pulp of the *portio mollis* or soft portion of the seventh pair of nerves, the *auditory* nerve, expands on the membrane that lines the walls of this cavity.

Sound is propagated far more intensely through water than through air; and therefore it is that an aqueous fluid occupies those chambers of the ear on the walls of which the auditory nerve is expanded.

THE EYE —The *Eye* is a most important organ, and comes next under consideration, as enclosed in the bones of the skull. The eye of the horse should be large, somewhat but not too prominent, and the eyelid fine and thin. If the eye is sunk in the head, and *apparently* little—for there is actually a very trifling difference in the size of the eye in animals of the same species and bulk, and that seeming difference arises from the larger or smaller opening between the lids—and the lid is thick, and especially if there is any puckering towards the inner corner of the lids, that eye either is diseased, or has lately been subject to inflammation; and, particularly, if one eye is smaller than the other, it has, at no great distance of time, been inflamed.

The eye of the horse enables us with tolerable accuracy to guess at his temper. If much of the white is seen, the buyer should pause ere he completes his bargain; for horses exhibiting this characteristic are usually found vicious-tempered.

The eyes are placed at the side of the head, but the direction of the conoid cavity which they occupy, and of the sheath by which they are surrounded within the orbit, gives them a prevailing direction forwards, so that the animal has a very extended field of vision.

The eye-ball is placed in the anterior and most capacious part of the orbit, nearer to the frontal than the temporal side, with a degree of prominence varying with different individuals, and the will of the animal. It is protected by a bony socket beneath and on the inside, but is partially exposed on the roof and on the outside. It is, however, covered and secured by thick and powerful muscles—by a mass of adipose matter which is distributed to va nous parts of the orbit, upon which the eye may be readily moved without friction and by a sheath of considerable density and firmness, and especially where it is most needed, on the external and superior portions.

In front, the eye is supported and covered by the lids, which closing rapidly, protect it from many an injury that threatens and supply it with that moisture which is necessary to preserve its transparency.

Extending round both lids, and, it may be almost said, having neither origin nor insertion, is a muscle called the *orbicularis*, or circular muscle. Its office is to close the lids in the act of winking or otherwise, but only while the animal is awake. When he sleeps, this is effected by another and very ingenious mechanism. The natural state of the eyelids is that of being closed ; and they are kept open by the energy of the muscles whose office it is to raise the upper lid. As sleep steals upon the animal, these muscles cease to act, and the lids close by the inherent elasticity of the membrane of which they are composed.

The skin of the lid is, like that of the ear, exceedingly fine, in order to prevent unnecessary weight and pressure on such a part, and to give more easy and extensive motion.

The horse has no *eye-brows*, and the eye-lashes are peculiarly arranged to guard against the ingress of too much light, or of insects, and therefore should never be clipped, as is the custom with some senseless grooms in England.

There is a beautiful contrivance about the horse's eye, to clear it of dust, insects, and other foreign matters. Concealed within its inner corner, or only the margin of it, black or pied, visible is a triangular-shaped cartilage, the *haw*, with its broad part forwards. It is concave within, exactly to suit the globe of the eye; it is convex without, acurately to adapt itself to the membrane lining the lid; and the base of it is reduced to a thin or almost sharp edge. At the will of the animal this is suddenly protruded from its hiding-place. It passes rapidly over the eye, and shovels up every nuisance mixed with the tears, and then, being speedily drawn back, the dust or insect is wiped away as the cartilage again passes under the corner of the eye.

The *haw* has no muscle attached to it to thrust it forward or draw it dack. When that powerful muscle which the horse possesses in common with other quadrupeds, for the purpose of drawing back the eye, or causing it to recede into its socket, when threatened with danger, is brought into action, the eye presses upon the fatty matter below it, and as a portion of that fatty matter is peculiarly accumulated about the inner corner of the eye, it is forced outward in that direction and drives the haw before it. Being pressed between the eye and a polished bone, it shoots out with the velocity of lightning, and guided by the lids, projects over the eye, and clears it of offending matter. When the muscle which draws in the eye ceases to act, the eye resumes its natural situation in the orbit. There is room for the fatty matter to return to its place, and it immediately returns by the elasticity of the membrane by which it is covered, and draws after it this cartilage with which it is connected, and whose return is as rapid as was the projection.

The old farriers strangely misunderstood the nature and design of the haw, and many at the present day do not seem to be much better informed. When, from sympathy with other parts of the eye laboring under inflammation, and becoming itself inflamed and increased in bulk, and the neighboring parts likewise thickened, it is either forced out of its place, or voluntarily protruded to defend the eye from the action of light and cannot return, they mistake it for some injurious excrescence or tumor, and proceed to cut it out. The "*haw* in the eye" is a disease well known to the majority of grooms, and this sad remedy for it is deemed the only cure. It is a barbarous practice, and if they were compelled to walk half a dozen miles in a thick dust, without being permitted to wipe or to cleanse the eye, they would feel the torture to which they doom this noble animal. A little patience having been exercised, and a few cooling applications made to the eye while the inflammation lasted, and afterwards some mild astringent ones, and other proper means being employed, the tumor would have disappeared, the haw would have returned to its place, and the animal would have discharged the duties required of him without inconvenience to himself, instead of the agony to which an unguarded and unprotected eye must now expose him.

The loss of blood occasioned by the excision of the haw may frequently relieve the inflammation of the eye; and the evident amendment which follows induces these wise men to believe that they have performed an excellent operation; but the same loss of blood by scarification of the overloaded vessels of the conjunctiva would be equally beneficial, and the animal would not be deprived of an instrument of admirable use to him.

The eye is of a globular figure, yet not a perfect globe. It is rather composed of parts of two globes; the half of one of them smaller and transparent in front, and of the other larger and the coat of it opaque, behind. We shall most conveniently begin with the coats of the eye.

The *conjunctiva*, *f* (Fig. 7), is that membrane which lines the lids, and covers the fore-part of the eye. It spreads over all that we can see or feel of the eye, and even the transparent part. It is itself transparent, and transmits the color of the parts beneath It is very susceptible of inflammation.

THE EYE.

Fig. 7.

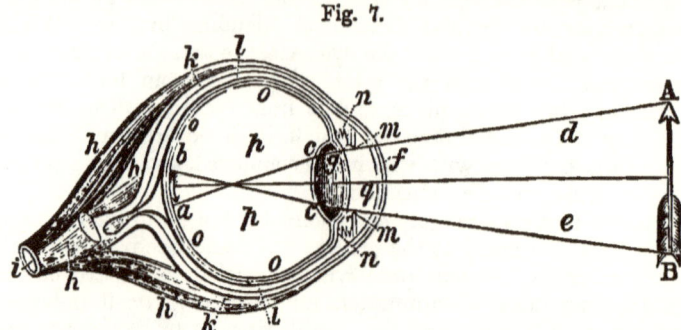

A B a supposed object viewed by the animal, and an inverted image of which, *a b*. is thrown on the retina at the back of the eye.
c c The points where the rays, having passed the cornea and lens, converge by the refractive power of the lens.
d e The rays proceeding from the extremities of the object to the eye.
f The *cornea*, or horny and transparent part of the eye, covered by the *conjunctiva*, uniting different parts together.
g The crystalline (crystal or glassy) lens, behind the pupil, and in front of the vitreous humor.
h h Muscles of the eye.
i The optic nerve, or nerve of sight.
k The *sclerotica* (hard firm coat) covering the whole of the eye except the portion occupied by the cornea, and being a seeming prolongation of the covering of the optic nerve.
l The *choroides* (receptacle or covering), or choroid coat, covered with a black secretion or paint.
m m The *iris* or rainbow-colored circular membrane under the cornea, in front of the eye, and on which the color of the eye depends. The duplicature behind is the *uvea*, from being colored like a grape. The opening in the centre is the pupil.
n n The ciliary (hair-like) processes.
o The *retina*, or net-like expansion of the optic nerve, spread over the whole of the choroides as far as the lens.
p The vitreous (glass-like) humor filling the whole of the cavity of the eye behind the lens.
q The aqueous (water-like) humor filling the space between the cornea and the lens.

Covering the back part of the eye, and indeed four fifths of the globe of it, is the *sclerotica*, *k*.

The *cornea* is, or we would wish it to be, the only visible part of the horse's eye. It fills up the vacuity which is left by the sclerotica in the fore-part of the eye, and, although closely united to the sclerotica, may be separated from it, and will drop out like a watch-glass. Its convexity or projection is a point of considerable importance, as we shall hereafter have occasion to see

It should be perfectly transparent. Any cloudiness or opacity is the consequence of disease. There is nothing that deserves attention from the purchaser of a horse more than its perfect transparency over the whole of its surface. The eye should be examined for this purpose both in front, and with the face of the examiner close to the cheek of the horse, under and behind the eye. The latter method of looking through the cornea is the most satisfactory, so far as the transparency of that part of the eye is concerned. During this examination the horse should not be in the open air, but in the stable standing in the doorway and a little within the door. If any small, faint, whitish lines appear to cross the cornea, or spread over any part of it, they are assuredly the remains of previous inflammation; or, although the centre and bulk of the cornea should be perfectly clear, yet if around the edge of it, where it unites with the sclerotica, there should be a narrow ring or circle of haziness, the conclusion is equally true, that the inflammation occurred at a more distant period. Whether however the inflammation has lately existed, or several weeks or months have elapsed since it was subdued, it is too likely to recur.

There is one caution to be added. The cornea in its natural state is not only a beautiful transparent structure, but it reflects, even in proportion to its transparency, many of the rays which fall upon it; and if there is a white object immediately before the eye, as a light waistcoat, or much display of a white neckcloth, the reflection may puzzle an experienced observer, and has misled many a careless one. The coat should be buttoned up, and the white cravat carefully concealed.

Within the sclerotica, and connected with it by innumerable minute fibres and vessels, is the *choroid coat, l.* It is a very delicate membrane, and extends over the whole of the internal part of the eye, from the optic nerve to the cornea. It secretes a dark-colored substance or paint, by which it is covered; the intention of which, like the inside of our telescopes and microscopes, is probably to absorb any wandering rays of light which might dazzle and confuse the vision. The different manner in which this colored matter is distributed in the horse's eye from that of the human being, and its different color, render the sight of the former less strong during the day, but much more acute in the night.

Perfectly white and cream-colored horses have a peculiar appearance of the eyes. The pupil is red instead of black. It is the choroid coat itself which we see in them; and the red appearance is caused by the numerous blood-vessels which are found on every part of that coat.

Tracing the choroides towards the fore-part of the eye, we perceive that it is reflected from the side to the edge of the lens, *n*, and has the appearance of several plaits or folds. They are actually foldings of the membrane. They prevent the passage of any rays of light on the outside of the lens, and which, proceeding forward in various directions, and uncondensed by the power of the lens, would render vision confused or imperfect These folds of the choroides are called the *ciliary processes*.

Within the cornea, and occupying the fore-part of the eye, is the *aqueous humor*, *p*, so termed from its resemblance to pure water. It is that by which the cornea is preserved in its protuberant and rounded form. It extends to the crystalline lens *q*, and therefore a portion of it, although a very small one, is behind the iris (*m*, Fig. 7). Floating in this fluid is a membrane, with an oblong aperture, called the *Iris*. It is that which gives color to the eye. The color varies little in the horse, except that it always bears some analogy to that of the skin. We rarely see it lighter than a hazel, or darker than a brown. Horses perfectly white, or cream-colored, have the iris white and the pupil red. When horses of other colors, and that are usually pied, have a white iris and a black pupil, they are said to be *wall-eyed*. Vulgar opinion has decided that a wall-eyed horse is never subject to blindness, but this is altogether erroneous.

The aperture in the iris is termed the *pupil*, and through it light passes to the inner chamber of the eye. The pupil is oblong, and variable in size. It differs with the intensity or degree of light that falls upon the eye.

This alteration of form in the pupil is effected by the muscular fibres that enter into the composition of the iris. When these fibres are relaxed, the pupil must proportionably diminish.

This dilatation or contraction of the pupil gives a useful method of ascertaining the existence of blindness in one eye or in both. The cornea and crystalline lens remain perfectly transparent, but the retina is palsied, and is not affected by light; and many persons have been deceived when blindness of this description has been confined to one eye. A horse blind in both eyes will usually have his ears in constant and rapid motion, directing them in quick succession to every quarter. He will likewise hang back in his halter in a peculiar way, and will lift his feet high as if he were stepping over some obstacle, when there is actually nothing to obstruct his passage, and there will be an evident uncertainty in the putting down of his feet. In blindness of one eye, little or nothing of this characteristic gait and manner can be perceived. Although a one-eyed horse may not be absolutely condemned for the common business of the carriage or the road, he is generally deteriorated as a hunter, for he cannot measure his distance, and will run into his leaps.

Let the size of both pupils be carefully noticed before the horse is removed from the stable, and, as he is led to the door, observe whether they both contract, and equally so, with the increase of light. If the horse should be first seen in the open air, let it be observed whether the pupils are precisely of the same size; then let the hand be placed over each eye alternately and held there for a little while, and let it be observed whether the pupil dilates with the abstraction of light, and equally in each eye.

In our cut, m gives a duplicature of the iris, or the back surface of it. This is called the *uvea*, and it is covered with a thick coat of black mucus, to arrest the rays of light, and to prevent them from entering the eye in any other way than through the pupil. The color of the iris is, in some unknown way, connected with this black paint behind. Wall-eyed horses, whose iris is white, have no uvea.

We now arrive at a body on which all the important uses of the eye mainly depend, the *crystalline lens*, g, so called from its resemblance to a piece of crystal, or transparent glass. It is of a yielding jelly-like consistence, thicker and firmer towards the centre, and convex on each side, but more convex on the inner than the outer side. It is enclosed in a delicate transparent bag or *capsule*, and is placed between the aqueous and the vitreous humors, and received into a hollow in the vitreous humor, with which it exactly corresponds. It has, from its density and its double convexity, the chief concern in converging the rays of light which pass into the pupil.

The lens is very apt to be affected from long or violent inflammation of the conjunctiva, and either its capsule becomes cloudy, and imperfectly transmits the light, or the substance of the lens becomes opaque. The examination of the horse, with a view to detect this, must either be in the shade, or at a stable door, where the light shall fall on the animal from above and in front; and in conducting this examination, we would once more caution the intended purchaser against a superfluity of white about his neck. Holding the head of the animal a little up, and the light coming in the direction that has been described, the condition of the lens will at once be evident. The confirmed *cataract*, or the opaque lens of long standing, will exhibit a *pearly* appearance, that cannot be mistaken, and will frequently be attended with a change of form—a portion of the lens being forced forwards into the pupil. Although the disease may not have proceeded so far as this, yet if there is the slightest cloudiness of the lens, either generally, or in the form of a minute spot in the centre, and with or without lines radiating from that spot, the horse is to be condemned; for, in ninety-nine cases out of a hundred, the disease will proceed, and cataract, or complete opacity of the lens, and absolute blindness, will be the result.

Behind the lens, and occupying four fifths of the cavity of the eye, is the *vitreous humor* (glassy, or resembling glass). It seems, when first taken from the eye, to be of the consistence of a jelly, and of beautiful transparency; but if it is punctured a fluid escapes from it as limpid and as thin as water, and when this has been suffered completely to ooze out, a mass of membraneous bags or cells remains.

Last of all, between the *vitreous humor* and the *choroid coat*, is the retina, *o*, or net-like membrane. It is an expansion of the substance, *g*, of the optic nerve.

On this expansion of nervous pulp, the rays of light from surrounding objects, condensed by the lens and the humors, fall, and producing a certain image corresponding with these objects, the animal is conscious of their existence and presence.

It may, however, so happen that from the too great or too little convexity of the eye or a portion of it, the place of most distinct vision may not be immediately on the retina, but a little before or behind it. In proportion as this is the case, the sight will be indistinct and imperfect; nor shall we be able to offer any remedy for this defect of sight. It is this that occasions *shying* in the horse, and as he grows older and the eye becomes less convex, the habit of shying will increase.

Nature has given seven muscles to the horse to enable him to turn his eye, so that he can command the whole of that extended field of view which the position of the organ enables it to take in. And that they may act with sufficient power and quickness, no fewer than six nerves are directed to the muscles of the eye generally, or to particular ones—while the eye rests on a mass of fat, that it may be turned with little exertion of power, and without friction.

Muscles of the Eye

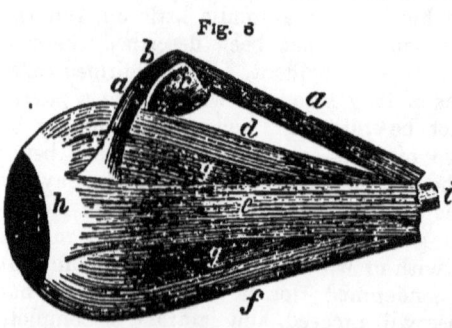

Fig. 8

There are four straight muscles, three of which, *d, e,* and *f,* are represented in our cut, rising from the back of the orbit, and inserted into the ball of the eye, opposite to, and at equal distances from, each other. One. *d,* runs to the upper part of the eye, just behind the transparent and visible portion of it, and its office is clearly to raise the eye. When it contracts, the eye must be drawn upwards. Another, *f,* is inserted exactly opposite, at the bottom of the eye; and its office is as clearly to depress the eye.

or enable the animal to look downwards. A third, *e*, is inserted at the outer corner, and by means of it the eye is turned outward, and, from the situation of the eye of the horse, considerably backward ; and the fourth is inserted at the inner corner, turning the eye inward. They can thus rotate or turn the eye in any direction the animal wishes, and by the action of one, or the combined power of any two of them, the eye can be immediately and accurately directed to every point.

These muscles also assist to support the eye in its place. They are aided in this, especially when the head is depressed, by the *retractor* (drawer back) muscle, *g*, which has already been alluded to. The power of this muscle is very great, and it renders some operations on the eye almost impossible. It is an admirable substitute for hands to defend the eye from many things that would injure it. Being partially separated into four divisions, it assists the straight muscles in turning the eye.

The muscles we have described, perform another important office. By drawing back the eye, and slightly flattening it, they bring the lens nearer the retina, and adapt the eye to the observation of more distant objects. There are two other muscles, used solely in turning the eye, called *oblique* muscles, because their course is obliquely across the eye. The upper one, *a*, *b*, is most curiously constructed. It comes from the back part of the orbit, and takes a direction upwards and towards the inner side, and there, just under the ridge of the orbit, it passes through a perfect mechanical pulley, and, turning round, proceeds across the eye, and is inserted rather beyond the middle of the eye, towards the outer side. Thus the globe of the eye is evidently directed inward and upward. Something more, however, is accomplished by this singular mechanism. When it is necessary to bring the eye forward in its socket, to enlarge the field of vision, the object is readily effected by this singular pulley, *b*, *c*. By the power of this muscle—the *trochlearis*, or pulley-muscle—and the straight muscles at the same time not opposing it, or only regulating the direction of the eye, it is really brought somewhat forward. The lower oblique muscle rises just within the lachrymal bone (*i*, Fig. 2), and, proceeding across the eye, is fixed into the part of the sclerotica opposite to the other oblique muscle, and it turns the eye in a contrary direction, assisting, however, the upper oblique in bringing the eye forward from its socket.

CHAPTER III.

INJURIES AND DISEASES OF THE SKULL—THE BRAIN—THE EARS—AND THE EYES.

We have now arrived at a convenient resting-place in our somewhat dry but necessary description of the structure of the horse, and we willingly turn to more practical matter. We will consider the injuries and diseases of the parts we have surveyed.

FRACTURE.

The skull of the horse is so strongly and admirably constructed, that a fracture of it is almost impossible. A blow of sufficient violence to break these bones, must likewise irreparably injure the brain, and remedies are out of the question.

The upper part of the orbit of the eye is sometimes fractured by falling, or by violent blows. The slightest examination will detect the loosened pieces; but a professional man alone can render effectual assistance.

EXOSTOSIS.

Bony enlargements of the orbital arch sometimes arise from natural predisposition or local injury. They should be attacked in the earliest stage, for they are too apt rapidly to increase. Some preparation of iodine, as described in the account of medicines, will be useful in this case.

CARIES.

Inflammation and enlargement of the injured bones, followed by abscess and the production of certain bony growths, are of occasional occurrence. A skilful practitioner can alone decide whether a cure should be attempted, or the sufferings of the animal terminated by death

COMPRESSION OF THE BRAIN.

Cysts containing a serous or viscid fluid, are occasionally found within the cranial cavity, and lying upon or imbedded in the brain. The following is a history of a case of this kind:—A horse exhibited symptoms of vertigo, or staggers, which disappeared after copious bleeding and purgatives. About twelve months afterwards the same complaint was evident. He carried his head low and inclined to the right side. He staggered as he walked, and the motion of his limbs was marked by a peculiar convulsive action, confined to the four extremities. He moved by a succession of spasmodic boundings. He was completely deaf; and rapidly lost flesh, though he ate and drank voraciously. He remained in this state, to the shame of the owner and the practitioner, several months, and then he had a fresh attack of vertigo, and died suddenly. On examination of the brain, its membranes were found to be completely reddened; and, between the two lobes of the brain, was a round cyst as large as a pullet's egg. The pressure of this was the manifest cause of the mischief.

PRESSURE ON THE BRAIN.

This may be produced by some fluid thrown out between the membranes, or occupying and distending the ventricles of the brain. In the full-grown horse it rarely occurs; but it is well known to breeders as an occasional disease of the foal, under the name of "water in the head." The head is either much enlarged, or stangely deformed, or both; and the animal dies, either in the birth, or a few days after it.

MEGRIMS.

This is another kind of pressure on the brain, resulting from an unusual determination or flow of blood to it. From various causes, of which the most common is violent exercise on a hot day, and the horse being fat and full of blood, more than the usual quantity is sent to the head; or, from some negligence about the harness—as the collar being too small, or the curb-rein too tight—the blood is prevented from returning from the head. The larger vessels of the brain will then be too long and injuriously distended; and, what is of more consequence, the small vessels that permeate the substance of the brain will be enlarged, and the bulk of the brain increased, so that it will press upon the origins of the nerves, and produce, almost without warning, loss of power and consciousness

The mildest affection of this kind is known as *Megrims* When the horse is driven rather quickly, he will, without any premonitory symptoms, suddenly stop, shake his head, and exhibit evident giddiness and half-unconsciousness. This will soon pass over, and he will go on as if nothing had happened.

When the attack is more serious, he will fall without the slightest warning, or suddenly run round once or twice and then fall. He will lie insensible, or struggle with the utmost violence. In five or ten minutes he will begin gradually to come to himself; he will get up and proceed on his journey, yet somewhat dull, and evidently affected and exhausted by what had happened, although not seriously or permanently ill.

At the moment of attack, three or four quarts of blood should be taken from the neck-vein, or the bars of the palate should be cut, in the manner hereafter described. The driver should treat him soothingly, loosen the curb-rein, ease the collar if practicable and drive slowly the rest of his journey. When he gets home, a dose of physic should be administered if the horse can be spared, the quantity of dry food lessened, and mashes given or green food, or he should have a run at grass. A predisposition to a second attack almost always remains, and it is a long time before the blood-vessels recover their former tone. Experience has shown that a horse that has had a *second* attack of the megrims is never to be trusted.*

APOPLEXY.

MEGRIMS is APOPLEXY under its mildest form. In the latter affection, the determination of blood, if not so sudden, is greater, or differently directed, or more lasting. It is seldom, however, that there are not timely warnings of its approach, if the carter or the groom had wit enough to observe them. The horse is a little off his feed—he is more than usually dull—there is a

---

* *Note by Mr. Spooner.*—Mr. Spooner speaks of a species of the disease the symptoms of which border on epilepsy, and appear to arise from disordered functions of the brain. He says:—

We have known some horses more liable to this disease in very cold frosty weather; in such instances the symptoms have been those of giddiness, without the severity of ordinary megrims; the animal has reeled, however, like a drunken man, and been extremely dangerous both to ride and drive. We have known an old horse thus continue almost useless throughout the winter, and gradually shake off the disease as warm weather came on. Now, it must be evident that the exciting causes of such instances must be altogether different from that of ordinary megrims; and, whilst the bleeding and purging are very proper, as recommended in the text for ordinary megrims, arising from plethora, it is not to be advised for that variety of disease to which we have called attention, and which is rather to be benefited by warmth, good grooming, and tonic medicine.

degree of stupidity about him, and, generally, a somewhat staggering gait. This goes off when he has been out a little while, but it soon returns under a more decided character, until, at length, it forces itself on the attention of the most careless.

The actual illness is perhaps first recognized by the horse standing with his head depressed. It bears upon, or is forced against the manger or the wall, and a considerable part of the weight of the animal is evidently supported by this pressure of the head. As he thus stands, he is balancing himself from one side to the other as if he were ready to fall; and it is often dangerous to stand near to him, or to move him, for he falls without warning. If he can get his muzzle into a corner, he will sometimes continue there motionless for a considerable time, and then drop as if he were shot; but, the next moment, he is up again, with his feet almost in the rack. He sleeps or seems to do so as he stands, or at least he is nearly or quite unconscious of surrounding objects. When he is roused, he looks vacantly around him. Perhaps he will take a lock of hay if it is offered to him, but ere it is half masticated, the eye closes, and he sleeps again with the food in his mouth. Soon afterwards he is, perhaps, roused once more. The eye opens, but it has an unmeaning glare. The hand is moved before him, but the eye closes not, he is spoken to, but he hears not. The last act of voluntary motion which he will attempt is usually to drink; but he has little power over the muscles of deglutition (swallowing), and the fluid returns through the nostrils.

He now begins to foam at the mouth. His breathing is laborious and loud. It is performed by the influence of the organic nerves, and those of animal life no longer lend their aid. The pulse is slow and oppressed—the jugular vein is distended almost to bursting—the muzzle is cold, and the discharge of the fæces involuntary. He grinds his teeth—twitchings steal over his face and attack his limbs—they sometimes proceed to convulsions, and dreadful ones, too, in which the horse beats himself about in a terrible manner; but there is rarely disposition to do mischief. In the greater number of cases these convulsions last not long. All the powers of life are oppressed, and death speedily closes the scene.

Post-mortem examination usually shows the whole venous system in a state of congestion, and the vessels of the brain, particularly, turgid with black blood. Occasionally, however, there is no inflammation of the brain or its membranes; but either the stomach contains a more than usual quantity of food, or the larger intestines are loaded with foul matter.

Apoplexy is a determination of blood to the head, and the cause is the over-condition of the animal, and too great fulness of blood. It used to be much more common, when it was customary to keep horses exceedingly fat, overwork them, and then suffer them to eat voraciously until their stomachs were preternaturally distended. The farmer used to keep his horses at the plough six or eight hours, then suffer them to overgorge themselves at will. The consequence was, that the farmer's horse was notoriously subject to fits of heaviness and sleepiness—to staggers, or *half-attacks* of staggers. And from the frequent pressure on the optic nerve and other parts, caused by oppression of the brain, they frequently became blind. A better division of labor, with properly distributed intervals for rest and feeding, have, comparatively speaking, banished *sleepy staggers*.

Old horses are more subject to staggers than young ones, their stomachs and digestive functions having been weakened by repeated abuses.

Hard-worked, and half-starved animals on being turned into rich pastures, are sometimes attacked. If the weather is hot, the sympathy of the brain with the undue labor of the stomach is more easily excited, and a determination of blood to the brain more readily effected.

There is nothing in the appearance of the horse which will lead to a discovery of the cause of staggers—no yellowness nor twitchings of the skin, no local swellings, as some have described; but the practitioner or owner must get at the truth of the matter as well as he can, and proceed accordingly.

As to the TREATMENT of staggers, whatever be the cause of the disease, bleeding is the first measure indicated—the over loaded vessels of the brain must be relieved. The jugular vein should be immediately opened. It is easily got at—it is large—the blood may be drawn from it in a full stream, and, being also the vessel through which the blood is returned from the head, the greater part of the quantity obtained will be taken immediately from the overloaded organ, and therefore will be most likely to produce the desired effect No definite quantity of blood should be ordered to be abstracted. The effect produced must be the guide, and the bleeding must be continued until the horse falters, or begins to blow—or, perhaps, with more assured success, until he falls. Some persons select the temporal artery. This is very unscientific practice. It is difficult, or impossible, to obtain from this vessel a stream that promises any decisive success. It is likewise difficult to stop the bleeding from this artery; and, after all, the blood is not drawn from the actual seat of the disease—the brain.

The second step is to ascertain what is the *cause* of the apoplexy. If produced by over-distention of the stomach, cathartics are of little avail. Recourse should be had to the *stomach pump* (one of the most valuable discoveries of modern times), and injections of warm water. The latter may be continued not only until the contents of the stomach are so far diluted as to escape by the anus, but until the obstruction to vomiting offered by the contracted entrance of the stomach is overcome, and a portion of the food is returned through the nostrils or mouth.

This being effected, or it having been ascertained that there was no extreme distention of the stomach, recourse should be had to aloes, and from eight to twelve drachms of it may be administered. It will be proper to add some stimulating medicine to the aloes, with a view of restoring the tone of the stomach, and inducing it to contract on its contents. Gentian and ginger are most likely to effect this purpose.

The after-treatment must be regulated by circumstances. For some time the horse should be put on a restricted diet; mashes should be given; green food in no great quantity; a moderate allowance of hay, and very little grain. When sufficiently recovered, he may be turned out with advantage on rather bare pasture. One circumstance, however, should never be forgotten —that the horse who has once been attacked with staggers is liable to a return of the complaint from causes that otherwise would not affect him. The distended vessels are weakened— the constitution is weakened, and prudence would dictate that such an animal cannot be too soon disposed of.

Let no one delude himself with the idea that apoplexy is contagious. It is so under no circumstances, though the same kind of mismanagement may produce repeated cases of it nearly at the same time, and in the same establishment.*

* *Note by Mr. Spooner.*—With regard to those diseases which come under the denomination of staggers, we have, certainly, three varieties, though neither of them are so prevalent as they were formerly.

Mad staggers is undoubtedly inflammation of the brain, and is characterized by those symptoms of extreme violence spoken of in the text. These symptoms may be preceded by the sleepy stage, or may occur without it. In sleepy staggers, as it used to be called, one of the most striking symptoms is a disposition to thrust the head forwards, and it is surprising with what force and determination this will be done. Thus resting his head, the horse will doze for hours. Now, there are certainly two diseases presenting these symptoms. One, which has been denominated stomach staggers, arises from distention of the viscus with food. Such is the sympathy between the stomach and the brain, that distention of the former will produce very similar symptoms to that when the brain is primarily diseased. We are, however, very much in the dark as to whether distention of the stomach with food is a cause or an effect; that is, whether it is caused by indigestion arising from a want of tone in the nervous system, or whether distention of the stomach with food is at once the cause of all the other symptoms.

Stomach staggers used formerly to be very prevalent, owing to the causes named in the text. In this disease there is a very great disposition to

PHRENITIS.

Primary inflammation of the brain or its membranes, or both, sometimes occurs, and of the membranes oftenest when both are not involved.

The early symptoms are almost precisely those of apoplexy, except that the phrenetic horse is not quite so lethargic. He sees a little better, will shrink more from the whip, and the disease runs its course more rapidly. In apoplexy, from distention of the stomach, twenty-four or thirty-six hours will elapse before cure, rupture of the stomach, or the destruction of the horse. If it proceeds merely from an oppression of the digestive organs and the sympathy which subsists between the stomach and brain, it may run on for two or three days. But the apoplexy of the phrenetic horse will often run its course in a few hours.

In a case of evident phrenitis, blood-letting and physic must be early carried to their full extent. The horse will often be materially relieved, and, perhaps, cured by this decisive treatment; but, if the golden hour has been suffered to pass, or if remedial measures have become ineffectual, the scene all at once changes, and the most violent reaction succeeds. The eye brightens—strangely so; the membrane of the eye becomes suddenly reddened, and forms a frightful contrast with the transparency of the cornea; the pupil is dilated to the utmost; the nostril, before scarcely moving, expands and quivers, and labors; the respiration becomes short and quick; the ears are force the head forwards, the pulse is slow and oppressed, and the abdomen generally distended, the bowels costive, and the dung usually slimy. This distention of the stomach is the principal distinction between this affection of the stomach, and the sleepy staggers, as it is called, which is primarily a disease of the brain. In this latter complaint, however, there is less disposition to thrust forward the head, and the abdomen is by no means distended.

Sleepy staggers is sometimes suddenly succeeded by mad staggers or inflammation of the brain; the symptoms of which are sufficiently detailed in the text. It is important to distinguish between these different diseases, as the treatment requires considerable modification.

Mad staggers, the symptoms of which are so extremely violent, must be met by the active bleedings and purgatives recommended in the text.

I would not, however, recommend the same active blood-letting for the stomach or the sleepy staggers, as in these diseases there appears a want of that nervous energy and excitation which abounds so much in the mad staggers, and which blood-letting is calculated to depress. In the stomach disease, oily purgatives and clysters, assisted by plenty of diluents, are called for; and, in those cases where lethargy and debility are present, tonics and mild stimulants are to be recommended.

I have never observed any connection to exist between staggers and amaurosis; the latter, it is true, may be caused by indigestion, but I have never met with an instance of its being produced by staggers.

erect, or bent forward to catch the slightest sound; and the horse, becoming more irritable every instant, trembles at the slightest motion. The irritability of the patient increases—it may be said to change to ferocity—but the animal has no aim or object in what he does. He dashes himself violently about, plunges in every direction, rears on his hind-legs, whirls round and round, and then falls backward with dreadful force. He lies for a while exhausted—there is a remission of the symptoms, but perhaps only for a minute or two, or possibly for a quarter of an hour.

In the intervals between the paroxysms, one or both jugulars should be opened; and all the blood abstracted that can be obtained. It is better not even to pin up the vein at all. The patient will never thus be lost, and it is indispensable to promptly relieve the brain and reduce the inflammation. Physic should be administered, and that which will most speedily act. The farina of the Croton nut will, perhaps, have the preference. Half a drachm or two scruples of it may be fearlessly administered. This medicine can be administered in the form of a little ball, or in drink, by means of the probang, or a stick, or the horn. Sometimes the phrenetic horse will drink with avidity, and thus repeated doses of purgative medicine may be given, and they should be continued until the bowels respond The forehead should be blistered, if it can in any way be accomplished; yet but little service is to be expected from this manipulation. The bowels having been well opened, digitalis should be administered. Its first and most powerful action is on the heart, diminishing both the number and strength of its pulsations. To this may be added emetic tartar and nitre, but not a particle of hellebore; for that drug, if it acts at all, produces an increased determination of blood to the brain.

The second paroxysm is more dreadful than the first. Again the animal whirls round and round, and plunges and falls. He seizes his clothing and rends it in pieces; perhaps, destitute of feeling and of consciousness, he bites and tears himself. He darts furiously at everything within his reach; but no mind, no design, seems to mingle with or govern his fury. These attacks and remissions follow for an uncertain period, until he becomes unable to rise. He pants—he foams—at length, completely exhausted, he dies.

While the disease continues, no attempt must be made to induce the horse to feed; and even when appetite returns with the abatement of inflammation, great caution must be exercised both with regard to the quantity and quality of the food.

The post-mortem appearances are altogether uncertain. There is usually very great injection and inflammation of the mem branes of the brain, and even of portions of the substance of the brain; but in other cases there is scarcely any trace of inflammation, or even of increased vascularity.

Phrenitis may be confounded with cholic and rabies. In cholic, the horse rises, falls, and kicks at his belly, but there is no involuntary spasm of any of the limbs, and he is *perfectly sensible* He looks piteously at his flanks, and the expression of his anxious countenance is altogether different from the fearfully excited one of the phrenetic horse. His pulse is also comparatively quiet, and his struggles and violence are tame in comparison with those of the other.

In rabies, there is even more violence than in phrenitis, but the horse is perfectly conscious, recognizes those about him, and seemingly exhibits more than his ordinary intelligence in his attempts to do mischief.

RABIES, OR MADNESS.

This is another and fearful disease of the nervous system. It results from the bite of a rabid animal, and, most commonly, of the companion and friend of the horse—the coach-dog.

The early symptoms of rabies in the horse have not been carefully observed or well recorded; but, in the majority of cases, so far as our records go, there will not often be premonitory symptoms sufficiently decisive to be noticed by the groom.

The horse goes out to his usual work, and, for a certain time and distance, performs it as well as he had been accustomed to do; then he stops all at once—trembles, heaves, paws, staggers, and falls. Almost immediately he rises, drags his load a little farther, and again stops, looks about him, backs, staggers, and falls once more. This is not a fit of megrims—it is not a sudden determination of blood to the brain, for the horse is not for a single moment insensible. The sooner he is led home the better, for the progress of the disease is as rapid as the first attack is sudden; and, possibly, he will fall twice or thrice before he reaches his stable.

In the great majority of cases—or rather, with very few exceptions—a state of excitation ensues, which is not exceeded by that of the dog under the most fearful form of the malady; but there are intervals when, if he had been naturally good-tempered and had been attached to his rider or his groom, he will recognize his former friend and seek his caresses, and bend on him one of those piteous, searching looks which, once observed will never be forgotten: but there is danger about this. Presently succeeds another paroxysm, without warning and without control; and there is no safety for him who had previously the most complete mastery over the animal.

I attended a rabid horse which the owner refused to have destroyed, and to which attendance I only consented on condition of the animal being slung. He had been bitten in the near hind-leg. When I approached him on that side, he did not attempt to bite me, and he could not otherwise injure me; but he was agitated and trembled, and struggled as well as he could; and if I merely touched him with my finger, the pulsations were quickened full ten beats in a minute. When, however, I went round to the off side, he permitted me to pat him, and I had to encounter his imploring gaze, and his head was pressed against me—and then presently would come the paroxysm; but it came on almost before I could touch him, when I approached him on the other side.

These mild cases, however, are exceptions to a general rule.

The symptoms of the malady of Mr. Moneyment's pony rapidly increased—he bit everything within his reach, even different parts of his own body—he breathed laboriously—his tail erect—screaming dreadfully at short intervals, striking the ground with his fore-feet, and perspiring most profusely. At length he broke the top of his manger, and rushed out of the stall with it hanging to his halter. He made immediately towards the medical attendant, and the spectators who were standing by. They fortunately succeeded in getting out of his way, and he turned in the next stall, and dropped and died.

A young veterinary friend of mine in fool-hardily attempting to administer a ball to a rabid horse, was seized by the hand, lifted from the ground, shaken as a terrier would shake a rat, and the ferocious animal was only compelled to relinquish his hold when attacked with pitchforks, and not before he had completely torn the flesh from the hand.

In the Museum of the Veterinary School at Alfort, is the lower jaw of a rabid horse, which was fractured in the violent efforts of the animal to do mischief.

There is also in the horse, whose attachment to his owner is often comparatively small, a degree of treachery which we rarely meet with in the nobler and more intellectual dog.

I have had occasion more than once to witness the evident pain of the bitten part, and the manner in which the horse in the intervals of his paroxysms employs himself in licking or gnawing the cicatrix. One animal had been bitten in the chest, and he, not in the intervals between the exacerbation, but when the paroxysm was most violent, would bite and tear himself until his breast was shockingly mangled, and the blood flowed from it in a stream.

The most interesting and satisfactory symptom is the evident dread of water which exists in the decided majority of cases, and the impossibility of swallowing any considerable quantity.

As the disease progresses, not only is the animal rapidly debilitated, but there is the peculiar staggering gait which is observable in the dog—referable to evident loss of power in the muscles of he lumbar region. Although this symptom is not often observed in the dog, it is a satisfactory identification of the disease, when it is so frequently seen in the horse, and so invariably in the human being.

The earliest and perhaps the most decisive symptom of the near approach of rabies in the horse, is a spasmodic movement of the upper lip, particularly of the angles of the lip. Close following on this, or contemporaneous with it, is the depressed and anxious countenance, and inquiring gaze, suddenly however lighted up and becoming fierce and menacing, from some unknown cause, or at the approach of a stranger. From time to time different parts of the frame—the eyes—the jaws—particular limbs—will be convulsed. The eye will occasionally wander after some imaginary object, and the horse will snap again and again at that which has no real existence. Then will come the irrepressible desire to bite the attendants or the animals within its reach. To this will succeed the demolition of the rack, the manger, and the whole furniture of the stable, accompanied by the peculiar dread of water which has been already alluded to.

Towards the close of the disease there is generally paralysis, usually confined to the loins and the hinder extremities, or involving those organs which derive their nervous influence from this portion of the spinal cord;—hence the distressing tenesmus (ineffectual attempt to stool) which is occasionally seen.

The disease rarely extends beyond the third day.

After death, there is uniformly found inflammation at the back part of the mouth, and at the top of the windpipe, and likewise in the stomach, and on the membrane covering the lungs, and where the spinal marrow first issues from the brain.

When the disease can be clearly connected with a previous bite, the sooner the animal is destroyed the better, for *there is no cure.* If the symptoms bear considerable resemblance to rabies, although no bite is suspected, the horse should at least be slung, and the medicine, if any is administered, given in the form of a drink, and with the hand well protected; for if it should be scratched in balling the horse, or the skin should have been previously broken, the saliva of the animal is capable of communicating the disease. Several farriers have lost their lives from being bitten or scratched in the act of administering medicine to a rabid horse.

If a horse is bitten by a dog under suspicious circumstances, he should be carefully examined, and every wound, and even the slightest scratch, well burned with the lunar caustic (nitrate of silver). The scab should be removed and the operation repeated on the third day. The hot iron does not answer so well, and other caustics are not so manageable. In the spring of 1827, four horses were bitten near Hyde Park, by a mad dog. To one of them the lunar caustic was twice severely applied—he lived. The red-hot iron was unsparingly used on the others, and they died. The caustic must reach every part of the wound. At the expiration of the fourth month, the horse may be considered to be safe.

TETANUS, OR LOCKED JAW.

TETANUS is one of the most dreadful and fatal, diseases to which the horse is subject. It is called LOCKED JAW, because the muscles of the jaw are earliest affected, and the mouth is obstinately and immovably closed. It is a constant spasm of all the voluntary muscles, and particularly of those of the neck, the spine, and the head. It is generally slow and treacherous in its attack. The horse, for a day or two, does not appear to be quite well; he does not feed as usual; he partly chews his food, and drops it; and he gulps his water. The owner at length finds that the motion of the jaws is considerably limited, and some saliva is drivelling from the mouth. If he tries he can only open the mouth a very little way, or the jaws are perfectly and rigidly closed; and thus the only period at which the disease could have been successfully combated is lost. A cut of a horse laboring under this disease is here given, which the reader will do well to examine carefully.

Fig. 9.

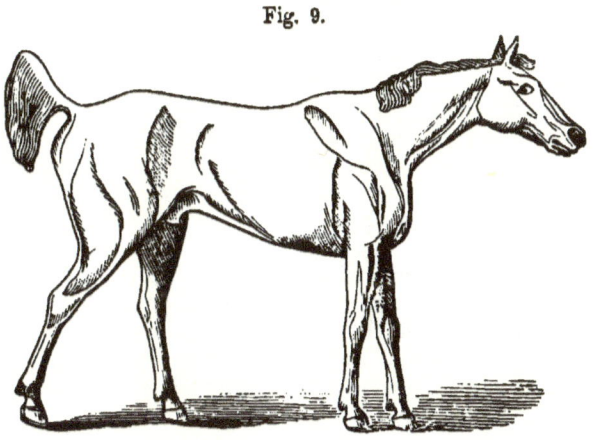

The first thing that strikes the observer is a protrusion of the muzzle, and stiffness of the neck; and, on passing the hand down it, the muscles will be found singularly prominent, distinct, hard, knotty, and unyielding. There is difficulty in bringing the head round, and still greater difficulty in bending it. The eye is drawn deep within the socket, and, in consequence of this, the fatty matter behind the eye is pressed forward; the haw is also protruded, and there is an appearance of strabismus, or squinting, in an outward direction.

The ears are erect, pointed forward, and immovable; if the horse is spoken to, or threatened to be struck, they change not their position. Considering the beautiful play of the ear of the horse when in health, and the kind of conversation which he maintains by the motion of it, there is not a more characteristic symptom of tetanus than this immobility of the ear. The nostril is expanded to the utmost, and there is little or no play of it, as in hurried or even natural breathing. The respiration is usually accelerated, yet not always so; but it is uniformly laborious. The pulse gives little indication of the severity of the disease. It is sometimes scarcely affected. It will be rapidly accelerated when any one approaches the animal and offers to touch him, but it presently quiets down again almost to its natural standard. After a while, however, the heart begins to sympathize with the general excitation of the system, and the pulse increases in frequency and force until the animal becomes debilitated, when it beats yet quicker and quicker, but diminishes in power, and gradually flutters and dies away.

The countenance is eager, anxious, haggard, and tells plainly enough what the animal suffers.

The stiffness gradually extends to the back. If the horse is in a narrow stall, it is impossible to turn him; and, even with room and scope enough, he turns altogether like a deal-board.

The extremities begin to participate in the spasm—the hinder ones generally first, but never to the extent to which it exists in the neck and back. The horse stands with his hind-legs straddling apart in a singular way. The whole of the limb moves, or rather is dragged on, together, and anxious care is taken that no joint shall be flexed more than can possibly be helped. The fore limbs have a singular appearance; they are as stiff as they can possibly be, but stretched forward and straddling They have not unaptly been compared to the legs of a form.

The abdominal muscles gradually become involved. They seem to contract with all the power they possess, and there is a degree of "hide-bound" appearance, and of tucking up of the belly, which is seen under no other complaint. The tail becomes in constant motion from the alternate and violent action of the muscles that elevate and depress it.

Constipation, and to an almost insurmountable degree, now appears. The abdominal muscles are so powerfully contracted, that no portion of the contents of the abdomen can pass on and be discharged.

By degrees the spasm extends and becomes everywhere more violent. The motion of the whole frame is lost, and the horse stands fixed in the unnatural posture which he has assumed The countenance becomes wilder and more haggard—its expression can never be effaced from the memory of him who cares about the feelings of a brute. The violent cramp of a single muscle, or set of muscles, makes the stoutest heart quail, and draws forth the most piteous cries—what, then, must it be for this torture to pervade the whole frame, and to continue, with little respite, from day to day, and from week to week! When his attendant approaches and touches him, he scarcely moves, but the despairing gaze, and the sudden acceleration of the pulse, indicate what he feels and fears

Tetanus is evidently an affection of the nerves, caused by an injury to some one of them, and the effect of that injury has spread to the origin of the nerve—the brain—and universal diseased action has followed.

If the disease terminates fatally, it is usually from the sixth to the eighth day. There are occasionally slight remissions in the spasm, but not sufficiently to enable the animal to eat or to drink. If these remissions return and increase in length, and particularly if there is more relaxation of the lower jaw, there is yet hope. If the horse recovers, it will be slowly, and he will be left sadly weak, and a mere walking skeleton.

On *post-mortem* examination the muscular fibre will exhibit sufficient proof of the labor which has been exacted from it. The muscles will appear as if they had been macerated—their texture will be softened, and they will be torn with the greatest ease. The lungs will, in the majority of cases, be highly inflamed, for they have been laboring long and painfully, to furnish arterial blood in sufficient quantity to support this great expenditure of animal power. The stomach will contain patches of inflammation, but the intestines, in most cases, will not exhibit much departure from the hue of health. The examination of the brain will be altogether unsatisfactory. There may be slight injection of some of the membranes, but, in the majority of cases, there will not be any morbid change worthy of record.

Tetanus most usually occurs from injuries to some nervous fibre of the foot—sometimes from a prick in shoeing. It is also connected with docking, nicking and castration (q. v.)

Severe over-exertion, or sudden exposure to cold after being heated by exercise, has also brought it on.

The treatment of tetanus is simple—*the system must be tranquillized.* The grand agent in accomplishing this is copious bleeding. The animal should be bled until he falls, or the pulse evidently falters. Twenty pounds of blood have been safely taken in such cases.

The profuse bleeding will generally relax the muscles of the jaw, so that a dose of physic can be administered. Eight or ten drachms of aloes should be given. If the remission of the spasm is slight, there is another purgative—not so certain in its action, but more powerful when it does act—the farina of the Croton nut.

Clysters will be useful in assisting the action of the purgative A solution of Epsom salts will constitute the safest and best injection. As to medicine, opium is not only a valuable drug, but it is that on which alone dependence can be placed in this disease. It will be borne in doses, from half a drachm to two drachms.

The application of sheep-skins warm from the animal, and applied along the whole course of the spine, may somewhat unload the congested vessels of the part, and diminish the sufferings of the animal. They should be renewed as soon as they become offensive, and the patient should be covered from the poll to the tail with double or treble clothing.

Gentle friction with the hand along the course of the spine, and the application of an opiate liniment, is highly useful.

Gruel should be placed within the reach of the horse, and he should also have thoroughly wet mashes placed before him. By means of a small horn, or bottle, gruel can sometimes be introduced in the stomach. This can be readily accomplished by means of the flexible tube accompanying Read's patent pump. A little food should be placed in the manger, and occasionally inserted between his grinders. The *effort* to eat will assist in breaking the chain of spasmodic action. Turn out the horse for a few hours in the middle of the day, in fine weather.*

CRAMP.

This is a sudden, involuntary, and painful spasm of a particular muscle. It occasionally attacks the muscles of organic

---

* *Note by Mr. Spooner.*—Successful treatment is principally confined to those cases in which the spasm is not universal, but confined to one part, as the neck or jaw, when it is denominated *trismus*. Purgatives, opiates, and antimonials, form, with blood-letting, the principal curative measures; but it should be borne in mind that, beyond all these, perfect quietude, and the absence of all excitement, is most essential. The animal should therefore be left alone as much as possible, without being harassed by frequent visits and the exhibition of medicines.

life, but in its most common form only affects the hind extremities, where it is observed by the temporary lameness and stiffness it produces, in the hardly worked horse, as he is first led out of the stable in the morning. If any lameness remains, which can be ascertained by pressing the parts, it should be removed by hard rubbing, or by giving the horse a wider and more comfortable stall, if that should appear to be the origin of the difficulty.

STRINGHALT.

This is a sudden and spasmodic action of some of the muscles of the thigh when the horse is first led from the stable. One or both legs are caught up at every step with great rapidity and violence, so that the fetlock sometimes touches the belly; but, after the horse has been out a little while, this usually goes off and the natural action of the animal returns. In a few cases it does not perfectly disappear after exercise, but the horse continues to be slightly lame.

Stringhalt is not a perfectly involuntary action of a certain muscle, or a certain set of muscles. The limb is flexed at the command of the will, but it acts to a greater extent and with more violence than the will had prompted.

Professor Spooner is of opinion that this peculiar affection is not referable to any diseased state of the brain or spinal cord, nor to any local affection of the muscles of the limbs, but simply to a morbid affection of the sciatic nerve. He has not dissected a single case of stringhalt in which he has not found disease of this nerve, which mainly contributes to supply the hind extremities with sensation and the power of voluntary motion.

Stringhalt is decided unsoundness; but generally speaking, it so little interferes with the services of the animal, that although an unsoundness, it would not weigh a great deal against other manifest valuable qualities.

CHOREA.

This is a convulsive, involuntary twitching of some muscle or set of muscles. A few, and very few, cases of it in the horse are recorded. Professor Gohier relates one in which it attacked both fore-legs, and especially the left, but the affection was not constant. During five or six minutes the spasms were most violent, so that the horse was scarcely able to stand. The convulsions then became weaker, the interval between them increased, and at length they disappeared, leaving a slight but temporary lameness. All means of cure were fruitlessly tried, and the disease continued until the horse died of some other complaint. In another case it followed sudden suppression of the discharge of glanders and disappearance of the enlarged glands. This also was intermittent during the life of the animal.

FITS, OR EPILEPSY.

The stream of nervous influence is sometimes rapid, or the suspensions are considerable. This is the theory of FITS, or EPILEPSY. Fortunately the horse is not often afflicted with this disease, although it is not unknown to the breeder. The attack is not sudden. The animal stops—trembles—looks vacantly around him, and falls. Occasionally the convulsions that follow are slight; at other times they are terrible. The head and forepart of the horse are most affected, and the contortions are very singular. In a few minutes the convulsions cease; he gets up; looks around him with a kind of stupid astonishment; shakes his ears; urines; and eats or drinks as if nothing had happened.

The only hope of cure consists in discovering the cause of the fits; and an experienced practitioner must be consulted, if the animal is valuable. Generally speaking, however, the cause is so difficult to discover, and the habit of having fits is so soon formed, and these fits will so frequently return, even at a great distance of time, that he who values his own safety, or the lives of his family, will cease to use an epileptic horse.

PALSY.

The stream of nervous influence is sometimes stopped, and thence results palsy. The power of the muscle is unimpaired, but the nervous energy is deficient. In the horse, palsy is usually general, and not confined to one side as commonly happens in the human subject. It generally attacks the hind extremities. The loins and the back oftenest exhibit the effects of palsy, because there are some of the most violent muscular efforts, and there is the greatest movement and the least support. It may consequently be taken as an axiom to guide the judgment of the practitioner that palsy in the horse almost invariably proceeds from disease or injury of the spine.

On inquiry it is almost invariably found that the horse had lately fallen, or had been worked exceedingly hard, or that covered with perspiration, he had been left exposed to cold and wet. It commences generally in one hind-leg, or perhaps both are equally affected. The animal can scarcely walk—he walks on his fetlocks instead of his soles—he staggers at every motion. At length he falls. He is raised with difficulty, or he never rises again. The sensibility of the part seems for a while to be dreadfully increased; but, in general, this gradually subsides—it sinks below the usual standard—it ceases altogether.

If he is examined after death, there will usually, about the region of the loins, be inflammation of the membranes of the spinal cord, or of the cord itself. The medullary matter will be found of a yellow color, or injected with spots of blood, or it will be softened, and have become semifluid.

The treatment is simple. It should commence with bleeding until the pulse begins to falter or the horse to reel. To this should follow a strong cathartic. The loins should be covered with a mustard poultice frequently renewed. The horse should be warmly clothed, supplied plentifully with mashes, but without a kernel of grain in them; and frequent injections administered. If favorable symptoms appear, the horse must not be in the slightest degree neglected, nor the medical treatment suspended, for in no disease is there a greater liability of relapse, and in none is a relapse more fatal. Palsy of the horse is an inflammatory complaint, and under no circumstances should grain or any tonic medicine be given.

If the heat and tenderness abate, and the animal regains a freer use of his limbs, or if it is becoming a case of chronic palsy, an extensive and stimulating charge over the loins should be immediately applied. It will accomplish three purposes: there will be the principle of counter-irritation—a defence against the cold—and a useful support of the limbs.

RHEUMATISM.

It is only of late years that this has been admitted into the list of the diseases of the horse, although it is in truth a very common affection. It is frequent in old horses that have been early abused, and among younger ones whose powers have been severely taxed. The lameness is frequently excessive, and the pain is evidently excruciating. The animal dares not to rest the slightest portion of its weight on the limb, or even to touch the ground with his toe. He is heaving at the flanks, sweating profusely, his countenance plainly indicative of the agony he feels; but there is at first no heat, or swelling, or tenderness. With proper treatment, the pain and the lameness gradually disappear; but in other instances the fasciæ of the muscles become thickened—the ligaments are also thickened and rigid—the capsules of the joint are loaded with a glairy fluid, and the joint is evidently enlarged. This is simply rheumatism; but if it is neglected, palsy soon associates itself with, or succeeds to, the complaint; and the loss of nervous power follows the difficulty or pain of moving.

Every horseman will recollect cases in which the animal that seemed on the preceding day to be perfectly sound becomes decidedly lame, and limps as though he had lost the use of his limbs; yet there is no thickening of the tendons, nor any external inflammatory action to show the seat of the complaint.

The attack is most common in winter, and in wet, cold weather. Good bleeding and sharp purging, the former aided if necessary by injections—and warm fomentations to the affected parts—constitute the proper treatment.

NEUROTOMY.

From the faulty construction of the shoe, the premature and cruel exaction of labor, and various other causes, the horse is subject to a variety of diseases of the foot—all of them accompanied with a greater or less degree of pain, often of a very intense character, and ceasing only with the life of the animal.

The division of the nerve as a remedy for intense pain in any part of the frame, was systematically practiced more than a century ago. Mr. Moorecroft has the honor of introducing this operation—neurotomy—into veterinary practice. He laid bare one of the metacarpal nerves, and divided it. It always immediately reduced the lameness, and, sometimes, the horse rose perfectly sound. This result was not always permanent, however, for the lameness returned in a few weeks, or on much active exertion. He next cut out a small piece of the nerve. The freedom from lameness was of longer duration, but eventually returned. He then tried a bolder experiment—the excision of a portion of the nerves going both to the inner and outer metacarpals, and found that the sensibility of the foot was thus destroyed.

Fig. 10 gives a view of the nerve on the inside of the leg, as it approaches the fetlock. It will be seen that branches are given off above the fetlock, which go to the fore-part of the foot and supply it with feeling. The continuation of the nerve below the fetlock is given principally to the quarters and hinder part of the foot. The grand consideration, then, with the operator is—does he wish to deprive the whole of the foot of sensation, or is the cause of lameness principally in the hinder part of the foot, so that he can leave some degree of feeling in the fore-part, and prevent that alteration in the tread and going of the horse, which the horseman so much dislikes?

The horse must be cast and secured, and the limb to be operated on removed from the hobbles and extended—the hair having been previously shaved from the part. The operator then feels for the throbbing of the artery, or the round firm body of the nerve itself, on the side of the shank bone or the larger pastern. The vein, artery, and nerve here run close together, the vein nearest to the front of the leg, then the artery, and the nerve behind. He cautiously cuts through the skin for an inch and a half in length. The vessels will then be brought into view, and the nerve will be distinguished from them by its lying behind the others, and by its whiteness. A crooked needle, armed with silk, is then passed under it, in order to raise it a little. It is dissected from the cellular substance beneath, and about three quarters of an inch of it cut out,—the first incision being made at the upper part, in which case the second incision will not be felt. The horse must then be turned, and the operation performed on the other side; for there is a nervous trunk on both sides. The wounds are now closed with strips of adhesive plaster, a bandage placed over them, the head tied up for a couple of days, and the animal kept rather low, and as quiet as possible. The incisions will generally rapidly heal; and in three weeks or a month, and sometimes earlier, the horse will be fit for work.

Fig. 10.

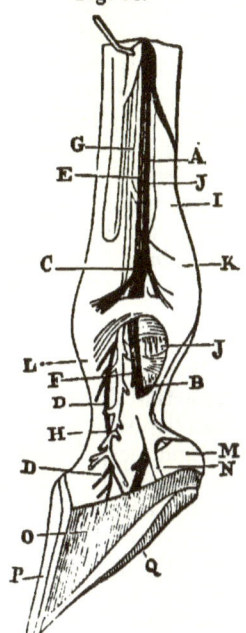

A The metacarpal nerve on the inside of the off leg at the edge of the shank bone, and behind the vein and artery.
B The continuation of the same nerve on the pastern, and proceeding downward to supply the back part of the foot with feeling.
C The division of the nerve on the fetlock joint.
D The branch which supplies with feeling the fore-part of the foot.
E The artery between the vein and nerve.
F The continuation of the artery on the pastern, close to, and before the nerve.
G The vein before the artery and nerve.
H The same vein spreading over the pastern
I One of the flexor tendons, the *perforatus* (perforated).
J The deeper flexor tendon, the *perforans* (perforating, contained within the other).
K The tendinous band in which the flexors work.
L One of the extensors of the foot.
M The internal or sensible frog.
N The posterior lateral ligament.
O The fleshy or sensible lamina covering the coffin bone, the horny crust being removed.
P The horny crust.
Q The sole.

For ring-bone—the side cartilages becoming bony, and there being partial stiffness of the pastern and coffin joints—the operation of nerving will probably be beneficial. The sense of pain being taken away, the animal will use these parts more, and they will gradually recover their natural action and motion. For the same reason, in old contraction of the feet, it is highly beneficial. The torture occasioned by the pressure of the horny crust on the sensible parts within being no longer felt, and the foot coming fully and firmly in contact with the ground, not only is lameness relieved, but the elasticity and form of the foot partially restored. Where lameness has long existed, unattended with heat of the foot or alteration of shape, and the seat of which could not be ascertained, although probably existing between the navicular bone and the back tendon that plays over it, neurotomy may be resorted to with decided advantage.

Mischief, however, will result from the operation if the pastern or coffin joints are perfectly stiff, because the concussion occasioned by the forcible contact of the foot with the ground, and unbroken by the play of the joints, must necessarily still more injure the bone. When the sole of the foot is convex or *pumiced*, the effect of neurotomy will be most destructive. The sole scarcely able to bear the pressure of the coffin-bone, even when pain induces the animal to put his foot as gently as possible on the ground, being forced below its natural situation, would be speedily worn through and destroyed. So if inflammation existed, although its pain might be removed, yet its progress would be quickened by the bruising to which the parts might be subjected; and more especially would this be the case, if there was any ulceration of the ligaments or cartilages.

The unfettered shoe of Mr. Turner being adopted, at least so far as we can have it unfettered—attached to the foot on one side alone, and the inner quarter being left free—the foot gradually regains its original healthy form, and when, in process of time, a new portion of nerve is produced, and the sensibility of the foot re-established, the horse continues to be sound. To some extent, immediate good effect is produced as it regards the actual disease. We remove that general constitutional irritability which long-continued pain occasions, and which heightens and perpetuates local disease. We obtain for the patient an interval of repose, and every local ailment soon subsides or disappears, and the whole constitution becomes invigorated.

Mr. Percival relates the case of a mare with contracted feet, that was never subject to periodical œstrum, and would not breed—and an incompetent stallion, with some disease of the feet—both of which procreated freely after being subjected to the operation of neurotomy.

Neurotomy having been performed, the veterinary surgeon will attempt to remove the original cause of the pain, and re store the foot, except so far as feeling is concerned, to its natural condition. In doing this, he is now permitted to use appliances which humanity would have prevented him from resorting to, before the sensibility of the part was destroyed. Some of these will be hereafter adverted to.

The principle of neurotomy is plain and simple—*it is the removal of pain*. In this light, it is a noble operation, and one in which every humane person will rejoice. But it may be abused. If no contemporaneous means are adopted to cure the disease of the foot—if in canker, or quittor, or inflammation of the laminæ, for example, no means are used to lessen the concussion and pressure—the destruction of the part, and the utter ruin of the horse, are the inevitable consequences. The primary result is the removal of pain. It is for the operator to calculate the bearing of this on the actual disease, and the future usefulness of the animal.

The excised portion of the nerve is again reproduced, but the time in which this is effected has not been tested by any definite experiments. With the restoration of the nerve, the lameness and pain return, unless the cause is removed.

Can the horse that has undergone the operation of neurotomy be afterwards passed as sound? Most certainly not.* [See Unsoundness.]

---

* *Note by Mr. Spooner.*—The operation has sometimes fallen into disrepute from having been performed on improper cases, or from the horse having afterwards been unduly worked. It should never be performed on a weak. flat, or convex foot, as the danger from concussion, pricks from shoeing. and other injuries, is great, and is still further increased by the operation in question. It also should not be performed for diseases of the fetlock joint, nor when the feet are exceedingly contracted; for, in the former case, the inflammation of the fetlock will soon extend above the seat of operation on the renewal of work; and, in the latter case, the disposition to expansion will be so great from the horse treading boldly on his heels that inflammation will result from the pressure of the soft parts against the horny crust, and enlargement and disorganization will be likely to follow. The best cases for the operation are those where the foot is strong and but little contracted. The horse should be worked moderately and steadily afterwards, either at a foot pace or a steady trot. He should not be used for hunting; as, in alighting from a leap, the diseased sinew, in passing over the navicular bone, to which it often becomes morbidly united, sometimes snaps or ruptures, and the horse is rendered useless. For the same reason, the horse should not be turned out to grass, as the same result may happen from playfulness. A result which sometimes attends this operation is, that when the horse has been previously disposed to overreach or clack his hind shoes against his fore ones, this disposition is afterwards greatly increased, from the leg operated on not being moved out of the way of the hind-leg so rapidly as it should be.

Neurotomy is usually performed a few inches above the fetlock joint. Some novices have performed it midway between the fetlock joint and the knee, and been much surprised to find that the lameness still continued,

INSANITY.

There is no doubt that the animals which we have subjugated possess many of the same mental faculties as the human being —volition, memory, attachment, gratitude, resentment, fear, and hatred. Who has not witnessed the plain and manifest display of these principles and feelings in our quadruped dependants? The simple possession of these faculties implies that they may be used for purposes good or bad, and that, as in the human being, they may be deranged or destroyed by a multitude of causes which it is not necessary to particularize.

The conduct of the horse laboring under insanity, is highly analogous to certain acts of insanity in man.

Professor Rodet, of Toulouse, gives an account of a horse remarkable for an habitual air of stupidity, and for a wandering expression of countenance, that when he saw or heard any sudden or unusual noise, or even when his grain was thrown into his manger without speaking to him or patting him, was frightened to an incredible degree; he recoiled precipitately, every limb trembled, and he struggled violently to escape. If unable to do so, he became so enraged that it was dangerous to approach him. This was followed by dreadful convulsions, which did not cease until he got free. He then would become calm, and suffer himself to be led back to his stall.

Professor Rodet also speaks of a mare belonging to a soldier, that had not the slightest fear of the sights and sounds of a field of battle, but had an insane aversion to paper! She distinguished it at once from all other objects, and even in the dark,

which was owing to the fact that the outer metacarpal nerve sends off a branch which passes obliquely over the back sinews, and joins the other several inches lower down; so that the section is made on one side below the place where the branch nerve leaves, and on the other above the spot where it joins the nerve; thus feeling is readily kept up by means of this branch nerve. Sometimes the operation is performed below, or immediately upon the fetlock joint; the effect of which is, that feeling is preserved to the front of the foot by means of two small branch nerves which are given off above the fetlock joint, whilst the navicular joint is deprived of all feeling. This would be a very desirable mode of performing the operation, were it always successful; but it often happens that, after some time, lameness again follows from the mischief extending itself within the sphere of the nerves that remain. In some instances, however, where the disease is entirely confined within the navicular joint, the horse has continued sound, and still preserved a certain degree of feeling. Another mode of operating is, to excise the nerve on the inside above the fetlock, and, on the outside, upon it; by which means a slight degree of feeling is preserved on the outside and front of the foot, and there is no danger of injury from cutting which is the case when the operation is performed immediately on the fetlock joint on both sides of the leg.

if two leaves were rubbed together—and her fright caused her several times to unhorse her rider.

Another mare, quiet in other respects, would invariably rush at another white or gray horse, and attempt to destroy it.

These instances are selected from various others, because they approach so nearly to what would be termed insanity in man. It is a species of monomania, and as decided insanity as ever the biped discovered. One of these horses, the second, was by long and kind attention divested of this insane terror, and became perfectly quiet and useful; but the others bid defiance to all means of cure, and to coercion among the rest.

DISEASES OF THE EYE.

The diseases of the eye constitute a very important, but a most unsatisfactory division of our work, for the maladies of this organ, although few in number, are frequent in their appearance. They are sadly obstinate, and often baffle all skill.

We have spoken of FRACTURE of the orbit, and its treatment Occasionally the substance round the eye is wounded by a fork or other sharp instrument, and inflammation ensues. This should be abated by poultices, and bleeding, and physic; but no probe should be used in such a place.

The eyelids are subject to occasional inflammation from blows or other injuries. Fomentation with warm water will be serviceable here.

The horse has occasionally a scaly eruption on the edges of the eyelids, attended with great itching, in the effort to allay which, by rubbing the part, the eye may be blemished. The nitrated ointment of quicksilver, mixed with an equal quantity of lard, may be slightly rubbed on the edges of the lids with considerable good effect.

The eyelids will sometimes become œdematous (puffed up with a serous humor). Horses fed in low wet pastures, old carriage-horses, &c., are subject to it. It is sometimes the result of badly treated inflammation. The lids should be well bathed with warm water mingled with an aromatic tincture.

Weakness and dropping of the upper lid is caused by diminution or loss of power in its muscles. Dry frictions and aromatic lotions will frequently restore the tone of the parts.

The eyelids are subject to occasional injury from their situation and office. In small incised (cut) wounds of them great care should be taken that the divided edges unite by the first intention. This will hasten the cure, and prevent deformity. If any of the muscles are divided, it is usually the ciliary or orbicularis palpebrarum. This lesion must be healed, if possible, by the first intention, and either by means of adhesive plaster or the suture (sewing). The suture is probably the preferable agent.

Suppurating wounds in the eyelids may be the consequence of the necessary abstraction of a considerable surface of the skin, in the removal of warts or tumors. The principal thing to be attended to is the frequent removal of the matter by means of tow or cotton wool. The rest may generally be left to nature.

Inversion of the lids is of very rare occurrence in the horse.

Warts are sometimes attached to the edges of the lids, and are a source of great irritation. When rubbed they bleed, and the common opinion is true—that they are propagated by the blood. They should be taken off with a sharp pair of scissors, and their roots touched with the lunar caustic.

The membrane which covers the Haw is subject to inflammation. It is, indeed, a continuation of the conjunctiva, the inflammation of which constitutes ophthalmia. An account of this inflammation will be better postponed until the nature and treatment of ophthalmia come under particular notice.

The Haw, or *Membrana Nictitans*, is subject to inflammation peculiar to itself, arising from the introduction of foreign bodies, or from blows or other accidents. The entire substance of the haw becomes inflamed. It swells and protrudes from the inner angle of the eye. The heat and redness gradually disappear, but the membrane often continues to protrude. The inflammation of this organ often assumes a chronic character in a very short time, on account of the structure of the parts, which are in general little susceptible of reaction.

The ordinary causes of this disease in the horse are repeated and periodical attacks of ophthalmia, and blows on the part. Young and old horses are most subject to it.

Emollient applications, bleeding, and restricted diet will be proper at the commencement of the disease, and, the inflammation being abated, slight astringents will be useful in preventing the engorgement of the part. Rose-water with subacetate of lead will form a proper eye-wash. If the protruding body does not diminish after proper means have been tried, and for a sufficient period, it must be removed with a curved pair of scissors. No danger will attend this operation if it is performed in time; but if it is neglected, ulceration of the part and the growth of fungous vegetations will give a serious character to the affair. A second operation may also be necessary, and even a third, and fungus hæmatodes will probably be established.

Ulceration and caries (decay) of the cartilage will sometimes be accompanied by ulceration of the conjunctiva. This will frequently prove a very serious affair, demanding, at least, the removal of the haw.

The Caruncula Lacrymalis, or Tubercle, by means of which the tears are directed into the canal through which they are to escape from the nostril, is sometimes enlarged in consequence of inflammation, and the Puncta Lacrymalia, or conduits into which the tears pass from the eye, are partially or completely closed The application of warm and emollient lotions will generally remove the collected mucus or the inflammation of the parts; but if the passage of a stylet or other more complicated means are required, the assistance of a veterinary surgeon should be immediately obtained. The lacrymal sac into which the tears pass from the puncta has occasionally participated in the inflammation, and been distended and ruptured by the tears and mucus. This lesion is termed *Fistula Lacrymalis*. It has occasionally existed in colts, and will require immediate and peculiar treatment.

COMMON INFLAMMATION OF THE EYE.

The conjunctiva is occasionally the seat of great disease, and that which is too often destructive to the eye. Inflammation of the eye may be considered under two forms—the common and manageable, and the specific and fatal. The *Common Inflammation* is generally sudden in its attack. The lids will be found swelled and the eyes partially closed, and some weeping. The inside of the lid will be red, some red streaks visible on the white of the eye, and the cornea slightly dim. This is occasionally connected with some degree of catarrh or cold; but it is as often unaccompanied by this, and depends on external irritation, as a blow, or the presence of a bit of hay-seed or oat-husk within the lid, and towards the outer corner where the haw cannot reach it: therefore the lids should always be carefully examined as to this possible source of the complaint. The health of the animal is generally unaffected—he feeds well, and performs his work with his usual spirit. Cooling applications to the eye, as the Goulard's extract or tincture of opium, with mash-diet, and gentle physic, will usually abate the evil; or the inflammation will subside without medical treatment.*

* *Note by Mr. Spooner.*—Unless this disease is connected with influenza, or some other malady affecting the whole system, it is usually produced by external violence, and in nine cases out of ten, may be distinguished from specific ophthalmia. When caused by a blow, there is in addition to swelling of the lids, and a large effusion of tears, a considerable dimness or opacity on the surface of the eye, whilst at the same time the interior is comparatively free from disease. In specific ophthalmia, there is a greater amount of disease in the interior of the eye, and little if any opacity of the cornea. When connected with influenza there is much swelling of the lids, and a great flow of tears, while the eye itself is tolerably free from injury; and when it proceeds from a cold, there is usually a thick matter, or mucus, dis-

SPECIFIC OPHTHALMIA, OR MOON-BLINDNESS.

Should three or four days pass, and the inflammation not be abated, we may begin to suspect that it is *Ophthalmia*, especially if the eye is very impatient of light, and the cornea is considerably clouded The aqueous humor then often loses its transparency—even the iris changes its color, and the pupil is exceedingly contracted. The veterinary surgeon has now an obstinate disease to combat, and one that will generally maintain its ground in spite of all his efforts. For three, or four, or five weeks, the inflammation will remain undiminished; or if it appears to yield on one day, it will return with redoubled violence on the next. At length, and often unconnected with any of the means that have been used, the eye begins to bear the light, the redness of the membrane of the lid disappears, the cornea clears up, and the only vestige of disease which remains is a slight thickening of the lids and apparent uneasiness when exposed to a very strong light.

If the owner imagines that he has got rid of the disease, he will be sadly disappointed, for, in the course of six weeks, or two months, either the same eye undergoes a second and similar attack, or the other one becomes affected. All again seems to pass over, except that the eye is not so perfectly restored, and a slight, deeply-seated cloudiness begins to appear; and after repeated attacks, and alternations of disease from eye to eye, the affair terminates in opacity of the lens or its capsule, attended with perfect blindness either of one eye or both. This affection was formerly known by the name of moon-blindness, from its periodical return, and some supposed influence of the moon. That body, however, has not, and cannot have, anything to do with it.

What is the practitioner doing all this while? He is an anxious and busy, but almost powerless spectator. He foments the eyes with warm water, or applies cold lotions, with the extract of lead or opium, or poultices to which these drugs may be added; he bleeds, not from the temporal artery, for that does not supply the orbit of the eye, but from the *angular vein* at the inner corner of the eye, or he scarifies the lining of the lid, or subtracts a considerable quantity of blood from the jugular vein. The scarifying of the conjunctiva, which may be easily accomplished without a twitch, by exposing the inside of the

charged from the corner of the eye after the first day or two. A cut from a whip generally leaves a streak on the surface of the eye (unless the injury is sufficient to involve the whole surface), and this streak sometimes becomes permanent.

lids, and drawing a keen lancet slightly over them, is the most effectual of all ways to abate inflammation, for we are then immediately unloading the distended vessels. He places his setons in the cheek, or his rowels under the jaw; and he keeps the animal low, and gives physic or fever medicine (digitalis, nitre and emetic tartar). The disease, however, ebbs and flows, re treats and attacks, until it reaches its natural termination, blind ness of one or both eyes.

The horse is more subject to this disease from the age of foui to six years. Every affection of the eye appearing about this age, should be regarded with suspicion. The eye should be most carefully observed at the time of purchase, and the examiner should be fully aware of the minute indications of disease. They are a slight thickening of the lids, or puckering towards the inner corner of the eye; a difference in the apparent size of the eyes; a cloudiness, although perhaps scarcely perceptible, of the surface of the cornea, or more deeply seated, or a hazy circle round its edge; a gloominess of eye generally, and dulness of the iris; or a minute, faint, dusky spot in the centre, with or without minute fibres or lines diverging from it.

There is undoubtedly a strong predisposition to this inflamma tion in the eye of the horse, but it is assisted by the heated and empoisoned air of many stables. The dung and urine of the horse, and the litter when becoming putrid, emit fumes of volatile alkali, or hartshorn. We need not wonder at the prevalence of inflammation in the eye of the stable horse, nor at the difficulty in abating it, while this organ continues much exposed to the effect of this pungent gas.

Dark stables are another cause of ophthalmia. Let the horse be led several times a day from a dark room into a full glare of light, and the sight will become disordered, the eyes weak, and disposed to take on sudden inflammation, with all its fatal results.

The disease is also in a high degree hereditary. A stallion with defective sight should never be employed.

The most frequent consequences of this disease are cloudiness of the eye, and cataract. The cloudiness is singular in its nature. It will change in twenty-four hours from the thinnest film to the thickest opacity, and, as suddenly, the eye will nearly regain its perfect transparency, but only to lose it, and as rapidly, a second time.

Chalk, salt, sugar, and even pounded glass have been introduced into the eye to remove the film, but we need not say that the effect of such remedies would be to recall the inflammation, and that they are utterly barbarous. Where the cloudiness can be removed, it will be best effected by first abating inflamma tion, and then exciting the absorbents to take up the gray deposit, by washing the eye with a very weak solution of corrosive sublimate.

Opacity of the lens is another consequence of inflammation. A white speck appears on the centre of the lens, which gradually spreads over it, and completely covers it. It is generally so white and pearly as not to be mistaken—at other times it is more hazy, deceiving the inexperienced, and occasioning doubt in the mind of professional men. We have seen many instances in which the sight has been considerably affected or almost lost, and yet the horse has been pronounced sound by very fair judges. The eye must be exposed to the light, and yet under the kind of shelter which has been already described, in order to discover the defect. The pupil of the horse is seldom black, like that of the human being, and its grayish hue conceals the recent or thin film that may be spreading over the lens.

Confirmed cataract in the eye of the horse admits of no remedy. But slight cataracts come and go, sometimes without any previous inflammation, and without leading to blindness. Still it is a serious thing at all times, and, although existing in the minutest degree, it is *unsoundness*, and very materially lessens the value of the horse.

Mr. Percival says the best way of distinguishing between this transient cataract, and that which is the consequence of ophthalmia, is the general appearance of the eye. If perfectly clear and healthy, we should infer it was the former, but the slightest trace of prior or present inflammation would lead us to suspect the latter.*

* *Note by Mr. Spooner.*—With regard to the causes of these diseases, we agree with the author in ascribing much to the ammoniacal fumes which escape from the urine, to which we would add high stimulating food and great exertion in harness. We believe, also, that improved stabling and better ventilation has lessened the frequency of these ocular cases. Horses with small *pig* eyes are much more liable to ophthalmia than those with large prominent eyes; and thus, as the former are more frequently found with horses deficient in breeding, it may account for the opinion which is popularly entertained, that black horses are more liable to blindness than others, these horses being generally deficient in breeding.

With regard to the treatment of these diseases, we have little to add to that detailed in the text. Inflammation is the leading feature in all, and therefore should be met by active antiphlogistic treatment. An active dose of physic should be given, as soon as the horse is prepared, by mashes and, in the meantime, three or four quarts of blood should be taken from the neck, on the same side as the affected eye. The eyelids should also be scarified, then well fomented with warm water; after which we have derived great assistance from putting linseed poultices, in linen bags, on the eyes, by means of leather blinds. These should be continued during the day, and may serve as the vehicle for the application of opiate or Goulard lotions, which, applied in the usual way, are but of little service. By this

GUTTA SERENA.

Another species of blindness, and of which mention was made when describing the retina, is Gutta Serena, commonly called *glass eye.* The pupil is more than usually dilated : it is immovable, and bright, and glassy. This is palsy of the optic nerve, or its expansion, the retina; and is usually produced by determination of blood to the head. It is the kind of blindness which we have described, as sometimes resulting from the pressure on the base of the brain, and the consequent injury to the function of the nerve, in staggers.

The treatment of Gutta Serena is quite as difficult as that of cataract. We have heard of successful cases, but we never saw one; nor should we be disposed to incur much expense in endeavoring to accomplish impossibilities. Reasoning from the cause of the disease, we should bleed and physic, and administer the strychnine in doses, commencing at half a grain, and not exceeding two grains, morning and night—very carefully watching it. If we succeed, it must be by constitutional treatment. As to local treatment, the seat of the disease is out of our reach.*

prompt and active treatment a great deal of good can be accomplished, and the loss of sight may be greatly postponed. It is useless to attempt half measures; we should either treat actively or not at all. After the violence of the inflammation has subsided, much benefit may be obtained by putting a few drops of the wine of opium into the eye twice a day

CATARACT.

Cataract may be either partial or complete; and again, it may either succeed the violent disease before spoken of, or it may gradually come on with very little previous inflammation. It admits also of another important division. It may be either a cataract of the lens itself, or merely of the membrane which covers it. The latter may come on without any noticeable inflammation; appearing as one or two small specks in the centre of the eye, about the size of a pin's head. It is very important to distinguish between these different kinds of cataracts, inasmuch as, whilst the former is irremovable, the latter is very frequently absorbed without any external treatment. Whilst the former is often pearly white, and completely opaque, so far as it exists, the latter is gray and less opaque. It requires a considerable amount of tact, as well as experience, to discover these small incipient cataracts, and to discriminate between the one kind and the other.

* *Note by Mr. Spooner.*—This disease is sometimes connected with diseased liver, particularly a rupture of its coats, when the blindness may shift from one eye to the other. Although this disease is generally but little under the influence of treatment, we have met with successful cases in young animals. The treatment should principally be directed to the removal of the cause which produces the disease.

DISEASES OF THE EAR.

Wounds of the ear are usually the consequence of careless or brutal treatment—often of the application of the twitch or the pliers. These bruises or wounds will generally speedily heal; but sinuses and abscesses are sometimes the result. A simple laceration of the cartilage is easily remedied. The divided edges are brought together, the head tied up closely a few days, and all is well; but where ulceration of the skin and subjacent parts, and caries of the cartilage take place, deep sinuses will be formed, and the wound will bid defiance to medical treatment. I had a case of this kind under my care for more than two months, and finally had to cut off the ear. The lunar caustic, or the muriate of antimony, or the heated iron, must be early employed, or all labor will be in vain.

I have seen two cases where the auditory passage was closed, and the hearing destroyed—the result of violent blows. When there is swelling about the root of the ear and the fluctuation of a fluid within can be detected, it should be opened with a lancet, and the purulent fluid liberated. The incision should be of considerable length, or the opening will soon close. It should not be permitted to close until the abscess is obliterated.

The size and carrying of the ear may be changed. The first is done by clipping them to the requisite size. If they hang down too much, a fold of the skin is pinched up and cut away, on either side of the occipital bone, and in a straight line forward and backward. The divided edges are then brought together, confined by two or three stitches, and they presently unite. If the ears are too close together, this fault may be corrected by another piece of cruelty. Similar slips of skin are cut away on the outside base of the ear, and in the same direction. The edges of the wound are then brought together, confined by stitches, and the ears are drawn further apart from each other, and have different directions given to them. A very slight examination of either of the horses will readily detect the imposition.

DEAFNESS.

Of the occasional existence of this in the horse, there is no doubt. The beautiful play of the ears has ceased, and the horse hears not the voice of his master, or the sound of the whip. Much of the apparent stupidity of a few horses is attributable to their imperfect hearing. It is the result of certain diseases, blows, and, as in other domesticated animals, is the certain accompaniment of old age. It is incurable.

CHAPTER IV.

THE ANATOMY OF THE DISEASES OF THE NOSE AND MOUTH

We now proceed to a description of the *face*, or lower part of the head of the horse. The *nasal bones*, or bones of the nose (*j j*, Fig. 2, and *a*, Fig. 3), are connected with the frontal bones above, and with the lacrymal, *i i*, and the bones of the upper jaw, *l l*, on either side. They are united together by a plain suture, which is a continuation of the frontal, and they terminate in a point at the nostril (*p*, Fig. 2). They are rounded and arched above, because they are exposed to occasional violence and injury, which the arch-form will enable them best to resist; and at the base of the arch, where the main strength should be, they are overlapped by the upper jaw-bone, as the temporal bone overlaps the base of the parietal. These bones form a principal part of the face; and the length, or shortness, and the character of the face, depend upon them. Sometimes there is an appearance of two little arches, with a depression between them along the sutures. This is often found in the blood-horse, with his comparatively broad head and face. The single elevated arch is found in the long and narrow face of the heavy draught-horse.

The profile of the horse has been supposed by many, and probably with some truth, to be indicative of his temper. The straight profile may be accompanied with a good or bad temper, but not often either in any great excess. The one with a prominent Roman nose, is usually an easy, good-tempered, hardy beast, ready enough to feed, not always, perhaps, so ready to work, but may be made to do his duty without any cruel urging, and having no extraordinary pretension to speed or blood. On the other hand, a depression across the centre of the nose generally indicates some breeding, especially if the head is small, but occasionally accompanied by a vicious, uncontrollable disposition.

There is another way, however, in which the nasal bones do more certainly indicate the breed, viz., by their comparative length or shortness. There is no surer criterion of a well-bred horse, than a broad angular forehead, prominent features, and a short face ; nor of a horse with little breeding, than a narrow forehead small features, and lengthened nose. The comparative development of the head and face indicates, with little error, the preponderance of the animal or intellectual principle.

Fracture of the nasal bones of the horse will sometimes occur from falling, or a kick from the companion, or the brutality of the attendant. It is generally followed by laceration of the lining membrane of the nostrils, and by hæmorrhage. The bleeding may usually be arrested by the application of cold water externally. In spontaneous hæmorrhage, this does not often succeed until a considerable quantity of blood is lost.

In cases of fracture of the nasal bones, the assistance of a veterinary surgeon is indispensable. He alone knows the precise anatomy of the parts, and will have recourse to the *elevator* or the *trephine*, as circumstances may require.

Ozena sometimes follows these wounds, or foundation may be laid for the appearance of glanders.

Spontaneous bleeding from the nose must be carefully attended to. It may proceed from an over fulness of the blood vessels of the membrane of the nose, consequent on very high condition, or from the lungs. If from the nostril alone, it will usually be confined to one side ; if from the lungs, the discharge is from both nostrils, and generally mingled with mucus or froth ; and there is also a quickened respiration, and more or less cough.

If it is apparently connected with some slight cause, a dose of physic and quietness for a day or two will be sufficient, and, if necessary, a slight solution of alum may be injected up the nostril. If the bleeding is apparently from the lungs, a more serious evacuation will be required.

These bones form the roof of an important cavity (see *a*, Fig. 3). The sides are constituted above by the nasal bones, and, lower down, by the upper jaw-bones (*superior maxillaries*), while plates from these latter bones project and compose the palate, which is both the floor of the nose and the roof of the mouth (*t*, Fig. 3.) Above (near 8), not visible in our cut, is a bone called the *palatine*, although it contributes very little to the formation of the palate. It is the termination of the palate, or the border of the opening where the cavities of the mouth and nose meet (8). The frontal sinuses, *b*, and large vacuities in the upper jaw-bone, and in the æthmoid, *l*, and sphenoid bones, k, communicate with and enlarge the cavity of the nose.

This cavity is divided into two parts by a cartilage called the *Septum* (see *r*, Fig. 3.) It is of considerable thickness and strength, and divides the cavity of the nose into two equal parts. It is placed in the centre for the purpose of strength, and it is

Fig. 11.

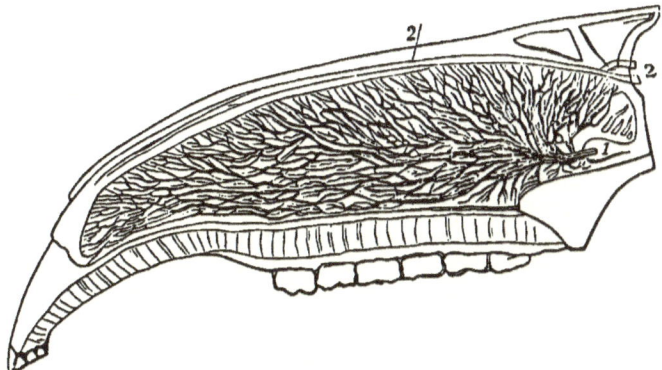

formed of cartilage, in order that, by its gradual yielding resistance, it may neutralize almost any force that may be applied to it.

When we open the nostril, we see the membrane lining the whole cavity of the nose, by the color of which, much more than by that of the lining of the eye-lids, we judge of the degree of fever, and particularly of inflammation of the lungs, or of any of the air passages. The cut above shows the ramification of the arterial and venous blood-vessels on this membrane. Certain ulcerations on it also betray the existence of glanders.

The nasal cavity is, on either side, occupied by two bones, which, from their being rolled up somewhat in the form of a turban, are called the *turbinated* or *turban-shaped* bones, (s s, Fig. 3.); part of the cartilage is cut away in our cut in order to display them. They are as thin as gauze, and perforated, like gauze, with a thousand holes. Between them are left sufficient passages for the air. Spread out, they would occupy a considerable surface. Over them is spread the substance or pulp of the olfactory nerves, which makes them the *seat of smell;* and they are thus expanded, because by the sense of smell, the horse must in a great degree supply the want of that of *touch*. They also enable him to distinguish his proper herbage, detect distant danger; and they, like the windings of a horn, give loudness to his voice.

The extension of the nostril at the lower part of these cavities is an important part of the face, and intimately connected with breeding, courage, and speed. The horse can breathe only through the nose. All the air which goes to and returns from the lungs, must pass through the nostrils. In the common act of breathing, these are sufficiently large; but when the animal is put on his speed, and the respiration is quickened, these passages must dilate, or he will be much distressed. The expanded nostril is a striking feature in the blood-horse, especially when he has been excited and not over-blown. The nostril should be proportioned to the kind of labor we require from the animal—larger in proportion to the *activity* of the labor, and the consequent liability of being blown.

Some very powerful muscles proceed from different parts of the face to the neighborhood of the nostrils, in order to draw them back and dilate them. Four of these are given in the following cut, which is inserted to complete our present subject, and which will be often referred to in the course of our work; *l*, *m*, *o*, and *p*, are muscles employed for this purpose.

THE MUSCLES, NERVES, AND BLOOD-VESSELS OF THE HEAD AND UPPER PART OF THE NECK.

Fig. 12.

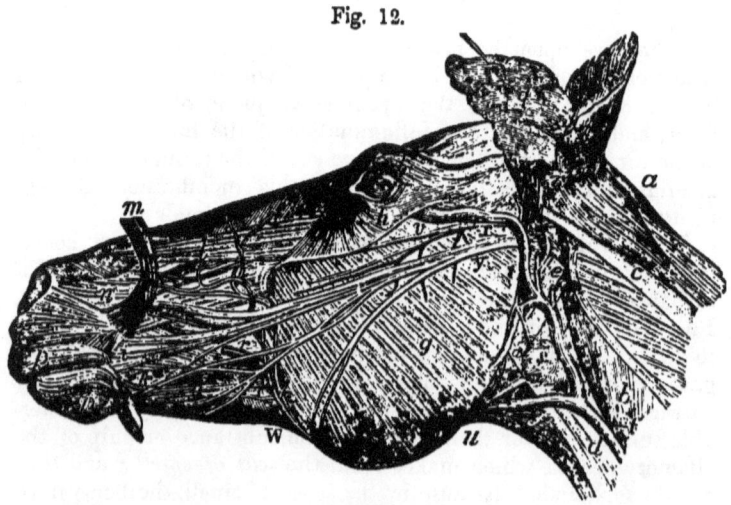

a The upper part of the ligament of the neck.
b The *levator humeri* (elevator of the shoulder), arising from the tubercle of the occiput, the mastoid (nipple-shaped) process of the temporal bone, and the transverse processes (cross projections) of the four first bones of the neck, and the ligament of the neck, and going to the muscles of the shoulders, and the upper bone of the arm; to draw forward the shoulder and arm; or turn the head and neck; and, when the two levators act, to depress the head.
c The tendon common to the *complexus major* (larger complicated), and *splenius* (splint-like): to the mastoid process of the temporal bone, to hold up the head, or, the muscles on one side alone acting, to turn it.
d The *sterno-maxillaris* (belonging to the breast-bone) and upper jaw, from the cartilage in front of the chest to the angle of the lower jaw: to bend the head, or, if one only acts, to bend it on one side.
e The *stylo-maxillaris*, from the styloid (pencil-shaped) or coracoid (beak-shaped) process of the occiput, to the angle of the jaw: to pull the jaw backward and open it.

MUSCLES, ETC., OF THE HEAD. 103

f The *subscapulo hyoideus*, from under the shoulder-blade, to the body of the *os hyoides* (the bone at the root of the tongue formed like a Greek *n*, υ) : to draw back that bone.

g The *masseter* (chewing) ; a most powerful muscle, constituting the cheek of the horse :—from the upper jaw bone into the rough surface round the angle of the lower : in conjunction with the temporal muscle to close the mouth and chew the food.

h The *orbicularis* (circular) surrounding the eye and closing the lids.

i The *zygomaticus*, from the zygomatic arch and masseter to the corner of the mouth, to draw back the angle of the mouth.

k The *buccinator* (trumpeter), from the inside of the mouth and cheeks, to the angle of the mouth, to draw it back.

l The *vasalis labii superioris* (belonging to the nose and upper lip), from a depression at the junction of the superior maxillary and malar bones, to the angle of the nostril : to raise the lip, and dilate the nostrils.

m Dilator *naris lateralis* (side dilator of the nostril), reversed to show the vessels and nerves which it covers, going from the covering of the nasal and frontal bones, to the angle of the mouth, and side of the nostril: to retract the upper lip and dilate the nostrils.

n Dilator *magnus* (great dilator), assisting in the same office.

o Depressor *labii inferioris* (puller down of the under lip), to the sides of the under lip : to pull it down.

p Orbicularis *oris* (circular muscle of the mouth), surrounding the mouth : to close the lips and dilate the nostrils.

q The upper portion of the parotid gland (gland near the ear) reversed, to show the blood-vessels and nerves beneath it.

r The parotid duct piercing the cheek, to discharge the saliva into the mouth.

s The maxillary gland (gland of the lower jaw) with its duct.

t The jugular (neck) vein, after the two branches have united.

u At this letter, the submaxillary artery, a branch of the jugular, and the parotid duct, pass under and within the angle of the lower jaw ; they come out again at *r*, and climb up the cheek to be distributed over the face.

v The vein and artery, passing under the zygomatic arch.

x A branch of the fifth pair, the sensitive nerve of the face, emerging from under the parotid gland.

y The main branch of the *portio dura* (hard portion) of the seventh pair, the *motor* (moving) nerve of the face coming out from beneath the parotid gland, to spread over the face.

z Branches of both nerves, with small blood-vessels.

There are also four distinct cartilages attached to the nostrils, which, by their elasticity, bring back the nostrils to their former dimensions, as soon as the muscles cease to act. The bones of the nose (*a a*, Fig. 2, and Fig. 3), are also sharpened off to a point, to give wider range for the action of the muscles ; while the cartilages are so contrived, as not only to discharge the office we have mentioned, but to protect this projection of bone from injury.

The membrane of the nose, as already stated, is an excellent guide to the degree and character of many diseases. In health, and uninfluenced by exercise, that portion of the membrane seen in the nostrils is a pale uniform pink. An increased blush of red betokens some excitement of the system—a streaked appearance, inflammation commenced—intense redness, acute inflammation—pale ground with patches of vivid red, half-subdued but still existing fever—uniform color, but somewhat redder than natural, a return to healthy circulation—paleness approaching to white, debility—and dark livid color, approaching stagnation of the vital current.

NASAL POLYPUS.

By the polypus, is meant an excrescence or tumor, varying in size, structure, and consistence, and attached by a pedicle to a mucous surface.

The nasal polypus usually adheres to some portion of the superior turbinated bone, or it has come from some of the sinuses connected with that cavity.

As it increases in weight, it elongates that sac of the schniderian membrane which invests it, and it descends in the nose. It is of a pear form, and differs in weight from a few drachms to three or four pounds.

When it descends so that it can fairly be got at with the fingers, the forceps, or (for it possesses little sensibility) the tentaculum, it must be carefully and gently drawn out, and a ligament passed tightly round the neck or pedicle of it, as high up as convenient, and then if practicable, it should be returned into the nostril. It will slough off in a few days, with very little inconvenience to the horse. If it cannot be returned, it should be cut off below the ligature. If the ligature is drawn sufficiently tightly, not much hemorrhage will often ensue. Cautery may be resorted to to stop bleeding, as a last resort, in case of obstinate hemorrhage, but it is objectionable on account of the degree of irritation it produces, and the difficulty of safely resorting to it in such a situation. In very bad cases, where the tumor cannot be drawn out, it may be necessary to slit up the side of the nostril, but in that case the false nostril should not be cut through, as from its thinness it is difficult to confine the edges securely together until they unite. The incision should be made along the lateral edge of the nasal bone, beginning at its point. The flap will then conveniently turn down, so as to expose the cavity, and there will be sufficient muscular substance to secure an almost certain union by the first intention, when stitched properly together.*

NASAL GLEET, OR DISCHARGE FROM THE NOSE.

There is a constant secretion of fluid to lubricate and moisten the membrane that lines the cavity of the nose, and which, un-

---

* *Note by Mr. Spooner.*—Still more rarely we find a bony tumor forming in the nostrils, nearly obstructing all passage, and causing a discharge somewhat resembling that of glanders. This, like the former, should be removed if possible by an operation.

der catarrh or cold, is increased in quantity, and altered in appearance and consistence. This will properly belong to the account of catarrh or cold; but that which is immediately under consideration, is a continued and oftentimes profuse discharge of thickened mucus, when every symptom of catarrh and fever has passed away. If the horse is at grass, the discharge is almost as green as the food on which he lives;—or if he is stabled, it is white, or straw-coloured, or brown, or even bloody, and sometimes purulent. It is either constantly running, or snorted out in masses many times a day; teazing the horse, and becoming a perfect nuisance in the stable, and to the rider. This has been known to continue several months, and eventually to destroy the horse.

If the discharge is not offensive to the smell, nor mixed wtih purulent matter, it is probably merely an increased and somewhat vitiated secretion from the cavities of the nose; and, all fever having disappeared, will frequently yield to small doses of blue vitriol, given twice in the day. If fever or cough remains, the cough medicine that will hereafter be described must be combined with the tonic. If the discharge is mingled with pus, and very offensive, the vegetable tonics, gentian and ginger, may be added to the copper; but there is now reason to apprehend that the discharge will not be controlled, and will terminate in glanders. Turning into a salt marsh will occasionally effect a cure, when both the mineral and the vegetable tonics have failed.*

OZENA.

Ozena is ulceration of the membrane of the nose, not always or often visible, but recognised by the discharge of muco-purulent matter, and the peculiar stench from which the disease derives its name. It resembles glanders, in being confined, in most instances, to one nostril, and the submaxillary gland on the same side being enlarged; but differs from it in the gland not being adherent, and the discharge, from its earliest stage, being purulent and stinking.

There is sometimes a fœtid discharge from the nostril, in consequence of inflammation of the lungs, or produced by some of the sequelæ of pheumonia; distinguished, however, from ozena,

* *Note by Mr. Spooner.*—It is exceedingly rare that the nasal discharge s ever so profuse as that described in the text, unless produced by strangles, or severe catarrh, or glanders: nor is it brown or bloody, unless connected with other active disease. It is, indeed, very rare, and is usually of a gray color and free from smell, and seems to arise from a relaxation of the secreting membrane of the nostrils. It should be treated by tonics internally, assisted by good feeding and grooming.

by its usually flowing irregularly, being coughed up in great quantities, more decidedly purulent, and the gland or glands seldom affected. The discharge from ozena is constant, mucopurulent, and attended by enlargement of the glands. It is of immense consequence that we should be enabled to distinguish the one from the other; for while ozena may, sometimes at least, be manageable, the other is too frequently the precursor of death.

The cause of ozena cannot always be discovered. Chronic inflammation of the membrane may assume another and malignant character. In severe catarrh, the membrane may become abraded, and the abrasions may degenerate into foul and fœtid ulcers. It is not an unfrequent consequence of epidemic catarrh. It has been produced by caustic applications to the lining membrane of the nose. It has followed hemorrhage, spontaneous, or the consequence of injury.

In some cases, and those as obstinate as any, it cannot perhaps be traced to any probable cause, and the health of the animal has not appeared to be in the slightest degree affected.

The steam of a bran-mash, scalding hot, could, by means of a nose-bag, be made to penetrate the cavities of the nose, and would cleanse the part. By means of the nose-bag and warm mash, chloride of lime might be introduced into the cavities, removing the stench and arresting the tendency to decomposition. The vapor of turpentine, or of resinous pine shavings, can by the same means be brought in contact with all parts of the membrane, and it has been found serviceable. A run at *spring grass* promises still better. It is the finest alterative, depurative, and restorative in the whole list of remedies; and if it is acceptable in the form of a salt-marsh, there is no better chance of doing good.*

* *Note by Mr. Spooner.*—When a nasal gleet is attended by much offensive smell, we may rest assured that it is not glanders, but that it either arises from external injury, or may be justly included under the designation *ozena*. This is a rare disease in a horse, and is generally produced by catarrh, particularly that of the epidemic kind. The discharge is usually thick, considerable, and very offensive. The treatment should consist of tonics, internally and externally, fumigations of chlorine gas by means of Read's inhaler, or with the common nose bag; or, if this does not succeed a solution of the chloride of lime may be syringed up the nostrils every day, or may be alternated with a weak solution of the sulphates of zinc and copper, and applied in the same manner. Nasal gleet, attended with fœtid smell, and proceeding from one nostril only, is usually produced by some blow, or external injury. This much resembles glanders, and has often been confounded with it.

GLANDERS.

The most formidable of all the diseases to which the horse is subject, is Glanders. It has been known from the earliest antiquity.

The earliest symptom of Glanders is an increased discharge from the nostril, small in quantity, constantly flowing, of an aqueous (watery) character, and a little mucus mingling with it.

It is a common and very mischievous error to suppose that this discharge is *sticky*, when it first makes its appearance. It is an aqueous or mucous, but small and constant discharge, and is thus distinguished from catarrh, or nasal gleet, or any other defluxion (discharge) from the nostril. If a horse is in the highest condition, yet has this small watery constant discharge, and especially from one nostril, no time should be lost in separating him from his companions. No harm will be done by this, although the defluxion should not ultimately betray lurking mischief of a worse character.

The peculiar stickiness and gluiness which is generally supposed to distinguish the discharge of glanders from all other mucous and prevalent secretions belongs to the second stage of the disease, and, for many months before this, glanders may have existed in an insidious and highly contagious form. It must be acknowledged, however, that, in the majority of cases, some degree of stickiness does characterise the discharge of glanders from a very early period.

It is a singular circumstance, for which no satisfactory account has yet been given, that when one nostril alone is attacked, it is, in a great majority of cases, the near, or left.

This discharge, in cases of infection, may continue, and in so slight a degree as to be scarcely perceptible, for many months, or even two or three years, unattended by any other disease, even ulceration of the nostril, and yet the horse being decidedly glandered from the beginning, and capable of propagating the malady. In process of time, however, pus (matter) mingles with the discharge, and then another and a characteristic symptom appears. Some of this is absorbed, and the neighbouring glands become affected. If there is discharge from both nostrils, the glands within the under jaw will be on both sides enlarged. If the discharge is from one nostril only, the swelled gland will be found on that side alone. Glanders, however, will frequently exist at an early stage without these swelled glands, and some other diseases, as catarrh, will produce them. Then we must look out for some peculiarity about these glands, and we shall readily find it. The swelling may be at first somewhat large and diffused, but the surrounding enlargement soon goes off, and one or two small distinct glands remain; and they are not in the centre of the channel, but *adhere closely to the jaw on the affected side.*

The membrane of the nose should now be examined, and will materially guide our opinion. It will either be of a dark purplish hue, or almost of a leaden colour, or of any shade between the wo; or if there is some of the redness of inflammation, it will have a purple tinge: but there will never be the faint pink blush of health, or the intense and vivid red of usual inflammation. Spots of ulceration will probably appear on the membrane covering the cartilage of the nose—not mere sore places, or streaks of abrasion, and quite superficial, but small ulcers, unusually approaching to a circular form, deep, and with the edges abrupt and prominent. When these appearances are observed, there can be no doubt about the matter. Care should be taken, however, to ascertain that these ulcers do actually exist, for spots of mucus adhering to the membrane have been more than once taken for them. The finger should, if possible, be passed over the supposed ulcer, in order to determine whether it can be wiped away; and it should be recollected, as was hinted when describing the duct that conveys the tears to the nose, that the orifice of that duct, just within the nostril, and on the inner side of it, has been mistaken for a chancrous ulcer. This orifice is on the continuation of the common skin of the muzzle which runs a little way up the nostril, while the ulcer of glanders is on the proper membrane of the nose above. The line of separation between the two is evident on the slightest inspection.

When ulcers begin to appear on the membrane of the nose, the constitution of the horse is soon evidently affected. The patient loses flesh—his belly is tucked up—his coat unthrifty, and readily coming off—the appetite is impaired—the strength fails—cough, more or less urgent, may be heard—the discharge from the nose will increase in quantity; it will be discoloured, bloody, offensive to the smell—the ulcers in the nose will become larger and more numerous, and the air-passages being obstructed, a grating, choking noise will be heard at every act of breathing. There is now a peculiar tenderness about the forehead. The membrane lining the frontal sinuses is inflamed and ulcerated, and the integument of the forehead becomes thickened and somewhat swelled. Farcy is now superadded to glanders, or glanders has degenerated into farcy, and more of the absorbents are involved.

At or before this time little tumours appear about the muscles, and face, and neck, following the course of the veins and the absorbents, for they run side by side; and these the tumours soon ulcerate. Tumours or buds, still pursuing the path of the absorbents, soon appear on the inside of the thighs. They are conaected together by a corded substance. This is the inflamed and enlarged lymphatic; and ulceration quickly follows the appearance of these buds. The deeper seated absorbents are next affected; and one or both of the hind-legs swell to a great size, and become stiff, and hot, and tender. The loss of flesh and strength is more marked every day. The membrane of the nose becomes of a dirty livid color. The membrane of the mouth is strangely pallid. The eye is infiltrated with a yellow fluid; and the discharge from the nose becomes more profuse, and insufferably offensive. The animal presents one mass of putrefaction, and at last dies, exhausted.

There are peculiarities about the enlargement of the submaxillary glands, already referred to, which deserve particular attention. They are rarely large, except at first, or hot, or tender; but they are characterised by a singular hardness, a proximity to the jaw-bone, and, frequently, actual adhesion to it. The adhesion is produced by the inflammatory action going forward in the gland, and the effusion of coagulable lymph. This hardness and adhesion accompanying discharge from the nostril, and being on the same side with the nostril whence the discharge proceeds, afford proof not to be controverted that the horse is glandered. But there are cases of glanders in which the glands are neither adherent nor much enlarged.

Glanders have often been confounded with *strangles*, and by those who ought to have known better. Strangles are peculiar to young horses. The early stage resembles common cold, with some degree of fever and sore throat—generally with distressing cough, or at least frequent wheezing, and when the enlargement appears beneath the jaw, it is not a single small gland, but a swelling of the whole of the substance between the jaws, growing harder towards the centre, and, after a while, appearing to contain a fluid, and breaking. In strangles, the membrane of the nose will be intensely red, and the discharge from the nose profuse and purulent, or mixed with matter almost from the first. When the tumor has burst, the fever will abate, and the horse will speedily get well.

Should the discharge from the nose continue, as it sometimes does, for a considerable time after the horse has recovered from strangles, there is no cause for fear. Simple strangles need never degenerate into glanders. Good keep, and small doses of tonic medicine, will gradually perfect the cure.

Glanders have been confounded with catarrh or cold; but the distinction between them is plain enough. Fever, and loss of appetite and sore throat, accompany cold—the quidding of the food and gulping of the water are sufficient indications of the latter of these; the discharge from the nose is profuse, and perhaps purulent; the glands under the jaw, if swelled, are moveable, there is a thickening around them, and they are tender and hot. With proper treatment the fever abates; the cough disappears; the swellings under the throat subside; and the discharge from the nose gradually ceases, or, if it remains it is usually very different from that which characterises glanders. In glanders, there is seldom cough of any consequence, and generally no cough at all.

A running from the nose, small in quantity, and, from the smallness of its quantity, drying about the edges of the nostril, and presenting some appearance of stickiness, will, in a few cases, remain after severe catarrh, and especially after the influenza of spring; and these have gradually assumed the character of glanders, and more particularly when they have been accompanied by enlarged glands and ulceration in the nose. Here the aid of a judicious veterinary surgeon is indispensable; and he will sometimes experience considerable difficulty in deciding the case. One circumstance will principally guide him. No disease will run on to glanders which has not, to a considerable and palpable degree, impaired and broken down the constitution; and *every disease that does this will run on to glanders.* He will look then to the general state and condition of the horse, as well as to the situation of the glands, the nature of the discharge, and the character of the ulceration.

If, after all, he is in doubt, an experiment may be resorted to, which wears indeed the appearance of cruelty, and which only the safety of a valuable animal, or of a whole team, can justify. He will inoculate an ass, or a horse already condemned to the hounds, with the matter discharged from the nose. If the horse is glandered, the symptoms of glanders or farcy will appear in the inoculated animal in the course of a few days.

The post mortem examination of the horse will remove every doubt as to the character of the disease. The nostril is generally more or less blanched, with spots or lines of inflammation of considerable intensity. Ulceration is almost invariably found, and of a chancrous character, on the septum, and also on the æthmoid and turbinated bones. The ulcers evidently follow the course of the absorbents, sometimes almost confined to the track of the main vessel, or, if scattered over the membrane generally, thickest over the path of the lymphatic. The æthmoid and turbinated bones are often filled with pus, and sometimes eaten through and carious; but, in the majority of cases, the ulceration is confined to the external membrane, although there may be pus within. In aggravated cases the disease extends through all the cells of the face and head.

The path of the disease down the larynx and windpipe is easily traced, and the ulcers follow one line—that of the absorbents. In aggravated cases, this can generally be traced on to the lungs. It produces inflammation in these organs, characterised in some cases by congestion; but in other cases, the congestion having gone on to hepatisation, in which the cellular texture of the lungs is obliterated. Most frequently, when the lungs are affected at all, tubercles are found—miliary tubercles—minute granulated spots on the surface, or in the substance of the lungs, and not accompanied by much inflammation. In a few cases there are larger tubercles, which soften and burst, and terminate in cavities of varying size.

In some cases, and showing that glanders is not essentially or necessarily a disease of the lungs, there is no morbid affection whatever in those organs.

The history thus given of the symptoms of glanders will clearly point out its nature.

It is inflammation, whether specific or common, of the lining membrane of the nose—possibly for months, and even for years, confined to that membrane, and even to a portion of it—the health and the usefulness of the animal not being in the slightest degree impaired. Then, from some unknown cause, not a new but an intenser action is set up, the inflammation more speedily runs its course, and the membrane becomes ulcerated. The inflammation spreads on either side down the septum, and the ulceration at length assumes that peculiar chancrous form which characterises inflammation of the absorbents. Even then, when the discharge becomes gluey, and sometimes after chancres have appeared, the horse is apparently well. There are hundreds of glandered horses about the country with not a sick one among them. For months or years this disease may do no injury to the general health. The inflammation is purely local, and is only recognised by the invariable accompaniment of inflammation and increased secretion. Its neighbors fall around, but the disease affects not the animal whence it came. At length a constitutional inflammation appears; farcy is established in its most horrible form, and death speedily closes the scene.

Glanders may be either bred in the horse, or communicated by contagion. What we have farther to remark on this malady will be arranged under these two heads.

Improper stable management we believe to be a far more frequent cause of glanders than contagion. The air which is necessary to respiration is changed and empoisoned in its passage through the lungs, and a fresh supply is necessary for the support of life. That supply may be sufficient barely to support life, but not to prevent the vitiated air from again and again passing to the lungs, and producing irritation and disease. The membrane of the nose, possessed of extreme sensibility for the purposes of smell, is easily irritated by this poison, and close and ill-ventilated stables oftenest witness the ravages of glanders. Professor Coleman relates a case which proves to demonstration the rapid and fatal agency of this cause. "In the expedition to Quiberon, the horses had not been long on board the transports before it became necessary to shut down the hatchways for a few hours; the consequence of this was, that some of them were suffocated, and that all the rest were disembarked either glandered or farcied."

The injurious gasses arising from the dung, urine, &c., in badly cleaned stables, are also powerful sources of the mischief.

Glanders may be produced by anything that injures, or for a length of time acts upon and weakens, the vital energy of this membrane. They have been known to follow a fracture of the bones of the nose. They have been the consequence of violent catarrh, and particularly the long-continued discharge from the nostrils, of which we have spoken. They have been produced by the injection of stimulating and acrid substances up the nostril. Everything that weakens the constitution generally will lead to glanders.

Among the causes of glanders are want of regular exercise, over-exertion, and the stimulating and debilitating cordials administered by senseless grooms.

Every exciting cause of disease exerts its chief and worst influence on the membrane of the nose, and there is not another disease which may not lay the foundation of glanders. A long time may elapse before it appears, but when at length the whole frame becomes excited or debilitated in some way, this debilitated portion is the first to yield to the attack.

Several strongly marked instances are on record showing the connection between the attack of this disease and exposure to the dampness of brick or stone stables, the walls of which were not yet dry, and in others subject to damp exhalations.

There is no doubt that glanders, or a predisposition to glanders, is sometimes hereditary.

Glanders are highly contagious. If the discharge from the nostrils of a glandered horse is rubbed on a wound, or on a mucous surface, like the nostrils, it will produce a similar disease. If the division between two horses were sufficiently high to prevent all smelling and snorting at each other, and contact of every kind, and they drank not out of the same pail, a sound horse might live for years, uninfected, by the side of a glandered one. The matter of glanders has been mixed up into a ball, and given to a healthy horse, without effect. Some horses have eaten the hay left by those that were glandered, and no bad consequence has followed; but others have been speedily infected. The glanderous matter must come in contact with a wound, or fall on some membrane, thin and delicate, like that of the nose, and through which it may be absorbed. It is easy, then, accustomed as horses are to be crowded together, and to recognize each other by the smell—eating out of the same manger, and drinking from the same pail—to imagine that the disease may be very readily communicated. One horse has passed another when he was in the act of snorting, and has become glandered. Some fillies have received the infection from the matter blown by the wind across a lane, when a glandered horse, in the opposite field, has claimed acquaintance by neighing or snorting. It is almost impossible for an infected horse to remain long in a stable with others without irreparable mischief.

If some persons underrate the danger, it is because the disease may remain unrecognised in the infected horse for some months, or even years, and therefore, when it appears, it is attributed to other causes, or to after inoculation. No glandered horse should be employed on any farm, nor should a glandered horse be permitted to work on any road, or even to pasture on any field He should be destroyed.

In a well settled case of glanders it is not worth while, except by way of experiment at a veterinary school, to attempt any remedies. The chances of cure are too remote, and the danger of infection too great.

If, however, remedial measures are resorted to, a pure atmosphere is that which should first be tried. Turn out the horse, and, if practicable, on a salt marsh,—but much caution is requisite, as the grass, and even the fences may receive the glanderous matter; and hardening on them, it may months afterward communicate the disease to horses; and there is not yet decided proof that sheep and cattle are not subject to the same malady.

Worse than all, the man who attends on that horse is in danger. The cases are now becoming far too numerous in which the groom or the veterinary surgeon attending on glandered horses becomes infected, and in the majority of cases dies.

Every portion of the stable, every vessel, &c., which have been within the reach of a nasal discharge of a glandered horse, should be well scraped, scoured with soap and water, then well washed with a solution of chloride of lime (a pint of the chloride to a pail full of water,) and the walls white-washed. His head gear should be burned—his clothing baked or washed—pails newly painted—and the iron work with which he has been in contact, should, where practicable, be exposed to a red heat.*

* *Note by Mr. Spooner.*—Mr. S.'s note contains nothing materially adding to Mr. Youatt's elaborate account; but the following is important:
The contagious character of glanders is very well known, and not only

FARCY

Farcy is intimately connected with glanders; they will run into each other, or their symptoms will mingle together, and before either arrives at its fatal termination its associate will almost invariably appear. An animal inocculated with the matter of farcy will often be afflicted with glanders, while the matter of glanders will frequently produce farcy. They are different types or stages of the same disease. There is, however, a very material difference in their symptoms and progress, and this most important one of all, that while glanders are generally incurable, farcy, in its early stage and mild form, may be successfully treated.

While the capillary vessels of the arteries are everywhere employed in building up the frame, the absorbents are no less diligently at work in selecting and carrying away every useless or worn-out portion or part of it. There is no surface on which thousands of these little mouths do not open. Opening on the surfaces of glanderous ulcers, they absorb a portion of the virus secreted by them, and as it passes through these little tubes, they become thickened and inflamed by means of its acrimonious qualities, and hence they received the name of *corded veins* from farriers who mistook them for the veins whose courses they follow.

At certain distances in the course of the absorbents are natural valves, or loose duplicatures of the lining membrane, which are pressed against the side of the vessel and permit the fluid to pass in a direction towards the chest, but belly out and impede or arrest its progress from the chest. The virus at these places, and the additional inflammation there excited, is to a greater or less degree evident to the eye and to the feeling. They are usually first observed about the lips, the nose, the neck and the thighs. They are very hard—even of a scirrhous hardness, more or less tender, and with perceptible heat about them.

The poisonous matter being thus confined and pressing on the part, suppuration and ulceration ensue. The ulcers have the

---

it so with regard to the horse, but it is capable of being communicated to the human being; and, indeed, there have been very many deaths from this cause, and most horrible deaths they are. It is generally by means of some cut or abrasion which comes in contact with the glandered matter, that the infection is communicated. The utmost caution should, therefore, be exercised by the attendants; and it is most unpardonable to keep glandered horses any length of time for the sake of their work; and we are scarcely justified in tampering long with them under the idea of effecting a cure, when the cases are decidedly glandered.

same character as the glanderous ones on the membrane of the nose. They are rounded, with an elevated edge and a pale surface. They are true chancres, and they discharge a virus as infectious and as dangerous as the matter of glanders. While they remain in their hard prominent state, they are called *buttons or farcy buds;* and they are connected together by the inflamed and *corded* veins.

In some cases the horse will droop for many a day before the appearance of the corded veins or buds—his appetite will be impaired—his coat will stare—he will lose flesh. The poison is evidently at work, but has not gained sufficient power to cause the absorbents to enlarge. In a few cases these buds do not ulcerate, but become hard and difficult to disperse. The progress of the disease is then suspended, and possibly for some months the horse will appear to be restored to health; but he bears the seeds of the malady about him, and in due time the farcy assumes its virulent form, and hurries him off. These buds have sometimes been confounded with the little tumors or lumps termed *surfeit.* They are generally higher than these tumors, and not so broad. They have a more knotty character, and are principally found on the inside of the limbs, instead of the outside. The *surfeit bumps* are pustular and end in desquamation (scaling off,) not in ulceration, and they do not follow the course of the absorbents, but are scattered irregularly over the skin.

Few things are more unlike, or more perplexing, than the different forms which farcy assumes at different times. One of the legs, and particularly one of the hinder legs, will suddenly swell to an enormous size. At night the horse will appear to be perfectly well, and in the morning one leg will be three times the size of the other, with considerable fever, and scarcely the power of moving the limb.

At other times the head will be subject to this enlargement, the muzzle particularly will swell, and an offensive discharge will proceed from the nose. Sometimes the horse will gradually lose flesh and strength; he will be hide-bound; many eruptions will appear in different parts; the legs will swell; cracks will be seen at the heels, and an inexperienced person may conceive it to be a mere want of condition, combined with grease.

By degrees the affection becomes general. The virus has reached the termination of the absorbents, and mingles with the general circulating fluid, and is conveyed with the blood to every part of the frame. There are no longer any valves to impede its progress, and consequently no knots or *buds*, but the myriads of capillary absorbents that penetrate every part become inflamed, and thickened, and enlarged, and cease to dis charge their function. Hence arises enlargement of the substance of various parts, swellings of the legs, and chest, and head—sudden, painful, enormous, and distinguished by a heat and tenderness, which do not accompany other enlargements.

Farcy cannot probably exist without previous glanders, and it is certain that it cannot long and extensively prevail without being accompanied by it. They are, in fact, stages of the same disease.

Farcy has been confounded with other diseases; but he must be careless or ignorant who mistook sprain for it. The inflammation is too circumscribed and too plainly connected with the joint or tendon.

It may be readily distinguished from grease or swelled legs. In grease there is usually some crack or scurfiness, a peculiar tenseness and redness and glossiness of the skin, some ichorous discharge, and a singular spasmodic catching up of the leg.

In farcy the engorgement is even more sudden than that of grease. The horse is well to-day, and to-morrow he is gorged from the fet-lock to the haunch, and although there is not the same redness or glossiness, there is great tenderness, a burning heat in the limb, and much general fever. It is simultaneous inflammation of all the absorbents of the limb.

Local dropsy of the cellular membrane, and particularly that enlargement beneath the thorax which has the strange appellation of *water-farcy*, have none of the characters of real farcy. It is general debility to a greater or less degree, and not inflammation of the absorbents.

Farcy, like glanders, springs from infection and from bad stable management. It is produced by all the causes which give rise to glanders, with this difference, that it is more frequently generated, and sometimes strangely prevalent in particular districts. The matter of farcy must come in contact with a wound or sore, in order to communicate the disease.

The treatment of farcy differs with the form that it assumes. As a general rule, and especially when the buttons or buds are beginning to appear, a mild dose of physic should first be administered. The buds should then be carefully examined, and if any of them have broken, the budding-iron, at a dull red heat, should be applied. If pus should be felt in them, showing that they are disposed to break, they should be penetrated with the iron. These wounds should be daily inspected, and if, when the slough of the cautery comes off, they look pale, and foul, and spongy, and discharge a thin matter, they should be frequently washed with a strong lotion of corrosive sublimate, dissolved in rectified spirit. When the wounds begin to look red, and the bottom of them is even and firm, and they discharge a thick white or yel low matter, the Friar's balsam will usually dispose them to heal.

As, however, the constitution is now tainted, local applications will not be sufficient, and the disease must be attacked by internal medicine, as soon as the physic has ceased to operate.

The most effectual constitutional remedy is the *diniodide of copper*. It is a stimulant of the absorbent vessels, and a tonic. The gentian root is usually combined with it. Cantharides, in small quantities, may be advantageously added. An indication of its influence is a soreness of the diseased parts, arising from the absorbent vessels being roused into increased action : the agent should then be for a time withheld.

The animal should be generously fed, have green food, if possible, and a free circulation of air.*

THE LIPS.

The *lips* of the horse are far more important organs than many suppose. They are the hands of the animal, and without them he could not convey his food to his mouth. The lips are composed of a muscular substance for the sake of strength, and a multitude of small glands, which secrete a fluid that covers the inside of the lips and the gums, in order to prevent friction, and likewise furnish a portion of the moisture so necessary for the proper chewing of the food.

The lips of the horse should be thin and well kept together : and the depth of the mouth should be considerable. The cor-

---

* *Note by Mr. Spooner.*—The cure of farcy materially depends on the extent to which the constitution is affected by the disease. If it be confined to a single extremity, particularly one of the hind ones, or if the superficial absorbents are alone affected, there is then a very reasonable prospect of establishing a cure. The application of the caustic, as advised in the text, is very proper ; but we may also materially assist the case by rubbing into any swollen part, or along the course of the absorbents, an ointment consisting of

Iodine	ʒ 1
Lard	ʒ 1
Mercurial ointment	ʒ 1

to be incorporated together.

Advantage will also be felt by the internal exhibition of five to ten grains daily of hydriodate of potash in combination with a mineral tonic, such as sulphate of iron, three drachms, and gentian, two drachms. The ointment as well as the ball must be continued for some time.

We have succeeded in many cases by this mode of treatment, though it must be acknowledged that there is no disease, to which the horse is liable, so deceptive as this. When the external symptoms are most favourable, the ulcers healed, and the swelling reduced, the disease will sometimes break out again, and prove rapidly fatal.

ners or angles of the lips are sometimes wounded by the tightness of the bearing-rein, or by sharp or badly formed bits. If inflammation or ulcers in the mouth follow contusions inflicted by the bit, a little cooling medicine may be administered; and to the ulcers themselves, tincture of myrrh, diluted with water, or alum dissolved in water, may be applied with advantage.

THE BONES OF THE MOUTH.

The bones, in and giving form to the mouth, are the superior maxillary or upper jaw (*b*, Fig. 1, and *l*, Fig. 2,) containing the grinders : the anterior maxillary, or lower part of the upper jaw, (*b*, Fig. 1, *n*, Fig. 2, *r*, Fig. 3,) containing the upper-nippers or cutting-teeth ; the palatine bone (below 8, Fig. 3,) and the posterior maxillary or under jaw (*a*, Fig. 1, and *w*, Fig. 3,) containing all the under-teeth.

The size of these, their connection with the other bones of the head, and their muscular attachments, will be sufficiently learned from a careful inspection of the cuts, Figs. 1, 2, 3, and 12.

THE PALATE.

Adhering to a portion of the three bones just described, and constituting the lining of the roof of the mouth, is the palate (*t*, Fig. 3,) composed of an elastic and dense substance, divided into several ridges called *bars*. The following cut gives a view of them.

Fig. 13.

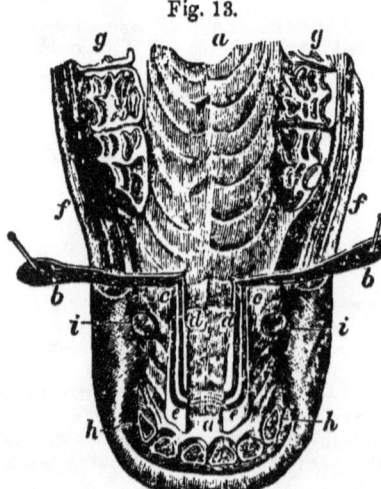

a The palate, divided into ridges or bars.
b A strip dissected up to show the vessels and nerve beneath.
c The palatine artery.
d The palatine vein.
e The palatine nerve, between the artery and the vein.
f The cheek divided, showing the direction of the muscular fibres.
g The grinders.
h The nippers.
i The tushes.

It will also point out the bleeding place, if it should occasionally be deemed advisable to abstract blood from the mouth; or, if the horse should be attacked with megrims on a journey, and the driver, having no lancet, should be compelled to make use of his knife, the incision should be made between the central and second nippers on either side, about an inch within the mouth, and cutting through the second bar. A stream of blood will be thus obtained, which will usually cease to flow when two or three quarts have escaped, or may generally be arrested by the application of a sponge filled with cold water.

Should the cut be made a little too much on one side, and about the middle of the second incisor tooth, the artery may be wounded longitudinally, but not divided, and there may be very great difficulty in stopping the blood. We recollect a horse which almost bled to death from the artery being thus wounded. If, however, a large and firm pledget of lint or tow be rolled round a piece of twine, and that tied firmly round the front teeth, the pressure on the part will effect the desired purpose; or, should this in a very few cases fail, a gag may be easily contrived to press upon the pledget, and the bleeding will immediately cease.

This, however, is a make-shift sort of bleeding, that may be allowable on a journey, and possibly in some cases of lampas, but which is decidedly objectionable as the usual mode of abstracting blood. The quantity withdrawn cannot be measured, the degree of inflammation cannot be ascertained by the manner in which it coagulates, and there may be difficulty to the operator, and annoyance and pain to the horse, in stopping the bleeding.

LAMPAS.

The bars occasionally swell, and rise to a level with, and even beyond the edge of, the teeth. They are very sore, and the horse feeds badly on account of the pain he suffers from the pressure of the food on them. This is called the LAMPAS. It may arise from inflammation of the gums, propagated to the bars, when the horse is shedding his teeth—and young horses are more subject to it than others—or from some slight febrile tendency in the constitution generally, as when a young horse has lately been taken up from grass, and has been over-fed, or not sufficiently exercised. At times, it appears in aged horses; for the process of growth in the teeth of the horse is continued during the whole life of the animal.

In the majority of cases, the swelling will soon subside without medical treatment; or a few mashes, and gentle alteratives, will relieve the animal. A few slight incisions across the bars with a lancet, or pen-knife, will remove the inflammation, and cause the swelling to subside; indeed, this scarification of the bars in lampas will seldom do harm, although it is far from being so necessary as is supposed. The brutal custom of the farrier, who sears and burns down the bars with a red-hot iron, is most objectionable. It is torturing the horse to no purpose, and rendering that part callous, on the delicate sensibility of which all the pleasure and safety of riding and driving depend. It may be prudent, in case of lampas, to examine the grinders, and more particularly the tushes, in order to ascertain whether either of them is making its way through the gum. If it is so, two incisions across each other should be made on the tooth, and the horse will experience immediate relief.*

THE LOWER JAW.

The posterior or lower jaw may be considered as forming the floor of the mouth (*a*, Fig. 1, or *w*, Fig. 3). The body, or lower part of it, contains the under cutting teeth and the tushes, and at the sides are two flat pieces of bone containing the grinders. [See the preceding cuts of the anatomy and tissues of the head]. The joint which connects the lower to the upper jaw, unlike that in carnivorous animals, is so constructed, that it not only admits of the simple motion of a hinge, but of a lateral or grinding motion, necessary to break down vegetable fibre, and fit it for the stomach.

* *Note by Mr. Spooner.*—It is almost impossible that the swelling of the bars of the mouth, denominated lampas, can interfere with the process of mastication, when the horse is in the stable and feeding on grain, for we well know that the food is ground as in a mill, by the *molar* teeth. It often happens, however, that connected with this lampas, there is an inability to masticate properly; the horse quids his food, as it is called, that is, throws it out of his mouth in rolls covered with saliva. On the same principle as "Tenterden steeple being the cause of Goodwin sands," the lampas has been regarded as the cause of this imperfect mastication. If we look farther, however, we shall almost invariably find that the gums are swelled generally, and particularly the membranous tissues covering the lower jaw-bone, between the molar and incisor teeth; so much so, that when the horse attempts to masticate, this membrane gets between the molar teeth and causes pain, and interrupts the process of mastication. This state of the parts is often overlooked, and the horse becomes weak and thin from not having sufficient nutriment. This disease, if it can be called so, is commonly termed the Bags, or Washes, and is relieved by cutting off a portion of the membrane by means of a pair of scissors; the bleeding relieves the inflammation, and the cicatrization of the wound causes the membrane to contract, so as to be put out of the way of further injury from the teeth. The horse should have mashes for some days after the operation, and care must be taken that the bit does not injure the denuded part.

PROCESS OF TEETHING.

The space beneath between the jaw-bones, called the *channel*, is of considerable consequence. It may be a little too wide, and then the face will have a clumsy appearance: but if it is too narrow, the horse will never be able to bend his head freely and gracefully; he will be always pulling or boring upon the hand, nor can he possibly be well reined in.

The jaws contain the teeth, which are the millstones employed in comminuting the food. The mouth of the horse at five years old contains forty teeth, viz.: six nippers or cutting-teeth in front, a tush on each side, and six molars, or grinding-teeth, above and below. The gums are singularly compact, that it may not be wounded by the hard or sharp particles of the food, and almost devoid of feeling, for the same purpose.

Seven or eight months before the foal is born, the germs or beginnings of the teeth are visible in the cavities of the jaws. At the time of birth, the first and second grinders have appeared, large compared with the size of the jaw, and seemingly filling it. In the course of seven or eight days the two central nippers are seen as in Fig. 14. They likewise appear to be large, and to fill the front of the mouth; although they will afterwards be found to be small, compared with the permanent teeth that follow. In the course of the first month the third grinder appears above and below, and, not long after, and generally before six weeks have expired, another incisor above and below will be seen on each side of the two first, which have now considerably grown, but not attained their perfect height. The second cut will represent the appearance of the mouth at that time.

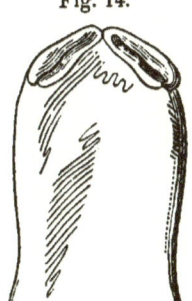

Fig. 14.

At two months, the central nippers will have reached their natural level, and between the second and third month the second pair will have overtaken them. They will then begin to wear away a little, and the outer edge, which was at first somewhat raised and sharp, is brought to a level with the inner one, and so the mouth continues until some time between the sixth and ninth month, when another nipper begins to appear on each side of the two first, making six above and below, and completing the colt's mouth; after which, the only observable difference, until between the second and third year, is in the wear of these teeth. See Fig. 15

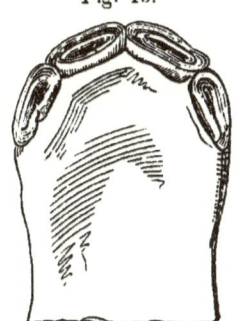

Fig. 15.

The teeth are covered with a polished and exceedingly hard substance, called the enamel. It spreads over that portion of the teeth which appears above the gum, and not only so, but as they are to be so much employed in nipping the grass, and gathering up the animal's food, and in such employment even this hard substance must be gradually worn away, a portion of it, as it passes over the upper surface of the teeth, is bent inward, and sunk into the body of the teeth, and forms a little pit in them. The inside and bottom of this pit being blackened by the food, constitutes the *mark* of the teeth, by the gradual disappearance of which, in consequence of the wearing down of the edge, we are enabled, for several years, to judge of the age of the animal.

The colt's nipping-teeth are rounded in front, somewhat hollow towards the mouth, and present at first a cutting surface, with the outer edge rising in a slanting direction above the inner edge. This, however, soon begins to wear down until both surfaces are level, and the *mark*, which was originally long and narrow, becomes shorter, and wider, and fainter. At six months the four nippers are beginning to wear to a level. The annexed cut will convey some idea of the appearance of the teeth at twelve months. The four middle teeth are almost level, and the corner ones becoming so. The mark in the two middle teeth is wide and faint; in the two next teeth it is darker, and longer, and narrower; and in the corner teeth it is darkest, and longest, and narrowest.

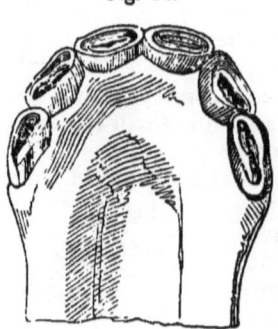

Fig. 16.

The back teeth, or grinders, will not guide us far in ascertaining the age of the animal, for we cannot easily inspect them; but there are some interesting particulars connected with them. The foal is born with two grinders in each jaw, above and below; or they appear within three or four days after the birth. Before the expiration of a month they are succeeded by a third, more backward. The crowns of the grinders are entirely covered with enamel on the top and sides, but attrition soon wears it away from the top, and there remains a compound surface of alternate layers of crusted petraser, enamel, and ivory, which are employed in grinding down the hardest portion of the food. Nature has, therefore, made an additional provision for their strength and endurance.

Fig. 17 represents a grinder sawed across. The five dark spots represent bony matter; the parts covered with lines, enamel; and the white spaces, a strong bony cement, uniting the other portions of the teeth.

Fig. 17.

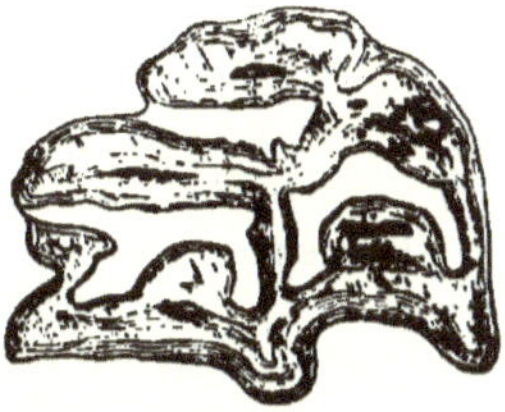

At the completion of the first year, a fourth grinder usually comes up, and the yearling has then, or soon afterwards, six nippers, and four grinders above and below in each jaw, which, with the alteration in the appearance of the nippers that we have just described, will enable us to calculate nearly the age of the foal, suject to some variations arising from the period of weaning, and the nature of the food.

At the age of one year and a-half, the mark in the central nippers will be much shorter and fainter; that in the two other pairs will have undergone an evident change, and all the nippers will be flat.

Fig. 18.

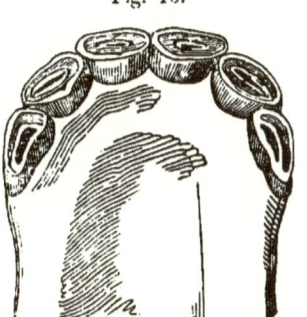

At two years this will be more manifest. The accompanying cut (Fig. 18,) deserves attention, as giving an accurate represention of the nippers in the lower jaw of a two-years-old colt.

About this period a fifth grinder will appear, and now, likewise, will commence another process. The first teeth are adapted to the size and wants of the young animal They are sufficiently large to occupy and fill the colt's jaws; but when these bones have expanded with the increasing growth of the animal, the teeth are separated too far from each other to be useful, and another and larger set is required. The second teeth then begin to push up from below, and the fangs of the first are *absorbed*, until the former approach the surface of the gum, when they drop out. Where the temporary teeth do not rise immediately under the milk-teeth, but by their sides, the latter being pressed sideway, are absorbed throughout their whole length. They grow narrow, are pushed out of place, and cause inconvenience to the gums, and sometimes the cheek. They are then called *wolf's-teeth*, and they should be extracted.*

The teeth which first appeared are first renewed, and there-

---

* *Note by Mr. Spooner.*—Although irregularities of the teeth sometimes occur, as mentioned in the text, yet the wolves' teeth are generally two very small supplementary teeth appearing in front of the molar teeth; and,

fore the front or first grinder is changed at the age of two years.

During the period between the falling out of the central milk nippers, and the coming up of the permanent ones, the colt, having a broken mouth, may find some difficulty in grazing. If he should fall away considerably in condition, he should be fed with mashes and corn, or cut feed.

The next cut (Fig. 19,) will represent a three-year-old mouth. The central teeth are larger than the others, with two grooves in the outer convex surface, and the mark is long, narrow, deep and black. Not having yet attained their full growth, they are rather lower than the others. The mark in the two next nippers is nearly worn out, and it is wearing away in the corner nippers. Is it possible to give this mouth to an early two-years-old? The ages of all horses used to be reckoned from May, but some are foaled even so early as January, and being actually four months over the two years, if they have been well nursed and fed, and are strong and large, they may, with the inexperienced, have an additional year put upon them. The central nippers are punched or drawn out, and the others appear three or four months earlier than they otherwise would. In the natural process, they could only rise by long pressing upon, and causing the absorption of, the first set. But opposition from the first set being removed, it is easy to imagine that their progress will be more rapid. Three or four months will be gained in the appearance of the teeth, and these three or four months may enable the breeder to term him a late colt of a preceding year. To him, however, who is accustomed to horses, the general form of the animal—the little development of the fore-hand—the continuance of the mark on the next pair of nippers—its more evident existence in the corner ones, some enlargement or irregularity about the gums from the violence used in forcing out the teeth—the small growth of the first and fifth grinders and the non-appearance of the sixth

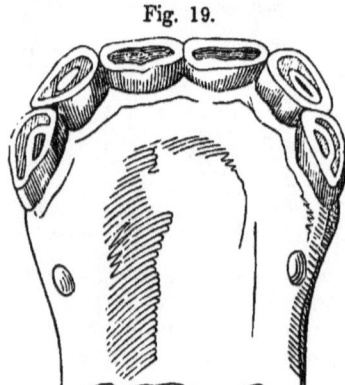

Fig. 19.

though supposed to have an injurious effect on the eyes, we have rarely, if ever, found that they produce any injurious effect, either on the eyes or the mouth, and, consequently, it is useless to interfere with them. When, however, the teeth grow irregularly, the permanent ones appearing by the side of the temporary, the latter should be removed.

grinder, which if it is not through the gum at three years old, is swelling under it, and preparing to get through—any or all of these circumstances, carefully attended to, will be a sufficient security against deception.

A horse at three years old ought to have the central permanent nippers growing—the other two pairs wasting—six grinders in each jaw, above and below—the first and fifth level with the others, and the sixth protruding. The sharp edge of the new incisors, although it could not be well expressed in the cut, will be very evident when compared with the neighboring teeth.

As the permanent nippers wear, and continue to grow, a narrower portion of the cone-shaped tooth is exposed to the attrition, and they look as if they had been compressed, but it is not so. The mark, of course, gradually disappears as the pit is worn away.

At three years and a half, or between that and four, the next pair of nippers will be changed, and the mouth at that time cannot be mistaken. The central nippers will have attained nearly their full growth. A vacuity will be left where the second stood, or they will begin to peep above the gum, and the corner ones will be diminished in breadth, worn down, and the mark becoming small and faint. At this period, likewise, the second pair of grinders will be shed. Previously to this may be the attempt of the dealer to give to his three-year-old an additional year, but the fraud will be detected by an examination similar to that which has been already described.

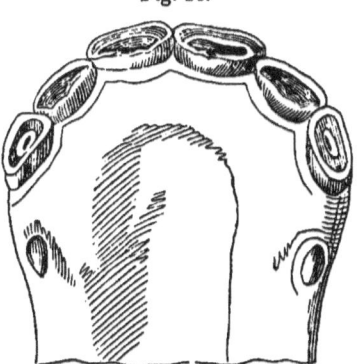

Fig. 20.

At four years, the central nippers will be fully developed; the sharp edge somewhat worn off, and the mark shorter, wider, and fainter. The next pair will be up, but they will be small, with the mark deep, and extending quite across them. The corner nippers will be larger than the inside ones, yet smaller than they were, and flat, and the mark nearly effaced. The sixth grinder will have risen to a level with the others, and the tushes will begin to appear.

Now, more than at any other time, will the dealer be anxious to put an additional year upon the animal, for the difference between a four-years-old colt, and a five-years-old horse, in strength, utility, and value, is very great; but, the want of wear in the other nippers—the small size of the corner ones—the little growth of the tush—the smallness of the second grinder—the low fore-hand—the legginess of the colt, and the thickness and little depth of the mouth, will, to the man of common experience among horses, at once detect the cheat.

The tushes (see Fig. 13,) are four in number, two in each jaw, situated between the nippers and the grinders—much nearer to the former than the latter, and nearer in the lower jaw than in the upper, but this distance increasing in both jaws with the age. It is conical, protrudes about an inch from the gum, and is sharp pointed and curved. Mares have the rudiments of them, and they usually appear externally in old age.

The appearance of the tush in the horse may vary from four years to four years and six months. It can only be accelerated a few weeks by cutting the gum over it.

At four years and a half, or between that and five, the last important change takes place in the mouth of the horse. The corner nippers are shed, and the permanent ones begin to appear The central nippers are considerably worn, and the next pair are commencing to show marks of usage. The tush has now protruded, and is generally a full half-inch in height; externally it has a rounded prominence, with a groove on either side, and it is evidently hollowed within. The reader needs not to be told that after the rising of the corner nipper, the animal changes its name—the colt becomes a horse, and the filly a mare.

At five years the horse's mouth is almost perfect, (see Fig. 21.)

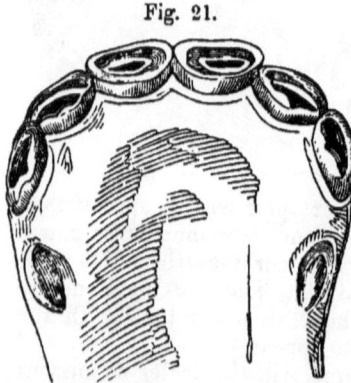

Fig. 21.

The corner nippers are quite up, with the long deep mark irregular on the inside; and the other nippers bearing evident tokens of increasing wearing. The tush is much grown—the grooves have almost or quite disappeared, and the outer surface is regularly convex. It is still as concave within, and with the edge nearly as sharp as it was six months before. The sixth molar is quite up, and the third molar is wanting. This last circumstance, if the general appearance of the animal, and particularly his forehead and the wearing of the centre nippers, and the growth and shape of the tushes, are likewise carefully attended to, will prevent deception if a late four-years-old is attempted to be substituted for a five The nippers may be brought up a few months before their time and the tushes a few weeks, but the grinder is with difficulty displaced. The three last grinders and the tushes are never shed.

At six years, (see Fig. 22,) the *mark* on the central nippers is worn out. There will still be a difference of color in the centre of the tooth. The cement filling up the hole, made by the dipping in of the enamel, will present a browner hue than the other part of the tooth, and it will be evidently surrounded by an edge of enamel, and there will even remain a little depression in the centre, and also a depression round the case of enamel: but the deep hole in the centre of the teeth, with the blackened surface which it presents, and the elevated edge of enamel, will have disappeared. Persons not much accustomed to horses have been puzzled here. They expected to find a plain surface of a uniform color, and knew not what conclusion to draw when there was both discoloration and irregularity.

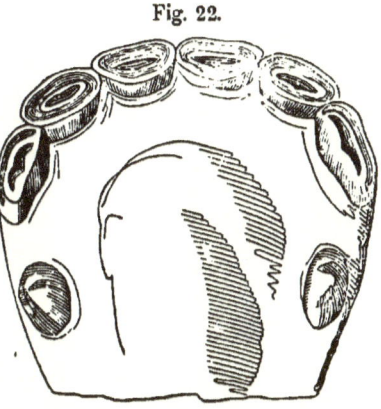

Fig. 22.

In the next incisors the mark is shorter, broader and fainter; and in the corner teeth the edges of the enamel are more regular, and the surface is evidently worn. The tush has attained its full growth, being nearly or quite an inch in length; convex outward, concave within; tending to a point, and the extremity somewhat curved. The third grinder is fairly up; and all the grinders are level.

The horse may now be said to have a perfect mouth. All the teeth are produced, fully grown, and have hitherto sustained no material injury. During these important changes of the teeth, the animal has suffered less than could be supposed possible. In children, the period of teething is fraught with danger. Dogs are subject to convulsions, and hundreds of them die, from the irritation caused by the cutting or shedding of their teeth; but the horse appears to feel little inconvenience. The gums and palate are occasionally somewhat hot and swollen; but the slightest scarification will remove this. The teeth of the horse are more necessary to him than those of the other animals are to them. The child may be fed, and the dog will bolt his food; but that of the horse must be well ground down, or the nutriment cannot be extracted from it.

At seven years, (see Fig. 23,) the mark, in the way in which we have described it, is worn out in the four central nippers, and fast wearing away in the corner teeth; the tush also is beginning to be altered. It is rounded at the point; rounded at the edges; still round without; and beginning to get round inside.

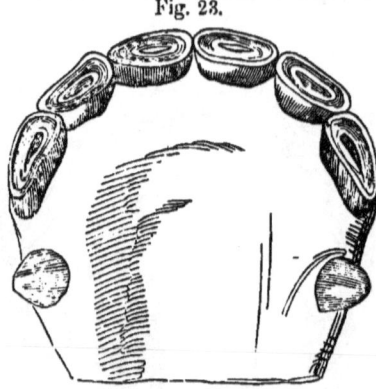
Fig. 23.

At eight years old, the tush is rounder in every way; the mark is gone from all the bottom nippers, and it may almost be said to be out of the mouth. There is nothing remaining in the bottom nippers that can afterwards clearly show the age of the horse, or justify the most experienced examiner in giving a positive opinion.

Dishonest dealers have been said to resort to a method of prolonging the mark in the lower nippers. It is called *bishoping*, from the name of the scoundrel who invented it. The horse of eight or nine years old, (see Fig. 24,) is thrown, and with an engraver's tool a hole is dug in the now almost plain surface of the corner teeth, and in shape and depth resembling the mark in a seven-years-old horse. The hole is then burned with a heated iron, and a permanent black stain is left. The next pair of nippers are sometimes lightly touched. An ignorant man would be very easily imposed on by this trick: but the irregular appearance of the cavity—the diffusion of the black stain around the tushes, the sharpened edges and concave inner surface of which can never be given again—the marks on the upper nippers, together with the general conformation of the horse, can never deceive the careful examiner

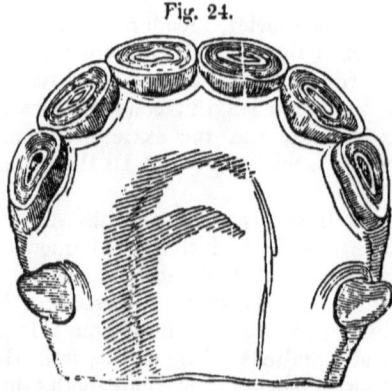
Fig. 24.

Horsemen, after the animal is eight years old, are accustomed to look to the nippers in the upper jaw, and some conclusion has been drawn from the appearances which they present. It cannot be doubted that the mark remains in them for some years after it has been obliterated from the nippers in the lower jaw.

There are various opinions as to the intervals between the disappearance of the marks from the different cutting-teeth in the upper jaw. Some have averaged it at two years, and others at one. The author is inclined to adopt the latter opinion, and then the age will be thus determined. at nine years, the mark will be worn out from the middle nippers—from the next pair at ten, and from all the upper nippers at eleven. During these periods, the tush is likewise undergoing a manifest change—it is blunter, shorter, and rounder In what degree this takes place in the different periods, long and most favorable opportunities for observation can alone enable the horseman to decide.

The alteration in the form of the tushes is frequently uncertain. It will sometimes be blunt at eight, and at others, remain pointed at eighteen.

After eleven, and until the horse is very old, the age may be guessed at, with some degree of confidence, from the shape of the upper surface or extremity of the nippers. At eight, they are all oval, the length of the oval running across from tooth to tooth; but as the horse gets older, the teeth diminish in size—and this commencing in their width, and not in their thickness. They become a little apart from each other, and their surfaces become round instead of oval. At nine, the centre nippers are evidently so; at ten, the others begin to have the oval shortened. At eleven, the second pair of nippers are quite rounded; and at thirteen, the corner ones have that appearance. At fourteen, the faces of the central nippers become somewhat triangular. At seventeen, they are all so. At nineteen, the angles begin to wear off, and the central teeth are again oval, but in a reversed direction, viz., from outward, inward; and at twenty-one, they all wear this form.

It would of course be folly to expect anything like certainty in an opinion of the exact age of an old horse, drawn from the above indications. Stabled horses have the marks sooner worn out than those that are at grass, and crib-biters still sooner. At nine or ten, the bars of the mouth become less prominent, and their regular diminution will designate increasing age. At eleven or twelve, the lower nippers change their original upright direction, and project forward or horizontally, and become of a yellow color.

The general indications of old age, independent of the teeth, are deepening of the hollows over the eyes; gray hairs, and particularly over the eyes and about the muzzle; thinness and hanging down of the lips; sharpness of the withers; sinking of the oack; lengthening of the quarters; and the disappearance of windgalls, spavins, and tumors of every kind.

Horses, kindly and not prematurely used, sometimes live to between thirty-five and forty years of age; and Mr. Percivall gives an account of a barge horse that died in his sixty-second year.*

DISEASES OF THE TEETH.

Of the diseases of the teeth in the horse, we know little. Carious or hollow teeth are occasionally, but not often, seen; but the edges of the grinders, from the wearing off of the enamel, or

* *Note by Mr. Spooner.*—We have little to add. There are exceptions, however, to the above rules. We have known a horse at twelve exhibit the same appearance as another at six. In such instances, the age must be judged by the length and shape of the teeth, and more particularly by the shape of the faces of the teeth.

A careful examination leads me to believe that the observation in the text, that the teeth are developed much earlier in young animals that are cornfed and taken early into the stable, and that in thorough-bred horses, consequently, the changes of the teeth are earlier than in animals that remain more in a state of nature, is erroneous. I think them, of the two, rather more backward. Many successful attempts have doubtless been made to run four year old horses for three year olds, as in the celebrated case of Running Rein, which obtained such notoriety. An incisor tooth, when it is first shed, and for some time afterwards, is higher on the outer or front edge, than the inner or back edge. After some time, this outer edge is worn down to the same level as the inner, and subsequently both edges wear equally, till the bottom of the hole which forms the mark is reached, when, of course, the mark disappears. It takes about three years to effect this process, that is, from the time the tooth is cut to the disappearance of the mark. In a four year old mouth, there are four permanent lower incisors, and two corner temporary teeth. The outer and inner edge of the central teeth are tolerably level, and the mark smaller than the middle teeth next them, which present the appearance of younger teeth. Now, in a three-year old mouth the central teeth have a younger appearance, the mark being larger, and the outer edge higher, than the inner, whilst the middle teeth are either in the act of being cut, or the temporary teeth have not yet disappeared. By careful examination, therefore, the difference between a three and four year old horse can be readily detected. The permanent teeth differ from the temporary, being larger, less white, and having more depth above the gums.

After the marks have disappeared, the age of the horse may be judged partly by the shape of the faces of the teeth, and partly by the horizontal position in which the teeth proceed from the jaw. If we take a young incisor tooth and saw it off below the bottom of the hole which forms the mark, and again at a similar distance lower down, we shall find that the several surfaces made by the sections resemble the shape of the face of the tooth in a horse in which a similar quantity of the tooth has been naturally worn down. The comparison also holds good with regard to the direction in which the teeth proceed from the lower jaw, being in the young animal upright or curved, and in the old one nearly horizontal. Although the teeth grow to supply the loss of that which wears away, yet the original shape remains, so that the face of an incisor tooth at different periods is owing to that particular part which, in its turn, reaches and forms the surface.

the irregular growth of the teeth, become rough, and wound the inside of the cheek; it is then necessary to adopt a summary, but effectual method of cure; namely, to rasp them smooth. Many bad ulcers have been produced in the mouth by neglect of this.

The teeth sometimes grow irregularly in length—particularly the grinders—from not meeting the proper opposition of the corresponding tooth in the other jaw. These sometimes penetrate the bars, causing ulceration; and at others, interfere partially or entirely with the grinding motion of the jaw. The teeth should be reduced to the level of the others with a saw, and occasionally looked to, because the difficulty will return. Horses often pine away from this unsuspected cause. Every horse that grows thin without apparent cause, especially if he *quids*, (partly chews and then drops his feed) should be looked to in this particular. Very irregular teeth lessen the value of a horse, and to all intents and purposes constitute unsoundness.

Decayed teeth should be removed to prevent injury to the other teeth and to the jaw. The hammer and punch should never be resorted to in this operation, but a keyed instrument, like that of the human subject, only on a larger scale.*

Fever, cough, catarrhal affections generally, disease of the eyes, cutaneous affections, diarrhœa, dysentery, loss of appetite, and general derangement, will frequently be traced by the careful observer to irritation from teething, in the colt.

It is a rule scarcely admitting of the slightest deviation, that, when young horses are laboring under any febrile affection, the mouth should be examined, and if the tushes are prominent and pushing against the gums, a crucial (in the form of a cross) incision should be made across them. Relief will often be immediate.

THE TONGUE.

The tongue is the organ of taste. It is also employed in disposing the food for being ground between the teeth, and afterwards collecting it together, and conveying it to the back part of the mouth, in order to be swallowed. It is likewise the main instrument in swallowing, and the canal through which the water passes in the act of drinking. Its form, attachments. &c., are too well known to require description.

* The keyed instrument is now banished from human practice, and the substitutes for it might probably be advantageously introduced into veterinary practice.—*American Editor.*

DISEASES OF THE TONGUE.

The tongue is frequently lacerated by carelessness in administering medicine, by the bit, and sometimes by being bitten by the animal itself. A little diluted tincture of myrrh, or alum dissolved in water, or, if the wound is not serious, unassisted nature, will heal the parts.

Purple-colored vesicles or bladders will sometimes appear along the under side of the tongue, and increase to considerable size; the tongue will be enlarged so that it becomes difficult to swallow; and a great quantity of ropy saliva will drivel from the mouth. Lance the vesicles freely and deeply from end to end and they will soon disappear, and any little fever that remains may be subdued by cooling medicine.

THE SALIVARY GLANDS.

In order that the food may be properly comminuted preparatory to digestion, it is necessary that it should be previously moistened. Nature has made a provision for this. She has placed in the neighborhood of the mouth various glands to secrete, and that plentifully, a limpid fluid, somewhat saline to the taste. This fluid is conveyed from the glands into the mouth, by various ducts, in the act of chewing, and, being mixed with the food, renders it more easily ground, more easily passed afterwards into the stomach, and better fitted for digestion.

The principal of these is the *parotid* gland (see Fig. 12). The quantity of fluid poured into the mouth, in the act of mastication, from each of these glands, amounts to a pint in half an hour.

The parotid gland sympathizes with every inflammatory affection of the upper part of the throat, and therefore it is found swollen, hot, and tender, in almost every catarrh or cold. The catarrh is to be treated in the usual way; while a stimulating application, almost amounting to a blister, well rubbed over the gland, will best subdue the inflammation of that body.

In bad strangles, and, sometimes, in violent cold, this gland will be much enlarged and ulcerated, or an obstruction will take place in some part of the duct, and the accumulating fluid will burst the vessel, and a fistulous ulcer will be formed that will be very difficult to heal. A veterinary surgeon alone will be competent to the treatment of either case; and the principle by which he will be guided, will be to heal the abscess in the gland as speedily as he can, and, probably, by the application of the heated iron: or, if the ulcer is in the duct, either to restore the passage through the duct, or to form a new one, or to cut off the flow of the saliva by the destruction of the gland.

A second source of the saliva is from the *submaxillary* glands. or the glands under the jaw. One of them is represented at s, Fig. 12. When the horse has catarrh or cold, these glands, like the parotid gland, enlarge. This is often to be observed after strangles, and several distinct kernels are to be felt under the jaw. The farriers call them VIVES, and often adopt cruel and absurd methods to disperse them,—as burning them with a lighted candle, or hot iron, or even cutting them out. They will, in the majority of instances, gradually disperse in proportion as the disease which produced them subsides; or they will yield to slightly stimulating embrocations; or, if they are obstinate in their continuance, they are of no further consequence, than as indicating that the horse has labored under severe cold or strangles.

During catarrh, the little protuberances marking the mouths of these ducts on either side of the bridle of the tongue, are apt to enlarge, and the mouth under the tongue is a little red, and hot, and tender. The farriers call these swellings BARBS or PAPS; and as soon as they discover them, mistaking the effect of disease for the cause of it, they set to work to cut them close off. The bleeding that follows this operation somewhat abates the local inflammation, and affords temporary relief; but the wounds will not speedily heal, and even when healed are apt to break out again for months or years afterwards. These paps disappear with the cold that caused them, and should not be meddled with.

The *sublingual glands*, resembling little folds in the integument on the lower side of the tongue, or on the bottom of the mouth, sometimes enlarge during catarrh, and are called *gigs*, *bladders*, or *flaps in the mouth*. Let them alone; and should any ulceration remain after that abatement of the swelling, use tincture of myrrh, or a solution of alum.

STRANGLES.*

This is a disease principally incident to young horses—usually appearing between the fourth and fifth year, and oftener in the spring than in any other part of the year. It is preceded by cough, and can at first be scarcely distinguished from common cough, except that there is more discharge from the nostril, of a yellowish color, mixed with pus, and generally without smell There is likewise a considerable discharge of ropy fluid from the mouth, and greater swelling than usual under the throat. This swelling increases with uncertain rapidity, accompanied by some fever, and disinclination to eat, partly arising from the fever, but more from the pain which the animal feels in the act of masti

* Usually termed "*Horse distemper*," in the United States.

cation. There is considerable thirst, but after a gulp or two the horse ceases to drink, yet is evidently desirous of continuing his draught. In the attempt to swallow, and sometimes when not drinking, a convulsive cough comes on, which almost threatens to suffocate the animal—and thence, probably, the name of the disease.

The tumor is under the jaw, and about the centre of the channel. It soon fills the whole of the space, and is evidently one uniform body, and may thus be distinguished from glanders, or the enlarged glands of catarrh. In a few days it becomes more prominent and soft, and evidently contains a fluid. This rapidly increases; the tumor bursts, and a great quantity of pus is discharged. As soon as the tumor has broken, the cough subsides, and the horse speedily mends, although some degree of weakness may hang about him for a considerable time. Few horses, possibly none, escape its attack; but, the disease having passed over, the animal is free from it for the remainder of his life. Catarrh may precede, or may predispose to, the attack, and, undoubtedly the state of the atmosphere has much to do with it, for both its prevalence and its severity are connected with certain seasons of the year and changes of the weather. There is no preventive for the disease, nor is there anything contagious about it. Many strange stories are told with regard to this; but the explanation of the matter is, that when several horses in the same form, or in the same neighborhood, have had strangles at the same time, they have been exposed to the same powerful but unknown exciting cause.

As soon as the tumor under the jaw is decidedly apparent, the part should be actively blistered. From the thickness of skin, poultices, fomentations, &c., are of little avail. The blister will also abate the internal inflammation and soreness of the throat, and thus lessen the cough and wheezing.

As soon as the swelling is soft on its summit, and evidently contains matter, it should be freely and deeply lanced. It is a bad, although frequent practice, to suffer the tumor to burst naturally, for a ragged ulcer is formed, very slow to heal, and difficult of treatment. If the incision is deep and large enough, no second collection of matter will be formed: and that which is already there may be suffered to run out slowly, all pressure with the fingers being avoided. The part should be kept clean, and a little friar's balsam daily injected into the wound.

The remainder of the treatment will depend on the symptoms. If there is much fever, and evident affection of the chest, and which should carefully be distinguished from the oppression and choking occasioned by the pressure of the tumor it will be proper to bleed In the majority of cases. however bleeding will not only be unnecessary, but injurious. It will delay the suppuration of the tumor, and increase the subsequent debility. A few cooling medicines, as nitre, emetic tartar, and perhaps digitalis, may be given, as the case requires. The appetite, or rather the ability to eat, will return with the opening of the abscess. Bran-mashes, or fresh-cut-grass or tares, should be liberally supplied, which will not only afford sufficient nourishment to recruit the strength of the animal, but keep the bowels gently open. If the weakness is not great, no farther medicine will be wanted, except a dose of mild physic in order to prevent the swellings or eruptions which sometimes succeed to strangles In cases of debility, a small quantity of tonic medicine, as chamomile, gentian, or ginger, may be administered.*

THE PHARYNX.

Proceeding to the back of the mouth, we find the PHARYNX (*carrying* or *conveying* the food towards the stomach). It commences at the root of the tongue (see 7, 8 and 9, Fig. 3.); is separated from the mouth by the soft palate (7), which hangs down from the palatine bone at 8, and extends to the epiglottis or covering to the windpipe.

In order to understand the diseases of these parts, the anatomy of the neck generally must be considered.

---

* *Note by Mr. Spooner.*—A blister is, unquestionably, the best topical application; but it should be washed off as soon as it rises, by which means it can be repeated in a day or two, and so the action can be kept up, which will greatly promote the suppurative process. After the abscess is lanced, a linseed poultice will be a very desirable application; and, with regard to injections, they may be omitted without injury. Although the ages from two to five are the usual period for strangles to appear, yet it occasionally attacks old animals; we have, indeed, known it affect a horse sixteen years old, and within the last month an animal eight years old, but such instances are rare.

It is a very desirable thing in strangles to get the submaxillary abscess to form and suppurate without much delay; for when it is suppressed, or does not form in this place, there is sometimes danger to be apprehended; occasionally, abscesses will form internally, and carry off the patient. The symptoms of these untoward cases are an unthrifty coat, occasional shivering fits, and a pulse rather accelerated.

When the glands remain hard, and do not suppurate, the disease is frequently termed *bastard strangles*, and may lead to glanders. The use of iodine, applied externally as an ointment, and internally as hydriodate of potass, in daily doses of five to ten grains combined with tonics, will be found useful.

CHAPTER V.

THE ANATOMY AND DISEASES OF THE NECK AND NEIGHBORING PARTS.

THE neck of the horse, and of every animal belonging to the class *mammalia*, except one species, is composed of seven bones called *vertebræ*, movable or turning upon each other (see Fig. 1). They are connected together by strong ligaments, and form so many distinct joints, in order to give sufficiently extensive motion to this important part of the body. The *atlas* has already been described. Its junction with the head is the seat of a very serious and troublesome ulcer, termed

POLL-EVIL.

From the horse rubbing and sometimes striking his poll against the lower end of the manger, or hanging back in the stall and bruising the part with the halter—or from the frequent and painful stretching of the ligaments and muscles by unnecessary tight reining, and, occasionally, from a violent blow on the poll, inflammation ensues, and a swelling appears, hot, tender, and painful. It used to be a disease of frequent occurrence, but it is now, from better treatment of the animal, of comparatively rare occurrence.

It has been stated, that the ligament of the neck passes over the atlas, or first bone, without being attached to it, and the seat of inflammation is between the ligament and the bone beneath; and being thus deeply situated, it is serious in its nature and difficult of treatment.

The first thing to be attempted is to abate the inflammation by bleeding, physic, and the application of cold lotions to the part. In a very early period of the case a blister might have considerable effect. Strong purgatives should also be employed. By these means the tumor will sometimes be dispersed. This system, however, must not be pursued too far. If the swelling ncreases, and the heat and tenderness likewise increase. matter will form in the tumor; and then our object should be to hasten its formation by warm fomentations, poultices, or stimulating embrocations. As soon as the matter is formed, which may be known by the softness of the tumor, and before it has time to spread around and eat into the neighboring parts, it should be evacuated. Now comes the whole art of treating poll-evil; *the opening into the tumor must be so contrived that all the matter shall run out*, and continue afterwards to run out as quickly as it is formed, and not collect at the bottom of the ulcer, irritating and corroding it. This can be effected by a seton alone. The needle should enter at the top of the tumor, penetrate through its bottom, and be brought out at the side of the neck, a little below the abscess. Without anything more than this, except frequent fomentation with warm water, in order to keep the part clean, and to obviate inflammation, poll-evil in its early stage will frequently be cured.

If the ulcer has deepened and spread, and threatens to eat into the ligaments of the joints of the neck, it may be necessary to stimulate its surface, and perhaps painfully so, in order to bring it to a healthy state, and dispose it to fill up. In extreme cases, some highly stimulating application may be employed. All measures, however, will be ineffectual, unless the pus or matter is, by the use of setons, perfectly evacuated. The application of these setons will require the skill and anatomical knowledge of the veterinary surgeon. In desperate cases, the wound cannot be fairly exposed to the action of the caustic without the division of the ligament of the neck. This may be effected with perfect safety; for although the ligament is carried on to the occipital bone, and some strength is gained by this prolongation of it, the main stress is on the second bone; and the head will continue to be supported. The divided ligament, also, will soon unite again, and its former usefulness will be restored when the wound is healed.*

* *Note by Mr. Spooner.*—All cooling applications to the poll-evil are useless, for when once the swelling which constitutes the disease has appeared we have never known it dispersed, but sooner or later it suppurates. It often takes many months before the matter reaches the surface; but the more complete the suppuration is, the easier it is to effect a cure. The injury, which generally arises from striking the poll against a low door-way, is deep-seated, and the surface of the bone is often diseased from the beginning.

It must be confessed that the poll-evil is very difficult to cure, a difficulty arising not from the character of the injury, but rather from its situation, and the nature of the surrounding parts. When matter forms in any situation it has a tendency to pass downwards, and to seek an exit where the least obstacles are offered to its passage. It consequently forms passages or sinuses (pipes) amongst the muscles, and, when these are filled, the matter points to the surface. This tendency continues after an external opening is

THE MUSCLES AND PROPER FORM OF THE NECK.

The bones of the neck serve as the frame-work to which numerous muscles concerned in the motions of the head and neck are attached. The weight of the head and neck is supported by the ligament without muscular aid, and without fatigue to the animal; but in order to raise the head higher, or to lower it, or to turn it in every direction, a complicated system of muscles is necessary.

The *splenius* muscle (*c*. Fig. 12) is the principal one concerned in this. It gives its bulk to the neck above, and the beauty of that member depends mainly upon it. It was admirably developed in the horse of whose neck the annexed cut (Fig. 25) gives an accurate delineation.

Fig. 25.

made, and deep sinuses are formed in various directions, rendering it almost impossible to get a depending opening.

The abscess should not be opened till the matter is thoroughly formed, and then a depending opening should be made, through which a seton may be passed. The great error frequently made in the treatment of poll-evil is, that these openings are not made half large enough, so that much of the pus flows in another direction, and there forms sinuses. Now, the chief art in the treatment of this disease is to use the bistoury freely, to lay all the sinuses open as much as possible, and to throw them together; then to make the lower opening extremely large, and as low down as possible, large enough, indeed, for two fingers to be inserted. If the bone is injured, it will be necessary to apply some caustic application, in order to cause a healthy slough. Pressure is found very useful in keeping the sides of the wound together, and preventing the formation of sinuses. With this view, it has been recommended to apply a tight compress, by means of bandages, round the part, but it is extremely inconvenient to apply them in consequence of the windpipe interfering.

If the curve were quite regular from the poll to the withers, we should call it a perfect neck. It is rather a long neck, and we do not like it the less for that. In the carriage-horse, a neck that is not half concealed by the collar is indispensable, so far as appearance goes; and it is only the horse with a neck of tolerable length that will bear to be reined up, so as to give this part the arched and beautiful appearance which fashion demands. It is no detriment to the riding-horse, and there are few horses of extraordinary speed that have not the neck rather long. The race-horse at the top of his speed not only extends it as far as he can, that the air-passages may be as straight as he can make them, and that he may therefore be able to breathe more freely, but the weight of the head and neck, and the effect increasing with their distance from the trunk, add materially to the rapidity of the animal's motion. It has been said, that a horse with a long neck will bear heavy on the hand; neither the length of the neck nor even the bulk of the head has any influence in causing this. They are both counterbalanced by the power of the ligament of the neck. The *setting on* of the head is most of all connected with heavy bearing on the hand, and a short-necked horse will bear heavily, because, from the thickness of the lower part of the neck, consequent on its shortness, the head cannot be rightly placed, nor, generally, the shoulder.

However fine at the top, the neck should be muscular at the bottom, or it generally indicates a weak and worthless animal. It is then called a *loose* neck.

The principal bulk of the lower part of the neck is composed of the *complexus major*, or larger complicated muscle. If its action is habitually too powerful, the muzzle is protruded, and the horse becomes what is technically called a *star-gazer*. He is heavy in hand, and even the martingale will not ordinarily remedy the difficulty.

Connected with this is another unsightly deformity. The horse is *ewe-necked;* i. e. the neck is hollowed above, and arched below. His head can never be fairly got down, and the bearing rein of harness is a source of constant torture to him.

The *mane* is a matter of some importance. In a wild state, the horse has many battles to fight, and his neck, deprived of the mane, would be a vulnerable part. The hair of the mane, the tail, and the legs, is not shed in the same manner as that on the body. It does not fall so regularly, nor so often; for, if all were shed at once, the parts would be for a long time defenceless.

The mane is generally dressed so as to lie on the right side— some persons divide it equally on both sides. For ponies, it used to be cut off near the roots, only a few stumps being left to stand perpendicularly. This was termed the hog-mane. The groom sometimes bestows a great deal of pains in getting the mane of his horse into good and fashionable order. It is wetted, and plaited, and loaded with lead; and every hair that is a little too long is pulled out. The mane and tail of the heavy draught-horse are seldom thin; but on the well-bred horse, the thin, well-arranged mane is very ornamental.

THE BLOOD-VESSELS OF THE NECK.

Running down the under part of the neck, are the principal blood-vessels, going to and returning from the head, with the windpipe and gullet. Our cut could not give a view of the *arteries* that carry the blood from the heart to the head, because they are too deeply seated. The external arteries are the *carotid*, of which there are two. They ascend the neck on either side, close to the windpipe, until they have reached the middle of the neck, where they sometimes diverge, and lie more deeply.

The vertebral arteries run through the bones of the neck, supplying the neighboring parts as they climb, and at length enter the skull at the large hole in the occipital bone, and ramify on and supply the brain.

It is rarely or never necessary to bleed from an *artery*. If an artery is opened in the direction in which it runs, there is usually great difficulty in stopping the bleeding, and it is sometimes necessary to tie the vessel to accomplish this: if cut across, it retracts, and after the first gush of blood, no more is obtained.

THE VEINS OF THE NECK.

The external veins which return the blood from the head to the heart are the jugulars. The horse has but one on either side. The human being and the ox have two. The jugular takes its rise from the base of the skull; it then descends, receiving other branches in its way towards the angle of the jaw and behind the parotid gland; and emerging from that, as seen at *t*, Fig. 12, and being united to a large branch from the face, it takes its course down the neck. Veterinary surgeons and horsemen have agreed to adopt the jugular, a little way below the union of these two branches, as the usual place for bleeding; and a very convenient one it is, for it is easily got at, and the vessel is large. The manner of bleeding, &c., will hereafter be adverted to. (See page 166.)

INFLAMMATION OF THE VEIN.

It is usual and proper, after bleeding, to bring the edges of the wound carefully together, and to hold them in contact by inserting a pin through the skin, with a little tow twisted round it. In ninety-nine cases out of a hundred, the wound quickly heals, and gives no trouble; but in a few instances, from using a blunt instrument, or a dirty or rusty one; or striking too hard, and bruising the vein; or, in the act of pinning up, pulling the skin too far from the neck, and suffering some blood to insinuate itself into the cellular texture; or neglecting to tie the horse up for a little while, and thus enabling him to rub the bleeding place against the manger and tear out the pin; or from the animal being worked immediately afterward; or the reins of the bridle rubbing against it; or several blows having been clumsily given, and a large and ragged wound made; or from some disposition to inflammation about the horse (for the bleeder is not always in fault) the wound does not heal, or, if it closes for a little while, it re-opens. A slight bleeding appears —some tumefaction commences—the edges of the orifice separate, and become swollen and red—a discharge of sanious, bloody fluid proceeds from the wound, followed, perhaps, in a few days, by purulent matter. The neck swells, and is hot and tender both above and below the incision. The lips of the wound become everted—the swelling increases, particularly above the wound, where the vein is most hard and cordy—the horse begins to loathe his food, and little abscesses form round the orifice. The cordiness of the vein rapidly increases. Not only the vein itself has become obstructed and its coats thickened, but the cellular tissue inflamed and hardened, and is an additional source of irritation and torture.

The thickening of the vein extends to the bifurcation above: it occupies both branches, and extends downward to the chest— even to the very heart itself, and the patient dies.

Of the means of cure it is difficult to speak confidently. The wound should be carefully examined—the divided edges brought into exact apposition, and any hair interposed between them removed—the pin withdrawn or not, according to circumstances— the part carefully and long fomented, and a dose of physic administered. If two or three days have passed and the discharge still remains, the application of the budding-iron—not too large or too hot—may produce engorgement of the neighboring parts, and union of the lips of the wound. This should be daily, or every second day, repeated, according to circumstances. A blister applied over the orifice, or as far as the mischief extends, will often be serviceable. Here, likewise, the parts will be brought into contact with each other, and pressed together, and union may be effected.

The owner of the horse will find it his interest to apply to a veterinary practitioner as soon as a case of inflamed vein occurs.

Should the vein be destroyed, the horse will not be irreparably injured, and perhaps at no great distance of time, scarcely injured at all.*

THE PALATE—(RESUMED).

At the back of the palate (see Fig. 3), and attached to the crescent-shaped border of the palatine bone, is a dense membranous curtain, called the *velum palati*, so arranged that the horse can breathe through his nostrils alone, and in the act of vomiting, the contents of the stomach are ejected the same way, and not by the mouth. On this account it is, and on account of the structure of the entrance of the stomach, that the horse can with great difficulty be excited to vomit.

THE LARYNX

Is placed on the top of the windpipe (see 1, Fig. 3) and is the inner guard of the lungs, if any injurious substance should penetrate so far; it is the main protection against the passage of food into the respiratory tubes, and it is at the same time the instrument of voice.

THE EPIGLOTTIS (see 2, Fig. 3), is a heart-shaped cartilage, placed at the extremity of the opening into the windpipe, with its back opposed to the pharynx, so that when a pellet of food passes the pharynx in its way to the œsophagus, it presses down the epiglottis, and by this means, as already described, closes the aperture of the larynx, and prevents any food from entering it. The food having passed over the epiglottis, from

---

* *Note by Mr. Spooner.*—This disease sometimes occurs when bleeding has been performed with the utmost care and skill.

The course of treatment which a considerable experience of the disease has induced us to adopt, is to avoid all setons, and dissecting out the vein, and above all, caustic injection, which we have known to produce a fatal result. First allay the superficial inflammation by cold applications, and then blister the part, washing off the effects of the blister the following day, and repeating it several times. The ointment of iodine may be alternated with the blister to advantage. During this time, the horse's head should be tied up to the rack, and he should be fed on such food as will not require any considerable action of the jaws, such as bran mashes, scalded oats, carrots, and but very little hay. In a few weeks the swelling will become reduced, the blood find new channels, and the horse will become as useful as ever. We have never known this treatment to fail. In a few instances it may be necessary to apply the iron to the edges of the wound, and use other methods to stop bleeding.

its own elasticity and that of the membrane at its base, and more particularly the power of the hyo-epiglotideus muscle, rises again and resumes its former situation.

THE THYROID CARTILAGE (see 1, Fig. 3) occupies almost the whole of the external part of the larynx, both anteriorly and laterally. It envelops and protects all the rest.

THE TRACHEA OR WINDPIPE.

The windpipe is composed of an elastic cartilage, divided into rings (50 or 52), sufficiently firm to resist ordinary pressure, and united together by means of an interposed highly elastic fibro-ligamentous substance, which, in effect, constitutes a joint between each ring, giving the necessary flexibility to all its motions, and admitting of elongation when the head is stretched upward or downward.

It is indisputable that the windpipe should be prominent and loose on the neck, in the horse from which active exertion is required, and which consequently is subjected to hurried respiration. It is not commonly found thus in large slow beasts, like the carthorse, nor is it necessary.

TRACHEOTOMY.

It has been found that when obstructions, not speedily removable enough for safety, occur in the windpipe of the horse, a portion of the trachea may be safely removed, on or below the point of obstruction, to admit of the continuance of respiration.

The operation must be performed while the horse is standing, and secured by a side-line, for he would, probably, be suffocated amidst the struggles with which he would resist the act of throwing. The twitch is then firmly fixed on the muzzle; the operator stands on a stool or pail, by which means he can more perfectly command the part, and an assistant holds a scalpel, a bistoury, scissors, curved needles armed, and a moist sponge.

The operator should once more examine the whole course of the windpipe, and the different sounds which he will be able to detect by the application of the ear, and likewise the different degrees of temperature and of tenderness which the finger will detect, will guide to the seat of the evil.

The hair is to be closely cut off from the part, the skin tightened across the trachea with the thumb and fingers of the left hand, and then a longitudinal incision cautiously made through the skin, three inches in length. This is usually effected when there is no express indication to the contrary on the fifth and sixth rings; a slip from which, and the connecting ligament above and below, about half the width of each ring, should be excised with the intervening ligament. The remaining portion will then be strong enough to retain the perfect arched form of the trachea.

If the orifice is only to be kept open while some foreign body is extracted, or tumor removed, or ulcer healed, or inflammation subdued, nothing more is necessary than to keep the lips of the wound a little apart, by passing some thread through each, and slightly everting them, and tying the threads to the mane.

If, however, there is any permanent obstruction, a tube will be necessary. It should be two or three inches long, curved at the top, and the external orifice turning downwards with a little ring on each side, by which, through the means of strings, it may be retained in its situation.

The purpose of the operation being answered, the flaps of integument must be brought over the wounds, the edges, if necessary, diminished, and the parts kept in apposition by a few stitches. The cartilage will be perfectly reproduced, only the rings will be a little thicker and wider.

THE BRONCHIAL TUBES.

After the windpipe has entered the chest, and continued through the mediastinum to the base of the heart, it divides into two tubes—the *Bronchial tubes*—which enter each lung, where they are again subdivided into smaller tubes carrying air to every portion and cell of the lungs. Before considering their diseases, we will pause and consider the structure and functions of the chest.

CHAPTER VI.

THE CHEST.

Fig. 26.

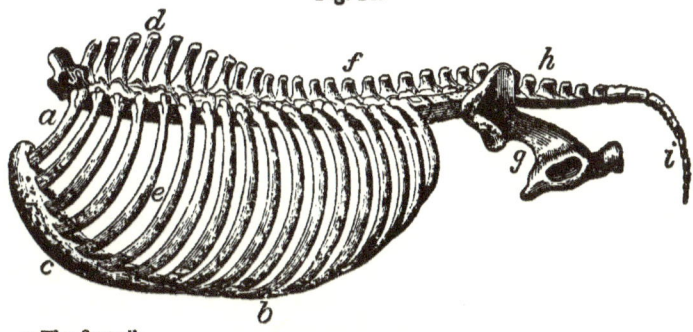

a The first rib.
b The cartilages of the eleven hindermost, or *false* ribs, connected together and uniting with that of the seventh or last *true* rib.
c The breast-bone.
d The top, or point, of the withers, which are formed by the lengthened spinous, or upright processes of the ten or eleven first bones of the back. The bones of the back are eighteen in number.
e The ribs, usually eighteen on each side; the seven first united to the breastbone by cartilage; the cartilages of the remaining eleven united to each other, as at *b*.
f That portion of the spine where the loins commence, and composed of five bones.
g The bones forming the hip, or haunch, and into the hole at the bottom of which the head of the thigh-bone is received.
  The portion of the spine belonging to the haunch, and consisting of five pieces.
  The bones of the tail, usually fifteen in number.

THE chest, in the horizontal position in which it is placed in the cut, is of a somewhat oval figure, with its extremities truncated (cut off). The spine is its roof; the sternum, or breast, its floor; the ribs, its sides; the trachea, œsophagus, and great blood-vessels passing through its anterior extremity and the diaphragm, being its posterior. It is contracted in front, broad and deep towards the central boundary, and again contracted posteriorly. It encloses the heart and the lungs, the origin of the arterial and the termination of the venous trunks and the collected vessels of the absorbents. The windpipe penetrates into it, and the œsophagus traverses its whole extent.

Most ingeniously and admirably is this whole structure contrived to fill its various purposes.

The ribs are eighteen in number on either side. Nine of them are perfect, and commonly called the *true*, or, more properly, *sternal* ribs, extending from the spine to the sternum. The remaining nine are posterior and shorter, and are only indirectly connected with the sternum.

The ribs are united to the corresponding vertebræ, or bones of the spine, so as to form perfect joints—or, rather, each rib forms two joints. Before the ribs reach the sternum, they terminate in a cartilaginous prolongation. The cartilage is united to the ribs and sternum by joints, and the cartilages of the posterior ribs are united to them in the same manner.

The *sternum*, or breast-bone, is a long, flat, spongy bone, forming the floor of the chest. It supports the ribs by the connecting cartilage. It is composed of from seven to nine pieces united together by cartilage. The point of the breast-bone is occasionally injured by blows, and has even been completely broken off. A kind of tumor on it, difficult to heal, has also been produced by some cruelty or violence.

The front of the chest is a very important consideration in the structure of the horse. It should be prominent and broad, and full, and the sides of it well occupied. When the breast is narrow, the chest has generally the same appearance: the animal is flat-sided, the proper cavity of the chest is diminished, and the stamina of the horse are materially diminished, although, perhaps, his speed for short distances may not be affected. When the chest is narrow, and the fore-legs are too close together, in addition to the want of bottom, they will interfere with each other, and there will be wounds on the fetlocks, and bruises below the knee.

A chest too broad is not desirable, but a fleshy and a prominent one: yet even this, perhaps, may require some explanation. When the fore-legs appear to recede, and to shelter themselves under the body, there is a faulty position of the fore limbs, a bend, or standing over, an unnatural lengthiness about the fore parts of the breast, sadly disadvantageous in progression.

The Intercostal Muscles.—The spaces between the ribs are occupied by muscles firmly attached to their edges, the fibres of which cross each other in the form of the letter X. By the prolongation thus obtained, they have a much greater latitude of action, than they would have if they ran straight from rib to rib

The ribs, while they protect the important viscera of the thorax from injury, are powerful agents in extending and contracting the chest in the alternate inspiration and expiration of air.

The Proper Form of the Chest.—This leads to a very important consideration, the most advantageous form of the chest for the proper discharge of the natural or extraordinary functions of the thoracic viscera. The contents of the chest are the lungs and the heart:—the first, to render the blood nutrient and stimulating, and to give or restore it to that vitality which will enable it to support every part of the frame in the discharge of its function, and devoid of which, the complicated and beautiful machine is inert and dead; and the second, to convey this purified arterialized blood to every part of the frame.

In order to produce, and to convey to the various parts, a sufficient quantity of blood, these organs must be large. If it amounts not to hypertrophy, the larger the heart and the larger the lungs, the more rapid the process of nutrition, and the more perfect the discharge of every animal function.

Then it might be imagined that, as a circle is a figure which contains more than any other of equal girth and admeasurement, a circular form of the chest would be most advantageous. Not exactly so; for the contents of the chest are alternately expanding and contracting. The circular chest could not expand, but every change of form would be a diminution of capacity.

That form of chest which approaches nearest to a circle, while it admits of sufficient expansion and contraction, is the best—certainly for some animals, and for all under peculiar circumstances, and with reference to the discharge of certain functions. This was the grand principle on which Mr. Bakewell proceeded, and on which all our improvements in the breeding of cattle were founded.

In the heavy draft-horse, the circular chest is no disadvantage, and it gives him, what we require, weight to oppose the weight of his load. Speed is not demanded of him.

Some of our saddle-horses and cobs have barrels round enough, and we value them on account of it, for they are always in condition, and they rarely tire. But when we look at them more carefully, there is just that departure from the circular form of which mention has been made—that happy medium between the circle and the ellipse, which retains the capacity of the one and the expansibility of the other. Such a horse is invaluable for common purposes, but he is seldom a horse of speed. If he is permitted to go his own pace, and that not a slow one, he will work on forever; but if he is too much hurried, he is soon distressed

The Broad Deep Chest.—Then for the usual purposes of the road, and more particularly for rapid progression, search is made for that form of the chest which shall unite, and to as great a degree as possible, considerable capacity in a quiescent state, and the power of increasing that capacity when the animal requires it. There must be the broad chest for the production of muscles and sinews, and the deep chest, to give the capacity or power of furnishing arterial blood equal to the most rapid exhaustion of vitality.

This form of the chest is consistent with lightness, or at least with all the lightness that can be rationally required. The broad-chested horse, or he that, with moderate depth at the girth, swells and barrels out immediately behind the elbow, may have as light a forehead and as elevated a wither as the horse with the narrowest chest; but the animal with the barrel approaching too near to rotundity is invariably heavy about the shoulders and low in the withers. It is to the mixture of the Arabian blood that we principally owe this peculiar and advantageous formation of the chest of the horse. The Arab is light; some would say too much so before : but immediately behind the arms the barrel almost invariably swells out, and leaves plenty of room, and where it is most wanted for the play of the lungs, and at the same time where the weight does not press so exclusively on the fore-legs, and expose the feet to concussion and injury.

Many horses with narrow chests, and a great deal of daylight under them, have plenty of spirit and willingness for work. They show themselves well off, and exhibit the address and gratify the vanity of their riders on the parade or in the park, but they have not the appetite nor the endurance that will carry them through three successive days' hard work.

Five out of six of the animals that perish from inflamed lungs, are narrow-chested. There are many other important points, but that which is most of all connected with the general health of the animal, and with combined fleetness or bottom, is a deep, and broad, and swelling chest, with sufficient lengthening of the sternum, or breast-bone, beneath.*

* *Note by Mr. Spooner.*—In speedy animals the chest is, no doubt, more capacious than in slower ones, and a greater quantity of atmospheric air is inspired, so as to afford a full supply for the purpose of respiration. This large capacity is gained, however, not by the greater rotundity of the chest, but by its increased depth and length, more particularly the former. It is very evident that a circular chest must present a very unfavorable surface for the attachment of the shoulder blade, and, indeed, must induce a rolling action which is inimical to speed; thus we find that animals with very circular chests, and with their fore-legs, in consequence, wide apart, are by no means speedy, but have a great predisposition to the accumulation of fat. In such animals a considerable quantity of fat is generally found round the heart and in other parts of the chest, so that, in point of fact, animals with circular chests have smaller lungs than those with deep and flat ribs. It is extremely desirable for a cart-horse to have a circular chest, as this de

The above remarks show the impropriety of tight-girthing, particularly where it is less necessary, as in the stable, or when the rider is off from the saddle.

A point of consequence is the length of the carcase and the ribbing home. If the horse has to carry a heavy weight, and has much work to do, he should be well ribbed home, i. e. there should be but little space between the last rib and the hip-bone.

If speed, however, is required, there must be room for the full action of the hinder limbs; and this can only exist where there is sufficient space between the last rib and the hip-bone.

The thorax, or chest, is formed by the spine *f*, above (Fig. 26) the ribs *e*, on either side; and the sternum, or breast-bone, *c*, beneath.

THE SPINE AND BACK.

The spine, or back, consists of a chain of bones from the poll to the extremity of the tail. It is made of twenty-three bones from the neck to the haunch; eighteen, called *dorsal vertebræ*, composing the back; and five *lumbar vertebræ*, occupying the loins. The structure and attachments of these are remarkably well calculated for easiness of carriage and strength. The hunter will carry a heavy man through a long chase without great fatigue or strain; but if the horse is over-weighted, or tasked too long, or too suddenly pulled upon his haunches, the ligaments uniting the vertebræ are strained, inflammation follows, and the ligaments become changed to bone. From hard service, and especially from being used *too young*, very many horses have some of the bones of the back or loins *anchylosed*—i. e. united by bony matter in the place of the natural ligament. When this exists to any considerable extent, the horse becomes unpleasant to ride, turns with difficulty in his stall, is indisposed to lie down, or being down, to rise, and has a singular straddling action.

The length of the back deserves attention. The long-backed horse will be easier in his paces, because the spring is longer; and he is formed for speed, for there is more room to bring his hinder legs under him. But he will be comparatively weak in the back, and more easily over-weighted.

For general purposes the horse with a short *carcase*, also, is to be preferred, as possessing greater health and hardiness. He will have sufficient easiness of action not to fatigue the rider, and speed

notes a disposition to make flesh, and thus to economize food; and, for the same reason, in other horses, a rather circular abdomen is approved of—in fact, one neither too wide nor too flat is the most desirable.

for every ordinary purpose. Length of back will always be desirable when there is more than usual substance generally, and particularly when the loins are wide, and the muscles of the loins large and swelling. The two requisites, strength and speed, will then probably be united.

The back should be depressed a little immediately behind the withers; and then continue in an almost straight line to the loins. This is the form most consistent with beauty and strength. Some horses have a very considerable hollow behind the withers. They are said to be *saddle-backed*. Such horses are evidently easy goers, but in the same proportion, they are weak and liable to sprain.

A few horses have the curve outward. They are said to be *roach-backed*, from the supposed resemblance to the arched back of a roach. This is a very serious defect;—altogether incompatible with beauty, and materially diminishing the usefulness of the animal. It is almost impossible to prevent the saddle from being thrown on the shoulders, or the back from being galled;—the elasticity of the spine is destroyed;—the rump is badly set on;—the hinder legs are too much under the animal;—he is continually overreaching, and his head is carried awkwardly low.

THE LOINS.

The loins are attentively examined by every good horseman. They can scarcely be too broad and muscular. The strength of the back, and especially the strength of the hinder extremities, will depend materially on this. The union of the back and loins should be carefully observed, for there is sometimes a depression between them. A kind of line is drawn across, which shows imperfection in the construction of the spine, and is regarded as an indication of weakness.

THE WITHERS.

The spinous processes of the vertebræ, above the upper part of the shoulder, form the elevated ridge called the withers. (See Figs. 1 and 26.)

High withers have been always, in the mind of the judge of the horse, associated with good action, and generally with speed. The reason is plain enough:—they afford larger surface for the attachment of the muscles of the back; and in proportion to the elevation of the withers, these muscles act with greater advantage. And as the rising of the fore-parts depends not only upon the muscles of the legs and shoulders, but on certain ones connecting the loins and the spinous processes, the longer the arm of the lever to which the power is applied, the easier and to the greater height will the weight be carried up. Good and high action, and speed, will not, therefore, be often found without this conformation.

FISTULOUS WITHERS.

When the saddle has been suffered to press long upon the withers, a tumor will be formed, hot and exceedingly tender. It may sometimes be dispersed by the cooling applications recommended in the treatment of poll-evil; but if, in despite of these, the swelling should remain stationary, and especially if it should become larger and more tender, warm fomentations and poultices, and stimulating embrocations, should be diligently applied, in order to hasten the formation of pus. As soon as that can be fairly detected, a seton should be passed from the top to the bottom of the tumor, so that the whole of the matter may be evacuated, and continue to be discharged as it is afterwards formed; or the knife may be freely used, in order to get at the bottom of every sinus. The knife has succeeded many a time when the seton has failed. The after treatment must be precisely that which was recommended for a similar disease in the poll.

In neglected fistulous withers the ulcer may be larger and deeper, and more destructive than in poll-evil. It may burrow beneath the shoulder blade, and the pus may appear at the point of the shoulder or the elbow; or the bones of the withers may become carious.

WARBLES, SITFASTS, AND SADDLE GALLS.

On other parts of the back, tumors and very troublesome ulcers may be produced by the same cause. Those resulting from the pressure of the saddle are called *warbles*, and, when they ulcerate, they frequently become *sitfasts*. Warbles are small circular bruises, or extravasations of blood, where there has been an undue pressure of the saddle or harness. If a horse is subject to these tumors, the saddle should remain on him two or three hours after he has returned to the stable. It is only for a certain time, however, that this will perfectly succeed, for by the frequent application of the pressure, the skin and the cellular substance are bruised or otherwise injured, and a permanent sore or tumor, of a very annoying description, takes place. The centre of the sore gradually loses its vitality. A separation takes place from the surrounding integument, and there is a circular piece of dried and hard skin remaining in the centre. No effort must be made to tear or dissect it off, but stimulating poultices or fomentations, or, if these fail, a mild blister will cause a speedy separation; and the wound will then readily heal by the use of turpentine dressings, more or less stimulating, according to circumstances.

Saddle galls are tumors, and sometimes galls or sores, arising also from the pressure and chafing of the saddle. They differ little from the warble, except that there is very seldom the separation of the dead part in the centre, and the sore is larger and varying in its form. The application of cold water, or salt and water, will generally remove excoriations of this kind.

CHEST-FOUNDER.

The muscles of the breast are occasionally the seat of an obscure disease, called by the old farriers *anticor* and *chest-founder*. The horse has considerable stiffness in moving, evidently not referable to the feet. There is tenderness about the muscles of the breast, and, occasionally, swelling. I believe it to be nothing more than rheumatism, produced by improper exposure. Sometimes a considerable degree of fever accompanies this; but bleeding, physic, a rowel in the chest, warm embrocations over the parts affected, warm stabling, and warm clothing, with occasional doses of antimonial powder, will soon subdue the complaint.*

* *Note by Mr. Spooner.*—The absorption or diminution of the muscles of the chest, alluded to in the text, and which used to be denominated chest founder, is neither more nor less than disease in the feet (the navicular disease, in fact), and which, existing in both feet, prevents the fore-legs being exercised to the same extent as before; and, consequently, the muscles, from being partially thrown out of use, become, to a certain extent, absorbed.

By the term anticor, we rather understand an abscess in the breast, or brisket, to which some horses are liable. It is a rare disease, and more frequently attacks heavy-chested horses. Foreign horses are more subject to this disease than English ones.

CHAPTER VII.

THE CONTENTS OF THE CHEST.

THE THYMUS GLAND.

At the entrance of the trachea into the thorax, and situated in the doubling of the anterior mediastinum, is an irregular glandular body, called the thymus gland, or "sweet-bread." It conveys a peculiar albuminous fluid to the veins, but its use in the system is unknown.

THE DIAPHRAGM.

The interposed curtain extending across the cavity of the chest, between the thorax and abdomen, is called the diaphragm (midriff). It is an irregular muscular expansion, proceeding from the inferior surface of the lumbar vertebræ posteriorly and superiorly, adhering to the ribs on either side, and extending obliquely forward and downward to the sternum ; or, rather it is a flattened muscle arising from all these points, with its fibres all converging towards the centre, and terminating there in an expansion of tendinous substance. It is lined anteriorly by the pleura or investing membrane of the thoracic cavity, and posteriorly by the peritoneum or investing membrane of the abdominal cavity.

The diaphragm is the main agent, both in ordinary and extraordinary respiration; it assists also in the expulsion of the urine, and it is a most powerful auxiliary in the act of parturition.

It is subject to injury and disease of a serious and varied character. Whatever may be the original seat of thoracic or abdominal ailment, the diaphragm soon becomes irritable and inflamed. This accounts for the breathing of the horse being so much affected under every inflammation or excitement of the chest or belly. The irritability of this muscle is often evinced by a singular spasmodic action of a portion, or the whole of it.

Opium should be administered in small doses, together with ammonia or nitric ether, and as soon as any reaction is observed, have recourse to bleeding.

RUPTURE OF THE DIAPHRAGM.

This may sometimes occur from any extraordinary exertion, particularly when the stomach is distended with food or gas.

In rupture of the diaphragm, the horse usually sits on his haunches, like a dog; but this is far from being an infallible symptom of the disease. It accompanies introsusception, as well as rupture of the diaphragm. [Mr. Youatt gives no remedy, and probably the case admits of none.]

THE PLEURA.

The walls of the chest are lined, and the lungs are covered, by a smooth glistening membrane, the *pleura*. It is a *serous* membrane, so called from the nature of its exhalation, in distinction from the *mucous secretion* yielded by the membrane of the air-passages. The serous membrane generally invests the most important organs, and always those that are essentially connected with life; while the mucous membrane lines the interior of the greater part of them. The pleura is the investing membrane of the lungs, and a mucous membrane the lining one of the bronchial tubes.

Among the circumstances principally to be noticed, with regard to the pleura, is the polish of its external surface. The glistening appearance of the lungs, and of the inside of the chest, is to be attributed to the membrane by which they are covered, and by means of which the motion of the various organs is freer and less dangerous. Although the lungs, and the bony walls which contain them, are in constant approximation with each other, both in expiration and inspiration, yet in the frequently hurried and violent motion of the animal, and, in fact, in every act of expiration and inspiration, of dilatation and contraction, much and injurious friction would ensue if the surfaces did not glide freely over each other by means of the peculiar polish of this membrane.

Every serous membrane has innumerable exhalent vessels upon its surface, from which a considerable quantity of fluid is poured out. In life and during health it exists in the chest only as a kind of dew, just sufficient to lubricate the surfaces. The pleura possesses very little sensibility in health, but it is otherwise when it is the seat of disease. In pleurisy, pneumonia, &c., it becomes susceptible of intense pain.

The pleura adheres intimately to the ribs and to the substance of the lungs. While the diseases of mucous membranes spread to other parts, those of serous membranes are generally isolated.

THE LUNGS.

The lungs form two distinct bodies, the right somewhat larger than the left, and are divided from each other by the duplicature of the pleura, which has been already described—the mediastinum. Each lung has the same structure, and properties, and uses. Each of them is subdivided, the right lobe consisting of three lobes, and the left of two. The intention of these divisions is probably to adapt the substance of the lungs to the form of the cavity in which they are placed, and to enable them more perfectly to occupy and fill the chest.

If one of these lobes is cut into, it is found to consist of innumerable irregularly formed compartments, to which anatomists have given the name of *lobules*, or little lobes. They are distinct from each other, and impervious. On close examination, they can be subdivided almost without end. There is no communication between them, or if perchance such communication exists, it constitutes the disease known by the name of *broken wind*.

On the delicate membrane of which these cells are composed, innumerable minute blood-vessels ramify. They proceed from the heart, through the medium of the *pulmonary artery*—they follow all the subdivisions of the bronchial tubes—they ramify upon the membrane of these multitudinous lobules, and at length return to the heart, through the medium of the pulmonary veins, the character of the blood which they contain being essentially changed. The mechanism of this, and the effect produced, must be briefly considered.

THE HEART.

The heart is placed between a doubling of the pleura—termed the *mediastinum;* by means of which it is supported in its natural situation, and all dangerous friction between these important organs is avoided. It is also surrounded by a membrane or bag of its own, called the *pericardium*, whose office is of a similar nature. By means of the heart, the blood is circulated through the frame.

It is composed of four cavities—two above, called *auricles*, from their supposed resemblance to the ear of a dog; and two below, termed *ventricles*, occupying the substance of the heart. In point of fact, there are two hearts—the one on the left side impelling the blood through the frame, the other on the right side conveying it through the pulmonary system; but, united in the manner in which they are, their junction contributes to their mu tual strength and both circulations are carried on at the same time.

The first is the arterial circulation. No function can be discharged—life cannot exist, without the presence of arterial blood The left ventricle that contains it contracts, and by the power of that contraction, aided by other means, which the limits of our work will not permit us to describe, the blood is driven through the whole arterial circulation—the capillary vessels and the veins —and returns again to the heart, but to the right ventricle. The other division of this viscus is likewise employed in circulating the blood thus conveyed to it, but is not the same fluid which was contained in the left ventricle It has gradually lost its vital power. As it has passed along, it has changed from red to black, and from a vital to a poisonous fluid. Ere it can again convey the principle of nutrition, or give to each organ that impulse or stimulus which enables it to discharge its function, it must be materially changed.

When the right ventricle contracts, and the blood is driven into the lungs, it passes over the gossamer membrane of which the lobules of the lungs have been described as consisting; the lobules being filled with the air which has descended through the bronchial tubes in the act of inspiration. This delicate membrane permits some of the principles of the air to permeate it. The oxygen of the atmosphere attracts and combines with a portion of the superabundant carbon of this blood, and the expired air is poisoned with carbonic acid gas. Some of the constituents of the blood attract a portion of the oxygen of the air, and obtain their distinguishing character and properties as arterial blood, and being thus revivified, it passes on over the membrane of the lobes, unites into small and then larger vessels, and at length pours its full stream of arterial blood into the left auricle, thence to ascend into the ventricle, and to be diffused over the frame.

DISEASES OF THE HEART.

The best place to examine the beating of the heart is immediately behind the elbow, on the left side. The hand applied flat against the ribs will give the number of pulsations. The ear thus applied will enable the practitioner better to ascertain the character of the pulsation. The stethoscope affords an uncertain guide, for it cannot be flatly and evenly applied.

PERICARDITIS.—The bag, or outer investing membrane of the heart ("heart case"), is liable to inflammation, in which the effused fluid becomes organized, and deposited in layers, increasing the thickness of the pericardium, and the difficulty of the expansion and contraction of the heart. The only symptom on which dependence can be placed, are a quickened and irregular respiration; a bounding action of the heart in an early stage of the disease; but that, as the fluid increases and becomes concrete, assuming a feeble and fluttering character.

HYDROPS PERICARDII is the term used to designate the presence of the fluid secreted in consequence of this inflammation, and varying from a pint to a gallon or more. In addition to the symptoms already described, there is an expression of alarm and anxiety in the countenance of the animal which no other malady produces. The horse generally sinks from other disease, or from constitutional irritation, before the cavity of the pericardium is filled; or if he lingers on, most dreadful palpitations and throbbings accompany the advanced stage of the disease. It is seldom or never that this disease exists alone, but is combined with dropsy of the chest or abdomen.

INFLAMMATION OF THE LINING OF THE HEART.—Mr. Simpson relates, in the Veterinarian for 1834, a case in which there were symptoms of severe abdominal pain; the respiration was much disturbed, and the action of the heart took on an extraordinary character. Three or four beats succeeded to each other, so violently as to shake the whole frame, and to be visible at the distance of several yards, with intervals of quietude for five minutes or more. At length this violent beating became constant.

On dissection both lungs were found to be inflamed, the serum in the pericardium increased in quantity, and the internal membrane of the heart violently inflamed, with spots of ecchymosis (livid spots occasioned by extravasated blood).

This would seem to be a case of inflammation of the heart; but in a considerable proportion of the cases of rabies, these spots of ecchymosis, and this general inflammation of the heart, are seen.

HYPERTROPHY is an augmentation or thickening of the substance of the heart; and although not dreamed of a few years ago, seems now to be a disease of no rare occurrence among horses. The heart has been known to acquire double its natural volume, or the auricle and venticle on one side have been thus enlarged.

DILATATION is increased capacity of the cavities of the heart, and the parietes being generally thinned. It is probable that this is a more frequent disease than is generally supposed; and from the circulating power being lessened, or almost suspended, on account of the inability of the cavities to propel their contents, it is accompanied by much and rapid emaciation.

OSSIFICATION OF THE HEART, AIR IN THE HEART, and ANEURISM of the aorta, sometimes occur.

THE ARTERIES.

The vessels which carry the blood from the heart are called arteries. The yielding of the artery to the gush of blood, forced into it by the contraction of the heart, constitutes

THE PULSE.

The pulse is a very useful assistant to the practitioner of human medicine, and much more so to the veterinary surgeon, whose patients cannot describe either the seat or degree of ailment or pain. The number of pulsations in any artery will give the number of the beatings of the heart, and so express the irritation of that organ, and of the frame generally. In a state of health, the heart beats in a farmer's horse about thirty-six times a minute. In the smaller, and in the thorough-bred horse, the pulsations are forty or forty-two. This is said to be the *standard* pulse—the pulse of health. It varies singularly little in horses of the same size and breed, and where it beats naturally there can be little materially wrong. The most convenient place to feel the pulse, is at the lower jaw (Fig. 1) a little behind the spot where the submaxillary artery and vein, and the parotid duct, come from under the jaw. There the number of pulsations will be easily counted, and the character of the pulse, a matter of fully equal importance, will be clearly ascertained. Many horsemen put the hand to the side. They can certainly count the pulse there, but they can do nothing more. We must be able to press the artery against some hard body, as the jaw-bone, in order to ascertain the manner in which the blood flows through it, and the quantity that flows.

When the pulse reaches fifty or fifty-five, some degree of fever may be apprehended, and proper precaution should be taken Seventy or seventy-five will indicate a dangerous state, and put the owner and the surgeon not a little on the alert. Few horses long survive a pulse of one hundred, for, by this excessive action the energies of nature are speedily worn out.

Some things, however, should be taken into account in forming our conclusion from the frequency of the pulse. Exercise, a warm stable, and fear, will wonderfully increase the number of pulsations.

When a careless, brutal fellow goes up to a horse and speaks hastily to him, and handles him roughly, he adds ten beats per minute to the pulse, and will often be misled in the opinion he may form of the state of the animal. A judicious person will approach the patient gently, and pat and soothe him, and even then the circulation, probably, will be a little disturbed. He should take the additional precaution of noting the number and quality of the pulse, a second time, before he leaves the animal.

If a *quick* pulse indicate irritation and fever, a *slow* pulse will likewise characterize diseases of an opposite description. It accompanies the sleepy stage of staggers, and every malady connected with deficiency of nervous energy.

The heart may not only be excited to more frequent, but also to more violent action. It may contract more powerfully upon the blood, which will be driven with greater force through the arteries, and the expansion of the vessels will be greater and more sudden. Then we have the *hard* pulse—the sure indicator of considerable fever, and calling for the immediate and free use of the lancet.

Sometimes the pulse may be hard and jerking, and yet *small*. The stream though forcible is not great. The heart is so irritable that it contracts before the ventricle is properly filled. The practitioner knows that this indicates a dangerous state of disease. It is an almost invariable accompaniment of inflammation of the bowels.

A *weak* pulse, when the arterial stream flows slowly, is caused by the feeble action of the heart. It is the reverse of fever, and expressive of debility.

The *oppressed* pulse is when the arteries seem to be fully distended with blood. There is obstruction somewhere, and the action of the heart can hardly force the stream along, or communicate pulsation to the current. It is the case in sudden inflammation of the lungs. They are overloaded and gorged with blood, which cannot find its way through their minute vessels. This accounts for the well-known fact of a copious bleeding increasing a pulse previously oppressed. A portion being removed from the distended and choked vessels, the remainder is able to flow on.

The state of the pulse should be carefully regarded during bleeding. The most experienced practitioner cannot tell what quantity of blood must be abstracted in order to produce the desired effect. The change of the pulse can alone indicate when the object is accomplished ; therefore, the operator should have his finger on the artery during the act of bleeding, and, comparatively regardless of the quantity, continue to take blood, until, in inflammation of the lungs, the oppressed pulse becomes fuller and more distinct, or the strong pulse of considerable fever is evidently softer, or the animal exhibits symptoms of faintness [See Bleeding.]*

* *Note by Mr. Spooner.*—The frequency of the pulse is certainly over rated in the text. There is not that difference in the pulsation of the cart-

INFLAMMATION.

Local inflammation is characterized by redness, swelling, heat, and pain.

If inflammation consists of an increased flow of blood to and through the part, the ready way to abate it is to lessen the quantity of blood. All other means are comparatively unimportant, contrasted with *bleeding*. Blood is generally abstracted from the jugular vein, and so the general quantity may be lessened; but if it can be taken from the neighborhood of the diseased part, it will be productive of tenfold benefit. One quart of blood abstracted from the foot in acute founder, by unloading the vessels of the inflamed part, and enabling them to contract, and, in that contraction, to acquire the tone and power to resist future distention, will do more good than five quarts taken from the general circulation. An ounce of blood obtained by scarifying the swelled vessels of the inflamed eye, will give as much relief to that organ as a copious bleeding from the jugular. It is a principle in the animal frame which should never be lost sight of by the veterinary surgeon, or the horseman, that if by bleeding the process of inflammation can once be checked,—if it can be suspended but for a little while,—although it may return, it is never with the same degree of violence, and in many cases it is got rid of entirely. Hence the necessity of bleeding early, and bleeding largely, in inflammation of the lungs or of the bowels, or of the brain, or of any important organ. Many horses are lost for want or insufficiency of bleeding, but we never knew one materially injured by the most copious extraction of blood in the *early* stage of acute inflammation. The horse will bear, and with advantage, the loss of an almost incredible quantity of blood,—four quarts taken from him, will be comparatively little more than one pound taken from the human being. We can scarcely conceive of a considerable inflammation of any part of the horse, whether proceeding from sprains, contusions, or any other cause in which bleeding, local (if possible), or general, or both, will not be of essential service.

Next in importance to bleeding, is purging. Something may

---

horse and the thorough bred, as there stated, and 36 or 37 a minute may be considered the standard pulse in the latter when in health and free from excitement. It is most important to distinguish between the pulse of fever and that of inflammation. We may have a pulse of the greatest rapidity, as in influenza, and yet no one part of the body much inflamed. We have known the pulse of the horse more than trebled, and the animal still recover; and, on the other hand, in cases of inflammation, a pulse of 60 has betokened great danger, and, in some cases, has been succeeded by death.

be removed from the bowels, the retention of which would increase the general irritation and fever. The quantity of blood will be materially lessened, for the serous or watery fluid which is separated from it by a brisk purge, the action of which in the horse continues probably more than twenty-four hours, is enormous. While the blood is thus determined to the bowels, less even of that which remains will flow through the inflamed part. While the purging continues, some degree of languor and sickness is felt; and the force of the circulation is thereby diminished, and the general excitement lessened. The importance of physic in every case of considerable external inflammation, is sufficiently evident. If the horse is laid by for a few days from injury of the foot, or sprain, or poll-evil, or wound, or almost any cause of inflammation, a physic-ball should be given.

In cases of internal inflammation, much judgment is required to determine when a purgative may be beneficial or injurious. In inflammation of the lungs or bowels, it should never be given.

The means of abating external inflammation are various, and seemingly contradictory. The heat of the part very naturally and properly led to the application of cold embrocations and lotions. Heat has a strong tendency to equalize itself, or to leave that substance which has a too great quantity of it, or little capacity to retain it, for another which has less of it, or more capacity. Hence the advantage of cold applications, by which a great deal of the unnatural heat is speedily abstracted from the inflamed part. The foot laboring under inflammation is put into cold water, or the horse is made to stand in water or wet clay. Various cold applications are also used to sprains. The part is wetted with diluted vinegar, or goulard, or salt and water. When benefit is derived from these applications, it is to be attributed to their coldness alone. Water, especially when cooled below the natural temperature, is as good an application as any that can be used. Nitre dissolved in water, will lower the temperature of the fluid many degrees; but the lotion must be applied immediately after the salt has been dissolved. A bandage may be afterwards applied to strengthen the limb, but during the continuance of active inflammation, it would only confine the heat of the part, or prevent it from benefiting by the salutary influence of the cold produced by the evaporation of the water.

Sometimes, however, we resort to warm fomentations, and if benefit is derived from their use, it is to be traced to the warmth of the fluid, more than to any medicinal property in it. Warm water will do as much good to the horse, who has so thick a skin, as any decoction of chamomile, or marsh-mallow, or poppy heads, or any nostrum that the farrier may recommend. Fomentations increase the warmth of the skin, and open the pores of it, and promote perspiration, and thus lessen the tension and swelling of the part, assuage pain, and relieve inflammation. Fomentations, to be beneficial, should be long and frequently applied, and at as great a degree of heat as can be used without giving the animal pain. Poultices are more permanent, or longer-continued fomentations. The part is exposed to the influence of warmth and moisture for many hours or days without intermission, and perspiration being so long kept up, the distended vessels will be very materially relieved. The advantage derived from a poultice is attributable to the heat and moisture, which, by means of it, can be long applied to the skin, and it should be composed of materials which will best retain this moisture and heat. The bran poultice of the farrier is, consequently, objectionable. It is never perfectly in contact with the surface of the skin, and it becomes nearly dry in a few hours, after which it is injurious rather than beneficial. Linseed-meal is a much better material for a poultice, for, if properly made, it will remain moist during may hours.

It is occasionally very difficult to decide when a cold or hot application is to be used, and no general rule can be laid down, except that in cases of superficial inflammation, and in the early stage, cold lotions will be preferable; but, when the inflammation is deeper seated, or fully established, warm fomentations will be most serviceable.

Stimulating applications are frequently used in local inflammation. When the disease is deeply seated, a stimulating application to the skin will cause some irritation and inflammation there, and lessen or sometimes remove the original malady: hence the use of rowels and blisters in inflammation of the chest. Inflammation to a high degree, cannot exist in parts that are near each other. If we can excite it in one, we shall abate it in the other, and also, by the discharge which we establish from the one, we shall lessen the determination of blood to the other.

Stimulating and blistering applications should never be applied to a part already inflamed. A fire is not put out by heaping more fuel upon it. Hence the mischief which the farrier often does by rubbing his abominable oils on a recent sprain, hot and tender. Many a horse has been ruined by this absurd treatment. When the heat and tenderness have disappeared by the use of cold lotions or fomentations, and the leg or sprained part remains enlarged, or bony matter threatens to be deposited, it might be right to excite inflammation of the skin by a blister, in order to rouse the deeper-seated absorbents to action, and enable them to take up this deposit; but, except to hasten the natural process and effects of inflammation, a blister, or stimulating application, should never be applied to a part already inflamed.

FEVER.

Fever is general increased arterial action, either without any local affection, or in consequence of the sympathy of the system with inflammation in some particular part.

The first is *pure fever*. Owing to bad stable management and general treatment, and the susceptibility of various parts of the horse to take on inflammation, this usually degenerates into inflammation. But pure fever is sometimes seen, and runs its course regularly.

It frequently begins with a cold or shivering fit, although this is not essential to fever. The horse is dull, unwilling to move, has a staring coat, and cold legs and feet. This is succeeded by warmth of the body; unequal distribution of warmth to the legs; one hot, and the other three cold, or one or more unnaturally warm, and the others unusually cold, but not the deathlike coldness of inflammation of the lungs; the pulse quick, soft, and often indistinct; the breathing somewhat laborious; but no cough or pawing, or looking at the flanks. The animal will scarcely eat, and is very costive. While the state of pure fever lasts, the shivering fit returns at nearly the same hour every day, and is succeeded by the warm one, and that often by a slight degree of perspiration; and these alternate during several days until local inflammation appears, or the fever gradually subsides. No horse ever died of pure fever. If he is not destroyed by inflammation of the lungs, or feet, or bowels succeeding to the fever, he gradually recovers.

Fever is general increased action of the heart and arteries, and therefore evidently appears the necessity for bleeding, regulating the quantity of blood by the degree of fever, and usually keeping the finger on the artery until some evident and considerable impression is made upon the system. The bowels should be gently opened; but the danger of inflammation of the lungs, and the uniformly injurious consequence of purgation in that disease, will prevent the administration of an active purgative. A small quantity of aloes may be given morning and night, with the proper fever medicine, until the bowels are slightly relaxed, after which nothing more of an aperient quality should be administered. Digitalis, emetic tartar, and nitre should be given morning and night, in proportions regulated by the circumstances of the case. The horse should be warmly clothed, but be placed in a cool and well-ventilated stable.

Symptomatic fever is increased arterial action, proceeding from some local cause. No organ of consequence can be much disordered or inflamed without the neighboring parts being disturbed, and the whole system gradually participating in the disturbance. Inflammation of the feet or of the lungs never existed long or to any material extent, without being accompanied by some degree of fever.

The treatment of symptomatic fever should resemble that of simple fever, except that particular attention must be paid to the state of the part originally diseased. If the inflammation which existed there can be subdued, the general disturbance will usually cease.*

THE VEINS.

These vessels carry back to the heart the blood which had been conveyed to the different parts by the arteries.

BOG AND BLOOD SPAVIN.

Attached to the extremities of most of the tendons, and between the tendons and other parts, are little bags containing a mucous substance to enable the tendons to slide over each other without friction, and to move easily on the neighboring parts. From violent exercise these vessels are liable to enlarge. Windgalls and thoroughpins are instances of this. There is one of

---

* *Note by Mr. Spooner.*—Pure fever does not of necessity require bloodletting, and, indeed, will often be removed better without the aid of depletion. The fact is well shown in cases of influenza, where great quickness of the pulse, with a hot mouth, and other tokens of fever, are present, and which symptoms may be often removed without the aid of bleeding. We decidedly object to bleeding in those cases of fever attended with a shivering fit; and, indeed, we have found that unless the pulse is full and strong, it is generally better to avoid bleeding. Fever is far more dependent on some irritation of the nervous system than is implied in the text, and bleeding is often calculated to increase this irritation. The administration of a diffusible stimulant that will act on the skin, such as the spirit of nitrous ether, is a far better mode of treatment, and will often cut short a case of fever, which the abstraction of blood would only prolong. In cases of fever the mucous membrane is very frequently in an irritable state, so that a purgative will greatly increase such irritation, and should therefore be avoided. If the bowels are costive, oily laxatives should be administered, and aloes carefully avoided, unless given in a liquid form, and as a single dose. It is a very dangerous practice to give small doses of aloes until the bowels are relaxed, for, from the long period required to relax the bowels in the horse, before this effect is produced a quantity will be taken sufficiently to endanger life, and, indeed, death has in many instances occurred from this practice. It is better therefore either to abstain altogether from giving aloes in such cases, or otherwise confine it to one moderate dose of two drachms.

them on the inside of the hock at its bending. This sometimes becomes considerably increased in size, and the enlargement is called a *bog-spavin*. A vein passes over the bag, which is pressed between the enlargement and the skin, and the passage of the blood through it is impeded; the vein is consequently distended by the accumulated blood, and the distention reaches from this bag as low down as the next valve. This is called *blood-spavin*. Blood-spavin then is the consequence of bog-spavin. It very rarely occurs, and is, in the majority of instances, confounded with bog-spavin.

Blood-spavin does not always cause lameness, except the horse is very hard worked; but this, as well as bog-spavin, constitutes unsoundness, and materially lessens the value of the horse. The proper treatment is to endeavor to promote the absorption of the contents of the bag. This may be attempted by pressure long applied. A bandage may be contrived to take in the whole of the hock, except its point; and a compress made of folded linen being placed on the bog-spavin, may confine the principal pressure to that part. It is, however, very difficult to adapt a bandage to a joint which admits of such extensive motion; therefore most practitioners apply two or three successive blisters over the enlargement, when it usually disappears. Unfortunately, however, it returns if any extraordinary exertion is required from the horse.*

* *Note by Mr. Spooner.*—Much error appears to have prevailed with regard to bog-spavins. We speak with confidence, and after numerous dissections, when we say, that this disease does not occur from the distention of any mucous bags, and, therefore, there is no possibility of cutting them out. A bog-spavin is neither more nor less than a distention of the capsular ligament of the joint itself; so that, if we cut into it, we open the joint, and endanger the life of the animal. There are different degrees of severity in which this disease may exist; it may be merely an increased secretion of synovia, so as to distend the ligament, and in such case it is readily curable; or, it may be, as it more frequently is, a rupture of the connections of the ligament with the bones, so as not only to distend, but actually to enlarge, the cavity of the joint. In the latter instance, though the disease may be temporarily removed, it generally recurs, with work. When lameness attends bog-spavin, there is usually no little degree of inflammation on the synovial membrane of the joint; and, in cases of long standing, the synovial fluid becomes solid, and causes permanent stiffness. *Thoroughpins*, are the same morbid affection as the bog-spavin, but affecting the upper and back part of the joint, and on each side.

With regard to the blood-spavin, the vein, as it passes up the leg, may certainly be somewhat obstructed by a bog-spavin: and, consequently, a little enlarged; but so slightly, that we believe that the bog and blood spavin of the old farriers were one and the same thing, the vein, from its proximity being supposed to feed the enlargement.

The best treatment for these enlargements is, next to the actual cautery, the repeated application of the iodide of mercury, which both operates as a blister, as well as specifically, on the absorbents.

BLEEDING.

This operation is performed with a fleam or a lancet. The first is the common instrument, and the safest, except in skilful hands. The lancet, however, has a more surgical appearance, and will be adopted by the veterinary practitioner. A bloodstick —a piece of hard wood loaded at one end with lead—is used to strike the fleam into the vein. This is sometimes done with too great violence, and the opposite side of the coat of the vein is wounded. Bad cases of inflammation have resulted from this. If the fist is doubled, and the fleam is sharp and is struck with sufficient force with the lower part of the hand, the bloodstick may be dispensed with.

For general bleeding the jugular vein is selected. The horse is blindfolded on the side on which he is to be bled, or his head turned well away. The hair is smoothed along the course of the vein with the moistened finger; then, with the third and little fingers of the left hand, which holds the fleam, pressure is made on the vein sufficient to bring it fairly into view, but not to swell it too much, for then, presenting a rounded surface, it would be apt to roll or slip under the blow. The point to be selected is about two inches below the union of the two portions of the jugular at the angle of the jaw (see Fig. 12). The fleam is to be placed in a direct line with the course of the vein, and over the precise centre of the vein, as close to it as possible, but its point not absolutely touching the vein. A sharp rap with the bloodstick or the hand on that part of the back of the fleam immediately over the blade, will cut through the vein, and the blood will flow. A fleam with a large blade should always be preferred, for the operation will be materially shortened, and this will be a matter of some consequence with a fidgety or restive horse. A quantity of blood drawn speedily will also have far more effect on the system than double the weight slowly taken, while the wound will heal just as readily as if made by a smaller instrument. There is no occasion to press so hard against the neck with the pail, or can, as some do; a slight pressure, if the incision has been large enough and straight, and in the middle of the vein, will cause the blood to flow sufficiently fast; or, the finger being introduced into the mouth between the tushes and the grinders, and gently moved about, will keep the mouth in motion, and hasten the rapidity of the stream by the action and pressure of the neighboring muscles.

When sufficient blood has been taken, the edges of the wound should be brought closely and exactly together, and kept together by a small sharp pin being passed through them. Round this a little tow, or a few hairs from the mane of the horse, should be wrapped, so as to cover the whole of the incision; and the head of the horse should be tied up for several hours to prevent his rubbing the part against the manger. In bringing the edges of the wound together, and introducing the pin, care should be taken not to draw the skin too much from the neck, otherwise blood will insinuate itself between it and the muscles beneath, and cause an unsightly and sometimes troublesome swelling.*

The blood should be received into a vessel, the dimensions of which are exactly known, so that the operator may be able to calculate at every period of the bleeding the quantity that is subtracted. Care likewise should be taken that the blood flows in a regular stream into the centre of the vessel, for if it is suffered to trickle down the sides, it will not afterwards undergo those changes by which we partially judge of the extent of inflammation. The pulse, however, and the symptoms of the case collectively, will form a better criterion than any change in the blood. Twenty-four hours after the operation, the edges of the wound will have united, and the pin should be withdrawn. When the bleeding is to be repeated, if more than three or four hours have elapsed, it will be better to make a fresh incision rather than to open the old wound.

For general bleeding the jugular vein is selected as the largest superficial one, and most easily got at. In every affection of the head, and in cases of fever or extended inflammatory action, it is decidedly the best place for bleeding. In local inflammation, blood may be taken from any of the superficial veins. In supposed affection of the shoulder, or of the fore-leg or foot, the *plate* vein, which comes from the inside of the arm, and runs upwards directly in front of it towards the jugular, may be opened. In affections of the hind extremity, blood is sometimes extracted from the *saphæna*, or thigh-vein, which runs across the inside of the thigh. In foot cases it may be taken from the coronet, or,

---

* *Note by Mr. Spooner.*—In performing this operation with the fleam, the blood-stick should never be loaded with lead, as there is no possible occasion for such extra weight. The lancet requires much greater skill; and, whilst the jugular vein of the near side is the most convenient situation for the fleam, the off side is the best for the lancet. In using the latter, the head of the horse should be elevated, so as to put the vein somewhat on the stretch, and prevent its rolling; the vein is then pressed with the fingers of the left hand, which, obstructing the current, causes the vein to swell: the lancet should then be dexterously thrust forwards and upwards, so as to open the vein with one incision. The lancet should not be too large—should be shaped like a human lancet, and about double its size, with a very sharp point. In bleeding from the arm or the thigh, the fleam is more convenient than the lancet.

In closing the orifice the pin should not be very large; and fine tow should be used to wind round it, and not hair, as the latter is so apt to slip.

much more safely, from the toe; not by cutting out, as the farrier does, a piece of the sole at the toe of the frog, which sometimes causes a wound difficult to heal, and followed by festering and even by canker; but cutting down with a fine drawing-knife called a searcher, at the union between the crust and the sole at the very toe until the blood flows, and, if necessary, encouraging its discharge by dipping the foot in warm water. The meshwork of both arteries and veins will be here divided, and blood is generally obtained in any quantity that may be needed. The bleeding may be stopped with the greatest ease, by placing a bit of tow in the little groove that has been cut, and tacking the shoe over it.*

* A great improvement has lately been introduced in the method of arresting arterial hemorrhage. The operation is very simple, and, with common care, successful. The instrument is a pair of artery forceps, with rather sharper teeth than the common forceps, and the blades held close by a slide. The vessel is laid bare, detached from the cellular substance around it, and the artery then grasped by the forceps, the instrument deviating a very little from the line of the artery. The vessel is now divided close to the forceps, and behind them, and the forceps are twisted four or five times round. The forceps are then loosened, and, generally speaking, not more than a drop or two of blood will have been lost. This method of arresting bleeding has been applied by several scientific and benevolent men with almost constant success. It has been readily and effectually practised in docking, and our patients have escaped much torture, and tetanus lost many a victim. The forceps have been introduced, and with much success, in castration, and thus the principal danger of that operation, as well as the most painful part of it, is removed. The colt will be a fair subject for this experiment. On the sheep and the calf it may be readily performed, and the operator will have the pleasing consciousness of rescuing many a poor animal from the unnecessary infliction of torture.

CHAPTER VIII.

WE now proceed to the consideration of the diseases of the respiratory system.

THE MEMBRANE OF THE NOSE.

The mucous membrane of the nose is distinguished from other mucous surfaces, not only by its thickness, but its vascularity. It is called the *Schneiderian* membrane. The importance of observing its color and appearance generally, as indicia of the different diseases to which the horse is subject, has been adverted to in speaking of the tissues of the head, (p. 103). Its characteristic appearance under all circumstances, should be attentively observed by every one who attempts to prescribe in the diseases of horses

CATARRH OR COLD.

Catarrh, or *Cold*, is attended by a slight discharge from the nose—now and then, a slighter weeping from the eyes, and some increased labor of breathing. When this is a simply local inflammation, attended by no loss of appetite or increased animal temperature, it may speedily pass over.

In many cases, however, the inflammation extends and involves the fauces, the lymphatic and some of the salivary glands, the throat, the parotid gland, and the membrane of the larynx. We have then increased discharge from the nose, greater redness of the membrane of the nose, more defluxion from the eyes, and loss of appetite, from a degree of fever associating itself with the local affection ; and there also being a greater or less degree of pain in the act of swallowing, and which, if the animal feels this, he will never eat. Cough now appears more or less frequent or painful ; but with no great acceleration of the pulse, or heaving of the flanks.

Catarrh frequently arises from exposures, or changes so trifling, that they would not be supposed of the least importance by one unaccustomed to horses.

In the majority of cases, a few warm mashes, warm clothing, and a *warm stable*—a fever-ball or two, with a drachm of aloes in each, and a little antimony in the evening, will set all right. In nineteen cases out of twenty, recovery would take place without any medicine, if the horse is kept free from the *cordials* which grooms are so fond of administering; but in the twentieth case, a neglected cough may be a precursor of bronchitis and pneumonia. These sometimes creep on before any danger is suspected. If there is the least fever, the horse should be bled. A common cold, attended by heat of the mouth or indisposition to feed, should never pass without the abstraction of blood. A physic-ball, however, should not be given in catarrh without much consideration. If inflammation of the lungs has set in, a dose of physic would be little better than a dose of poison. If there is no danger of this, small doses of aloes may be united with the other medicine with advantage.

If catarrh is accompanied by sore throat—if the submaxillary glands are enlarged—if the horse should quid his feed and gulp his water, this will be an additional reason for bleeding, and also for warm clothing and a comfortable stable.

Some stimulating liniment may be applied over the inflamed gland, consisting of turpentine or tincture of cantharides, diluted with spermaceti or neat's-foot oil—strong enough to produce considerable irritation on the skin, but not to blister, or to destroy the hair. An embrocation sufficiently powerful, and yet that never destroys the hair, consists of equal parts of hartshorn, oil of turpentine, and camphorated spirit, with a small quantity of laudanum.*

INFLAMMATION OF THE LARYNX.

Strictly speaking, this refers to inflammation confined to the larynx; but either catarrh or bronchitis, or both, frequently accompany the complaint.

Its approach is often insidious, scarcely to be distinguished from catarrh, except by being attended with more soreness of throat, and less enlargement of the parotid glands. There are also more decided and violent paroxysms of coughing than in common catarrh, attended by a gurgling noise, which may be heard at a little distance from the horse, and which, by auscultation, is decidedly referable to the larynx. The breathing is

* *Note by Mr. Spooner.*—In catarrh, if there is cough, the throat should be blistered, or stimulated by the tincture of cantharides.

shorter and quicker, and evidently more painful than catarrh; the membrane of the nose is redder; it is of a deep modena color; and the horse shrinks, and exhibits great pain when the larynx is pressed upon. The paroxysms of coughing become more frequent and violent, and the animal appears at times almost suffocated.

As the soreness of the throat proceeds the head of the animal is projected, and the neck has a peculiar stiffness. There is also much difficulty of swallowing. Considerable swelling of the larynx and the pharynx ensue, and also of the parotid, sublingual, and submaxillary glands. As the inflammation increases, the cough becomes hoarse and feeble, and in some cases altogether suspended. At the commencement, there is usually little or no running at the nose; but the secretion soon appears, either pure or mixed with an unusual quantity of saliva.

Auscultation is a very important aid in the discovery of the nature, and serious or trifling character of this disease. It cannot be too often repeated, that it is one of the most valuable means which we possess of detecting the seat, intensity, and results of the maladies of the respiratory passages. No instrument is required; the naked ear can be applied evenly and flatly, and with a very slight pressure, on any part that it is of importance to examine. The healthy sound, when the ear is applied to the windpipe, is that of a body of air passing uninterruptedly through a smooth tube of somewhat considerable calibre: it very much resembles the sound of a pair of forge bellows, when not too violently worked.

He who is desirous of ascertaining whether there is any disease in the larynx of a horse, should apply his ear to the lower part of the windpipe. If he finds that the air passes in and out without interruption, there is no disease of any consequence either in the windpipe or the chest; for it would immediately be detected by the loudness or the interruption of the murmur Then let him gradually proceed up the neck, with his ear still upon the windpipe. Perhaps he soon begins to recognize a little gurgling, grating sound. As he continues to ascend, that sound is more decisive, mingled with an occasional wheezing, whistling noise. He can have no surer proof that here is the impediment to the passage of the air, proceeding from the thickening of the membrane and diminution of the passage, or increased secretion of mucus, which bubbles and rattles as the breath passes. By the degree of the rattling or whistling, the owner will judge which cause of obstruction preponderates—in fact, he will have discovered the seat and the state of the disease, and the sooner he has recourse to professional advice the better.

Chronic laryngitis is of more frequent occurrence than acute

Many of the coughs that are most troublesome are to be traced to this source.

In violent cases laryngitis terminates in suffocation; in others, in thick wind or in roaring. Occasionally it is necessary to have recourse to the operation of tracheotomy.

In acute laryngitis the treatment to be pursued is sufficiently plain. The blood must be abstracted, and that from the jugular vein, for there will then be the combined advantage of general and local bleeding. The blood must be somewhat copiously withdrawn, depending on the degree of inflammation—the practitioner never for a moment forgetting that he has to do with inflammation of a mucous membrane, and that what he does he must do quickly. He will have lost the opportunity of struggling successfully with the disease when it has altered its character and debility has succeeded. The cases must be few and far between when the surgeon makes up his mind to any determinate quantity of blood, and leaves his assistant or his groom to abstract it; he must himself bleed, and until the pulse flutters or the constitution is evidently affected.

Next must be given the fever medicine already recommended: the digitalis, nitre, and emetic tartar, with aloes. Aloes may here be safely given, because the chest is not yet implicated. To this must be added, and immediately, a blister, and a sharp one. The surgeon is sure of the part, and he can bring his counter-irritant almost into contact with it.

INFLAMMATION OF THE TRACHEA.

Inflammation of the membrane of the larynx, and especially when it has run on to ulceration, may rapidly spread, and involve the greater part or the whole of the lining membrane of the trachea. A blister must reach as low as the rattling sound can be detected, and somewhat beyond this. The fever medicines must be administered in somewhat increased doses; and the bleeding must be repeated, if the state of the pulse does not indicate the contrary.

ROARING.

The present will be the proper place to speak of that singular impairment of the respiratory function recognized by this name It is an unnatural, loud, grunting sound made by the animal in the act of breathing, when in quick action or on any sudden exertion. On carefully listening to the *sound*, it will appear that the roaring is produced in the act of inspiration, and not in that of expiration. If the horse is briskly trotted on a level surface, and more particularly if he is hurried up hill, or if he is suddenly threatened with a stick, this peculiar sound will be heard and cannot be mistaken.

Roaring is manifest unsoundness. It proceeds from obstruction in some portion of the respiratory canal.

Bands of Coagulated Lymph in the trachea are a frequent cause of roaring. Thickening of the membrane is a more frequent cause. In some morbid specimens this is treble its natural thickness, and covered with ulcerations. This is particularly annoying in the upper part of the windpipe, where the passages, in their natural state, are narrow. Thus it is that roaring is the occasional consequence of strangles and catarrh, and other affections of the superior passages.

Chronic cough occasionally terminates in roaring.

The Disease of Draught-Horses generally.—There can be no doubt of the fact, that the majority of roarers are draught-horses, and horses of quick draught. They are not only subject to the usual predisposing causes of this obstruction, but there is something superadded,—the system of tight-reining. To a certain extent, the curb-rein is necessary. Without it there would be scarcely any command over a wilful horse, and it would need a strong arm occasionally to guide even the most willing. But curbing too tight, particularly when the horse is young, leads to frequent injuries to the larynx, which result in inflammation, and ultimately cause roaring.

Facts have established the hereditary predisposition to roaring, beyond the possibility of doubt, and therefore a stallion that is a roarer should never be bred from.

It is probably useless to attempt to cure confirmed roaring, but if it is of recent date, and the seat of the obstruction can be detected by auscultation, or otherwise, it might be well to bleed, purge, and most certainly to blister over the affected part. The physic having set, a course of fever medicine should be commenced. It should be considered as a case of chronic inflammation, and to be subdued by a continuance of moderate depletory measures. Probably blood should again be abstracted in less quantity; a second dose of physic should be given, and, most certainly, the blister should be repeated, or kept discharging by means of some stimulating unguent. The degree of success which attends these measures would determine the farther pursuit of them. If no relief is obtained after a fortnight or three weeks, perhaps the experimenter would ponder on another mode of treatment. He would again carefully explore the whole extent of the trachea, and if he could yet refer the rattling or wheezing to the same point at which he had before observed it, he would boldly propose *tracheotomy*, for he could certainly cut upon the seat of disease.

If he found one of these organized bands, the removal of it would afford immediate relief; or if he found merely a thickened membrane, no harm would be done; or the loss of blood might abate the local inflammation. No one would eagerly undertake case of roaring; but, having undertaken it, he should give the measures that he adopts a fair trial, remembering that, in every chronic case like this, the only hope of success depends on perseverance.*

BRONCHOCELE.

Mr. Percival is almost the only author who takes notice of enlargement of the thyroid glands—two oval bodies below the larynx, and attached to the trachea. The use of them has never been satisfactorily explained. They sometimes grow to the size of an egg, or larger, but are unattended by cough or fever, and are nothing more than an eye-sore. The iodine ointment has occasionally been applied with success. The blister or the seton may also be useful.

* *Note by Mr. Spooner.*—This disease is not always so easily discovered as is implied by the statement in the text. In some cases, the symptoms of roaring are only developed after a short gallop; and, in many, roarers will not grunt when suddenly alarmed. It is generally very old and confirmed cases that exhibit this symptom. There are not only a variety of degrees in which roaring may exist, but there are many different causes which produce the noise which gives a name to the disease. Several of these have been stated in the text; but one, and by no means an unfrequent one, has been omitted, which is the absorption and paralyzation of the muscles, on one side, which assist in opening and enlarging the entrance to the larynx, by pulling back the arytenoid cartilages, as they are termed. The consequence of this is, that an obstruction takes place; and, although the air can enter with sufficient rapidity when the animal is at rest, yet when respiration is hurried by exertion, a great noise is occasioned by the air passing through the narrow aperture with great rapidity.

The greater number of the cases of roaring certainly occur with carriage horses and are connected with the practice of tight reining. It is not, however, the sudden reining in which causes the mischief, but the long-continued position of the windpipe when thus distorted. When the breathing is greatly distressed, either from over-exertion or from inflammation of the lungs, the horse stretches out his head, and extends the nostrils, and by this means places the air-passages in a straight line, and admits their greatest expansion. When, however, the neck is much arched, there is a great angle formed at the throat, and the upper ring of the windpipe is forced up so as to form an obstruction to the passage of air. This position of the windpipe, at first temporary, at length becomes permanent, and thus proves a frequent cause of roaring.

EPIDEMIC CATARRH, OR INFLUENZA.

Various names are given to this disease—influenza, distemper, catarrhal fever, and epidemic catarrh. Its usual history is as follows:

In the spring of the year—a cold, wet spring—and that succeeding to a mild winter, and especially among young horses, and those in high condition, or made up for sale, or that have been kept in hot stables, or exposed to the usual causes of inflammation, this disease principally, and sometimes almost exclusively, prevails. Those that are in moderate work, and that are correspondingly fed, generally escape; or even when it appears in most of the stables in a narrower or wider district, horses in barracks, regularly worked and moderately fed, although not entirely exempt, are comparatively seldom diseased.

If it has been observed from the beginning, it will be found that the attack is usually sudden, ushered in by shivering, and that quickly succeeded by acceleration of pulse, heat of mouth, staring coat, tucked-up belly, diminution of appetite, painful but not loud cough, heaving at the flanks, redness of the membrane of the nose, swelled and weeping eye, dejected countenance-these are the symptoms of catarrh, but under a somewhat aggravated form.

It clearly is not inflammation of the lungs; for there is no coldness of the extremities, no looking at the flanks, no stiff immovable position, no obstinate standing up. It is not simple catarrh; for as early as the second day there is evident debility The horse staggers as he walks.

It is inflammation of the respiratory passages generally. It commences in the membrane of the nose, but it gradually involves the whole of the respiratory apparatus. Before the disease has been established four-and-twenty hours, there is frequently sore throat. The horse quids his hay, and gulps his water. There is no great enlargement of the glands; the parotids are a little tumefied, the submaxillary somewhat more so, but not at all equivalent to the degree of soreness. That soreness is excessive, and day after day the horse will obstinately refuse to eat. Discharge from the nose soon follows in considerable quantity: thick, very early purulent, and sometimes fetid. The breathing is accelerated and laborious at the beginning, but does not always increase with the progress of the disease—nay, sometimes a deceitful calm succeeds, and the pulse, quickened and full at first, soon loses its firmness, and although it usually maintains its unnatural quickness, yet it occasionally deviates from this, and subsides to little more than its natural standard. The extremities continue to be comfortably warm, or at least the temperature is variable, and there is not in the manner of the animal, or in any one symptom, a decided reference to any particular part or spot, as the chief seat of disease.

Thus the malady proceeds for an uncertain period: occasionally for several days—in not a few instances through the whole of its course, and the animal dies exhausted by extensive or general irritation: but in other cases the inflammation assumes a local determination, and we have bronchitis or pneumonia, but of no very acute character, yet difficult to treat, from the general debility with which it is connected. Sometimes there are considerable swellings in various parts, as the chest, the belly, the extremities, and particularly the head. The brain is occasionally affected; the horse grows stupid; the conjunctiva is alarmingly red; the animal becomes gradually unconscious, and delirium follows. A curious thickening, that may be mistaken for severe sprain, is sometimes observed about the tendons. It is seen under the knee or about the fetlock. It is hot and tender, and the lameness is considerable. The feet occasionally suffer severely. There is a determination of fever to them far more violent than the original disease, and separation of the laminæ and descent of the sole ensue.

The most decided character in this disease is debility. Not the stiff, unwilling motion of the horse with pneumonia, and which has been mistaken for debility—every muscle being needed for the purposes of respiration, and therefore imperfectly used in locomotion—but actual loss of power in the muscular system generally. The horse staggers from the second day. He threatens to fall if he is moved. He is sometimes down, permanently down, on the third or fourth day. The emaciation is also occasionally rapid and extreme.

At length the medical treatment which has been employed succeeds, or nature begins to rally. The cough somewhat subsides; the pulse assumes its natural standard; the countenance acquires a little more animation; the horse will eat a small quantity of some choice thing; and health and strength slowly, very slowly indeed, return: but at other times, when there has been no decided change during the progress of the disease, no manageable change of inflammation while there was sufficient power left in the constitution to struggle with it, a strange exasperation of symptoms accompanies the closing scene. The extremities become deathly cold; the flanks heave; the countenance betrays greater distress; the membrane of the nose is of an intense red, and inflammation of the substance of the lungs, and congestion and death speedily follow.

At other times the redness of the nostril suddenly disappears:

it becomes purple, livid, dirty brown, and the discharge is bloody and fetid, the breath and all the excretions becoming fetid too The mild character of the disease gives way to malignant typhus; swellings, and purulent ulcers, spread over different parts of the frame, and the animal is soon destroyed.

Post-mortem Examination.—Examination after death sufficiently displays the real character of the disease, inflammation first of the respiratory passages, and, in fatal or aggravated cases, of the mucous membranes generally. From the pharynx, to the termination of the small intestines, and often including even the larger ones, there will not be a part free from inflammation; the upper part of the trachea will be filled with adhesive spume, and the lining membrane thickened, injected, or ulcerated; the lining tunic of the bronchial tubes will exhibit unequivocal marks of inflammation; the substance of the lungs will be engorged, and often inflamed; the heart will partake of the same affection; its external coat will be red, or purple, or black, and its internal one will exhibit spots of ecchymosis; the pericardium will be thickened, and the pericardiac and pleuritic bags will contain an undue quantity of serous, or bloody-serous, or purulent fluid.

The œsophagus will be inflamed, sometimes ulcerated—the stomach always so; the small intestines will uniformly present patches of inflammation or ulceration. The liver will be inflamed—the spleen enlarged—no part, indeed, will have escaped; and if the malady has assumed a typhoid form in its latter stages, the universality and malignancy of the ulceration will be excessive.

This disease is clearly attributable to atmospheric influence. It is most prevalent in cold, ungenial weather, and is most frequent in the spring. It is both *epidemic* and *endemic*—sometimes raging over large districts so that scarcely a stable escapes, and at others, being confined to a neighborhood. It is much more liable to make its appearance in stables where a number of horses are kept, than in smaller ones.

The disease is beyond all doubt contagious.

With regard to the treatment of epidemic catarrh, there may be, and is at times, considerable difficulty. It is a disease of the mucous membrane, and thus connected with much debility; but it is also a disease of a febrile character, and the inflammation is occasionally intense. The veterinary surgeon, therefore, must judge for himself. Is the disease in its earliest stage marked by evident inflammatory action? Is there much redness of the membrane of the nose—much acceleration of the pulse—much heaving of the flanks? If so, blood must be abstracted. The orifice should be large, that the blood may flow quickly, and the circulation be sooner affected; and the medical attendant should be present at this first venesection, that he may close the orifice as soon as the pulse begins to falter. This attention to the first bleeding is indispensable. It is the carelessness with which it is performed—the ignorance of the object to be accomplished, and the effect actually produced, that destroys half the horses that are lost from this malady. The first falter of the pulse is the signal to suspend the bleeding. Every drop lost afterwards may be wanted.

If there is no appearance of febrile action, or only a very slight one, small doses of aloes may be given, combined with the fever medicines recommended for catarrh. As soon as the fæces are pultaceous, or even before that, the aloes should be omitted and the fever medicine continued. It will rarely be prudent to continue the aloes beyond the third drachm.

A stricter attention must be paid to diet than the veterinarian usually enforces, or the groom dreams of. No corn must be allowed, but mashes and thin gruel. The water should be entirely taken away, and a bucket of gruel suspended in the box. This is an excellent plan with regard to every sick horse that we do not wish to reduce too much ; and when he finds that the morning and evening pass over, and his water is not offered to him, he will readily take to the gruel, and drink as much of it as is good for him. Green meat should be early offered, such as grass, tares (the latter especially), lucerne, and, above all, carrots. If these cannot be procured, a little hay may be wetted, and offered morsel after morsel by the hand. Should this be refused, the hay may be damped with water slightly salted, and then the patient will generally seize it with avidity.

Should the horse refuse to eat during the two or three first days, there is no occasion to be in a hurry to drench with gruel ; it will make the mouth sore, and the throat sore, and tease and disgust : but if he should long continue obstinately to refuse his food, nutriment must be forced upon him. Good thick gruel must be horned down, or, what is better, given by means of Read's pump.

The practitioner will often and anxiously have recourse to auscultation. He will listen for the mucous rattle, creeping down the windpipe, and entering the bronchial passages. If he cannot detect it below the larynx, he will apply a strong blister, reaching from ear to ear, and extending to the second or third ring of the trachea. If he can trace the rattle in the windpipe, he must follow it,—he must blister as far as the disease has spread. This will often have an excellent effect, not only as a counter-irritant, but as rousing the languid powers of the constitution. A rowel of tolerable size between the fore-legs cannot do harm. It may act as a derivative, or it may take away a disposition to inflammation in the contiguous portion of the chest.

The inflammation which characterizes the early stage of this disease is at first confined to the membrane of the mouth and the fauces   Can fomentations be applied? Yes, and to the very part, by means of a hot mash, not thrown into the manger over which the head of the horse cannot be confined, but placed in that too-much-undervalued and discarded article of stable-furniture, the nose-bag. The vapor of the water will, at every inspiration, pass over the inflamed surface. In the majority of cases relief will speedily be obtained, and that suppuration from the part so necessary to the permanent removal of the inflammation —a copious discharge of mucus or purulent matter from the nostrils—will be hastened. If the discharge does not appear so speedily as could be wished, a stimulant should be applied to the part. The vapor impregnated with turpentine arising from fresh yellow deal saw-dust, used instead of bran, will have very considerable effect in quickening and increasing the suppuration. It may even be resorted to almost from the beginning, if there is not evidently much irritability of membrane.

A hood is a useful article of clothing in these cases. It increases the perspiration from the surface covering the inflamed part—a circumstance always of considerable moment.

An equable warmth should be preserved, if possible, over the whole body. The hand-brush should be gently used every day, and harder and more effectual rubbing applied to the leg. The patient should, if possible, be placed, in a loose box, in which he may toddle about, and take a little exercise, and out of which he should rarely, if at all, be taken. The exercise of which the groom is so fond in these cases, and which must in the most peremptory terms be forbidden, has destroyed thousands of horses. The air should be fresh and uncontaminated, but never chilly; for the object is to increase and not to repress cutaneous perspiration; to produce, if possible, a determination of blood to the skin, and not to drive it to the part already too much overloaded. In order to accomplish this, the clothing shou'd be rather warmer than usual.

The case may proceed somewhat slowly, and not quite satisfactorily to the practitioner or his employer. There is not much fever—there is little or no local inflammation; but there is great emaciation and debility, and total loss of appetite. The quantity of the sedative may then be lessened but not omitted altogether; for the fire may not be extinguished, although for a little while concealed. There are no diseases so insidious and treacherous as these. Mild and vegetable tonics, such as gentian and ginger, may be given. Two days after this the sedative may be altogether omitted, and the tonic gradually increased.

The feeding should now be sedulously attended to. Almost

every kind of green meat that can be obtained should be given, particularly carrots, nicely scraped and sliced. The food should be changed as often as the capricious appetite prompts; and occasionally, if necessary, the patient should be forced with gruel as thick as it will run from the horn, but the gradual return of health should be well assured, before one morsel of corn is given.*

Note by Mr. Spooner.—Though this disease often occurs in the form described in the text, yet influenza may, and often does occur, as a severe epidemic both with and without the peculiarities of catarrh. The diseases, therefore, though bordering, and often running into each other, are yet distinct and require separate notice.

With reference to the treatment of catarrhal fever, we should recommend great caution with regard to blood-letting; and, if much weakness is manifested, it should not be practised at.all. Equal caution should be observed with regard to purgative medicines; but, if the bowels are constipated, a pint of linseed oil, or two or three drachms of aloes in solution, may be given, but not repeated. This may be assisted by injections.

The influenza very extensively prevailed as an epidemic in this country in the years 1836 and 1840. A very full account of this disease as it prevailed during these periods, may be found in a small treatise on the subject published by the present writer. The symptoms in 1840 were very similar to those of the epizootic of 1836, sufficiently so to justify us in denominating it the same disease. The first symptom in that of 1840 which awakened attention was the sudden failure of the appetite (either total or partial); the horse, perhaps, might have appeared perfectly well in the morning, and at noon refused his feed. At this stage we usually found the mouth hot and the pulse quickened, varying, however, from 42 to 80, being sometimes full and strong, but more frequently soft and weak. There was generally a somewhat dull appearance of the animal at first, although nothing compared to what afterwards supervened; the coat was often staring, and when so the attack usually became more severe. This symptom, however, was far from being universal, and the extremities were rarely cold. In the course of six or twelve hours, the symptoms became more aggravated, the pulse increased in frequency, the appetite was more diminished, and probably the legs and eyelids were considerably swollen. In some cases the respiration became quickened, and in others there was cough and sore throat, but, in the majority of patients, there was no bronchial affection whatever.

In a few instances, the disease quickly reached its acmé, but, generally, the symptoms increased in severity for two or three days; when, supposing judicious treatment had been employed, they gradually declined, and at length totally disappeared, the animal slowly regaining his former health and spirits.

The bowels, generally speaking, were not apparently much deranged, but their mucous coat was particularly susceptible to the action of aperient medicines, and the fæces were frequently enveloped in thin slimy mucus, and often softer than in a state of health.

In some cases the affection of the eyes was so violent as to occasion temporary blindness, and in others pneumonia was present, but more frequently severe bronchitis. In many patients the œdematous swelling of the legs was enormous, and continued obstinate when the other symptoms had abated. But commonly, in proportion as the legs and eyes were much affected, the internal viscera were free from disease, and *vice versâ.* This rule, however

THE MALIGNANT EPIDEMIC.

Continental veterinarians describe a malignant variety or termination of epidemic catarrh, and Britain is not without its records of it. It prevailed in 1815, and three horses out of five attacked by it died. It reappeared in 1823, but was not so fatal. In 1714, a malignant epidemic was imported from the continent, and in the course of a few months destroyed 70,000 horses and cattle. It continued to visit other countries, with but short intervals, for fifty years afterwards.

The malignant epidemic was almost uniformly ushered in by inflammation of the mucous membrane of the respiratory passages, but soon involving other portions, and then ensued a

was by no means universal, for, in several instances, severe cephalic and thoracic symptoms were present in the same subject and at the same time.

When an animal had been previously suffering from some chronic disease, such as broken wind, or hepatized lungs, the influenza was nearly sure to light up afresh the embers of the former fire; and this local disease generally proved troublesome and obstinate. So, likewise, when, from the idiosyncrasy of the animal, an organ was in a weak and susceptible state, inflammation in that part was quickly excited by the general fever present in the system.

Treatment.—Whenever the pulse was full and strong, blood was abstracted with the best effect. In such instances I observed the blood slow in coagulating, and invariably presenting a buffy coat; great care, however, was taken not to abstract too large a quantity; and I found I could produce the required influence by half the quantity which, in ordinary inflammatory affections, it would be necessary to take. The amount of blood withdrawn was always determined by its effect on the pulse, taking care, as soon as its character was materially altered, becoming softer and less perceptible, to pin up the orifice. This alteration was sometimes produced by the loss of four pounds of blood, oftener by six, occasionally by eight, and in a few instances, ten pounds were required to be taken. In two or three cases, where there appeared to be severe internal inflammation, the blood-letting was repeated on the following day, and in one case on the same; but, as a general rule, even in cases where the pulse had on the following day regained its strength and fulness, I abstained from a second bleeding, trusting to medicine and the progress of the disease to soften the pulse, a result which usually followed on the second or third day.

Recourse was had to local venesection still more frequently than to general bleeding; indeed, whenever the eyes were much inflamed, or the lids swollen, I scarified the latter with a lancet, and opened the angular veins, which course of procedure was attended with the best results, for the local inflammation usually subsided in the course of twelve or twenty-four hours, whether I bled generally before or not.

On referring to some fifty cases, it appears that in twenty-three I employed general bleeding; in the remainder I did not; but in twenty-five cases I bled locally, either from the eyelids and eye veins, or the bars of the mouth. The majority of these were cases which had not been bled previously, and the minority belonged to those in which I had before em

diarrhœa, which no art could arrest. The fever, acute at first, rapidly passed over, and was succeeded by great prostration of strength. The inflammation then spread to the cellular texture, and there was a peculiar disposition to the formation of phlegmonous tumors: sometimes there were pustular eruptions, but, oftener, deep-seated tumors rapidly proceeding to suppuration. Connected with this was a strong tendency to decomposition, and unless the animal was relieved by some critical flux or evacuation, malignant typhus was established, and the horse speedily sunk.

The most satisfactory account of one of these epidemics is given us by Professor Brugnone, of Turin It commenced with loss of appetite, staring coat, a wild and wandering look, and a ployed venesection. More than one half of the horses that were bled generally were from the same stable, and were mostly young cart-horses that had been recently purchased, and afterwards worked very hard. They had also been allowed a considerable quantity of beans, a diet to which they had not previously been accustomed. Among these horses I found my severest cases, which were often complicated with pneumonia, bronchitis, and other visceral derangement. In them, too, the blood presented a thick buffy coat, and the pulse was strong and full.

The usual treatment in the way of medicines consisted in administering the following:—

(RECIPE.) Oil of Croton . . . . . . 5 drops.
Nitrate of potassa . . . . 4 to 6 drachms.
Potassio-tartrate of antimony . 1 drachm.
Spirit of nitric ether . . . . 4 drachms to 1 ounce.
Solution of acetate of ammonia 2 to 4 ounces.
Warm water sufficient to make a draught.

Sometimes four drachms of bi-tartrate of potassa was added to the above; and, when the head appeared much affected, a drachm of camphor. This draught was generally administered once, but sometimes twice a day, the croton oil being omitted after the first dose: after the first day, in by far the greater number of cases, two drachms of powdered gentian were added; and after the second or third day, a ball was substituted for the draught, consisting of:—

(RECIPE.) Nitrate of potassa . . . . . 3 drachms.
Potassio-tartrate of antimony . 1 "
Powdered gentian root . . . 2 "
Powdered pimento berries . . 1 "
Treacle sufficient to form a ball.

Counter-irritation.—In by far the greater number of cases, there was no inflammation of the air-passages; but whenever it was denoted, I blistered the throat, the course of the windpipe, and the breast, or inserted setons or rowels, as the particular case appeared to demand.

The above treatment I found successful, not only in conquering the disease, but in restoring health and strength in a short space of time.

staggering from the very commencement. The horse would continually lie down and get up again, as if tormented by colic; and he gazed alternately at both flanks. In the moments of comparative ease, there were universal twitchings of the skin, and spasms of the limbs. The temperature of the ears and feet was variable. If there happened to be about the animal any old wound or scar from setoning or firing, it opened afresh and discharged a quantity of thick and black blood. Very shortly afterwards the flanks, which were quiet before, began to heave, the nostrils were dilated, the head extended for breath. The horse had by this time become so weak that, if he lay or fell down, he could rise no more; or if he was up, he would stand trembling, staggering, and threatening to fall every moment. The mouth was dry, the tongue white, and the breath fetid; a discharge of yellow or bloody fetid matter proceeded from the nose, and fetid blood from the anus. The duration of the disease did not usually exceed twelve or twenty-four hours; or if the animal lingered on, swellings of the head and throat, and sheath, and scrotum (testicle bag) followed, and he died exhausted or in convulsions.

Black spots of extravasation were found in the cellular membrane, in the tissue of all the membranes, and on the stomach. The mesenteric and lymphatic glands were engorged, black, and gangrenous. The membrane of the nose and the pharynx was highly injected, the lungs were filled with black and frothy blood, or with black and livid spots. The brain and its meninges (enveloping membranes) were unaltered.

It was found to be highly contagious.

M. Brugnone found that bleeding only accelerated the death of the patient. He afterwards tried, and ineffectually, acids, cordials, purgatives, vesicatories, and the actual cautery; and he frankly attributes to the power of nature the recovery of the few who survived.

If seen at its outset the practitioner would probably bleed; but if a few hours only had elapsed, he would find that bleeding would only hasten the catastrophe. Stimulants should be administered mingled with opium, and the spirit of nitrous ether in doses of three or four ounces, with an ounce or more of laudanum. The quantity of opium should be regulated by the spasms and the diarrhœa. These medicines should be repeated in a few hours, combined, perhaps, with ginger and gentian. If these failed, there is little else to be done. Deep incisions into the tumors, or blisters over them, might be proper measures; but the principal attention should be directed to the arresting of the contagion. The infected should be immediately removed from the healthy. All offensive matter should be carefully cleared away, and no small portion of chloride of lime used in washing the animal, and particularly his ulcers. It might with great propriety be administered internally, while the stable, and everything that belonged to the patient, should undergo a careful ablution with the same powerful disinfectant.

BRONCHITIS.

This is not generally a primary disease. That inflammation of the superior respiratory passages, constituting catarrh, gradually creeps downwards and involves the larynx and the trachea, and at length, possibly, the farthest and the minutest ramifications of the air-tubes. When it is found to be thus advancing, its progress should be carefully watched by the assistance of auscultation. The distant murmur of the healthy lung cannot be mistaken, nor the crepitating (crackling) sound of pneumonia; and in bronchitis the blood may be heard filtering or breaking through the divisions of the lobes, and accounting for that congestion or filling of the cells with mucus and blood, which is found after intense inflammation. Inflammation precedes this increased discharge of mucus. Even that may be detected. The inflamed membrane is thickened and tense. It assumes an almost cartilaginous structure, and the murmur is not only louder, but has a kind of snoring sound. Some have imagined that a sound like a metallic ring is mingled with it; but this is never very distinct.

The interrupted whizzing sound has often and clearly indicated a case of bronchitis, and there are many corroborative symptoms which should be regarded. The variable temperature of the extremities will be an important guide—not deathly cold as in pneumonia, nor of increased temperature, as often in catarrh, but with a tendency to coldness, yet this varying much. The pulse will assist the diagnosis—more rapid than in catarrh, much more so than in the early stage of pneumonia: not so hard as in pleurisy, more so than in catarrh, and much more so than in pneumonia. The respiration should next be examined, abundantly more rapid than in catarrh, pneumonia, or pleurisy; generally as rapid and often more so than the pulse, and accompanied by a wheezing sound, heard at some distance. Mr. Percivall relates a case in which the respiration was more than one hundred in a minute.

In addition to these clearly characteristic symptoms, will be observed a haggard countenance, to which the anxious look of the horse laboring under inflammation of the lungs cannot for a moment be compared; also an evident dread of suffocation expressed, not by inability to move, as in pneumonia, but frequently an obstinate refusal to do so; cough painful in the extreme; breath hot, yet no marked pain in the part, and no looking at the side or flanks.

As the disease proceeds, there will be considerable discharge from the nostrils, much more than in catarrh, because greater extent of membrane is affected. It will be muco-purulent at first, but will soon become amber-colored or green, or grayish green; and that not from any portion of the food being returned, but from the peculiar hue of the secretion from ulcers in the bronchial passages. Small organized pieces will mingle with the discharge,—portions of mucus condensed and hardened, and forced from the inside of the tube. If the disease proceeds, the discharge becomes bloody, and then, and sometimes earlier, it is fetid.

The natural termination of this disease, if unchecked, is in pneumonia.

Like every other inflammation of the respiratory passages, bronchitis is clearly epidemic. It has not, however, yet been proved to be contagious.

Here again the first step will be to bleed; and here too will be the paramount necessity of the personal attendance of some well-informed person while the animal is bled. This is a disease of a mucous—and an extended mucous surface; and while our measures must be prompt, there is a tendency to debility which we should never forget. Although the horse may be distressed quite to the extent which Mr. Percivall describes, yet he would not bear the loss of four pounds of blood without fainting. No determinate quantity of blood will therefore be taken, but the vein will not be closed until the pulse falters, and the animal staggers, and in a minute or two would fall. This may probably effect the desired object; if it does not, it is possible that the practitioner may not have a second opportunity.

The medical attendant should be cautious in the administration of *purgatives*, for the reasons that have again and again been stated; but if the bowels are evidently constipated, small doses of aloes must be given with the febrifuge medicine, and their speedy action promoted by injections, so that a small quantity may suffice.

A blister is always indicated in bronchitis. It can never do harm, and it not unfrequently affords decided relief. It should extend over the brisket and sides, and up the trachea to the larynx. The food, if the horse is disposed to eat, should be mashes. No grain should be offered, nor should the horse be coaxed to eat.*

* *Note by Mr. Spooner.*—In addition to the treatment mentioned in the text, the use of setons in the brisket, or as near the termination of the

PNEUMONIA—INFLAMMATION OF THE LUNGS.

The intimate structure of the lungs has never been satisfactorily demonstrated. They appear, however, to be composed of minute cells or pouches, into which the air is at length conducted, and over the delicate membrane constituting the divisions of which myriads of minute blood-vessels are ramifying. The blood is not merely permeating them, but it is undergoing a vital change in them; there is a constant decomposition of the air, or of the blood, or of both; and, during the excitement of exercise, that decomposition proceeds with fearful rapidity. Then it can readily be conceived that a membrane so delicate as this must be in order that its interposition shall be no hindrance to the arterialization of the blood; so fragile also, and so loaded with blood-vessels, will be exceedingly subject to inflammation, and that of a most dangerous character.

Inflammation of the substance of the lungs is the not unfrequent consequence of all the diseases of the respiratory passages that have been treated on. Catarrh, influenza, bronchitis, if neglected or badly managed or, sometimes in spite of the most skilful treatment, will spread along the mucous membrane, and at length involve the termination of the air-passages. At other times, there is pure pneumonia. This cellular texture is the primary seat of inflammation. It is often so in the over-worked horse. After a long and hard day's hunt, it is very common for horses to be attacked by pure pneumonia.

The following are the most frequent causes of pneumonia. A sudden transition from heat to cold; a change from a warm stable to a colder one; a neglect of the usual clothing; a neglect even of some little comforts; riding far and fast against a cold wind, especially in snowy weather; and loitering about when unusual perspiration has been excited.

It has not unfrequently happened that when horses have been turned out too early to grass, or without gradual preparation, pneumonia has supervened. Few are, under any management, so subject to pneumonia as those which, in poor condition and without preparation, are turned into salt-marsh.

windpipe as possible, are of material service; and if the inflammation extends up the windpipe, the setons should also so extend, or the course of the windpipe may be blistered. Physic should be avoided. With regard to bleeding, this must depend entirely upon the state of the pulse. Sometimes its weakness entirely forbids depletion, and, on the other hand, several bleedings have been required. As a general rule, however, the blood-letting should not be very copious.

On the other hand, a sudden and considerable change from cold to heat may be followed by inflammation of the lungs.

Whether it is the consequence of previous disease of the respiratory passages, or that inflammation first appears in the cellular texture of the lungs, pneumonia is usually ushered in by a shivering fit. The horse is cold all over; this, however, soon passes off, and we have general warmth, or heat of the skin above the usual temperature, but accompanied by coldness of the extremities—intense deathy coldness. *This is a perfectly characteristic symptom. It will never deceive.* It is an early symptom. It is found when there is little or no constitutional disturbance; when the pulse is scarcely affected, and the flanks heave not at all, but the horse is merely supposed to be dull and off his feed. It is that by which the progress of the disease may be unhesitatingly marked, when many scarcely suspect its existence.

The pulse is *not* always at first much increased in rapidity, and but rarely or never hard; but it is obscure, oppressed.

It is only, however, in the early insidious stage that the flanks are occasionally quiet. If the compressibility of the lungs is diminished by the thickening of the membrane, or the engorgement of the vessels, or the filling of the cells, it will be harder work to force the air out; there must be a stronger effort, and that pressure which cannot be accomplished by one effort is attempted over and over again. The respiration is quickened—laborious; the inspiration is lengthened; the expiration is rapid; and when, after all, the lungs cannot be compressed by the usual means, every muscle that can be brought to bear upon the part is called into action. Hence the horse will not lie down, for he can use the muscles of the spine and the shoulder with most advantage as he stands; hence, too, the very peculiar stiffness of position—the disinclination to move. The horse with decided pneumonia can scarcely be induced to move at all; he cannot spare for a moment the assistance which he derives from certain muscles, and he will continue obstinately to stand until he falls exhausted or dying. How eagerly does the veterinarian ask when he goes into the stable—"Was he down last night?" And he concludes that much progress has not been made towards amendment in the case when the answer is in the negative. When the patient, wearied out, lies down, it is only for a moment; for if the inflammation is not subdued, he cannot dispense with the auxiliary muscles. He frequently, and with doleful expression, looks at his sides—at one side or at both, accordingly as one or both are involved. There is not, however, the decidedly haggard countenance of bronchitis; and in bronchitis the horse rarely or never gazes at his flanks. His is a dread of suffocation more than a feeling of pain. The head is protruded, and the nostrils distended, and the mouth and the breath intensely hot. The nose is injected from the earliest period; and soon afterwards there is not merely injection, but the membrane is uniformly and intensely red. The variation in this intensity is anxiously marked by the observant practitioner; and he regards with fear and despair the livid or dirty brownish hue that gradually creeps on.

The unfavorable symptoms are, increased coldness of the ears and feet, if that be possible; partial sweats, grinding of the teeth, evident weakness, staggering, the animal not lying down. The pulse becomes quicker, and weak and fluttering; the membrane of the nose paler, but of a dirty hue; the animal growing stupid, comatose. At length he falls, but he gets up immediately. For awhile he is up and down almost every minute, until he is no longer able to rise; he struggles severely; he piteously groans; the pulse becomes more rapid, fainter, and he dies of suffocation. The disease sometimes runs its course with strange rapidity. A horse has been destroyed by pure pneumonia in twelve hours The vessels ramifying over the cells have yielded to the fearful impulse of the blood, and the lungs have presented one mass of congestion.

The favorable symptoms are, the return of a little warmth to the extremities—the circulation beginning again to assume its natural character, and, next to this, the lying down quietly and without uneasiness; showing us that he is beginning to do without the auxiliary muscles. These are good symptoms, and they will rarely deceive.

Congestion is a frequent termination of pneumonia. Not only are the vessels gorged—the congestion which accompanies common inflammation—but their parietes are necessarily so thin, in order that the change in the blood may take place although they are interposed, that they are easily ruptured, and the cells are filled with blood. This effused blood soon coagulates, and the lung, when cut into, presents a black, softened, pulpy kind of appearance, termed by the farrier and the groom, *rottenness*, and being supposed by them to indicate an old disease. It proves only the violence of the disease, the rupture of many a vessel surcharged with blood; and it also proves that the disease is of recent date, for in no great length of time, the serous portion of the blood becomes absorbed, the more solid one becomes organized, the cells are obliterated, and the lung is hepatized— i. e. assumes the appearance of *liver*.

In every case of pneumonia, early and anxious recourse should be had to auscultation. Here, again, is the advantage of being perfectly acquainted with the deep distant murmur presented by

INFLAMMATION OF THE LUNGS. 189

the healthy lung. This sound is most distinct in the young horse, and especially if he is a little out of condition. On such a horse the tyro should commence his study of the exploration of the chest. There he will make himself best acquainted with he respiratory murmur in its full state of development. He should next take an older and somewhat fatter horse; he will there recognize the same sound, but fainter, more distant. In still older animals, there will sometimes be a little difficulty in detecting it at all. Repeated experiments of this kind will gradually teach the examiner what kind of healthy murmur he should expect from every horse that is presented to him, and thus he will be better enabled to appreciate the different sounds exhibited under disease.

If pneumonia exists to any considerable degree, this murmur is soon changed for, or mingled with, a curious crepitating sound, which having been once heard, cannot afterwards be mistaken. It is caused by the infiltration of blood into the air-cells. Its loudness and perfect character will characterize the intensity of the disease, and the portion of the chest at which it can be distinguished will indicate its extent.

The whole lung, however, is not always affected, or there are only portions or patches of it in which the inflammation is so intense as to produce congestion and hepatization. Enough remains either unaffected, or yet pervious for the function of respiration to be performed, and the animal lingers on, or perhaps recovers. By careful examination with the ear, this also may be ascertained. Where the lung is impervious—where no air passes—no sound will be heard, not even the natural murmur. Around it the murmur will be heard, and loudly. It will be a kind of rushing sound; for the same quantity of blood must be arterialized, and the air must pass more rapidly and forcibly through the remaining tubes.

A horse with any portion of the lungs hepatized cannot be sound. He cannot be capable of continued extra exertion.

Another consequence of inflammation of the substance of the lungs is the formation of tubercles. A greater or smaller number of distinct cysts are formed—cells into which some fluid is poured in the progress of inflammation: these vary in size from a pin's point to a large egg. By degrees the fluid becomes concrete or hardened; and so it continues for a while—the consequence and the source of inflammation. It occupies a space that should be employed in the function of respiration, and by its pressure it irritates the neighboring parts, and exposes them to inflammation.

By and by, however, another process, never sufficiently explained, commences. The tubercle begins to soften at its centre,—a process of suppuration is set up, and proceeds until the contents of the cyst become again fluid, but of a different character, for they now consist of pus. The pus increases; the cyst becomes more and more distended; it encroaches on the substance of the lungs; it comes into contact with other tubercles, and the walls opposed to each other are absorbed by their mutual pressure; they run together, and form one cyst, or regular excavation, and this sometimes proceeds until a considerable portion of the lung is, as it were, hollowed out. By and by, however, the vomica (tumor) presses upon some bronchial passage; the cyst gives way, and the purulent contents are poured into the bronchiæ, and got rid of by the act of coughing. At other times the quantity is too great to be thus disposed of, and the animal is suffocated. Occasionally it will break through the pleuritic covering of the lung, and pour its contents into the thorax.

Abscesses may exist for a considerable time in the lungs undiscovered.

The resolution or gradual abatement of inflammation is the termination most to be desired in this state of the disease, for then the engorgement of the vessels will gradually cease, the effusion into the cells be absorbed, and the lungs will gradually resume their former cellular texture, yet not perfectly; for there will be some induration, slight but general; or some more perfect induration of certain parts; or the rupture of some of the air-cells; or an irritability of membrane predisposing to renewed inflammation. The horse will not always be as useful as before; there will be chronic cough, thick wind, broken wind.

The first thing to do in pneumonia is to bleed until the pulse falters, and the animal bears heavy on the pail. The orifice in the vein should be large, that the blood may be extracted as quickly as possible. This is the secret of treating the inflammation of a vital organ.

Next comes purging, if we dared; but experience teaches that in pneumonia there is such a fatal tendency in the inflammation to spread over every mucous membrane, that purging is almost to a certainty followed by inflammation, and that inflammation bids defiance to every attempt to arrest it. It may be said with perfect confidence that, in the majority of cases, a physic-ball would be a dose of poison to a horse laboring under pneumonia.

May we not relax the bowels? Yes, if we can stop there We may, after the inflammation has evidently a little subsided, venture upon, yet very cautiously, small doses of aloes in our fever medicine, and we may quicken their operation by frequent injections of warm soap and water; omitting the purgative, however the moment the fæces are becoming softened. We must, however, be assured that the inflammation is subsiding, and there must be considerable constipation, or the purgative had better be let alone.

If we must not give physic, we must endeavor to find some other auxiliary to the bleeding, and we have it in the compound of *digitalis, nitre*, and *emetic tartar*, which has been so often recommended.

The greatest care should be taken of the patient laboring under this complaint. His legs should be well hand-rubbed, in order to restore, if possible, the circulation to the extremities. Comfortable flannel rollers should encase the legs from the foot to the knee. He should be covered up warm. There cannot be a doubt about this. As for air, in warm weather he cannot have too much. In cold weather, his box must be airy, but not chilly. We want to determine the blood to the extremities and the skin but not all the clothing in the world will keep our patient warm if he is placed in a cold and uncomfortable situation.

As for food, we think not of it. In nine cases out of ten he will not touch anything; or if he is inclined to eat, we give him nothing but a bran-mash, or a little green feed, or a few carrots

We now look about us for some counter-irritant. Therefore we blister the sides and the brisket, and produce all the irritation we can on the skin; and in proportion as we do so, we abate, or stand a chance of abating, the inflammation within.

We have recourse to a blister in preference to a seton; and decidedly so, for our stimulus can be spread over a larger surface, —there is more chance of its being applied to the immediate neighborhood of the original inflammation—and, most assuredly, from the extent of surface on which we can act, we can employ a quantity of stimulus beyond comparison greater than a seton would permit us to do. *Rowels* are frequently excellent adjuvants (aids) to the blister, but should not be depended upon alone.

In the *latter* stage of disease the blister will not act, because the powers of nature are exhausted. We must repeat it,—we must rouse the sinking energies of the frame, if we can, although the effort will generally be fruitless. The not rising of a blister, in the latter stage of the disease, may, too often, be regarded as the precursor of death, especially if it is accompanied by a livid or brown color of the membrane of the nose.

Pneumonia, like bronchitis, requires anxious watching. The first object is to subdue the inflammation, and our measures must be prompt and decisive. If the mouth continues hot, and the extremities cold, and the nose red, we must bleed again and again, and that in rapid succession. The good which we can do must be done at first, or not at all.

When we have obtained a little returning warmth to the extremities, we must continue to administer our sedative medicines without one grain of a carminative or a tonic ; and the return of the deathy-cold foot will be a signal for farther depletion.

* The commencement of the state of convalescence requires the same guarded practice, as in bronchitis. As many horses are lost by impatience now, as by want of decision at first. If we have subdued the disease, we should let well alone. We should guard against the return of the foe by the continued administration of our sedatives in smaller quantities ; but give no tonics unless debility is rapidly succeeding. When we have apparently weathered the storm, we must still be cautious ; we must consider the nature and the seat of the disease, and the predisposition to returning inflammation. If the season will permit, two or three months' run at grass should succeed our medical treatment ; but if this is impracticable, we must put off the period of active work as long as it can be delayed, and even after that permit the horse to return as gradually as may be to his usual employment and food.*

* *Note by Mr. Spooner.*—The diseases of the lungs have been recently carefully investigated, and we are enabled to detect three important varieties in the inflammatory affections of the lungs and chest, viz., congestive inflammation of the lungs, or *pulmonary apoplexy*—*pneumonia*, or true inflammation of the lungs—and *pleurisy*, or pleuritis. The first consists in the distention of the small vessels of the lungs with dark venous blood, and is generally produced by over-exertion, particularly if the animal, when attacked, is not in proper condition for work. The symptoms are rapid breathing, cold extremities, and short duration of the disease, ending either in death or recovery. When death supervenes, the lungs are black, as stated in the text. With regard to treatment, bleeding should be adopted if the pulse is distinct as well as rapid ; if not, a diffusible stimulant should first be given and bleeding should follow.

True pneumonia is longer in its duration, but the symptoms are often obscure at first. There is considerable distress, but there does not appear to be any active pain ; and in this respect it may generally be distinguished from *pleurisy*. The pulse is full, strong, and rapid—pain, sometimes acute but varying from time to time, and the blood presenting a considerable quantity of buff, or fibrine. The tendencies of the disease are either the deposition of water in the chest, or else fibrous flakes, and sometimes both conjoined.

Sometimes pneumonia and pleurisy are combined together, causing *pleuropneumonia*, and then the danger is increased at the same time, as the symptoms are rendered more obscure.

Blood-letting is one of the first of our remedial measures for these diseases, but is called for in a more marked degree in pleurisy than in pneumonia. The pulse, however, in both cases must be our guide as to the quantity to be taken ; and, as stated in the text, a decided effect should be obtained. Repetition of bleeding, too, may be had recourse to with greater freedom, in pleurisy than in pneumonia. In the latter disease, we must take care tnat we do not shipwreck the vital powers by repeated and too copious bleeding, or mistake the effects produced by bleeding for the symptoms of the disease itself. It is only by the conjoint aids of science and experi

CHRONIC COUGH.

It would occupy too much space to treat all the causes of this obstinate cough. Irritability of the air-passages, occasioned by previous inflammation, is the most frequent. It is sometimes connected with worms; it is sometimes caused by glanders. It is the necessary attendant of thick or broken wind.

If a harsh hollow cough is accompanied by a staring coat, and the appearance of worms,—a few worm-balls may expel the worms, and remove the irritation of the intestinal canal. If it proceeds from irritability of the air-passages, which will be discovered by the horse coughing after drinking, or when he first goes out of the stable in the morning, or by his occasionally snorting out thick mucus from the nose, medicines may be given, and sometimes with advantage, to diminish irritation generally. Small doses of digitalis, emetic tartar, and nitre, administered every night, frequently have a beneficial effect, especially when mixed with tar, which seems to have a powerful influence in allaying the irritation. These balls should, if necessary, be regularly given for a considerable time. They are sufficiently powerful to quiet slight excitement of this kind, but not to nauseate the horse, or interfere with his food or his work. A blister, extending from the root of one ear to that of the other, taking in the whole of the channel, and reaching six or eight inches down

---

ence that these nice discriminations can be made; it is therefore the height of folly for the inexperienced owner to attempt to treat such cases himself.

When pleurisy and pneumonia are combined, the symptoms, though extremely severe. are yet very obscure, and the chances of successful treatment are much diminished. The water in the chest spoken of in the text, is the termination of pleurisy, and becomes fatal in a majority of cases (particularly if, in addition to this serous fluid, flakes of lymph are also thrown out). In some cases where water in the chest has supervened early, and the inflammation has otherwise subsided, relief has been obtained by tapping.

We have little to add with regard to the treatment of these inflammatory diseases, except that we do not approve of the many repeated bleedings advised in the text. It is rarely the case that more than one bleeding is desirable, but this in general should be very copious. The best guide as to the propriety of bleeding is the strength of the pulse and not its frequency. If some hours after the first bleeding the pulse is still strong and full, as well as quick, then bleeding is most probably called for again, and more particularly if the blood has exhibited a thick buffy coat. If the first bleeding has exhibited no buff on the surface, then a repetition of bleeding is rarely demanded. Aloes should be always eschewed, and diuretics should not be continued after twelve drachms, or two ounces of nitre or resin have been taken. We have also found very good effects from the administration of small doses of calomel and opium, twice a day, two scruples of the former, and one of the latter, being sufficient for a dose; and we have also found an ounce or two of the spirit of nitrous ether very serviceable in the early stage of the disease, particularly if the legs and ears are cold.

the windpipe, has been tried, and often with good effect, on the supposition that the irritation may exist at the roots of the tongue or the larynx. The blister has sometimes been extended through the whole course of the windpipe, until it enters the chest.

Feeding has much influence on this complaint. Too much dry feed, and especially chaff, increase it. It is aggravated when the horse is suffered to eat his litter; and is often relieved when spring tares are given. Carrots afford decided relief.

The seat of the disease, however, is so uncertain, and all our means and appliances so inefficacious, and the cough itself so little interfering, and sometimes interfering not at all with the health of the animal, that it is scarcely worth while to persevere in any mode of treatment that is not evidently attended with benefit.

When chronic cough chiefly occurs after eating, the seat of the disease is evidently in the substance of the lungs. In the violent effort of the lungs to discharge their functions, when laboring under congestion, irritation is produced, and the act of coughing is the consequence.*

THICK-WIND.

When treating of pneumonia, it was observed, that not only are the vessels which spread over the delicate membrane of the air-cells gorged with blood, but they are sometimes ruptured, and the cells are filled with blood. The black, softened, pulpy appearance of the lungs thus produced, has been adverted to. If the horse is not destroyed by this injury to the structure of the lungs, the serous portion of the effused blood is absorbed, and the lung becomes organized in that solid form. Its appearance and structure then much resemble that of a liver, and it is said to be *hepatized*. This may occur in patches, or it may involve a considerable portion of the lung.

If a portion of the lung is thus rendered impervious, the remainder will have additional work to perform. The same quantity of blood must be supplied with air; and if the working part of the machine is diminished, it must move with great velocity as well as force—the respiration must be quicker and more laborious. This quick and labored breathing can be detected even when the animal is at rest; and it is indicated plainly enough by his sad distress when he is urged to unusual

---

* *Note by Mr. Spooner.*—Chronic cough is generally caused by long-continued or neglected catarrh, or sore throat. One of the best remedies for an obstinate cough that bids fair to become chronic is a seton under the throat which should be kept in seven or eight weeks.

or continued speed. The inspirations and the expirations are shorter, as well as more violent; the air must be more rapidly admitted, and more thoroughly pressed out; and this is accompanied by a peculiar sound that can rarely be mistaken.

The inflammatory stage of the disease having passed, the horse is restored to comparative health, but in a *thick-winded* state. Auscultation will indicate the amount of the hepatization, and it will enable us to distinguish between this cause of thick-wind and that thickening of the air-passages which sometimes results from bronchitis.

Of the *treatment*, little can be said. We know not by what means we can excite the absorbents to take up the solid organized mass of hepatization, or restore the membrane of the cells, and the minute vessels ramifying over them, now confounded and lost. We have a somewhat better chance, and yet not much, in removing the thickening of the membrane, for counter-irritants, extensively and perseveringly applied to the external parietes of the chest, may do something. If thick-wind immediately followed bronchitis, it would certainly be justifiable practice to blister the brisket and sides, and that repeatedly; and to administer purgatives, if we dared, or diuretics, more effectual than the purgatives, and always safe.

Our attention must be principally confined to diet and management. A thick-winded horse should have his full proportion, or rather more than his proportion of grain, and a diminished quantity of less nutritious food, in order that the stomach may never be overloaded, and press upon the diaphragm, and so upon the lungs, and increase the labor of these already over-worked organs. Particular care should be taken that the horse is not worked immediately after a full meal. The overcoming of the pressure and weight of the stomach, will be a serious addition to the extra work which the lungs already have to perform from their altered structure.

Thick-wind may be to some extent *palliated* by daily exercising the horse to the fair extent of his power, and without seriously distressing him.

Thick-wind, however, is not always the consequence of disease. There are certain cloddy, round-chested horses, that are naturally thick-winded, at least to a certain extent. They are capable of that slow exertion for which nature designed them, but they are immediately distressed if put a little out of their usual pace. A circular chest, whether the horse is large or small, indicates thick wind.

BROKEN-WIND.*

This is immediately recognizable by the manner of breathing The inspiration is performed in somewhat less than the natural time, and with an increased degree of labor; but the expiration has a peculiar difficulty accompanying it. It is accomplished by a double effort, in the first of which, as Mr. Blaine has well explained it, "the usual muscles operate; and in the other, the auxiliary muscles, particularly the abdominal, are put on the stretch to complete the expulsion more perfectly; and that being done, the flank falls, or the abdominal muscles relax with a kind of jerk or spasm."

This is attributable to an emphysematous state of the lungs. The inner membrane of the bronchial tubes swells and partly obstructs them. The powerful muscles of inspiration, however, overcome that obstruction, and fill the cells of the lungs with air. But there are no such muscles to aid expiration—to force the air out again. It is left chiefly to the elasticity of the parts—sufficient when the bronchial tubes are in their ordinary unobstructed condition, but not sufficient when they are so obstructed as to require considerable force to press the air through them. Accordingly the air remains imprisoned in the cells, and every succeeding inspiration introduces more air into them until they are ruptured, or the dilated condition becomes permanent.

Broken-wind is preceded or accompanied by cough—a cough perfectly characteristic, and by which the horseman would, in the dark, detect the existence of the disease. It is short—seemingly cut short—grunting, and followed by wheezing. When the animal is suddenly struck or threatened, there is a low grunt of the same nature as that of roaring, but not so loud. Broken-wind is usually preceded by cough; the cough becomes chronic, leads on to thick-wind, and then there is but a step to broken-wind. It is the consequence of the cough which accompanies catarrh and bronchitis oftener than that attending or following pneumonia; and of inflammation, and probably, thickening of the membrane of the bronchiæ, rather than of congestion of the air-cells.

A troublesome cough, and sometimes of long continuance, is the foundation of the disease, or indicates that irritable state of the bronchial membrane with which broken-wind is almost necessarily associated. Horses that are greedy feeders, or devour large quantities of slightly nutritious food, or are worked with a stomach distended by this food, are very subject to broken-wind. More depends upon the management of the food and exercise than is generally supposed. The post-horse, the coach-horse, and the

* Called *Heaves* in the United States.

racer, are comparatively seldom broken-winded. They are fed, at stated periods, on nutritious food that lies in little compass, and their hours of feeding and of exertion are so arranged that they seldom work on a full stomach. The agricultural horse is too often fed on the very refuse of the farm, and his hours of feeding, and his hours of work, are frequently irregular ; and the carriage-horse, although fed on more nutritious food, is often summoned to work, by his capricious master, the moment his meal is devoured.

A rapid gallop on a full stomach has often produced broken-wind ; but generally, probably, there has been some gradual preparation for the result. There has been chronic cough, more than usually disturbed respiration after exercise, &c. Galloping after drinking has been censured as a cause of broken-wind, but it is not half so dangerous as galloping with a stomach distended with food.

It is said that broken-winded horses are foul feeders, because they devour almost everything that comes in their way, and thus impede the play of the lungs ; but there is so much sympathy between the respiratory and digestive systems, that one cannot be much deranged without the other evidently suffering. Flatulence, and a depraved appetite, may be the consequence as well as the cause of broken-wind ; and there is no pathological fact of more frequent occurrence than the co-existence of indigestion and flatulence with broken-wind.

The narrow-chested horse is more subject to broken-wind than the broader and deeper chested one, for there is not so much room for the lungs to expand when rapid progression requires the full discharge of their function.

Is broken-wind hereditary ? We believe so. It may be referred to hereditary conformation—to a narrower chest, and more fragile membrane—and predisposition to take on those inflammatory diseases which end in broken-wind ; and the circular chest, which cannot enlarge its capacity when exertion requires it, must render both thick and broken-wind of more probable occurrence.

Is there any cure for broken-wind ? None ! No medical skill can repair the broken-down structure of the lungs.

If, however, we cannot cure, we may in some degree palliate broken-wind ; and, first of all, we must attend carefully to the feeding. The food should lie in little compass—plenty of oats and little hay, but no chaff. Chaff is particularly objectionable, from the rapidity with which it is devoured, and the stomach distended Water should be given in moderate quantities, but the horse should not be suffered to drink as much as he likes until the day's work is over. Green feed will always be serviceable. Carrots are particularly useful. They are readily digested, and appear to have a peculiarly beneficial effect on the respiratory system.

Many horses become broken-winded even in the straw-yard. Keeping the stomach constantly distended to get enough nutriment from such poor feed, and consequently habitually pressing on the lungs, the latter are easily ruptured when the horse plays with his companions.

The pursive or broken-winded horse should be exercised daily By attention to this and to his feeding he may be rendered comfortable to himself, and no great nuisance to his owner. Occasional physic, or alterative medicine, will often give considerable relief where the broken-winded animal has been urged unprepared, or with a stomach full of food, on a journey, and is suffering the consequences of it.

Thick-wind and broken-wind exist in various degrees, and with many shades of difference. They have assumed various names.

Pipers make a shrill noise when in quick action. This is a species of *roaring*. The *wheezer* utters a sound not unlike that of an asthmatic person when a little hurried. This can be heard even when the horse is at rest in the stable. The *whistler* utters a shriller sound than the wheezer, but only when in exercise, and that of some continuance. A sharp gallop up hill will speedily detect it. It is a great nuisance to the rider, and such a horse becomes speedily distressed.

When the obstruction seems to be principally in the nose, the horse loudly puffs and blows, and the nostrils are dilated to the utmost, while the flanks are comparatively quiet. This animal is said to be a HIGH-BLOWER.* With all his apparent distress, he often possesses great speed and endurance. The sound is unpleasant, but the lungs may be perfectly sound.

Every horse violently exercised on a full stomach, or when overloaded with fat, will grunt almost like a hog; but there are some horses who will at all times emit it, if suddenly touched with the whip or spur. They are called GRUNTERS, and should be avoided. It is the consequence of previous disease, and is frequently followed by thick or broken-wind, or roaring.†

---

* Eclipse (the English horse of that name), perhaps as good a horse as ever run, was a high-blower.—AM. ED.

† *Note by Mr. Spooner.*—The term *piper* is applied solely to a broken-winded horse, and not to any variety of roarer. The terms *wheezing* and *whistling* are simply varieties of roaring, and express the noise made in the act of respiration. [Mr. Spooner's description of the pathology and treatment of broken-wind offers nothing of importance that is not found in the text.]

PHTHISIS PULMONALIS, OR CONSUMPTION.

This fatal complaint is usually connected with, or the consequence of, pneumonia or pleurisy, and especially in horses of a peculiar formation or temperament.

If a narrow-chested, flat-sided horse is attacked by inflammation of the lungs, or severe catarrhal fever, experience tells us that we shall have more difficulty in subduing the disease in him, than in one deeper in the girth or rounder in the chest.

When this disease has been properly treated, and apparently subdued, this horse cannot be quickly and summarily dismissed to his work. He is sadly emaciated—he long continues so—his coat stares—his skin clings to his ribs—his belly is tucked up, notwithstanding that he may have plenty of mashes, and carrots, and green meat, and medicine—his former gaiety and spirit do not return, or if he is willing to work he is easily tired, sweating on the least exertion, and the sweat most profuse about the chest and sides—his appetite is not restored, or, perhaps, never has been good, and the slightest exertion puts him completely off his feet.

"We observe him more attentively, and, even as he stands quiet in his stall, the flanks heave a little more laboriously than they should do, and that heaving is painfully quickened when sudden exertion is required. He coughs sorely, and discharges from the nose a mucus tinged with blood, or a fluid decidedly purulent—the breath becomes offensive—the pulse is always above 40, and strangely increased by the slightest exertion.

When many of these symptoms are developed, the animal will exhibit considerable pain on being gently struck on some part of the chest; the cough then becomes more frequent and painful; the discharge from the nose more abundant and fetid, and the emaciation and consequent debility more rapid, until death closes the scene.

The lesions that are presented after death are very uncertain Generally there are tubercles; sometimes very minute, at other times large in size. They are in different states of softening, and some of them have burst into the bronchial passages, and exhibit abscesses of enormous bulk. Other portions of the lungs are shrunk, flaccid, indurated or hepatized, and of a pale or red-brown color; and there are occasional adhesions between the lungs and the sides of the chest.

There is some difficulty in deciding whether consumption is hereditary; but those conformations which lead to this disease *are* hereditary, and thus far the disease is.

If the horse is not very bad, and it is spring of the year, a *run at grass* may be tried. But the apparent amelioration is often transient.

The medical treatment, if any is tried, will depend on two simple and unerring guides, the pulse and the membrane of the nose. If the first is quick and hard, and the second streaked with red, bleeding should be resorted to, Small bleedings of one or two quarts, omitted when the pulse is quieted and the nostril is pale, may be effected. *Counter-irritants* will rarely do harm. They should be applied in the form of blisters, extending over the sides, and thus brought as near as possible to the affected part. *Sedative medicines* should be perseveringly administered: and here, as in acute inflammation, the chief dependence will be placed on *digitalis*. It should be given in small doses until a slightly intermittent pulse is produced, and that state of the constitution should be maintained by a continued exhibition of the medicine. *Nitre* may be added as a diuretic, and *pulvis antimonialis* as a diaphoretic.

Any *tonics* here? Yes, the tonic effect of mild and nutritious food—green food of almost every kind, carrots particularly, mashes, and now and then a malt mash.

But anything like a cure in confirmed phthisis is out of the question, and all the practitioner can do is to detect the disease in its earliest state, and allay the irritation which causes or accompanies the growth of the tubercles.

PLEURISY.

The prevailing causes of pleurisy are the same as those which produce pneumonia—exposure to wet and cold, sudden alterations of temperature, partial exposure to cold, riding against a keen wind, immersion as high as the chest in cold water, drinking cold water, and extra work of the respiratory machine. To these may be added, wounds penetrating into the thorax and lacerating the pleura, fracture of the ribs, or violent contusions on the side, the inflammation produced by which is propagated through the parietes of the chest.

It is sometimes confined to one side, or to one of the pleura on either side, or even to patches on that pleura, whether pulmonary (of the lungs), or costal (of the ribs).

The first symptom is *rigor* (chill) followed by increased heat and partial sweats: to these succeed loss of appetite and spirits, and a low and painful cough. The inspiration is a short, sudden effort, and broken off before it is fully accomplished, indicating the pain felt from the distention of the irritable, because inflamed, membrane. This symptom is exceedingly characteristic. In the human being it is well expressed by the term *stitch*, and an exceedingly painful feeling it is. The expiration is retarded as much as possible, by the use of all the auxiliary muscles which the animal can press into the service; but it at length finishes abruptly in a kind of spasm. This peculiarity of breathing, once carefully observed, cannot be forgotten. The next character is found in the tenderness of the sides when the costal pleura is affected. This tenderness often exists to a degree scarcely credible. If the side is pressed upon, the horse will recede with a low painful grunt; he will tremble, and try to get out of the way before the hand touches him again. Then comes another indication, both of pain and the region of that pain,—the intercostal muscles, affected by the contiguous pleura, and in their turn affecting the subcutaneous muscular expansion without—there are twitchings of the skin on the side —corrugations (wrinkles) —waves creeping over the skin. This is never seen in pneumonia. There is, however, as we may expect, the same disinclination to move, for every motion must give intense pain.

The pulse should be anxiously studied. It presents a decided difference of character from that of pneumonia. It is increased in rapidity, but instead of being oppressed and sometimes almost unappreciable, as in pneumonia, it is round, full, and strong. Even at the last, when the strength of the constitution begins to yield, the pulse is wiry, although small.

The extremities are never deathly cold; they may be cool, they are oftener variable, and they sometimes present increased heat. The body is far more liable to variations of temperature; and the cold and the hot fit more frequently succeed each other. The mouth is not so hot as in pneumonia, and the breath is rarely above its usual temperature.

A difference of character in the two diseases is here particularly evident on the membrane of the nose. Neither the crimson nor the purple injection of pneumonia is seen on the lining of the nose, but a somewhat darker, dingier hue.

Both the pneumonic and pleuritic horse will look at his flanks, thus pointing out the seat of disease and pain; but the horse with pneumonia will turn himself more slowly round, and long and steadfastly gaze at his side, while the action of the horse with pleurisy is more sudden, agitated, spasmodic. The countenance of the one is that of settled distress; the other brightens up occasionally. The pang is severe, but it is transient, and there are intervals of relief. While neither will lie down or willingly move, and the pneumonic horse stands fixed as a statue, the pleuritic one shrinks, and crouches almost to falling. If he lies down, it is on the affected side, when the disease is confined to one side only. The head of the horse with inflammation of the substance of the lungs, hangs heavily; that of the other is protruded.

We here derive most important assistance from *Auscultation*. In a case of pleurisy we have no crepitating, crackling sound. referable to the infiltration of the blood through the gassamer membrane of the air-cells; we have not even a louder and distincter murmur. Perhaps there is no variation from the sound of health, or, if there is any difference the murmur is fainter; for the pleural membrane is thickened, and its elasticity is impaired, and the sound is not so readily transmitted. There is sometimes a slight rubbing sound, and especially towards the superior region of the chest, as if there was friction between the thickened and indurated membranes.

To this may be added the different character of the cough, sore and painful enough in both, but in pneumonia generally hard, and full, and frequent. In pleurisy it is not so frequent, but faint, suppressed, cut short, and rarely attended by discharge from the nose.

These are sufficient guides in the early stage of the disease, when it is most of all of importance to distinguish the one from the other.

If after a few days the breathing becomes a little more natural, the inspiration lengthened and regular, and the expiration, although still prolonged, is suffered to be completed—if the twitchings are less evident and less frequent—if the cough can be fully expressed—if the pulse softens, although it may not diminish in frequency, and if the animal begins to lie down, or walks about of his own accord, there is hope of recovery. But if the pulse quickens, and, although smaller, yet possesses the wiry character of inflammation—if the gaze at the flanks, previously by starts, becomes fixed as well as anxious, and the difficulty of breathing continues (the difficulty of *accomplishing* it, although the efforts are oftener repeated)—if patches of sweat break out, and the animal gets restless—paws—shifts his posture every minute—is unable longer to stand, yet hesitates whether he shall lie down,—determines on it again and again, but fears, and at length drops, rather than lies gently down, a fatal termination is at hand. For some time before his death the effusion and its extent will be evident enough. He not only walks unwillingly, but on the slightest exercise his pulse is strangely accelerated; the feeling of suffocation comes over him, and he stops all of a sudden, and looks wildly about and trembles; but he quickly recovers himself and proceeds. There is also, when the effusion is confirmed, œdema (swelling from a dropsical humour) of some external part, and that occasionally to a very great extent. This is oftenest observed in the abdomen, the chest and the point of the breast.

The immediate cause of death is effusion in the chest, com

pressing the lungs on every side, rendering expiration difficult and at length impossible, and destroying the animal by suffocation. The very commencement of effusion may be detected by auscultation. There will be the cessation of the respiratory murmur at the sternum, and the increased grating—not the crepitating, crackling noise as when congestion is going on—not the feebler murmur as congestion advances; but the absence of it, beginning from the bottom of the chest.

It is painfully interesting to watch the progress of the effusion—how the stillness creeps up, and the murmur gets louder above, and the grating sound louder too, until at length there is no longer room for the lungs to play, and suffocation ensues.

The fluid contained in the chest varies in quantity as well as appearance and consistence. Many gallons have been found in the two sacs, pale, or yellow, or bloody, or often differing in the two sides of the thorax; occasionally a thick adventitious coat covering the costal or the pulmonary pleura—rarely much adhesion, but the lungs purple-colored, flaccid, compressed, not one-fourth of their usual size, immersed in the fluid, and rendered incapable of expanding by its pressure.

Here, as in pneumonia, the bleeding should be prompt and copious. Next, and of great importance, aperient medicine should be administered—that, the effect of which is so desirable, but which we do not dare to give when the mucous membrane of the respiratory passages is the seat of disease. Here we have to do with a serous membrane, and there is less sympathy with the mucous membranes of either cavity. Small doses of aloes should be given with the usual fever medicine, and repeated morning and night until the dung becomes pultaceous, when it will always be prudent to stop. The sedative medicine is that which has been recommended in pneumonia, and in the same doses. Next should follow *a blister* on the chests and sides. It is far preferable to setons, for it can be brought almost into contact with the inflamed surface, and extended over the whole of that surface. An airy, but a comfortable box, is likewise even more necessary than in pneumonia, and the practice of exposure, uncovered, to the cold, even more absurd and destructive. The blood, repelled from the skin by the contractile, depressing influence of the cold, would rush with fatal impetus to the neighboring membrane, to which it was before dangerously determined. Warm and comfortable clothing cannot be dispensed with in pleurisy.

The sedative medicines, however, should be omitted much sooner than in pneumonia, and succeeded by diuretics. The common turpentine is as good as any, made into a ball with linseed meal, and given in doses of two or three drachms twice in the day. If the constitution is much impaired, tonics may be cautiously given, as soon as the violence of the disease is abated. The spirit of nitrous ether is a mild stimulant and a diuretic. Small quantities of gentian and ginger may be added, but the turpentine must not be omitted.

By auscultation and other modes of examination, the existence f water in the chest is perhaps ascertained, and, possibly, it is increasing. Is there any mechanical way of getting rid of it? There is one to which recourse should be had as soon as it is evident that there is considerable fluid in the chest. The operation of *Paracentesis*, or tapping, should be performed; it is a very simple one. The side-line may be had recourse to, or the twitch alone may be used. One of the horse's legs being held up, and, counting back from the sternum to between the seventh and eighth ribs, the surgeon should pass a moderate-sized trochar into the chest immediately above the cartilages. He will not have selected the lowest situation, but as near it as he could with safety select; for there would not have been roon between the cartilages if the puncture had been lower; and there would have been injured in the forcing of the instrument between them, or, what is worse, there would have been great hazard of wounding the pericardium, for the apex of the heart rests on the sternum. Through this aperture, close to the cartilages, the far greater part of the fluid may be evacuated. The operator will now withdraw the stilette, and let the fluid run through the canula. He will not trouble himself afterwards about the wound; it will heal readily enough; perhaps too quick, for, could it be kept open a few days, it might act as a very useful drain. *It should be attempted early.* Recourse should be had to the operation as soon as it is ascertained that there is considerable fluid in the chest, for the animal will at least be relieved for a while, and some time will have been given for repose to the overlabored lungs. and for the system generally to be recruited. The fluid will be evacuated before the lungs are too much debilitated by laborious action against the pressure of the water, and a state of collapse brought on, from which they will be incapable of recovering They only who have seen the collapsed and condensed state of the lung that had been long compressed by the fluid, can conceive of the extent to which this is carried.

Few cases of tapping have been permanently successful, but the reason has been that they have not been early enough resorted to.

If there is fluid in both cavities of the thorax, but one side should be operated on at once, and the other one, the succeeding day.

There is in pleurisy a far greater tendency to relapse than in pneumonia. Edematous swellings, cough, disinclination to work, pleuritic stitches, which might easily be mistaken for colicky pains, often succeed it.

There is a greater disposition to metastasis or shifting of the seat of the inflammation, than in pneumonia. It attacks almost every part. Dropsy is the most frequent change—effusion in the abdomen is substituted for effusion in the chest or thorax.

CHAPTER IX.

THE ABDOMEN AND ITS CONTENTS.

THE STOMACH.

Fig. 27.

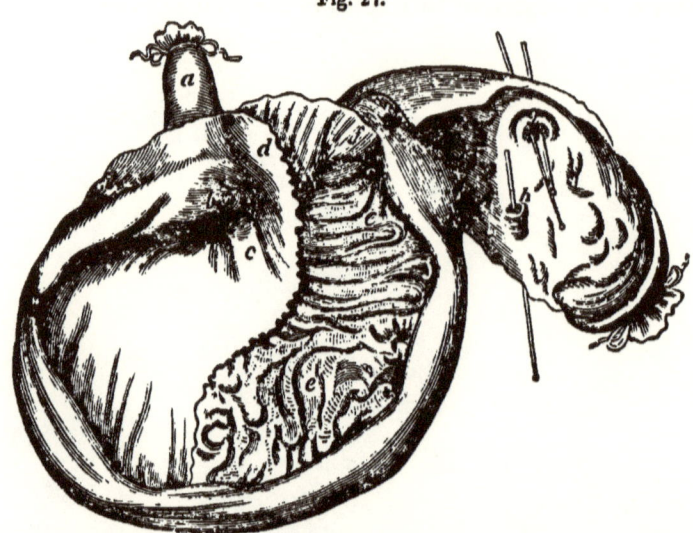

a   The œsophagus or gullet, extending to the stomach.
b   The entrance of the gullet into the stomach. The circular layers of the muscles are very thick and strong, and which, by their contractions, help to render it difficult for the food to be returned or vomited.
c   The portion of the stomach which is covered by cuticle, or insensible skin.
d d   The margin, which separates the cuticular from the villous portion.
e e   The mucous, or villous (velvet) portion of the stomach, in which the food is principally digested.
f   The communication between the stomach and the first intestine.
g   The common orifice through which the bile and the secretion from the pancreas pass into the first intestine. The two pins mark the two tubes here united.
h   A smaller orifice, through which a portion of the secretion of the pancreas enters the intestines.

The œsophagus (gullet) extends from the mouth down the left side of the neck, and enters the stomach in a somewhat curved direction. It is so constructed at its entrance into the stomach, that a return of the food by vomiting is almost impossible.

The stomach of the horse is so situated that it must be displaced and driven back by every contraction of the diaphragm (midriff) or act of inspiration; and in proportion to the fulness of the stomach will be the weight to be overcome, and the labor of the diaphragm, and the exhaustion of the animal. Hence the frequency and labor of the breathing, and the quickness with which such a horse is blown, or possibly destroyed. Hence also the folly of giving too full a meal, or too much water, before the horse starts on a journey or for the chase.

The stomach has four coats. The outermost is the lining of the cavity of the belly, and the common covering of all the intestines—that by which they are confined in their respective situations, and from which a fluid is secreted that prevents all friction between them. This is called the *peritoneum*—that which stretches round the inside of the stomach.

The second is the muscular coat, consisting of two layers of fibres, one running lengthways, and the other circularly, and by means of which a constant gentle motion is communicated to the stomach, mingling the food more intimately together, and preparing it for digestion, and by the pressure of which the food when properly prepared is urged on into the intestines.

The third, or cuticular (*skin-like*) coat, c, covers but a portion of the inside of the stomach. It is a continuation of the lining of the gullet. There are numerous glands on it, which secrete a mucous fluid; and it is probably intended to be a reservoir in which a portion of the food is retained for a while, and softened and better prepared for the action of the other or true digestive portion of the stomach. The cuticular coat occupies nearly one half of the inside of the stomach.

The fourth coat is the mucous or villous (velvet) coat, e, where the work of digestion properly commences. The mouths of numerous little vessels open upon it, pouring out a peculiar fluid, the *gastric* (stomach) juice, which mixes with the food already softened, and converts it into a fluid called *chyme*. As this is formed, it passes out of the other orifice of the stomach, the *pylorus* (doorkeepers), f, and enters the first small intestine; the harder and undissolved parts being turned back to undergo farther action.

The stomach is occasionally subject to inflammation and various other injuries.

The symptoms, however, are obscure and frequently mistaken. They resemble those of colic more than anything else, and should be met by bleeding, oily purges, mashes, warm gruel, and the application of the stomach-pump: but when, in addition to the colicky pains, there appear indistinctness of the pulse—and a very characteristic symptom that is—pallidness of the membranes, coldness of the mouth, frequent lying down, and in such position that the weight of the horse may rest on the chest, frequently pointing with his muzzle at the seat of pain, and, especially, if these symptoms are accompanied or followed by vomiting, rupture of the stomach is plainly indicated. The horse does not necessarily die as soon as this accident occurs. In a case related by Mr. Rogers, the animal died in about four hours after the accident, but in one that occurred in the practice of the author, three days elapsed between the probable rupture of the stomach, from a sudden and violent fall, and the death of the animal, and in which interval he several times ate a little food.

Wisely considering the shocks and dangers to which it is exposed, the stomach is extremely insensible.

BOTS.

In the spring and early part of the summer, horses are much troubled by a grub or caterpillar, which crawls out of the anus, fastens itself under the tail, and seems to cause a great deal of itching or uneasiness. Grooms are sometimes alarmed at the appearance of these insects. Their history is curious, and will dispel every fear with regard to them. We are indebeted to Mr. Bracy Clark for almost all we know of the bot.

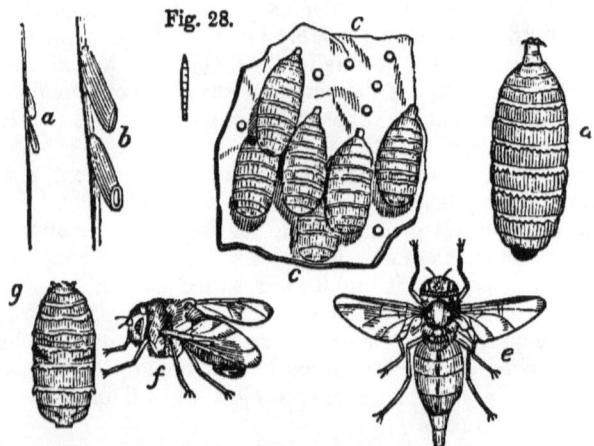

Fig. 28.

a and *b* The eggs of the gad-fly, adhering to the hair of the horse.
    c The appearance of the bots on the stomach, firmly adhering by their hooked mouths. The marks or depressions are seen which are left on the coat of the stomach when the bots are detached from their hold
    d The bot detached.
    e The female of the gad-fly, of the horse, prepared to deposit her eggs.
    f The gad-fly by which the red bots are produced
    g The sn... or red bot

A species of gad-fly, *e*, the œtrus equi, is in the latter part of the summer exceedingly busy about the horse. It is observed to be darting with great rapidity towards the knees and sides of the animal. The females are depositing their eggs on the hair, and which adhere to it by means of a glutinous fluid with which they are surrounded (*a* and *b*). In a few days the eggs are ready to be hatched, and the slightest application of warmth and moisture will liberate the little animals which they contain. The horse in licking himself touches the egg; it bursts, and a small worm escapes, which adheres to the tongue, and is conveyed with the food into the stomach. There it clings to the cuticular portion of the stomach, *c*, by means of a hook on either side of its mouth; and its hold is so firm and so obstinate, that it must be broken before it can be detached. It remains there feeding on the mucus of the stomach during the whole of the winter, and until the end of the ensuing spring; when, having attained a considerable size, *d*, and being destined to undergo a certain transformation, it disengages itself from the cuticular coat, is carried into the villous portion of the stomach with the food, passes out of it with the chyme, and is evacuated with the dung.

The *larva* or maggot seeks shelter in the ground, and buries itself there; it contracts in size, and becomes a chrysalis or grub, in which state it lies inactive for a few weeks, and then, bursting from its confinement, assumes the form of a fly. The female, becoming impregnated, quickly deposits her eggs on those parts of the horse which he is most accustomed to lick, and thus the species is perpetuated.

There are several plain conclusions to be drawn from this history. The bots cannot, while they inhabit the stomach of the horse, give the animal any pain, for they have fastened on the cuticular and insensible coat. They cannot be injurious to the horse, for he enjoys the most perfect health when the cuticular part of his stomach is filled with them, and their presence is not even suspected until they appear at the anus. They cannot be removed by medicine, because they are not in that part of the stomach to which medicine is usually conveyed; and if they were, their mouths are too deeply buried in the mucus for any medicine, that can be safely administered, to affect them; and, last of all, in due course of time they detach themselves, and come away. Therefore, the wise man will leave them to themselves, or content himself with picking them off when they collect under the tail and annoy the animal.

The smaller bot, *f* and *g*, is not so frequently found.

Of inflammation of the stomach of the horse, except from poisonous herbs, or drugs, we know little. It rarely occurs. It can with difficulty be distinguished from inflammation of the bowels; and, in either case, the assistance of the veterinary surgeon is required.

Few horses are destroyed by poisonous plants in our meadows. Natural instinct teaches the animal to avoid the greater part of those that would be injurious.

THE INTESTINES.

The food having been partially digested in the stomach, and converted into chyme, passes through the pyloric orifice into the intestines.

Fig. 29.

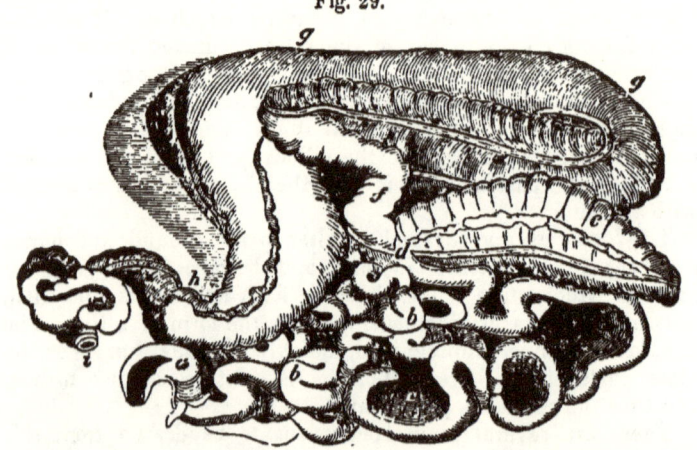

a The commencement of the small intestines. The ducts which convey the bile and the secretion from the pancreas are seen entering a little below.
b b The convolutions or winding of the small intestines.
c A portion of the mesentery.
d The small intestines, terminating in the cæcum.
e The cæcum, or blind gut, with the bands running along it, puckering and dividing it into numerous cells.
f The beginning of the colon.
ç g The continuation and expansion of the colon, divided, like the cæcum, into cells.
h The termination of the colon in the rectum.
i The termination of the rectum at the anus.

The intestines of a full-grown horse are not less than ninety feet in length. They are divided into the small and large intestines; the former of which occupy about sixty-six feet, and the latter twenty-four.

The intestines, like the stomach, are composed of three coats viz., the peritoneum, the middle coat, and the mucous or villous one inside of the others.

The intestines are chiefly retained in their relative positions by the *mesentery*, c, (middle of the intestines), which is a doubling of the peritoneum, including each intestine in its folds, and also inclosing in its duplicatures the arteries, the veins, the nerves, and the vessels which convey the nutriment from the intestines to the circulation.

The first of the small intestines, and commencing from the right extremity of the stomach, is the *duodenum*, a. It is the largest and shortest of all the small intestines. It receives the food partially converted into chyme by the digestive power of the stomach, and in which it undergoes another and very important change; a portion of it being converted into *chyle*. It is here mixed with the bile and the secretion from the pancreas which enter this intestine about five inches from its commencement. The bile seems to be the principal agent in this change, for no sooner does it mingle with the chyme than that fluid begins to be separated into two distinct ingredients—a white, thick liquid termed chyle, and containing the nutritive part of the food, and a yellow, pulpy substance, the innutritive portion, which, when the chyle is all pressed from it, is evacuated through the rectum.

The next portion of the small intestines is the *Jejunum*, so called because it is generally found to be empty. It is smaller in bulk and paler in color than the duodenum. It is more loosely confined in the abdomen—floating comparatively unattached in the cavity of the abdomen, and the passage of the food being comparatively rapid through it.

There is no separation or distinction between it and the next intestine—the *Ileum*. Together they form that portion of the intestinal tube which floats in the umbilical region: the latter, however, is said to occupy three-fifths, and the former two-fifths, of this portion of the intestines, and the five would contain about eleven gallons of fluid. The ileum diminishes in size as it approaches the larger intestines.

These two intestines are attached to the spine by a loose doubling of the peritoneum, and float freely in the abdominal cavity.

The large intestines are three in number:—the *cæcum*, the *colon*, and the *rectum*. The first of them is the *cæcum* (blind gut), e,—it has but one opening into it, and consequently everything that passes into it, having reached the blind or closed end, must return, in order to escape. It is not a continuation of the ileum, but the ileum pierces the head of it, as it were, at right angles (d) and projects some way into it, and has a valve—the valvula coli—at its extremity, so that what has traversed the ileum and entered the head of the colon, cannot return into the ileum. Along the outside of the cæcum run three strong bands each of them shorter than that intestine, and thus puckering it up, and forming it into three sets of cells, as shown in the accompanying side cut.

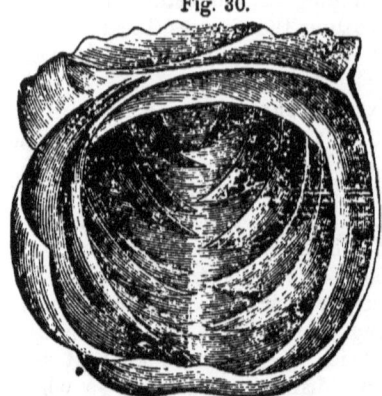

Fig. 30.

That portion of the food which has not been taken up by the lacteals or absorbent vessels of the small intestines, passes through this valvular opening of the ileum, and a part of it enters the colon, while the remainder flows into the cæcum. Then, from this being a blind pouch, and from the cellular structure of this pouch, the food must be detained in it a very long time; and in order that, during this detention, all the nutriment may be extracted, the cæcum and its cells are largely supplied with blood-vessels and absorbents. It is principally the fluid part of the food that seems to enter the cæcum. A horse will drink at one time a great deal more than his stomach will contain; or even if he drinks a less quantity, it remains not in the stomach or small intestines, but passes on to the cæcum, and there is retained, as in a reservoir, to supply the wants of the system. The cæcum will hold four gallons.

The *colon* is an intestine of exceedingly large dimensions, and is capable of containing no less than twelve gallons of liquid or pulpy food. It has likewise, in the greater part of its course, three bands like the cæcum, which also divide it, internally, into the same description of cells. The intention of this is evident,— to retard the progress of the food, and to give a more extensive surface on which the vessels of the lacteals may open; and therefore, in the colon, all the chyle is finally separated and taken up. The food does not require to be much longer detained, and the mechanism for detaining it is gradually disappearing. The colon, also, once more contracts in size, and the chyle having been all absorbed, the remaining mass, being of a harder consistence, is moulded into pellets or balls in its passage through these shallower cells.

At the termination of the colon, the *rectum* (straight gut) commences. It is smaller in circumference and capacity than the colon, although it will contain at least three gallons of water. It serves as a reservoir for the dung until it is evacuated The fæces descend to the rectum, which somewhat enlarges to receive them; and when they have accumulated to a certain extent, the animal, by the aid of the diaphragm and the muscles of the belly, presses upon them, and they are evacuated. A curious circular muscle, and always in action, called the *sphincter* (constrictor muscle), is placed at the anus, to prevent the constant and unpleasant dropping of the fæces, (dung) and to retain them until the horse is disposed voluntarily to expel them.

THE LIVER.

Between the stomach and the diaphragm—its right lobe or division in contact with the diaphragm, the duodenum and the right kidney, and the middle and left divisions with the stomach —is the liver. It is an irregularly-shaped, reddish-brown substance, of considerable bulk, and performs a very singular and important office.

The blood brought back by the veins from the stomach, intestines, spleen, pancreas, and mesentery, instead of flowing directly to the heart, pass first through the liver. As the blood traverses this organ, the *bile* is separated from it, and discharged through the *hepatic duct* directly into the duodenum, without the intervention of any gall-bladder, as is found in most animals. The bile is probably a kind of excrement, the continuance of which in the blood would be injurious, and it doubtless aids in the process of digestion.

THE PANCREAS.

In the domestic animals which are used for food, this organ is called the *sweet-bread*. It lies between the stomach and left kidney. It secretes a fluid which is carried into the intestines by a duct which enters at the same aperture with that from the liver. The specific use of this fluid is unknown, but is clearly employed in aiding the process of digestion.

THE SPLEEN.

This organ, often called the *melt*, is a long, bluish-brown substance, broad and thick at one end, and tapering at the other; lying along the left side of the stomach, and between it and the short ribs. The particular use of this organ has never been clearly ascertained, for in some cruel experiments it has been removed without apparent injury to digestion or any other function.

THE OMENTUM.

Or *cawl*, is a doubling of the peritoneum, or rather consists of four layers of it. It has been supposed to have been placed between the intestines and the walls of the belly, in order to prevent concussion and injury during the rapid movement of the animal. That, however, cannot be its principal use in the horse, from whom the most rapid movements are required; for in him it is unusually short, extending only to the pancreas and a small portion of the colon. Being, however, thus short, the horse is exempt from a very troublesome, and occasionally, fatal species of rupture, when a portion of the omentum penetrates through some accidental opening in the covering of the belly.

CHAPTER X.

THE DISEASES OF THE INTESTINES.

THESE form a very important and mysterious class of ailments. They will be considered in the order in which the various contents of the abdomen have been described.

THE DUODENUM.

This intestine is subject to many more diseases than are included in the present imperfect veterinary nosology. The passage of the food through it has been impeded by *stricture*. The symptoms resemble those of colic and end in death. It has been perforated by bots, which have escaped into the abdomen, causing death.

The diseases of the jejunum and the ileum consist either of spasmodic affection or inflammation.

SPASMODIC COLIC.

The passage of the food through the intestinal canal is effected by the alternate contraction and relaxation of the muscular coat of the intestines. When that action is simply increased through the whole of the canal, the food passes more rapidly, and purging is produced; but the muscles of every part of the frame are liable to irregular and spasmodic action, and the muscular coat of some portion of the intestines may be thus affected. The spasm may be confined to a very small part of the canal. The gut has been found, after death, strangely contracted in various places, but the contraction not exceeding five or six inches in any of them. In the horse, the ileum is the usual seat of this disease. It is of much importance to distinguish between spasmodic colic and inflammation of the bowels, for the symptoms have considerable resemblance, although the mode of treatment should be very different.

The attack of colic is usually very sudden. There is often

not the slightest warning. The horse begins to shift his posture, look round at his flanks, paw violently, strike his belly with his feet, and crouch in a peculiar manner, advancing his hind limbs under him; he will then suddenly lie, or rather fall down, and balance himself upon his back, with his feet resting on his belly. The pain now seems to cease for a little while, and he gets up, and shakes himself, and begins to feed; the respite, however, is but short—the spasm returns more violently—every indication of pain is increased—he heaves at the flanks, breaks out into a profuse perspiration, and throws himself more recklessly about. In the space of an hour or two, either the spasms begin to relax, and the remissions are of longer duration, or the torture is augmented at every paroxysm; the intervals of ease are fewer and less marked, and inflammation and death supervene. The pulse is but little affected at the commencement, but it soon becomes frequent and contracted, and at length is scarcely tangible.

It will presently be seen that many of the symptoms very closely resemble those of inflammation of the mucous membrane of the bowels: it may therefore be useful to point out the leading distinctions between them.

COLIC.	INFLAMMATION OF THE BOWELS.
Sudden in its attack.	Gradual in its approach, with previous indications of fever.
Pulse rarely much quickened in the early period of the disease, and during the intervals of ease; but evidently fuller.	Pulse very much quickened, but small, and often scarcely to be felt.
Legs and ears of the natural temperature.	Legs and ears cold.
Relief obtained from rubbing the belly.	Belly exceedingly tender and painful to the touch.
Relief obtained from motion.	Motion evidently increasing the pain.
Intervals of rest.	Constant pain.
Strength scarcely affected.	Rapid and great weakness.

Among the causes of colic are, the drinking of cold water when the horse is heated. There is not a surer origin of violent spasm than this. Hard water is very apt to produce this effect. Colic will sometimes follow the exposure of a horse to the cold air or a cold wind after strong exercise. Green feed, although, generally speaking, most beneficial to the horse, yet, given in too large a quantity, or when he is hot, will frequently produce gripes. Doses of aloes, both large and small, are not unfrequent causes of colic. In some horses there seems to be a constitutional predisposition to colic. They cannot be hardly worked, or exposed to unusual cold, without a fit of it. In many cases, when these horses have died, calculi have been found in some part of the alimentary canal. Habitual costiveness and the presence of calculi are frequent causes of spasmodic colic. The seat of colic is occasionally the duodenum, but oftener the ileum or the jejunum; sometimes, however, both the cæcum and colon are affected.

Fortunately we are acquainted with several medicines that allay these spasms; and the disease often ceases almost as suddenly as it appeared. Turpentine is one of the most powerful remedies, especially in union with opium, and in good warm ale. The account that has just been given of the cæcum will not be forgotten here. A solution of aloes will be advantageously added to the turpentine and opium.

If relief is not obtained in half an hour, it will be prudent to bleed, for the continuance of violent spasm may produce inflammation. Some practitioners bleed at first, and it is far from bad practice; for although the majority of cases will yield to turpentine, opium, and aloes, an early bleeding may occasionally prevent the recurrence of inflammation, or at least mitigate it. If it is clearly a case of colic, half of the first dose may be repeated, with aloes dissolved in warm water. The stimulus produced on the inner surface of the bowels by the purgative may counteract the irritation that caused the spasm. The belly should be well rubbed with a brush or warm cloth, but not bruised and injured by the broom-handle rubbed over it, with all their strength, by two great fellows. The horse should be walked about, or trotted moderately. The motion thus produced in the bowels, and the friction of one intestine over the other, may relax the spasm, but the hasty gallop might speedily cause inflammation to succeed to colic. Clysters of warm water, or containing a solution of aloes, should be injected. The patent syringe will here be exceedingly useful. A clyster of tobacco-smoke may be thrown up as a last resort.

When relief has been obtained, the clothing of the horse, saturated with perspiration, should be removed, and fresh and dry clothes substituted. He should be well littered down in a warm stable or box, and have bran mashes and lukewarm water for the next two or three days.

Some persons give gin, or gin and pepper, or even spirit of pimento, in cases of gripes. This course of proceeding is, however, exceedingly objectionable. It may be useful, or even sufficient in ordinary cases of colic; but if there should be any inflammation, or tendency to inflammation, it cannot fail to be highly injurious.*

* *Note by Mr. Spooner.*—It is very important to discriminate accurately between colic and inflammation of the bowels. The principal distinctive

FLATULENT COLIC.

This is altogether a different disease from the former. It is not spasm of the bowels, but inflation of them from the presence of gas emitted by undigested food. Whether collected in the stomach, or small or large intestines, all kinds of vegetable matter are liable to ferment. In consequence of this fermentation, gas is evolved to a greater or less extent—perhaps to twenty or

symptoms are these: in colic, although the pain is excessive, there are yet occasional remissions of the paroxysms; whilst in inflammation of the bowels, the agony continues without remission, but varying in severity according to the violence of the disease. The pulse, too, in the latter disease is rapid, and often small and thready; whilst in the former, though it becomes more rapid during the paroxysms, it subsides during the intervals of ease. A careful examination of these distinctions will generally be sufficient to prevent any mistake with regard to the character of the disease. Indeed, we must not rely on any others.

There appears to be three varieties of colic, *spasmodic, flatulent,* and *stercoral,* or that which proceeds from constipation or obstruction in the bowels. The symptoms vary with the situation of the disease—whether in the stomach, the small, or the large intestines. Flatulent colic generally affects either the stomach or the large intestines. When the former, it is extremely dangerous, and yet is relieved with greater rapidity than when elsewhere existing. In a case that proved fatal before any remedy was resorted to, the stomach was found by the present writer distended to three times its ordinary size. Flatulent may be distinguished from spasmodic colic principally by the great distention of the abdomen which takes place; whilst stercoral colic is marked by the less violent, though more obstinate, continuance of the symptoms of pain.

For flatulent colic one of the best remedies is sulphuric ether, combined with the tincture of opium, and even in other cases it is preferable to the spirits of turpentine, which is apt to irritate and inflame the throat whilst being administered, and the bowels likewise, if there is any accession of inflammation. If relief is not obtained in the course of an hour, bleeding should be resorted to; and, if constipation is present, a watery infusion of aloes, or a dose of oil, should be given with the antispasmodic. In stercoral colic, dependence must be placed on relieving the obstruction, and at the same time keeping down pain and irritation by means of an opiate. For these purposes large doses of linseed oil, such as a pint three times a day, with an ounce of the tincture of opium, should be given until the desired object is attained. It is better, however, after the exhibition of a few doses, to substitute the watery infusion of opium for the spirit, as being less likely to produce inflammation. By steadily pursuing this system of treatment, we have, in many of the most obstinate and formidable cases, succeeded in establishing a cure. Other means, however, such as repeated and copious injections, should be had recourse to in addition; and, as soon as the bowels become relaxed, means should be used to counteract the excessive purgation which follows, which, if effected by ordinary medicines, would be exceedingly dangerous, but when produced by means of linseed oil, is comparatively without danger. Drenches of thick flour gruel should be given; with two ounces of prepared chalk, and two drachms of tincture of opium, to stay the bowels.

thirty times the bulk of the food. This may take place in the stomach; and if so, the life of the horse is in immediate danger, for, as will plainly appear from the account that has been given of the œsophagus and upper orifice of the stomach, the animal has no power to expel this dangerous flatus (wind) by eructation (belching.)

This extrication of gas usually takes place in the colon and cæcum, and the distention may be so great as to rupture either the one or the other, or sometimes to produce death, without either rupture or strangulation, and that in the course of from four to twenty-four hours.

An overloaded stomach is one cause of it, and particularly so when water is given either immediately before or after a plentiful meal, or food to which the horse has not been accustomed is given.

The symptoms, according to Professor Stewart, are, "the horse suddenly slackening his pace—preparing to lie down, or falling down as if he were shot. In the stable he paws the ground with his fore-feet, lies down, rolls, starts up all at once, and throws himself down again with great violence, looking wistfully at his flanks, and making many fruitless attempts to void his urine."

Hitherto the symptoms are not much unlike spasmodic colic, but the real character of the disease soon begins to develope itself. It is in one of the large intestines, and the belly swells all round, but mostly on the right flank. As the disease proceeds, the pain becomes more intense, the horse more violent, and at length death closes the scene.

The treatment is considerably different from that of spasmodic colic. The spirit of pimento would be here allowed, or the turpentine and opium drink; but if the pain, and especially the swelling, do not abate, the gas, which is the cause of it, must be got rid of, or the animal is inevitably lost.

This is usually, or almost invariably, a combination of hydrogen with some other gas. It has a strong affinity for chlorine. Then if some compound of chlorine—the chloride of lime—dissolved in water, is administered in the form of a drink, this gives speedy relief.

Where these two medicines are not at hand, and the danger is imminent, the trochar may be used, in order to open a way for the escape of the gas. The trochar should be small, but longer than that which is used for the cow, and the puncture should be made in the middle of the right flank, for there the large intestines are most easily reached. In such a disease it cannot be expected that the intestines shall always be found precisely in their natural situations, but usually the origin of the ascending portion of the colon, or the base of the cæcum will be pierced. The author of this work, however, deems it his duty to add, that it is only when the practitioner despairs of otherwise saving the life of the animal that this operation should be attempted. Much of the danger would be avoided by using a very small trochar, and by withdrawing it as soon as the gas has escaped. The wound in the intestines will then probably close, from the innate elasticity of the parts.

INFLAMMATION OF THE BOWELS.

There are two varieties of this malady. The first is inflammation of the external coats of the intestines, accompanied by considerable fever, and usually costiveness. The second is that of the internal or mucous coat, and almost invariably connected with purging.

ENTERITIS.

The muscular coat is that which is oftenest affected. Inflammation of the external coats of the stomach, wehther the peritoneal or muscular, or both, is a very frequent and fatal disease. It speedily runs its course, and it is of great consequence that its early symptoms should be known. If the horse has been carefully observed, restlessness and fever will have been seen to precede the attack. In many cases a direct shivering fit will occur: the mouth will be hot, and the nose red. The animal will soon express the most dreadful pain by pawing, striking at his belly, looking wildly at his flanks, groaning, and rolling. The pulse will be quickened and small; the ears and legs cold; the belly tender, and some times hot; the breathing quickened; the bowels costive; and the animal becoming rapidly and fearfully weak.

The reader will probably here recur to the sketch given in page 216, of the distinction between spasmodic colic and inflammation of the bowels, or enteritis.

The causes of this disease are, first of all and most frequently sudden exposure to cold. If a horse that has been highly fed carefully groomed, and kept in a warm stable, is heated with exercise, and has been during some hours without food, and in this state of exhaustion is suffered to drink freely of cold water, or is drenched with rain, or have his legs and belly washed with cold water, an attack of inflammation of the bowels will often follow An over-fed horse, subjected to severe and long-continued exertion, if his lungs were previously weak, will probably be attacked by inflammation of them; but if the lungs were sound, the bowels will on the following day be the seat of disease. Stones in the intestines are an occasional cause of inflammation, and colic neglected or wrongly treated will terminate in it.

The horse paws and stamps as in colic, but without the intervals of ease that occur in that disease. The pulse also is far quicker than in colic. The breathing is more hurried, and the indication of suffering more evident. "The next stage," in the graphic language of Mr. Percival, "borders on delirium. The eye acquires a wild, haggard, unnatural stare—the pupil dilates—his heedless and dreadful throes render approach to him quite perilous. He is an object not only of compassion but of apprehension, and seems fast hurrying to his end; when, all at once, in the midst of agonizing torments, he stands quiet, as though every pain had left him, and he were going to recover. His breathing becomes tranquillized—his pulse sunk beyond all perception—his body bedewed with a cold, clammy sweat—he is in a tremor from head to foot, and about the legs and ears has even a death-like feel. The mouth feels deadly chill; the lips drop pendulous; and the eye seems unconscious of objects. In fine, death, not recovery, is at hand. Mortification has seized the inflamed bowel—pain can no longer be felt in that which, a few minutes ago, was the seat of exquisite suffering. He again becomes convulsed, and in a few more struggles, less violent than the former, he expires."

The treatment of inflammation of the bowels, like that of the lungs, should be prompt and energetic. The first and most powerful means of cure will be bleeding. From six to eight or ten quarts of blood, in fact, as much as the horse can bear, should be abstracted as soon as possible; and the bleeding repeated to the extent of four or five quarts more, if the pain is not relieved and the pulse has not become rounder and fuller. The speedy weakness that accompanies this disease should not deter from bleeding largely. That weakness is the consequence of violent inflammation of these parts; and if that inflammation is subdued by the loss of blood, the weakness will disappear. The bleeding should be effected on the first appearance of the disease, for there is no malady that more quickly runs its course.

A strong solution of aloes should immediately follow the bleeding, but, considering the irritable state of the intestines at this period, guarded by opium. This should be quickly followed by back-raking, and injections consisting of warm water, or very thin gruel, in which Epsom salts or aloes have been dissolved; and too much fluid can scarcely be thrown up. If the common ox-bladder and pipe is used, it should be frequently replenished; but with Read's patent pump, already referred to, sufficient may be injected to penetrate beyond the rectum, and reach to the colon and cæcum, and dispose them to evacuate their contents. The horse should likewise be encouraged to drink plentifully of warm water or thin gruel; and draughts, each containing a couple of drachms of dissolved aloes, with a little opium, should be given every six hours, until the bowels are freely opened.

It will now be prudent to endeavor to excite considerable external inflammation as near as possible to the seat of the internal disease, and therefore the whole of the belly should be blistered. In a well-marked case of this disease, no time should be lost in applying fomentations, but the blister at once resorted to. The tincture of Spanish flies, whether made with spirit of wine or turpentine, should be thoroughly rubbed in. The legs should be well bandaged in order to restore the circulation in them, and thus lessen the flow of blood to the inflamed part; and, for the same reason, the horse should be warmly clothed; but the air of the stable or box should be cool.

No corn or hay should be allowed during the disease, but bran mashes, and green feed if it can be procured. The latter will be the best of all food, and may be given without the slightest apprehension of danger. When the horse begins to recover, a handful of grain may be given two or three times in the day; and, if the weather is warm, he may be turned into a paddock for a few hours in the middle of the day. Clysters of gruel should be continued for three or four days after the inflammation is beginning to subside, and good hand-rubbing applied to the legs.

The second variety of inflammation of the bowels affects the internal or mucous coat, and is generally the consequence of physic in too great quantity, or of an improper kind. The purging is more violent and continues longer than was intended; the animal shows that he is suffering great pain; he frequently looks round at his flanks; his breathing is laborious, and the pulse is quick and small—not so small, however, as in inflammation of the peritoneal coat, and, contrary to some of the most frequent and characteristic symptoms of that disease, the mouth is hot and the legs and ears are warm. Unless the purging is excessive, and the pain and distress great, the surgeon should hesitate at giving any astringent medicine at first; but he should plentifully administer gruel or thin starch, or arrow-root, by the mouth and by clyster, removing all hay and corn, and particularly green feed. He should thus endeavor to soothe the irritated surface of the bowels, while he permits all remains of the purgative to be carried off. If, however, twelve hours have passed, and the purging and the pain remain undiminished, he should continue the gruel, adding to it chalk, catechu, and opium, repeated every six hours. As soon as the purging begins to subside, the astringent medicine should be lessened in quantity, and gradually discontinued. Bleeding will rarely be necessary, unless the inflammation is very great, and attended by symptoms of general fever. The horse should be warmly clothed, and placed in a comfortable stable, and his legs should be hand-rubbed and bandaged

Violent purging, and attended with much inflammation and fever, will occur from other causes. Green feed will frequently purge. A horse worked hard upon green feed will sometimes scour. The remedy is change of diet, or less labor. Young horses will often be strongly purged, without any apparent cause. Astringents should be used with much caution here. It is probably an effort of nature to get rid of something that offends A few doses of gruel will assist in effecting this purpose, and the purging will cease without astringent medicine.

Many horses that are not *well-ribbed home*—having too great space between the last rib and the hip-bone—are subject to purging if more than usual exertion is required from them. They are recognized by the term of *washy* horses. They are often free and fleet, but destitute of continuance. They should have rather more than the usual allowance of grain, with beans, when at work. A cordial ball, with catechu and opium, will often be serviceable either before or after a journey.*

* *Note by Mr. Spooner.*—When this disease occurs, as it is usually in the most violent form, and is more frequently fatal than otherwise, bleeding is called for most assuredly; but we should endeavor previously to bring warmth to the skin and extremities, and also to raise the pulse. Two ounces of spirit of nitrous ether, in which a drachm of opium has been infused, may be administered in a pint and a half of linseed-oil. This will enable us to take a much larger quantity of blood than we should otherwise be enabled to abstract. It is of great importance to bleed largely in the first instance, but of very doubtful benefit to repeat the blood-letting. Warm fomentations to the abdomen are of much importance, and should be continued almost without remission, whilst the pain continues; thus applied, the heat of hot water will be more efficacious than any external stimulants. The oil may be repeated in doses of one pint until the bowels are opened, and the last dose should contain a scruple of powdered opium. Copious draughts of linseed gruel should also be given, and injections of the same frequently thrown up.

Inflammation of the peritoneum seldom occurs as an independent disease. When it does, it usually follows castration, or some injury external to the bowels. The treatment should resemble that previously described. It sometimes exists in unison with pleurisy, and also with the inflammation of the bowels (*enteritis*) just described.

Inflammation of the mucous coat of the intestines is also a very dangerous disease. It may be produced by cold, or by over-exertion, particularly in hot weather, or, more frequently than either, by an overdose of physic, or an ordinary or weak dose while the membrane is either in a state of irritation, or liable to become so from sympathy with some other important part, such as the lungs, more particularly their lining or mucous membrane.

Bleeding in this disease is seldom of service, the weak and almost imperceptible state of the pulse forbidding it. Our endeavors must be devoted to bringing warmth to the skin and extremities, and gradually stopping the irritation of the bowels and sheathing its internal mucous membrane. We may venture on powdered chalk with small doses of opium administered in thick wheat flour gruel.

PHYSICKING.

Physicking the horse is often necessary—but it has injured the constitution and destroyed thousands of animals when unnecessarily or improperly resorted to. When the horse comes from grass to dry feed, or from the open air to the heated stable, a dose or two of physic may be necessary to prevent the tendency to inflammation. To a horse that is becoming too fat, or has surfeit, or grease, or mange, or is out of condition from inactivity of the digestive organs, a dose of physic is serviceable; but the periodical physicking of all horses in the spring and autumn, the severe course of physic thought necessary to train them for work, and the too frequent method of treating the animal when under the operation of physic, cannot be too strongly condemned.

A horse should be carefully prepared for the action of physic. Two or three bran mashes given on that or the preceding day are far from sufficient when a horse is about to be physicked. Mashes should be given until the dung becomes softened. Five drachms of aloes, given when the dung has thus been softened, will act much more effectually and much more safely than seven drachms, when the lower intestines are obstructed by hardened dung.

On the day on which the physic is given, the horse should have walking exercise, or may be gently trotted for a quarter of an hour twice in the day; but after the physic begins to work, he should not be moved from his stall. Exercise would then produce gripes, irritation, and, possibly, dangerous inflammation. The common and absurd practice is to give the horse most exercise after the physic has begun to operate.

A little hay may be put into the rack. As much mash should be given as the horse will eat, and as much water, with the coldness of it taken off, as he will drink. If, however, he obstinately refuses to drink warm water, it is better that he should have it cold, than to continue without taking any fluid; but in such case he should not be suffered to take more than a quart at a time, with an interval of at least an hour between each draught.

When the purging has ceased, or *the physic is set*, a mash should be given once or twice every day until the next dose is taken, between which and the *setting* of the first there should be an interval of a week. The horse should recover from the languor and debility occasioned by the first dose, before he is harassed by a second.

Eight or ten tolerably copious motions will be perfectly sufficient to answer every good purpose, although the groom or the carter may not be satisfied unless double the quantity are procured. The consequence of too strong purgation will be, that weakness will hang about the animal for several days or weeks and inflammation will often ensue from the over-irritation of the intestinal canal.

Long-continued custom has made ALOES the almost invariable purgative of the horse, and very properly so; for there is no other at once so sure and so safe. The Barbadoes aloes, although sometimes very dear, should alone be used. The dose, with a horse properly prepared, will vary from four to seven drachms. The preposterous doses of nine, ten, or even twelve drachms, are now, happily for the horse, generally abandoned. Custom has assigned the form of a ball to physic, but good sense will in due time introduce the solution of aloes, as acting more speedily, effectually and safely.

The only other purgative on which dependence can be placed is the CROTON. The farina or meal of the nut is generally used; but from its acrimony it should be given in the form of ball, with linseed meal. The dose varies from a scruple to half a drachm. It acts more speedily than the aloes, and without the nausea which they produce; but it causes more watery stools, and, consequently, more debility.

LINSEED-OIL is an uncertain but safe purgative, in doses from a pound to a pound and a half. OLIVE-OIL is more uncertain, but safe; but CASTOR-OIL, that mild aperient in the human being, is both uncertain and unsafe. EPSOM-SALTS are inefficacious, except in the immense dose of a pound and a half, and then they are not always safe.*

* *Note by Mr. Spooner.*—We have little to add under this head. We condemn, with the author, the reckless administration of violent doses, by which very many horses have been killed. The mucous coat of the intestines of the horse appears to be more irritable than that of man; besides which it relatively occupies a larger extent of surface.

Barbadoes aloes is certainly the best purgative with which we are acquainted. A drachm of ginger may be advantageously combined with it to prevent griping. A ball is certainly the best and safest mode of giving ordinary physic to a horse. It is necessary to give a much stronger dose in the form of a draught than that of a ball, which is probably owing to the fact, that with a ball a considerable amount of action is produced at one spot where the ball is dissolved, and the irritation there produced spreads by sympathy to the adjacent parts, whilst the liquid being spread at once over a large surface, a less amount of irritation is produced at any one particular spot. The exercise on the day following the administration of the physic should depend on the effect produced. If the purging is copious, no exercise should be given; but, if otherwise, it will much assist our operations by giving a greater or lesser amount of exercise, as may be required.

CALCULI, OR STONES, IN THE INTESTINES.

These are a cause of inflammation in the bowels of the horse and more frequently of colic. They are generally found in the cæcum or colon, varying considerably in shape, and varying in weight from a few grains to several pounds. From the horizontal position of the horse's body, the stone does not tend downward as in the human being, and continues increasing until it becomes the source of fatal irritation. It is a fruitful cause of colic. Little advance has been made or can be made to procure their expulsion, or even to determine their existence.*

INTROSUSCEPTION OF THE INTESTINES.

A portion of an intestine is sometimes slid into the contiguous portion, producing a fold or doubling. The irritation produced by it soon forms an obstruction which no power can overcome. There are no symptoms to indicate the presence of this, except continued and increasing pain; or, if there were, all our means of relief would here fail.

ENTANGLEMENT OF THE BOWELS.

This is produced by colic, by the abominable and poisonous drinks of the farrier, and by other causes.

When the animal rolls and throws himself about, portions of the intestine become so entangled as to be twisted into nooses and knots, drawn together with a degree of tightness scarcely credible. Nothing but the extreme and continued torture of the animal can lead us to suspect that this has taken place, and, could we ascertain its existence, there would be no cure.

Fig. 31.

The following cut shows an entanglement of the bowels of a horse that died from the effects of it. The parts are a little loosened in order better to show the entanglement of the intestines, but in the animal they were drawn into a tight knot, and completely intercepted all passage.

* *Note by Mr. Spooner.*—When colic arises from stones or concretions in the intestines, the pain is usually very severe, until, by rolling about, the stone is dislodged from the position in which it was fixed, and then, becoming free, the pain ceases. We may presume such to be the nature of the case if the horse lies much on his back, and rolls over from side to side, with an evident desire to relieve himself from some painful pressure. After repeated attacks of this kind the case at length becomes fatal, the calculus accumulates, becomes firmly fixed, obstructing all passage, inflammation supervenes, and the animal dies.

WORMS.

Worms of different kinds inhabit the intestines; but, except when they exist in very great numbers, they are not so hurtful as is generally supposed, although the groom or carter may trace to them, hidebound, and cough, and loss of appetite, and gripes, and megrims, and a variety of other ailments.

The long white worm much resembles the common earth-worm. It is from six to ten inches long, and inhabits the small intestines. If there are too many of them, they may consume more than can be spared of the nutritive part of the food, or the mucus of the bowels. A tight skin, and rough coat, and tucked-up belly, are sometimes connected with their presence. They are then, however, voided in large quantities. A dose of physic will sometimes bring away almost incredible quantities of them. Calomel is frequently given as a vermifuge. The seldom r this drug is administered to the horse the better. When the horse can be spared, a strong dose of physic is an excellent vermifuge, so far as the long round worm is concerned; but a better medicine, and not interfering with either the feeding or work of the horse, is emetic tartar, with ginger, made into a ball with linseed meal and treacle, and given every morning, half an hour before the horse is fed.

A smaller, darker-colored worm, called the needle-worm, inhabits the large intestines. Hundreds of them sometimes descend into the straight gut, and immense quantities have been found in the blind gut. These are a more serious nuisance than the former, for they cause a very troublesome irritation about the fundament, which sometimes sadly annoys the horse. Their existence can generally be discovered by a small portion of mucus, which, hardening, is found adhering to the anus. Physic will sometimes bring away great numbers of these worms; but when there is much irritation about the tail, and much of this mucus, indicating that they have descended into the straight gut, an injection of linseed oil, or of aloes dissolved in warm water, will be a more effectual remedy.

The tape-worm is seldom found in the horse.

HERNIA, OR RUPTURE.

A portion of the intestine protrudes out of the cavity of the belly, either through some natural or artificial opening. In some cases it may be returned, but, from the impossibility of applying a truss or bandage, it soon escapes again. At other times, the opening is so narrow, that the gut, gradually distended by dung, or thickened by inflammation, cannot be returned, and *strangu-*

lated hernia is then said to exist. The seat of hernia is either in the testicle bag of the perfect horse, or the groin of the gelding. The causes are violent struggling when under operations, overexertion, kicks, or accidents. The assistance of a veterinary surgeon is here indispensable.*

DISEASES OF THE LIVER.

Horses dying when not more than five years old of other complaints, usually show a healthy liver, but when they reach eight or nine, the liver is frequently increased in size—is less elastic—has assumed a more granulated or broken down appearance—the blood does not so readily pass through its vessels—and at length, blood begins to ooze from it into its membraneous covering, or into the cavity of the belly. The horse feeds well, is in apparent health, in good condition, and capable of constant work; but, at length, the peritoneal covering of the liver suddenly gives way, and the contents of the abdomen are deluged with blood.

* *Note by Mr. Spooner.*—In congenital hernia (that appearing at birth), in the testicle bag, the remedy consists in castration by the covered operation, that is, without cutting into the hernial sac, but placing wooden claws on the cord and the peritoneal membrane, and at the same time, forcing the gut gently upwards towards the abdomen. In the course of a few days the testicles will slough off, or may be removed. The writer purchased a colt a few years since for a trifle, being abandoned by its owner as worthless, on which the operation was successfully performed, and the colt sold afterwards at a good price.

When the hernia is strangulated, violent pain and great danger is the result; the opening through which the gut has escaped is generally very small, being in fact, the inguinal ring. In such cases, if the hernia cannot be reduced by the hand, or the taxis, as it is called, it is necessary to open the hernial sac, and by means of a bistoury, enlarge the opening sufficiently to put back the gut—an operation of great difficulty and danger, and requiring much skill.

Abdominal hernia may occur in different situations, and are usually caused by external violence, such as the horn of a cow, or jumping over and across a post. The muscular and other covering of the abdomen is broken through, whilst the skin, from its greater looseness, remains entire; and, indeed, is the only object between the bowels and the air. If the case is recent, the hernia may be reduced, and the hernial sac opened, and the sides of the opening brought together by sutures of metallic wire. Where, however, the injury is of long standing or natural, as, for instance, in mares, when the abdominal ring is unusually large, we cannot succeed by this means; but yet the case is not always hopeless. The gut being forced back, an incision is made in the skin, and one or more wooden skewers passed through it, so that a good portion of the skin can be embraced by some strong waxed twine, the skewers preventing it slipping off the skin thus embraced, which sloughs off, and a cicatrix forming the surrounding skin becomes tighter and thicker than before—sufficiently so to keep the gut, for the most part, within the abdomen.

The symptoms of this sudden change are—pawing, shifting the posture, distention of the belly, curling of the upper lip, sighing frequently and deeply, the mouth and nostrils pale and blanched, the breathing quickened, restlessness, debility, fainting, and death.

On opening the abdomen, the intestines are found to be deluged with dark venous blood. The liver is either of a fawn, or light yellow, or brown color—easily torn by the finger, and, in some cases, completely broken down.

If the hemorrhage has been slight at the commencement, and fortunately arrested, yet a singular consequence will frequently result. The sight will gradually fail; the pupil of one or both eyes will gradually dilate, the animal will have *gutta serena*, and become perfectly blind. This will almost assuredly take place on a return of the affection of the liver. Little can be done in a medical point of view. Astringent and styptic medicines may, however, be tried. Turpentine, alum, or sulphuric acid, will afford the only chance.*

JAUNDICE,

Commonly called the THE YELLOWS, is a more frequent, but more tractable disease. It is the introduction of bile into the general circulation. This is usually caused by some obstruction in the ducts or tubes that convey the bile from the liver to the intestines. The yellowness of the eyes and mouth, and of the skin, where it is not covered with hair, mark it sufficiently plainly.

---

* *Note by Mr. Spooner.*—The symptoms which we have noticed as attending this disease are, a heavy dull appearance, loss of appetite, and respiration somewhat quickened, but not distressed as in inflammation of the lungs; the pulse is distinct and somewhat quickened, perhaps from fifty to sixty in the minute. The membranes of the eyelids are yellow, or at any rate pale. It is a very obstinate disease, often becoming fatal, even when the symptoms at first do not appear to denote danger. In such instances they gradually increase in severity, and symptoms of severe pain become connected with those of distress previously existing, and, in the course of six to ten days, the case becomes fatal.

Bleeding is required in the first instance, but not to the same extent as in inflammation of the lungs. Recourse should then be had to mercurial alteratives. Calomel two scruples, with opium one scruple, should be given twice a day for several days, until the system appears to be affected by the mercury. The relaxation of the bowels should be promoted by a pint of linseed oil, repeated twice or thrice. The hair should be cut off the side opposite the liver, and mercurial or blistering ointment rubbed in. If the horse refuses to eat mashes, plenty of linseed or oatmeal gruel should be given with the horn.

The hepatirrhœa, or rupture and bleeding from the liver, mentioned in the text, is uniformly fatal, if not at the first, at the second or third attack. It is sometimes attended with amaurosis, or paralysis of the optic nerve. Treatment is comparatively useless.

The dung is small and hard; the urine highly colored; the horse languid, and the appetite impaired. If he is not soon relieved, he sometimes begins to express considerable uneasiness; at other times he is dull, heavy, and stupid. A characteristic symptom is lameness of the right fore leg, resembling the pain in the right shoulder of the human being in liver affections. The principal causes are over-feeding or over-exertion in sultry weather, or too little work, generally speaking, or inflammation or other disease of the liver itself.

It is sometimes caused by the sympathy of the liver with some other diseased part, and in this case, the removal of that disease will remove it. If there is no other apparent disease to any great extent, an endeavor to restore the natural passage of the bile by purgatives may be tried, not consisting of large doses, lest there should be some undetected inflammation of the lungs or bowels, in either of which a strong purgative would be dangerous; but, given in small quantities, repeated at short intervals. and until the bowels are freely opened. Bleeding should always be resorted to, regulated according to the apparent degree of inflammation, and the occasional stupor of the animal. Plenty of water, slightly warmed, or thin gruel, should be given. The horse should be warmly clothed, and the stable well ventilated, but not cold. Carrots or green food will be very beneficial. Should the purging, when once excited, prove violent, we need not be in any haste to stop it, unless inflammation is beginning to be connected with it, or the horse is very weak. The medicine recommended under diarrhœa may then be given. A few slight tonics should be given when the horse is recovering from an attack of jaundice.*

THE KIDNEYS.

The kidneys are two large glandular bodies, placed under the loins, of the shape of a kidney-bean, of immense size. The right kidney is most forward, lying under the liver; the left is pushed more backward by the stomach and spleen. A large artery runs to each, carrying not less than a sixth part of the whole of the blood that circulates through the frame. This artery is divided into innumerable little branches, most curiously complicated and coiled upon each other; and the blood, traversing these convolu-

---

* *Note by Mr. Spooner.*—Jaundice very seldom occurs unconnected with inflammation of the liver; when it does, it is denoted by the yellowness of the membranes, and the absence of any of the symptoms of inflammation. It is best treated by the same internal medicines as those we advised under the head of "Inflammation of the liver" (in note); or aloes may also be given in moderate quantities.

tions, has its watery parts, and others, the retaining of which would be injurious, separated from it.

The fluid thus separated (the urine), varies materially in quantity and composition during health. There is no organ in the horse so much under our command ; and there are no medicines so useful, or may be so injurious, as diuretics (those which increase the evacuation of urine), such as nitre and digitalis. They stimulate the kidneys to separate more watery fluid from the blood, and thus reduce the circulation, lowering inflammation and calming excitement. They cause the removal of that fluid in the cellular substance of the legs of the horse, which causes them so often to swell. The legs of many horses cannot be rendered fine, or kept so, without the use of diuretics ; nor can grease—often connected with these swellings, producing them or caused by them —be otherwise subdued. It is on this account that diuretics are ranked among the most useful of veterinary medicines.

In injudicious hands, however, these medicines are sadly abused. Among the absurdities of stable management, there is nothing so injurious as the frequent use of diuretics. Not only are the kidneys often over-excited, weakened, and disposed to disease, but the whole frame becomes debilitated. There is likewise one important fact of which the groom or the horseman seldom thinks, viz :—That when he is removing these humors by the imprudent use of diuretics, he is only attacking a symptom or a consequence of disease, and not the disease itself. The legs will fill again, and the grease will return. While the cause remains, the effect will be produced.

In the administration of diuretics, one thing should be attended to, and the good effect of which the testimony of every intelligent man will confirm : *the horse should have plenty to drink.* Not only will inflammation be prevented, but the operation of the medicine will be much promoted.

INFLAMMATION OF THE KIDNEYS.

This is no uncommon disease in the horse, and is more unskilfully and fatally treated than almost any other. The early symptoms are those of fever generally, but the seat of the disease soon becomes evident. The horse looks anxiously round at his flanks ; stands with his hinder legs wide apart ; is unwilling to lie down ; straddles as he walks ; expresses pain in turning ; shrinks when the loins are pressed, and some degree of heat is felt there. The urine is voided in small quantities : frequently it is high-colored, and sometimes bloody. The attempt to urinate becomes more frequent, and the quantity voided smaller, until the animal strains painfully and violently, but the discharge is nearly or quite suppressed. The pulse is quick and hard; full in the early stage of the disease, but rapidly becoming small, yet not losing its character of hardness. These symptoms clearly indicate an affection of the urinary organs; but they do not distinguish inflammation of the kidney from that of the bladder In order to effect this, the hand must be introduced into the rectum. If the bladder is felt full and hard under the rectum, there is inflammation of the neck of it; if it is empty, yet on the portion of the intestines immediately over it there is more than natural heat and tenderness, there is inflammation of the body of the bladder; and if the bladder is empty, and there is no increased heat or tenderness, there is inflammation of the kidney.

Too powerful or too often repeated diuretics induce inflammation of the kidney, or a degree of irritation and weakness of that organ that disposes to inflammation from causes that would otherwise have no injurious effect. If a horse is sprained in the loins by being urged on, far or fast, by a heavy rider, or compelled to take too wide a leap, or by being suddenly pulled up on his haunches, the inflammation of the muscles of the loins is often speedily transferred to the kidneys, with which they lie in contact. Exposure to cold is another frequent origin of this malady, especially if the horse is drenched with rain, or the wet drips upon his loins; and, more particularly, if he was previously disposed to inflammation, or these organs had been previously weakened.

The treatment will only vary from that of inflammation of other parts by a consideration of the peculiarity of the organ affected. Bleeding must be promptly resorted to, and carried to its full extent. An active purge should next be administered; and a counter-inflammation excited as nearly as possible to the seat of disease. For this purpose the loins should be fomented with hot water, or covered with a mustard-poultice—the horse should be warmly clothed; but no cantharides or turpentine should be used, and, most of all, no diuretic be given internally. When the groom finds this difficulty or suppression of staling, he immediately has recourse to a diuretic ball to force on the urine; and by thus needlessly irritating a part already too much excited, he adds fuel to fire, and frequently destroys the horse. The action of the purgative having begun a little to cease, white hellebore may be administered in small doses, with or without emetic tartar. The patient should be warmly clothed; his legs well bandanged; and plenty of water offered to him. The food should be carefully examined, and anything that could have excited or that may prolong the irritation carefully removed.*

* *Note by Mr. Spooner*—This disease is readily distinguished from

DIABETES, OR PROFUSE STALING

Is a comparatively rare disease. It is generally the consequence of undue irritation of the kidney by bad food or strong diuretics, and sometimes follows inflammation of that organ. It can seldom be traced in the horse to any disease of the digestive organs. The treatment is obscure, and the result often uncertain. It is evidently increased action of the kidneys, and therefore the most rational plan of treatment is to endeavor to abate that action. In order to effect this, the same course should be pursued in the early stage of diabetes as in actual inflammation; but the lowering system must not be carried to so great an extent. To bleeding, purging, and counter-irritation, medicines of an astringent quality should succeed, as catechu, the powdered leaf of the whortleberry (uva ursi,) and opium. Very careful attention should be paid to the food. The hay and oats should be of the best quality. Green feed, and especially carrots will be very serviceable.*

BLOODY URINE—HÆMATURIA.

The discharge of urine of this character is of occasional occurrence. Pure blood is sometimes discharged which immediately coagulates—at other times it is more or less mixed with the urine, and does not coagulate. The cause of its appearance and the source whence it proceeds cannot always be determined, but it is probably the result of some strain or blow. It may or may not be accompanied by inflammation.

Should it be the result of strain or violence, or be evidently attended by inflammation, soothing and depleting measures should be adopted. Perhaps counter-irritation on the loins might

---

others, from the great tenderness of the loins when pressed, and the high color of the urine, which is sometimes almost black.

The bleeding, as stated in the text, should be very copious, and repeated if necessary. One of the best applications to the loins is a fresh sheep-skin, the skin side inwards. This will very soon cause, and keep up, a considerable perspiration, which may be continued by means of a fresh skin in the course of twelve hours. With regard to internal medicines, one of the best sedatives is the white hellebore, in doses of a scruple twice a-day. The bowels should be opened by means of an aperient draught, and abundance of linseed tea should be given, so as to sheath the irritated parts.

* *Note by Mr. Spooner.*—Diabetes is almost invariably produced by unwholesome food, such as mow-burnt hay, or kiln-dried oats. It causes excessive debility and loss of flesh. We do not approve of blood-letting, as recommended in the text; but astringents, such as opium and catechu, combined with sulphate of iron, in doses of a drachm twice a-day, are of much service. The cause of the disease, should of course be removed.

be useful. If there is no apparent inflammation, some gentle stimulus may be administered internally.

ALBUMINOUS URINE.

A peculiar mucous state of the urine of some horses has lately attracted attention. It has been associated with stretching out of the legs, stiffness, disinclination to move, a degree of fever, and costiveness. Slight bleeding, mild physic, the application of gentle stimulants to the loins, quietness, and gentle opiates, have been of service.

THE BLADDER.

The urine separated from the blood is discharged by the minute vessels, of which we have spoken, into some larger canals, which terminate in a cavity or reservoir in the body of each kidney, designated its *pelvis*. Thence it is conveyed by a duct called the *ureter*, to a large reservoir, the *bladder*.

INFLAMMATION OF THE BLADDER.

There are two varieties of this disease, inflammation of the body of the bladder, and of its neck. The symptoms are nearly the same with those of inflammation of the kidney, except that there is rarely a total suppression of urine, and there is heat felt in the rectum over the situation of the bladder. The causes are the presence of some acrid or irritant matter in the urine, or of calculus or stone in the bladder. With reference to inflammation of the body of the bladder, mischief has occasionally been done by the introduction of cantharides or some other irritating matter, in order to hasten the period of horsing in the mare. The treatment in this case will be the same as in inflammation of the kidneys, except that it is of more consequence that the animal should drink freely of water or thin gruel.

In inflammation of the neck of the bladder there is the same frequent voiding of urine in small quantities, generally appearing in an advanced stage of the disease, and often ending in almost total suppression. There is also this circumstance which can never be mistaken by him who will pay sufficient attention to the case, that the bladder is distended with urine, and can be distinctly felt under the rectum. It is spasm of the part, closing the neck of the bladder so powerfully that the contraction of the bladder and the pressure of the muscles are unable to force out the urine.

Here the object to be attempted is sufficiently plain. This spasm must be relaxed, and the most likely means to effect it is to bleed largely, and even to fainting. This will sometimes succeed, and there will be at once an end to the disease. To the exhaustion and loss of muscular power occasioned by copious bleeding, should be added the nausea consequent on physic. Should not this speedily have effect, another mode of abating spasm must be tried—powdered opium, made into a ball or drink, should be given every two or three hours; while an active blister is applied externally. The evacuation of the bladder, both in the mare and the horse, should be effected through the medium of a veterinary surgeon.*

STONE IN THE BLADDER.

The symptoms of stone in the bladder much resemble those of spasmodic colic, except that, on careful inquiry, it will be found that there has been much irregularity in the discharge of urine and occasional suppression of it. When fits of apparent colic frequently return, and are accompanied by any peculiarity in the appearance or the discharge of the urine, the horse should be carefully examined. For this purpose he must be thrown. If there is stone in the bladder, it will, while the horse lies on its back, press on the rectum, and may be distinctly felt if the hand is introduced into the rectum. Several cases have lately occurred of successful extraction of the calculus; but to effect this it will always be necessary to have recourse to the aid of a veterinary practitioner.†

The catheter invented by Mr. Taylor is made of polished round iron, three feet long, one and a half inch in circumference, and with eight joints at its farther extremity. The solid

---

* *Note by Mr. Spooner.*—This is a very rare but exceedingly dangerous disease, the irritation being so great that it is almost impossible to keep any soothing application in the bladder, the contents of which are being continually ejected. Recourse therefore must be had to very copious bleeding, so as to endeavor to check both the inflammation which exists, as well as to assuage the irritation which forbids topical (local) measures. It will assist to administer calomel combined with opium and tartarized antimony, two scruples of each being given three times a day. The same means may be adopted when inflammation attacks the neck of the bladder, and the spasm prevents its evacuation. As stated in the text the bladder of a mare may be readily evacuated by means of a catheter; and, by the aid of the elastic and flexible catheter, the bladder of the gelding can also be discharged, though the operation requires some tact and skill.

† *Note by Mr. Spooner.*—In cutting for the stone, the horse is cast and turned on his back, and supported in that position. A whalebone or wooden staff is then passed up the urethra, and when it is felt at the perineum just under the anus, is cut down upon. A pair of forceps is next passed through the wound thus made, into the bladder, with which the calculus must be removed. The bladder then should be washed out with tepid water, and the wound sewed up.

part between each joint is one and a quarter inch in length, and one and a half in circumference, the moveable part being ten inches, and the solid part two feet two inches. The joints are on the principle of a half joint, so that the moveable part would only act in a straight line, or curve in one direction. The joints are perfectly rounded and smooth when acting either in a straight line or a curve. It is represented both in its straight and curved state in the following cuts.

Fig. 32.

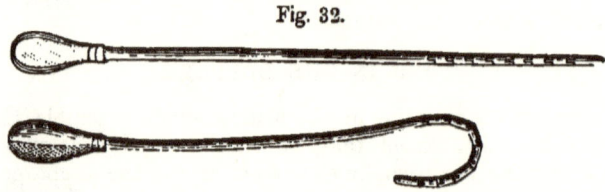

Many horses occasionally void a considerable quantity of gravel, sometimes without inconvenience, and at others with evident spasm or pain. A diuretic might be useful in such case, as increasing the flow of urine, and possibly washing out the concretions before they become too numerous or bulky.

The urine having passed the neck of the bladder, flows along the urethra, and is discharged. The sheath of the penis is sometimes considerably enlarged. When at the close of acute disease, there are swellings and effusions of fluid, under the chest and belly, this part seldom escapes. Diuretics, with a small portion of cordial medicine, will be beneficial, but in extreme cases slight scarifications may be necessary. The inside of the sheath is often the seat of disease. The mucous matter, naturally secreted there to defend the part from the acrimony of the urine, accumulates and becomes exceedingly offensive, and produces swelling, tenderness, and even excoriation, with considerable discharge. Fomentation with warm water, and the cleansing of the part with soap and water, aided perhaps by the administration of a diuretic ball, will speedily remove every inconvenience.

CHAPTER XI.

BREEDING, CASTRATION, ETC.

Our observations on this will be of a general nature, and very simple. The first axiom that we would lay down, is that "like will produce like," and that the progeny will inherit the general or mingled qualities of the parents. There is scarcely a disease by which either of the parents is affected that the foal does not often inherit, or at least occasionally show a predisposition to it. Even the consequences of ill usage or hard work will descend to the progeny. There has been proof upon proof, that blindness, roaring, thick-wind, broken-wind, spavins, curbs, ringbones, and founder, have been bequeathed to their offspring, both by the sire and the dam. It should likewise be recollected that although these blemishes may not appear in the immediate progeny, they frequently do in the next, or even more distant generation. Hence the necessity of some knowledge of the parentage both of the sire and the dam.

Peculiarity of form and constitution will also be inherited. This is a most important but neglected consideration; for, however desirable or even perfect may have been the conformation of the sire, every good point may be neutralized or lost by the defective structure of the mare. The essential points should be good in both parents, or some minor defect in either be met, and got rid of, by excellence in that particular point in the other. The unskilful or careless breeder too often so badly pairs the animals, that the good points of each are almost lost: the defects of both increased, and the produce is far inferior to both sire and dam.

The mare is sometimes put to the horse at too early an age; or, what is of more frequent occurrence, the mare is incapacitated for work by old age. The owner is unwilling to destroy her, and he determines that she shall bear a foal, and thus remunerate him for her keep. What is the consequence? The foal exhibits an unkindliness of growth,—a corresponding weakness,—and there is scarcely an organ that possesses its natural and proper strength.

That the constitution and endurance of the horse are inherited, no sporting man ever doubted. The qualities of the sire or the dam descend from generation to generation, and the excellences or defects of certain horses are often traced, and justly so, to some peculiarity in a far-distant ancestor.

It may, perhaps, be justly affirmed, that there is more difficulty in selecting a good mare to breed from than a good horse, because she should possess somewhat opposite qualities. Her carcase should be long, in order to give room for the growth of the fœtus, and yet with this there should be compactness of form and shortness of leg. What can they expect whose practice it is to purchase worn-out, spavined, foundered mares, about whom they fancy there have been some good points, and send them far into the country to breed from, and, with all their variety of shape, to be covered by the same horse? In a lottery like this there may be now and then a prize, but there must be many blanks.

As to the shape of the stallion, little satisfactory can be said. It must depend on that of the mare, and the kind of horse wished to be bred; but if there is one point absolutely essential, it is "compactness"—as much goodness and strength as possible condensed into a little space.

Next to compactness, the inclination of the shoulder will be regarded. A huge stallion, with upright shoulders, never got a capital hunter or hackney. From him the breeder can obtain nothing but a cart or dray horse, and that, perhaps, spoiled by the opposite form of the mare. On the other hand, an upright shoulder is desirable, if not absolutely necessary, when a mere slow draught-horse is required.

From the time of covering, to within a few days of the expected period of foaling, the cart-mare may be kept at moderate labor, not only without injury, but with decided advantage. It will then be prudent to release her from work, and keep her near home, and under the frequent inspection of some careful person.

When nearly half the time of pregnancy has elapsed, the mare should have a little better food. She should be allowed one or two feeds of grain in the day. This is about the period when they are accustomed to slink their foals, or when abortion occurs: the eye of the owner should, therefore, be frequently upon them. Good feeding and moderate exercise will be the best preventives of this mishap. The mare that has once aborted, is liable to a repetition of the accident, and therefore should never be suffered to be with other mares between the fourth and fifth months: for such is the power of imagination or of sympathy in the mare, that if one suffers abortion, others in the same pasture will too often share the same fate. Farmers wash, and paint, and tar their stables, to prevent some supposed infection;—the infection lies in the imagination.

The thorough-bred mare—the stock being intended for sporting purposes—should be kept quiet, and apart from other horses, after the first four or five months. When the period of parturition is drawing near, she should be watched and shut up during the night in a safe yard or loose box.

If the mare, whether of the pure or common breed, be thus taken care of, and be in good health while in foal, little danger will attend the act of parturition. If there is false presentation of the fœtus, or difficulty in producing it, it will be better to have recourse to a well-informed practitioner, than to injure the mother by the violent and injurious attempts that are often made to relieve her.

The parturition being over, the mare should be turned into some well-sheltered pasture, with a hovel or shed to run into when she pleases; and if she has foaled early, and grass is scanty, she should have a couple of feeds of grain daily. The breeder may depend upon it, that nothing is gained by starving the mother and stinting the foal at this time. It is the most important period of the life of the horse; and if, from false economy, his growth is arrested, his puny form and want of endurance will ever afterwards testify the error that has been committed. The grain should be given in a trough on the ground, that the foal may partake of it with the mother. When the new grass is plentiful, the quantity of corn may gradually be diminished.

The mare will usually be found again at heat at or before the expiration of a month from the time of foaling, when, if she is principally kept for breeding purposes, she may be put again to the horse. At the same time, also, if she is used for agricultural purposes, she may go again to work. The foal is at first shut in the stable during the hours of work; but as soon as it acquires sufficient strength to toddle after the mare, and especially when she is at slow work, it will be better for the foal and the dam that they should be together. The work will contribute to the health of the mother; the foal will more frequently draw the milk, and thrive better, and will be hardy and tractable, and gradually familiarized with the objects among which it is afterwards to live. While the mother, however, is thus worked, she and the foal should be well fed; and two feeds of corn, at least, should be added to the green food which they get when turned out after their work, and at night.

In five or six months, according to the growth of the foal, it may be weaned. It should then be housed for three weeks or a month, or turned into some distant rick-yard. There can be no better place for the foal than the latter, as affording, and that without trouble, both food and shelter. The mother should be put to harder work, and have drier food. One or two urine-balls, or a physic-ball, will be useful, if the milk should be troublesome or she should pine after her foal.

There is no principle of greater importance than the liberal feeding of the foal during the whole of his growth, and at this time in particular. Bruised oats and bran should form a considerable part of his daily provender. The farmer may be assured that the money is well laid out which is expended on the liberal nourishment of the growing colt; yet while he is well fed, he should not be rendered delicate by excess of care.

A racing colt is often stabled; but one that is destined to be a hunter, a hackney, or an agricultural horse, should have a square rick, under the leeward side of which he may shelter himself; or a hovel, into which he may run at night, and out of the rain.

The process of breaking-in should commence from the very period of weaning. The foal should be daily handled, partially dressed, accustomed to the halter when led about, and even tied up. The tractability, and good temper, and value of the horse, depend a great deal more upon this than breeders are aware.

Everything should be done, as much as possible, by the man who feeds the colt, and whose management of him should be always kind and gentle. There is no fault for which a breeder should so invariably discharge his servant as cruelty, or even harshness, towards the rising stock; for the principle on which their after usefulness is founded, is early attachment to, and confidence in man, and obedience, implicit obedience, resulting principally from this.

After the second winter the work of breaking-in may commence in good earnest. The colt may be bitted, and a bit selected that will not hurt his mouth, and much smaller than those in common use. With this he may be suffered to amuse himself, and to play, and to champ it for an hour, on a few successive days.

Having become a little tractable, portions of the harness may be put upon him, concluding with the blind winkers; and, a few days afterwards, he may go into the team. It would be better if there could be one horse before, and one behind him, besides the shaft horse. There should at first be the mere empty wagon. Nothing should be done to him, except that he should have an occasional pat or kind word. The other horses will keep him moving, and in his place; and no great time will pass, sometimes not even the first day, before he will begin to pull with the rest. The load may then be gradually increased.

The agricultural horse is sometimes wanted to ride as well as to draw. Let his first lesson be given when he is in the team

Let his feeder, if possible, be first put upon him. He will be too much hampered by his harness, and by the other horses, to make much resistance; and, in the majority of cases, will quietly and at once submit. We need not to repeat, that no whip or spur should be used in giving the first lessons in riding.

When he begins a little to understand his business, backing—the most difficult part of his work—may be taught him; first to back well without anything behind him, and then with a light cart, and afterwards with some serious load—always taking the greatest care not seriously to hurt his mouth. If the first lesson causes much soreness of the gums, the colt will not readily submit to a second. If he has been previously rendered tractable by kind usage, time and patience will do everything that can be wished. Some carters are in the habit of blinding the colt when teaching him to back. This may be necessary with a restive and obstinate one, but should be used only as a last resort.

The colt having been thus partially broken-in, the necessity of implicit obedience must be taught him, and that not by severity, but by firmness and steadiness. The voice will go a great way, but the whip or the spur is sometimes indispensable—not so severely applied as to excite the animal to resistance, but to convince him that we have the power to enforce submission. Few, it may almost be said, no horses, are naturally vicious. It is cruel usage which has first provoked resistance. That resistance has been followed by greater severity, and the stubbornness of the animal has increased. Open warfare has ensued, in which the man has seldom gained advantage, and the horse has been frequently rendered unserviceable. Correction may, or must be used, to enforce implicit obedience after the education has proceeded to a certain extent, but the early lessons should be inculcated with kindness alone. Young colts are sometimes very perverse. Many days will occasionally pass before they will permit the bridle to be put on, or the saddle to be worn; and one act of harshness will double or treble this time: patience and kindness, however, will always prevail. On some morning, when he is in a better humor than usual, the bridle may be put on, or the saddle may be worn; and, this compliance being followed by kindness and soothing on the part of the breaker, and no inconvenience or pain being suffered by the animal, all resistance will be at an end.

The same principles will apply to the breaking-in of the horse for the road or the chase. The handling, and some portion of instruction, should commence from the time of weaning. The future tractability of the horse will much depend on this. At two years and a half, or three years, the regular process of breaking-in should commence. If it is delayed until the animal is four years old, his strength and obstinacy will be more difficult to overcome The plan usually pursued by the breaker cannot perhaps be much improved, except that there should be much more kindness and patience, and far less harshness and cruelty, than these persons are accustomed to exhibit, and a great deal more attention to the form and natural action of the horse. A headstall is put on the colt, and a cavesson (or apparatus to confine and pinch the nose) affixed to it, with long reins. He is first accustomed to the rein, then led round a ring on soft ground, and at length mounted and taught his paces. Next to preserving the temper and docility of the horse, there is nothing of so much importance as to teach him every pace, and every part of his duty, distinctly and thoroughly. Each must constitute a separate and sometimes long-continued lesson, and that taught by a man who will never suffer his passion to get the better of his discretion.

After the cavesson has been attached to the headstall, and the long reins put on, the colt should be quietly led about by the breaker—a steady boy following behind, by occasional threatening with the whip, but never by an actual blow, to keep him moving. When the animal follows readily and quietly, he may be taken to the ring, and walked round, right and left, in a very small circle. Care should be taken to teach him this pace thoroughly, never suffering him to break into a trot. The boy with his whip may here again be necessary, but not a single blow should actually fall.

Becoming tolerably perfect in the walk, he should be quickened to a trot, and kept steadily at it; the whip of the boy, if needful, urging him on, and the cavesson restraining him. These lessons should be short. The pace should be kept perfect, and distinct in each; and docility and improvement rewarded with frequent caresses, and handfuls of corn. The length of the rein may now be gradually increased, and the pace quickened, and the time extended, until the animal becomes tractable in' these his first lessons, towards the conclusion of which, crupper-straps, or something similar, may be attached to the clothing. These, playing about the sides and flanks, accustom him to the flapping of the coat of the rider. The annoyance which they occasion will pass over in a day or two; for when the animal finds that no harm comes to him, he will cease to regard them.

Next comes the bitting. The bits should be large and smooth, and the reins buckled to a ring on either side of the pad. There are many curious and expensive machines for this purpose, but the simple rein will be quite sufficient. It should at first be slack, and then very gradually tightened. This will prepare for the more perfect manner in which the head will be afterwards got into its proper position, when the colt is accustomed to the saddle

Occasionally the breaker should stand in front of the colt, and take hold of each side rein near to the mouth, and press upon it, and thus begin to teach him to stop and to back on the pressure of the rein, rewarding every act of docility, and not being too eager to punish occasional carelessness or waywardness.

The colt may now be taken into the road or street, to be gradually accustomed to the objects among which his services will be required. Here, from fear or playfulness, a considerable degree of starting and shying may be exhibited. As little notice as possible should be taken of it. The same or a similar object should be soon passed again, but at a greater distance. If the colt still shies, let the distance be still farther increased until he takes no notice of the object. Then he may be gradually brought nearer to it, and this will be usually effected without the slightest difficulty: whereas, had there been an attempt to force him close to it in the first instance, the remembrance of the contest would have been associated with every appearance of the object, and the habit of shying would have been established.

Hitherto, with a cool and patient breaker, the whip may have been shown, but will scarcely have been used; the colt must now, however, be accustomed to this necessary instrument of authority. Let the breaker walk by the side of the animal, and throw his right arm over his back, holding the reins in his left, occasionally quickening his pace, and at the moment of doing this, tapping the horse with the whip in his right hand, and at first very gently. The tap of the whip and the quickening of the pace will soon become associated in the mind of the animal. If necessary, these reminders may gradually fall a little heavier, and the feeling of pain be the monitor of the necessity of increased exertion. The lessons of reining in and stopping, and backing on the pressure of the bit, may continue to be practised at the same time.

He may now be taught to bear the saddle. Some little caution will be necessary at the first putting of it on. The breaker should stand at the head of the colt, patting him and engaging his attention, while one assistant, on the off-side, gently places the saddle on the back of the animal; and another, on the near-side, slowly tightens the girths. If he submits quietly to this, as he generally will when the previous process of breaking-in has been properly conducted, the ceremony of mounting may be attempted on the following, or on the third day. The breaker will need two assistants in order to accomplish this. He will remain at the head of the colt, patting and making much of him. The rider will put his foot into the stirrup, and bear a little weight upon it, while the man on the off-side presses equally on the other stirrup-leather; and, according to the docility of the animal, he will gradually increase the weight, until he balances himself on the stirrup. If the colt is uneasy or fearful, he should be spoken kindly to and patted, or a mouthful of grain be given to him; but if he offers serious resistance, the lessons must terminate for that day. He may probably be in better humor on the morrow.

When the rider has balanced himself for a minute or two, he may gently throw his leg over, and quietly seat himself in the saddle. The breaker will then lead the animal round the ring, the rider sitting perfectly still. After a few minutes he will take the reins, and handle them as gently as possible, and guide the horse by the pressure of them; patting him frequently, and especially when he thinks of dismounting; and, after having dismounted, offering him a little grain, or green feed. The use of the rein in checking him, and of the pressure of the leg and the touch of the heel in quickening his pace, will soon be taught, and his education will be nearly completed.

The horse having thus far submitted himself to the breaker, these pattings and rewards must be gradually diminished, and implicit obedience mildly but firmly enforced. Severity will not often be necessary. In the great majority of cases it will be altogether uncalled for: but should the animal, in a moment of waywardness, dispute the command of the breaker, he must at once be taught that he is the slave of man, and that we have the power, by other means than those of kindness, to bend him to our will. The education of the horse should be that of the child. Pleasure is, as much as possible, associated with the early lessons; but firmness, or, if need be, coercion, must establish the habit of obedience. Tyranny and cruelty will, more speedily in the horse than even in the child, provoke the wish to disobey; and, on every practicable occasion, the resistance to command. The restive and vicious horse is, in ninety-nine cases out of a hundred, made so by ill-usage, and not by nature. None, but those who will take the trouble to make the experiment, are aware how absolute a command the due admixture of firmness and kindness will soon give us over any horse.

CASTRATION.

The period at which this operation may be best performed depends much on the breed and form of the colt, and the purpose for which he is destined. For the common agricultural horse the age of four or five months will be the most proper time, or, at least before he is weaned. Few horses are lost when cut at that age. Care, however, should be taken that the weather is not too hot, nor the flies too numerous.

If the horse is designed either for the carriage or for heavy draught, the farmer should not think of castrating him until he is at least a twelvemonth old ; and, even then, the colt should bo carefully examined. If he is thin and spare about the neck and shoulders, and low in the withers, he will materially improve by remaining uncut another six months; but if his fore-quarters are fairly developed at the age of a twelvemonth, the operation should not be delayed, lest he become heavy and gross before, and perhaps has begun too decidedly to have a will of his own. No specific age, then, can be fixed ; but the castration should be performed rather late in the spring or early in the autumn, when the air is temperate, and particularly when the weather is dry.

No preparation is necessary for the sucking colt, but it may be prudent to bleed and to physic one of more advanced age. In the majority of cases, no after treatment will be necessary, except that the animal should be sheltered from intense heat, and more particularly from wet. In temperate weather, he will do much better running in the field, than nursed in a close and hot stable. The moderate exercise that he will take in grazing will be preferable to perfect inaction.

The old method of opening the scrotum (testicle bag), on either side, and cutting off the testicles, and preventing bleeding by a temporary compression of the vessels, while they are seared with a hot iron, must not, perhaps, be abandoned ; but there is no necessity of that extra pain, when the spermatic cord (the blood-vessels and the nerve) is compressed between two pieces of wood as tightly as in a vice, and there left until the following day, or until the testicle drops off.

The practice of some farmers of *twitching* * their colts at an early period, exposes the animal to much unnecessary pain, and is accompanied with considerable danger.,

Another method of castration is by *Torsion*. An incision is made into the scrotum, and the *vas deferens* is exposed and divided. The artery is then seized by a pair of forceps contrived for the purpose, and twisted six or seven times round. It retracts without untwisting the coils, and bleeding ceases. The testicle is removed, and there is no sloughing or danger. The most painful part of the operation—the operation of the firing-iron or the clams—is avoided, and the wound readily heals.†

* Termed cording in the United States.—Am. Ed.
† *Note by Mr. Spooner.*—We agree with the author, that the old method of operating, by opening the scrotum with the knife, cutting the clams on the cord, and searing it off with the hot iron, is as safe and unobjectionable as any. We have, however, in performing this operation, found the use of chloroform very beneficial, both in removing all pain, and also preventing that severe struggling which often takes place, and which has sometimes been followed with very dangerous consequences. With this assistance we have safely performed the operation in seven minutes, without any pain to the animal.

CHAPTER XII.

THE FORE LEGS.

WE arrive now at those parts of the frame which are most essentially connected with the action and value of the horse, and oftenest, and most annoyingly, the subjects of disease.

SPRAIN OF THE SHOULDER.

The muscles of the shoulder-blade are occasionally injured by some severe shock. This is effected oftener by a slip or side-fall, than by fair, although violent exertion. It is of considerable importance to be able to distinguish this shoulder-lameness from injuries of other parts of the fore extremity. There is not much tenderness, or heat, or swelling. If, on standing before the horse, and looking at the size of the two shoulders, or rather their points, one should appear evidently larger than the other, this must not be considered as indicative of sprain of the muscles of the shoulder. It probably arises from bruise of the point of the shoulder, which a slight examination will determine.

In sprain of the shoulder the horse evidently suffers extreme pain while moving, and, the muscle underneath being inflamed and tender, he will extend it as little as possible. *He will drag his toe along the ground.* It is in the lifting of the foot that the shoulder is principally moved. If the foot is lifted high, let the horse be ever so lame, the shoulder is little, if at all affected.

In shoulder-lameness, the toe alone rests on the ground. The circumstance which most of all characterises this affection is, that when the foot is lifted and then brought considerably forward the horse will express very great pain, which he will not do if the lameness is in the foot or the leg.

In sprain of the internal muscles of the shoulder, few local measures can be adopted. The horse should be bled from the vein on the inside of the arm (the plate vein), because the blood is then abstracted more immediately from the inflamed part. A dose of physic should be given, and fomentations applied, and principally on the inside of the arm, close to the chest, and the horse should be kept as quiet as possible. The injury is too deeply seated for external stimulants to have very great effect, yet a blister will properly be resorted to, if the lameness is not speedily removed.*

SLANTING DIRECTION OF THE SHOULDER.

It will be observed, that (see G and J, Fig. 1.) the shoulder-blade and the lower bone of the shoulder are not connected together in a straight line, but form a very considerable angle with each other. This will be more evident from the following cut, which represents the fore and hind extremities in the situations which they occupy in the horse.

Fig. 33.

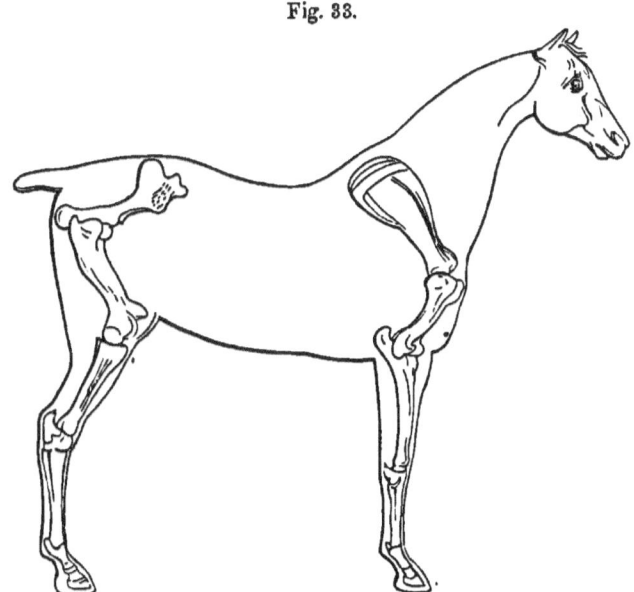

This angular construction of the limbs reminds us of the similar arrangement of the springs of a carriage, and the ease of motion, and almost perfect freedom from jolting, which are thereby obtained.

* *Note by Mr. Spooner.*—The symptoms of shoulder lameness as pointed out in the text, are for the most part correct. A horse, however, never points in this disease, but will sometimes keep the lame limb further back than the other. The pain is almost entirely felt in motion, and not in sustaining the weight; whilst, in strains of the flexor tendons, there is no pain in extending the limb, but only when the weight comes upon it; so that a horse, in the latter case, steps short with the sound leg and long with the lame one, and the very reverse in shoulder lameness. Bleeding from the arm, and mildly blistering the shoulder, generally succeeds in effecting a cure.

The obliquity or slanting direction of the shoulder effects other very useful purposes. That the stride in the gallop, or the space passed over in the trot, may be extensive, it is necessary that the fore part of the animal should be considerably elevated. The shoulder, by means of the muscles which extend from it to the inferior part of the limb, is the grand agent in effecting this. Had the bones of the shoulder been placed more upright than we see them, they could not then have been of the length which they now are,—their connection with the chest could not have been so secure,—and their movements upon each other would have been comparatively restricted.

The slanting shoulder accomplishes a most useful object. The muscles extending from the shoulder-blade to the lower bone of the shoulder are the powers by which motion is given to the whole of the limb. The extent and energy of that motion depend much on the force exerted or the strength of the muscle; but there are circumstances in the relative situations of the different bones which have far greater influence.

Let it be supposed that, by means of a lever, some one is endeavoring to raise a certain weight.

A is a lever, resting or turning on a pivot B; C is the weight to be raised; and D is the power, or the situation at which the power is applied. If the strength is applied in the direction perpendicular to the lever, as represented by the line E, the power which must be exerted can easily be calculated.

Fig. 34.

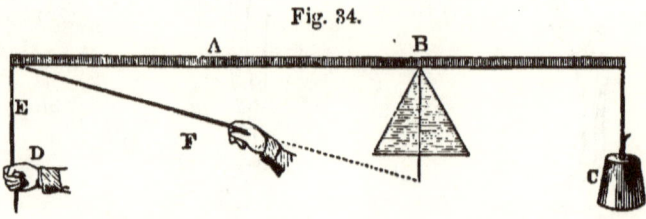

In proportion as the distance of the power from the pivot or centre of motion exceeds that of the weight from the same place, so will be the advantage gained. The power here is twice as far from the center as the weight is, and therefore advantage is gained in the proportion of two to one: or if the weight is equal to 200lbs., a force of 100lbs. will balance it. If the direction in which the power is applied is altered, and it is in that of the line F, will 100lbs. effect the purpose? No; nothing like it. How, then, is the necessary power to be calculated? The line of direction must be prolonged, until another line, falling perpendicularly from the lever, and commencing at the center of motion, will cut it; and the length of that line will give the actual effect of the strength employed. Now, this new line is but half as long as the distance of the weight from the centre of motion, and therefore advantage is lost in the proportion of two to one; or a strength equal to 400lbs. must be exerted to raise the 200lbs., and so in proportion to the deviation from the right or perpendicular line.

Let the shoulder of the horse be considered. The point of the shoulder—the shoulder joint—is the pivot or centre of motion; the leg attached to the bone of the arm is the weight; the shoulder-blade being more fixed is the part whence the power emanates; and the muscles extending from the one to the other are the lines in which that power is exerted. These lines approach much more nearly to a perpendicular in the oblique than in the upright shoulder (see Fig. 33). In the upright one, the shoulder-blade and the bones of the arm are almost in a straight line, and the real action and power of the muscles are most strangely diminished. In this point of view the oblique shoulder is most important. It not only gives extensive action, but facility of action. The power of the muscles is more than doubled by being exerted in a line approaching so much nearer to a perpendicular.

The oblique shoulder is less exposed to concussion, particularly n rapid action. The horse is less likely to trip. Nature, as if to supply the deficiency of action and of power in an upright shoulder, invariably accumulates on it more muscle, and therefore the upright shoulder is proverbially thick and cloddy.

Then, ought every horse to have an oblique shoulder? No! The question has relation to those horses that are designed to ride pleasantly, or from which extensive and rapid action is required. In them it has been said that an oblique shoulder is indispensable: but there are others which are seldom ridden; whose pace is slow, and who have nothing to do but to throw as much weight as possible into the collar. To them an upright shoulder is an advantage, because its additional thickness gives them additional weight to throw into the collar, which the power of their hinder quarters is fully sufficient to accomplish; and because the upright position of the shoulder gives that direction to the collar which enables the horse to act upon every part of it, and that inclination of the traces which will enable his weight or power to be most advantageously employed.

An improved breed of our heavy draught-horses has of late years been attempted, and with much success. Sufficient uprightness of shoulder is retained for the purposes of draught, while a slight degree of obliquity has materially quickened the pace and improved the appearance.

k

CUT 2 THE MUSCLES ON THE OUTSIDE OF THE SHOULDER.

a and *b*, in Fig. 35, represent a portion of the *Trapezius* muscle. Its use is to elevate and support the shoulder-blade—to raise it and likewise to draw it backward. A portion of it is represented as turned back, to show the muscles beneath.

Fig. 35.

A moment's consideration will convince the reader that although a low forehand and thick shoulder are very properly objected to, yet still some fullness and fleshiness are necessary, even about the withers; otherwise, although there may be height of withers, and obliquity of shoulder, to give extensive action, there will not be sufficient muscular power to work the machine with either quickness or continuance.

At *c* is a portion of the *levator humeri* (the raiser of the shoulder). It is a muscle of immense power and great utility, raising and drawing forward the shoulder and the arm, or, when these are fixed, turning the head and neck if one only acts, and depressing them if the muscles on both sides act at the same time.

At *d* is a portion of the *serratus magnus* muscle, between the shoulder and side of the chest, and constituting the bulk of the lower part of the neck.

At *e* is a small portion of the splenius muscle, *f*, represents a muscle sometimes described as a portion of the *levator humeri*

MUSCLES OF THE SHOULDER.

At *g* is a portion of the *sterno maxillaris*, or muscle common to the fore part of the chest and the lower jaw.

h designates the principal portion of this muscle, extending from the shoulder to the humerus, and employed in drawing this bone towards the shoulder-blade, and bending the whole of the limb.

The muscle *i*, *antea spinatus*, is situated on the outer and anterior part of the shoulder, below and behind the muscle next mentioned; and its office is to extend the lower bone of the shoulder on the shoulder-blade.

The muscle *j*, *postea spinatus*, behind the spine or ridge, occupies that space of the shoulder. It draws this bone outward and upward.

At *k*, is a muscle common to the breast and the shoulder-blade, and called *the pectoralis parvus*. Its action, in common with that of a larger muscle, seen at *m*, *the great pectoral*, is to draw the head of the shoulder backward, and also the lower part of the shoulder-blade, and to give the latter a more upright position.

At *q*, is the tendon of a very important muscle, the *extensor longus* of the arm. At *r* and *s*, are the three divisions of another muscle concerned in the same office.

1, 2 and 3 designate the places of the principal artery, nerve, and vein of the leg; 4 gives the subcutaneous vein running within the arm; and 5 the subcutaneous vein of the side of the chest.

Fig. 36 represents the muscles on the inside of the shoulder and fore-arm. *a* is a very prominent one. It is called the *pectoralis transversus* (the muscle crossing the breast). The use of this muscle is obvious and important. It binds the arm to the side of the horse; it keeps the legs straight before the horse when he is at speed, that the weight of the body may be received on them in a direction most easy and safe to the horse and to the rider, and most advantageous for the full play of all the muscles concerned in progression. Considering the unevenness of surface over which a horse often passes, and the rapid turnings which are sometimes necessary, these muscles have enough to do; and when the animal is pushed beyond his strength, and these muscles are wearied, and the fore-legs spread out, and the horse is "*all abroad*," the confused and unpleasant manner of going, and the sudden falling-off in speed, are well known to

Fig. 36.

every rider. The lines above represent, in the order from the front, the principal nerves, arteries, and veins of the shoulder and arm ; and, on the muscles, *k* represents the principal subcutaneous vein of the inside of the arm, and *i* the artery by which it is accompanied.

THE HUMERUS, OR LOWER BONE OF THE SHOULDER.

Forming a joint with the shoulder-blade, at the point of the shoulder, is the *humerus*. It is a short, strong bone, slanting backward in an opposite direction to the shoulder-blade. At the upper part it has a large round head, received into the shallow cavity of the shoulder-blade. In a well-formed horse this bone can scarcely be too short.

THE ARM.

The *arm* extending from the elbow to the knee (see K and L, Fig. 1, and also Fig. 35), consists, in the young horse, of two distinct bones. The long and front bone, called the *radius*, is nearly straight, receiving into its upper end the lower heads of the humerus ; and the lower end corresponding with the upper layer of the bones of the knee. The short and hinder bone is called the *ulna*. It has a very long and powerful projection, received between the heads of the humerus, and called the elbow ; it then stretches down, narrowing by degrees (see L, Fig. 1, and the Fig. 35), to below the middle of the front bone, where it terminates in a point. The two bones are united together by cartilage and ligament ; but these are by degrees absorbed and changed to bone, and before the horse becomes old the whole of the arm consists of one bone only.

The strength of the horse, so far as his fore limbs are concerned, resides principally in those muscles which give size to the arm.

A full and swelling fore-arm is the characteristic of every thorough-bred horse. Whatever other good points the animal may possess, if the arm is narrow in front and near the shoulder, flat on the side, and altogether deficient in muscular appearance, that horse is radically defective. He can neither raise his knee for rapid action, nor throw his legs sufficiently forward.

The arm should likewise be long. In proportion to the length of the muscle is the degree of contraction of which it is capable ; and in proportion also to the degree of contraction will be the extent of motion in the limb beneath.

Enlargements sometimes appear about the elbow, either the consequence of a violent blow, or from the calks of the shoes injuring this part when the horse sleeps with his legs doubled under him. If a seton is passed through the tumor, it will sometimes rapidly diminish, and even disappear; but if it is of considerable magnitude, the skin should be opened along the middle of the swelling, and the tumor dissected out.

The elbow-joint is sometimes punctured, either accidentally, or through the brutality of the groom or carter. The swelling is often rapid and extensive, and fatal inflammation may ensue. Rest, and the closure of the wound, are the most important considerations.

There are other muscles of the fore-arm employed in extending the limb. At x, Fig. 35, is the principal one, called the *extensor metacarpi*. Its office is to extend the leg.

The next muscle in situation and importance is seen at w, and called the *extensor pedis*.

At u, Fig. 35, is the tendon of another extensor muscle, and at z a curious oblique one, passing over the tendon of x, confining it in its situation, and likewise assisting in extending or straightening the leg.

The muscles employed in bending the leg are both numerous and powerful. Two of the superficial ones are given in Fig. 36. The first is at t, Fig. 35; it is also seen at b, Fig. 35. It is called the *flexor medius metacarpi*, because its office is to bend the leg. The other is seen at v, Fig. 35. It is called the *flexor metacarpi externus*, and is also designed to flex the leg.

The internal flexor is seen at e. Its office is also to bend the leg.

A portion of one of the most powerful of the flexor muscles, and powerful indeed they must be, is delineated at c, Fig. 35. It is the *flexor brachii*. It is the muscle by which, almost alone, the whole of the leg below the arm is bent, and carried forward and upward. [There are other muscles of the leg and foot, not necessary to be named here.]

THE KNEE.

To avoid the effects of concussion in so exposed a part, six distinct bones, each covered above and below with a thick coating of cartilage, connected together by strong ligaments, but separated by interposed fluids and membranes, form the knee.

The knee should be broad. It should present a very considerable width, compared with the arm above, or the shank below. In proportion to the breadth of the knee is the space for the attachment of muscles, and for the accumulation of ligamentous expansions and bands. In proportion to the breadth of the knee there will be more strength; and likewise the direction of some muscles will be less oblique, and the course of others will be more removed from the centre of motion, in either of which cases much power will be gained.

BROKEN KNEES.

The treatment of broken knees is a subject of considerable mportance, for many horses are sadly blemished, and others are destroyed, by wounds in the knee-joint. The horse, when falling, naturally throws his knees forward; they receive all his weight, and are sometimes very extensively lacerated. The first thing to be done is, by very careful washing with warm water, to cleanse the wound from all gravel and dirt. It must then be ascertained whether the joint is penetrated. The grating of the probe on one of the bones of the knee, or the depth to which the probe enters the wound, will too plainly indicate that the joint has been opened. Should any doubt exist, a linseed-meal poultice must be applied. This will at least act as a fomentation to the wound, and will prevent or abate inflammation; and when, twelve hours afterwards, it is taken off, the *synovia* or *joint-oil*, in the form of a glairy, yellowish, transparent fluid, will be seen, if the capsular ligament has been penetrated. Should doubt remain after the first poultice, a second ought to be applied.

It having been ascertained that the interior of the joint is not injured, attention must be paid to the wound that is actually made. The horse should wear a cradle to prevent his getting at the wound. A stimulating application—the common black-oil of the farrier is as good as any—should be lightly applied every day, until healthy pus is produced on the wound, and then a little friar's balsam will probably effect a cure.

The opening of the joint, however, being ascertained, the first and immediate care is to close the orifice; for the fluid which separated and lubricated the bones of the knee being suffered to escape, they will be brought into contact with and will rub upon each other; the delicate membrane with which they are covered will be highly inflamed; the constitution will be speedily affected, and a degree of fever will ensue that will destroy the horse: while, in the meantime, of all the tortures that can be inflicted on the poor animal, none can equal that which accompanies inflammation of the membranes lining the joints.

The manner of closing the orifice must be left to the judgment of the veterinary surgeon, who alone is capable of properly treating such a case. It may be effected by a compress enclosing the whole of the wound, and not to be removed for many days; or it may be attempted by the old and generally successful method of applying the hot iron over the wound, and particularly over the spot where the ligament appears to be lacerated. A poultice may then be placed on the part, and the case treated as a common wound. The surgeon will find no difficulty in determining whether the sharp edge of the common firing-iron should be used—as would be the case if the laceration is considerable, or whether the budding-iron should be resorted to After the use of the cautery, the application of a blister may, in some cases, be serviceable. Should the joint-oil continue to flow, the iron may be applied a second, or even a third time. By its application, so much swelling is produced on the immediate puncture, and in the neighboring parts, as mechanically to close up and plug the orifice.

If, however, the opening into the joint is extensive, and the joint-oil continues to flow, and the horse is evidently suffering much pain, humanity will dictate that he should be destroyed The case is hopeless. A high degree of fever will ere long carry him off, or the inflammation will cause a deposit of matter in the cavity of the joint that will produce incurable lameness.*

* *Note by Mr. Spooner.*—The knee is subject to a variety of injuries from falls. Sometimes, though the wound is large and apparently formidable, it is yet but an ordinary wound, and will heal readily with common treatment. At other times, partly from the width and extent of the wound, and partly from the restlessness of the animal, a wide and deep fissure takes place, which opens every time the horse bends his knee, and the sides of the chap growing at the same time, the wound becomes deeper and wider, and is extremely difficult to heal. The best mode of treatment is to cut away the sides and edges of the fissure to its full depth, thereby converting it into one simple wound, which may be healed with little difficulty. When the joint is opened the treatment must be conducted on very different principles from that of an ordinary wound; whereas, in the latter case, fomentations and poultices are very proper, in order to cleanse the wound, and to keep down inflammation. When the joint is opened, these measures are to be avoided, as they increase irritation, by keeping open the joint, and encouraging the flow of synovia (joint-oil), and the entrance of the air.

In a case of open joint, our principal endeavor must be to close the joint with all possible despatch; but even with judicious treatment our chances of success will materially depend on one or two circumstances, viz., the size of the wound, the cavity opened, and the fact as to whether inflammation is already set up in the joint or not. If the latter be the case, our chances of success are very slight, for the joint will, in all probability, become anchylosed or stiff. We may in great measure ascertain the existence of inflammation by the animal placing the limb in a bent position, and keeping it in motion by pawing from uneasiness. There are various methods of closing an open joint. A simple, and often a very effective one, is by means of a solution of bichloride of mercury in a solution of spirits of wine, and applied to the wound several times a day by means of a feather, till the synovia ceases to flow. Another is the application of the hot iron. The object in both these modes is to coagulate the synovia, so as to form a temporary plug to the joint, till nature has time to close it more permanently. If either of these methods are adopted, it will not do to apply a poultice afterwards, as stated in the text, as this would wash

THE LEG.

The part of the limb between the knee and the fetlock consists of three bones—a large one before, called the *cannon* or *shank*, and two smaller or *splint* bones behind (see N, Fig. 1).

The smaller bones are placed behind the larger ones on either side. They are united to the larger bone by a ligamentous substance. They reach from one-half to two-thirds of the length of the shank-bone, and, through their whole extent, are united to it by this substance; but, from the animal being worked too soon, or too violently, inflammation ensues—bony matter is deposited in the room of the ligamentous, and a bony union takes place instead of the natural one. There is no doubt that the ease of motion is somewhat lessened by this substitution of bone, but other elastic principles are probably called into more powerful action, and the value of the horse is not perceptibly impaired, although it is hard to say what secret injury may be done to the neighboring joints, and the cause of which, the lameness not appearing until a distant period, is not suspected.

In this process, however, mischief does often immediately extend to the neighboring parts. The disposition to deposit bone reaches beyond the space between the larger and smaller bones of the leg, and a tumor, first callous, and afterwards bony, is found, with part of its base resting on the line of union between these bones. This is called a

SPLINT.

The splint is invariably found on the outside of the small bones and generally on the inside of the leg (*c*, *Fig*. 41). The inner bone receives the whole weight transmitted to the small bone of the knee; and the absurd practice of many smiths of raising the outer heel of the shoe to an extravagant degree, throws still more of the weight of the horse on the inner splint-bone.

Bony tumors occasionally appear on other parts of the shank bone, being the consequence of violent blows or other external injuries, and are commonly called splints.

away the plug which we have sought to form. Another method of treatment is to apply compresses of bandages and paste, letting them continue on for a length of time, so as to close the joint mechanically. Over these bandages we may apply linseed poultices with advantage, as by so doing we keep down inflammation without washing congulated synovia from the wound. By this means we may succeed even in formidable wounds, if inflammation has not been previously set up in the joint. It is very desirable that the horse should keep the limb in a straight position; lying down should therefore be avoided, and it is often necessary to support the animal in slings.

When the splint of either sort is forming, the horse is frequently lame, for the periosteum or membrane covering the bone is painfully stretched; but when this membrane has accommodated itself to the tumor that extended it, the lameness subsides, and altogether disappears, unless the splint be in a situation in which it interferes with the action of some tendon or ligament, or in the immediate neighborhood of a joint. Pressing upon a ligament or tendon, it may cause inflammation of those substances; or, being close to a joint, it may interfere with its action. Splints, then, do not necessarily cause unsoundness, and may not lessen in the slightest degree the action or value of the horse. All depends on their situation.

The treatment of splints, if it is worth while to meddle with them, is exceedingly simple. The hair should be closely shaved off round the tumor; a little strong mercurial ointment rubbed in for two days; and this followed by an active blister. If the splint is of recent formation, it will generally yield to this, or to a second blister. Should it, however, resist these applications, it not unfrequently happens, that it will afterwards, and at no great distance of time, begin rapidly to lessen, and quite disappear. There is also a natural process by which the greater part of splints disappear when the horse grows old.

The hydriodate of potash, made into an ointment with lard, and a small quantity of mercurial ointment being added, will frequently cause the disappearance of a splint of either sort.*

SPEEDY CUT.—The inside of the leg, immediately under the knee, and extending to the head of the inner splint-bone, is subject to injury from what is termed the *speedy cut*. A horse with high action, and in the fast trot, violently strikes this part, either with his hoof or the edge of the shoe. Sometimes bony enlargement is the result; at others, great heat and tenderness; and the pain from the blow seems occasionally to be so great, that the horse drops as if he were shot. The only remedy is to take care that no part of the shoe projects beyond the foot; and to let the inner side of the shoe—except the country is very deep, or the horse used for hunting—have but one nail, and that near the toe. This part of the hoof, being unfettered with nails, will expand when it comes in contact with the ground, and contract when in

---

* *Note by Mr. Spooner.*—The best remedy for splints is unquestionably *subcutaceous periosteotomy*, an operation which consists in making a small incision through the skin at the lower part of the splint, and passing up a small knife made for the purpose under the skin, and so dividing the periosteum, as the membrane which covers the bone is termed. This relieves the tension, and thus puts a stop to the irritation, and its consequence, the bony deposition. A small seton is left in the wound for a fortnight, which keeps it open and produces some counter irritation.

air and relieved from the pressure of the weight of the body; and, although this contraction is to no great extent, it will be sufficient to carry the foot harmlessly by the leg. Care should likewise be taken that the shoe is of equal thickness at the heel and the toe, and that the bearing is equal on both sides.

TIED IN BELOW THE KNEE.—Immediately under the knee, is one of those ligamentous rings by which the tendons are so usefully bound down and secured; but if the hinder bone of the knee, the *trapezium*, described at p. 250, is not sufficiently prominent, this ring will confine the flexor tendons of the foot too tightly, and the leg will be very deficient in depth under the knee. This is called being *tied in below the knee* (*b*, Fig. 41). Every horseman recognizes it as a most serious defect. It is scarcely compatible with speed, and most assuredly not with continuance. Such a horse cannot be ridden far and fast, without serious sprain of the back sinews. There are few more serious defects than this tying-in of the tendons immediately below the knee. The foreleg may be narrow in front, but it must be deep at the side, in order to render the horse valuable; for then only will the tendons have free action, and the muscular force be exerted in the most advantageous direction. There are few good race-horses whose legs are not deep below the knee. If there are exceptions, it is because their exertion, although violent, is but of short continuance.

In a perfect leg, and towards its lower part, there should be three distinct and perfect projections visible to the eye, as well as perceptible by the finger—the sides of the shank-bone being the most forward of the three; next, the suspensory ligament; and, hindermost of all, the flexor tendons. When these are not to be distinctly seen or felt, or there is considerable thickening about them and between them (*d*, Fig. 41), and the leg is round instead of flat and deep, there has been what is commonly, but improperly, called*

SPRAIN OF THE BACK-SINEWS.

These tendons are enclosed in a sheath of dense cellular substance, in order to confine them in their situation, and to defend them from injury. Between the tendon and the sheath, there is

---

* *Note by Mr. Spooner.*—We cannot agree with the author when he says that there are few good race-horses but what are deep in the leg below the knee. Very many first class race-horses have very faulty fore-legs, being slight and tottering below the knee. It is well known to trainers that such legs often stand their work very well, for race horses require strength rather in the extensors than in the flexors of the limb. Their action should be long and low, not high and round, which high withers and strong flexor muscles are calculated to produce. Thus what would be a grievous fault in almost every other kind of horse, is not, with a horse kept purely for the turf.

a mucous fluid to prevent friction; but when the horse has been over-worked, or put to sudden or violent exertion, the tendon presses upon the delicate membrane lining the sheath, and inflammation is produced. A different fluid is then thrown out, which *coagulates*, and adhesions are formed between the tendon and the sheath, and the motion of the limb is more difficult and painful. At other times, from violent or long-continued exertion, some of the fibres which confine the tendons are ruptured. A slight injury of this nature is called a sprain of the back-sinews or tendons; and, when it is more serious, the horse is said to have *broken down*. It should be remembered, however, that the *tendon* can never be sprained, because it is inelastic and incapable of extension; and the tendon, or its sheath, are scarcely ever ruptured, even in what is called breaking down. The first injury is confined to inflammation of the sheath, or rupture of a few of the attaching fibres. This inflammation, however, is often very great, the pain intense, and the lameness excessive. The anguish expressed at every bending of the limb, and the local swelling and heat, will clearly indicate the seat of injury.

In every serious affection of this kind, care should be taken that the local inflammation does not produce general disturbance of the system; and, therefore, the horse should be bled and physicked. The bleeding may be at the toe, by which an important local, as well as general, effect will be produced. The vessels of the heart will be relieved, while fever will be prevented. [For directions for bleeding at the toe, see Art. "Bleeding," p. 190.]

As a local application, no hot farrier's oil should come near the part, but the leg should be well fomented with warm water two or three times in the day, and half an hour at each time. Between the fomentations, the leg should be enclosed in a poultice of linseed-meal. Any herb that pleases the owner may be added to the fomentation, or vinegar or Goulard's extract to the poultice; for the beneficial effect of both depends simply on the warmth of the water and the moisture of the poultice. All stimulating applications will infallibly aggravate the mischief.

The horse beginning to put his foot better to the ground, and to bear pressure on the part, and the heat having disappeared, the object to be accomplished is changed. Recurrence of the inflammation must be prevented, the enlargement must be got rid of, and the parts must be strengthened. The two latter purposes cannot be better effected than by using an elastic bandage—one of thin flannel will be the best. This will sustain and support the limb, while by few means are the absorbents sooner induced to take up the effused coagulable matter of which the swelling is composed, than by moderate pressure. If the bandage is kept wet with vinegar—to each pint of which a quarter of a pint of spirit of wine has been added—the skin will be slightly stimulated and contracted, and the cold produced by the constant evaporation will tend to subdue the remaining and deep-seated inflammation. This bandage should be daily tightened in proportion as the parts are capable of bearing increased pressure, and the treatment should be persisted in for a fortnight. If, at the expiration of that period, there is no swelling, tenderness, or heat, the horse may gradually, and very cautiously, be put to his usual work.

Should there, however, remain the slightest lameness or considerable enlargement, the leg must be blistered, and, indeed, it would seldom be bad practice to blister after every case of severe sprain, for the inflammation may lie deep in the sheath of the tendons, and the part once sprained may long remain weak, and subject to renewed injury, not only from unusual, but even ordinary exertion. If a blister is resorted to, time should be given for it to produce its gradual and full effect, and the horse should be afterwards turned out for one or two months. We must here be permitted to repeat, that a blister should never be used while any heat or tenderness remains about the part, otherwise the slightest injury may be, and often is, converted into incurable lameness.

Very severe sprains, or much oftener, sprains badly treated, may require the application of the cautery. If from long-continued inflammation the structure of the part is materially altered—if the swelling is becoming callous, or the skin is thickened and prevents the free motion of the limb, no stimulus short of the heated iron will be sufficient to rouse the absorbents to remove the injurious deposit. The firing should be applied in straight lines, because the skin, contracting by the application of the cautery, and gradually regaining its elastic nature, will thus form the best bandage over the weakened part. It should likewise be as deep as it can be applied without penetrating the skin. Here, even more particularly than in the blister, time should be given for the full action of the firing. Many weeks pass away before it is perfectly accomplished; and, after firing, the horse should have at least a six months', and it would be better if he could be given a twelve months' run at grass.*

* *Note by Mr. Spooner.*—In the original description of the anatomy of these parts in the text there are one or two omissions which it is necessary to supply. The office of these tendons is two-fold, viz., to flex the limb and also to sustain a great portion of the animal's weight. They therefore act both as sinews and as ligaments. In the latter office they are greatly assisted by a strong ligamentous substance which is attached to the common bone above, and to the perforans tendon below, for which, indeed, it forms a sheath. In those strains of the tendons where the enlargement takes place, just under the knee, this ligament is the seat of mischief; and the effect is, if not early subdued, to cause a contraction of the sinews, and con-

In examining a horse for the purchase, the closest attention should be paid to the appearance of the flex or tendons. If there is any thickening of the substance around them, it shows that the horse has been strained, and is not sound. He has been patched up for awhile, but will fail again when severe exertion is required from him.

WIND-GALLS.

In the neighborhood of the fetlock there are occasionally found considerable enlargements, oftener on the hind-leg than the fore-one, which are denominated, *wind-galls*, (e, Fig. 41). Between the tendons and other parts, and wherever the tendons are exposed to pressure or friction, and particularly about their extremities, little bags or sacs are placed, containing and suffering to ooze slowly from them a mucous fluid to lubricate (make slippery) the parts. From undue pressure, and that most fresequently produce first a straight or knuckling, and afterwards an over shot fetlock, so that the animal is rendered useless, and requires, in order to restore him to any degree of usefulness, the performance of an operation denominated

Division of the Flexor tendons, the purpose of which is actually to lengthen the sinews, and thus restore the fetlock to its original position. The operation is performed midway between the knee and the fetlock, there being there no sheath of any consequence, and no synovial cavity to to be opened. The tendons being divided recede to the extent of from one to two inches, which space is, in the course of a month, filled up with new tendinous substance thrown out from the divided extremities of the sinews.

In the ordinary strains of the flexor tendons the seat of injury is usually either midway between the knee and the fetlock, or somewhat nearer the latter joint than the former. There is every possible variety as to the amount of injury, varying from a slight lameness and a trivial enlargement to a very considerable swelling, and excessive pain, inflammation, and lameness. It has been doubted whether the sinews themselves are actually enlarged, many supposing that the swelling is confined to their sheathy investments. The writer, however, is assured from numerous dissections, as well as from the operation before alluded to of dividing the sinews, that they actually become both inflamed and enlarged.

When the lameness and enlargement are excessive, the mischief is denominated in racing stables a *break-down;* but in such instances this serious mischief is nearly always preceded by a slight strain, which is allowed to pass either unobserved or neglected, for we often find that no men are so careless and neglectful in this respect as those who are intrusted with the most valuable of all horses.

In these very severe cases the most energetic measures should be adopted, such as copious bleeding from the arm, repeated if necessary once or twice; constant warm fomentations for some hours at a time; physic, and after some days, cold applications to the leg, continued without intermission. By such treatment, the writer has succeeded in restoring the animal to hunting work, when strained to such a degree as to be incapable of standing on the leg for a week.

quently caused by violent action and straining of the tendons, or, often, from some predisposition about the horse, these little sacs are injured. They take on inflammation, and sometimes become large and hardened. There are few horses perfectly free from them. When they first appear, and until the inflammation subsides, they may be accompanied by some degree of lameness; but otherwise, except when they attain a great size, they do not interfere with the action of the animal, or cause any considerable unsoundness. The farriers used to suppose that they contained wind—hence their name, wind-galls; and hence the practice of opening them, by which dreadful inflammation was often produced, and many a valuable horse destroyed. It is not uncommon for wind-galls entirely to disappear in aged horses.

A slight wind-gall will scarcely be subjected to treatment; but if these tumors are numerous and large, and seem to impede the motion of the limb, they may be attacked first by bandage. The rollers should be of flannel, and soft pads should be placed on each of the enlargements, and bound down tightly upon them. The bandage should also be wetted with the lotion recommended for sprain of the back-sinews. The wind-gall will often diminish or disappear by this treatment, but will too frequently return when the horse is again hardly worked. A blister is a more effectual, but too often temporary remedy. Wind-galls will return with the renewal of work. Firing is still more certain, if the tumors are sufficiently large and annoying to justify our having recourse to measures so severe; for it will not only effect the immediate absorption of the fluid, and the reduction of the swelling, but, by contracting the skin, will act as a permanent bandage, and therefore prevent the reappearance of the tumor. The iodine and mercurial ointments have occasionally been used with advantage in the proportion of three parts of the former to two of the latter.*

* *Note by Mr. Spooner.*—Numerous dissections of these wind-galls have enabled us to give a different explanation from that stated in the text. They appear to be of two kinds, those situated between the suspensory ligaments and the flexor tendons, and which are the most common, and those formed between the suspensory ligaments and the bone in front, in each case immediately above the fetlock joint. Now the former wind-galls consist in an extension of the investment of the sheath of the flexor perforans formed for it by the perforatus, and the latter a distension of the capsular ligaments of the joint itself. In each a synovial cavity is effected, and consequently the wind-gall cannot be opened without considerable danger. They rarely occasion lameness unless attended with considerable inflammation or ossification of the neighboring parts, or a solidification of the synovia (joint oil). When this is the case the treatment advised in the text should be adopted.

THE PASTERNS

Fig. 37.

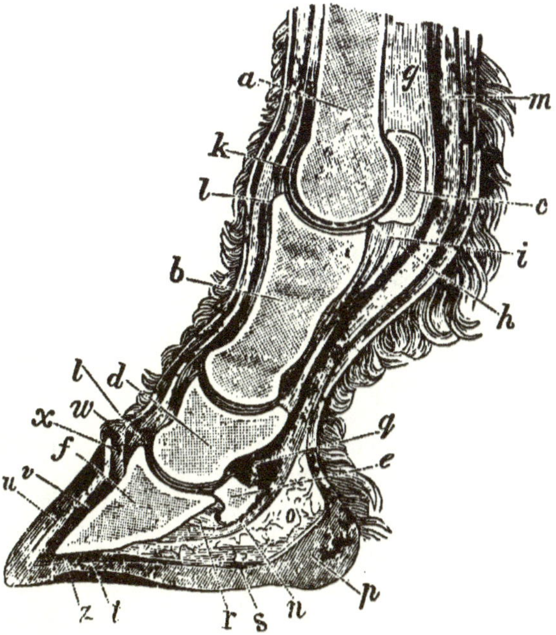

a The shank-bone.
b The upper and larger pastern-bone.
c The sessamoid-bone.
d The lower or smaller pastern-bone.
e The navicular or shuttle-bone.
f The coffin-bone, or bone of the foot.
g The suspensory ligament, inserted into the sessamoid-bone.
h A continuation of the suspensory ligament, inserted into the smaller pastern-bone.
i The small inelastic ligament, tying down the sessamoid-bone to the larger pastern-bone.
k A long ligament reaching from the pastern-bone to the knee.
l The extensor tendon inserted into both the pasterns and the coffin-bone.
m The tendon of the performing flexor inserted into the coffin-bone, after having passed over the navicular bone.
n The seat of the navicular joint lameness.
o The inner or sensible frog.
p The cleft of the horny frog.
q A ligament uniting the navicular bone to the smaller pastern.
r A ligament uniting the navicular bone to the coffin-bone.
s The sensible sole, between the coffin-bone and the horny sole.
t The horny sole.
u The crust or wall of the foot.
v The sensible laminæ to which the crust is attached.
w The coronary ring of the crust.
x The covering of the coronary ligament from which the crust is secreted.
z Place of bleeding at the toe.

At the back of the shank just below the knee, and in the space between the splint bones, is the *suspensory* ligament, admirably adapted to prevent concussion. It originates from the head of the shank-bone, and is inserted in the sessamoids. The pasterns (see Fig. 37) are united to the shank in an oblique direction, differing in degree in the different breeds of horses, and in each adapted to the purpose for which that breed was designed. The weight falls upon the pastern in the direction of the shank-bone, and the pastern being set on obliquely, a portion of that weight must be communicated to the sessamoids. Much concussion is saved by the yielding of the pasterns, in consequence of their oblique direction; and the concussion which would be produced by that portion of weight which falls on the sessamoid bones is completely destroyed, for there is no bone underneath to receive it. They are suspended by this ligament—an *elastic* ligament, which gradually yields to, and is lengthened by, the force impressed upon it, and in this gradual yielding and lengthening, materially lessening, or generally preventing, all painful or dangerous concussion.

The length and obliquity of the pastern vary in the different breeds of horses, and on it depends the elastic action of the animal, and the easiness of his paces. The pastern must be long in proportion to its obliquity, or the fetlock will be too close to the ground, and, in rapid action, come violently into contact with it. In proportion as the pastern is oblique or slanting, two consequences will follow, less weight will be thrown on the pastern, and more on the sessamoid, and, in that proportion, concussion will be prevented.

Every advantage, however, has, to a certain extent, its corresponding disadvantage. The long, slanting pastern has less strength, and will be more subject to strains.

The long and slanting pastern is advantageous in the racehorse, from the springiness of action and greater extent of stride by which it is accompanied. A less degree of it is given in the hunter who is to unite continuance of exertion with ease of pace. For the hackney there should be sufficient obliquity to give pleasantness of going, but not enough to endanger continuance and strength. In the cart-horse the pasterns are short and upright. Except a horse for general purposes, and particularly for riding, is very hardly used, a little too much obliquity is a far less evil than a pastern too upright. While the jolting of the upright pastern is an insufferable nuisance to the rider, it is injurious and most unsafe to the horse, and produces many diseases in the feet and legs, and particularly ringbone, ossification of the cartilages and contracted feet.

INJURIES TO THE SUSPENSORY LIGAMENT.

The suspensory ligament is sometimes strained and even ruptured by extraordinary exertion. The sessamoids, which in their natural state are suspended by it, and from which function its name is derived, are in the latter case let down, and the fetlock almost touches the ground. This is generally mistaken for rupture of the flexor tendon ; but one circumstance will sufficiently demonstrate that it is the suspensory ligament which is concerned, viz. : that the horse is able to bend his foot. Rupture of this ligament is a bad, and almost desperate case. The horse is frequently lame for life, and never becomes perfectly sound. Keeping him altogether quiet, bandaging the leg, and putting on a high-heeled shoe, will afford the most probable means of relief.

The common injury to this ligament is sprain, indicated by lameness, and swelling, and heat, more or less severe in proportion as the neighboring parts are involved. This will sometimes yield to rest and cooling treatment; but if the care is obstinate, 't will be necessary to have recourse to firing.

THE FETLOCK.

The fetlock-joint is a very complicated one, and from the stress which is laid on it, and its being the principal seat of motion below the knee, it is particularly subject to injury. There are not many cases of sprain of the back-sinew that are not accompanied by inflammation of the ligaments of this joint ; and numerous supposed cases of sprain higher up are simple affections of the fetlock. It requires a great deal of care, and some experience, to distinguish the one from the other. The heat about the part, and the point at which the horse least endures the pressure of the finger, will be the principal guides. Occasionally, by the application of cooling lotions, the inflammation may be subdued, but, at other times, the horse suffers dreadfully, and is unable to stand A serious affection of the fetlock-joint demands treatment more prompt and severe than that of the sheaths of the tendons.

GROGGINESS.

The peculiar knuckling of the fetlock-joint, and the tottering of the whole of the fore-leg, known by the name of *grogginess*, and which is so often seen in old and over-worked horses, is seldom an affection of either the fetlock or the pastern-joints simply. In deed it is difficult to fix on any particular joint, unless it is that which is deep in the foot, and where the flexor tendon runs over the navicular bone. It seems oftenest to be a want of power in the ligaments of the joints generally, produced by frequent and severe sprains, or by ill-judged and cruel exertion. Professor Stewart very truly says, that "it is common among all kinds of fast workers, and long journeys at a fast pace will make almost any horse groggy. Bad shoeing and want of stable care may help to increase, but never can alone produce grogginess. It is one of the evils of excessive work." In the majority of cases it admits of no remedy.*

CUTTING.

The inside of the fetlock is often bruised by the shoe or the hoof of the opposite foot. Many expedients used to be tried to remove this; the inside heel has been raised and lowered, and the outside raised and lowered; and sometimes one operation has succeeded, and sometimes the contrary; and there was no point so involved in obscurity, or so destitute of principles to guide the practitioner. The most successful remedy, and that which in the great majority of cases supersedes all others, is Mr. Turner's shoe, of equal thickness from heel to toe, and having but one nail, and that near the toe on the inside of the shoe; care being taken that the shoe shall not extend beyond the edge of the crust, and that the crust shall be rasped a little at the quarters.

There are some defects, however, in the natural form of the horse, which are the causes of cutting, and which no contrivance will remedy; as when the legs are placed too near to each other, or when the feet are turned inward or outward. A horse with these defects should be carefully examined at the inside of the fetlock, and if there are any sore or callous places from cutting, there will be sufficient reason for rejecting the animal. Some horses will cut only when they are fatigued or lame, and old; many colts will cut before they arrive at their full strength.†

THE PASTERNS.

A consideration of the pasterns will throw more light upon this and other diseases of the extremities.

* *Note by Mr. Spooner.*—The term *grogginess* is applied by horsemen to slight lameness, which goes off with exercise, and which is shown in the stable by the animal pointing the affected foot. The seat of the disease is the navicular joint, and it is altogether unconnected with that knuckling of the fetlock which is often seen in horses much worked, and which appears to be owing to weakness of the sinews, principally of the extensors.

† *Note by Mr. Spooner.*—This evil is sometimes removed by shoeing the horse very thin on the inside, or even giving him a three-quarter shoe, the tendency of which plan is to make the horse carry his feet wider apart; but, in some cases the very opposite plan is found the best.

THE PASTERNS.

The *upper pastern* bone (*b*, Fig. 37, and *a*, in Fig. 38, and *b*, in Fig. 39,) receives the lower pulley-like head of the shank-bone, and forms a hinge-joint admitting only of bending and extension, but not of side motion; it likewise forms a joint with the sessamoid-bones. Its lower head has two rounded protuberances, which are received into corresponding depressions in the lower pastern. On either side, above the pastern-joint, are roughened projections for the attachment of very strong ligaments, both in capsular ligaments, and many cross ligaments, which render the joint between the two pasterns sufficiently secure.

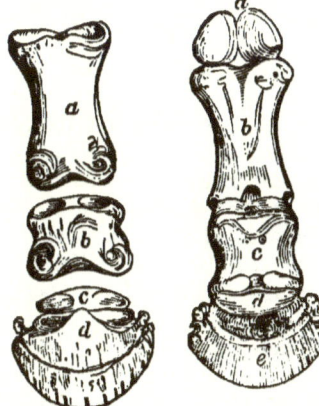

Fig. 38.   Fig. 39.

Fig. 38.
a The upper pastern.
b The lower pastern.
c The navicular bone.
d The coffin-bone.

Fig. 39.
a The sessamoid-bone.
b The upper pastern.
c The lower pastern.
d The navicular bone.
e The coffin-bone, with the horny laminæ.

The *lower pastern* (*d*, Fig. 37, and *b*, in the first figure, and *c*, in the second in this cut,) is a short and thick bone, with its larger head downward. Its upper head has two depressions to receive the protuberances on the lower head of the upper bone, bearing some resemblance to a pully, but not so decidedly as the lower head of the shank-bone. Its lower head resembles that of the other pastern, and has also two prominences, somewhat resembling a pulley, by which it forms a joint with the coffin-bone; and a depression in front, corresponding with a projection in the coffin-bone. There are also two slight depressions behind, receiving eminences of the navicular bone. Neither of these joints admits of any lateral motion. The ligaments of this joint, both the capsular and the cross ones, are, like those of the pastern-joint, exceedingly strong. The tendon of the extensor muscle is inserted into

Fig. 40.

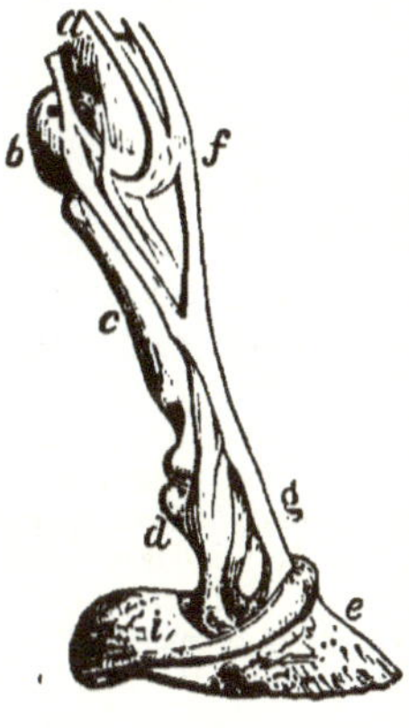

the fore-part, both of the upper and lower pastern-bones, as well as into the upper part of the coffin-bone (*l*, Fig. 57); and at the back of these bones the suspensory ligament is expanded and inserted, while a portion of it goes over the fore-part of the upper pastern to reach the extensor tendon. These attachments in front of the bones are seen in Fig. 40, in which *a* represents the lower part of the shank-bone; *b* the sessamoid-bones; *c* the upper pastern; *d* the lower pastern; and *e* the coffin-bone; *f* are the branches of the suspensory ligaments going to unite with the extensor tendon; *g* the long extensor tendon; *h* ligaments connecting the two pastern-bones together; and *i* the lateral cartilages of the foot.

SPRAIN OF THE COFFIN-JOINT.

The proof of this is when the lameness is sudden, and the heat and tenderness are principally felt round the coronet. Bleeding at the toe, physic, fomentation, and blisters are the usual means adopted. This lameness is not easily removed, even by a blister; and if removed, like sprains of the fetlock and of the back sinews, it is apt to return, and finally produce a great deal of disorganization and mischief in the foot. Sprain of the coffin-joint sometimes becomes a very serious affair. Not being always attended by any external swelling, and being detected only by heat round the coronet, the seat of the lameness is often overlooked by the groom and the farrier; and the disease is suffered to become confirmed before its nature is discovered.

From violent or repeated sprains of the pastern or coffin-joints, or extension of the ligaments attached to other parts of the pastern-bones, inflammation takes place in the periosteum, and bony matter is formed, which often rapidly increases, and is recognized by the name of*

RINGBONE.

Ringbone is is a deposit of bony matter in one of the pasterns, and usually near the joint. It rapidly spreads, and involves not only the pastern-bones, but the cartilages of the foot, and spread-

---

* *Note by Mr. Spooner.*—Sprain of the coffin-joint is extremely rare, the joint being so well secured from injury by the horny box in which it is cased. Its ligaments are, however, occasionally strained, which may be detected by heat at the coronet and tenderness, when the joint is wrenched laterally. When these symptoms are absent, we may safely conclude the disease exists elsewhere. It is not this, but the navicular disease, which is often mistaken for shoulder lameness. This disease, when it does occur often occasions ossifications of, and near, the side cartilages of the foot.

ing around the pasterns and cartilages, thus derives its name. When the first deposit is on the lower pastern, and on both sides of it, and produced by violent inflammation of the ligaments of the joints, it is recognized by a slight enlargement, or bony tumor on each side of the foot, and just above the coronet, (See *f*, Fig. 41.) Horses with short upright joints, and with small feet and high action, are oftenest, as may be supposed, the subjects of this disease, which is the consequence either of concussion or sprain of the pastern-joints. It is also more frequent in the hind foot than the fore, because, from the violent action of the hind legs in propelling the horse forward, the pasterns are more subject to legamentary injury behind than before: yet the lameness is not so great there, because the disease is confined principally to the ligaments, and the bones have not been injured by concussion; while from the position of the fore limbs, there will generally be in them injury of the bones to be added to that of the ligaments. In its early stage, and when recognized only by a bony enlargement on both sides of the pastern-joint, or in some few cases on one side only, the lameness is not very considerable, and it is not impossible to remove the disease by active blistering, or by the application of the cautery; but there is so much wear and tear in this part of the animal, that the inflammation and the disposition to the formation of bone rapidly spread. The pasterns first become connected together by bone instead of ligament, and thence results what is called an anchylosed or fixed joint. From this joint the disease proceeds to the cartilages of the foot, and to the union between the lower pastern, and the coffin and navicular bones. The motion of these parts likewise is

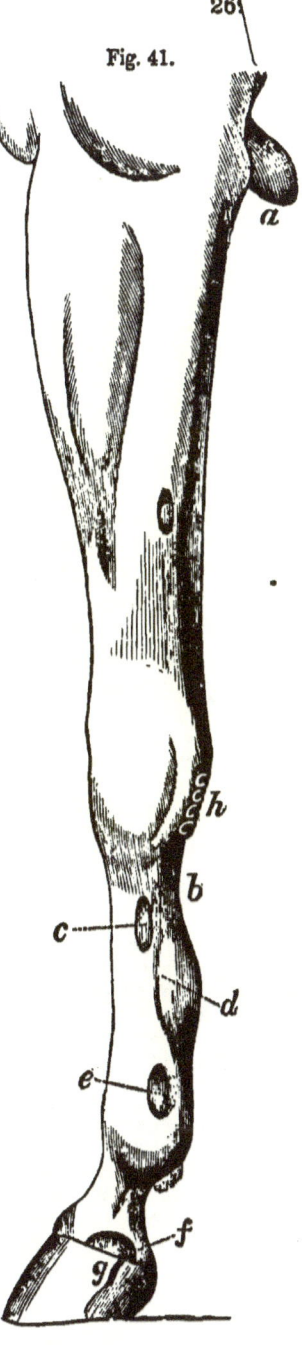

Fig. 41.

impeded or lost, and the whole of the foot becomes one mass of spongy bone. From a disposition to spread, and at first around the pastern-joint, which is situated just above the coronet, the disease has acquired the name of ringbone.*

We have introduced a bird's-eye view of some of the principal lamenesses to which the fore extremities of the horse are subject.

At *a* is a representation of the capped hock, or enlargement of the joint of the elbow.

b is the tying-in of the leg below the knee.

c is the most frequent situation of splint on the side of the shank-bone, and not producing lameness after its first formation, because it does not interfere wtih the motion of the knee, nor injure the supensory ligament.

d is the situation and appearance of the enlargement accompanying sprain of the back sinews. This, however, is an aggravated case; and the sprain may be great, and the lameness distressing, without all this swelling.

e is the place of wind-gall.

f gives the appearance of ringbone when it first appears on the side of the pastern, about the joint, and where there is naturally some prominence of bone.

g is the situation of sand-crack in the fore-leg.

h the situation of mallenders.

* *Note by Mr. Spooner.*—This disease, so termed because it constituted bony growth round the pastern-bones, is of two kinds, which are distinguished by horsemen as true and false ringbones. The former occurs at the pastern joint, and generally arises from strain of these ligaments; but the latter consists in ossification of the cartilages of the sides of the foot, which become enlarged, as well as converted into bone. This is less frequently the consequence of strains than the other disease, and it is oftener found with heavy cart-horses than with lighter horses. Indeed, with many horses there seems a predispositin to change their cartilaginous strucure into bone. The exciting cause of these false ringbones is concussion, produced by the weight of the animal and the hardness of the road or pavement. Thus, on the London stones the disease is very common; for the same reason, it is the fore limbs where the disease occurs, in nine cases out of ten. Indeed, we have found that all ringbones are more common in the fore feet than in the hind ones.

The best treatment for ringbones of either kind is, after the inflammation has been in great measure removed by cooling applications, to fire the part, or otherwise well rub in the iodide of mercury ointment, washing off the effects on the following day, and thus repeating it again and again. We have by such means succeeded in removing the lameness, diminishing the enlargement, and restoring the animal, in many cases, to a state of usefulness.

CHAPTER XIII.

THE HIND LEGS.

THE HAUNCH.

THE haunch (see O, p. Fig. 1, and Fig. 33,) is composed of three bones. The first is the ilium, principally concerned in the formation of the haunch. Its extended branches behind the flanks are prominent in every horse. When they are more than usually wide, the animal is said to be *ragged-hipped*. A branch runs up to the spine at the commencement of the sacral vertebræ (E), and here the haunch-bones are firmly united with the bones of the spine. The ischium, or hip-bone, is behind and below the ilium. Its tuberosities or prominences are seen under the tail (Fig. 1). The pubis unites with the two former below and behind.

From the loins to the setting-on of the tail a line should be carried on almost straight, or rounded only in a slight degree. Thus the haunch-bones will be most oblique, and will produce a corresponding obliquity, or slanting direction, in the thigh-bone—a direction in which, as stated when the fore legs were described, the muscles act with most advantage. This direction of the haunch is characteristic of the thorough-bred horse; and by the degree in which it is found, we judge to a considerable extent of the breeding of the animal. If the bones at D and E, (Fig. 1,) take a somewhat arched form, as they do in the cart-horse, it is evident that the haunch-bone O would be more upright. The thigh-bone P would likewise be so. The stifle Q would not be so far under the body, and the power of the horse would be considerably impaired. The oblique direction of the haunch and thigh-bones, produced by the straightness of the line of the spine, does not, as is commonly supposed, afford increased surface for the attachment of muscles, but places the muscles in a direction to act with great advantage. It is in the advantageous direction, quite as much as in the bulk of the muscle, that the strength of the horse consists.

Width of haunch is a point of great consequence, for it evidently affords more room for the attachment of muscles; and even though it should be so wide as to subject the horse to the charge of being *ragged-hipped*, and may somewhat offend the eye, it will not often be any detriment to action. If the loins are broad and the horse well ribbed home, the protuberances of the hip-bones can scarcely be too far apart. Many a ragged-hipped horse has possessed both fleetness and strength, while but few that were narrow across the haunch could boast of the latter quality.

The only portion of these bones exposed to injury or fracture are the prominences of the haunch. A fall or blow may chip off or disunite a portion of them, and, if so, there are no means of forcibly bringing the disunited parts together again, and retaining them in their natural position. The power of nature, however, will gradually unite them, but that union will be attended by deformity and lameness. A *charge*, or very strong adhesive plaster, across the haunch may be useful, as helping, in some slight degree, to support the parts, and hold them together. [See "charge" in list of medicines.]

THE THIGH.

In the lower and fore part of the hip-bones is a deep cavity or cup to receive the head of the thigh-bone. The thigh-bone is both the largest and strongest in the frame. Its lower extremity is complicated in its form. It consists of two prominences, which are received into corresponding depressions in the next bone, and a hollow in front, in which the bone of the knee or stifle plays as over a perfect pully.

The muscles of the hinder extremity are more powerful than those in any other part of the frame, and they are covered by a strong tendinous coat or membrane, intended to confine them in their places. Another, thicker and firmer, lies below, and is intended to tighten and strengthen the first. It is represented at *a* in Fig. 42, raised and turned back. For practical purposes, and therefore for the purposes of this abridgment, the names of the muscles of the hinder parts—to identify the localities of injuries and diseases—is all that is necessary, and is all therefore that will be given.

MUSCLES OF THE THIGH. 273

CUT OF THE MUSCLES, ETC., OF THE INSIDE OF THE THIGH

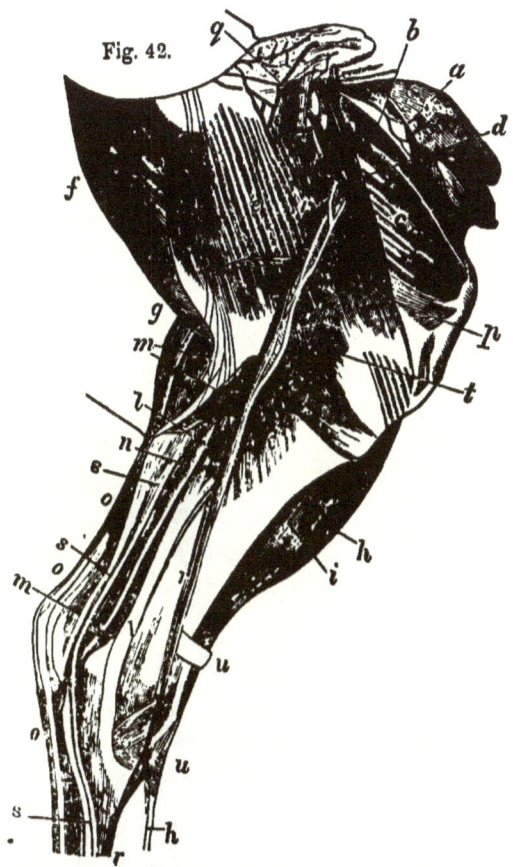

Fig. 42.

a Inner tendinous coat raised and turned back.
b The rectus, or straight muscle.
c The vastus, or great muscle.
d The sartorius, or tailor's muscle.
e The gracilis muscle.
f The pectineus muscle.
h The extensor pedis, or extendor of the foot.
i The flexor metatarsi, or bender of the leg.
k The popliteus muscle.
l The peronæus muscle.
m A portion of *j* in the next cut.
n Inside view of the flexor, or perforatus of the foot.
o The flexor perforatus, or perforating flexor of the foot.
p The course of the principal artery.
q Blood-vessels belonging to the groin.
r The large cutaneous vein.
s The principal nerves on the posterior part of the inside of the thigh
t Principal nerves of the fore part of the inside of the thigh.
u The ligamentous bands confining the tendons at the bending of the hock
18

274 MUSCLES OF THE THIGH.

We now turn to some of the muscles, &c., that are evident to the eye on the outside of the thigh.

CUT OF THE MUSCLES, ETC., OF THE OUTSIDE OF THE THIGH

Fig. 43.

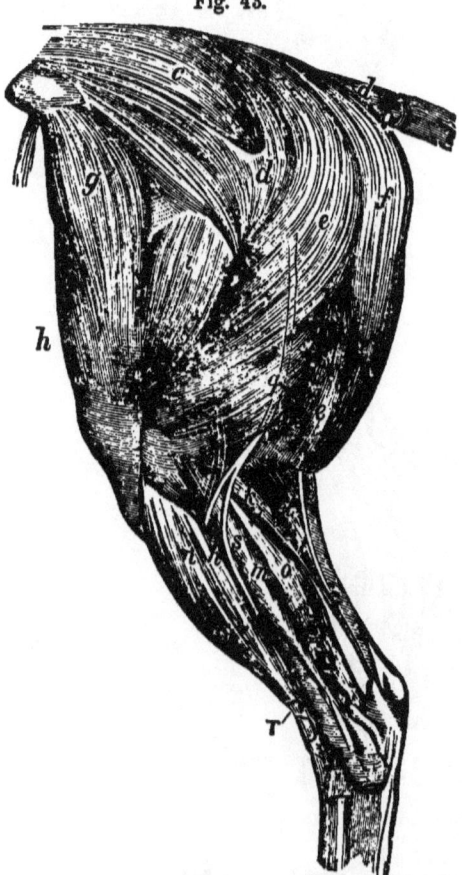

c The great glutæus muscle.
e Biceps femoris, or two-headed muscle.
f Is a continuation of the membrane seen at *a*, in the preceding cut.
i Glutæus externus.
j A powerful muscle to extend the hock.
k A slender muscle arising from the head of the fibula, its tendon uniting with that of the perforating muscle.
m The peronæus muscle.
n Extensor pedis, or extendor of the foot.
o Flexor pedis, or bender of the foot.
p Gives the course of the anterior arteries.
q Gives the course of the principal nerves.

The Os Femoris, or Thigh Bone (see P, Fig. 1), is long and cylindrical, taking an oblique direction from above, downwards, and from behind, forwards. At its upper extremities, and projecting from the body, is a thick flattened neck, terminating in a large smooth hemispherical head, adapted to a hollow, in the superior point of the haunch.

This bone is commonly called the *Round Bone*. It has, in some rare instances, been dislocated and fractured. It is much oftener sprained, but not so frequently as the groom or farrier imagines. There is nothing peculiar in the lameness to detect injury of this part, except, that the horse will drag his leg after him. Injury of the round bone will be principally discovered by heat and tenderness in the situation of the joint.

A part so deeply situated is treated with difficulty. Fomentions should at first be used to abate the inflammation, and, after that, an active blister should be applied. Strains of this joint are not always immediately relieved, and the muscles of the limb in some cases waste considerably: it therefore may be necessary to repeat the blister, while absolute rest should accompany every stage of the treatment. It may even be requisite to fire the part, —or, as a last resort, a *charge* may be placed over the joint, and the horse turned out for two or three months.*

THE STIFLE.

The stifle joint and the patella (answering to the knee-pan in the human subject) are seen at p. 45, Fig. 1.

The stifle joint is not often subject to sprain. The heat and tenderness will guide to the seat of injury. Occasionally, dislocation of the patella has occurred, and the horse drags the injured limb after him, or rests it on the fetlock; the aid of a veterinary surgeon is here requisite. The muscles of the inside of the thigh have sometimes been sprained. This may be detected by diffused heat, or heat on the inside of the thigh above the stifle.

* *Note by Mr. Spooner.*—This disease is so extremely rare that we have seldom met with an instance. The joint is so strong, so firmly secured, and so well protected, that it is almost impossible to become injured without dislocation occurring. Unless we can detect heat or tenderness about the part, we are by no means justified in supposing that the round bone is the seat of injury. For, although it used to be the case that all obscure lamenesses in the hind extremity were referred to some supposed disease in this joint, we are now well assured by *post mortem* examinations that in these obscure lamenesses the seat of disease is the hock joint.

When the neighborhood of the hip joint is injured, there is external tenderness, evinced on pressure, and the mischief is produced by external causes

Rest, fomentations, bleeding, and physic, will be the proper means of cure.*

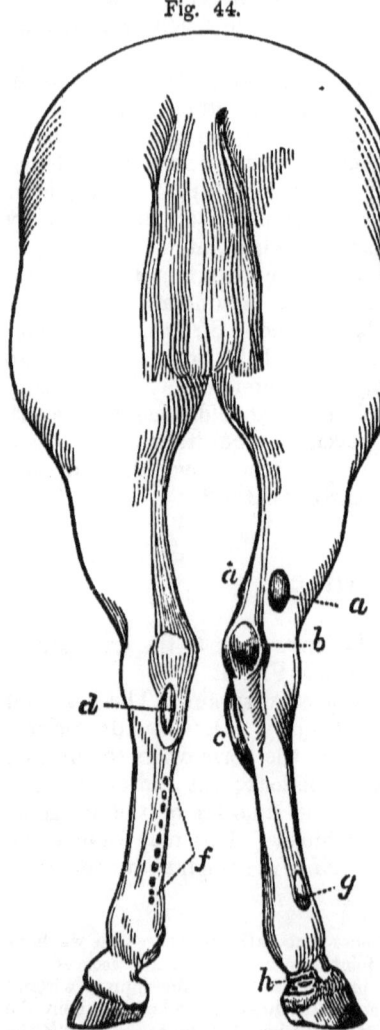

CUT OF THE HAUNCH AND HIND LEGS.
Fig. 44.

The lower bone of the thigh is double. The larger portion, in front, extending from the stifle to the hock, is called *the Tibia*. The smaller bone, or *fibula*, behind (see R, Fig. 1), reaches not more than a third of the way down. It is united to the shank-bone, like the splint-bone, by a cartilaginous substance, which is soon changed into a bony one. Of the use of these little bones we cannot speak.

The lower bone of the thigh forms an angle with the upper one, being the reverse of that which exists between the upper bone and the pelvis. In proportion to the acuteness of the angle between these two bones, and the degree consequently in which the stifle is brought under the horse, will be the direction given to the muscles favorable to their powerful action. [But, to prevent any misapprehension as to the external form of the parts which indicates what is here laid down as the proper directions of these bones, see the remarks on the Haunch in the beginning of this chapter.—Am. Ed.]

There is much difference in this in different horses,

* *Note by Mr. Spooner.*—This joint and its connections are much more frequently the seat of disease than the joint above. From its situation, it is rather exposed to blows from the horse running through a narrow gateway, and thus striking his stifle against the post. Swelling, and heat, and tenderness, will point out the injured part, in addition to which the horse will

and the construction of this part of the frame is a matter worthy of more regard than is generally paid to it.

This part of the thigh should likewise be long. In proportion to the length of the muscle is the degree of contraction of which it is capable; and also in proportion to the contraction of the muscle is the extent of motion in the limb; but it is still more necessary that this part of the thigh should have considerable muscle, in order that strength may be added to such extent or compass of motion. Much endurance would not be expected from a horse with a thin arm. A horse with thin and lanky thighs will not possess the strength which considerable exertion would sometimes require.

THOROUGH-PIN.

Mention has been made of *wind-galls* and their treatment. A similar enlargement is found above the hock, between the tendons of the flexor of the foot and the extensor of the hock. As from its situation it must necessarily project on both sides of the hock, in the form of a round swelling, it is called a *thorough-pin*, a Fig. 44. It is an indication of considerable work, but is rarely attended by lameness. The mode of treatment must resemble that for wind-galls. Although thorough-pin cannot, perhaps, be pronounced to be unsoundness, it behoves the buyer to examine well a horse that is disfigured by it, and to ascertain whether undue work may not have injured him in other respects.*

THE HOCK.

This is a most important joint, occasionally the evident, and much oftener the unsuspected seat of lameness, and the proper

step very short with the affected limb, being unable to extend it. The latter symptom will be also present when the ligaments of this joint have been strained, which, though very unfrequent, is yet occasionally the case.

The treatment in these cases consists in applying fomentations and cooling applications to the part affected, until the inflammation is subdued; which, if severe, may be further assisted by bleeding from the vein inside the thigh, and so relieving the vessels in the neighborhood of the joint. When the inflammation is subdued, a blister on the joint will be desirable in cases of strains, but will rarely be required when a blow is the cause of injury.

* *Note by Mr. Spooner.*—The usual seat of thorough-pins is below, and in advance of the point of the hock, and it consists of distension of the capsular ligament at this part, and often a giving way or rupture of its connections. It precisely resembles bog-spavin, which occurs at the lower and front part of the same joint. These affections may occur independently, but more frequently are found together. Though seldom productive of lameness, a weakness and stiffness of the part is often the consequence. The best treatment is either the application of the firing-iron, or the repeated rubbing in of the ointment of oidine and mercury. A seton over the part has been found useful.

278   THE HOCK.

formation of which is essentially connected with the value of the horse. It answers to the ancle in the human being.

Fig. 45.

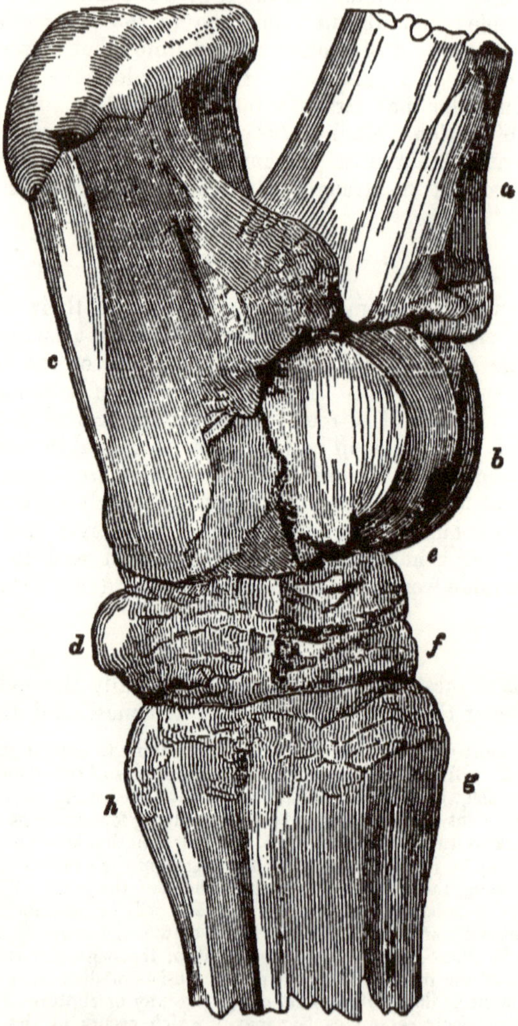

a. The fibia.
b. The astragalus.
c. Os calchis, or bone of the heel.
d. Os cuboides, or cube-formed bone.
e. The larger cuneifom, or wedge-spaped bone.
f. The two smaller wedge-shaped bones.
g. The shank-bone.
h. The splint-bones.

These bones are all connected together by very strong ligaments which prevent dislocation, but allow a slight degree of motion between them, and the surfaces which are opposed to each other are thickly covered by elastic cartilage.

Much more depends, than they who are not well accustomed to horses imagine, on the length of the os calcis or projection of the hock. In proportion to the length of this bone will two purposes be effected. The line of direction will be more advantageous, for it will be nearer to a perpendicular, and the arm of the lever to which the power is applied will be lengthened, and thus mechanical advantage will be gained to an almost incredible extent. The slightest lengthening of the point of the hock will wonderfully tell in the course of a day's work, and therefore it is that the character of the os calcis is of such immense importance.

The line of direction of the legs beneath the hocks should not be disregarded. The leg should descend perpendicularly to the fetlock. The weight and stress will thus be equally diffused, not only over the whole of the hock, but also the pasterns and the foot. Some horses have their hocks closer than usual to each other. The legs take a divergent direction outward, and the toes also are turned outward. These horses are said to be *cat-* or *cow-hocked*. They are generally supposed to possess considerable speed. But this advantage is more than counterbalanced by many evils. The increased contraction of the muscles is an expenditure of animal power; and, as already stated, the weight and the concussion being so unequally distributed by this formation of the limbs, some part must be over-strained and over-worked, and injury must ensue. On this account it is that the cow-hocked horse is more subject than others to thorough-pin and spavin; and is so disposed to curbs, that these hocks are denominated by horsemen *curby* hocks. The mischief extends even farther than this. Such a horse is peculiarly liable to wind-gall, sprain of the fetlock, cutting, and knuckling.

A slight inclination to this form in a strong powerful horse may not be very objectionable, but a horse decidedly cow-hocked should never be selected.

ENLARGEMENT OF THE HOCK.

First, there is inflammation, or *sprain of the hock-joint generally*, arising from sudden violent concussion, by some check at speed, or overweight, and attended with enlargement of the whole joint, and great tenderness and lameness. This, however, like other diffused inflammations, is not so untractable as an intense one of a more circumscribed nature, and by rest and fomentation, or, perchance, firing, the limb recovers its action, and the horse becomes fit for ordinary work.

The swelling, however, does not always subside. Enlargement, spread over the whole of the hock-joint, remains. A horse with an enlarged hock must always be regarded with suspicion. In truth, he is unsound. The parts, altered in structure, must be, to a certain degree, weakened. The animal may discharge his usual work during a long period, without return of lameness; but if one of those emergencies should occur when all his energies require to be exerted, the disorganised and weakened part will fail.

CURB.

There are often injuries of particular parts of the hock-joint. *Curb* is an affection of this kind. It is an enlargement at the back of the hock, three or four inches below its point. It is represented at *d*, Fig. 44, and is either a strain of the ring-like ligament which binds the tendons in their place, or of the sheath of the tendons; oftener, however, of the ligament than of the sheath. Any sudden action of the limb of more than usual violence may produce it, and therefore horses are found to 'throw out curbs' after a hardly-contested race, an extraordinary leap, a severe gallop over heavy ground, or a sudden check in the gallop. Young horses are particularly liable to it, and horses that are *cow-hocked* (vide Fig. 44),—whose hocks and legs resemble those of the cow, the hocks being turned inward, and the legs forming a considerable angle outwards. This is intelligible enough; for in hocks so formed, the annular ligament must be continually on the stretch, in order to confine the tendon.

Curbs are generally accompanied by considerable lameness at their first appearance, but the swelling is not always great. They are best detected by observing the leg sideway.

The first object in attempting the cure is to abate inflammation, and this will be most readily accomplished by cold evaporating lotions frequently applied to the part. Equal portions of spirit of wine, water, and vinegar, will afford an excellent application. It will be almost impossible to keep a bandage on. If the heat and lameness are considerable, it will be prudent to give a dose of physic, and to bleed from the subcutaneous vein, whose course is represented at *r*, Fig. 42; and whether the injury is of the annular ligament, or the sheath of the tendon, more active means will be necessary to perfect the cure. Either a liquid blister should be rubbed on the part, consisting of a vinous or turpentine tincture of cantharides, and this daily applied until some considerable swelling takes place; or, what is the prefer able plan, the hair should be cut off, and the part blistered as soon as the heat has been subdued. The blister should be repeated until the swelling has disappeared, and the horse goes sound. In severe cases it may be necessary to fire; but a fair trial, however, should be given to milder measures. If the iron is used, it should be applied in straight lines.

There are few lamenesses in which the absolute and long-continued rest is more requisite. It leaves the parts materially weakened, and, if the horse is soon put to work again, the lameness will frequently return. No horse that has had curbs, should be put even to ordinary work in less than a month after the apparent cure; and, even then, he should very gradually resume his former habits.

A horse with a curb is manifestly unsound. A horse with the vestige of curb, should be regarded with much suspicion, or generally condemned as unsound.

Curb is also an hereditary complaint, and therefore a horse that has once suffered from it should always be regarded with suspicion, especially if either of the parents has exhibited it.*

BOG SPAVIN.

The hock is plentifully supplied with reservoirs of mucus, to lubricate (make slippery) the different portions of this compli-

* *Note by Mr. Spooner.*—The seat of this injury is usually the flexor tendon of the leg, as it passes through a sheath at the back of the hock. It therefore resembles a strain of the back sinews, as they are commonly called, although the injury is seldom so severe or so difficult to be cured. There are many degrees as to the amount and extent of the injury and the corresponding lameness. It is by far the best plan to take a horse out of work immediately on his showing lameness, as by that means the cure can be more expeditiously and perfectly effected; and there is much less enlargement left afterwards than when a horse is patched up by the application of stimulants, and worked on, thereby renewing the strain again and again. After the inflammation has been quite subdued by the means pointed out in the text, we have found that the firing-iron effects the most perfect cure, and secures the animal, in nine cases out of ten, from a return of the lameness. The marks of the iron, in cases of curbs, need not be great, and never operate to the animal's disadvantage. We have always found that a horse which has been fired for a curb, will realize as much, or more, than another which has thrown out a curb, but has not been fired for it We have also frequently found that a horse fired for a curb has remained sound, while in the course of a twelvemonth he has thrown out a curb on the other hock, even though he had been fired with a view of preventing it, showing that, though firing may act as a cure, it does not act as a preventative.

In the examination of horses for soundness, we have not hesitated to pass a horse with a curb, requiring, however, a special warranty that should the curb cause lameness within a reasonable time, the seller shall be responsible.

cated joint. Some of these are found on the inside of the joint, which could not be represented in Fig. 45. From over exertion of the joint, they become inflamed, and considerably enlarged. They are wind-galls of the hock. The subcutaneous vein passes over the inside of the hock, and over some of these enlarged mucous reservoirs, and is compressed between them and the external integument—the course of the blood is partially arrested, and a portion of the vein below the impediment, and between it and the next valve, is distended, and causes the soft tumor on the inside of the hock, called *Bog* or *Blood spavin*.

This is a very serious disease, attended with no great, but often permanent lameness, and too apt to return when the enlargement has subsided under medical treatment. It must be considered as decided unsoundness. In a horse for slow draught, it is scarcely worth while even to attack it. And in one destined to more rapid action, the probability of a relapse should not be forgotten, when the chances of success and the expenses of treatment are calculated.

The cause of the disease—the enlarged mucous sack or capsule—lies deep, and is with difficulty operated upon. Uniform pressure would sometimes cause the absorption of the fluid contained in cysts or bags like these, but in a joint of such extensive motion as the hock, it is difficult, or almost impossible, to confine the pressure on the precise spot at which it is required. Could it be made to bear on the enlarged bag, it would likewise press on the vein, and to a greater degree hinder the passage of the blood, and increase the swelling below the obstruction. The old and absurd method of passing a ligature above and below the enlarged portion of the vein, and then dissecting out the tumor, is not, in the advanced stage of veterinary science, practised by any surgeon who regards his reputation. The only method of relief which holds out any promise even of temporary success, is exciting considerable inflammation on the skin, and thus rousing the deeper-seated absorbents to carry away the fluid effused in the enlarged bag. For this purpose, blisters or firing may be tried : but in the majority of cases, the disease will bid defiance to all appliances, or will return and baffle our hopes when we had seemed to be accomplishing our object.

A horse with bog spavin will do for ordinary work. He may draw in a cart, or trot fairly in a lighter carriage, with little detriment to his utility; but he will never do for hard or rapid work.*

---

* *Note by Mr. Spooner.*—Our observations under the head of thoroughpins equally apply here; only that bog spavins are generally more serious, the capsular ligament having a larger amount of surface at the lower part of the hock than at the upper It must not be forgotten that it is the joint itself that is affected, and not the parts exterior to it.

BONE SPAVIN.

A still more formidable disease ranks under the name of *Spavin*, and is an affection of the bones of the hock-joint. It has been stated that the bones of the leg, the shank-bone, *g*, Fig. 45, and the two small splint-bones behind, *h*, support the lower layer of the bones of the hock. The cube-bone, *d*, rests principally on the shank-bone, and in a slight degree on the outer splint-bone. The middle wedge-bone, *f*, rests entirely upon the shank-bone, and the smaller wedge-bone presses (not seen in the cut) in a very slight degree on the shank-bone, but principally, or almost entirely, on the inner splint-bone. Then the splint-bones sustain a very unequal degree of concussion and weight. Not only is the inner one placed more under the body, and nearer the centre of gravity, but it has almost the whole of the weight and concussion communicated to the smaller cuneiform bone carried on it. It is not therefore to be wondered at that the inner splint-bone, or its ligaments, or the substance which connects it with the shank-bone should receive injury, particularly in young horses, before the limbs have become properly knit. The smith frequently greatly increases this tendency, by raising the outer heel higher than the inner one, to prevent cutting (interfering).

The weight and concussion being thrown principally on the inner splint-bone, produce inflammation of the cartilaginous substance that unites it to the shank-bone. In consequence of it, the cartilage is absorbed, and bone deposited; the union between the splint-bone and the shank becomes bony, instead of cartilaginous; the degree of elastic action between them is destroyed, and there is formed a splint of the hind leg. As in the fore leg, the disposition to form bony matter having commenced, and the cause which produced it continuing to act, bone continues to be deposited, and it generally appears in the form of a tumor, where the head of the splint-bone is united with the shank, and in front of that union. It is seen at *c*, Fig. 44. This is called BONE SPAVIN. Inflammation of the ligaments of any of the small bones of the hock, proceeding to bony tumor, would equally class under the name of spavin; but, commonly, the disease commences on the precise spot that has been described.

While spavin is forming, there is always lameness, and that frequently to a very great degree: but when the membrane of the bone has accommodated itself to the tumor that extended it, the lameness subsides or disappears, or depends upon the degree in which the bony deposit interferes with the motion of the joint. It is well known to horsemen, that many a hunter, with spavin that would cause his rejection by a veterinary surgeon, stands his work without lameness. Horses with exceedingly large spavins, are often seen that are only slightly lame, or that merely have a stiffness in their gait at first starting, but which gradually goes off after a little motion; while others, with the bony tumor comparatively small, have the lameness so great as to destroy the usefulness of the horse. There is always this peculiarity in the lameness of spavin, that it abates, and sometimes disappears, on exercise; and, therefore, a horse, with regard to which there is any suspicion of this affection, should be examined when first in the morning it is taken from the stable.

If the spavin continues to increase, the bony deposit first spreads over the lower wedge-bones, then the larger wedge-bones, and even to the cuboid bones on the other side, [see Fig. 45.] Up to this point, it may not produce much lameness, because there is very little motion in these parts of the joint. But when it extends to the union of the *tibia* and *astragalus*, in which is the chief motion of the hock, the lameness becomes severe, and the horse becomes nearly or quite useless.

Spavined horses are generally capable of slow work and often improve on the farm. For fast work, and for work that must be regularly performed, spavined horses are not well calculated; for this lameness behind produces great difficulty in rising, and the consciousness that he will not be able to rise without painful effort occasionally prevents the horse from lying down at all; and the animal that cannot rest well cannot long travel far or fast.

The treatment of spavin is simple enough, but far from being always effectual. The owner of the horse will neither consult his own interest, nor the dictates of humanity, if he suffers the chisel and mallet, or the gimlet, or the pointed iron, or arsenic, to be used; yet measures of considerable severity must be resorted to. Repeated blisters will usually cause either the absorption of the bony deposit, or the abatement or removal of the inflammation of the ligaments, or, as a last resource, the heated iron may be applied.*

---

* *Note by Mr. Spooner.*—Bone spavin, as stated in the text, is one of the most serious by which the horse is affected. In the majority of cases it must be confessed that treatment does not succeed in removing lameness When the disease is a simple ossification, on or below the small bones of the hock, the lameness may generally be removed; but it is more frequently the case that the disease extends itself between the small bones of the hock, causing ulceration of the synovial membrane and cartilage forming the articulating surfaces, and even extending to the substance of

The account of the diseases of the hock is not yet completed. It is well known that the horse is frequently subject to lameness behind, when no ostensible cause for it can be found, and there is no external heat or enlargement to indicate the seat of it. It is often pronounced an affection of the stifle, or of the round bone; or, if there is a stiffness about the hock, the commencement of spavin. Yet in the latter case, the joint may be of its natural size and neither heat nor tenderness perceptible; and months and years elapse without any appearance of spavin. Repeated dissections have shown that in these cases of incurable lameness behind, where there are no indications, during life, to point out the seat of it, it is occasioned by injuries to the delicate and sensible membranes with which the upper and lower wedge-bones are invested. Ulceration of the synovial membrane between the upper and lower wedge-shaped bones sometimes takes place, and the bones themselves become carious or ulcerated.

CAPPED HOCK.

The point of the hock is sometimes swelled. A soft, fluctuating tumor appears on it. This is an enlargement of one of the mucous bags of which mention has been made, and that surrounds the insertion of the tendons into the point of the hock.

It is seldom accompanied by lameness, and yet it is a some-

the bones themselves. When such is the nature of the case, treatment will, to a great extent, prove unavailing. The amount of enlargement that may exist, therefore, offers no criterion as to the greater or lesser seriousness of the case, for a large exostosis may occur without this ulceration, which latter may exist in some instances with very little enlargement, and, in others, none whatever. Indeed, as stated in the text, in the greater number of cases of lameness of the hind extremities, where no cause is externally perceptible, the seat of injury is the hock. In the majority of cases, the synovial surfaces of the small bones of the hock are affected, in others the larger articulation between the tibia and astragalus is the seat of mischief, the synovial membrane and cartilage being similarly affected.

With regard to the treatment of these hock cases, as we before observed, the result is extremely uncertain and unsatisfactory. If any external inflammation is present, we cannot do better than commence by abstracting blood from the vein above, and use cooling applications to the hock; after which we may resort either to the blister, the seton, or the iron. The first is the milder remedy, and if resorted to, should be repeated several times. With regard to the seton, and the iron, we have both succeeded and failed with each. It may be urged in favor of the seton that the marks and blemishes of the iron are avoided.

In otherwise incurable lameness of the hock, the operation of neurotomy has been adopted with success, excising the nerve on the inside only a few inches above the hock. The merit of this operation is principally due to Professor Spooner, of the Royal Veterinary College of London, who was the first to perform and introduce it.

what serious business, for it is usually produced by blows and mostly by the injuries which the horse inflicts upon himself in the act of kicking : therefore it is that a horse with a capped hock is very properly regarded with a suspicious eye. The whole of the hock should be carefully examined, in order to discover whether there are other marks of violence, and the previous history of the animal should be carefully inquired into. Does he kick in harness or in the stall, or has he been lying on a thin bed, or on no bed at all; and thus may the hock have been bruised, and the swelling produced?

It is exceedingly difficult to apply a bandage over a capped hock; and puncturing the tumor, or passing a seton through it, would be a most injudicious practice. Blisters, or iodine, repeated as often as may be necessary, are the best means to be employed. Occasionally the tumor will spontaneously disappear; but at other times it will attain a large size, or assume a callous structure, that will bid defiance to all the means that can be employed.*

MALLENDERS AND SALLENDERS.

On the inside of the hock, or a little below it, as well as at the oend of the knee (*h*, Fig. 41), there is occasionally a surfy eruption, called *mallenders* in the fore-leg, and *sallenders* in the hind-leg. They seldom produce lameness; but if no means are taken to get rid of them, a discharge proceeds from them which it is afterwards difficult to stop. They usually indicate bad stable management.

A diuretic ball should be occasionally given, and an ointment of sugar-of-lead and tar, with treble the quantity of lard, rubbed over the part. Should this fail, a weak mercurial ointment may be used. Iodine has here also been useful.

---

* *Note by Mr. Spooner.*—The actual seat of this injury is between the skin and the tendons inserted in, and passing over, the point of the hock. The skin is very loose at this part, and, to facilitate the motions of the hock, there is much cellular membrane. A capped hock is a serous tumor or abscess; that is, the parts are inflamed and irritated from blows, and serum is thrown out between the skin and the cellular membrane, and the tumor is circumscribed. The vice of kicking against the stall-post is, in nearly every case, the cause of this disease. We should endeavor to remove the swelling by cooling measures, followed by a blister, or the application of iodine ointment; but if these means fail, and the tumor is large, we may pass a seton through it with impunity, for there is no joint or tendinous sheath opened The seton should be kept in until the discharge becomes slightly purulent, or otherwise the tumor will soon fill again with serum.

SWELLED LEGS

The fore-legs, but oftener the hind ones, and especially in coarse horses, are sometimes subject to considerable enlargement. Occasionally, when the horse does not seem to labor under any other disease, and sometimes from an apparent shifting of disease from other parts, the hind-legs suddenly swell to an enormous degree from the hock, and almost from the stifle to the fetlock, attended by a greater or less degree of heat, and tenderness of the skin, and sometimes excessive and peculiar lameness. The pulse likewise becomes quick and hard, and the horse evidently labors under considerable fever. It is acute inflammation of the cellular substance of the legs, and that most sudden in its attack, and most violent in its degree, and therefore attended by the effusion of a considerable quantity of fluid into the cellular membrane. It occurs in young horses, and in those which are over-fed and little exercised. Fomentations, diuretics, or purgatives, or, if there is much fever, a moderate bleeding will often relieve the distention almost as suddenly as it appeared.

Sometimes the legs are swelled without lameness. At other times there is a great degree of stiffness and pain. Occasionally they become tremendously swollen in a single night, and exhibit great tenderness. Many horses, if suffered to remain several days without exercise, will have swelled legs. If the case is neglected, abscesses appear in various parts of the legs; the heels are attacked by grease, and, if proper measures are not adopted, the horse has an enlarged leg for life.

The cure, when the case has not been too long neglected, is sufficiently plain. Physic or diuretics, or both, must be had recurse to. Mild cases will generally yield to their influence; but, if the animal has been neglected, the treatment must be decisive. If the horse is in high condition, these should be preceded or accompanied by bleeding; but if there are any symptoms of debility, bleeding would only increase the want of tone in the vessels.

Horses taken from grass and brought into close stables very speedily have swelled legs, because the difference of food and increase of nutriment rapidly increase the quantity of the circulating fluid, while the want of exercise takes away the means by which it might be got rid of. The remedy here is sufficiently plain. Swelled legs, however, may proceed from general debility. They may be the consequences of starvation, or disease that has considerably weakened the animal; and these parts, being farthest from the centre of circulation, are the first to show the loss of power by the accumulation of fluid in them. Here the means of cure would be to increase the general strength, with which the extremities would sympathize. Mild diuretics and tonics would therefore be evidently indicated.

Horses in the spring and fall are subject to swelled legs. The powers of the constitution are principally employed in providing a new coat for the animal, and the extremities have not their share of vital influence. Mingled cordials and diuretics are indicated here—the diuretic to lessen the quantity of the circulating fluid, and the cordial to invigorate the frame.

Swelled legs are often teasing in horses that are in tolerable or good health : but where the work is somewhat irregular, the cure consists in giving more equal exercise, walking the horse out daily when the usual work is not required, and using plenty of friction in the form of hand-rubbing. Bandages have a greater and more durable effect, for nothing tends more to support the capillary vessels, and rouse the action of the absorbents, than moderate pressure. Hay-bands will form a good bandage for the agricultural horse, and their effect will probably be increased by previously dipping them in water.

The physic, or the diuretic ball may occasionally be used, but very sparingly : and only when they are absolutely required. In the hands of the owner of the horse, or the veterinary surgeon, they may be employed with benefit; but in those of the carter or the groom they will do far more harm than good. The frequent and undue stimulus of the urinary organs by the diuretic ball, will be too often followed by speedy and incurable debility. If the swelling bids defiance to exercise, and friction, and bandage, the aid of the diuretic may be resorted to, but never until these have failed, unless there is an evident tendency to humor or grease.

GREASE.*

Swelled legs, although distinct from grease, is a disease that is apt to degenerate into it. Grease is a specific inflammation of the skin of the heels, sometimes of the fore-feet, but oftener of the hinder ones. It is not a contagious disease, as some have asserted, although when it once appears in a stable it frequently attacks almost every horse in it. Bad stable management is the true cause of it.

There is a peculiarity about the skin of the heel of the horse. In its healthy state there is a secretion of greasy matter from it, in order to prevent excoriation and chapping, and the skin is soft and pliable. Too often, however, from bad management, the secretion of this greasy matter is stopped, and the skin of the heel becomes red, and dry, and scurfy. The joint still continuing to be

---

* A variety of this is termed "SCRATCHES" in the United States.—AM. ED

extended and flexed, cracks of the skin begin to appear, and these, if neglected, rapidly extend, and the heel becomes a mass of soreness, ulceration, and fungus.

The distance of the heel from the centre of circulation, and the exposure and changes to which the part is subjected, render it a matter of little wonder that it is frequently attacked by inflammation.

Grease is a local complaint. It is produced principally by causes that act locally, and it is most successfully treated by local applications. Diuretics and purgatives may be useful in abating inflammation; but the grand object is to get rid of the inflammatory action which exists in the skin of the heel, and to heal the wounds, and remedy the mischief which it has occasioned.

The first appeaaance of grease is usually a dry and scurfy state of the skin of the heel, with redness, heat, and itchiness. The heel should be well but gently washed with soap and water, and as much of the scurf detached as is easily removable. An ointment, composed of one part plum. diacet. and seven of adeps suillæ will usually supple, and cool, and heal the part.

When cracks appear, the mode of treatment will depend on their extent and depth. If they are but slight, a lotion, composed plumbi sulph. ℨij. et aluminis ℨiiij., dissolved in a pint of water, will often speedily dry them up, and close them. There is sometimes considerable caprice in the application of this lotion, which has induced Professor Morton to have recourse to alumen et terebinthinus vulgaris one part each, and adeps suillæ three parts, made into an ointment.

If the cracks are deep, with an ichorous discharge and considerable lameness, it will be necessary to poultice the heel. A poultice of linseed meal will be generally effective, unless the discharge is thin and offensive, when an ounce of finely-powdered charcoal should be mixed with the linseed meal; or a poultice of carrots, boiled soft and mashed. The efficacy of a carrot-poultice is seldom sufficiently appreciated in cases like this.

When the inflammation and pain have evidently subsided, and the sores discharge good matter, the calamine ointment may be applied with advantage; and the cure will generally be quickened if a very diluted vitriolic or alum solution is applied.

The best medicine will consist of mild aloetic balls; gentle diuretics being given towards the close of the treatment.

After the chaps or cracks have healed, the legs will sometimes continue gorged and swelled. A flannel bandage, evenly applied over the whole of the swelled part, will be very serviceable; or, should the season admit of it, a run at grass, particularly spring grass, should be allowed. A blister is inadmissible, from the dan ger of bringing back the inflammation of the skin, and the discharge from it; but the actual cautery, special care being taken not to penetrate the skin, may occasionally be resorted to.

In some cases the cracks are not confined to the centre of the heels, but spread over them, and extend on the fetlock, and even up the leg, while the legs are exceedingly swelled, and there is a watery discharge from the cracks, and an apparent oozing through the skin at other places. The legs are exceedingly tender and sometimes hot, and there is an appearance which the farrier thinks very decisive as to the state of the disease, and which the better informed man should not overlook—*the heels smoke*—the skin is so hot, that the watery fluid partly evaporates as it runs from the cracks or oozes through the skin.

There will be great danger in suddenly stopping this discharge. Inflammation of a more important part has rapidly succeeded to the injudicious attempt. The local application should be directed to the abatement of the inflammation. The poultices just referred to should be diligently used night and day, and especially the carrot-poultice; and when the heat, and tenderness, and stiffness of motion have diminished, astringent lotions may be applied—either the alum lotion, or a strong decoction of oak-bark, changed, or used alternately, but not mixed. The cracks should likewise be dressed with the ointment above-mentioned; and, the moment the horse can bear it, a flannel bandage should be put on, reaching from the coronet to three or four inches above the swelling.

The medicine should be confined to mild diuretics, mixed with one-third part of cordial mash; or, if the horse is gross, and the inflammation runs high, a dose of physic may be given. If the horse is strong, and full of flesh, physic should always precede and sometimes supercede the diuretics. In cases of much debility, diuretics, with aromatics or tonics, will be preferable.

The feeding should likewise vary with the case, but with these rules, which admit of no exception, that green meat should be given, and more especially carrots, when they are not too expensive, and mashes, if the horse will eat them, and never the full allowance of corn.

Walking exercise should be resorted to as soon as the horse is able to bear it, and this by degrees may be increased to a gentle trot.

From bad stable management at first, and neglect during the disease, a yet worse kind of grease occasionally appears. The ulceration extends over the skin of the heal and the fetlock, and a fungus springs from the surface of both, highly sensible, bleeding at the slightest touch, and interspersed with scabs. By degrees, portions of the fungus begin to be covered with a horny substance protruding in the form of knobs, and collected together in bunches.

These are known by the name of *grapes*. A fœtid and very peculiar exudation proceeds from nearly the whole of the unnatural substance. The horse evidently suffers much, and is gradually worn down by the discharge. The assistance of a veterinary surgeon is here indispensable.

Some horses are more subject to grease than others, particularly draft horses, both heavy and light, but especially the former, and if they have no degree of blood in them. It was the experience of this which partly contributed to the gradual change of coach and other draught horses to those of a lighter breed. In the great majority of cases, grease arises from mismanagement and neglect.

Want of exercise, high feeding and want of exercise, want of cleanliness, and dirty stables are among the causes of it. The absurd practice of washing the feet and legs of horses when they come from their work, and either carelessly sponging them down afterwards, or leaving them to dry as they may, is, however, the most common origin of grease.

When the horse is warmed by his work, and the heels share in the warmth, the momentary cold of washing may not be injurious, if the animal is immediately rubbed dry; yet even this would be better avoided: but to wash out the heels, and then leave them partially dry or perfectly wet, and suffering from the extreme cold that is produced by evaporation from a moist and wet surface, is the most absurd, dangerous, and injurious practice that can be imagined. It is worse when the post-horse or the plough-horse is plunged up to his belly in the river or pond, immediately after his work. The owner is little aware how many cases of inflammation of the lungs, and bowels, and feet, and heels follow. After they have been suffered to stand for twenty minutes in the stable, during which time the horse-keeper or the carter may be employed in taking care of the harness, or carriage, or beginning to dress the horse, the greater part of the dirt which had collected about the heels may be got rid of with a dry brush; and the rest will disappear a quarter of an hour afterwards under the operation of a second brushing. The trouble will not be great, and the heels will not be chilled and subject to inflammation.

Their has been some dispute as to the propriety of cutting the hair from the heels. Custom has very properly retained the hair on our farm-horses. Nature would not have given it, had it not been useful. It guards the heel from being injured by the inequalities of the ploughed field; it prevents the dirt in which the heels are constantly enveloped, from reaching and caking on, and irritating the skin; it hinders the usual moisture which is mixed with the clay and mould from reaching the skin, and it preserves an equal temperature in the parts. If the hair is suffered to remain on the heels of the farm-horses, there is greater necessity for brushing and hand-rubbing the heels, and never washing them.

Fashion and utility have removed the hair from the heels of our hackney and carriage horses. When the horse is carefully tended after his work is over, and his legs quickly and completely dried, the less hair he has about them the better, for then both the skin and the hair can be made perfectly dry before evaporation begins, or proceeds so far as to deprive the legs of their heat.*

Note by Mr. Spooner.—In the treatment of this disease and those analagous cases of humors or swellings of the legs by which it is preceded, blood-letting will be generally desirable, with a dose of physic; for it is while the system is under the cooling effects of these depletive agents that local measures are attended with the greatest benefit. Poultices either of linseed meal or carrots, may be applied, and astringent lotions added to them so as to remove the irritation, and check the discharge at the same time.

CHAPTER XIV.

THE FOOT.

Fig. 46.

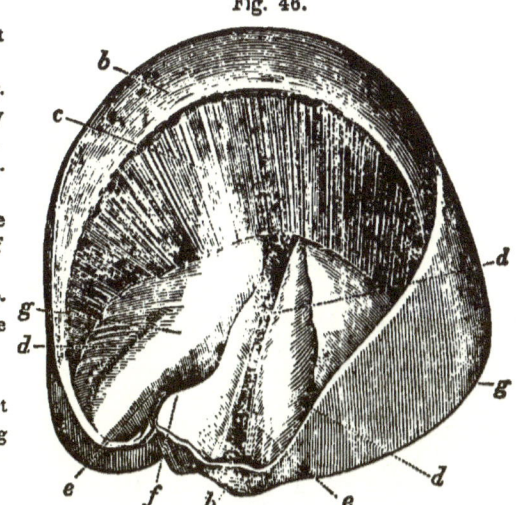

a The external crust seen at the quarter.
b The coronary ring.
c The little horny plates lining the crust.
d The same continued over the bars.
e e The two concave surfaces of the inside of the horny frog.
f That which externally is the cleft of the frog.
g The bars.
h The rounded part of the heels, belonging to the frog.

This cut exhibits, in as satisfactory a manner, the mechanism and structure of the base of the foot.

Fig. 47.

a a The frog.
b The sole.
c c The bars.
d d The crust.

The foot is composed of the horny box that covers the extremities of the horse, and the contents of that box. The hoof or box is composed of the crust or wall, the coronary ring and band, the bars, the horny laminæ, the sole, and the horny frog.

THE CRUST OR WALL OF THE HOOF.

The crust, or *wall*, is that portion which is seen when the foot is placed on the ground, and reaches from the termination of the hair to the ground. It is deepest in front, where it is called the toe, measuring there about three inches and a half in depth, (see Fig 48,) shallower at the sides, which are denominated the quarters, and of least extent behind, where it is seldom more than an inch and a half in height, and is termed the heel. The crust in the healthy foot presents a flat and narrow surface to the ground, ascending obliquely backwards, and possessing different degrees of obliquity in different horses. In a sound hoof the proper degree of obliquity is calculated at forty-five degrees, or the fourth part of a semicircle, at the front of the foot. When the obliquity is greater than this, it indicates undue flatness of the sole, and the crust is said to have "fallen in." If the obliquity is very much increased, the sole projects, and is said too be pumiced or convex.

If the foot is more upright, or forms a greater angle than forty-five degrees, it indicates much contraction, and a sole too concave; and this difference of obliquity is often so great, that the convexity or concavity of the sole may be affirmed without the trouble of raising the foot for the purpose of examination.

It is of some importance to observe where the depth of the crust appears rapidly or slowly to decrease from the front to the heel. If the decrease is little, and even at the heel the crust is high and deep, this indicates a foot liable to contraction, sand-crack, thrush, and inflammation. The pasterns are upright, the paces of that horse are not pleasant. On the other hand, if the crust rapidly diminishes in depth and the heels are low, this is accompanied by too great slanting of the pastern, and disposition to sprain in the back sinew. The foot, generally, is liable to be weak and flat, and bruised, and there is more tendency to the frequent, but obscure lameness, of which there will presently be occasion to treat—the navicular-joint disease.

The crust is composed of numerous horny fibres, connected together by an elastic membranous substance, and extending from the coronet to the base of the hoof. It differs materially in its texture, its elasticity, its growth, and its occasional brittleness according to the state in which it is kept, and the circumstances that are acting upon it.

The outside of the hoof should be smooth and level. Protuberances or rings round the crust indicate that the horse has had inflammation in the feet, and that to such a degree, as to produce an unequal growth of horn, and probably to leave some injurious consequences in the internal part of the foot. If there is a depression or hollow in front of the foot, it betrays a sinking of the coffin-bone, and a flat or pumiced sole. If there is a hollow at the quarters, it is the worse system of bad contraction.

The thickness of the crust, in the front of the foot, is rather more than half an inch; it becomes gradually thinner towards the quarters and heels, but this often varies to a considerable extent. In some hoofs, it is not more than half the above thickness. If however there is not, in the majority of horses, more than half an inch for nail-hold at the toe, and not so much at the quarters, it will not appear surprising that these horses are occasionally wounded in shoeing, and especially as some of them are very unmanageable while undergoing this process.

While the crust becomes thinner towards both quarters, it is more so at the inner quarter than at the outer, because more weight is thrown upon it than upon the outer. It is more under the horse. It is under the inner splint-bone, on which so much more of the weight rests than on the outer; and, being thinner, it is able to expand more. Its elasticity is called more into play, and concussion and injury are avoided. When the expansion of the quarters is prevented by their being nailed to an unbending shoe, the inner quarter suffers most. Corns are oftenest found there; contraction begins there; sand-crack is seated there. Nature meant that this should be the most yielding part, in order to obviate concussion, because on it the weight is principally thrown, and therefore when its power of yielding is taken away it must be the first to suffer.

A careful observer will likewise perceive that the inner quarter is higher than the outer. While it is thin to yield to the shock, its increased surface gives it sufficient strength.

On account of its thinness, and the additional weight which it bears, the inner heel wear saway quicker than the outer; a circumstance that should never be forgotten by the smith. His object is to give a plane and level bearing to the whole of the crust. To accomplish this, it will be often scarcely necessary to remove any thing from the inner heel, for this has already been done by the wear of the foot. If he forgets this, as he too often seems to do, and cuts away with his knife or his buttress an equal portion all round, he leaves the inner or weaker quarter lower than the outer; he throws an uneven bearing upon it; and produces corns and sand-cracks and splints, which a little care and common sense might have avoided.

THE CORONET, OR CORONARY RING.

The crust does not vary much in thickness until near the top where it rapidly gets thin. It is in a manner scooped or hollowed out. It likewise changes its color and consistence, and seems almost like a continuation of the skin, but is easily separated from it by muceration, (steeping or soaking in a fluid,) or by disease. The upper and thin part is called the coronary ring, *x* Fig. 37. It extends round the upper portion of the hoofs, and receives, within it, or covers, a thickened or bulbous prolongation of the skin, called the *coronary ligament* (see *b*, in the accompanying cut). This prolongation of the skin—it is nothing more—is thickly supplied with blood-vessels. It is almost a mesh of blood-vessels connected together by fibrous texture, and many of them are employed in secreting or forming the crust or wall of the foot. Hence it is, that in sand-crack, quitor, and other diseases in which strips of the crust are destroyed, it is so long in being renewed, or *growing down*. It must proceed from the coronary ligament, and so gradually creep down the foot with the natural growth or lengthening of the horn, of which, as in the human nail, a supply is slowly given to answer to the wear and tear of the part.

Fig. 48.

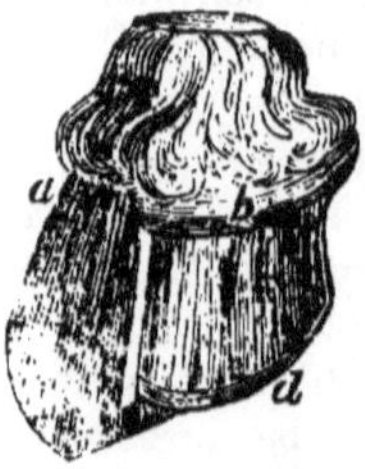

THE BARS.

At the back part of the foot the wall of the hoof, instead of continuing round and forming a circle, is suddenly bent in as in Fig. 47, where *d* represents the base of the crust, and *e* its inflection or bending at the heel. The bars are, in fact, a continuation of the crust, forming an acute angle, and meeting at a point at the toe of the frog—see *a*, *b*, and *c*, in Fig. 47, and the inside of the bars, like the inside of the crust, (see Fig. 46.) presents a continuance of the horny leaves, showing that it is a part of the same substance, and helping to discharge the same office.

It needs only the slightest consideration of the cut, or of the natural hoof, to show the importance of the bars. The arch which these form on either side, between the frog and the quarters, is admirably contrived both to admit of, and to limit to its proper extent, the expansion of the foot. When the foot is placed on the ground, and the weight of the animal is thrown on the leaves of the inside of the bars, these arches will shorten and widen, in order to admit of the expansion of the quarters—the bow returning to its natural curve, and powerfully assisting the foot in regaining its usual form. It can also be conceived that these bars must form a powerful protection against the contraction, or *wiring in*, of the quarters. A moment's inspection (*g*, Fig. 46) will show that, if the bars are taken away, there will be nothing to resist the contraction or falling in of the quarters, when the foot is exposed to any disease, or bad management, that would induce it to contract. One moment's observation of them will also render evident the security which they afford to the frog (*f*), and the effectual protection which they give to the lateral portions of the foot.

Then appears the necessity of passing lightly over them, and leaving prominent, when the foot is pared for shoeing, that which so many smiths cut perfectly away. They imagine that it gives a more open appearance to the foot of the horse. Horses shod for the purpose of sale, have usually the bars removed with this view; and the smiths in the neighborhood of the metropolis and large towns, shoeing for dealers, too often habitually pursue, with regard to all their customers, the injurious practice of removing the bars. The horny frog, deprived of its guard, will speedily contract, and become elevated and thrushy; and the whole of the heel, having lost the power of reaction which the curve between the bar *c* and the crust *d* gave it (vide Fig. 47.), will speedily fall in.

THE HORNY LAMINÆ, OR LEAVES.

The inside of the crust is covered by thin horny leaves (*c*, Fig 46), extending all round it, and reaching from the coronary ring to the toe. They are about five hundred in number, broadest at their base, and terminating in the most delicate expansion of horn. They not a little resemble the inner surface of a mushroom. In front, they run in a direction from the coronet to the toe, and towards the quarters they are more slanting from behind forwards They correspond, as will be presently shown, with similar cartilaginous and fleshy leaves on the surface of the coffin-bone, and form a beautiful elastic body, by which the whole weight of the horse is supported.

THE SOLE

Is under, and occupies the greater portion of the concave and elastic surface of the foot (see *b*, Fig. 47), extending from the crust to the bars and frog. It is not so thick as the crust, because, notwithstanding its situation, it does not support so much weight as the crust; and because it was intended to expand, in order to prevent concussion, when, by the descent of the bone of the foot, the weight was thrown upon it. It is not so brittle as the crust, and it is more elastic than it. It is thickest at the toe (see *l*, Fig 37), because the first and principal stress is thrown on that part. The coffin-bone, *f*, is driven forward and downward in that direction. It is likewise thicker where it unites with the crust than it is towards the centre, for a similar and evident reason, because there the weight is first and principally thrown.

In a state of nature it is, to a certain degree, hollow. The reason of this is plain. It is intended to descend or yield with the weight of the horse, and by that gradual descent or yielding, most materially lessen the shock which would result from the sudden action of the weight of the animal in rapid and violent exercise; and this descent can only be given by a hollow sole. A flat sole, already pressing upon the ground, could not be brought lower; nor could the functions of the frog be then discharged; nor would the foot have so secure a hold. Then if the sole is naturally hollow, and hollow because it must descend, the smith should not interfere with this important action. When the foot will bear it, he must pare out sufficient of the horn to preserve the proper concavity; also a small portion at the toe and near the crust, and cutting deeper towards the centre. He must put on a shoe which shall not prevent the descent of the sole, and which not only shall not press upon it, but shall leave sufficient room between it and the sole to admit of this descent. If the sole is pressed upon by the coffin-bone during the lengthening of the elastic laminæ, and the shoe will not permit its descent, the sensible part between the coffin-bone and the horn will necessarily be bruised, and inflammation and lameness will ensue. It is from this cause, that if a stone insinuates itself between the shoe and the sole, it produces so much lameness. Of the too great concavity of the sole, or the want of concavity in it, we shall treat when we arrive at diseases of the foot.

THE FROG.

In the space between the bars, and accurately filling it, is the FROG. It is a triangular portion of horn, projecting from the sole, almost on a level with the crust, and covering and defending a soft and elastic substance called the *sensible frog*. Its shape all are familiar with. It is firmly united to the sole, but is perfectly distinct from it. It is softer and far more elastic. It discharges various duties besides the one above named. It comes in contact with the ground and prevents the horse from slipping, especially when the heel comes first to the ground, as in galloping. It assists materially in the expansion of the foot. To discharge these various duties, it must come in contact with the ground, and in the unshod horse is always so. The practice of cutting much of it away in shoeing, is therefore highly improper.

The rough and detached parts should be cut off at each shoeing, and the substance of the frog itself, so as to bring it just *above or within the level of the shoe*. It will then, in the descent of the sole, when the weight of the horse is thrown upon it in the putting down of the foot, descend likewise, and pressing upon the ground, do its duty; while it will be defended from the wear, and bruise, and injury that it would receive if it came upon the ground with the first and full shock of the weight. This will be the proper guide to the smith in shoeing, and to the proprietor in the direction which he gives.

THE COFFIN-BONE.

The interior part of the foot must now be considered. The lower pastern, a small portion of which (see d, Fig. 37) is contained in the horny box, has been already described, p. 267.—Beneath it, and altogether inclosed in the hoof, is the coffin-bone, or proper bone of the foot, (see f, Fig. 37, and d, Fig. 38). It is fitted to, and fills the fore part of the hoof, occupying about half of it. It is of a light and spongy structure (see d, Fig. 38), and filled with numerous minute foramina (holes or pores). Through these pass the blood-vessels and nerves of the foot, which are necessarily numerous, considering the important and various secretions there carrying on, and the circulation through the foot which could not possibly be kept up if these vessels did not run through the substance of the bone. Considering the manner in which this bone is inclosed in the horny box, and yet the important surfaces around and below it that are to be nourished with blood, the circulation which is thus carried on within the very body of the bone is one of the most beautiful provisions of nature that is to be found in the whole frame. No inconvenience can arise from occasional or constant pressure, but the bone allows free passage to the blood, and protects it from every possible obstruction.

Its shape and position within the foot will be seen by inspecting Fig. 37.

On the front and sides of the coffin-bone are laminæ or leaves —cartilaginous fleshy plates—running down between the horny leaves of the crust. The substance which connects these leave with the coffin-bone is highly elastic—and necessarily so—as while the horse is at rest, his whole weight is supported by them. This has been proved by experiment. The sole, bars, and frog were removed from the foot of a horse, and yet as he stood, the coffin-bone did not in the slightest degree descend. But when the horse is moving, both sets of leaves—those of the coffin-bone and the superior portion of the crust, gradually lengthen, and suffer the coffin-bone to press on the sole. The sole then descends, and in descending, expands; and so, by an admirable mechanism, the violent shock which would be produced by the pressure of such a weight as that of the horse, and the velocity with which it descends, is lessened or destroyed, and the complicated apparatus of the foot remains uninjured.

THE SENSIBLE SOLE.

Between the coffin-bone and the horny sole is situated the sensible sole, (Fig. 37,) formed above of a substance of a ligamentous or tendinous nature, and below of a cuticular or skin-like sub stance, plentifully supplied with blood-vessels. It was placed between the coffin-bone and the sole, by its yielding structure to assist in preventing concussion, and also to form a supply of horn for the sole. It extends beyond the coffin-bone, but not at all under the frog. Leaving a space for the frog, it proceeds over the bars, and there is covered by some laminæ, to unite with those that have been described, page 293, as found in the bars. It is here likewise thicker, and more elastic, and by its elasticity is evidently assisting in obviating concussion. It is supplied with nervous fibres, and is highly sensible, as the slightest experience in horses will evince. The lameness which ensues from the pressure of a stone, or of the shoe, on the sole is caused by inflammation of the sensible sole. Corns result from bruise and inflammation of the sensible sole, between the crust and the bar.

THE SENSIBLE FROG.

The coffin-bone does not occupy more than one-half of the hoof. The posterior part is filled by a soft mass, partly ligamentous, and partly tendinous (*o*, Fig. 37). Its shape below corresponds with the cavities of the horny frog; in front it is attached to the inferior part of the coffin-bone; and farther back, it adheres to the lower part of the cartilages of the heels, where they begin to form the rounded protuberances that constitute the heel of the foot. It occupies the whole of the back part of the foot above the horny frog and between the cartilages. Running immediately above the frog, and along the greater part of it, we find the perforans flexor tendon, which passes over the navicular bone, *e*, Fig. 37, and is inserted into the heel of the coffin-bone

THE NAVICULAR-BONE

Is placed behind and beneath the lower pastern-bone, and behind and above the heel of the coffin-bone, *e*, Fig. 37, so that it forms a joint with both bones, and answers a very important office in strengthening the union between these parts, in receiving a portion of the weight which is thrown on the lower pastern and in enabling the flexor tendon to act with more advantage. Supposing that this tendon were inserted into the coffin-bone without the intervention of the navicular bone, it would act at great mechanical disadvantage in bending the pastern, for it is inserted near the end of the coffin-bone, and the weight, concentrated about the middle of the bone, is far off, and requires a great power to raise it; but when the navicular-bone is interposed, the centre of motion becomes the posterior edge of that bone, where it is in contact with the tendon, and then it will be seen that the distance of the power from the centre of motion is nearly or quite the same as the weight, and very great expenditure of muscular power will be saved. In the one case, the power must be at least double the weight, in the other they will be nearly equal; and also the angle at which the tendon is inserted, is considerably more advantageous. Perhaps this is the principal use of the navicular-bone; yet at the same time we are aware of the benefit which accrues (see Fig. 37) from a portion of the weight being taken from the coffin-bone, and thrown on the navicular-bone, and from it on the tendon, and the tendon resting on the elastic frog underneath.

THE CARTILAGES OF THE FOOT.

There is a groove extending along the upper part of the coffin-bone and on either side, except at the protuberance which receives the extensor tendon *e*, Fig. 37, occupied by cartilage, which, like the crust, is convex outwards and concave inwards. It extends to the very posterior part of the foot, rising about the quarters half an inch or more above the hoof, and diminishing in height forward and backward. These cartilages occupy a greater portion of the foot than does the coffin-bone, as will be seen in Fig. 40, where they are represented as extending far behind the coffin-bone. They are held in their situation not merely by this groove, but by other connections with the coffin-bone, the navicular bone, and the flexor tendon, and are thus perfectly secured.

Below are other cartilages connected with the under edges of the former, and on either side of the frog.

Between these cartilages is the sensible frog, filling up the whole of the space, and answering several important purposes.

CHAPTER XV.

THE DISEASES OF THE FOOT.

Of these there is a long list. That will not be wondered at by those who have duly considered the complicated structure of the foot, the duty it has to perform, and the injuries to which it is exposed. It will be proper to commence with that which is the cause of many other diseases of the foot, and connected with almost all.

INFLAMMATION OF THE FOOT, OR ACUTE FOUNDER.

The sensible laminæ, or fleshy plates on the front and sides of the coffin-bone, being replete with blood-vessels, are, like every other vascular (filled with blood-vessels) part, liable to inflammation, from its usual causes, and particularly from the violence with which, in rapid and long-continued action, these parts are strained and bruised. When battered and bruised by severe races or journeys, it will be no wonder if inflammation of the over-worked parts should ensue; and the occurrence of it may probably be produced, and the disease aggravated by the too prevalent absurd mode of treating the animal. If a horse that has been ridden or driven hard is suffered to stand in the cold, or if his feet are washed and not speedily dried, he is very likely to have "fever in the feet." There is no more fruitful source of inflammation in the human being, or the brute, than these sudden changes of temperature. This has been explained as it regards grease, but it bears more immediately on the point now under consideration. The danger is not confined to change from heat to cold. Sudden transition from cold to heat is as injurious, and therefore it is that so many horses, after having been ridden far in frost and snow, and placed immediately in a hot stable, and littered up to the knees, are attacked by this malady.

Sometimes there is a sudden change of inflammation from one organ to another. A horse may have labored for several days under evident inflammation of the lungs; all at once that will subside, and the disease will appear in the feet, or inflammation of the feet may follow similar affections in the bowels or the eyes. In cases of severe inflammation of the lungs, it may not be bad practice to remove the shoes and poultice the feet.

To the attentive observer the symptoms are clearly marked, and yet there is no disease so often overlooked by the groom and the carter, and even by the veterinary surgeon. The disease may assume an acute or chronic form. The earliest symptoms of fever in the feet are fidgetiness, frequent shifting of the fore-legs, but no pawing, much less any attempt to reach the belly with the hind-feet. The pulse is quickened, the flanks heaving, the nostrils red, and the horse, by his anxious countenance, and possibly moaning, indicating great pain. Presently he looks about his litter, as if preparing to lie down, but he does not do so immediately; he continues to shift his weight from foot to foot; he is afraid to draw his feet sufficiently under him for the purpose of lying down: but at length he drops. The circumstance of his lying down at an early period of the disease will sufficiently distinguish inflammation of the feet from that of the lungs, in which the horse obstinately persists in standing until he drops from mere exhaustion. His quietness when down will distinguish it from colic or inflammation of the bowels, in both of which the horse is up and down, and frequently rolling and kicking when down. When the grievance is in the feet, the horse experiences so much relief, from getting rid of the weight painfully distending the inflamed and highly sensible laminæ, that he is glad to lie as long as he can. He will likewise, as clearly as in inflammation of the lungs or bowels, point out the seat of disease by looking at the part. His muzzle will often rest on the feet or the affected foot. He must be inattentive who is not aware of what all this indicates.

If the feet are now examined, they will be found evidently hot. The patient will express pain if they are slightly rapped with a hammer, and the artery at the pastern will throb violently. No great time will now pass, if the disease is suffered to pursue its course, before he will be perfectly unable to rise; or, if he is forced to get up, and one foot is lifted, he will stand with difficulty on the other, or perhaps drop at once from intensity of pain.

The treatment will resemble that of other inflammations, with such differences as the situation of the disease may suggest.

Bleeding is indispensable; and that to its fullest extent. If the disease is confined to the fore-feet, four quarts of blood should be taken as soon as possible from the toe of each at the situation pointed out, fig. z, page 263, and in the manner already described; care being taken to open the artery as well as the vein. The feet may likewise be put into warm water, to quicken the flow of the blood, and increase the quantity abstracted. Poultices of linseed meal, made very soft, should cover the whole of the foot and pastern, and be frequently renewed, which will promote evaporation from the neighboring parts, and possibly through the pores of the hoof, and by softening and rendering supple the hoof, will relieve its painful pressure on the swelled and tender parts beneath. More fully to accomplish this last purpose, the shoe should be removed, the sole pared as thin as possible, and the crust, and particularly the quarters, well rasped. All this must be done gently, and with a great deal of patience, for the poor animal can scarcely bear his feet to be meddled with. There used to be occasional doubt as to the administration of physic, from fear of metastasis (shifting) of inflammation which has sometimes occurred, and been generally fatal. When, however, there is so much danger of losing the patient from the original attack, we must run the risk of the other. Sedative and cooling medicines should be diligently administered, consisting of digitalis, nitre, and emetic tartar.

If no amendment is observed, three quarts of blood should be taken from each foot on the following day. In extreme cases, a third bleeding of two quarts may be justifiable, and, instead of the poultice, clothes kept wet with water in which nitre has been dissolved *immediately before*, and in the proportion of an ounce of nitre to a pound of water, may be wrapped round the feet. About the third day a blister may be tried, taking in the whole of the pastern and the coronet; but a cradle must previously be put on the neck of the horse, and the feet must be covered after the blister, or they will probably be sadly blemished. The horse should be kept on mash diet, unless green meat can be procured for him; and even that should not be given too liberally, nor should he, in the slightest degree, be coaxed to eat. When he appears to be recovering, his getting on his feet should not be hurried. It should be left perfectly to his own discretion; nor should even walking exercise be permitted until he stands firm on his feet. When that is the case, and the season will permit, two months' run at grass will be very serviceable.

It is not always, however, or often, that inflammation of the feet is thus easily subdued; and, if it is subdued, it sometimes leaves after it some fearful consequences. The loss of the hoof is not an unfrequent one. About six or seven days from the first attack, a slight separation will begin to appear between the coronet and the hoof. This should be carefully attended to, for the separated horn will never again unite with the parts beneath, but the disunion will extend, and the hoof will be lost. It is true that a new hoof will be formed, but it will be smaller in size and weaker than the first, and will rarely stand hard work. When this separation is observed, it will be a matter of calculation with the proprietor of the horse whether he will suffer the medical treatment to proceed.*

CHRONIC FOUNDER.

This is a species of founder, insidious in its attack, and destructive to the horse. It is a milder form of the preceding disease. There is lameness, but it is not so severe as in the former case. The horse stands as usual. The crust is warm, and that warmth is constant, but it is not often probably greater than in a state of health. The surest symptoms is the action of the animal. It is diametrically opposite to that in the navicular disease. The horse throws as much of his weight as he can, on the posterior parts of his feet.

The treatment should be similar to that recommended for the acute disease—blood-letting, soultices, fomentations, and blisters, and the last much sooner and much more frequently than in the former disease.

PUMICED FEET.

The sensible and horny little plates which were elongated and partially separated during the intensity of the inflammation of founder, will not always perfectly unite again, or will have lost

---

* *Note by Mr. Spooner.*—*Laminitis*, or inflammation of the laminæ of the feet (or acute founder), though often occasioned by long-continued exertion on the hard road, is not produced by galloping on the turf, and, indeed, scarcely ever affects race-horses. Heavier breeds are more liable, and particularly when the feet are weak in proportion to the weight of the animal. When horses work on soft ground, the sole and the frog bear some proportion of the weight, but on the hard road the shoe alone comes in contact with the ground, and consequently the crust and the laminæ bear the whole of the weight, and thus are exposed to inflammatory action from this cause. Some relief, however, is obtained by the feet being alternately in the air and on the ground; but when horses are confined many days in a standing posture, as on board ship, the laminæ are almost constantly on the stretch; this disease, therefore, very frequently follows a voyage, and has often attacked troop-horses, particularly when the voyage has been rough and of undue continuance. When, however, *laminitis* suspenses as a secondary disease, the prior disorder affects a similar tissue as the other; thus it is when pleurisy is succeeded with *laminitis*, both the pleura and the laminæ being fibrous tissues and of the same character. Such likewise is the case when acute rheumatism is the prior disease.

With regard to *treatment*, the most energetic measures must be adopted, as advised in the text. It is not however judicious to bleed a second time in the feet, but better to repeat the bleeding from the arms or the coronets. When a blister is applied its effects should be washed off the following day, by doing which it can be repeated several times. Bleeding, however, is the sheet-anchor, and there is generally a capability of bearing a large depletion.,   20

much of their elasticity, and the coffin-bone, no longer fully supported by them, presses upon the sole, and the sole becomes flattened, or convex, from this unnatural weight, and the horse acquires a PUMICED FOOT. This will also happen when the animal is used too soon after an attack of inflammation of the feet, and before the laminæ have reigained sufficient strength to support the weight of the horse, or to contract again by their elastic power when they have yielded to the weight. When the coffin-bone is thus thrown on the sole, and renders it pumiced, the crust at the front of the hoof will "*fall in*," leaving a kind of hollow about the middle of it.

Pumiced feet, especially in horses with large, wide feet, are frequently produced without this acute inflammation. Undue work, and especially much battering of the feet on the pavement, will extend and sprain these laminæ so much, that they will not have the power to contract, and thus the coffin-bone will be thrown backward on the sole. A very important law of nature will unfortunately soon be active here. When pressure is applied to any part, the absorbents become busy in removing it; so, when the coffin-bone begins to press upon the sole, the sole becomes thin from the increased wear and tear to which it is subjected by contact with the ground, and also because these absorbents are rapidly taking it away.

This is one of the diseases of the feet for which there is no cure. No skill is competent to effect a reunion between the separated fleshy and horny laminæ, or to restore to them the strength and elasticity of which they have been deprived, or to take up that hard, horny substance which speedily fills the space between the crust and the receding coffin-bone.

All that can be done in the way of palliation is by shoeing. Nothing must press on the projecting and pumiced part. If the projection is not considerable, a thick bar-shoe is the best thing that can be applied; but should this sole have much descended, a shoe with a very wide web, bevelled off so as not to press on the part, may be used. These means of relief, however, are only temporary, the disease will proceed; and, at no great distance of time, the horse will be useless.*

* *Note by Mr. Spooner.*—When this disease follows that previously treated of in the preceding article, the horse is rendered completely unserviceable, the laminæ become disorganized, the coffin-bone separates from the crust and descends on the sensible sole, which, unable to bear the pressure, becomes bruised and diseased, and in fact the horse is incurably lame. When, however, a convex foot is gradual in its approach, and the sole becomes *pumiced* by degrees, there is some palliation to be offered; in such instances there is usually a weak foot previously, giving a predisposition to the disease. In this case likewise the toe of the bone recedes from the crust, a horny substance is thrown out between them, which is however of

CONTRACTION.

Fig. 47, will give a fair idea of the young and healthy foot, approaching nearly to a circle, and of which the quarters form the widest part, and the inner quarter (this is the near foot) rather wider than the outer. This shape is not long preserved in many horses, but the foot increases in length, and narrows in the quarters, and particularly at the heel, and the frog is diminished in width, and the sole becomes more concave, and the heels higher, and lameness, or at least a shortened and feeling action, ensues.

It must be premised that there is a great deal more horror of contracted heels than there is occasion for. Many persons reject a horse at once if the quarters are *wiring in;* but the fact is, that although this is an unnatural form of the hoof, it is slow of growth, and nature kindly makes that provision for the slowly altered form of the hoof which she does in similar cases—she ac commodates the parts to the change of form. As the hoof draws in, the parts beneath, and particularly the coffin-bone, and especially the heels of that bone, diminish; or, after all, it is more a change of form than of capacity. As the foot lengthens in proportion as it narrows, so does the coffin-bone, and it is as perfectly adjusted as before to the box in which it is placed. Its laminæ are in as intimate and perfect union with those of the crust as before the hoof had begun to change. On this account it is that many horses, with very contracted feet, are perfectly sound, and no horse should be rejected merely because he has contraction. He should undoubtedly be examined more carefully, and with considerable suspicion; but if he has good action, and is otherwise unexceptionable, there is no reason that the purchase should not be made. A horse with contracted feet, if he goes sound, is better than another with open but weak heels.

The opinion is perfectly erroneous that contraction is the ne-

---

no use as a support; the front of the foot, usually the strongest, now becomes the weakest, and the horse goes mostly upon his heels. A cure being out of the question, we must endeavor to palliate as best we can, and this we shall do by means of shoeing. A bar-shoe should be nailed on, well hollowed out, so as not to press on the sole in the slightest degree, and a rim of leather should be put under the shoe to diminish concussion, but should not extend over the sole. The bar should be put on so as to be within the eighth of an inch from the frog, by which means pressure only will be given it when the foot is on the ground, and it will thus be enabled to support a moderate share of the superincumbent weight, and so relieve the crust of it. The hoof should be frequently anointed with a mixture of tar and grease, and if the horse is rested for some time the coronets may be blistered

cessary consequence of shoeing. There can be no doubt that an inflexible iron ring being nailed to the foot prevents, to a very considerable degree, the descent of the sole and the expansion of the heels below; and it is likewise probable, that when the expansion of the heels is prevented they often begin to contract. But here, as before stated, nature makes provision for the change. Some gentlemen who are careful of their horses have driven them twenty years, and principally over the rough pavement of towns, without a day's lameness. Shoeing may be a necessary evil, but it is not the evil which many speculative persons have supposed it, and notwithstanding its effects, the foot ordinarily lasts longer than the legs; nay, horsemen tell us that one pair of good feet is worth two pairs of legs.

There is nothing in the appearance of the feet which would enable us to decide when contraction is or is not destructive to the usefulness of the animal; his manner of going, and his capability for work, must be our guides. Lameness usually accompanies the beginning of contraction; it is the invariable attendant on rapid contraction, but it does not always exist when the *wiring in* is slow, or of long standing.

A very excellent writer, particularly when treating of the foot of the horse, Mr. Blaine, has given us a long and correct list of the causes of injurious contraction, and most of them are, fortunately, under the control of the owner of the animal. He places at the head of them, *neglect of paring*. The hoof is continually growing, the crust is lengthening, and the sole is thickening. This is a provision for the wear and tear of the foot in an unshod state; but when it is protected by a shoe, and none of the horn can be worn away by coming in contact with the ground, and the growth of horn continues, the hoof grows high, and the sole gets thick, and, in consequence of this, the descent of the sole and the expansion of the heels are prevented, and contraction is the result. The smith might lessen, if not prevent the evil, by carefully thinning the sole and lowering the heels at each shoeing; but the first of these is a matter of considerable labor, and the second could not be done effectually without being accompanied by the first, and therefore they are both neglected. Owners should often stand by and see that this is properly done.

Wearing the shoes too long, especially when nails are placed nearer than they should be to the quarters to make the shoes hold, is another cause of contraction. There is no rule which admits of so little exception as that, once in about every three weeks, the growth of horn which the natural wear of the foot cannot get rid of, should be pared away—the toe should be shortened in most feet—the sole should be thinned, and the heels lowered Every one who has carefully observed the shape of the horse's foot, must have seen that in proportion to its height or neglected growth, it contracts and closes round the coronet. A low-heeled horse might have other serious defects, of which it will be our duty to speak, but he has seldom a contracted foot.

Another source of contraction is the want of natural moisture. The hoof of the stable-horse kept from moisture becomes dry and unelastic, and, consequently, is rendered more subject to this disease. Hence the propriety of stopping the feet where there is the least tendency to contraction. The intelligent and careful groom will not omit it a single night. Cow-dung, with a small portion of clay to give it consistence, is a common and very good stopping. A better one is a piece of thick felt, cut to the shape of the sole, and soaked in water. The common stopping of tar and grease is peculiarly objectionable, for it closes the pores of the feet, and ultimately increases the dryness and brittleness which it was designed to remedy.

Thrushes aid sometimes in producing contraction, but they are much oftener the consequence than the cause.

The removal of the bars takes away a main impediment to contraction. Their use in assisting the expansion of the foot has been already stated, and should a disposition to contraction be produced by any other cause, the cutting away of the bars would hasten and aggravate the evil; but the loss of the bar would not of itself produce contraction.

The contraction, however, that is connected with permanent lameness, although increased by the circumstances which we have mentioned, usually derives its origin from a different source, and from one that acts violently and suddenly. Inflammation of the little plates covering the coffin-bone is the most usual cause; and a degree of inflammation not sufficiently intense to be characterized as acute founder, but quickly leading to sad results, may and does spring from causes almost unsuspected. Something may depend upon the breed. Blood-horses are particularly liable to contraction. Not only is the foot naturally small, but it is disposed to become narrower at the heels. On the other hand, the broad, flat foot of the cart-horse is subject to diseases enough, but contraction is seldom one of the number. In horses of equal blood, not a little seems to depend upon the color, and the dark chestnut is proverbially prone to contraction.

Whatever is the cause of that rapid contraction or narrowing of the heels which is accompanied by severe lameness, the symptoms may be easily distinguished. While standing in the stable, the horse will point with, or place forward, the contracted foot; or if both feet are affected, he will alternately place one before the other. When he is taken out of the stable, his step will be peculiarly short and quick, and the feet will be placed gently and tenderly on the ground, or scarcely lifted from it in the walk or the trot. It would seem as if the slightest irregularity of surface would throw the animal down, and so it threatens to do, for he is constantly tripping and stumbling. If the fore-feet are carefully observed, one or both of them will be narrowed across the quarters and towards the heels. In a few cases, the whole of the foot appears to be contracted and shrunk; but in the majority of instances, while the heels are narrower, the foot is longer. The contraction appears sometimes in both heels: at other times in the inner heel only; or, if both are affected, the inner one is *wired in* the most, either from the coronet to the base of the foot, or only or principally at the coronet—oftener near the base of the foot—but in most cases the hollow being greatest about mid-way between the coronet and the bottom of the foot. This irregularity on contraction, and uncertainty as to the place of it, prove that it is some internal disorganization, the seat of which varies with the portion of the attachment between the hoof and the foot that was principally strained or injured. In every recent case, the contracted part will be hotter than the rest of the foot, and the sole will, in the majority of cases, be unnaturally concave.

Of the treatment of contraction attended with lameness, little that is satisfactory can be said. There have been various mechanical contrivances, such as clips of a peculiar form, and a jointed shoe, which, when the foot was softened, was gradually pressed asunder at the heels by a screw; but all have proved of no avail, for the disease speedily returned when the ordinary shoe was again applied to enable the horse to work, and work was required of him.

If the action of the horse is not materially impaired, it is better to let the contraction alone, be it as great as it will. If the contraction has evidently produced considerable lameness, the owner of the horse will have to calculate between his value, if cured, the expense of the cure, and the probability of failure.

The medical treatment should alone be undertaken by a skilful veterinary surgeon, and it will principally consist in abating any inflammation that may exist, by local bleeding and physic, paring the sole to the utmost extent that it will bear; rasping the quarters as deeply as can be, without their being too much weakened, or the coronary ring (see *b*, Fig. 37), injured; rasping deeply likewise at the toe, and perhaps scoring at the toe. The horse is afterwards made to stand during the day in wet clay, placed in one of the stalls. He is at night moved into another stall, and his feet bound up thickly in wet cloths; or he is turned out into wet pasturage, with tips, or, if possible, without them, and his feet are frequently pared out, and the quarters lightly rasped. In five or six months the horn will generally have grown down, when he may be taken up, and shod with shoes unattached by nails on the inner side of the foot, and put to gentle work. The foot will be found very considerably enlarged, and the owner will, perhaps, think that the cure is accomplished. The horse may, possibly, for a time stand very gentle work, and the inner side of the foot being left at liberty, its natural expansive process may be resumed: the internal part of the foot, however, has not been healthily filled up with the expansion of the crust. If that expansion has been effected forward on the quarters, the crust will no longer be in contact with the lengthened and narrowed heels of the coffin-bone. There will not be the natural adhesion and strength, and a very slight cause, or even the very habit of contraction, will, in spite of all care and the freedom of the inner quarter, in very many instances, cause the foot to wire in again as badly as before.*

THE NAVICULAR-JOINT DISEASE.

Many horses with well-formed and open feet become sadly and permanently lame, and veterinary surgeons have been puzzled to discover the cause. The farrier has had his convenient explanation "the shoulder;" but the scientific practitioner may not have been able to discover an ostensible cause of lameness in the whole limb. There is no one accustomed to horses who does not recollect an instance of this.

By reference to c, Fig. 37, it will be seen that, behind and beneath the lower pastern-bone, and behind and above the heel of the coffin-bone, is a small bone called the navicular or shuttle-bone. It is so placed as to strengthen the union between the lower pastern and the coffin-bone, and to enable the flexor tendon, which passes over it in order to be inserted into the bottom of the coffin-bone, to act with more advantage. It forms a kind of joint with that tendon. There is a great deal of weight thrown on the navicular-bone, and from the navicular-bone on

---

* *Note by Mr. Spooner.*—A vast amount of error has been written in various books with regard to the subject of contraction. For our own parts, we believe that it is in the greater number of instances the consequence rather than the cause of lameness; and the dissection of a great number of diseased feet, has assured us that when lameness is present there is disease of the navicular-joint, of the pressure of which there cannot be better proof than the symptom of pointing alluded to in the text. It is quite true that some horses will point from gait or habit, without any disease being present; but when lameness exists, and the horse also points, we may take the latter symptom as presumptive evidence that the case is one of navicular-joint disease.

the tendon; and there is a great deal of motion or play between them in the bending and extension of the pasterns.

It is very easy to conceive that, from sudden concussion, or from rapid and overstrained motion, and that, perhaps, after the animal has been sometime a trest, and the parts have not adapted themselves for motion, there may be too much play between the bone and the tendon—the delicate membrane which covers the bone, or the cartilage of the bone, may be bruised, and inflamed, and destroyed; that all the painful effects of an inflamed and opened joint may ensue, and the horse be irrecoverably lame. Numerous dissections have shown that this joint, formed by the tendon and the bone, has been the frequent, and the almost invariable, seat of these obscure lamenesses. The membrane covering the cartilage of the bone has been found in an ulcerated state; the cartilage has been ulcerated and eaten away; the bone has become carious or decayed, and bony adhesions have taken place between the navicular and the pastern and the coffin-bones, and this part of the foot has often become completely disorganized and useless. This joint is probably the seat of lameness, not only in well-formed feet, but in those which become lame *after* contraction.

The cure of navicular disease is difficult and uncertain. The first and all-important point is, the removal of the inflammation in this very susceptible membrane. Local bleeding, poulticing, and physic will be our principal resources. If there is contraction, this must, if possible, be removed by the means already pointed out. If there is no contraction, it will nevertheless be prudent to get rid of all surrounding pressure, and to unfetter, as much as possible, the inside heel of the coffin-bone, by paring the sole and rasping the quarters, and using the shoe without nails on the inner quarter, and applying cold poultices to the coronet and the whole of the foot. This is a case, however, which must be turned over to the veterinary surgeon, for he alone, from his knowledge of the anatomy of the foot, and the precise seat of the disease, is competent to treat it. If attacked on its earliest appearance, and before ulceration of the membrane of the joint has taken place, it may be radically cured: but ulceration of the membrane will be with difficulty healed, and decay of the bone will for ever remain.

Blistering the coronet will often assist in promoting a cure by diverting the inflammation to another part, and it will materially quicken the growth of the horn. A seton passed through the frog by a skilful operator, and approaching as nearly as possible to the seat of disease, has been serviceable.

Neurotomy (see p. 86) may be profitably resorted to in this disease, but if the lameness is extreme. either with or without contraction, and especially if there is heat about the foot, the operation is dangerous. There is, probably, ulceration of the membrane—possibly, decay of the bone; and the additional friction to which the parts would be subjected, by the freer ac tion of the horse, the sense of pain being removed, would cause that ulceration or decay to proceed more rapidly until the foot would be completely disorganized, or the tendon would be gradually worn through by rubbing against the roughened surface of the bone.*

* *Note by Mr. Spooner.*—Navicular-joint disease is one of the most frequent lamenesses by which the horse is afflicted, and one of the most insidious and incurable. It sometimes comes on suddenly from a sudden jar or strain, and then the lameness is often very severe, and there is no contraction previous to the lameness, although afterwards, from the pointing of the foot, and the consequent absence of the usual weight upon it, contraction is sure to follow; more frequently, however, this disease is gradual in its approach, the horse points previous to the lameness, and, if the foot is attentively examined, contraction in some degree will be discovered. Thus the symptoms are Lameness, Pointing, and Contraction, each of which demands separate consideration, in order that we may understand the true nature of this very deceptive disease, and the more so as it has not been treated at much length in the text.

The Lameness.—The degree of lameness in navicular disease admits of a variety of shades. In some cases we find it manifested the first hundred yards only; in some it may continue for a mile or two and then go off; in others, again, it may continue throughout a journey, but not so severely as at first. This circumstance is common to some other lamenesses, but not so uniformly the case as in navicular disease. So important a symptom is it that, on ascertaining its existence, it of itself leads us strongly to suspect the nature of the lameness. It is customary to say of a groggy horse, "Oh! he will go sound enough when he gets a little warm." This peculiarity, which is common to many lamenesses, but more particularly to the navicular disease, is ascribed to the attention of the horse being called away from the injured part: this in a great measure is the case, but we must add that, in the disease in question, the secretion of synovia becomes increased by exercise, and the horse is enabled so to dispose his weight as to rest but very lightly on the injured joint. In some cases the lameness is so slight that the utmost tact of the practitioner is required to detect it: or the horse may show it on the stones and go sound on gravel. Should the horse be slightly lame in both feet the difficulty is still greater, and he may go a long time in this state before the owner thinks him actually lame. When both feet are thus equally affected, however, the action of the horse becomes altered in proportion to the extent of mischief; he no longer bends the knee with the same freedom as before, his action becomes shorter, the heels of the foot scarcely touch the ground, and the shoe will exhibit the toe almost worn away, whilst the heels continue undiminished in thickness. These circumstances, whether one leg or both be affected, will at all times materially assist our diagnosis. After the disease has existed in both feet for a considerable period, the horse brings his hind-legs under his body, and makes them sustain the greater part of his weight, and in the stable he almost constantly lies down.

Pointing.—We should be cautious of giving an opinion of the cause of lameness until we have seen the horse in the stable, where, if there be any doubt of the matter, we should leave him for a while undisturbed. In many cases, on asking the question, "Does the horse point?" the groom will reply "Oh yes, he has done so for a long time." The ascertainment of the length of this time will inform us how long the disease has been coming on. In other cases, on asking the same question, we are told he never points. The former reply we may generally depend on, but the latter we must never trust to; for, unless the lame foot is thrust out nearly a yard in front of the other, the groom does not consider that the horse points. In a case of this sort (supposing all the time that it is one of navicular disease,) we shall probably find, on noticing the horse, that the affected foot is advanced in some degree beyond the other, that there is very little weight resting on it, and none whatever on the heels. In navicular disease the horse always, or at least in ninety-nine cases in a hundred, points, either little or much, although it may be unnoticed by the attendants; it is, indeed, one of the most striking characteristics of the disease. We must not, however, always conclude that because a horse points he must necessarily have the disease, although in the majority of instances we may expect its approach, either early or late; but some horses have been known to point for years without going lame: either the horse has pointed from habit, or the alteration of structure in the foot may be sufficient to occasion pointing, and yet by careful treatment prevented from being so bad as to produce lameness. Some persons, having witnessed a case in which a horse may have pointed for a lengthened period without being lame, immediately conclude that it is of no consequence, thus confidently drawing an inference from the narrow limits of their own experience, and allowing it to influence their conduct. We may, however, safely aver that pointing, if a habit, is, at best, a wretched bad one, having so much the semblance of disease; and from its so frequently being the precursor of lameness, it materially lessens the value of an animal.

If a horse is lame and points, must we necessarily conclude that he has navicular disease? No; he may point from corns or from other injury at the posterior part of the foot, but then this pointing is different from that of navicular disease. In the latter the foot is generally set out straight; in the former it is not extended so far, but the heels are more elevated. In the former, the animal having put his foot in the easiest position, turns his attention to other objects, whilst in the latter the solicitude of the horse is evidently directed more continually to the part, and if a horse points from corns, the lameness and pain are unusually severe.

Contraction.—This is a symptom that, either generally or partially, we usually find attending navicular disease. It is, however, by no means universally the case; indeed we occasionally find navicular lameness without any contraction, and, on the other hand, quite as frequently extensive contraction without any lameness whatever. Contraction is more frequently the consequence than the cause of lameness, arising, as it does most commonly, from resting or favoring the foot which the lameness induces. There are different sorts as well as different degrees of contraction. Putting aside the natural oblong narrow mule's-shape foot, which often exists through life unattended with lameness, we may have the heels drawn in, the crust and bars approaching with scarcely any space in the commissures, and the frog much diminished, hard, dry, and preternaturally elevated. In other cases the contraction may be only on one side, or the foot may appear altogether free from contraction, which may be only found to exist by comparing it with the other foot. There are other cases in which there may be no apparent contraction, and yet the parts are by no means in a natural or proper position the horny sole is preternaturally arched and thick, and the consequence is the navicular joint is driven up higher in the horny box, and instead of having a comparatively flat and elastic surface to repose on, it has a hard ur yielding ridge formed by the commissures.

Having given the leading symptoms attending the disease, it would be well perhaps, here to mention the morbid appearances of the joint which accompany them, and which post-mortem examinations of the malady in its different stages, exhibit. Among some morbid specimens in my possession, one merely shows a slight indentation on the ridge of the navicular-bone, and when recent the corresponding portion of the sinew was roughened. The horse had pointed a long time prior to his death, and was lame for a mile or so on first going off.

Another specimen exhibits holes in the navicular-bone somewhat like a carious tooth, together with very diminutive bone deposits on different parts of the surface of the bone. The mare to which it had belonged had been lame for several years in both feet, which were much contracted, and got gradually worse until she was only fit to go to plough.

Another case developes still greater disease on both navicular-bones, which are ulcerated in a great degree, and present also numerous long spiculi on their corticular surface, besides which there is an ossification of the inferior cartilage, so that although the bones have been boiled the navicular-bone rests securely on the ossified parts, which must therefore have materially saved the diseased tendon. The bones had belonged to a very old horse and favorite hunter, that had been lame for many years, and had consequently been used for agricultural labor.

Another morbid specimen is that of the feet of an old horse that had been groggy for some years. The navicular bones in both feet were closely united to the flexor tendons, and on tearing them apart the fibres of the sinew were lacerated; the greater part of the posterior surface of these bones was denuded of cartilage, and presented a rough appearance, and the bones themselves were situated higher up in the hoof than natural, assuming a more vertical or less horizontal position. Although this was the position of the bones, yet the foot by a common observer would have been pronounced well-shaped; the sole, however, I found enormously thick.

From a review of the various circumstances which attend the domestication of the horse, we may, I think, justly conclude that most of them operate in inducing the disease in question. The foot in its natural state has a disposition to contract when at rest, and expand when pressed upon. In a weak foot there is a greater tendency to spread than contract, but in a strong one we may consider these two antagonist principles as equivalent to each other. When, however, the horse becomes domesticated, every means is used to aid the contraction and to neutralize the disposition to expansion. The shoe is nailed to the foot when the latter is in its most contracted state, and the horse is confined in a stall the greater part of the day. On a sudden he is taken out of the stable, and, without having prepared his joints and limbs by preliminary exercise, he is driven as fast as he can trot for the space of an hour or upwards, on the hard road, and then during the remainder of the twenty-four hours consigned to the stable. What is the result of this unnatural system? By the joint effects of the shoe, hot litter, and standing in the stable so long, the foot so contracts that the sole is dri'd upwards, and with it the navicular-bone, which thus, as we have before noticed, has a hard unyielding substance to rest upon; and the joint having been in a quiescent state for many hours, there is probably a diminished secretion of synovia (joint oil). In this unprepared state the feet are battered on the hard road,* and the result is in many cases a bruise of the synovial membrane, which may either be sufficient to produce sudden and severe lameness, or so moderate as to occasion the slightest lameness only.

---

* The reader will bear in mind that Mr. Spooner speaks of the hard metal roads of England. Our roads, hard only when they are dry, do not produce these effects in a so great degree.—Am. Ed.

So far as my experience goes, horses used for racing are not so often affected as others, and this circumstance must, I think, be attributed to the fact of their taking a great deal of exercise on the soft ground, where the various parts of the feet meet the soil. They are not taken out of the stable and compelled to proceed at once with speed, but even during severe training are first walked for a considerable period before they take their gallops, which thus gradually prepares the joints for the severer exertions they are about to perform. Hunters, too, as we have before remarked, although exposed to sudden concussions and severe exertions, more perhaps than any other horses, are yet much more exempt from the disease than horses used on the road. How is this, but because they take much walking exercise every day, and particularly on the day of hunting, before their severe exertions commence, and these exertions are taken, in great measure, on the soft soil, where the frog, bars, and sole all meet the ground, and greatly assist in diminishing concussion and preserving the feet in a healthy state. It is a fact, too, that few will gainsay who have made extensive observations, that when hunters are affected with navicular disease, it is much more frequently than with other horses, attended by sudden and acute lameness: the horse goes out perfectly sound and comes home dead lame.

From these circumstances we are disposed to draw the following conclusions:—

First—That navicular lameness may be produced suddenly by a bruise on the synovial membrane, without any predisposing cause existing, but that this is by no means frequent.

Secondly—That well-bred horses with strong feet are most subject to the disease.

Thirdly—That the lameness is usually preceded by an alteration in the structure of the foot, whereby the navicular-bone is somewhat displaced, and has a hard unyielding surface to rest on instead of an elastic cushion.

Fourthly—That this contraction may be either apparent or obscure.

Fifthly—That in feet thus contracted the lameness itself is yet produced by a sudden bruise.

Sixthly—That contraction is not a direct cause of lameness itself, although usually considered so by authors, inasmuch as the dissection of morbid feet clearly developes the disease elsewhere; but that, although not an exciting cause, it is yet a predisposing agent.

Seventhly—That contraction is more frequently a consequence than a cause of lameness, being produced by any circumstance that induces the horse to abstain from bearing his weight upon the foot.

Treatment.—In endeavoring to cure the navicular disease, much, indeed almost everything, will depend on the length of time the horse has been lame. If the lameness came on suddenly, and but a short time has elapsed, we may then set about our treatment with a reasonable prospect of success; but if, on the other hand, the mischief has been slowly coming on, and preceded by pointing for some time, we may then afford some palliation, but a *permanent* cure we are seldom able to accomplish. In seeking a remedy our endeavors should be directed, first, to the removal of the inflammation in the joint; and, secondly, to the restoration of the various parts of the foot to their natural and proper position. If the injury has been suddenly produced our treatment will be principally confined to antiphlogistic measures.

The shoe being removed, the foot must be pared out and the sole thinned, more particularly that part opposite the navicular joint; the commissures should also be well cut out and thinned. This being done the foot must be bled freely from the toe; four quarts of blood may be taken, and the foot should then be placed in a linseed-meal poultice, or one made of bran and meal. The poultice should be wetted several times and changed once a day, and the bleeding may be repeated in the course of a few days, if required. The poultice is to be continued for eight or ten days, and then, when the utmost benefit has been derived from it that it is capable of affording, we may have recourse to counter-irritation.

The importance of venesection in every case of navicular disease must be apparent to every one, for there can be no case requiring treatment but what must be attended with some degree of inflammation, and in some cases the injury may be confined to inflammation alone. Where we have reason to infer that such is the case we may indeed confine our treatment to the bleeding and poulticing. The benefit of poultice is inferior only to blood-letting. It softens the horn, changing it from a hard, dry, and almost inelastic substance, to a soft, yielding, and elastic material. The degree of paring that may be necessary must depend upon the alteration of structure that has taken place in the foot.

Having pushed our antiphlogistic (tending to reduce inflammation) treatment as far as we well can, we may next seek the aid of counter-irritation. Shall we blister the coronet, or insert a frog seton? The latter is, I think, in every respect preferable; we create artificial inflammation and suppuration very near the seat of the disease, and we may keep this up almost as long as we please; a month, however, of active suppuration is generally long enough. The only objection to the seton is that the horse must be kept in the stable; he cannot be turned out, or into a soft, moist place during the time it remains in the foot. Before the seton is inserted, a shoe should be placed on the foot, nailed on the outside quarter only, which will much assist the expansion of the foot. By the judicious employment of the treatment we have recommended, varied or modified according to the nature of the case, we may in many instances effect a cure; but a love of truth obliges us to confess, that in a majority of cases, taking them as they come, no treatment will succeed. In chronic cases of navicular disease, in which there is no probability of effecting a cure, and but little of relieving the animal to any considerable extent, we have to determine whether we shall work the animal lame (if he is able to work at all), or remove sensation from the feet by the operation of neurotomy. It is a matter of much consequence that when a horse is submitted to the preceding course of treatment, every chance should be given it by allowing a long rest, viz., from two to four months.

SAND-CRACK.

This, as its name imports, is a *crack* or division of the hoof from above downward, and into which *sand* and dirt are too apt to insinuate themselves. It is so called, because it most frequently occurs in sandy districts, the heat of the sand applied to the feet giving them a disposition to crack. It occurs both in the fore and the hind feet. In the fore feet it is usually found in the inner quarter (see *g*, Fig. 41), but occasionally in the outer quarter, because there is the principal stress or effort towards expansion in the foot, and the inner quarter is weaker than the outer. In the hind feet the crack is almost invariably found in the front, because in the digging of the toe into the ground in the act of drawing, the principal stress is in front.

This is a most serious defect. It indicates a brittleness of the crust, sometimes natural, but oftener the consequence of mis management or disease, which, in spite of every means adopted, will probably be the source of future annoyance. On a hoof that has once been thus divided, no dependence can be placed, unless, by great care, the natural suppleness of the horn has been restored and is retained.

Sand-crack may happen in an instant, from a false step or over-exertion, and therefore a horse, although he may spring a sand-crack within an hour after the purchase, cannot be returned on that account.

The crack sometimes does not penetrate through the horn. It then causes no lameness; nevertheless, it must not be neglected. It shows that there is brittleness, which should induce the purchaser to pause; and, if proper means are not taken, it will generally soon penetrate to the quick. It should be pared or rasped fairly out, and if the paring or rasping has been deep the foot should be strengthened by a coating of pitch, with coarse tape bound over it, and a second coating of pitch covering this.

If the crack has penetrated through the crust, and lameness has ensued, the case is more serious. It must be carefully examined, in order to ascertain that no dirt or sand has got into it; the edges must be more considerably thinned, and if any fungus (proud-flesh) is beginning to protrude through the crack, and is imprisoned there, it must be destroyed by the application of the butyr (chloride) of antimony. This is preferable to the cautery (hot-iron) because the edges of the horn will not be thickened or roughened, and thus become a source of after-irritation. The firing iron must then be run deeply across, above, and below the crack; a pledget of dry tow being placed in the crack, in and over it, and the whole bound down as tightly as possible. On the third day the part should be examined, and the caustic again applied, if necessary: but if the crack is dry, and defended by a hard horny crust, the sooner the pitch plaster is put on the better.

The most serious case is, when, from *tread* or neglect, the coronet is divided. The growth of horn proceeds from the coronary ligament, and unless this ligament is sound, the horn will grow down disunited. The method to be here adopted, is to run the back of the firing-iron over the coronet where it is divided. Some inflammation will ensue; and when the scab produced by the cautery peels off, as it will in a few days, the division will be obliterated, and sound and united horn will grow down. When there is sufficient horn above the crack, a horizontal line should be drawn with a firing-iron between the sound horn and the crack. The connexion between the sound part and the crack will thus be prevented, and the new horn will gradually and safely descend, but the horse should not be used until sufficient horn has grown down fairly to isolate the crack. When the horn is divided at the coronet, it will be five or six months before it will grow fairly down, and not before that, should the animal be used even for ordinary work. When, however, the horn is grown an inch from the coronet, the horse may be turned out—the foot being well defended by the pitch plaster, and that renewed as often as it becomes loose —a bar-shoe being worn, chambered so as not to press upon the hoof immediately under the crack, and that shoe being taken off, the sole pared out, and any bulbous projection of new horn being removed once in every three weeks.

To remedy the undue brittleness of the hoof, there is no better application than that recommended in page 304, the sole being covered at the same time with the common cow-dung, or felt stopping.*

TREAD AND OVER-REACH.

Under these terms are comprised bruises and wounds of the coronet, inflicted by the other feet.

A TREAD is said to have taken place, when the inside of the coronet of one hind foot is struck by the calkin of the shoe of the other, and a bruised or contused wound is inflicted.

A tread, or wound of the coronet, must never be neglected, lest gravel should insinuate itself into the wound, and form deep ulcerations, called *sinuses* or *pipes*, and which constitute *quittor*. Although some mildly stimulating caustic may be occasionally required, the caustic, too frequently used by farriers, should be carefully avoided, not only lest quittor should be formed, but lest the coronary ligament should be so injured as to be afterwards incapable of secreting perfect horn. When properly treated, a tread is seldom productive of much injury. If the dirt is well

---

* *Note by Mr. Spooner.*—When lameness attends sand-crack, it is owing to the crack extending from the horn to the quick above. If the horse is worked on, this injury is repeated again and again until the coronary substance becomes so injured as to produce a false quarter. When a horse throws out a sand-crack he must be rested a month or more in order to effect a cure, to do which effectually the foot should be poulticed for a week in order to encourage the growth of horn, and the coronet for the same reason may be stimulated. In the course of a month the sound horn will be grown down for the space of a quarter of an inch, and then, and not till then, the firing-iron should be drawn transversely above the crack, so as to cut off the communication between the fissure and the sound horn above, which will gradually grow down. A plaster of pitch or shoe-maker's wax may then be placed on the crack, and a strap fastened round the foot, so as to prevent too much motion taking place. A bar-shoe is indispensable, in order that the weak quarter may be secured from the pressure.

washed out of it, and a pledget of tow, dipped in Friar's balsam bound over the wound, it will in the majority of cases, speedily heal. Should the bruise be extensive, or the wound deep, a poultice may be applied for one or two days, and then the Friar's balsam, or digestive ointment. Sometimes a soft tumour will form on the part, which will be quickly brought to suppuration by a poultice; and when the matter has run out, the ulcer will heal by the application of the Friar's balsam, or a weak solution of blue vitrol.

An OVER-REACH is a tread upon the heel of the coronet of the fore foot by the shoe of the corresponding hind foot, and either inflicted by the toe, or by the inner edge of the inside of the shoe. The preventive treatment is the bevelling, or rounding off, of the inside edge or rim of the hind shoes. The cure is, the cutting away of the loose parts, the application of Friar's balsam, and protection from the dirt.

Some horses, particularly young ones, overreach so as to strike the toes of the hind shoes against the fore ones, which is termed *clinking*. Keeping up the head of the horse does something to prevent this; but the smith may do more by shortening the toe of the hind shoes, and having the web broad. When they are too long, they are apt to be torn off—when too narrow, the hind foot may bruise the sole of the fore one, or may be locked fast between the branches of the fore shoe.

FALSE QUARTER.

If the coronary ligament, by which the horn of the crust is secreted, is divided by some cut or bruise, or eaten through by any caustic, there will occasionally be a division in the horn as it grows down, either in the form of a permanent sand-crack, or one portion of the horn overlapping the other. It occasionally follows neglected sand-crack, or it may be the consequence of quittor. This is exteriorly an evident fissure in the horn, and extending from the coronet to the sole, but not always penetrating to the laminæ. It is a very serious defect, and exceedingly difficult to remedy; for occasionally, if the horse is over weighted or hurried on his journey, the fissure will open and bleed, and very serious inconvenience and lameness may ensue. Grit and dirt may insinuate itself into the aperture, and penetrate to the sensible laminæ. Inflammation will almost of necessity be produced; and much mischief will be effected. While the energies of the animal are not severely taxed, he may not experience much inconvenience or pain; but the slightest exertion will cause the fissure to expand, and painful lameness to follow

The coronary ligament must be restored to its perfect state, or at least to the discharge of its perfect function. Much danger would attend the application of the caustic in order to effect this. A blister is rarely sufficiently active: but the application, not too severely, of a heated flat or rounded iron to the coronet at the injured part affords the best chance of success—the edges of the horn on either side of the crack being thinned, the hoof supported, and the separated parts held together by a firm encasement of pitch, as described when speaking of the treatment of sand-crack. The coronet must be examined at least once in every fortnight, in order to ascertain whether the desired union has taken place; and, as a palliative during the treatment of the case, or if the treatment should be unsuccessful, a bar-shoe may be used, and care taken that there be no bearing at or immediately under the separation of the horn. This will be best effected, when the crust is thick and the quarters strong, by paring off a little of the bottom of the crust at the part, so that it will not touch the shoe; but if the foot is weak, an indentation or hollow should be made in the shoe. Strain or concussion on the immediate part will thus be avoided, and, in sudden or violent exertion, the crack will not be so likely to extend upward to the coronet, when whole and sound horn has begun to be formed there.

QUITTOR.

This has been described as being the result of neglected or bad tread or over-reach; but it may be the consequence of any wound in the foot, and in any part of the foot. In the natural process of ulceration, matter is thrown out from the wound. It precedes the actual healing of the part. The matter which is secreted in wounds of the foot is usually pent up there, and, increasing in quantity, and urging its way in every direction, it forces the little fleshy plates of the coffin-bone, from the horny ones of the crust or the horny sole from the fleshy sole, or even eats deeply into the internal parts of the foot. These pipes or sinuses run in every direction, and constitute the essence of *quittor*.

If it arises from a wound in the bottom of the foot, the aperture may speedily close up, and the matter which continues to be secreted is confined within, separating the horny from the fleshy sole, until it forces its way upward and appears at the coronet (usually at the quarter) and there slowly oozes out. The opening and the quantity of matter discharged are so small, that although over a great part of the quarter and sole the horn may have separated from the coffin-bone, and the matter may have penetrated even under the cartilages and ligaments, and into the coffin-joint, but little mischief would be suspected by an unexperienced person. The pressure of the matter wherever it has gone has formed ulcerations that are indisposed to heal, and that require the application of strong and painful stimulants to induce them to heal; and, worse than this, the horn, once separated from the sensible parts beneath, will never again unite with them. Quittor may occur in both the fore and the hind feet.

It may be necessary to remove much of the horny sole, which will be speedily reproduced when the fleshy surface beneath can be brought to a healthy condition; but if much of the horn at the quarters must be taken away, five or six months may probably elapse before it will be sufficiently grown down again to render the horse useful.

Measures of considerable severity are indispensable. The application of some caustic will alone produce a healthy action on the ulcerated surfaces; but on the ground of interest and of humanity, we protest against that brutal practice, or at least the extent to which it is carried, and is pursued by many ignorant smiths, of coring out, or deeply destroying the healthy as well as the diseased parts—and parts which no process will again restore. When any portion of the bone can be felt by the probe, the chances of success are diminished, and the owner and the operator should pause. When the joints are exposed, the case is hopeless, although, in a great many instances, the bones and the joints are exposed by the remedy and not by the disease. One hint may not be necessary to the practitioner, but it may guide the determination and hopes of the owner; if, when a probe is introduced into the fistulous on the coronet, the direction of the *sinuses* or *pipes* is backward, there is much probability that a perfect cure may be effected; but if the direction of the sinuses is forward, the cure is at best doubtful. In the first instance, there is neither bone nor joint to be injured; in the other, the more important parts of the foot are in danger, and the principal action and concussion are found.

Neglected bruises of the sole sometimes lay the foundation for quittor. When the foot is flat, it is very liable to be bruised if the horse is ridden fast over a rough and stony road; or, a small stone, insinuating itself between the shoe and the sole, or confined by the curvature of the shoe, will frequently lame the horse. The heat and tenderness of the part, the occasional redness of the horn, and the absence of puncture, will clearly mark the bruise. The sole must then be thinned, and particularly over the bruised part, and, in neglected cases, it must be pared even to the quick, in order to ascertain whether the inflammation has run on to suppuration. Bleeding at the toe will be clearly indicated; and poultices, and such other means as have either been described under "Inflammation of the Feet," or will be pointed out under the next head. The principal causes of bruises of the foot are leaving the sole too much exposed by means of a narrow-webbed shoe, or the smith paring out the sole too closely, or the pressure of the shoe on the sole, or the introduction of gravel or stones between the shoe and the sole.

Th author subjoins the mode of cure in this disease, as it has been practised by two veterinary surgeons. They are both excellent, and, so far as can well be the case, satisfactory.

Mr. Percival says :—" The ordinary mode of cure consists in the introduction of *caustic* into the sinus ; and so long as the cartilage preserves its integrity—by which I mean, is free from decay—this is perhaps the most prompt and effectual mode of proceeding. The farrier's practice is to mix about half a drachm of corrosive sublimate in powder with twice or thrice the quantity of flour, and make them into a paste with water. This he takes up by little at a time with the point of his probe, and works it about into the sinus until the paste appears rising in the orifice above. After this is done, he commonly has the horse walked about for an hour or two, or even sent to slow work again, which produces a still more effectual solution of the caustic, at the same time that it tends greatly to its uniform and thorough diffusion into every recess and winding of the sinus. The consequence of this sharp caustic dressing is a general slough from the sinus. Every part of its interior surface is destroyed, and the dead particles become agglutinated, and cast off along with the discharges in the form of a dark, firm curdled mass, which the farrier calls the core ; and so it commonly proves, for granulations follow close behind it, and fill up the sinus."

The other mode of treatment is that of Mr. Newport, a surgeon of long standing :—" After the shoe has been removed, thin the sole until it will yield to the pressure of the thumb ; then cut the under parts of the wall in an oblique direction from the heel to the anterior part, immediately under the seat of complaint, and only as far as it extends, and rasp the side of the wall thin enough to give way to the pressure of the over-distended parts, and put on a bar-shoe rather elevated from the frog. Ascertain with a probe the direction of the sinuses, and introduce into them a *saturated solution of sulphate of zinc*, by means of a small syringe. Place over this dressing the common poultice, or the turpentine ointment, and renew the application every twenty-four hours. I have frequently found three or four such applications complete a cure. I should recommend that when the probe is introduced, in order to ascertain the progress of cure, that it be gently and carefully used, otherwise it may break down the new-formed lymph. I have found the solution very valuable, where the synovial fluid (joint-oil) has escaped, but not to be if the inflammation of the parts is great."*

PRICK OR WOUND IN THE SOLE OR CRUST.

This is the most frequent cause of quittor. It is evident that the sole is very liable to be wounded by nails, pieces of glass, or even sharp flints. Every part of the foot is subject to injuries of this description. The usual place at which these wounds are found, is in the hollow between the bars and the frog, or in the frog itself. In the fore-feet the injury will be generally recognized on the inner quarter, and on the hind-feet near the toe. In fact, these are the thinnest parts of the fore and hind-feet. Much more frequently the laminæ are wounded by the nail in shoeing; or if the nail does not penetrate through the internal surface of the crust, it is driven so close to it that it presses upon the fleshy parts beneath, and causes irritation and inflammation, and at length ulceration. When a horse becomes suddenly lame, after the legs have been carefully examined, and no cause of lameness appears in them, the shoe should be taken off. In many cases the offending substance will be immediately detected, or the additional heat felt in some part of the foot will point out the seat of injury; or, if the crust is rapped with the hammer all round, the flinching of the horse will discover it; or pressure with the pincers will render it evident.

When the shoe is removed for this examination, the smith should never be permitted to wrench it off, but each nail should be drawn separately, and examined as it is drawn, when some moisture appearing upon it will not unfrequently reveal the spot at which matter has been thrown out.

Sudden lameness occurring within two or three days after the

* *Note by Mr. Spooner.*—This disease is much less common than it used to be, in consequence of the improvement in shoeing and the discontinuance of calkin (calks). It is generally caused by a tread or an external bruise, the injury inflicted being deep-seated. It is also often produced by a festered corn, the matter from which having no depending opening, spreads upwards between the horn and the bone, and forms sinuses about the coronet in different directions, and under and within the cartilages of the foot. With regard to the cure, the first thing is to poultice well, after which an injection of the solution of sulphate of zinc will often effect a cure. In other cases it is necessary to lay open the sinuses or insert setons, bringing them out in some depending position. We have successfully inserted setons at the coronet, bringing them out severally at the heels and the bars of the foot. When the cartilage is in a state of caries, it is desirable to produce a slough by means of corrosive sublimate. By the adoption of these remedial measures, a cure can generally be effected; for our own part, we have scarcely ever yet met with a case of quittor which we have been unable to cure, though sometimes the treatment has been very protracted and troublesome.

horse has been shod, will lead to the suspicion that the smith has been in fault; yet no one who considers the thinness of the crust, and the difficulty of shoeing many feet, will blame him for sometimes pricking the animal. His fault will consist in concealing or denying that of which he will almost always be aware at the time of shoeing, from the flinching of the horse, or the dead sound, or the peculiar resistance that may be noticed in the driving of the nail.

When the seat of mischief is ascertained, the sole should be thinned round it, and at the nail-hole, or the puncture, it should be pared to the quick. The escape of some matter will now probably tell the nature of the injury, and remove its consequences. If it be puncture of the sole effected by some nail, or any similar body, picked up on the road, all that will be necessary is a little to enlarge the opening, and then to place on it a fledget of tow dipped in Friar's balsam, and over that a little common stopping. If there is much heat and lameness, a poultice should be applied.

A puncture near the centre of the sole is most dangerous, from its liability to wound the flexor tendon where it is inserted in the coffin-bone, from which much action is required; or it may even penetrate the joint between the navicular and coffin-bone.

If pricked by a nail, the treatment above described will usually soon effect a cure. It may, however, be prudent to keep the foot stopped for a few days. If the accident has been neglected, and matter begins to be formed, and to be pent up, and to press on the neighboring parts, and the horse evidently suffers extreme pain, and is sometimes scarcely able to put his foot to the ground, and much matter is poured out when the opening is enlarged, further precautions must be adopted. The fact must be recollected that the living and dead horn will never unite, and every portion of the horny sole that has separated from the fleshy sole above must be removed. *The separation must be followed as far as it reaches.* Much of the success of the treatment depends on this. No small strip or edge of separated horn must be suffered to press upon any part of the wound. The exposed fleshy sole must then be touched, but not too severely, with the butyr (chloride) of antimony, some soft and dry tow being spread on the part, the foot stopped, and a poultice placed over all if the foot seems to require it. On the following day a thin pellicle of horn will frequently be found over a part or the whole of the wound. This should be, yet very lightly, again touched with the caustic; but if there is an appearance of fungus sprouting from the exposed surface, the application of the butyr must be more severe, the tow being again placed over it, so as to afford considerable yet uniform pressure. Many days do not often elapse before the new horn covers the whole of the wound. In these extensive openings the Friar's balsam will not always be successful, but the cure must be effected by the judicious and never-too-severe use of the caustic. Bleeding at the toe, and physic, will be resorted to as useful auxiliaries when much inflammation arises.

CORNS.

In the angle between the bars (*c*, Fig. 47) and the quarters, the horn of the sole has sometimes a red appearance, and is more spongy and softer than at any other part. The horse flinches when this portion of the horn is pressed upon, and occasional or permanent lameness is produced. This disease of the foot is termed CORNS : bearing this resemblance to the corn of the human being, that it is produced by pressure, and is a cause of lameness. When corns are neglected, so much inflammation is produced in that part of the sensible sole, that suppuration follows; and to that, quittor succeeds, and the matter either undermines the horny sole, or is discharged at the coronet.

The pressure hereby produced manifests itself in various ways. When the foot becomes contracted, the part of the sole inclosed between the external crust that is wiring in, and the bars that are opposing that contraction (see Fig. 47), is placed in a kind of vice, and becomes inflamed; hence it is rare to see a contracted foot without corns. When the shoe is suffered to remain on too long, it becomes embedded in the heel of the foot : the external crust grows down on the outside of it, and the bearing is thrown on this angular portion of the sole. No part of the sole can bear continued pressure, and inflammation and corns are the result. From the length of wear, the shoe sometimes becomes loosened at the heels, and gravel insinuates itself between the shoe and the crust, and accumulates in this angle, and sometimes seriously wounds it.

The bars are too frequently cut away, and then the heel of the shoe must be bevelled inward, in order to answer to this absurd and injurious shaping of the foot. By this slanting direction of the heel of the shoe inward, an unnatural disposition to contraction is given, and the sole must suffer in two ways,—in being pressed upon by the shoe, and squeezed between the outer crust and the external portion of the bar. The shoe is often made unnecessarily narrow at the heels, by which this angle, seemingly less disposed to bear pressure than any other part of the foot, is exposed to accidental bruises. If, in the paring out of the foot, the smith should leave the bars prominent, he too frequently neglects to pare away the horn in the angle between the bars and the external crust; or if he cuts away the bars, he scarcely touches the horn at this point; and thus, before the horse has been shod a fortnight, the shoe rests on this angle, and produces corns. The use of a shoe for the fore feet, thickened at the heels, is, and especially in weak feet, a source of corns, from the undue bearing there is on the heels, and the concussion to which they are subject.

Corns are most frequent and serious in horses with thin horn and flat soles, and low weak heels. They do not often occur in the outside heel. It is of a stronger construction than the inside one. The method adopted by shoeing-smiths to ascertain the existence of corn by the pain evinced when they pinch the bar and crust with their irons, is very fallacious. If the horn is naturally thin, the horse will shrink under no great pressure although he has no corn, and occasionally the bars are so strong as not to give way under any pressure.

The cure of old corns is difficult; for as all shoeing has some tendency to produce pressure here, the habit of throwing out this diseased horn is difficult to get rid of when once contracted; recent corns, however, will yield to good shoeing.

The first thing to be done is well to pare out the angle between the crust and the bars. Two objects are answered by this: the extent of the disease will be ascertained, and one cause of it removed. A very small drawing-knife must be used for this purpose. The corn must be pared out to the very bottom, taking care not to wound the sole. It may then be discovered whether there is any effusion of blood or matter underneath. If this is suspected, an opening must be made through the horn, the matter evacuated, the separated horn taken away, the course and extent of the sinuses explored, and the treatment recommended for quittor adopted. Should there be no collection of fluid, the butyr of antimony should be applied over the whole extent of the corn, after the horn has been thinned as closely as possible. The object of this is to stimulate the sole to throw out more healthy horn. In bad cases a bar-shoe may be put on, so chambered, that there shall be no pressure on the diseased part. This may be worn for one or two shoeings, but not constantly, for there are few frogs that would bear the constant pressure of the bar-shoe; and the want of pressure on the heel, generally occasioned by their use, would produce a softened and bulbous state of the heels, that would of itself be an inevitable source of lameness.

The cause of corn is a most important subject of inquiry, and which a careful examination of the foot and the shoe will easily discover. The cause being ascertained, the effect may, to a great extent, be afterwards removed. Turning out to grass, after the horn is a little grown, first with a bar-shoe, and afterwards with the shoe fettered on one side, or with tips, will often be serviceable. A horse that has once had corns to any considerable extent should, at every shoeing, have the seat of corn well pared out, and the butyr of antimony applied. The *seated* shoe (hereafter to be described) should be used, with a web sufficiently thick to cover the place of corn, and extending as far back as it can be made to do without injury to the frog.

Low weak heels should be rarely touched with the knife, or anything more be done to them than lightly to rasp them, in order to give them a level surface. Where corns exist of any consequence, they are a disgrace to the smith, the groom, and to the owner.

THRUSH.

This is a discharge of offensive matter from the cleft of the frog. It is inflammation of the lower surface of the sensible frog, and during which pus is secreted together with, or instead of horn. When the frog is in its sound state, the cleft sinks but a little way into it; but when it becomes contracted or otherwise diseased, it extends in length, and penetrates even to the sensible horn within, and through this unnaturally deepened fissure the thrushy discharge proceeds. A very full and fleshy state of the body may be a predisposing cause of thrush, but the immediate and grand cause is moisture. This should never be forgotten, for it will lead a great way towards the proper treatment of the disease. If the feet are habitually covered with any moist application—his standing so much on his own dung is a fair example—thrush will inevitably appear. It is caused by anything that interferes with the healthy structure and action of the frog. We find it in the hinder feet oftener and worse than in the fore, because in our stable management the hinder feet are too much exposed to the pernicious effects of the dung and the urine, moistening, or as it were macerating, and at the same time irritating them.

In the fore-feet, thrushes are usually connected with contraction. We have stated that they are both the cause and the effect of contraction. The pressure on the frog from the wiring in of the heels will produce pain and inflammation; and the inflammation, by the increased heat and suspended function of the part, will dispose to contraction. Horses of all ages, and in almost all situations, are subject to thrush. The unshod colt is frequently thus diseased.

Thrushes are not always accompanied by lameness. In a great many cases the appearance of the foot is scarcely, or not at all altered, and the disease can only be detected by close examination, or the peculiar smell of the discharge. The frog may not appear to be rendered in the slightest degree tender by it, and therefore the horse may not be considered by many as unsound. Every disease, however, should be considered as legal unsoundness, and especially a disease which, although not attended with present detriment, must not be neglected, for it will eventually injure and lame the horse.

The progress of a neglected thrush, although sometimes slow, is sure. The frog begins to contract in size—it becomes rough, ragged, brittle, tender—the discharge is more copious and more offensive—the horn gradually disappears—a mass of hardened mucus usurps its place—this easily peels off, and the sensible frog remains exposed—the horse cannot bear it to be touched—fungous granulations spring from it—they spread around—the sole becomes under-run, and canker steals over the greater part of the foot.

If a young colt, fat and full of blood, has a bad thrush, with much discharge, it will be prudent to accompany the attempt at cure by a dose of physic or a course of diuretics. A few diuretics may not be injurious when we are endeavoring to dry up thrush in older horses.

There are many recipes to stop a running thrush. Almost every application of an astringent, but not of too caustic nature, will have the effect. The common Ægyptiacum (vinegar boiled with honey and verdigris) is a good liniment; but the most effectual and the safest—drying up the discharge speedily, but not suddenly—is a paste composed of blue vitriol, tar, and lard, in proportions according to the virulence of the canker. A pledget of tow, covered with it, should be introduced as deeply as possible, yet without force, into the cleft of the frog every night, and removed in the morning before the horse goes to work. Attention should at the same time, as in other diseases of the foot, be paid to the apparent cause of the complaint, and that cause should be carefully obviated or removed. Before the application of the paste, the frog should be examined, and every loose part of the horn or hardened discharge removed; and if much of the frog is then exposed, a larger and wider piece of tow, covered with the paste, may be placed over it, in addition to the pledget introduced into the cleft of the frog. It will be necessary to preserve the frog moist while the cure is in progress, and this may be done by filling the feet with tow, covered by common stopping, or using the felt pad, likewise covered with it. Turning out, would be prejudicial rather than of benefit to thrushy feet, except the dressing is continued, and the feet defended from moisture.

CANKER

Is a separation of the horn from the sensible part of the foot, and the sprouting of the fungous matter (proud-flesh) instead of it, occupying a portion or even the whole of the sole and frog. It is the occasional consequence of bruise, puncture, corn, quittor, and thrush, and is exceedingly difficult to cure. It is more frequently the consequence of neglected thrush than of any other disease of the foot, or rather it is thrush involving the frog, the bars, and the sole, and making the foot in one mass of rank putrefaction.

It is often found in, and is almost peculiar to, the heavy breed of cart-horses, and partly resulting from constitutional predisposition. Horses with white legs and thick skins, and much hair upon their legs—the very character of many dray-horses—are subject to canker, especially if they have an attack of grease, or their heels are habitually thick and greasy. The disposition to canker is certainly hereditary.

Although canker is a disease most difficult to remove, it is easily prevented. Attention to the punctures to which these heavy horses, with their clubbed feet and brittle hoofs, are more than any others subject in shoeing, and to the bruises and treads on the coronet, to which, from their awkwardness and weight, they are so liable, and the greasy heels which a very slight degree of negligence will produce in them, and the stopping of the thrushes, which are so apt in them to run on to the separation of the horn from the sensible frog, will most materially lessen the number of cankered feet.

The cure of canker is the business of the veterinary surgeon, and a most painful and tedious business it is. The principles on which he proceeds are, first of all, to remove the extraneous fungous growth; and for this purpose he will need the aid of the knife and the caustic, or the cautery, for he should cut away every portion of horn which is in the slightest degree separated from the sensible parts beneath. He will have to discourage the growth of fresh fungus, and to bring the foot into that state in which it will again secrete healthy horn. A slight and daily application of the chloride of antimony, and that not where the new horn is forming, but on the surface which continues to be diseased, and accompanied by as firm but equal pressure as can be made—the careful avoidance of the slightest degree of moisture—the horse being exercised or worked in the mill, or wherever the foot will not be exposed to wet. and that exercise adopted as early as possible, and even from the beginning, if the malady is confined to the sole and frog—

these means will succeed, if the disease is capable of cure. It is proper to resort to neurotomy, if the means of cure are persisted in. Medicine is not of much avail in the cure of canker, but as it sometimes alternates with other diseases, a course of alteratives or diuretics may be administered, when the cure is nearly completed.

OSSIFICATION OF THE CARTILAGES.

The cartilages embedded in the heels of the feet from bruises, sprains, &c., are subject to inflammation, and the result of that inflammation is that the cartilages are absorbed, and bone substituted in their stead. This is common in heavy draught-horses, particularly as they are used on paved streets.

No evident inflammation of the foot, or great, or perhaps even perceptible lameness, accompanies this change; a mere slight degree of stiffness may have been observed, which, in a horse of more rapid pace, would have been lameness. Even when the change is completed, there is not in many cases anything more than a slight increase of stiffness, little or not at all interfering with the usefulness of the horse. When this altered structure appears in the lighter horse, the lameness is more decided, and means should be taken to arrest the progress of the change. These are blisters or firing; but, after the parts have become bony, no operation will restore the cartilage. Some benefit, however, will be derived from the use of leather soles. Advantage has resulted from bar-shoes in conjunction with leather.

Connected with ringbone the lameness may be very great This has been spoken of in page 268.

WEAKNESS OF THE FOOT.

This is more accurately a bad formation, than a disease; often, indeed, the result of disease, but in many instances the natural construction of the foot. The term *weak foot* is familiar to every horseman, and the consequence is too severely felt by all who have to do with horses. In the slanting of the crust from the coronet to the toe, a less angle is almost invariably formed, amounting probably to not more than forty instead of forty-five degrees; and, after the horse has been worked for one or two years the line is not straight, but a little indented or hollow, midway between the coronet and the toe. This has been described as the accompaniment of pumiced feet, but it is often seen in weak feet, that, although they might become pumiced by severity of work, do not otherwise have the sole convex. The crust is not only less oblique than 't ought to be, but it has not the smooth, even appearance of the good foot. The surface is sometimes irregularly roughened, but it is much oftener roughened in circles or rings. The form of the crust likewise presents too much the appearance of a cone; the bottom of the foot is unnaturally wide in proportion to the coronet; and the whole of the foot is generally, but not always larger than it should be.

When the foot is lifted, it will often present a round and cirular appearance, with a fullness of frog, and would mislead the inexperienced, and indeed be considered as almost the perfection of structure; but, being examined more closely, many glaring defects will be seen. The sole is flat, and the smith finds that it will bear little or no paring. The bars are small in size. They are not cut away by the smith, but they can be scarcely said to have any existence. The heels are low, so low that the very coronet seems almost to touch the ground; and the crust, if examined, appears scarcely thick enough to hold the nails.

Horses with these feet can never stand much work. They will be subject to corns, to bruises of the sole, to convexity of the sole, to punctures in nailing, to breaking away of the crust, to inflammation of the foot, and to sprain and injury of the pastern, and the fetlock, and the flexor tendon.

These feet admit of little improvement. Shoeing as seldom as may be, and with a light yet wide concave web; little or no paring at the time of shoeing, and as little violent work as possible, and especially on rough roads, may protract for a long period the evil day, but he who buys a horse with these feet will sooner or later have cause to repent his bargain.

CHAPTER XVI.

FRACTURES.

Accidents of this description are not of unfrequent occurrence, but when they do happen it is not always that the mischief can be repaired; occasionally however, and much more frequently than is generally imagined, the life of a valuable animal might be saved if the owner, or the veterinary surgeon, would take a little trouble, and the patient is fairly tractable, and that, in the majority of cases, he will soon become, with kind treatment.

With the exception of accidents that occur in casting the animal for certain operations, and his struggles during the operation, the causes of FRACTURE are usually blows, kicks, or falls, and the lesion may be considered as *simple*, confined to one bone, and not protruding through the skin—or *compound*, the bone or bones protruding through the skin—or *complicated*, where the bone is broken or splintered in more than one direction. The duty of the veterinary surgeon resolves itself into the replacing of the displaced bones in their natural position, the keeping of them in that position, the healing of the integument, and the taking of such measures as will prevent any untoward circumstances from afterwards occurring.

In the greater number of cases of fracture, it will be necessary to place the horse under considerable restraint, or even to suspend or sling him.

Fig. 49 contains a view of the suspensory apparatus used by Mr. Percivall. A broad piece of sail-cloth, furnished with two breechings, and two breast-girths, is placed under the animal's belly, and, by means of ropes and pulleys attached to a cross beam above, he is elevated or lowered as circumstances may require. It will seldom be necessary to lift the patient quite off the ground, and the horse will be quietest, and most at his ease, when his feet are suffered just to touch it. The head is confined by two collar ropes, and the head-stall well padded. Many horses may plunge about and be difficult to manage at first, but generally speaking, it is not long ere they become perfectly passive.

334 FRACTURES.

The use of the different buckles and straps which are attached to the sail-cloth will be evident on inspection. If the horse exhibits more than usual uneasiness, other ropes may be attached to the corners of the sail-cloth. This will afford considerable relief to the patient, as well as add to the security of the bandages.

Fig. 49.

In many cases the fracture, although a simple one, may be visible on the slightest inspection; in others, there may be merely a suspicion of its existence. In detecting it, will be exhibited the skill and humanity of the educated surgeon, or the recklessness and brutality of the ignorant pretender.

Heat, swelling, tenderness, fearfulness of the slightest motion, crepitus, (crackling) and especially change of the natural position of the limb, are the most frequent indications of the fracture.

The probability of reunion of the parts depends upon the depth of the wound connected with the fracture—the contusion of the soft parts in the immediate neighborhood of it—the blood-vessels, arterial or venous, that have been wounded—the nearness of some large joint to which the inflammation may be communicated—dislocation of the extremities of the fractured joint—injuries of the periosteum—the existence of sinuses, caries, or ne crosis, (diseased bones), or the fracture being compound, or broken into numerous spiculæ or splinters.

In a horse that is full of flesh, the cure of fracture is difficult; likewise in an old or worn-out horse—or when the part is inaccessible to the hand or to instruments—or when separation has taken place between the parts that were beginning to unite—or when the surrounding tissues have been or are losing their vitality—or when the patient is already afflicted with any old or permanent disease.

It may be useful briefly to review the various seats of fracture.

FRACTURE OF THE SKULL.—Fracture of the skull is generally accompanied by stupidity, convulsive motions of the head or limbs, laborious breathing, and a staggering walk. The eyes are almost or quite closed, the head is carried low, and the lower lip hangs down. There are various instances on record of a portion of the depressed bone being removed and the animal recovering; and in some instances, a reunion of the depressed bones has taken place, leaving a permanent depression of the outer surface of the skull.

FRACTURE OF THE NASAL BONES.—This will sometimes occur from falling, or be produced by a kick from another horse, or the brutality of the attendant or the rider. A fracture of this kind is generally accompanied by a laceration of the membrane of the nose, and considerable hemorrhage, (flow of blood,) which, however, may generally be arrested by the application of cold water. The fractured portion of bone is usually depressed, and, the space for breathing being diminished, difficulty of respiration occurs.

If there is fracture of the nasal bones, with depression, and only a little way from the central arch and the section between the nostrils, a slightly curved steel rod may be cautiously introduced into the passage, and the depressed portions carefully raised. If this cannot be effected, the trephine must be applied a little above or below the fracture, and the elevator, or steel rod, be introduced through the aperture. If the fracture is in any other part of the bone, it will be impossible to reach it with the elevator, for the turbinated bones are in the way. The trephine must then be resorted to in the first instance. The wound, if there is any, must be covered, and a compress kept on it.

THE SUPERIOR MAXILLARY, OR UPPER JAW-BONE, will occasionally be fractured. Mr. Cartwright had a case in which it was fractured by a kick at the situation where it unites with the lacrymal and malar bones. He applied the trephine, and removed many small pieces of bone. The wound was then covered by adhesive plaster, and in a month the parts were healed.

Mr. Clayworth speaks of a mare which, being ridden almost at speed, fell and fractured the upper jaw, three inches above the corner incisors. The front teeth and jaw were turned like a hook, completely within the lower ones. She was cast, a balling iron put into her mouth, and the surgeon, exerting considerable force, pulled the teeth outward into their former and proper situation. She was then tied up, so that she could not rub her muzzle against anything, and was well fed with bean-meal, and linseed tea. Much inflammation ensued, but it gradually subsided, and, at the expiration of the sixth week, the mouth was quite healed, and scarcely a vestige of the fracture remained.

THE MAXILLARY BONE, OR LOWER JAW, is more subject to fracture, and particularly in its branches between the tushes and the lower teeth, and at the symphysis (union by cartilage) between the two branches of the jaw. Its position, its length, and the small quantity of muscle that covers it, especially anteriorly, are among the causes of its fracture, and the same circumstances combine to render a reunion of the divided parts more easy to be accomplished. Mr. Blaine relates that, in a fracture of the lower jaw, he succeeded by making a strong leather frame that exactly encased the whole jaw. The author of this volume has effected the same object by similar means.

In the majority of these cases of simple fracture, a cure might be effected, or should, at least, be attempted, by means of well-adapted bandages around the muzzle, confined by straps. It will always be prudent to call in veterinary aid, and it is absolutely necessary in case of compound fracture of the lower jaw.

FRACTURE OF THE SPINE.—This accident, fortunately for the horse, is not of frequent occurrence, but it has been uniformly fatal. It sometimes happens in the act of falling, as in leaping a wide ditch; but it oftener occurs while a horse is struggling during a painful operation. It is generally sufficiently evident while the horse is on the ground. Either a snap is heard, indicative of the fracture, or the struggles of the hind-limbs suddenly and altogether cease. In a few cases, the animal has been able to get up and walk to his stable; in others, the existence of the fracture has not been apparent for several hours: showing that the vertebræ, although fractured, may remain in their place for a certain period of time. The bone that is broken, is usually one of the posterior dorsal or anterior lumbar vertebræ. There is no satisfactory case on record of reunion of the fractured parts.

FRACTURE OF THE RIBS.—These fractures are not always easily recognized. Those that are covered by the scapula (shoulder-blade) may exist for a long time without being detected, and those that are situated posteriorly are so thickly covered by muscles as to render the detection of the injury almost impossible.

The ordinary causes of fracture are kicks and blows, or falls. The fractures are generally about their middle, and, in the true ribs, commonly oblique. They are occasionally broken into splinters, and if those splinters are directed inward, they may seriously wound the pleura or lungs. In order most certainly to detect the situation and extent of these fractures, it may be necessary to trace the rib through its whole extent, and, should there be any irregularity, to press firmly upon it above and below in order to ascertain the nature and extent of the injury.

If fracture is detected, it is not often that much essential good can be done. If there is little or no displacement, a broad roller should be tightly drawn round the chest, in order to prevent as much as possible the motion of the ribs in the act of breathing, and to throw the labor on the diaphragm and the abdominal muscles until the fractured parts are united. If the fractured parts protrude outwards, a firm compress must be placed upon them. If they are depressed, it will always be advisable to place a firm bandage over the seat of fracture, although, perhaps, there may be scarcely the possibility of elevating them to any considerable degree. Should much irritation be the consequence of the nature or direction of the fracture, proper means must be adopted to allay the constitutional disturbance that may be produced. General or local bleedings will be most serviceable.

FRACTURE OF THE PELVIS.—This is not of frequent occurrence, on account of the thickness of the soft parts which surround the pelvis, and protect it from injury, but it is of a serious character when it does take place, on account of the violence which must have been necessary to produce it. The usual cases are falls from a considerable height, or heavy blows on the pelvis. The injury may have reference to the internal or external portion of the pelvis. In the first case, the danger may not be discovered until irreparable mischief is produced. When it is chiefly external, the altered appearance of the hip speaks for itself. It is rarely in our power to afford any assistance in cases like this, except when there are fractured portions of the bone that may be partially or entirely removed, or the projecting spine of the ilium is only partially fractured.

FRACTURE OF THE TAIL.—This accident is not of frequent occurrence, except from accidental entanglement, or the application of brute force. The fracture is easily recognized, frequently by the eye and always by the fingers. If the tail is not amputated, a cord passed over a pulley, and with a small weight attached to it, will bring the separated bones again into apposition, and in about a month the natural cartilage of the part will be sufficiently reinstated.

FRACTURES OF THE LIMBS.—These, fortunately, are of rare occurrence in the horse, for although their divided edges might be easily brought again into apposition, it would be almost in-possible to retain them in it, for the slightest motion would displace them. A rapid survey of each may not, however, be altogether useless.

FRACTURE OF THE SHOULDER.—The author is not aware of the successful treatment of this accident by any English veterinary surgeon.

It is not at all times easy to discover the existence and precise situation of fracture of the humerus. The lameness is very great —the animal will not bear at all upon the broken limb—he will drag it along the ground—he will move slowly and with difficulty, and his progression will consist of a succession of short leaps The lifting of the foot will give very great pain. If he is roughly handled, he will sometimes rear, or throw himself suddenly down. By careful application of the hand, a crepitus (crackling sound) will more or less distinctly be heard.

FRACTURE OF THE ARM.—This accident is not of unfrequent occurrence. It commonly takes an oblique direction, and is usually first discovered by the displacement of the limb. Mr. Gloag, of the 10th Hussars, gives an interesting account of a case that occurred in his practice. "An entire black cart-horse was grazing in a field, into which some mares were accidentally turned. One of them kicked him severely a little above the knee. He, however, contrived to get home, and being carefully examined, there was found a simple fracture of the radius, about an inch and a half above the knee. The ends of the fractured bone could be heard distinctly grating against each other, both in advancing the leg and turning it sideway from the body. He was immediately placed in a sling not completely elevated from the ground, but in which he could occasionally relieve himself by standing. The leg was well bathed with warm water, and the ends of the bone brought as true to their position as possible. Some thin slips of green wood were then immersed in boiling water until they would readily bend to the shape of the knee, and they were tied round the joint, reaching about nine inches above and six below the knee, the ends of them being tied round with tow.

A fortnight afterwards he became very troublesome, knocking his foot on the ground, and when, at the expiration of the sixth week, he was taken from the slings, there was a considerable bony deposit above the knee. This, however, gradually subsided as the horse regained his strength, and, with the exception of turning the leg a little outwards, he is as useful as ever for common purposes."

FRACTURE OF THE ELBOW.—This is far more exposed to danger than the two last bones, and is oftener fractured. The fracture is generally an oblique one, and about two-thirds from the summit of the limb. It is immediately detected by the altered action, and different appearance of the limb. It is not so difficult of reduction as either the humerus or the scapula, when the fracture is towards the middle of the bone. A great quantity of tow saturated with pitch must be placed around the elbow, and confined with firm adhesive plasters, the ground being hollowed away in the front of the injured leg, so that no pressure shall be made by that foot.

FRACTURE OF THE FEMUR.—Considering the masses of muscle that surround this bone, and the immense weight which it supports, it would naturally be deemed impossible to reduce a real fracture of the femur. If the divided bones are ever united, it is a consequence of the simple repose of the parts, and their tendency to unite.

FRACTURE OF THE PATELLA.—This does occasionally, though very seldom, occur. It is usually the consequence of violent kicks, or blows, and if this singular bone is once disunited, no power can bring the divided portions of the bone together again.

FRACTURE OF THE TIBIA.—This affection is of more frequent occurrence, and of more serious consequence, than we were accustomed to imagine it to be.

Mr. J. S. Mayer gives an interesting account of the successful treatment of a case of fracture of the tibia. The simplicity of the process will, we trust, encourage many another veterinary surgeon to follow his example.

"A horse received a blow on the tibia of the near leg; but little notice was taken of it for two or three days. When, however, we were called in to examine him, we found the tibia to be obliquely fractured about midway between the hock and the stifle, and a small wound existing on the inside of the leg. It was set in the following manner:—The leg, from the stifle down to the hock, was well covered with an adhesive compound; it was then wrapped round with fine tow, upon which another layer of the same adhesive mixture was laid, the whole being well splinted and bandaged up, so as to render what was a slightly compound fracture a simple one. The local inflammation and sympathetic fever that supervened were kept down by antiphlogistic measures. At the end of six weeks the bandages and splints were removed, and readjusted in a similar way as before, and at the termination of three months from the time of the accident he was discharged, cured, the splints being wholly taken off, and merely an adhesive stay kept on the leg. The horse is now at work and quite sound, there being merely a little thickening, where the callus is formed."

FRACTURE OF THE HOCK.—This is not of frequent occurrence, but very difficult to treat, from the almost impossibility of finding means to retain the bone in its situation. A case, however, somewhat simple in its nature, occurred in the practice of Mr. Cartwright. A colt, leaping at some rails, got his leg between them, and, unable to extricate himself, hung over on the other side. After being liberated it appeared, on examination, that there was a simple horizontal fracture of the whole of the os calcis about the middle. A splint was contrived so as to reach from the middle of the tibia to that of the cannon bone, and this was applied to the front of the leg, keeping the hock from its usual motion, and relaxing the muscles inserted into the os calcis. Underneath this splint a charge was applied about the part, in order to form a level surface for the splint to rest upon. The whole was bound together by proper adhesive bandages, and he was ordered to be kept quiet in the stable, but not to be slung. In about two months the hock was fired and became perfectly sound.

FRACTURE OF THE CANNON OR SHANK BONE.—This is of more frequent occurrence than that of any other bone, on account of the length of the leg, and the danger to which it is exposed There is rarely any difficulty in detecting its situation, but there is sometimes a great deal in bringing the divided edges of the bone again into apposition. A kind of windlass, or a power equal to it, is occasionally necessary to produce sufficient extension in order to effect the desired purpose: but the divided edges being brought into apposition are retained there by the force of the muscles above. Splints reaching from the foot to above the knee should then be applied. The horse should be racked up during a fortnight, after which, if the case is going on well, the animal may often be turned out.

In cases of compound fracture the wounds should be carefully attended to: but Mr. Percivall says that he knows one or two old practitioners, who are in the habit of treating these cases in a very summary and generally successful manner. They employ such common support, with splints and tow and bandages, as the case seems to require, and then the animal with his leg bound up is turned out, if the season permits; otherwise he is placed in a yard or box, where there is not much straw to incommode his movements. The animal will take care not to impose too much weight on his fractured limb; and, provided the parts are well secured, nature will generally perform the rest.

FRACTURE OF THE SESAMOID BONES.—There are but two instances of this on record.

FRACTURE OF THE UPPER PASTERN.—Thick and strong, and movable as this bone seems to be, it is occasionally fractured. This has been the consequence of a violent effort by the horse to save himself from falling, when he has stumbled,—it has happened when he has been incautiously permitted to run down a steep descent—and has occurred when a horse has been travelling on the best road, and at no great pace.

The existence of fracture in this bone is, generally speaking, easily detected. The injured foot is, as lightly as possible, permitted to come in contact with the ground. As little weight as may be is thrown on it, or, if the animal is compelled to use it, the fetlock is bent down nearly to the ground, and the toe is turned upward. If the foot is turned sideways a crackling sound is generally heard, though this is not always the case.

The probability of success in the treatment of this fracture, depends on its being a simple or compound one. If it runs laterally across the bone, it may be readily and successfully treated—if it extends to the joints above and below, it will probably terminate in anchylosis (bony union), and if the bone is shivered, as it too frequently is, into various parts, there would scarcely seem the possibility of a successful treatment of the case. The instances, however, are numerous in which the case terminates successfully. Hurtrel d'Arboval recommends that a bandage steeped in some adhesive matter should be applied from the coronet to the middle of the leg. On this some wet pasteboard is to be moulded, enveloped afterwards in a linen bandage. A small splint is now to be applied before and behind and on each side, and the hollow places are filled with tow, in order to give them an equal bearing. If this does not appear to be sufficiently secure, other splints, thicker and broader, are placed over those extending to the knee or the hock.

The case related by M. Levrat was treated in this way. It will be comparatively seldom that it will be necessary to suspend the patient. The animal, under the treatment of M. Levrat, kept his foot in the air for nearly three weeks. At the end of that period he now and then tried to rest his toe on the litter. Six weeks after the accident, he began to throw some weight on the foot; and a few days afterwards he was able to go to a pond, about fifty paces from his stable, and where, of his own accord, he took a foot-bath for nearly an hour at a time. At the expiration of another month he was mounted, and went well at a walking pace; he was, however, still lame when he was trotted.

FRACTURE OF THE LOWER PASTERN.—Although this bone is much shorter than the upper pastern, there are several instances of fracture of it. The fractures of this bone are commonly longitudinal, and often extend from the larger pastern to the coffin-bone. It is frequently splintered, the splinters taking this longitudinal direction. Hutrel d'Arboval relates three cases of this, and in one of them the bone was splintered into four pieces. In several instances, however, this bone has been separated into eight or ten distinct pieces. When the fracture of the bone is neither compound nor complicated, it may be perfectly reduced by proper bandaging, and, in fact, there have been cases, in which union has taken place with slight assistance from art beyond the application of a few bandages.

FRACTURE OF THE COFFIN-BONE.—This is an accident of very rare occurrence, and difficult to distinguish from other causes of lameness. The animal halts very considerably—the foot is hot and tender—the pain seems to be exceedingly great, and none of the ordinary causes of lameness are perceived. According to Hurtrel D'Arboval, it is not so serious an accident as has been represented. The fractured portions cannot be displaced, and in a vascular bone like this, the union of the divided parts will be readily effected.

FRACTURE OF THE NAVICULAR BONE has been sufficiently considered under the article "Navicular Joint Disease," p. 311.

CHAPTER XVII.

ON SHOEING, ETC.

The period when the shoe began to be nailed to the foot of the horse is uncertain. William the Norman introduced it into our country.

Far more than is generally imagined, do the comfort and health of the horse, and the safety of his rider, depend upon shoeing.

In taking off the old shoe, the clenches of the nails should always be carefully raised or filed off; and, where the foot is tender, or the horse is to be examined for lameness, each nail should be partly punched out.

The edges of the crust are then to be rasped to detect whether any stubs remain in the nail-holes, and to remove the crust into which dirt and gravel have insinuated themselves.

Next comes the important process of paring out, with regard to which it is almost impossible to lay down any specific rules. This, however, is undoubted, that far more injury has been done by the neglect of paring, than by carrying it to too great an extent. The act of paring is a work of much more labor than the proprietor of the horse often imagines. The smith, except he is overlooked, will frequently give himself as little trouble about it as he can; and that portion of horn which, in the unshod foot, would be worn away by contact with the ground, is suffered to accumulate month after month, until the elasticity of the sole is destroyed, and it can no longer descend, and its other functions are impeded, and foundation is laid for corn, and contraction, and navicular disease, and inflammation. That portion of horn should be left on the foot, which will defend the internal parts from being bruised, and yet suffer the external sole to descend How is this to be ascertained? The strong pressure of the thumb of the smith will be the best guide. The buttress, that most destructive of all instruments, being, except on very particular occasions, banished from every respectable forge, the smith sets to work with his drawing-knife, and removes the growth of horn, until the sole will yield, although in the slightest possible degree, to the strong pressure of his thumb. The proper thickness of horn will then remain.

The quantity of horn to be removed, in order to leave the proper degree of thickness, will vary with different feet. From the strong foot, a great deal must be taken. From the concave foot, the horn may be removed until the sole will yield to a moderate pressure. From the flat foot, little needs be pared; while the pumiced foot should be deprived of nothing but the ragged parts.

The crust should be reduced to a perfect level all round, but left a little higher than the sole, or the sole will be bruised by its pressure on the edge of the seating.

The heels will require considerable attention. From the stress which is thrown on the inner heel, and from the weakness of the quarter there, the horn usually wears away considerably faster than it would on the outer one, and if an equal portion of horn were pared from it, it would be left lower than the outer heel. The smith should therefore accommodate his paring to the comparative wear of the heels, and be exceedingly careful to leave them precisely level.

The portion of the heels between the inflection of the bar and the frog should scarcely be touched—at least, the ragged and detached parts alone should be cut away. The foot may not look so fair and open, but it will last longer without contraction.

The bar, likewise, should be left fully prominent, not only at its first inflection, but as it runs down the side of the frog. The heel of the shoe is designed to rest partly on the heel of the foot and partly on the bar, for reasons that have been already stated. If the bar is weak, the growth of it should be encouraged; and it should be scarcely touched when the horse is shod, unless it has attained a level with the crust.

It will also be apparent, that the horn between the crust and the bar should be carefully pared out. Every horseman has observed the relief which is given to the animal lame with corns, when this angle is well thinned.

The degree of paring to which the frog must be subjected, will depend on its prominence, and on the shape of the foot. The principle has already been stated, that it must be left so far projecting and prominent, that it shall be just within and above the lower surface of the shoe; it will then descend with the sole sufficiently to discharge the functions that have been attributed to it. If it is lower, it will be bruised and injured; if it is higher, it cannot come in contact with the ground, and thus be enabled to do its duty. The ragged parts must be removed, and especially those occasioned by thrush, but the degree of paring must depend entirely on the principle just stated.

PUTTING ON THE SHOE.

The shoe should accurately fit the size of the foot; if too small, and the foot is rasped down to fit the shoe, the crust is thinned where it receives the nail, and the danger of puncture, and of pressure upon the sole, is increased; and a foot so artificially diminished in size, will soon grow over the shoe, to the hazard of considerable or permanent lameness.

The shoe should be properly bevelled off, that the dirt, gravel, &c., which gets between it and the foot may be shaken out.

The web of the shoe is likewise of that thickness, that when the foot is properly pared, the prominent part of the frog shall lie just within and above its ground surface, so that in the descent of the sole, the frog shall come sufficiently on the ground to enable it to act as a wedge, and to expand the quarters, while it is defended from the wear and injury it would receive, if it came on the ground with the first and full shock of the weight.

The nail-holes are, on the ground side, placed as near the outer edge of the shoe as they can safely be, and brought out near the inner edge of the seating. The nails thus take a direction inwards, resembling that of the crust itself, and have firmer hold, and the weight of the horse being thrown on a flat surface, contraction is not so likely to be produced.

It is expedient not only that the foot and ground surface of the shoe should be most accurately level, but that the crust should be exactly smoothed and fitted to the shoe. Much skill and time are necessary to do this perfectly with the drawing-knife. The smith has adopted a method of more quickly, and more accurately adapting the shoe to the foot. He pares the crust as level as he can, and then he brings the shoe to a heat somewhat below a red heat, and applies it to the foot, and detects any little elevations by the deeper color of the burned horn. This practice has been much inveighed against; but it is the abuse, and not the use of the thing which is to be condemned. If the shoe is not too hot, nor held too long on the foot, an accuracy of adjustment is thus obtained, which the knife would be long in producing, or would not produce at all. If, however, the shoe is made to burn its way to its seat, with little or no previous preparation of the foot, the heat must be injurious both to the sensible and insensible parts of the foot.

The heels of the shoe should be examined as to their proper width. Whatever is the custom of shoeing the horses of dealers, and the too prevalent practice in the metropolis of giving the foot an open appearance, although the posterior part of it is thereby exposed to injury, nothing is more certain than that, in the horse destined for road-work, the heels, and particularly the seat of corn, can scarcely be too well covered. Part of the shoe projecting externally can be of no possible good, but will prove an occasional source of mischief, and especially in a heavy country. A shoe, the web of which projects inward as far as it can without touching the frog, affords protection to the angle between the bars and he crust.

Of the manner of attaching the shoe to the foot the owner can scarcely be a competent judge; he can only take care that the shoe itself shall not be heavier than the work requires—that, for work a little hard the shoe shall still be light, with a bit of steel welded into the toe—that the nails shall be as small, and as few, and as far from the heels as may be consistent with the security of the shoe; and that, for light work at least, the shoe shall not be driven on so closely and firmly as is often done, nor the points of the nails be brought out so high up as is generally practised.

CALKINS.*

There are few cases in which the use of calkins (a turning up or elevation of the heel) can be admissible in the fore-feet, except in frosty weather, when it may in some degree prevent unpleasant or dangerous slipping. If, however, calkins are used, they should be placed on both sides. If the outer heel only is raised with the calkin, as is too often the case, the weight cannot be thrown evenly on the foot, and undue straining and injury of some part of the foot or of the leg must be the necessary consequence.

CLIPS.

These are portions of the upper edge of the shoe, hammered out, and turned up so as to embrace the lower part of the crust and which is usually pared out a little, in order to receive the clip. They are very useful, as more securely attaching the shoe to the foot, and relieving the crust from that stress upon the nails which would otherwise be injurious. A clip at the toe is almost necessary in every draught-horse, and absolutely so in the horse of heavy draught, in order to prevent the shoe from being loosened or torn off by the pressure which is thrown upon the toe in the act of drawing. A clip on the outside of each shoe, at the beginning of the quarters, will give security to it. Clips are likewise necessary on the shoes of all heavy horses, and of all others who are disposed to stamp, or violently paw with their feet, and thus incur the danger of displacing the shoe; but they are evils

---

* Called " calks," or vulgarly, " corks," in the U. S.—*Am. Ed*

inasmuch as they press upon the crust as it grows down, and they should only be used when circumstances absolutely require them. In the hunter's shoe they are not required at the sides. One at the toe is sufficient.

THE HINDER SHOE.

In forming the *hinder* shoes it should be remembered that the hind limbs are the principal instruments in progression, and that in every act of progression, except the walk, the toe is the point on which the whole frame of the animal turns, and from which it is propelled. This part, then, should be strengthened as much as possible ; and, therefore, the hinder shoes are made broader at the toe than the fore ones. Another good effect is produced by this, that, the hinder foot being shortened, there is less danger of *over-reaching, forging*, or *clinking*, and especially if the shoe is wider on the foot surface than on the ground one. The shoe is thus made to slope inward, and is a little within the toe of the crust.

The shape of the hinder foot is somewhat different from that of the fore foot. It is straighter in the quarters, and the shoe must have the same form. For carriage- and draught-horses generally calkins may be put on the heels, because the animal will be thus enabled to dig his toe more firmly into the ground, and urge himself forward, and throw his weight into the collar with greater advantage : but the calkins must not be too high, and they must be of an equal height on each heel, otherwise, as has been stated with regard to the fore feet, the weight will not be fairly distributed over the foot, and some part of the foot or the leg will materially suffer. The nails in the hinder shoe may be placed nearer to the heel than in the fore shoe, because, from the comparatively little weight and concussion thrown on the hinder feet, there is not so much danger of contraction.

DIFFERENT KINDS OF SHOES.

The shoe must vary in substance and weight with the kind of foot, and the nature of the work. A weak foot should never wear a heavy shoe, nor any foot a shoe that will last longer than a month. Here, perhaps, we may be permitted to caution the horse-proprietor against having his cattle shod by contract, unless he binds his farrier or veterinary surgeon to remove the shoes once at least in every month ; for if the contractor, by a heavy shoe, and a little steel, can cause five or six weeks to intervene between the shoeings, he will do so, although the feet of the horse must necessarily suffer. The shoe should never be heavier than the work requires, for an ounce or two in the weight of the shoe will sadly tell at the end of a hard day's work. This is acknowledged in the hunting-shoe, which is narrower and lighter than that of the hackney, although the foot of the hackney is smaller than that of the hunter. It is more decidedly acknowledged in the racer, who wears a shoe only sufficiently thick to prevent it from bending when it is used.

THE CONCAVE SEATED SHOE.

A cut is subjoined of a shoe which is useful and valuable for general purposes. It is employed in many of our best forges, and promises gradually to supersede the flat and the simple concave shoe, although it must, in many respects, yield to the unilateral shoe.

It presents a perfectly flat surface to the ground, in order to give as many points of bearing as possible, except that, on the outer edge, there is a groove or *fuller*, in which the nail-holes are punched, so that, sinking into the fuller, their heads project but a little way, and are soon worn down level with the shoe.

Fig. 50.

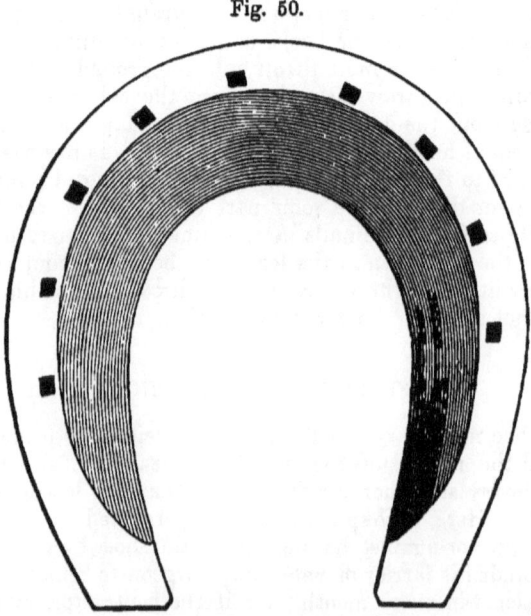

The web of this shoe is of the same thickness throughout, from the toe to the heel; and it is sufficiently wide to guard the sole from bruises, and, as much so as the frog will permit, to cover the seat of corn.

On the foot side it is *seated*. The outer part of it is accurately flat, and of the width of the crust, and designed to support the crust, for by it the whole weight of the horse is sustained.

Towards the heel this flattened part is wider and occupies the whole breadth of the web, in order to support the heel of the crust and its reflected part—the bar; thus, while it defends the horn included within this angle from injury, it gives that equal pressure from the bar and the crust, which is the best preventive against corns, and a powerful obstacle to contraction.

It is fastened to the foot by nine nails—five on the outside, and four on the inner side of the shoe; those on the outside extending a little farther down towards the heel, because the outside heel is thicker and stronger, and there is more nail-hold; the last nail on the inner quarter being farther from the heel, on account of the weakness of that quarter. For feet not too large, and where moderate work only is required from the horse, four nails on the outside, and three on the inside, will be sufficient; and the last nail being far from the heels, will allow more expansion there.

The inside part of the web is bevelled off, or rendered concave, that it may not press upon the sole. Notwithstanding the shoe, the sole does, although to a very inconsiderable extent, descend when the foot of the horse is put on the ground. It is unable to bear constant or even occasional pressure, and if it came in contact with the shoe, the sensible sole between it and the coffin-bone would be bruised, and lameness would ensue. Many of our horses, from too early and undue work, have the natural concave sole flattened, and the disposition to descend, and the degree of descent, are thereby increased. The concave shoe prevents, even in this case, the possibility of much injury, because the sole can never descend in the degree in which the shoe is or may be bevelled. A shoe bevelled still farther is necessary to protect the projecting or pumiced foot.

THE UNILATERAL, OR ONE SIDE NAILED SHOE.

This is a material improvement in the art of shoeing, for which we are indebted to Mr. Turner.

What was the state of the foot of the horse a few years ago? An unyielding iron hoof was attached to it by four nails in each quarter, and the consequence was, that in nine cases out of ten the foot underwent a very considerable alteration in its form and in its usefulness. Before it had attained its full developement—before the animal was five years old, there was, in a great many cases, an evident contraction of the hoof. There was an alteration in the manner of going. The step was shortened, the sole was hollowed, the frog was diseased, the general elasticity of the foot was destroyed—there was a disorganization of the whole horny cavity, and the value of the horse was materially diminished. What was the grand cause of this? It was the restraint f the shoe. The firm attachment of it to the foot by nails in ach quarter, and the consequent strain to which the quarters and every part of the foot were exposed, produced a necessary tendency to contraction, from which sprang almost all the maladies to which the foot of the horse is subject.

The unilateral shoe has this great advantage: it is identified with the grand principle of the expansibility of the horse's foot, and of removing or preventing the worst ailments to which the foot of the horse is liable. It can be truly stated of this shoe, that while it affords to the whole organ an iron defence equal to the common shoe, it permits, what the common shoe never did or can do, the perfect liberty of the foot.

We are enabled to present our readers with the last improvement of the unilateral shoe.

Fig. 51.

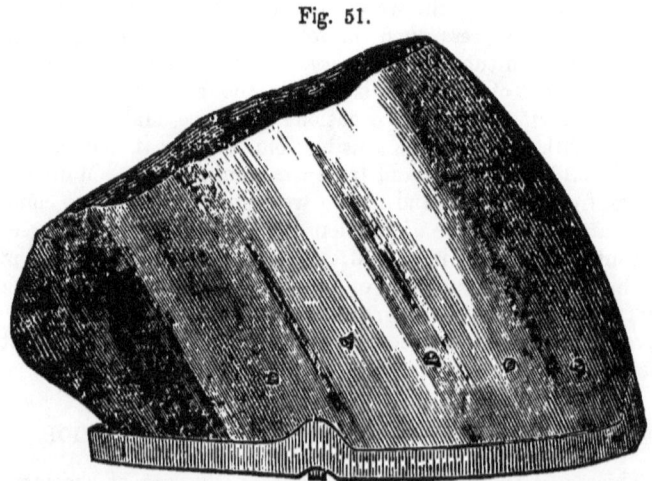

The above cut gives a view of the outer side of the off or right unilateral shoe. The respective situations of the five nails will be observed; the distance of the last from the heel, and the proper situations at which they emerge from the crust. The two clips will likewise be seen—one in the front of the foot, and the other n the side between the last and second nail.

Fig. 52 gives a view of the inner side of the unilateral shoe. The two nails near the toe are in the situation in which Mr. Turner directs that they should be placed, and behind them is no other attachment, between the shoe and the crust. The portion of the crust which is rasped off from the inner surface of the shoe, is now, we believe, not often removed from the side of the foot; it has an unpleasant appearance, and the rasping is somewhat unnecessary. The heel of this shoe exhibits the method which Mr. Turner has adopted, and with considerable success, for the cure of corns; he cuts away a portion of the ground surface at the heel, and injurious compression or concussion is rendered in a manner impossible.

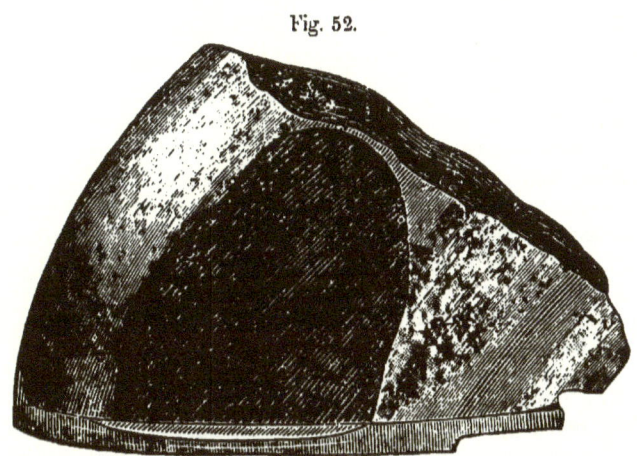

Fig. 52.

There can be no doubt that this one-sided nailing has been exceedingly useful. It has, in many a case that threatened a serious termination, restored the elasticity of the foot, and enabled it to discharge its natural functions. It has also restored to the foot, even in bad cases, a great deal of its natural formation, and enabled the horse to discharge his duty with more ease and pleasure to himself, and greater security to his rider.

THE HUNTING SHOE.

The hunter's shoe is different from that commonly used, in form as well as in weight. It is not so much bevelled off as the common concave-seated shoe. Sufficient space alone is left for the introduction of a picker between the shoe and the sole, otherwise, in going over heavy ground, the clay would insinuate itself, and by its tenacity loosen, and even tear off the shoe. The heels likewise are somewhat shorter, that they may not be torn off by the toe of the hind-feet when galloping fast, and the outer heel is frequently but injuriously turned up to prevent slipping. If calkins are necessary both heels should have an equal bearing.

THE BAR-SHOE.

A bar-shoe is often exceedingly useful. It is the continuation of the common shoe round the heels, and by means of it the pressure may be taken off from some tender part of the foot, and thrown on another which is better able to bear it, or more widely and equally diffused over the whole foot. It is principally resorted to in cases of corn, the seat of which it perfectly covers— in pumiced feet, the soles of which may be thus elevated above the ground and secured from pressure,—in sand-crack, when the pressure may be removed from the fissure, and thrown on either side of it, and in thrushes, when the frog is tender, or is become cankered, and requires to be frequently dressed, and the dressing can by this means alone be retained. In these cases the bar-shoe is an excellent contrivance, if worn only for one or two shoeings, or as long as the disease requires it to be worn, but it must be left off as soon as it can be dispensed with. If it is used for the protection of a diseased foot, however, it may be chambered and laid off the frog, it will soon become flattened upon it; or if the pressure of it is thrown on the frog in order to relieve the sand-crack or the corn, that frog must be very strong and healthy which can long bear the great and continued pressure. More mischief is often produced in the frog than previously existed in the part that was relieved. It will be plain that in the use of the bar-shoe for corn or sand-crack, the crust and the frog should be precisely on a level; the bar also should be the widest part of the shoe, in order to afford as extended bearing as possible on the frog and therefore less likely to be injurious. Bar-shoes are evidently not safe in frosty weather. They are never safe when much speed is required from the horse, and they are apt to be wrenched off in a heavy, clayey country.

TIPS.

Tips are short shoes, reaching only half round the foot, and worn while the horse is at grass, in order to prevent the crust being torn by the occasional hardness of the ground, or the pawing of the animal. The quarters at the same time being free, the foot disposed to contract has a chance of expanding and regaining its natural shape.

THE EXPANDING SHOE.

Our subject would not be complete if we did not describe the supposed expanding shoe, although it is now almost entirely out of use. It is either seated or concave like the common shoe, with a joint at the toe, by which the natural expansion of the foot is said to be permitted, and the injurious consequences of shoeing prevented. There is, however, this radical defect in the jointed shoe, that the nails occupy the same situation as in the common shoe, and prevent, as they do, the gradual expansion of the sides and quarters, and allow only of the hinge-like motion at the toe. It is a most imperfect accommodation of the expansion of the foot to the action of its internal parts, and even this accommodation is afforded in the slightest possible degree, if it is afforded at all. Either the nails fix the sides and quarters as in the common shoe, and then the joint at the toe is useless: or, if that joint merely opens like a hinge, the nail-holes near the toe can no longer correspond with those in the quarters, which are unequally expanding at every point. There will be more stress on the crust at these holes, which will not only enlarge them and destroy the fixed attachment of the shoe to the hoof, but often tear away portions of the crust. This shoe, in order to answer the intended purpose, should consist of many joints, running along the sides and quarters, which would make it too complicated and expensive and frail for general use.

While the shoe is to be attached to the foot by nails, we must be content with the concave-seated or unilateral one, taking care to place the nail-holes so far from the heels, and particularly from the inner heel, as the state of the foot and the nature of the work will admit; and where the country is not too heavy nor the work too severe, omitting all but two on the inner side of the foot.

FELT OR LEATHER SOLES.

When the foot is bruised or inflamed, the concussion or shock produced by the hard contact of the elastic iron with the ground gives the animal much pain, and aggravates the injury or disease. A strip of felt or leather is, therefore, sometimes placed between the seating of the shoe and the crust, which, from its want of elasticity, deadens or materially lessens the vibration or shock, and the horse treads more freely and is evidently relieved. This is a good contrivance while the inflammation or tenderness of the foot continues, but a very bad practice if constantly adopted. The nails cannot be driven so surely or securely when this substance is interposed between the shoe and the foot. The contraction and swelling of the felt or leather from the effect of moisture or dryness will soon render the attachment of the shoe less firm—there will be too much play upon the nails—the nail-holes will enlarge, and the crust will be broken away.

After wounds or extensive bruises of the sole, or where the sole is thin and flat and tender, it is sometimes covered with a piece f leather, fitted to the sole, and nailed on with the shoe. This may be allowed as a temporary defence of the foot; but there is the same objection to its permanent use for the insecurity of fastening, and the strain on the crust, and the frequent chipping of it. There are also these additional inconveniences, that if the hollow between the sole and the leather is filled with stopping and tow, it is exceedingly difficult to introduce them so evenly and accurately as not to produce partial or injurious pressure. A few days' work will almost invariably so derange the padding, as to cause unequal pressure. The long contact of the sole with stopping of almost every kind, will produce not a healthy, elastic horn, but that of a scaly, spongy nature—and if the hollow is not thus filled, gravel and dirt will insinuate themselves, and eat into and injure the foot.*

---

* *Note by Mr. Spooner.*—[Mr. Spooner's note contains nothing not given more fully in the text. After some remarks on the diversities of opinion on the subject of shoeing, he expresses the following opinions:] Some horses have so strong a development of the horny structure of the foot, that a considerable portion requires to be removed at each shoeing, whilst others require, if it were possible, horn to be added, for in them the wear is greater than the growth. Some horses have a tendency to high heels, others to low ones; some require the toe of the foot to be reduced every month, in others there is not a particle to spare. In some horses the frog is so large and gross that it requires considerable paring, in others it can only be very carefully removed. We find the sole in some horses so thin and flat, that the shoe must be seated considerably to prevent its pressing on the sole, whilst in others the sole is so strong and concave, that it is a matter of indifference whether the shoe is seated at all, except for the purpose of rendering it lighter. With this endless diversity in horses' feet, how is it possible to lay down any fixed plan for shoeing all horses alike? All that can be done is to take an average foot, and consider what sort of shoe is best suited for it, and so alter or modify such shoe as to adapt it to other feet according to their peculiarities.

There is no better shoe for a saddle or light harness horse on the road than one of moderate weight, rather less than an inch in breadth, seated on the foot surface, with five nails on the outside quarter and toe, and two or three on the inside and near the toe. A clip at the toe and another at the outer quarter will be a useful addition; and if the shoe is required to be light, then one or even two nails may be dispensed with. By means of such a shoe the foot will be secured from contraction, and the inside heel in great measure from corns. The shoe should be of equal thickness at the heel as at the toe, and the web should be narrower at the former than the latter situation. If the heels of the foot are very low, it will be prudent to make the heels of the shoe somewhat thicker than the toe, and vice versa.

STOPPING THE FEET.

The general habit of stopping the feet requires some consideration. It is a very good or very bad practice, according to circumstances. When the sole is flat and thin it should be omitted, except on the evening before shoeing, and then the application of a little moisture may render the paring of the foot safer and more easy. If it were oftener used it would soften the foot, and not only increase the tendency to descent, but the occasional occurrence of lameness from pebbles or irregularities of the road.

Professor Stewart gives a valuable account of the proper application of stopping. "Farm horses seldom require any stopping. Their feet receive sufficient moisture in the fields, or, if they do not get much, they do not need much. Cart-horses used in the town should be stopped once a week, or oftener during winter, and every second night in the hot weeks of summer Groggy horses, and all those with high heels, concave shoes, or hot and tender feet, or an exuberance of horn, require stopping almost every night. When neglected, especially in dry weather, the sole becomes hard and rigid, and the horse goes lame, or becomes lame if he were not so before."

One of two substances, or a mixture of both, is generally used for stopping the feet—clay and cow-dung. The clay used alone is too hard, and dries too rapidly. Many horses have been lamed by it. If it is used in the stable, it should always be removed before the horse goes to work. It may, perhaps, be applied to the feet of heavy draught-horses, for it will work out before much mischief is done.

Cow-dung is softer than the clay, and it has this good property, that it rarely or never becomes too hard or dry. For ordinary work, a mixture of equal parts of clay and cow-dung will be the best application; either of them, however, must be applied with a great deal of caution, where there is any disposition to thrush. Tow used alone, or with a small quantity of tar, will often be serviceable.

If the sole is inclined to be flat, it will be desirable to make the shoe somewhat broader in the web, unless a leather sole is used, which for such fee is extremely useful,—indeed a leather sole is at all times desirable during the summer season. It secures the sole from injury from stones, and saves many a fall and broken knee; it materially lessens concussion, diminishes both the wear of the horn and of the shoe, and keeps applied to the sole a stopping of grease and tar spread on tow, which preserves the horn in a moist and healthy state. It is objectionable for hunters by rendering the shoes more liable to cast; and if required, on account of lameness, for horses going on the soft ground, it should be merely a narrow rim of leather between the bearing part of the shoe and the foot.

In the better kind of stables, a felt pad is frequently used. It keeps the foot cool and moist, and is very useful, when the sole has a tendency to become flat. For the concave sole, tow would be preferable.

THE SANDAL.

The shoe is sometimes displayed when the horse is going at an ordinary pace, and more frequently during hunting; and no person who is a sportsman needs to be told in what a vexatious predicament every one feels himself who happens to loose a shoe in the middle of a chase, or just as the hounds are getting clear away with their fox over the open country.

Mr. Percivall has invented a sandal which occupies a very small space in the pocket, can be buckled on the foot in less than two minutes, and will serve as a perfect substitute for the lost one, on the road, or in the field; or may be used for the race-horse when travelling from one course to another; or may be truly serviceable in cases of diseased feet that may require at the same time exercise and daily dressing. The following is a short sketch of the horse sandal.

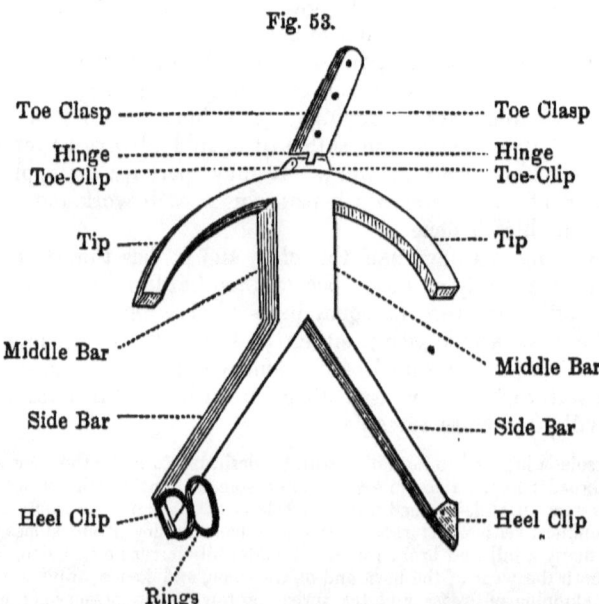

Fig. 53.

From an inspection of the above cut, it will be seen that the shoe, or iron part of the sandal, consists of three *principal* parts, to which the others are appendages; which are, the *tip* so called from its resemblance to the horse-shoe of that name; the *middle bar*, the broad part proceeding backward from the tip; and the *side bars*, or branches of the middle bar, extending to the heels of the hoof. The *appendages* are, the *toe-clasp*, the part projecting from the front of the tip, and which moves by a hinge upon the *toe-clip*, which toe-clasp is furnished with two *iron loops*. The *heel-clips* are two clips at the heels of the side bars, which correspond to the toe-clip; the latter embracing the toe of the crust, whilst the former embrace its heels. Through the heel-clips run *the rings*, which move and act like a hinge, and are double, for the purpose of admitting both the straps. In the plate, the right ring only is represented; the left being omitted, the better to show the heel-clip. The *straps*, which are composed of web, consist of a *hoof-strap* and a *heel and coronet-strap*.

The *hoof-strap* is furnished with a buckle, whose office it is to bind the shoe to the hoof; for which purpose it is passed through the lower rings, and both loops of the shoe, and is made to encircle the hoof twice.

The *heel and coronet-strap* is furnished with two pads and two sliding loops; one, a movable pad, reposes on the heel, to defend that part from the pressure and friction of the strap; the other, a pad attached to the strap near the buckle, affords a

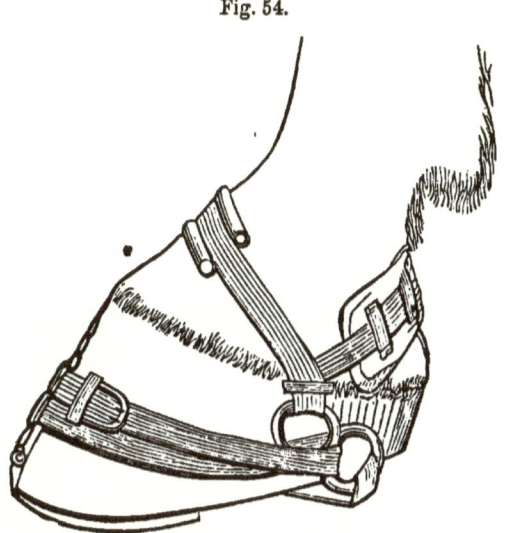

Fig. 54.

similar defence, to the coronet in front. The heel-strap runs through the upper rings, crosses the heel, and encircles the coronet; and its office is to keep the heels of the shoe closely applied to the hoof, and to prevent them from sliding forward.

In the application of the sandal, the foot is taken up with one hand, and the shoe slipped upon it with the other. With the same hand, the shoe is retained in its place, while the foot is gradually let down to rest on the ground. As soon as this is done, the straps are drawn as tight as possible, and buckled.

Fig. 54, on the preceding page, represents an accurate delineation of the sandal, when properly fastened to the foot.

TO MANAGE A FALLEN HORSE

Horses occasionally fall from bad riding, or bad shoeing, or overreaching, or an awkward way of setting on the saddle. The head, the neck, the knees, the back, or the legs will oftenest suffer. It is often difficult to get the animal on his legs again, especially if he is old, or exhausted, or injured by the fall. The principal object is, to support the head, and to render it a fixed point from which the muscles may act in supporting the body.

If the horse is in harness, it is seldom that he can rise until he is freed from the shafts and traces. The first thing is to secure the head, and to keep it down, that he may not beat himself against the ground. Next, the parts of the harness connected with the carriage must be unbuckled—the carriage must then be backed a little way, so that he may have room to rise. If necessary, the traces must be taken off; and after the horse gets up, he must be steadied a little, until he collects himself.

CHAPTER XVIII.

OPERATIONS.

THESE belong more to the veterinary surgeon than to the proprietor of the horse, but a short account of the manner of conducting the principal ones should not be omitted.

It is frequently necessary to bind the human patient, and in no painful or dangerous operation should this be omitted. It is more necessary to bind the horse, who is not under the control of reason, and whose struggles may not only be injurious to himself, but dangerous to the operator.

The *trevis* is a machine indispensable in every continental forge; even the quietest horses are there put into it to be shod.

The *side-line* is a very simple and useful method of confining the horse, and placing him in sufficient subjection, for the operations of docking, nicking, and slight firing. The long line of the *hobbles*, or a common cart-rope, with a noose at the end, is fastened on the pastern of the hind-leg that is not to be operated on. The rope attached to it is then brought over the neck and round the withers, and there tied to the portion that comes from the leg. The leg may thus be drawn so far forward that, while the horse evidently cannot kick with that leg, he is disarmed of the other for he would not have sufficient support under him, if he attempted to raise it: neither can he easily use his fore-legs; or, if he attempts it, one of them may be lifted up, and then he becomes nearly powerless. If necessary, the aid of the twitch, or the barnacles, may be resorted to.

For every minor operation, and even for many that are of more importance, this mode of restraint is sufficient, especially if the operator has active and determined assistants; and we confess that we are no friends to the casting of horses, if it can possibly be prevented. When both legs are included in the hobble, or rope—as in another way of using the side-line—the horse may appear to be more secure; but there is greater danger of his falling in his violent struggles during the operation.

For castrating and severe firing, the animal must be thrown. The safety of the horse, and of the operator, will require the use of the *improved* hobbles, by which any leg may be released from confinement, and returned to it at pleasure ; and, when the operation is ended, the whole of the legs may be set at liberty at once, without danger. The method of putting the legs as closely together as possible before the pull—the necessity of the assistants all pulling together—and the power which one man standing at the head, and firmly holding the snaffle-bridle, and another at the haunch, pushing the horse when he is beginning to fall, have in bringing him on the proper side, and on the very spot on which he is intended to lie, need not to be described. It will generally be found most convenient to throw the patients on the off side, turning them over when it is required. This, however, is a method of securing the horse to which we repeat that we are not partial, and to which we should not resort, except necessity compelled ; for in the fact of falling, and in the struggles after falling, many accidents have occurred, both to the horse and to the surgeon.

Among the minor methods of restraint, but sufficient for many purposes, are the *twitch* and the *barnacles*. The former consists of a noose passed through a hole at the end of a strong stick, and in which the muzzle is inclosed. The stick being turned round, the muzzle is securely retained, while the horse suffers considerable pain from the pressure—sufficiently great, indeed, to render him comparatively inattentive to that which is produced by the operation ; at the same time he is afraid to struggle, for every motion increases the agony caused by the twitch, or the assistant has power to increase it by giving an additional turn to the stick.

The degree of pain produced by the application of the twitch should never be forgotten or unnecessarily increased. In no case should it be resorted to when milder measures would have the desired effect. Grooms and horse-keepers are too much in the habit of having recourse to it when they have a somewhat troublesome horse to manage. The degree of useless torture which is thus inflicted in large establishments is dreadful : and the temper of many a horse is too frequently completely spoiled.

The *barnacles* are the handles of the pincers placed over and inclosing the muzzle, and which, being compressed by the assistant, give pain almost equal to that of the twitch. These may appear to be barbarous modes of enforcing submission, but they are absolutely indispensable. In a few instances the blindfolding of the horse terrifies him into submission ; but this is not to be depended upon. The twitch should be resorted to when the least resistance is offered ; and when that, as it occasionally does, renders the horse more violent, recourse must be had to the sideline or the hobbles.

In the painful examination of the fore-leg or foot while on the ground, the other foot should be held up by an assistant; or, if his aid is required in an operation, the knee may be fully bent, and the pastern tied up to the arm. When the hind-leg is to be examined in the same way, the fore-leg on that side should be held or fastened up.*

BLEEDING.

The operation of bleeding has been already described (p. 166), but we would remind our readers of the necessity, in every case of acute inflammation, of making a large orifice, and abstracting the blood as rapidly as possible, for the constitution will thus be the more speedily and beneficially affected.

The change which takes place in the blood after it is drawn from the vein, is diligently noticed by many practitioners, and is certainly deserving of some attention. The blood coagulates soon after it is taken from the vein. The coagulable part is composed of two substances: that which gives color to the blood, and that in which the red particles float. These, by degrees, separate from

* *Note by Mr. Spooner.*—For the operations of nerving, firing, and many others, where it is necessary to be exact, we prefer casting the horse, as we have him then completely in our own power; whereas, by the other restraints, the operator is, in a great measure, at the mercy of the animal, who can effectually resist if he pleases. Besides which, in a case of lameness, there is great danger of injury arising from the plunging of the animal. If a soft bed is made, with dung at the bottom and straw at the top, there is but little risk in casting. During the last nineteen years, in many hundreds of operations, we have only met with two cases of injury from casting, and these were in very old horses, whose spines proved to be anchylosed or set, and were thus much more liable to fracture. Where the object is to perform an otherwise painful operation without the infliction of pain, the use of sulphuric ether or of chloroform may be had recourse to. It is unnecessary to trace the history of these substances, so much having been of late written on the subject. The writer has used both with success, but the chloroform is preferable from its greater strength. The horse, however, requires a large quantity before the powers of sensation are temporarily destroyed, viz., from two to four ounces. It may be applied by a simple sponge, but better by means of apparatus, by which expiration is permitted, and at the same time sufficient air admitted to prevent dangerous effects following. The chloroform may be administered while the horse is in a standing position, and in some cases he will quietly fall or lie down; but as, in other instances, he will resist with determination, and stand even after sensation is gone, it is the better plan, in order to save the chloroform, and shorten the time during which the horse is under its influence, to cast the animal first, when the chloroform can be immediately applied, and the operation commenced as soon as sensation is removed. Or the chloroform can be applied when the horse is in a standing position, and the hobbles affixed at the same time, when, by means of the latter, the animal can be quietly thrown as soon as the former begins to act. This method will effect a saving of time. The use of chloroform is more suitable for short operations, such as nerving or castration, and the removal of tumors, than for those occupying considerable time.

P

each other, and the red particles sink to the bottom. If the coagulation takes place slowly, the red particles have more time to sink through the fluid, and there appears on the top a thick, yellowish, adhesive substance, called the buffy coat. The slowness of the coagulation and the thickness of buffy coat are indicative of inflammation, and of the degree of inflammation.

In a healthy state of the system the coagulation is more rapid, the red particles have not time to fall through, and the buffy coat is thin. When the horse is exhausted, and the system nearly broken up, the blood will sometimes not coagulate, but be of one uniform black color and loose texture. When the blood runs down the side of the vessel in which it is received, the coagulation will be very imperfect. When it is drawn in a full stream, it coagulates slowly, and when procured from a smaller orifice, the coagulation is more rapid. Every circumstance affecting the coagulation and appearance of the blood, the pulse, and the general symptoms, should be most attentively regarded.

BLISTERING.

We have spoken of the effect of BLISTERS, when treating of the various diseases to which they are applicable. The principle on which they act is, that no two intense inflammations can exist in neighboring parts, or perhaps in the system, at the same time.

Blisters have likewise the property of increasing the activity of the neighboring vessels: thus we blister to bring the tumor of strangles more speedily to a head—to rouse the absorbents generally to more energetic action, and cause the disappearance of tumors, and even callous and bony substances.

The judgment of the practitioner will decide whether the desired effect will be best produced by a sudden and violent action, or by the continuance of one of a milder character. Inflammation should be met by active blisters; old enlargements and swellings will be most certainly removed by milder stimulants—by the process which farriers call *sweating down*.

There is no better or more effectual blister than an ointment composed of one part of powdered Spanish flies and four of lard and one of resin. The lard and the resin should be melted together, and the powdered flies afterwards added. The best liquid or sweating blister is an infusion of the fly in spirit of turpentine, and that lowered with neat's foot oil, according to the degree of activity required.

In preparing the horse for blistering, the hair should be clipped or shaved as closely as possible, and the ointment thoroughly rubbed in. Much fault is often found with the ointment if the blister does not rise, but the failure is generally to be attributed to the idleness of the operator.

The head of the horse should be tied up during the first two days; except that, when the sides are blistered, the body-clothes may be so contrived as to prevent the animal from nibbling and blemishing the part, or blistering his muzzle. At the expiration of twenty-four hours, a little olive or neat's foot oil should be applied over the blister, which will considerably lessen the pain and supple the part, and prevent cracks in the skin that may be difficult to heal. The oil should be applied morning and night, until the scabs peel off. When they begin to loosen, a lather of soap and water applied with a sponge may hasten their removal, but no violence must be used.

Every particle of litter should be carefully removed from the stall, for the sharp ends of the straw coming in contact with a part rendered so tender and irritable by the blister, will cause a very great annoyance to the animal. After the second day the horse may be suffered to lie down; but the possibility of blemishing himself should be prevented by a *cradle* or wooden necklace, consisting of round strips of wood, strung together, reaching from the lower jaw to the chest, and preventing him from sufficiently turning or bending his head to get at the blistered part.

A blister thus treated will rarely produce the slightest blemish. When the scabs are all removed, the blister may be repeated, if the case should appear to require it, or the horse may be turned out.

In inflammations which threaten life, a blister can scarcely be too active or extensive. In inflammation of the lungs, it should reach over the whole of the sides, and the greater part of the brisket, for, should a portion of the fly be absorbed, and produce *strangury* (inflammation, or spasmodic affection of the neck of the bladder,) even this new irritation may assist in subduing the first and more dangerous one. In blistering, however, for injuries or diseases of the legs or feet, some caution is necessary. When speaking of the treatment of sprain of the back-sinews, p. 260, it was stated, that "a blister should never be used while any heat or tenderness remained about the part," for we should then add to the superficial inflammation, instead of abating the deeper-seated one, and enlargements of the limb and extensive ulcerations might follow, which would render the horse perfectly unserviceable. When there is a tendency to grease, a blister is a dangerous thing, and has often aggravated the disease. In winter, the inflammation of the skin produced by blistering is apt to degenerate into grease; therefore, if it should be necessary to blister the horse during that season, great care must be taken that he is not exposed to cold, and, particularly, that a current of cold air does not come upon the legs.

The inhuman practice of blistering *all round* at the same time, and perhaps high on the legs, cannot be too strongly reprobated. Many a valuable horse has been lost through the excessive general irritation which this has produced, or its violent effect on the urinary organs; and that has been particularly the case, when corrosive sublimate has entered into the composition of the blister.

If strangury should appear, the horse should be plentifully supplied with linseed tea, which is thus best prepared—a gallon of boiling water is thrown on half a pound of linseed; the infusion suffered to stand until nearly cold, and the clean mucilaginous fluid then poured off. Three-quarters of a pound of Epsom salts should also be given, dissolved in a quart of water, and, after that, a ball every six hours, containing opium and camphor, with linseed meal and treacle.

Half a pound or a pound of good mustard powder, made into a paste with boiling water, and applied hot, will often produce as good a blister as cantharides. It is a preferable one, when, as in inflammation of the kidneys, the effect of cantharides on the urinary organs is feared. Hartshorn is not so effectual. Tincture of croton makes an active liquid blister, and so do some of the preparations of iodine.*

FIRING.

Whatever seeming cruelty may attend this operation, it is in many cases indispensable. The principle on which we have recourse to it is similar to that which justifies the use of a blister— by producing superficial inflammation we may be enabled to get rid of a deeper-seated one, or we may excite the absorbents to

---

* *Note by Mr. Spooner.*—There has been a vast deal of puffing and humbug mixed up with the subject of blistering:—ointments and liniments have been sold under various captivating titles, and professing to be so amiable in their effects, as to require no tying up of the horse's head when the animal is submitted to the operation. Now, it should be borne in mind, that the effect of a blister being to stimulate violently the sensitive cutis and cause it to throw up the scarf skin in the form of bladders, this cannot be accomplished without pain and irritation. Of course, if from the weakness of the application a lesser effect is produced, the irritation is so much the less. Cantharides is the base of nearly all blisters, and its action is pretty much the same, whether applied in the usual blistering ointment or in some unguent of peculiar and astonishing efficacy, distinguished alike for the most opposite virtues,—combining the strength of the lion with the mildness of the dove. It is a fact that nine horses out of ten will not attempt to blemish themselves; and it is the knowledge of this fact that induces the puffers of these blisters to state that the animal does not require his head to be tied up. The careful veterinary surgeon will, however, use proper precautions in all cases, though only one in ten may actually require it. The writer has known a horse tear up the stones under his feet from the irritation produced by James's blister.

remove an unnatural bony or other tumor. It raises more intense external inflammation than we can produce by any other means. It may be truly said to be the most powerful agent that we have at our disposal. Humanity, however, will dictate that on account of the inflammation which it excites, and the pain it inflicts, it should only be had recourse to when milder means rarely succeed.

Some practitioners blister immediately after firing. As a general usage it is highly to be reprobated. It is wanton and useless cruelty. It may be required in bony tumors of considerable extent, and long standing, and interfering materially with the action of the neighboring joint. Spavin accompanied by much lameness, and ring-bone spreading round the coronet and involving the side cartilages or the pastern joint, may justify it. The inflammation is rendered more intense, and of considerably longer duration. In old affections of the round bone it may be admitted, but no excuse can be made for it in slighter cases of sprain or weakness, or staleness.

On the day after the operation, it will be prudent gently to rub some neat's foot oil, or lard, over the wound. This will soften the skin, and render it less likely to separate or ulcerate. A bandage would add to the irritation of the part. Any cracks of the skin, or ulcerations that may ensue, must be treated with the calamine ointment.

It will be evident that there is an advantage derived from firing to which a blister can have no pretension. The skin, partially destroyed by the iron, is reinstated and healed, not merely by the formation of some new matter filling up the vacuity, but by the gradual drawing together and closing of the separated edges. The skin, therefore, is lessened in surface. It is tightened over the part, and it acts, as just described, as a salutary and permanent bandage. Of the effect of pressure in removing enlargements of every kind, as well as giving strength to the part to which it is applied, we have repeatedly spoken; and it is far from being the least valuable effect of the operation of firing, that, by contracting the skin, it affords a salutary, equable, and permanent pressure. For whatever reason the horse is fired, he should, if possible, be turned out, or soiled in a loose box, for three or four months at least. The full effect intended to result from the external irritation is not soon produced, and the benefit derived from pressure proceeds still more slowly.

The firing in every case should be either in longitudinal or parallel lines. On the back sinews, the fetlocks, and the coronet, this is peculiarly requisite, for thus only will the skin contract so as to form the greatest and most equable pressure. The lines should be about half an inch from each other.*

* *Note by Mr. Spooner.*—Notwithstanding its seeming cruelty, it cannot

SETONS

Are pieces of tape or cord, passed, by means of an instrument resembling a large needle, either through abscesses, or the base of ulcers with deep sinuses, or between the skin and the muscular or other substances beneath. They are retained there by the nds being tied together, or by a knot at each end. The tape is moved in the wound twice or thrice in the day, and occasionally wetted with spirit of turpentine, or some acrid fluid, in order to increase the inflammation which it produces, or the discharge which is intended to be established.

In abscesses, such as occur in the withers or the poll, and when passed from the summit to the very bottom of the swelling, setons are highly useful, by discharging the purulent fluid, (pus or matter), and suffering any fresh quantity of it that may be secreted to flow out; and, by the degree of inflammation which they excite on the interior of the tumor, stimulating it to throw out healthy granulations which gradually occupy and fill the hollow. In deep fistulous wounds they are indispensable, for except some channel is made through which the matter may flow from the bottom of the wound, it will continue to penetrate deeper into the part, and the healing process will never be accomplished. On these accounts, a seton passed through the base of the ulcer in poll-evil and fistulous withers is of so much benefit.

Setons are sometimes useful by promoting a discharge in the neighborhood of an inflamed part, and thus diverting and carrying away a portion of the fluids which distend or overload the vessels of that part: thus a seton is placed with considerable advantage in the cheek, when the eyes are much inflamed. We confess, however, that we prefer a rowel under the jaw.

With this view, and to excite a new and different inflammation in the neighborhood of a part already inflamed, and especially so deeply seated and so difficult to be reached as the navicular joint, a seton has occasionally been used with manifest benefit, but we must peremptorily object to the indiscriminate use of the frog-seton for almost every disease of the frog or the foot.

In inflammations of extensive organs, setons afford only feeble aid. Their action is too circumscribed. In inflammation of the chest or the intestines, a rowel is preferable to a seton; and a blister is far better than any of them.

be denied that this operation often succeeds when all the other methods of cure have failed. We have little or nothing to add as to the mode of performing the operation, only that we prefer the lines to be made in the oblique or feather form, simply because it is as effectual as the perpendicular firing, as regards the bandage, and leaves a lesser blemish as the lines become covered by the hair growing from above.

On the principle of exciting the absorbents to action for the removal of tumors, as spavin or splent, a blister is quicker in its action, and far more effectual than any seton Firing is still more useful.*

DOCKING.

The shortening of the tail of the horse is an operation which fashion and the convenience of the rider require to be performed on most of these animals.

The operation is simple. That joint is searched for which is the nearest to the desired length of tail. The hair is then turned up, and tied round with tape for an inch or two above this joint, and that which lies immediately upon this joint is cut off. The horse is fettered with the side-line, and then the veterinary surgeon with his docking-machine, or the farmer with his carving-knife and mallet, cuts through the tail at one stroke.

The bleeding which ensues is rarely injurious, but as it would occasionally continue some hours and weaken the animal, it is customary to stop it by the application of a hot iron.

A large hole is made in the centre of the iron, that the bone may not be seared, which would exfoliate (scale off) if it were burned with any severity, or drop off at the joint above, and thus shorten the dock. The iron rests on the muscular parts round the bone, and is brought into contact with the bleeding vessels, and very speedily stops the bleeding. Care should be taken that the iron is not too hot—and that it is not held too long or too forcibly on the part, for many more horses would be destroyed by severe application of the cautery, than by the bleeding being left to its own course.

Powdered resin sprinkled on the stump, or indeed any other application, is worse than useless. It causes unnecessary irritation, and sometimes extensive ulceration; but if the simple iron is moderately applied, the horse may go to work immediately after the operation, and no dressing will be afterwards required If a slight bleeding should occur after the cautery, it is much better to let it alone than to run the risk of inflammation or locked-jaw, by re-applying the iron with greater severity.

Some farmers dock their colts a few days after they are dropped. This is a commendable custom on the score of humanity No colt was ever lost by it; and neither the growth of the hair nor the beauty of the tail, is in the least impaired.

* *Note by Mr. Spooner.*—We are more favorable than our author to the use of setons; they are equally effectual and far more cleanly than rowels, and a deep-seated and continued action may be kept up with little or no pain to the animal. They are often preferable to other methods of treatment for diseases of the hocks, and we have found the use of the frog seton, in many instances, extremely beneficial.

NICKING.

This barbarous operation was once sanctioned by fashion, and the breeder and the dealer even now are sometimes tempted to inflict the torture of it in order to obtain a ready sale for their colts. It is not, however, practised to the extent that it used to be, nor attended by so many circumstances of cruelty.

The operation is thus performed. The side-line is put on the horse, or some persons deem it more prudent to cast him, and that precaution we should be disposed to recommend. The hair at the end of the tail is securely tied together, for the purpose of afterwards attaching a weight to it. The operator then grasps the tail in his hand, and, lifting it up, feels for the *centre* of one of the bones—the prominences at the extremities will guide him—from two to four inches from the root of the tail, according to the size of the horse. He then, with a sharp knife, divides the muscles deeply from the edge of the tail on one side to the centre, and, continuing the incision across the bone of the tail, he makes it as deep on the other side. One continued incision, steadily yet rapidly made, will accomplish all this. If it is a blood-horse that is operated on, this will be sufficient. For a hunter, two incisions are usually made, the second being about two inches below the first, and likewise as nearly as possible in the centre of one of the bones.

On a hackney, or *cocktail*, a third incision is made; for fashion has decided that his tail shall be still more elevated and curved Two incisions only are made in the tail of a mare, and the second not very deep.

When the second incision is made, some fibres of the muscles between the first and second will project into the wound, and must be removed by a pair of curved scissors. The same must be done with the projecting portions from between the second and third incisions. The wound should then be carefully examined, in order to ascertain that the muscles have been equally divided on each side, otherwise the tail will be carried awry. This being done, pledgets of tow must be introduced deeply into each incision, and confined, but not too tightly, by a bandage. A very profuse bleeding will alone justify any tightness of bandage, and the ill consequences that have resulted from nicking are mainly attributable to the unnecessary force that is used in confining these pledgets. Even if the bleeding, immediately after the operation, should have been very great, the roller must be loosened in two or three hours, otherwise swelling and inflammation, and even death, may possibly ensue. Twenty-four hours after the operation, the bandage must be quite removed; and then, all that is necessary, so far as the healing of the incisions is concerned, is to keep them clean.

The wounds must remain open, and that can only be accomplished by forcibly keeping the tail curved back during two or three weeks. For this purpose a cord, one or two feet in length, is affixed to the end of the hair, which terminates in another divided cord, each division going over a pully on either side of the back of the stall. A weight is hung at either extremity sufficient to keep the incisions properly open, and regulated by the degree in which this is wished to be accomplished. The animal will thus be retained in an uneasy position, although, after the first two or three days, probably not of acute pain. It is barbarous to increase this uneasiness or pain by affixing too great a weight to the cords; for it should be remembered that the proper elevated curve is given to the tail, not by the weight of keeping it in a certain position for a considerable time, but by the depth of the first incisions, and the degree in which the wounds are kept open.

The dock should not—for the first three or four days—be brought higher than the back. Dangerous irritation and inflammation would probably be produced. It may, after that, be gradually raised to an elevation of forty-five degrees. The horse should be taken out of the pulleys, and gently exercised once or twice every day; but the pulleys cannot finally be dispensed with until a fortnight after the wounds have healed, because the process of contraction, or the approach of the divided parts, goes on for some time after the skin is perfect over the incisions, and the tail would thus sink below the desired elevation.

If the tail has not been unnecessarily extended by enormous weights, no bad consequences will usually follow; but if considerable inflammation should ensue, the tail must be taken from the pulley and diligently fomented with simple warm water, and a dose of physic given. Locked-jaw has in some rare instances followed, under which the horse generally perishes. The best means of cure in the early state of this disease is to amputate the tail at the joint above the highest incision. In order to prevent the hair from coming off, it should be unplaited and combed out every fourth or fifth day.

p

CHAPTER XIX.

THE VICES AND DISAGREEABLE OR DANGEROUS HABITS OF THE HORSE.

THE horse has many excellent qualities, but he has likewise defects, and these occasionally amounting to vices. Some of them may be attributed to natural temper, for the human being scarcely discovers more peculiarities of habit and disposition than does the horse. The majority of them, however, as perhaps in the human being, are the consequences of a faulty education. Their early instructor has been ignorant and brutal, and they have become obstinate and vicious.

RESTIVENESS.

At the head of all the vices of the horse is RESTIVENESS, the most annoying and the most dangerous of all. It is the produce of bad temper and worse education; and, like all other habits founded on nature and stamped by education, it is inveterate. Whether it appears in the form of kicking, or rearing, plunging, or bolting, or in any way that threatens danger to the rider or the horse, it rarely admits of cure. A determined rider may to a certain extent subjugate the animal; or the horse may have his favorites, or form his attachments, and with some particular person he may be comparatively or perfectly manageable; but others cannot long depend upon him, and even his master is not always sure of him. It is a rule, that admits of very few exceptions, that he neither displays his wisdom nor consults his safety, who attempts to conquer a restive horse.

BACKING OR GIBBING.*

One of the first kinds of restiveness, taking them in alphabetical order, is backing or gibbing. These are so closely allied that we hardly know how to separate them. Some horses have the

---

* Termed "balking" in the United States, and the horse accustomed to it is said to be "balky."—Am. Ed

habit of backing at first starting, and that more from playfulness than desire of mischief. A moderate application of the whip will usually be effectual. Others, even after starting, exhibit considerable obstinacy and viciousness. This is frequently the effect of bad breaking. Either the shoulder of the horse had been wrung when he was first put to the collar, or he had been foolishly accustomed to be started in the break *up-hill*, and, therefore, all his work coming upon him at once, he gradually acquired this dangerous habit.

A hasty and passionate breaker will often make a really good-tempered young horse an inveterate gibber. Every young horse is at first shy of the collar. If he is too quickly forced to throw his weight into it, he will possibly take a dislike to it, that will occasionally show itself in the form of gibbing as long as he lives. The judicious horse-breaker will resort to no severity, even if the colt should go out several times without even touching collar. The example of his companion will ultimately induce him to take it voluntarily and effectually.

A large and heavy stone should be put behind the wheel before starting, when the horse, finding it more difficult to back than to go forward, will gradually forget this unpleasant trick. It will likewise be of advantage as often as it can be managed, so to start that the horse shall have to back up-hill. The difficulty of accomplishing this will soon make him readily go forward. A little coaxing, or leading, or moderate flagellation, will assist in accomplishing the cure.

When, however, a horse, thinking he has had enough of work, or has been improperly checked or corrected, or beginning to feel the painful pressure of the collar, swerves, and gibs, and backs, it is a more serious matter. Persuasion should first be tried; and, afterwards, reasonable coercion, but no cruelty: for the brutality which is often exercised to compel a gibbing horse to throw himself habitually into the collar, never yet accomplished the purpose. The horse, may, perhaps, be whipped into motion; but if he has once begun to gib, he will have recourse to it again whenever any circumstance displeases or annoys him, and the habit will be so rapidly and completely formed, that he will become insensible to all severity.

Sometimes a horse not often accustomed to gib, betrays a reluctance to move, or a determination not to move. Before resorting to severity, the cause, if practicable, should be ascertained. The horse may be overtaxed, his withers may be wrung, or he may be insupportably galled or pained by the harness. These things should be examined into, and, if possible, rectified; for, under such circumstances, cruelty may produce obstinacy and vice, but not willing obedience.

They who are accustomed to horses know what seemingly trivial circumstances occasionally produce this vice. A horse, whose shoulders are raw, or have frequently been so, will not start with a cold collar. When the collar has acquired the warmth of the parts on which it presses, the animal will go without reluctance. Some determined gibbers have been reformed by constantly wearing a false collar, or strip of cloth round the shoulders, so that the coldness of the usual collar should never be felt; and others have been cured of gibbing by keeping the collar on night and day, for the animal is not able to lie down completely at full length, which the tired horse is always glad to do. When a horse gibs, not at starting, but while doing his work, it has sometimes been useful to line the collar with cloth instead of leather; the perspiration is readily absorbed, the substance which presses on the shoulder is softer, and it may be far more accurately eased off at a tender place.

BITING.

This is either the consequence of natural ferocity, or a habit acquired from the foolish and teasing play of grooms and stable-boys. When a horse is tickled and pinched by thoughtless and mischievous youths, he will first pretend to bite his tormentors; by degrees he will proceed farther, and actually bite them, and very soon after that, he will be the first to challenge to the combat, and, without provocation, seize some opportunity to gripe the incautious tormentor. At length, as the love of mischief is a propensity too easily acquired, this war, half playful and half in earnest, becomes habitual to him, and degenerates into absolute viciousness.

It is seldom that anything can be done in the way of cure. Kindness will aggravate the evil, and no degree of severity will correct it. "I have seen," says Professor Stewart, "biters punished until they trembled in every joint, and were ready to drop, but have never in any case known them cured by this treatment, or by any other. The lash is forgotten in an hour, and the horse is as ready and determined to repeat the offence as before. He appears unable to resist the temptation, and in its worst form biting is a species of insanity."

Prevention, however, is in the power of every proprietor of horses. While he insists on gentle and humane treatment of his cattle, he should systematically forbid this horse-play.

GETTING THE CHEEK OF THE BIT INTO THE MOUTH.

Some horses that are disposed to be mischievous try to do this, and are very expert at it. They soon find what advantage it gives them over their driver, who by this manœuvre loses almost all command. Harsh treatment is here completely out of the question. All that can be done, is, by some mechanical contrivance, to render the thing difficult or impossible, and this may be managed by fastening a round piece of leather on the inside of the cheek of the bit.

KICKING.

This, as *a vice*, is another consequence of the culpable habit of grooms and stable-boys of teasing the horse. That which is at first an indication of annoyance at the pinching and tickling of the groom, and without any design to injure, gradually becomes the expression of anger, and the effort to do mischief. The horse likewise too soon recognizes the least appearance of timidity, and takes advantage of the discovery. There is no cure for this vice; and he cannot be justified who keeps a kicking horse in his stable.

Some horses acquire, from mere irritability and fidgetiness, a habit of kicking at the stall or the bail, and particularly at night. The neighboring horses are disturbed, and the kicker gets swelled hocks, or some more serious injury. This is also a habit very difficult to correct if suffered to become established. Mares are far more subject to it than horses.

Before the habit is inveterately established, a thorn-bush or a piece of furze fastened against the partition or post will sometimes effect a cure. When the horse finds that he is pretty severely pricked, he will not long continue to punish himself. In confirmed cases it may be necessary to have recourse to the log, but the legs are often not a little bruised by it. A rather long and heavy piece of wood attached to a chain has been buckled above the hock, so as to reach about half-way down the leg. When the horse attempts to kick violently, his leg will receive a severe blow: this, and the repetition of it, may, after a time, teach him to be quiet.

A much more serious vice is kicking in harness. From the least annoyance about the rump or quarters, some horses will kick at a most violent rate, and destroy the bottom of the chaise, and endanger the limbs of the driver. Those that are fidgety in the stable are most apt to do this. If the reins should perchance get under the tail, the violence of the kicker will often be most outrageous; and while the animal presses down his tail so tightly that it is almost impossible to extricate the reins, he continues to plunge until he has demolished everything behind him.

This is a vice standing foremost in point of danger, and which no treatment will always conquer. It will be altogether in vain to try coercion. If the shafts are very strong and without flaw, or if they are plated with iron underneath, and a stout kicking-strap resorted to which will barely allow the horse the proper use of his hind limbs in progression, but not permit him to raise them sufficiently for the purpose of kicking, he may be prevented from doing mischief; or if he is harnessed to a heavy cart, and thus confined, his efforts to lash out will be restrained: but it is frequently a very unpleasant thing to witness these attempts, though ineffectual, to demolish the vehicle, for the shafts or the kicking-strap may possibly break, and extreme danger may ensue. A horse that has once begun to kick, whatever may have been the original cause of it, can never be depended upon again, and he will be very unwise who ventures behind him. The man, however, who must come within reach of a kicker should come as close to him as possible. The blow may thus become a push, and seldom is injurious.

UNSTEADINESS WHILE BEING MOUNTED.

When this merely amounts to eagerness to start—very unpleasant, indeed, at times, for many a rider has been thrown from his seat before he was fairly fixed in it—it may be remedied by an active and good horseman. We have known many instances in which, while the elderly, and inactive, and fearful man has been making more than one ineffectual attempt to vault into the saddle, the horse has been dancing about to his annoyance and danger; but the animal had no sooner been transferred to the management of a younger and more agile rider than he became perfectly subdued. Severity will here, more decidedly than in any other case, do harm. The rider should be fearless—he should carelessly and confidently approach the horse, mount at the first effort, and then restrain him for a while; patting him, and not suffering him to proceed until he becomes perfectly quiet. Horses of this kind should not be too highly fed, and should have sufficient daily exercise.

When the difficulty of mounting arises, not from eagerness to start, but unwillingness to be ridden, the sooner that horse is disposed of the better. He may be conquered by a skilful and determined horseman; but even he will not succeed without frequent and dangerous contests that will mar all the pleasure of the ride.

REARING.

This sometimes results from playfulness, carried indeed, to an unpleasant and dangerous extent; but it is oftener a desperate and occasionally successful effort to unhorse the rider, and consequently a vice. The horse that has twice decidedly and dangerously reared, should never be trusted again, unless, indeed, it was the fault of the rider, who had been using a deep curb and a sharp bit. Some of the best horses will contend against these, and then rearing may be immediately and permanently cured by using a snaffle-bridle alone.

The horse-breaker's remedy, that of pulling the horse backward on a soft piece of ground, should be practised by reckless and brutal fellows alone. Many horses have been injured in the spine, and others have broken their necks, by being thus suddenly pulled over; while even the fellow who fears no danger, is not always able to extricate himself from the falling horse. If rearing proceeds from vice, and is unprovoked by the bruising and laceration of the mouth, it fully partakes of the inveteracy which attends the other divisions of restiveness.

RUNNING AWAY.

Some headstrong horses will occasionally endeavor to bolt with the best rider. Others with their wonted sagacity endeavor thus to dislodge the timid or unskilful one. Some are hard to hold, or bolt only during the excitement of the chase; others will run away, prompted by a vicious propensity alone. There is no certain cure here. The method which affords any probability of success is, to ride such a horse with a strong curb and sharp bit; to have him always firmly in hand; and, if he will run away, and the place will admit of it, to give him (sparing neither curb, whip, nor spur) a great deal more running than he likes.

VICIOUS TO CLEAN.

It would scarcely be credited to what an extent this exists in some horses that are otherwise perfectly quiet. It is only at great hazard that they can be cleansed at all. The origin of this is probably some maltreatment. There is, however, a great difference in the sensibility of the skin in different horses. Some seem as if they could scarcely be made to feel the whip, while others cannot bear a fly to light on them without an expression of annoyance. In young horses the skin is peculiarly delicate. If they have been curried with a broken comb, or hardly rubbed with an uneven brush, the recollection of the torture they have felt makes them impatient, and even vicious, during every succeeding operation of the kind. Many grooms, likewise, seem to delight in producing these exhibitions of uneasiness and vice;

although, when they are carried a little too far, and at the hazard of the limbs of the groom, the animals that have been almost tutored into these expressions of irritation are brutally kicked and punished.

This, however, is a vice that may be conquered. If the horse is dressed with a lighter hand, and wisped rather than brushed, and the places where the skin is most sensitive are avoided as much as thorough cleanliness will allow, he will gradually lose the recollection of former ill-treatment, and become tractable and quiet.*

VICIOUS TO SHOE.

The correction of this is more peculiarly the business of the smith; yet the master should diligently concern himself with it, for it is oftener the consequence of injudicious or bad usage than of natural vice. It may be expected that there will be some difficulty in shoeing a horse for the first few times. It is an operation that gives him a little uneasiness. The man to whom he is most accustomed should go with him to the forge; and if another and steady horse is shod before him, he may be induced more readily to submit. It cannot be denied that, after the habit of resisting this necessary operation is formed, force may sometimes be necessary to reduce our rebellious servant to obedience; but we unhesitatingly affirm that the majority of horses *vicious to shoe* are rendered so by harsh usage, and by the pain of correction being added to the uneasiness of shoeing. It should be a rule in every forge that no smith should be permitted to strike a horse, much less to twitch or to gag him, without the master-farrier's order; and that a young horse should never be twitched or struck. There are few horses that may not be gradually rendered manageable for this purpose by mildness and firmness in the operator. They will soon understand that no harm is meant, and they will not forget their usual habit of obedience; but if the remembrance of corporal punishment is connected with shoeing, they will always be fidgety, and occasionally dangerous.†

* *Note by Mr. Spooner.*—In some instances the skin is so irritable that the horse really endures a great deal of misery every time he is cleaned, besides expending a great deal of muscular exertion needlessly. The remedy for this is very simple; instead of being currycombed and wiped, he should be simply washed over with warm water on his coming in warm from a journey, then gently scraped and covered with a rug. The warmth of the body will very soon dry the skin.

† *Note by Mr. Spooner.*—This is certainly a very bad vice, and one, indeed, that very materially diminishes the value of the horse, for it is a habit that generally gets worse at each time of shoeing. It is not so much the kicking of the horse that is to be feared, but the animal will bear his whole

SWALLOWING WITHOUT GRINDING.

Horses have many unpleasant habits in the stable and on the road, which cannot be said to amount to vice, but which materially lessen their value.

Some greedy horses habitually swallow their grain without properly grinding it, and the power of digestion not being adequate to the dissolving of the husk, no nutriment is extracted, and the oats are voided whole. This is particularly the case when horses of unequal appetite feed from the same manger. The greedy one, in his eagerness to get more then his share, bolts a portion of his grain whole. If the farmer, without considerable inconvenience, could contrive that every horse shall have his separate division of the manger, the one of smaller appetite and slower feed would have the opportunity of grinding at his leisure, without the fear of the greater share being stolen by his neighbor.

Some horses, however, are naturally greedy feeders, and will not, even when alone, allow themselves time to chew or grind their grain. In consequence of this they carry but little flesh, and are not equal to severe work. If the rack was supplied with hay when the grain was put into the manger, they will continue to eat on, and their stomachs will become distended with half-chewed and indigestible food. In consequence of this they will be incapable of considerable exertion for a long time after feeding, and, occasionally, dangerous symptoms of staggers will occur.

The remedy is, not to let such horses fast too long. The nosebag should be the companion of every considerable journey. The food should likewise be of such a nature that it cannot be rapidly bolted. Chaff should be plentifully mixed with the grain, and, in some cases, and especially in horses of slow work, it should, with the grain, constitute the whole of the food. This will be treated on more at large under the article " Feeding."

In every case of this kind the teeth should be carefully examined. Some of them may be unduly lengthened, particularly the first of the grinders: or they may be ragged at the edges, and may abrade and wound the cheek. In the first place the horse cannot properly masticate his food; in the latter he will not,

weight on the foot required to be shod, so that the smith is unable to lift it up, or afterwards to support it; besides which the animal will keep continually kicking or endeavoring to get the foot away, to the imminent danger of the limbs of the unfortunate operative. This deplorable and vicious habit is greatly increased, if not altogether produced, by rough usage at the early shoeings, and it generally gets worse at each time of shoeing, so that the horse is often rendered at last completely worthless

for these animals, as too often happens in sore-throat, would rather starve than put themselves to much pain.

CRIB-BITING.

This is a very unpleasant habit, and a considerable defect, although not so serious a one as some have represented. The horse lays hold of the manger with his teeth, violently extends his neck, and then, after some convulsive action of the throat, a slight grunting is heard, accompanied by a sucking or drawing in of air. It is not an effort at simple eructation, arising from indigestion. It is the inhalation of air. It is that which takes place with all kinds of diet, and when the stomach is empty as well as when it is full.

The effects of crib-biting are plain enough. The teeth are injured and worn away, and that, in an old horse, to a very serious degree. A considerable quantity of grain is often lost, for the horse will frequently crib with his mouth full of it, and the greater part will fall over the edge of the manger. Much saliva escapes while the manger is thus forcibly held, the loss of which must be of serious detriment in impairing the digestion. The crib-biting horse is notoriously more subject to colic than other horses, and to a species difficult of treatment and frequently dangerous. Although many a crib-biter is stout and strong, and capable of all ordinary work, these horses do not generally carry so much flesh as others, and have not their endurance. On these accounts crib-biting has very properly been decided to be unsoundness. We must not look to the state of the disease at the time of purchase. The question is, does it exist at all? A case was tried before Lord Tenterden, and thus decided; "a horse with crib-biting is unsound."

It is one of those tricks which are exceedingly contagious. Every companion of a crib-biter in the same stables is likely to acquire the habit, and it is the most inveterate of all habits. The edge of the manger will in vain be lined with iron, or with sheep-skin, or with sheep-skin covered with tar or aloes, or any other unpleasant substance. In defiance of the annoyance which these may occasion, the horse will persist in the attack on his manger. A strap buckled tightly round the neck, by compressing the wind-pipe, is the best means of preventing the possibility of this trick; but the strap must be constantly worn, and its pressure is too apt to produce a worse affection, viz., an irritation in the windpipe, which terminates in roaring.

Some have recommended turning out for five or six months; but this has never succeeded except with a young horse, and then rarely. The old crib-biter will employ the gate for the same purpose as the edge of his manger, and we have often seen him galloping across a field for the mere object of having a gripe at a rail. Medicine will be altogether thrown away in this case.

The only remedy is a muzzle, with bars across the bottom; sufficiently wide to enable the animal to pick up his corn and to pull his hay, but not to grasp the edge of the manger. If this is worn for a considerable period, the horse may be tired of attempting that which he cannot accomplish, and for a while forget the habit, but in a majority of cases, the desire of crib-biting will re turn with the power of gratifying it.

The causes of crib-biting are various, and some of them beyond the control of the proprietor of the horse. It is often the result of imitation; but it is more frequently the consequence of idleness. The high-fed and spirited horse must be in mischief if he is not usefully employed. Sometimes, but we believe not often, it is produced by partial starvation, whether in a bad straw-yard, or from unpalatable food. An occasional cause of crib-biting is the frequent custom of grooms, even when the weather is not severe, of dressing them in the stable. The horse either catches at the edge of the manger, or at that of the partition on each side, if he has been turned, and thus he forms the habit of laying hold of these substances on every occasion.

WIND-SUCKING.

This bears a close analogy to crib-biting. It arises from the same causes; the same purpose is accomplished; and the same results follow. The horse stands with his neck bent; his head drawn inward; his lips alternately a little opened and then closed, and a noise is heard as if he were sucking. If we may judge from the same comparative want of condition and the flatulence which we have described under the last head, either some portion of wind enters the stomach, or there is an injurious loss of saliva. This diminishes the value of the horse almost as much as crib-biting; it is as contagious, and it is as inveterate. The only remedies, and they will seldom avail, are tying the head up, except when the horse is feeding, or putting on a muzzle with sharp spikes towards the neck, and which will prick him whenever he attempts to rein his head in for the purpose of wind-sucking.

CUTTING.

Of this habit, mention has been made at page 266; and we would advise the owner of a cutting horse, without trying any previous experiments of raising or lowering the heels, to put on the cutting foot a shoe of even thickness from heel to toe, not projecting in the slightest degree beyond the crust, and the crust itself being rasped a little at the quarters. The shoe should be fastened as usual, on the outside, but with only one nail on the inside, and that almost close to the toe. The principle on which this shoe acts, has been explained at page 350

NOT LYING DOWN.

It not uncommonly happens that a horse will seldom or never lie down in the stable. He sometimes continues in apparent good health, and feeds and works well; but generally his legs swell, or he becomes fatigued sooner than another horse. If it is impossible to let him loose in the saddle, or to put him into a spare box, we know not what is to be done. No means, gentle or cruel, will force him to lie down. The secret is that he is tied up, and either has never dared to lie down through fear of the confinement of the halter, or he has been cast in the night and severely injured. If he can be suffered to range the stable, or have a comfortable box in which he may be loose, he will usually lie down the first night. Some few horses, however, will lie down in the stable, and not in a loose box. A fresh, well made bed, will generally tempt the tired horse to refresh himself with sleep.*

OVERREACH.

This unpleasant noise, known also by the term "clicking," arises from the toe of the hind-foot knocking against the shoe of the fore-foot. The consequences of it, and the treatment of the wounds resulting from it, have been sufficently given on page 320

If the animal is young, the action of the horse may be materially improved; otherwise nothing can be done, except to keep the toe of the hind foot as short and as round as it can safely be, and to bevel off and round the toe of the shoe, like that which has been worn off by a stumbling horse, and perhaps, to lower the heel of the fore-foot a little.

PAWING.

Some hot and irritable horses are restless even in the stable, and paw frequently and violently. Their litter is destroyed, the

---

* *Note by Mr. Spooner.*—It should not be forgotten that the basis of support afforded by the four extremities is so considerable in the horse, that he is able to sleep in a standing position, and we have known some horses preserve their health, strength, and condition, although they have never been known to lie down. At the same time, it must be confessed that an animal that will quietly lie down and take his rest, generally preserves his condition, and is better fitted for exertion.

floor of the stable broken up, the shoes worn out, the feet bruised, and the legs sometimes sprained. If this habit does not exist to any great extent, yet the stable never looks well. Shackles are the only remedy, with a chain sufficiently long to enable the horse to shift his posture, or move in his stall; but these must be taken off at night, otherwise the animal will seldom lie down. Except, however, the horse possesses peculiar value, it will be better to dispose of him at once, than to submit to the danger and inconvenience that he may occasion.

QUIDDING.

A horse will sometimes partly chew his hay, and suffer it to drop from his mouth. If this does not proceed from irregular teeth, which it will be the business of the veterinary surgeon to rasp down, it will be found to be connected with sore-throat, and then the horse, will exhibit some other symptoms of indisposition, and particularly, the swallowing of water will be accompanied by a peculiar gulping effort. In this case, the disease (catarrh, with sore-throat) must be attacked, and the quidding will cease.

ROLLING.

This is a very pleasant and perfectly safe amusement for a horse at grass, but cannot be indulged in the stable without the chance of his being dangerously entangled with the collar-rein (halter) and being cast. Yet, although the horse is cast, and bruised, and half-strangled, he will roll again on the following night and continue to do so as long as he lives. The only remedy is not a very pleasant one for the horse, nor always quite safe; yet it must be had recourse to, if the habit of rolling is inveterate. "The horse," says Mr. Castley, "should be tied with length enough of halter to lie down, but not to allow of his head resting on the ground; because, in order to roll over, a horse is obliged to place his head quite down upon the ground."

SHYING.

We have briefly treated of the cause of this vice at page 66, and observed that while it is often the result of cowardice, or playfulness, or want of work, it is at other times the consequence of a defect of sight. It has been remarked, and we believe very truly, that shying is oftener a vice of half or quarter-bred horses, than of those who have in them more of the genuine racing blood.

In the treatment of shying, is it of great importance to distinguish between that which is the consequence of defective sight.

and what results from fear, or newness of objects, or mere affectation or skittishness. For the first, the nature of which we have explained at page 66, every allowance must be made, and care must be taken that the fear of correction is not associated with the imagined existence of some terrifying object. The severe use of the whip and the spur cannot do good here, and are likely to aggravate the vice ten-fold. A word half encouraging and half scolding, with a slight pressure of the heel, or a slight touch of the spur, will tell the horse that there was nothing to fear, and will give him confidence in his rider on a future occasion.

The shying from skittishness or affectation is quite a different affair, and must be conquered: but how? Severity is altogether out of place. If he is forced into contact with the object by dint of correction, the dread of punishment will afterwards be associated with that object, and, on the next occasion, his startings will be more frequent and more dangerous. The way to cure him is to go on, turning as little as possible out of the road, giving a harsh word or two, and a gentle touch with the spur, and then taking no more notice of the matter. After a few times, whatever may have been the object which he chose to select as the pretended cause of affright, he will pass it almost without notice.

In page 243, under the head "breaking in," we described how the colt may be cured of the habit of shying from fear or newness of objects; and, if he then is accustomed as much as possible to the objects among which his services will be required, he will not possess this annoying vice when he grows to maturer age.

It is now generally admitted by all riding-masters and colt-breakers, that a great deal more is to be effected by lenient than by harsh treatment. Rewards are found to operate more beneficially than punishments; and therefore the most scientific and practised riding-masters adopt methods based upon the former.

Let us not be understood to mean that the animal is to receive any encouragement to shy; for by no other expression can be characterized that erroneous and foolish practice of patting the horse, or "making much of him," either just before or during the time he evinces shyness. The former is bad, because it draws the attention of the animal to the object he dreads; the latter is worse, because it fills him with the impression either that the object itself is really terrific, or that he has acted right in shying at it, and ought to do so again.

Whether we are approaching the frightful object, or the horse is actually shying, "we should let him alone"—"we should take no notice whatever of him"—neither letting him perceive that we are aware that we are advancing towards anything he dislikes; nor do more with him, while in the act of shying, than is necessary for due restraint with a steady hand upon the rein. We may depend upon it, that battling on our part will only serve to augment affright and arouse resistance on his, and that the most judicious course we can pursue is to persevere in mild forbearant usage.

Shying on coming out of the stable is a habit that can rarely or never be cured. It proceeds from the remembrance of some ill-usage or hurt which the animal has received in the act of proceeding from the stable, such as striking his head against a low door-way, or entangling the harness.

When the cure, however, is early attempted, it may be so far overcome that it will be unattended with danger or difficulty. The horse should be bridled when led out or in. He should be held short and tight by the head, that he may feel he has not liberty to make a leap, and this of itself is often sufficient to restrain him. Punishment, or a threat of punishment, will be highly improper. It is only timid or high-spirited horses that acquire this habit, and rough usage invariably increases their agitation and terror.*

SLIPPING THE COLLAR OR HALTER.

This is a trick at which many horses are so clever, that scarcely a night passes without their getting loose. It is a very serious habit, for it enables the horse sometimes to gorge himself with food, to the imminent danger of staggers; or it exposes him, as he

---

* *Note by Mr. Spooner.*—This vice or habit—for it ranges between the one and the other—exists in every variety of degree. There are more horses that shy than do not: when the practice exists in a slight degree, it is a matter of no consequence, but when the animal, instead of merely looking at the object of alarm and dwelling a little in his pace as he approaches it, stops suddenly, or turns round, or swerves considerably, the habit becomes a dangerous vice, and is exceedingly objectionable. There is more affectation than real fear about this habit, the horse making use of every unusual object as an excuse for the indulgence of his skittishness, or his obstinacy. There are often some strange eccentricities connected with it. Horses will often pass a frightful object without the least fear; but if, perchance, there is a puddle in the road, or a stick of timber lying beside it, imagination appears to paint the object in the most hideous colors or portentous forms. Horses shy most in the country, where there are but few objects to meet; and they rarely exhibit this propensity in the crowded streets of the metropolis. The objects are there far too numerous to allow an excuse for shying, or would soon weary them of the habit; indeed the very best method of curing the vice is to use the animal in crowded streets. Though shying is often connected with imperfect vision, it is rarely produced by actual disease, and, therefore, its existence does not augur unsound eyes. Too great convexity of the eye is certainly often connected with shying, so that objects are refracted too quickly, and thus are imperfectly painted on the retina.

Shying horses are frequently made much worse by rough usage; instead of which they should always be treated with gentleness and firmness, which system, in many instances, will succeed in effecting a cure.

wanders about, to be kicked and injured by the other horses, while his restlessness will often keep the whole team awake. If the web of the halter, being first accurately fitted to his neck, is suffered to slip only one way, or a strap is attached to the halter and buckled round the neck, but not sufficiently tight to be of serious inconvenience, the power of slipping the collar will be taken away.

TRIPPING.

He must be a skilful practitioner or a mere pretender who promises to remedy this habit. If it arises from a heavy fore-hand, and the fore-legs being too much under the horse, no one can alter the natural frame of the animal: if it proceeds from tenderness of the foot, grogginess, or old lameness, these ailments are seldom cured. Also if it is to be traced to habitual carelessness and idleness, no whipping will rouse the drone. A known stumbler should never be ridden, or driven by any one who values his safety or his life. A tight hand or a strong-bearing rein are precautions that should not be neglected, although they are generally of little avail; for the inveterate stumbler will rarely be able to save himself, and this tight rein may sooner and farther precipitate the rider. If, after a trip, the horse suddenly starts forward, and endeavors to break into a short trot or canter, the rider or driver may be assured that others before him have fruitlessly enleavored to remedy the nuisance.

If the stumbler has the foot kept as short, and the toe pared as close as safety will permit, and the shoe is rounded at the toe, or has that shape given to it which it naturally acquires in a fortnight from the peculiar action of such a horse, the animal may not stumble quite so much; or if the disease which produced the habit can be alleviated, some trifling good may be done, but in almost every case a stumbler should be got rid of, or put to slow and heavy work. If the latter alternative is adopted, he may trip as much as he pleases, for the weight of the load and the motion of the other horses will keep him upon his legs.

WEAVING

This consists in a motion of the head, neck, and body, from side to side, like the shuttle of a weaver passing through the web, and hence the name which is given to this peculiar, and incessant, and unpleasant action. It indicates an impatient, irritable temper, and a dislike to the confinement of the stable. A horse that is thus incessantly on the fret will seldom carry flesh, or be safe to ride or drive. There is no cure for it, but the close tying-up of the animal, or at least allowing him but one loose rein, except at feeding-time.

CHAPTER XX.

THE GENERAL MANAGEMENT OF THE HORSE.

This is a most important part of our subject, even as it regards the farmer, although there are comparatively few glaring errors in the treatment of the agricultural horse; but it comes more especially home to the gentleman, who is too often, and too implicitly, under the guidance of an idle, and ignorant, and designing groom.

We will arrange the most important points of general management under the following heads :—

AIR.

The breathing of pure air is necessary to the existence and the health of man and beast. It is comparatively lately that this has been admitted even in the management of our best stables. They have been close, and hot, and foul, instead of airy, and cool, and wholesome.

The stable should be as large, compared with the number of horses that it is destined to contain, as circumstances will allow A stable for six horses should not be less than forty feet in length, and thirteen or fourteen feet wide.* If there is no loft above, the inside of the roof should always be plastered in order to prevent direct currents of air and occasional droppings from broken tiles. The heated and foul air should escape, and cool and pure air be admitted, by elevation of the central tiles; or by large tubes carried through the roof, with caps a little above them, to prevent the beating in of the rain; or by gratings placed high up in the walls. These latter apertures should be as far above the horses as they can conveniently be placed, by which means all injurious draught will be prevented.

If there is a loft above the stable, the ceiling should be plastered, in order to prevent the foul air from penetrating to the hay above, and injuring both its taste and its wholesomeness;

---

* It will be borne in mind that the author is speaking of the close stone or brick stables of England.—*Am. Ed.*

and no openings should be allowed above the racks, through which the hay may be thrown into them; for they will permit the foul air to ascend to the provender, and also in the act of filling the rack, and while the horse is eagerly gazing upward for his food, a grass seed may fall into the eye, and produce considerable inflammation. At other times, when the careless groom has left open the trap-door, a stream of cold air beats down on the head of the horse.

The stable with a loft over it should never be less than twelve feet high, and proper ventilation should be secured, either by tubes carried through the roof, or by gratings close to the ceiling. These gratings or openings should be enlarged or contracted by means of a covering or shutter, so that spring, summer, and autumn, the stable may possess nearly the same temperature with the open air, and in winter a temperature of not more than ten degrees above that of the external atmosphere.

A hot stable has, in the mind of the groom, been long connected with a glossy coat. The latter, it is thought, cannot be obtained without the former.

To this we should reply, that in winter a thin, glossy coat is not desirable. Nature gives to every animal a warmer clothing when the cold weather approaches. The horse—the agricultural horse especially—acquires a thicker and a lengthened coat, in order to defend him from the surrounding cold. Man puts on an additional and a warmer covering, and his comfort is increased and his health preserved by it. He who knows anything of the farmer's horse, or cares about his enjoyment, will not object to a coat a little longer, and a little roughened when the wintry wind blows bleak. The coat, however, needs not to be so long as to be unsightly; and warm clothing, even in a cool stable, will, with plenty of honest grooming, keep the hair sufficiently smooth and glossy to satisfy the most fastidious. The over-heated air of a close stable saves much of this grooming, and therefore the idle attendant unscrupulously sacrifices the health and safety of the horse. When we have presently to treat of the hair and skin of the horse, this will be placed in a somewhat different point of view.

If the stable is close, the air will not only be hot, but foul. The breathing of every animal contaminates it; and when, in the course of the night, with every aperture stopped, it passes again and again through the lungs, the blood cannot undergo its proper and healthy change; digestion will not be so perfectly performed, and all the functions of life are injured. Let the owner of a valuable horse think of his passing twenty or twenty-two out of the twenty-four hours in this debilitating atmosphere! Nature does wonders in enabling every animal to accommodate itself to the situation in which it is placed, and the horse that lives in the stable-oven suffers less from it than would scarcely be conceived possible; but he does not, and cannot, possess the power and the hardihood which he would acquire under other circumstances.

The air of the improperly close and heated stable is still further contaminated by the urine and dung, which rapidly ferment there, and give out stimulating and unwholesome vapors. When a person first enters an ill-managed stable, and especially early in the morning, he is annoyed, not only by the heat of the confined air, but by a pungent smell, resembling hartshorn; and can he be surprised at the inflammation of the eyes, and the chronic cough, and the disease of the lungs, by which the animal, who has been all night shut up in this vitiated atmosphere, is often attacked; or if glanders and farcy should occasionally break out in such stables? It has been ascertained by chemical experiment that the urine of the horse contains in it an exceedingly large quantity of hartshorn; and not only so, but that, influenced by the heat of a crowded stable, and possibly by other decompositions that are going forward at the same time, this ammoniacal vapor begins to be rapidly given out almost immediately after the urine is voided.

When disease begins to appear among the inhabitants of these ill-ventilated places, is it wonderful that it should rapidly spread among them, and that the plague-spot should be, as it were, placed on the door of such a stable? When distemper appears in spring or in autumn, it is in very many cases to be traced to such a pest-house. It is peculiarly fatal there. The horses belonging to a small establishment, and rationally treated, have it comparatively seldom, or have it lightly; but among the inmates of a crowded stable it is sure to display itself, and there it is most fatal. The experience of every veterinary surgeon, and of every large proprietor of horses, will corroborate this statement.

Every stable should possess within itself a certain degree of ventilation. The cost of this would be trifling, and its saving in the preservation of valuable animals may be immense. The apertures need not be large, and the whole may be so contrived that no direct current of air shall fall on the horse.

A gentleman's stable should never be without a thermometer. The temperature should seldom exceed 70° in the summer, or sink below 40° or 50° in the winter.

LITTER.

Having spoken of the vapor of hartshorn, which is so rapidly and so plentifully given out from the urine of a horse in a heated stable, we next take into consideration the subject of litter. The first caution is frequently to remove it. The early extrication of gas shows the rapid putrefaction of the urine; and the consequence of which will be the rapid putrefaction of the litter that has been moistened by it. Everything hastening to decomposition should be carefully removed where life and health are to be preserved. The litter that has been much wetted or at all softened by the urine, and is beginning to decay, should be swept away every morning; the greater part of the remainder may then be piled under the manger; a little being left to prevent the painful and injurious pressure of the feet on the hard pavement during the day. The soiled and soaked portion of that which was left should be removed at night. In the better kind of stables, however, the stalls should be completely emptied every morning.

No heap of fermenting dung should be suffered to remain during the day in the corner or in any part of the stable. With regard to this, the directions of the master should be peremptory.

The stable should be so contrived that the urine shall quickly run off, and the offensive and injurious vapor from the decomposing fluid and the litter will thus be materially lessened, but if this is effected by means of gutters and a descending floor, the descent must be barely sufficient to cause the fluid to escape, as if the toes are kept higher than the heels, it will lead to lameness, and is also a frequent cause of contraction of the foot. Stalls of this kind certainly do best for mares; but for horses we much prefer those with a grating in the centre, and a slight inclination of the floor on every side towards the middle. A short branch may communicate with a larger drain, by means of which the urine may be carried off to a reservoir outside the stable. Traps are now contrived, and may be procured at little expense, by means of which neither any offensive smell nor current of air can pass through the grating.

Humanity and interest, as well as the appearance of the stable, should induce the proprietor of the horse to place a moderate quantity of litter under him during the day.*

LIGHT.

This neglected branch of stable-management is of far more consequence than is generally imagined; and it is particularly neglected by those for whom these treatises are principally designed. The farmer's stable is frequently destitute of any glazed window, and has only a shutter, which is raised in warm weather, and closed when the weather becomes cold. When the horse is

---

* It will be remembered the author is speaking of paved floors.—*Am. Ed.*

in the stable only during a few hours in the day, this is not of so much consequence, nor of so much, probably, with regard to horses of slow work; but to carriage-horses and hackneys, so far, at least, as the eyes are concerned, a dark stable is little less injurious than a foul and heated one. In order to illustrate this, reference may be made to the unpleasant feeling, and the utter impossibility of seeing distinctly, when a man suddenly emerges from a dark place into the full blaze of day. The sensation of mingled pain and giddiness is not soon forgotten; and some minutes pass before the eye can accommodate itself to the increased light. If this were to happen every day, or several times in the day, the sight would be irreparably injured, or possibly blindness would ensue. Can we wonder, then, that the horse, taken from a dark stable into a glare of light, feeling, probably, as we should do under similar circumstances, and unable for a considerable time to see anything around him distinctly, should become a starter, or that the frequently repeated violent effect of sudden light should induce inflammation of the eye so intense as to terminate in blindness? There is, indeed, no doubt that horses kept in dark stables are frequently notorious starters, and that abominable habit has been properly traced to this cause.

If plenty of light is admitted, the walls of the stable, and especially that portion of them which is before the horse's head, must not be of too glaring a color. The color of the stable should depend on the quantity of light. Where much can be admitted, the walls should be of a gray hue. Where darkness would otherwise prevail, frequent whitewashing may in some degree dissipate the gloom.

For another reason, it will be evident that the stable should not possess too glaring a light: it is the resting-place of the horse. The work of the farmer's horse, indeed, is confined principally to the day. The hour of exertion having passed, the animal returns to his stable to feed and to repose, and the latter is as necessary as the former, in order to prepare him for renewed work. Something approaching to the dimness of twilight is requisite to induce the animal to compose himself to sleep. This half-light more particularly suits horses of heavy work. In the quietness of a dimly-lighted stable, they obtain repose, and accumulate flesh and fat.

GROOMING.

Of this much need not be said to the agriculturist, since custom, and apparently without ill effect, has allotted so little of the comb and brush to the farmer's horse. The animal that is worked all day, and turned out at night, requires little more to be done to him than to have the dirt brushed off his limbs. Regular grooming, by rendering his skin more sensible to the alteration of temperature, and the inclemency of the weather, would be prejudicial. The horse that is altogether turned out, needs no grooming. The dandriff, or scurf, which accumulates at the roots of the hair, is a provision of nature to defend him from the wind and the cold.

It is to the stabled horse, highly fed, and little or irregularly worked, that grooming is of so much consequence. Good rubbing with the brush, or the curry-comb, opens the pores of the skin, circulates the blood to the extremities of the body, produces free and healthy perspiration, and stands in the room of exercise. No horse will carry a fine coat without either unnatural heat or dressing. They both effect the same purpose ; they both increase the insensible perspiration : but the first does it at the expense of health and strength, while the second, at the same time that it produces a glow on the skin, and a determination of blood to it, rouses all the energies of the frame. It would be well for the proprietor of the horse if he were to insist—and to see that his orders are really obeyed—that the fine coat in which he and his groom so much delight, is produced by honest rubbing, and not by a heated stable and thick clothing, and most of all, not by stimulating or injurious spices. The horse should be regularly dressed every day, in addition to the grooming that is necessary after work.

When the weather will permit the horse to be taken out, he should never be groomed in the stable, unless he is an animal of peculiar value, or placed for a time under peculiar circumstances. Without dwelling on the want of cleanliness, when the scurf and dust that are brushed from the horse lodge in his manger, and mingle with his food, experience teaches, that if the cold is not too great, the animal is braced and invigorated to a degree that cannot be attained in the stable, from being dressed in the open air. There is no necessity, however, for half the punishment which many a groom inflicts upon the horse in the act of dressing ; and particularly on one whose skin is thin and sensible. The curry-comb should at all times be lightly applied. With many horses, its use may be almost dispensed with ; and even the brush needs not to be so hard, nor the points of the bristles so irregular, as they often are. A soft brush, with a little more weight of the hand, will be equally effectual, and a great deal more pleasant to the horse. A hair-cloth, while it will seldom irritate and tease, will be almost sufficient with horses that have a thin skin, and that have not been neglected. After all, it is no slight task to dress a horse as it ought to be done. It occupies no little time, and demands considerable patience, as well as dexterity. It will be readily ascertained whether a horse has been well dressed by rubbing him with one of the fingers. A greasy stain will detect the idleness of the groom When, however, the horse is changing his coat, both the curry-comb and the brush should be used as lightly as possible.

Whoever would be convinced of the benefit of friction to the horse's skin, and to the horse generally, needs only to observe the effects produced by well hand-rubbing the legs of a tired horse. While every enlargement subsides, and the painful stiffness disappears, and the legs attain their natural warmth, and become fine, the animal is evidently and rapidly reviving; he attacks his food with appetite, and then quietly lies down to rest.

EXERCISE.

Our observations on this important branch of stable-management must have only a slight reference to the agricultural horse. His work is usually regular, and not exhausting. He is neither predisposed to disease by idleness, nor worn out by excessive exertion. He, like his master, has enough to do to keep him in health, and not enough to distress or injure him: on the contrary, the regularity of his work prolongs life to an extent rarely witnessed in the stable of the gentleman. Our remarks on exercise, then, must have a general bearing, or have principal reference to those persons who are in the middle stations of life, and who contrive to keep a horse for business or pleasure, but cannot afford to maintain a servant for the express purpose of looking after it. The first rule we would lay down is, that every horse should have daily exercise. The animal that, with the usual stable feeding stands idle for three or four days, as is the case in many establishments, must suffer. He is predisposed to fever, or to grease, or most of all, diseases of the foot; and if, after three or four days of inactivity, he is ridden far and fast, he is almost sure to have inflammation of the lungs or of the feet.

A gentleman's or a tradesman's horse suffers a great deal more from idleness than he does from work. A stable-fed horse should have two hours' exercise every day, if he is to be kept free from disease. Nothing of extraordinary, or even of ordinary labor, can be effected on the road or in the field, without sufficient and regular exercise. It is this alone which can give energy to the system, or develope the powers of any animal.

In training the hunter and the race-horse, regular exercise is the most important of all considerations, however it may be forgotten in the usual management of the stable. The exercised horse will discharge his task, and sometimes a severe one, with ease and pleasure; while the idle and neglected one will be fatigued ere half his labor is accomplished, and, if he is pushed a little too far, dangerous inflammation will ensue. How often, nevertheless, does it happen, that the horse which has stood inactive in the stable three or four days, is ridden or driven thirty or forty miles in the course of a single day! This rest is often purposely given to prepare for extra-exertion;—to lay in a stock of strength for the performance of the task required of him: and then the owner is surprised and dissatisfied if the animal is fairly knocked up, or possibly becomes seriously ill. Nothing is so common and so preposterous, as for a person to buy a horse from a dealer's stable, where he has been idly fattened for sale for many a day, and immediately to give him a long run after the hounds, and then to complain bitterly, and think that he has been imposed upon, if the animal is exhausted before the end of the chase, or is compelled to be led home suffering from violent inflammation. Regular and gradually increasing exercise would have made the same horse appear a treasure to his owner.

Exercise should be somewhat proportioned to the age of the horse. A young horse requires more than an old one. Nature has given to young animals of every kind a disposition to activity, but the exercise must not be violent. A great deal depends upon the manner in which it is given. To preserve the temper, and to promote health, it should be moderate, at least at the beginning and the termination. The rapid trot, or even the gallop, may be resorted to in the middle of the exercise, but the horse should be brought in cool.

FOOD.

The system of manger-feeding is becoming general among farmers. There are few horses that do not habitually waste a portion of their hay; and by some the greater part is pulled down and trampled under foot, in order first to cull the sweetest and best locks, and which could not be done while the hay was enclosed in the rack. A good feeder will afterwards pick up much of that which was thrown down; but some of it must be soiled and rendered disgusting, and, in many cases, one-third of this division of their food is wasted. Some of the oats and beans are imperfectly chewed by all horses, and scarcely at all by hungry and greedy ones. The appearance of the dung will sufficiently evince this.

The observation of this induced the adoption of manger-feeding, or of mixing a portion of chaff (i. e., cut feed) with the grain and beans. By this means the animal is compelled to chew his food; he cannot, to any great degree, waste the straw or hay; the chaff is too hard and too sharp to be swallowed without sufficient mastication, and while he is forced to grind that down, the oats and beans are ground with it, and yield more nourishment; the stomach is more slowly filled, and therefore acts better on its contents, and is not so likely to be overloaded; and the increased quantity of saliva thrown out in the lengthened maceration of the food, softens it, and makes it more fit for digestion.

Chaff may be composed of equal quantities of clover or meadow hay, and wheaten, oaten, or barley straw, cut into pieces of a quarter or half an inch in length, and mingled well together; the allowance of oats or beans is afterwards added, and mixed with the chaff. Many farmers very properly bruise the oats or beans. The whole oat is apt to slip out of the chaff and be lost; but when it is bruised, and especially if the chaff is a little wetted, it will not readily separate; or, should a portion of it escape the grinders, it will be partly prepared for digestion by the act of bruising. The prejudice against bruising the oats is, so far as the farmer's horse, and the wagon horse, and every horse of slow draught, are concerned, altogether unfounded. The quantity of straw in the chaff will always counteract any supposed purgative quality in bruised oats. Horses of quicker draught, except they are naturally disposed to scour, will thrive better with bruised than with whole oats; for a greater quantity of nutriment will be extracted from the food, and it will always be easy to apportion the quantity of straw or beans to the effect of the mixture on the bowels of the horse. The principal alteration that should be made in the horse of harder and more rapid work, such as the post-horse, and the stage-coach horse, is to increase the quantity of hay, and diminish that of straw. Two trusses of hay may be cut with one of straw.

Some gentlemen, in defiance of the prejudice and opposition of the coachman or the groom, have introduced this mode of feeding into the stables of their carriage-horses and hackneys, and with manifest advantage. There has been no loss of condition or power, and considerable saving of provender. This system is not, however, calculated for the hunter or the race-horse. Their food must lie in smaller bulk, in order that the action of the lungs may not be impeded by the distention of the stomach; yet many hunters have gone well over the field who have been manger-fed, the proportion of grain, however, being materially increased.

For the agricultural and cart-horse, eight pounds of oats and two of beans should be added to every twenty pounds of chaff. Thirty-four or thirty-six pounds of the mixture will be sufficient for any moderate-sized horse, with fair, or even hard work. The dray and wagon horse may require forty pounds. Hay in the rack at night is, in this case, supposed to be omitted altogether. The rack, however, may remain, as occasionally useful for the sick horse, or to contain tares or other green feed.

Horses are very fond of this provender. The majority of them, after having been accustomed to it, will leave the best oats given to them alone, for the sake of the mingled chaff and grain. We would, however, caution the farmer not to set apart too much damaged hay for the manufacture of the chaff. The horse may be thus induced to eat that which he would otherwise refuse; but if the nourishing property of the hay has been impaired, or it has acquired an injurious principle, the animal will either lose condition, or become diseased. Much more injury is done by eating damaged hay or musty oats than is generally imagined. There will be sufficient saving in the diminished cost of the provender by the introduction of the straw, and the improved condition of the horse, without poisoning him with the refuse of the farm. For old horses, and for those with defective teeth, chaff is peculiarly useful, and for them the grain should be broken down as well as the fodder.

While the mixture of chaff with the grain prevents it from being too rapidly devoured and a portion of it swallowed whole, and therefore the stomach is not too loaded with that on which, as containing the most nutriment, its chief digestive power should be exerted, yet, on the whole, a great deal of time is gained by this mode of feeding, and more is left for rest. When a horse comes in wearied at the close of the day, it occupies, after he has eaten his grain, two or three hours to clear his rack. On the system of manger-feeding, the chaff being already cut into small pieces, and the beans and oats bruised, he is able fully to satisfy his appetite in an hour and a half. Two additional hours are therefore devoted to rest. This is a circumstance deserving of much consideration even in the farmer's stable, and of immense consequence to the post-master, the stage-coach proprietor, and the owner of every hard worked horse.

Manger food will be the usual support of the farmer's horse during the winter, and while at constant or occasional hard work; but from the middle of April to the end of July, he may be fed with this mixture in the day and turned out at night, or he may remain out during every rest-day. A team in constant employ should not, however, be suffered to be out at night after the end of July.

The farmer should take care that the pasture is thick and good; and that the distance from the yard is not too great, or the fields too large, otherwise a very considerable portion of time will be occupied in catching the horse in the morning. He will likewise have to take into consideration the sale he would have for his hay, and the necessity for sweet and untrodden pasture for his cattle. On the whole, however, turning out in this way, when cicrumstances will admit of it, will be found to be more beneficial for the horse, and cheaper than soiling in the yard.

The horse of the inferior farmer is sometimes fed on hay or grass alone, and the animal, although he rarely gets a feed of grain, maintains himself in tolerable condition, and does the work that is required of him : but hay and grass alone, however good in quality, or in whatever quantity allowed, will not support a horse under hard work. Other substances containing a large proportion of nutriment in a smaller compass, have been added. They shall be briefly enumerated, and an estimate formed of their comparative value.

In almost every part of Great Britain, OATS have been selected as that portion of the food which is to afford the principal nourishment. They contain seven hundred and forty-three parts out of a thousand of the nutritive matter. They should be about or somewhat less than a year old, heavy, dry, and sweet. New oats will weigh ten or fifteen per cent. more than old ones; but the difference consists principally in watery matter, which is gradually evaporated. New oats are not so readily ground down by the teeth as old ones. They form a more glutinous mass, difficult to digest, and, when eaten in considerable quantities, are apt to occasion colic and even staggers. If they are to be used before they are from three to five months old, they would be materially improved by a little kiln-drying. There is no fear for the horses from simple drying, if the corn was good when it was put into the kiln. The old oat forms, when chewed, a smooth and uniform mass, which readily dissolves in the stomach, and yields the nourishment which it contains. Perhaps some chemical change may have been slowly effected in the old oat, disposing it to be more readily assimilated. Oats should be plump, bright in color, and free from unpleasant smell or taste. The musty smell of wetted or damaged grain is produced by a fungus which grows upon the seed, and which has an injurious effect on the urinary organs, and often on the intestines, producing profuse staling, inflammation of the kidneys, colic, and inflammation of the bowels.

This musty smell is removed by kiln-drying the oat; but care is here requisite that too great a degree of heat is not employed. It should be sufficient to destroy the fungus without injuring the life of the seed. A considerable improvement would be effected by cutting the unthrashed oat-straw into chaff, and the expense of thrashing would be saved. Oat-straw is better than that of barley, but does not contain so much nutriment as that of wheat

When the horse is fed on hay and oats, the quantity of the oats must vary with his size and the work to be performed. In winter, four feeds, or from ten to fourteen pounds of oats in the day, will be a fair allowance for a horse of fifteen hands one or two inches high, and that has moderate work. In summer, half the quantity, with green food will be sufficient. Those which work on the farm have from ten to fourteen pounds, and the hunter from twelve to sixteen. There are no efficient and safe substitutes for good oats; but, on the contrary, we are much inclined to believe that they possess an invigorating property which is not found in other food.

Oatmeal will form a poultice more stimulating than one composed of linseed-meal alone—or they may be mingled in different proportions, as circumstances require. In the form of gruel it constitutes one of the most important articles of diet for the sick horse—not, indeed, forced upon him, but a pail containing it being slung in his box, and of which he will soon begin to drink when water is denied. Few grooms make good gruel; it is either not boiled long enough, or a sufficient quantity of oatmeal has not been used. The proportions should be, a pound of meal thrown into a gallon of water, and kept constantly stirred until it boils, and five minutes afterwards.

White-water, made by stirring a pint of oatmeal in a pail of water, the chill being taken from it, is an excellent beverage for the thirsty and tired horse.

BARLEY is a common food of the horse on various parts of the Continent, and, until the introduction of the oat, seems to have constituted almost his only food. It is more nutritious than oats, containing nine hundred and twenty parts of nutritive matter in every thousand. There seems, however, to be something necessary besides a great proportion of nutritive matter, in order to render any substance wholesome, strengthening, or fattening: therefore it is that, in many horses that are hardly worked, and, indeed, in horses generally, barley does not agree with them so well as oats. They are occasionally subject to inflammatory complaints, and particularly to surfeit and mange.

When barley is given, the quantity should not exceed a peck daily. It should always be bruised, and the chaff should consist of equal quantities of hay and barley-straw, and not cut too short. If the farmer has a quantity of spotted or unsaleable barley that he wishes thus to get rid of, he must very gradually accustom his horses to it, or he will probably produce serious illness among them. For horses that are recovering from illness, barley, in the form of malt, is often serviceable, as tempting the appetite and recruiting the strength. It is best given in mashes—water, considerably below the boiling heat, being poured upon it, and the vessel or pail kept covered for half an hour.

Grains fresh from the mash-tub, either alone, or mixed with oats or chaff, or both, may be occasionally given to horses of slow draught; they would, however, afford very insufficient nourishment for horses of quicker or harder work.

WHEAT is, in Great Britain, more rarely given than barley

contains nine hundred and fifty-five parts of nutritive matter When farmers have a damaged or unmarketable sample of wheat, they sometimes give it to their horses, and, being at first used in small quantities, they become accustomed to it, and thrive and work well: it must, however, always be bruised and given in chaff. Wheat contains a greater portion of *gluten*, or sticky, adhesive matter, than any other kind of grain. It is difficult of digestion, and apt to cake and forms obstructions in the bowels This will oftener be the case if the horse is suffered to drink much water soon after feeding upon wheat.

Fermentation, colic, and death, are occasionally the consequence of eating any great quantity of wheat. A horse that is fed on wheat should have very little hay. The proportion should not be more than one truss of hay to two of straw. Wheaten flour, boiled in water to the thickness of starch, is given with good effect in over-purging, and especially if combined with chalk and opium.

BRAN, or the ground husk of the wheat, used to be frequently given to sick horses on account of the supposed advantage derived from its relaxing the bowels. There is no doubt that it does operate gently on the intestinal canal, and assists in quickening the passage of its contents, when it is occasionally given; but it must not be a constant, or even frequent food. Mr. Ernes attended three mills at which many horses were kept, and there were always two or three cases of indigestion from the accumulation of bran or pollard in the large intestines. Bran may, however, be useful as an occasional aperient in the form of a mash, but never should become a regular article of food.

BEANS.—These form a striking illustration of the principle, that the nourishing or strengthening effects of the different articles of food depend more on some peculiar property which they possess, or some combination which they form, than on the actual quantity of nutritive matter. Beans contain but five hundred and seventy parts of nutritive matter, yet they add materially to the vigor of the horse. There are many horses that will not stand hard work without beans being mingled with their food, and these not horses whose tendency to purge it may be necessary to restrain by the astringency of the bean. There is no traveller who is not aware of the difference in the spirit and continuance of his horse whether he allows or denies him beans on his journey. They afford not merely a temporary stimulus, but they may be daily used without losing their power, or producing exhaustion. They are indispensable to the hard-worked coach-horse. Washy horses could never get through their work without them; and old horses would often sink under the task imposed upon them. They should not be given to the horses whole or split, but crushed. This will make a material difference in the quantity of nutriment that will be extracted. They are sometimes given to turf-horses, but only as an occasional stimulant. Two pounds of beans may, with advantage, be mixed with the chaff of the agricultural horse, during the winter. In summer the quantity of beans should be lessened, or they should be altogether discontinued. Beans are generally given whole. This is very absurd: for the young horse whose teeth are strong, seldom requires them; while the old horse, to whom they are in a manner necessary, is scarcely able to masticate them, swallows many of them which he is unable to break, and drops much corn from his mouth in the ineffectual attempt to crush them. Beans should not be merely split, but crushed; they will even then give sufficient employment to the grinders of the animal. Some post-masters use chaff with beans instead of oats. With hardly-worked horses they may possibly be allowed; but, in general cases, beans, without oats, would be too binding and stimulating, and would produce costiveness, and probably megrims or staggers.

Beans should be at least a twelvemonth old before they are given to the horse, and they should be carefully preserved from damp and mouldiness, which at least disgust the horse if they do no other harm, and harbor an insect that destroys the inner part of the bean.

The straw of the bean is nutritive and wholesome, and is usually given to the horses. Its nutritive properties are supposed to be little inferior to those of oats. The small and plump bean is generally the best.

PEAS are occasionally given. They appear to be in a slight degree more nourishing than beans, and not so heating. They contain five hundred and seventy-four parts of nutritive matter. For horses of slow work they may be used; but the quantity of chaff should be increased, and a few oats added. They have not been found to answer with horses of quick draught. It is essential that they should be crushed; otherwise, on account of their globular form, they are apt to escape from the teeth, and many are swallowed whole. Exposed to warmth and moisture in the stomach, they swell considerably, and may painfully and injuriously distend it. The peas that are given to horses should be sound, and at least a twelve-month old.

In some northern counties pea-meal is frequently used, not only as an excellent food for the horse, but as a remedy for diabetes.

LINSEED is sometimes given to sick horses—raw, ground, and boiled. It is supposed to be useful in cases of catarrh.

Hay is most in perfection when it is about a twelve-month old The horse perhaps would prefer it earlier, but it neither so wholesome nor so nutritive, and often has a purgative quality. When it is about a year old, it retains or should retain somewhat of its green color, its agreeable smell and its pleasant taste. It has undergone the slow process of fermentation, by which the sugar which it contains is developed, and its nutritive quality is fully exercised. Old hay becomes dry and tasteless, and innutritive and unwholesome. After the grass is cut, and the hay stacked, a slight degree of fermentation takes place in it. This is necessary for the developement of the saccharine principle; but occasionally it proceeds too far and the hay becomes *mowburnt*, in which state it is injurious, or even poisonous. The horse soon shows the effect which it has upon him. He has diabetes to a considerable degree—he becomes hidebound—his strength is wasted—his thirst is excessive, and he is almost worthless.

Where the system of manger-feeding is not adopted, or where hay is still allowed at night, and chaff and corn in the day, there is no error into which the farmer is so apt to fall as to give an undue quantity of hay, and that generally of the worst kind. If the manger system is good, there can be no necessity for hay, or only for a small quantity of it; but if the rack is overloaded, the greedy horse will be eating all night, instead of taking rest—when the time for the morning feed arrives, his stomach will be already filled, and he will be less capable of work from the want of sleep, and from the long-continued distention of the stomach rendering it impossible for the food to be properly digested.

It is a good practice to sprinkle the hay with water in which salt has been dissolved. It is evidently more palatable to the animal, who will leave the best unsalted hay for that of an inferior quality that has been moistened with brine; and there can be no doubt that the salt very materially assists the process of digestion. The preferable way of salting hay is to sprinkle it over the different layers as the rick is formed. From its attraction for water, it would combine with that excess of moisture which, in wet seasons, is the cause of too rapid and violent fermentation, and of the hay becoming mowburnt, or the rick catching fire, and it would become more incorporated with the hay. The only objection to its being thus used is, that the color of the hay is not so bright; but this will be of little consequence for home consumption.

Of the value of TARES, as forming a portion of the late spring and summer food of the stabled and agricultural horse, there can be no doubt. They are cut after the pods are formed, but a considerable time before the seeds are ripe.—They supply a larger quantity of food for a limited time than almost any other forage-crop. The *vicia sativa* is the more profitable of the tare. It is very nutritive, and acts as a gentle aperient. When surfeit-lumps appear on the skin, and the horse begins to rub himself against the divisions of the stall, and the legs swell, and the heels threaten to crack, a few tares, cut up with the chaff, or given instead of a portion of the hay, will afford considerable relief. Ten or twelve pounds may be allowed daily, and half that weight of hay subtracted. It is an erroneous notion, that, given in moderate quantities, they either roughen the coat or lessen the capability for hard work.

RYE GRASS affords a valuable article of food, but is inferior to the tare. It is not so nutritive. It is apt to scour, and, occasionally, and late in the spring, it has appeared to be injurious to the horse.

CLOVER, for soiling the horse, is inferior to the tare and the rye grass, but nevertheless, is useful when they cannot be obtained. Clover hay is, perhaps, preferable to meadow hay for chaff. It will sometimes tempt the sick horse, and may be given with advantage to those of slow and heavy work: but custom seems properly to have forbidden it to the hunter and the hackney.

LUCERN, where it can be obtained, is preferable even to tares, and SAINFOIN is superior to lucern. Although they contain but a small quantity of nutritive matter, it is easily digested, and perfectly assimilated. They speedily put both muscle and fat on the horse that is worn down by labor, and they are almost a specific for hide-bound. Some farmers have thought so highly of lucern as to substitute it for oats. This may be allowable for the agricultural horse of slow and not severe work, but he from whom speedier action is sometimes required, and the horse of all work, must have a portion of hard meat within him.

THE SWEDISH TURNIP is an article of food the value of which has not been sufficiently appreciated, and particularly for agricultural horses. Although it is far from containing the quantity of nutritive matter which has been supposed, that which it has seems to be capable of easy and complete digestion. It should be sliced with chopped straw, and without hay. It quickly fattens the horse, and produces a smooth glossy coat and a loose skin. It will be good practice to give it once a day, and that at night when the work is done.

CARROTS.—The virtues of this root are not sufficiently known, whether as contributing to the strength and endurance of the sound horse, or the rapid recovery of the sick one. To the healthy horse they should be given sliced in his chaff. Half a bushel will be a fair daily allowance. There is little provender of which the horse is fonder. The following account of the value of the carrot is not exaggerated. " This root is held in much esteem. There is none better, nor perhaps so good. When first given it is slightly diuretic and laxative; but as the horse becomes accustomed to it, these effects cease to be produced. They also improve the state of the skin. They form a good substitute for grass, and an excellent alterative for horses out of condition. To sick and idle horses they render grain unnecessary. They are beneficial in all chronic diseases connected with breathing. and have a marked influence upon chronic cough and broken wind. They are serviceable in diseases of the skin, and in combination with oats they restore a worn horse much sooner than oats alone

POTATOES have been given, and with advantage, in their raw state, sliced with the chaff; but, where it has been convenient to boil or steam them, the benefit has been far more evident. Purging has then rarely ensued. Some have given boiled potatoes alone, and horses, instead of rejecting them, have soon preferred them even to the oat; but it is better to mix them with the usual manger feed, in the proportion of one pound of potatoes to two and a half pounds of the other ingredients   The use of the potato must depend on its cheapness, and the facility for boiling it. Half a dozen horses would soon repay the expense of a steaming boiler in the saving of provender, without taking into the account their improved condition and capability for work.* A horse fed on potatoes should have his quantity of water materially curtailed.

FURZE has sometimes been given during the winter months. There is considerable trouble attending the preparation of it, although its plentifulness and little value for other purposes would, on a large farm, well repay that trouble. The furze is cut down at about three or four years' growth; the green branches of that and the preceding year are bruised in a mill, and then given to the horses in the state in which they come from the mill, or cut up with the chaff. Horses are very fond of it. If twenty pounds of the furze are given, five pounds of straw, the beans, and three pounds of the oats, may be withdrawn.

The times of feeding should be as equally divided as convenience will permit; and when it is likely that the horse will be kept longer than usual from home, the nose-bag should invariably be taken. The small stomach of the horse is emptied in a few hours; and if he is suffered to remain hungry much beyond his accustomed time, he will afterwards devour his food so voraciously as to distend the stomach and endanger an attack of staggers.

When extra work is required from the animal, the system of management is often injudicious, for a double feed is put before him, and as soon as he has swallowed it, he is started. It would be far better to give him a double feed on the previous evening, which would be digested before he is wanted, and then he

---

* Professor Low says that 15 lbs. of potatoes yield as much nourishment as four pounds and a half of oats. Von Thayer asserts that three bushels are equal to 112 lbs. of hay; and Curwen, who tried potatoes extensively in the feeding of horses, says that an acre goes as far as four acres of hay.

might set out in the morning after a very small portion of grain has been given to him, or perhaps only a little hay One of the most successful methods of enabling a horse to get well through a long journey, is to give him only a little at a time while on the road, and at night to indulge him with a double feed of grain and a full allowance of beans.

WATER.—This is a part of stable management little regarded by the farmer. He lets his horses loose morning and night, and they go to the nearest pond or brook and drink their fill, and no harm results, for they obtain that kind of water which nature designed them to have, in a manner prepared for them by some unknown influence of the atmosphere, as well as by the deposition of many saline admixtures. The difference between *hard* and *soft* water is known to every one. In hard water, soap will curdle, vegetables will not boil soft, and the saccharine matter of the malt cannot be fully obtained in the process of brewing. There is nothing in which the different effect of hard and soft water is so evident, as in the stomach and digestive organs of the horse. Hard water, drawn fresh from the well, will assuredly make the coat of a horse unaccustomed to it stare, and it will not unfrequently gripe and otherwise injure him. Instinct or experience has made even the horse himself conscious of this, for he will never drink hard water if he has access to soft, and he will leave the most transparent and pure water of the well for a river, although the stream may be turbid, and even for the muddiest pool.* He is injured, however, not so much by the hardness of the well-water as by its coldness—particularly by its coldness in summer, and when it is in many degrees below the temperature of the atmosphere. The water in the brook and the pond being warmed by long exposure to the air, as well as having become soft, the horse drinks freely of it without danger.

If the horse were watered three times a day, and especially in summer, he would often be saved from the sad torture of thirst, and from many a disease. Whoever has observed the eagerness with which the over-worked horse, hot and tired, plunges his muzzle into the pail, and the difficulty of stopping him until he has drained the last drop, may form some idea of what he had previously suffered, and will not wonder at the violent spasms, and inflammation, and sudden death, that often result.

There is a prejudice in the minds of many persons against the

---

* Some trainers have so much fear of hard or strange water, that they carry with them to the different courses the water that the animal has been accustomed to drink, and that which they know agrees with it.

horse being fully supplied with water. They think that it injures his wind, and disables him for quick and hard work. If he is galloped, as he too often is, immediately after drinking, his wind may be irreparably injured; but if he were oftener suffered to satiate his thirst at the intervals of rest, he would be happier and better. It is a fact unsuspected by those who have not carefully observed the horse, that if he has frequent access to water, he will not drink so much in the course of the day as another will do, who, to cool his parched mouth, swallows as fast as he can, and knows not when to stop.

On a journey a horse should be liberally supplied with water. When he is a little cooled, two or three quarts may be given to him, and after that his feed. Before he has finished his corn, two or three quarts more may be offered. He will take no harm if this is repeated three or four times during a long and hot day.

It is a judicious rule with travellers, that when a horse begins to refuse his food, he should be pushed no farther that day. It may, however, be worth while to try whether this does not proceed from thirst, as much as from exhaustion, for in many instances his appetite and his spirits will return soon after he has partaken of the refreshing draught.

MANAGEMENT OF THE FEET.—This is the only division of stable management that remains to be considered, and one sadly neglected by the carter and groom. The feet should be carefully examined every morning, for the shoes may be loose and the horse would have been stopped in the middle of his work; or the clenches may be raised, and endanger the wounding of his legs; or the shoe may begin to press upon the sole or the heel, and bruises of the sole, or corn, may be the result; and, the horse having stood so long in the stable, every little increase of heat in the foot, or lameness, will be more readily detected, and serious disease may often be prevented.

When the horse comes in at night, and after the harness has been taken off and stowed away, the heels should be well brushed out. Hand-rubbing will be preferable to washing, especially in the agricultural horse, whose heels, covered with long hair, can scarcely be dried again. If the dirt is suffered to accumulate in that long hair, the heels will become sore, and grease will follow; and if the heels are washed, and particularly during the winter, grease will result from the coldness occasioned by the slow evaporation of the moisture. The feet should be stopped—even the feet of the farmer's horse, if he remains in the stable. Very little clay should be used in the stopping, for it will get hard and press upon the sole. Cow-dung is the best stopping to preserve the feet cool and elastic; but before the stopping is applied, the picker should be run round the whole of the foot, between the shoe and the sole, in order to detect any stone that may have insinuated itself there, or a wound on any other part of the sole. For the hackney and hunter stopping is indispensable. After several days' hard work it will afford very great relief to take the shoes off, having put plenty of litter under the horse, or to turn him, if possible, into a loose-box; and the shoes of every horse, whether hardly worked or not, should be removed or changed once in every three weeks.

CHAPTER XXI.

THE SKIN AND ITS DISEASES.

The skin of the horse consists of three layers. Externally is the cuticle, epidermis, or scarf-skin, composed of innumerable thin transparent scales, like those of a fish. They are raised in the form of pellucid bladders in blistering, and are thrown off in hard, dry, white scales, in mange and some other diseases. The scarf-skin is permeated by innumerable pores, for the passage of the hair, perspiration, and unctuous secretions, and for the inhalation of gasses and fluids. It is destitute of nerves and blood-vessels, is insensible, and its principal use seems to be to protect the true skin, and to moderate its occasional morbid sensibility. There is a constant alteration and renewal of every part of it, but it adheres to the true skin through the medium of the pores, and also numerous little eminences, or projections, which seem to be prolongations of the nerves of the skin.

Beneath the cuticle is a thin, soft substance, through which the pores and eminences of the true skin pass. It is termed the *rete mucosum*, from its web-like structure, and its soft mucous consistence. Its office is to cover the minute vessels and nerves in their way from the cutis to the cuticle. It is also connected with the color of the skin.

The *cutis*, or true skin, lies beneath the rete mucosum. It is decidedly of a fibrous texture, elastic, but with difficulty lacerated —exceedingly vascular, and highly sensitive.

The skin answers the double purpose of protection and strength. Where it is necessary that the parts should be bound and knit together, it adheres so tightly that we can scarcely raise it. Thus the bones of the knees and the pasterns and the tendons of the legs, on which so much stress is frequently thrown, are securely tied down and kept in their places.

Of its strength we have abundant proof, both in the living and dead animal.

It is, while the animal is alive, one of the most elastic bodies with which we are acquainted. It not only perfectly adapts itself to the slow growth or decrease of the body, and appears equally to fit, whether the horse is in the plumpest condition or reduced to a skeleton ; but, when a portion of it is distended to an extraordinary degree, in the most powerful action of the muscles, it, in a moment, again contracts to its usual dimensions.

It is principally indebted for this elasticity to almost innumerable minute glands which pour out an oily fluid that softens and supplies it. When the horse is in health, and every organ discharges its proper functions, a certain quantity of this unctuous matter is spread over the surface of the skin, and is contained in all the pores that penetrate its substance ; and the skin becomes pliable, easily raised from the texture beneath, and presenting that peculiar yielding softness and elasticity which experience has proved to be the best proofs of the condition, or in other words, the general health of the animal. Then, too, from the oilness and softness of the skin, the hair lies in its natural and proper direction, and is smooth and glossy. When the system is deranged, and especially the digestive system, and the vessels concerned in the nourishment of the animal feebly act, those of the skin evidently sympathize. This oily secretion is no more thrown out; the skin loses its pliancy ; it seems to cling to the animal, and we have that peculiar appearance which we call hide-bound. This, however, requires attentive consideration.

We observe a horse in the summer. We find him with a thin, smooth, glossy coat, and his extremities clean and free almost from a single rough and misplaced hair. We meet with him again towards the winter, when the thermometer has fallen almost or quite to the freezing point, and we scarcely recognize him in his thick, rough, coarse, colorless coat, and his legs enveloped in long, shaggy hair. The health of the horse is, to a certain degree, deranged. He is dull, languid, easily fatigued. He will break into a sweat with the slightest exertion, and it is almost imposssble thoroughly to dry him. He may perhaps feed as well as usual, although that will not generally be the case, but he is not equal to the demands which we are compelled to make upon him.

This process goes on for an uncertain time, depending on the constitution of the animal, until nature has effected a change, and then he once more rallies ; but a great alteration has taken place in him—the hair has lost its soft and glossy character, and is become dry and staring. The skin ceases to secrete that peculiar unctuous matter which kept it soft and flexible, and becomes dry and scaly ; and the exhalents on the surface, having become relaxed, are frequently pouring out a profuse perspiration, without any apparent adequate cause for it.

So passes the approach to winter, and the owner complains sadly of the appearance of his steed, and, according to the old custom, gives him plenty of cordial balls,—perhaps too many of them,—on the whole not being unserviceable at this critical period, yet not productive of a great deal of good. At length the animal rallies of himself, and although not so strong and full of spirits as he ought to be, is hardier and more lively than he was, and able to struggle with the cold of the coming winter.

What a desideratum in the management of the horse would be a course of treatment that would render all this unnecessary! The desideratum has been found—a free escape of perspiration, a moist and softened state of the skin, an evident increase of health, and capability of enduring fatigue, and working on shorter supply of food than he could before. This is said to be performed by the clipping and singeing systems.

Mr. Thomas Turner, who was almost one of the earliest advocates of these systems, states that during the months of October and November an inordinate growth of hair is observed over the whole surface of the body, and in many horses as early as the beginning of September, and almost invariably prevails, more or less, in every horse that is not thorough-bred. The debilitating effects thereby induced are profuse perspiration on the least possible exertion—depression of the animal spirits, and temporary loss of appetite. The immediate removal of all the superfluous hair by close clipping, instantly proves so powerful a tonic to the animal, that he unhesitatingly affirms it to be inferior to none at present known in our pharmacopæia. Mr. Turner adds,—" Now, signal as the success of clipping has been, I do entertain a hope, and am of opinion that, in the majority of instances, it may be superseded by singeing under certain modifications."

We may not, perhaps, be able satisfactorily to explain the apparently magical effects of clipping and singeing on the general constitution, and particularly the wind of the horse, or the respiratory functions generally, but there is no doubt of their existence. An increased tone is given to the system generally; and probably, in some way not yet sufficiently developed, the increased current of the electric fluid may have much to do with it.

HIDE-BOUND.

This is not so much a diminution of the cellular or fatty substance between the skin and the muscles beneath, as it is an alteration in the skin itself. It is a hardness and unyieldingness of the skin from the want of the oily matter on its surface and its substance. It is the difference that is presented to the feeling by well curried and supple leather, and that which has become dry and unyielding.

The surface of the skin becoming dry and hard, the scales of the cuticle are no longer penetrated by the hair, but separating themselves in every direction, give that peculiar roughness to the coat which accompanies want of condition. It betokens impaired function of the vessels everywhere, and particularly those of the stomach and bowels. Hide-bound is not so much a disease as a symptom of disease, and particularly of the digestive organs; and our remedies must be applied not so much to the skin—although we have, in friction and in warmth, most valuable agents in producing a healthy condition of the integuments—as to the *cause* of the hide-bound, and the state of the constitution generally. Every disease that can affect the general system may produce this derangement of the functions of the skin. Glanders, when become constitutional, is strongly indicated by the unthrifty appearance of the coat. Chronic cough, grease, farcy, and founder, are accompanied by hide-bound; and diet too sparing, and not adequate to the work exacted, is an unfailing source of it. If the cause is removed, the effect will cease.

Should the cause be obscure, as it frequently is—should the horse wear an unthrifty coat, and his hide cling to his ribs, without any apparent disease, we shall generally be warranted in tracing it to sympathy with the actual, although not demonstrable, suspension of some important secretion or function, either of the alimentary canal or the respiratory functions. A few mashes, and a mild dose of physic, are first indicated, and, simple as they appear to be, they often have a very beneficial effect. The regular action of the bowels being re-established, that of all the organs of the frame will speedily follow. If the horse cannot be spared for physic, alteratives may be administered. There is no better alterative for hide-bound and an unthrifty coat, than that which is in common use, pulverized antimony, nitre, and sulphur. The peculiar effect of the antimony and sulphur, and electric influence on the skin, with that of the sulphur on the bowels, and of the nitre on the urinary organs, will be here advantageously combined.

Should the horse not feed well, and there is no indication of fever, a slight tonic may be added, as gentian or ginger; but in the majority of cases, attended by loss of condition and an unthrifty coat, and hide-bound, tonics and aromatics should be carefully avoided.

The cause of the impaired action of the vessels being removed, the powers of nature will generally be sufficient, and had better be left to themselves. There are not any more dangerous medicines in common use in the stable, and especially in cases like these, than tonics and cordials. They often arouse to fatal action a tendency to fever that would otherwise have slept, or they produce a state of excitement near akin to fever, and apt to degenerate into it. By the stimulus of a cordial, the secretions may be suddenly roused, and among them, this unctuous secretion from the pores of the skin, so necessary to apparent condition ; but the effect soon passes over, and a repetition of the stimulus is necessary—the habit is soon formed—the dose must be gradually increased, and in the mean time the animal is kept in a state of dangerous excitement, by which the powers of nature must be eventually impaired.

Friction may be employed with advantage in the removal of hidebound. It has repeatedly been shown that this is one of the most efficacious instruments we can use, to call into exercise the suspended energies either of the absorbent or secreting vessels. Warmth may likewise be had recourse to—not warmth of stable, which has been shown to be so injurious, but warmth arising from exercise, and the salutary, although inexplicable, influence of clipping and singeing.

PORES OF THE SKIN.

Besides the openings already mentioned, through which proceeds the unctuous fluid that supplies and softens the skin, there are others more numerous, by means of which a vast quantity of aqueous fluid escapes, and perspiration is carried on.

This process of perspiration is not, however, so far under the control of medicine as in the human being.*

We are not aware of any drugs that will certainly produce it. Warm clothing seems occasionally to effect it, but this is more in appearance than reality. The insensible perspiration cannot escape through the mass of clothing, and assumes a visible form. There are, however, a few medicines, as antimony and sulphur, that have an evident and very considerable effect on the skin, in opening its pores and exciting its vessels to action.

Of the existence of absorbent vessels on the skin, or those which take up some fluid or substance, and convey it into the circulation, we have satisfactory proof. A horse is even more easily salivated than the human being. Salivation has been produced by rubbing a splint with mercurial ointment, previous to blistering ; and a very few drachms rubbed on the inside of the thighs, will probably produce a greater effect than the practitioner desires.

* *Note by Mr. Spooner.*—Although the same medicines will not produce this effect, yet those that come under the designation of diffusible stimulants, will. Thus, a large dose of spirit of nitrous ether will often produce perspiration; and so, likewise, will the spirit of hartshorn, and even vinegar.

MOULTING.

Twice in the year, the hair of the body of the horse is changed. The short, fine coat of summer would afford little protection against the winter, and that of the winter would be oppressive to the animal, if it appeared during the summer. The hair of the mane and tail remains. The bulbous root of the hair does not die, but the pulpy matter seems to be removed from the root of the hair, which, thus deprived of its nourishment, perishes and drops off, and a new hair springs at its side from the same bulb. The hair which is produced in the autumn, is evidently different from that which grows in the spring; it is coarser, thicker, and not so glossy as the other. As moulting is a process extending over the whole of the skin, and requiring a very considerable expenditure of vital power, the health of the animal is generally affected at these times. That energy, and nervous vital influence, which should support the whole of the frame, is to a great degree determined to the skin, and the animal is languid, and unequal to much hard work. He perspires greatly with the least unusual exertion, and if he is pressed beyond his strength, becomes seriously ill.

The treatment which the groom in this case adopts, is most absurd and dangerous. The horse, from the deranged distribution of vital power, is disposed to fever, or he labors under a slight degree of fever, sufficiently indicated by the increased quickness of pulse, redness of nose, and heat of mouth. The lassitude and want of appetite which are the accompaniments of this febrile state, are mistaken for debility; and cordials of various kinds, some of them exceedingly stimulating, are unsparingly administered. At length, with regard to the hunter, the racer, and even in the hackney and the carriage-horse, the scissors or the lamp are introduced, and a new method is established of guarding against this periodical debility, setting at defiance the occasional exposure to cold, and establishing a degree of health and strength previously unknown. Friction may be allowed, to assist the falling off of the old hair, and to loosen the cuticle for the appearance of the new hair, but it is somewhat more gently applied than it used to be. The curry-comb is in a great measure banished, and even the brush is not applied too hard or too long. The old hair is not forced off before the young hair is ready to take its place.

Nature adapts the coat to the climate and to the season. The Sheltie has one as long and thick as that of a bear; and, as the summer is short and cold in those northern islands, the coat is rough and shaggy during the whole of the year. In the southern parts of our country, the short, and light and glossy coat of summer gradually yields to the close and heavy, and warm clothing of winter. In the deserts of Arabia, where the winter is rarely cold, the coat remains short and glossy throughout the year. These are wise and kind provisions of nature, and excite our admiration.*

COLOR.

The color of the hair admits of every variety, and each color becomes in turn fashionable. Like that of the skin, it is influenced by, or depends on, the mucous mesh-work under the cuticle. There are comparatively few perfectly white horses now remaining. The majority of white horses are those that have become so. Light-grey colts begin to grow white before they are five years old, especially if they have not much dark mixture about the joints.

Grey horses are of different shades, from the lightest silver to a dark iron-grey. The silver-grey reminds the observer of the palfrey, improved by an admixture of Arab blood. He does not often exceed fourteen hands and a half in height, and is round carcassed—thin-legged—with oblique pasterns, calculated for a light carriage, or for a lady's riding—seldom subject to disease—but not very fleet, or capable of hard work.

The iron-grey is usually a larger horse; higher in the withers, deeper and thinner in the carcass, more angular in all his proportions, and in many cases a little too long in the legs. Some of these greys make good hackneys and hunters, and especially the Irish horses; but they are principally used for the carriage. They have more endurance than the flatness of their chest would promise; but their principal defect is their feet, which are liable to contraction, and yet that contraction not so often accompanied by lameness as in many other horses.

The dappled grey is generally a handsomer and a better horse

---

* *Note by Mr. Spooner.*—We must protest against the idea that a horse with a long coat, however fed and trained, is in as good condition, or capable of as great exertion, as a horse with a sleek glossy coat. As well may a man with a great coat on attempt to run a race with another stripped almost to the skin. This fact it is which has led to the now general practice of clipping or singeing, by which the coats of coarse-skinned horses are removed, and the horses put on a par with sleek skinned animals, without the necessity of very hot stables, and a long course of preparatory treatment. The advantages of clipping are great; perspiration is considerably lessened, the horse is soon brought into condition, and grooming is greatly facilitated, without unnecessary irritation; indeed, the quickest method is to wash the skin while the animal is somewhat warm, with warm water (and soap if necessary), and then scrape the skin, and throw a horse-cloth on the body, which, in the course of ten minutes, will be found dry and comfortable.

All the angular points of the iron-grey are filled up, and with that which not only adds to symmetry, but to use. Whether as a hackney, or, the larger variety, a carriage-horse, there are few better, especially since his form has been so materially improved, and so much of his heaviness got rid of, by the free use of foreign blood. There are not, however, so many dappled greys as there used to be, since the bays have been bred with so much care. The dappled grey, if dark at first, generally retains his color to old age.

Some of the greys approach to a nutmeg, or even bay color. Many of these are handsome, and most of them are hardy.

The roans, of every variety of color and form, are composed of white mixed with bay, or red, or black. In some it seems to be a natural mixture of the colors; in others it appears as if one color was powdered or sprinkled over another. They are pretty horses for ladies or light carriages, and many of them easy in their paces, but they do not usually display much blood, nor are they celebrated for endurance. If they should have white fore legs, with white hoofs, they are too often tender-footed, or become so with even a little hard work.

The strawberry horse is a mixture of sorrel with white; usually handsome and pleasant, but more celebrated for these qualities than for strength and endurance.

The pied horse is one that has distinct spots or patches of different colors, but generally of white with some other color. They are not liked as hackneys, on account of their peculiarity of color, nor in teams of horses; but they look well when tolerably matched in a phæton or light carriage. Their value must depend on their breed. Of themselves they have no peculiar character, except that a white leg and foot is as suspicious in them as it is in the roan.

The dun, of the Galloway size, and with considerable blood, is often attached to the curricle or the phæton. The larger variety is a true farmer's or miller's horse, with no great speed or extraordinary strength, yet a good-tempered, good-feeling, good-constitutioned, useful horse enough. Varieties of the dun, shaded with a darker color, or dappled, and with some breeding, and not standing too high, are beautiful animals, and much sought after for light carriages.

The cream-color, of Hanoverian extraction, with his white iris and red pupil, is appropriated to royal use. Attached to the state-carriage of the monarch, he is a superb animal. His bulky, yet perfectly-formed body, his swelling crest, and his proud and lofty action, as if conscious of his office, qualify him for the service that is exacted from him, but we have little experience how far he would suit other purposes.

Of the chestnuts there are three varieties—the pale red or the sorrel, usually with some white, either on the face or the legs—generally lightly made, yet some of them bulky enough for the heaviest loads. Their color is generally objectionable, and they are supposed to be somewhat deficient in endurance.

The light chestnut, with less red and a little more bay or brown, is considered a preferable animal, especially if he has little or no white about him; yet even he, although pleasant to ride, is sometimes irritable, and generally weak. We must except one variety, the Suffolk punch; a heavy horse, and adapted for slow work, but perfect of his kind—whom no labor can daunt, no fatigue overcome. This is a breed now, unfortunately, nearly extinct. The present variety, however crossed, is not equal to the old Suffolk.

The dark chestnut is as different a horse from the hackney-like chestnut as can be well imagined; round in the carcase; powerful in the quarters, but rather fine in the legs; possessed of great endurance, and with a constitution that rarely knows an ailment, except that the feet are small and disposed to contraction, and the horse is occasionally of a hot and unmanageable temper.

Of the bays, there are many varieties, and they include the very best of our horses of every description. The bright yellow bay, although very beautiful, and especially if his mane and tail are black, is the least valuable—the lightness of his color seems to give him some tenderness of constitution. The pure bay, with no white about him, and black from the knees and hocks to the feet, is the most desirable of all. He has generally a good constitution, and good feet; and, if his conformation is not faulty, will turn out a valuable horse for almost every purpose.

The bay-brown has not always so much show and action, but, generally, more strength and endurance, and usefulness. He has greater substance than the lighter bay, and more depth of leg; and, if he had the same degree of breeding, he would be as handsome and more valuable.

When, however, we arrive at the browns, it is necessary to examine the degree of breeding. This color is not so fashionable, and therefore these horses have been considerably neglected. There are many good ones, and those that are good are valuable; others, probably, are only half or a quarter bred, and therefore comparatively coarse, yet useful for the saddle and for harness—for slow work, and, occasionally, for that which is more rapid.

The black-brown is generally more neglected so far as its breed is concerned, and should be more carefully examined. It is valuable if it retains the goodness of constitution of the brown and bay-brown.

Of the black, greater care has been taken. The heavy black of Lincolnshire and the midland counties is a noble animal, and would be almost beyond price if he could be rendered more active. The next in size constitute the majority of our wagon-horses, and perhaps our best; and, on a smaller breed, and to the improvement of which much attention has been devoted, many of our cavalry are mounted. A few black thorough-bred horses and black hunters are occasionally seen, but the improvement of horses of this color has not been studied, except for the purposes that have been mentioned. Their peculiar high action, while not objectionable for draught, and desirable for the parade, would be unbearable in the roadster. Black horses have been said to be more subject to vice, disease, and blindness, than those of any other color. This charge is not true to its full extent; but there certainly are a great many worthless black horses in in every part of the country.

After all, there is an old saying, that a good horse cannot be a bad color; and that it is far more necessary to attend to the conformation and points of the animal than to his color. The foregoing observations, however, although they admit of many exceptions, may be useful in guiding to the judicious purchase of the horse.*

* *Note by Mr. Spooner.*—Color.—We do not consider that the size, conformation, and qualifications of horses depend so much on the color as the text would imply. We have found both good and bad horses of every color, and the only rule we can admit as correct is, that certain colors denote deficient breeding, and therefore such animal is not likely to be so good as he looks, but is probably deficient in bottom or the powers of endurance. These colors are black, which prevails so much with cart-horses, and sorrel, dun, piebald, &c.; the possessors of which come from the north, and possess no eastern blood. Black horses, unless evidently high bred, are very often soft and sluggish, with breeding insufficient for their work; the pedigree of the majority of them may be dated from the plough-tail, whatever admixtures there may have been since. White hair denotes a thin skin, which is objectionable, when it prevails on the legs of horses, as such animals are more disposed to swelled legs and cracked heels than others. Bay horses with black legs are greatly esteemed, and yet we have known many determined slugs of this hue. Their constitution is, however, almost invariably good. Chestnut is the prevailing color with our race-horses, and consequently chestnut horses are generally pretty well bred, and possess the good and bad qualities which obtain most amongst thorough-breds. The Suffolk cart-horse is also distinguished by his light chestnut color: and it is no small recommendation to find that this breed has, for several years past, carried away the principal prizes at the annual shows of the Royal Agricultural Society of England.

Gray is a very good color, and one which has become very fashionable for carriage and phæton horses during the present reign. Her Majesty's ponies, as they are still called, although they have increased in height from thirteen to fifteen hands, are beautiful specimens of this color, and have rendered the color fashionable for harness purposes. These horses have a

SURFEIT.

Large pimples or eruptions often appear suddenly on the skin of the horse, and especially in the spring of the year. Occasionally they disappear as quickly as they came. Sometimes they seem to be attended with great itching, but at other times, the annoyance is comparatively little. When these eruptions have remained a few days, the cuticle frequently peels off, and a small scaly spot—rarely a sore—is left. This is called a surfeit, from its resemblance to some eruptions on the skin of the human being when indigestible or unwholesome food has been taken. The surfeit is, in some cases, confined to the neck; but it oftener spreads over the sides, back, loins, and quarters. The cause is enveloped in some obscurity. The disease most frequently appears when the skin is irritable during or after the process of moulting, or when it sympathizes with any disorder of the stomach. It has been known to follow the eating of poisonous herbs or mowburnt hay, but, much oftener, it is to be traced to exposure to cold when the skin was previously irritable and the horse heated by exercise. It has also been attributed to the immoderate drinking of cold water when the animal was hot. It is obstruction of some of the pores of the skin and swelling of the surrounding substance, either from primary affection of the skin, or a plethoric state of the system, or sympathy with the digestive organs.

The state of the patient will sufficiently guide the surgeon as to the course he should pursue. If there is simple eruption, without any marked inflammatory action, alteratives should be resorted to, and particularly those recommended for hide-bound in page 407. They should be given on several successive nights. The night is better than the morning, because the warmth of the stable will cause the antimony and sulphur to act more powerfully on the skin. The horse should be warmly clothed—half an

---

considerable admixture of eastern blood, and most of them are immediately derived from an Arab or a Turkish horse. This, indeed, is the principal or only use of the eastern horse in this country. It is vain to expect any improvement in the speed of our race-horses from foreign admixture, for every attempt of the kind for some years past has been unsuccessful. The circular carcase, arched neck, good shoulders and fore legs, high and excellent trotting action, are, however, qualifications which our thorough-breds cannot supply, and are truly valuable in animals required for getting carriage-horses. The white Arabian horse is, therefore, the very animal required for getting phæton horses, and, if put to large mares, are also well adapted for perpetuating handsome and valuable carriage-horses. There are also some excellent cart-horses of a gray color; some of massive proportions, and others of moderate size, and more active. The iron grays and roans are generally cleaner about the legs, and more compact than the mottled greys.

hour's walking exercise should be given, an additional rug thrown over him—such green feed as can be procured should be used in moderate quantities, and the chill should be taken from the water.

Should the eruption continue or assume a more violent character, bleeding and aloes must be had recourse to, but neither should be carried to any extreme. The physic having set, the alteratives should again be had recourse to, and attention should be paid to the comfort and diet of the horse.

If the eruption, after several of these alternative appearances and disappearances, should remain, and the cuticle and the hair begin extensively to peel off, a worse affection is to be feared, for surfeit is too apt to precede, or degenerate into, mange. This disorder, therefore, must next be considered.

MANGE

Is a pimpled or vesicular eruption. After a while the vesicles break, or the cuticle and the hair fall off, and there is, as in obstinate surfeit, a bare spot covered with scurf—some fluid oozing from the skin beneath, and this changing to a scab, which likewise soon peels off, and leaves a wider spot. This process is attended by considerable itching and tenderness, and thickening of the skin, which soon becomes more or less folded, or puckered. The mange generally first appears on the neck at the root of the mane, and its existence may be suspected even before the blotches appear, and when there is only considerable itchiness of the part, by the ease with which the short hair at the root of the mane is plucked out. From the neck it spreads upward to the head, or downward to the withers and back, and occasionally extends over the whole carcass of the horse.

One cause of it, although an unfrequent one, has been stated to be neglected or inveterate surfeit. Several instances are on record in which poverty of condition, and general neglect of cleanliness, preceded or produced the most violent mange. A remark of Mr. Blaine is very important:—"Among the truly healthy, so far as my experience goes, it never arises spontaneously, but it does readily form a spontaneous origin among the unhealthy." The most common cause is contagion. Amidst the whole list of diseases to which the horse is exposed, there is not one more highly contagious than mange. If it once gets into a stable, it spreads through it, for the slightest contact seems sufficient for the communication of this noisome complaint.

If the same brush and currycomb is used on all the horses, the propagation of mange is assured; and horses feeding in the same pasture with a mangy one rarely escape, from the propensity they have to nibble one another. Mange in cattle has been propagated to the horse, and from the horse to cattle. There are also some well-authenticated instances of the same disease being communicated from the dog to the horse, but not from the horse to the dog.

Mange has been said to originate in want of cleanliness in the management of the stable. The comfort and the health of the horse demand the strictest cleanliness. The eyes and the lungs frequently suffer from the noxious fumes of the putrifying dung and urine; but, in defiance of common prejudice, there is no authentic instance of mange being the result. Poverty and starvation are fruitful sources of mange, but it does not appear that filth has much to do with it, although poverty and filth generally go hand in hand.

The propriety of bleeding in cases of mange depends on the condition of the patient. If mange is the result of poverty, and the animal is much debilitated, bleeding will increase the evil, and will probably deprive the constitution of the power of rallying. Physic, however, is indispensable in every case. A mercurial ball will be preferable to a common aloetic one, as more certain and effectual in its operation, and the mercury probably having some influence in mitigating the disease. In this, however, mange in the horse resembles itch in the human being—medicine alone will never effect a cure. There must be some local application. There is this additional similarity—that which is most effectual in curing the itch in the human being must form the basis of every local application for the cure of mange in the horse. Sulphur is indispensable in every ointment for mange. It is the sheet-anchor of the veterinary surgeon. In an early and not very acute state of mange, equal portions of sulphur, turpentine, and train-oil, gently but well rubbed on the part, will be applied with advantage. Farriers are fond of the black sulphur, but that which consists of earthy matter, with the mere dregs of various substances, cannot be so effectual as the pure sublimed sulphur. A tolerably stout brush, or even a curry-comb, lightly applied, should be used, in order to remove the dandriff or scurf, wherever there is any appearance of mange. After that, the horse should be washed with strong soap and water as far as the disease has extended; and, when he has been thoroughly dried, the ointment should be well rubbed in with the naked hand, or with a piece of flannel. More good will be done by a little of the ointment being well rubbed in, than by a great deal being smeared over the part. The rubbing should be daily repeated.

During the application of the ointment, and as soon as the physic has set, an alterative ball or powder, similar to those recommended for the other affections of the skin, should be daily given. If, after some days have passed, no progress should appear to have been made, half a pound of sulphur should be well mixed with a pint of oil of tar, or, if that is not to be obtained, a pint of Barbaboes tar, and the affected parts rubbed, as before. On every fifth or sixth day, the ointment should be washed off with warm soap and water. The progress towards cure will thus be ascertained, and the skin will be cleansed, and its pores opened for the more effectual application of the ointment.

The horse should be well supplied with nourishing, but not stimulating food. As much green feed as he will eat should be given to him, or, what is far better, he should be turned out, if the weather is not too cold. It may be useful to add, that, after the horse has been once well dressed with either of these liniments, the danger of contagion ceases. It is necessary, however, to be assured that every mangy place has been anointed. It will be prudent to give two or three dressings after the horse has been apparently cured, and to continue the alteratives for ten days or a fortnight.

The cure being completed, the clothing of the horse should be well soaked in water, to which a fortieth part of the saturated solution of the chloride of lime has been added; after which it should be washed with soap and water, and again washed and soaked in a solution of the chloride of lime. Every part of the harness should undergo a similar purification. The curry-comb may be scoured but the brush should be burned. The rack and manger, and partitions, and every part of the stable which the horse could possibly have touched, should be well washed with a hair-broom—a pint of the chloride of lime being added to three gallons of water. All the wood-work should then be scoured with soap and water, after which a second washing with the chloride of lime will render all secure.

Every case of itchiness of the skin should be regarded with suspicion. When a horse is seen to rub the root of his tail, or his head, or neck, against the manger, the parts should be carefully examined. Some of the hair may have been rubbed or torn off, but if the roots remain firmly adherent, and there is only redness and not scurfiness of the skin, it probably is not mange, but only inflammation of the skin, from too great fulness of blood. A little blood should be abstracted—a purgative administered—and the alteratives given. The mange ointment cannot do harm, and may possibly prevent this heat of the skin from degenerating into mange, or arrest the progress of mange if it has commenced. If a scurfiness of the skin should appear on any of the points that are pressed upon by the collar or harness, the veterinary surgeon will do right to guard against danger by alterative medicine and the use of the ointment.*

* *Note by Mr. Spooner.*—We have only to remark, that the administration

WARTS.

These are occasionally found on all parts of the horse. There are some caustics available, but frequently they must be removed by an operation. If the root is very small, it may be snipped asunder, close to the skin, with a pair of scissors, and touched with the lunar caustic. If the pedicle or stem is somewhat larger, a ligature of waxed silk should be passed firmly round it, and tightened every day. The source of nutriment being thus removed, the tumor will, in a short time, die and drop off. If the warts are large, or in considerable clusters, it will be necessary to cast the horse, in order to cut them off close to the skin: the root should then be seared with a red-hot iron. Unless these precautions are used, the warts will speedily sprout again.

VERMIN.

Both the biped and the quadruped are subject to the visitation of insects that fasten on the skin, and are a constant nuisance from the itchiness which they occasion. If the horse, after being turned out for the winter, is taken up in the spring long and rough in his coat, and poor in condition, and with evident hide-bound, he will almost invariably be afflicted with vermin.

In our present imperfect acquaintance with natural history, it is difficult to account for the appearance of certain insects, and of those alone, on the integument of one animal, while others of an altogether different character are found on its neighbor. Each one has a tormentor peculiar to itself.

The vermin of the horse is destroyed by an infusion of tobacco or a solution of corrosive sublimate, the latter requiring the greatest caution. The skin being once cleansed of them, an attention to cleanliness will prevent their reappearance.

of mercurial physic requires extreme caution in this disease. We have known horses very low in condition killed by this means, and we doubt the necessity of the purge. Topical treatment is the principal remedy, and it is also well to administer sulphur internally at the same time.

There is a disease very much resembling the mange, which we occasionally meet with. The horse is affected with the most violent itching, and the hair is often rubbed off, but the skin does not become wrinkled, as in mange. Though this disease often appears to yield to the same topical treatment as the mange, yet, in some instances, it is incurable, and continues through life.

CHAPTER XXII.

ON SOUNDNESS, AND THE PURCHASE AND SALE OF HORSES.

[This chapter is given nearly entire, as in the original, and in the remarks on WARRANTY, &c., entire, because it is believed to give a luminous exposition of what EQUITY in all cases demands in regard to the matters of which it treats. It constitutes therefore the proper basis of amicable settlement between *gentlemen*, in all countries, where the purchaser of the horse alleges a violation of warranty; and the basis of proper adjudication where an action is commenced for fraud. In some of the States of the Union, there may be statutes or judicial decisions which would vary from the English ones cited on the subject of warranty, fraud, and as to what constitutes unsoundness,—but probably in most cases, they will be found substantially the same.—Am. Ed.]

There are few sources of greater annoyance both to the purchaser and the seller of the horse than disputes with regard to the soundness of the animal.

That horse is sound in whom there is no disease, and no alteration of structure that impairs, or is likely to impair, his natural usefulness. The horse is unsound that labors under disease, or has some alteration of structure which does interfere, or is likely to interfere, with his natural usefulness.* The term "*natural usefulness*" must be borne in mind. One horse may possess great speed, but is soon knocked up; another will work all day, but cannot be got beyond a snail's pace: a third with a heavy

---

* Since the publication of our first edition, this definition or rule as to soundness or unsoundness has received very high judicial sanction. *Coates* v. *Stephens*, 2 Moody and Robinson, 157; *Scholefield* v. *Robb*, id. 210. We shall adhere to it as our test of soundness or unsoundness throughout this chapter, not forgetting what is said in the following extract from a note to one of these cases. "As it may now be considered as settled law, that the breach of a warranty or soundness does not entitle the purchaser to return the horse, but only to recover the difference of value of the horse with or without the particular unsoundness, the question of temporary maladies, producing no permanent deterioration of the animal, would, generally speaking, only involve a right to damages merely nominal."

forehand is liable to stumble, and is continually putting to hazard the neck of his rider; another, with an irritable constitution and a loose, washy form, loses his appetite and begins to scour if a litte extra work is exacted from him. The term unsoundness must not be applied to either of these; it would be opening far too widely a door to disputation and endless wrangling. The buyer can discern, or ought to know, whether the form of the horse is that which will render him likely to suit his purpose, and he should try him sufficiently to ascertain his natural strength, endurance, and manner of going. Unsoundness, we repeat, has reference only to disease, or to that alteration of structure which is connected with, or will produce disease, and lessen the usefulness of the animal.

These principles will be best illustrated by a brief consideration of the usually supposed appearances or causes of unsoundness.

BROKEN KNEES certainly do not constitute unsoundness, after the wounds are healed, unless they interfere with the action of the joint; for the horse may have fallen from mere accident, or through the fault of the rider, without the slightest damage more than the blemish. No person, however, would buy a horse with broken knees, until he has thoroughly tried him, and satisfied himself as to his form and action.

CAPPED HOCKS may be produced by lying on an unevenly paved stable, with a scanty supply of litter, or by kicking generally, in neither of which cases would they constitute unsoundness, although in the latter they would be an indication of vice; but, in the majority of instances, they are the consequence of sprain, or of latent injury of the hock, and accompanied by enlargement of it, and would constitute unsoundness. A special warranty should always be taken against capped hocks.*

CONTRACTION is a considerable deviation from the natural form of the foot, but not necessarily constituting unsoundness. It requires, however, a most careful examination on the part of the purchaser or veterinary surgeon, in order to ascertain that there is no heat about the quarter, or ossification of the cartilage—that the frog, although diminished in size, is not diseased—that

---

* *Note by Mr. Spooner.—Capped hocks.*—In nine cases out of ten these enlargements are occasioned by kicking in the stall, a vice altogether different from that of spitefulness, which appears to arise more from restlessness than anything else. The swelling consists of an effusion of serum or water in the cellular bag which is found beneath the skin at the point of the hock, placed there for the purpose of giving facility of motion.

It is never occasioned by strains, therefore, although a sad blemish, it should not be regarded as an unsoundness, unless accompanied with other indications of disease.

the horse does not step short and go as if the foot were tender, and that there is not the slightest trace of lameness. Unless these circumstances, or some of them, are detected, a horse must not be pronounced to be unsound because his feet are contracted; for many horses with strangely contracted feet do not suffer at all in their action. A special warranty, however, should be required where the feet are at all contracted.

CORNS manifestly constitute unsoundness. The portion of the foot in which bad corns are situated will not bear the ordinary pressure of the shoe; and accidental additional pressure from the growing down of the horn, or the introduction of dirt or gravel, will cause serious lameness. They render it necessary to wear a thick and heavy shoe, or a bar-shoe, in order to protect the weakened and diseased part; and they are very seldom radically cured. There may be, however, and frequently is, a difference of opinion as to the actual existence or character of the corn. They are sometimes, too, so slight that they do not diminish the value of the horse, and will disappear on the horse being shod with ordinary skill and care, even without any alteration in the shoe.

COUGH.—This is a disease, and consequently unsoundness. However slight may be its degree, and of whatever short standing it may be, although it may sometimes scarcely seem to interfere with the usefulness of the horse, yet a change of stabling or slight exposure to wet and cold, or the least over-exertion, may, at other times, cause it to degenerate into many dangerous complaints. A horse, therefore, should never be purchased with a cough upon him, without a special warranty; or if—the cough not being observed—he is purchased under a general warranty, that warranty is thereby broken. It is not law, that a horse may be returned on breach of the warranty. The seller is not bound to take him back, unless he has contracted so to do; but he is liable to damages. Lord Ellenborough has completely decided this matter. "I have always held," said he, "that a warranty of soundness is broken, if the animal, at the time of sale, had any infirmity upon him that rendered him less fit for present service. It is not necessary that the disorder should be permanent or incurable. While he has a cough, he is unsound, although that may either be temporary or prove mortal."

In deciding on another case, the same judge said, "I have always held it that a cough is a breach of the warranty. On that understanding I have always acted, and think it quite clear." It was argued on the other hand that two-thirds of the horses in London had coughs, yet still the judge maintained that the cough was a breach of warranty. When it was farther argued that the horse had been hunted the day after the purchase, and the cough might have been increased by this, the reply was singular, but decisive. "There is no proof that he would have got well if he had not been hunted." This doctrine is confirmed by Parke, B., in the first case cited in p. 420.

ROARING, WHEEZING, WHISTLING, HIGH-BLOWING, and GRUNTING, being the result of alteration of structure, or disease in some of the air-passages, and interfering with the perfect freedom of breathing, especially when the horse is put on his speed, without doubt constitute unsoundness. There are decisions to the contrary, which are now universally admitted to be erroneous. BROKEN-WIND is still more decidedly unsoundness.*

CRIB-BITING.—Although some learned judges have asserted that crib-biting is simply a trick or bad habit, it must be regarded as unsoundness. This unnatural sucking in of the air must, to a certain degree injure digestion. It must dispose to colic, and so interfere with the strength, and usefulness, and health of the horse. Some crib-biters are good goers, but they probably would have possessed more endurance had they not acquired this habit; and it is a fact well established, that, as soon as a horse becomes a crib-biter, he, in nine cases out of ten, loses condition. In its very early stage it may be a mere trick—confirmed, it must have produced morbid deterioration. The wear of the front teeth, and the occasional breaking of them, make a horse old before his time, and sometimes render it difficult or impossible for him to graze, when the state of the animal or the convenience of the owner requires that he should be turned out.†

* *Note by Mr. Spooner.*—*Roaring, wheezing,* and *whistling* may be considered as modifications of the same disease, viz., an obstruction to the passage of air to and from the lungs; and as the nature and amount of this obstruction necessarily varies, so must the noise thereby produced, and which is consequently expressed by the terms in question; all, however, being decidedly *unsoundness.*

Grunting is the noise which many roarers will evince when suddenly alarmed by a real or pretended blow. It is the common horse-dealer's method of discovering a roarer, but by no means one that can be depended on, as many moderate roarers, particularly if they have lately become so, will not grunt. With regard to high-blowing, we by no means consider it an unsoundness, understanding by this term, however, the noise, often very considerable, which some horses make on being first excited, or put into motion. This noise is produced by the false nostrils, which either possess greater laxity than common, or else it is owing to the nervousness of the horse. It begins at once if the horse is excited, and, instead of increasing with exertion, like roaring, it diminishes or goes off. This is, or ought to be, the proper test of soundness.

Broken wind is of course decided unsoundness, and equally so is *thick wind,* or quickened respiration, which often arises from consolidation of a portion of the lungs, and sometimes merely from thickening of the membrane of the air passages.

† *Note by Mr. Spooner.*—*Crib-biting* has often been the subject of dispute

CURB constitutes unsoundness while it lasts, and perhaps while the swelling remains, although the inflammation may have subsided; for a horse that has once thrown out a curb is, for a while at least, very liable to do so again, to get lame in the same place on the slightest extra exertion; or, at all events, he would there first fail on extraordinary exertion. A horse, however, is not returnable, although he should spring a curb five minutes after the purchase; for it is done in a moment, and does not necessarily indicate any previous unsoundness or weakness of the part.*

CUTTING, as rendering a horse liable to serious injury of the legs, and indicating that he is either weak, or has an awkwardness of gait inconsistent with safety, produces, rather than this, unsoundness. Many horses go lame for a considerable period after cutting themselves severely; and others have dropped from the sudden agony, and endangered themselves and their riders. As some doubt, however, exists on this subject, and as it is a very material objection to a horse, cutting, when evident, should have its serious consequences provided against by a special warranty.†

ENLARGED GLANDS.—The enlargement of the glands under the jaw has not been so much considered as it ought to have been in

as to whether it constitutes unsoundness or not, which is not to be wondered at, seeing that many crib-biters will perform their work for many years without hindrance or inconvenience. Crib-biting is now, however, regarded as an unsoundness, on the principle that though at the present time the horse may be equal to his work, yet, at a future period, it may render him unequal to its performance, by causing indigestion, loss of flesh, and weakness. It is better that the question should be thus set at rest, as the value of the animal is very materially diminished by being a crib-biter, which is owing not so much to real injury, as to the disagreeable habit, and to the fact that if the animal is in a stable with other horses, they are very likely to learn the habit.

Wind-sucking must come under the same rules as crib-biting, which resembles it so far as the swallowing of air is concerned, the animal, however, being enabled to do it without the necessity of laying hold of the manger.

* *Note by Mr. Spooner.*—Curb constitutes unsoundness, unless it is well known that the horse has stood the ordeal of work for some months since the curb was thrown out, or any treatment adopted for it. As this information, however, can seldom be satisfactorily obtained, the possible effects of a curb should be guarded against by a special warranty.

† *Note by Mr. Spooner.*—We cannot agree with the text in considering this an unsoundness. It is a visible defect, and therefore can readily be observed, and pointed out, and objected to, in proportion to the amount of the evil which may be very severe and unlikely to be remedied, or slight, and owing either to improper shoeing, or youth, awkwardness, or weakness. To consider it, therefore, as an unsoundness, there being neither alteration of structure nor function, would be to open the door to perpetual disputes, and render the already vexed question of soundness still more vexatious. At the same time, if the cutting is considerable, and evidently arises from naturally defective action, and is of such a nature as not to admit of a remedy, we should not hesitate, in such a case, to pronounce the animal unsound.

our estimate of the soundness of the horse. Simple catarrh will occasionally, and severe affection of the chest will generally, be accompanied by swelling of these glands, which does not subside for a considerable time after the cold or fever has apparently been cured. To slight enlargements of the glands under the jaw much attention need not be paid; but if they are of considerable size, and especially if they are tender, and the glands at the root of the ear partake of the enlargement, and the membrane of the nose is redder than it should be, we should hesitate in pronouncing that horse to be sound. We must consider the swelling as a symptom of disease.

ENLARGED HOCK.—A horse with enlarged hock is unsound, the structure of this complicated joint being so materially affected that, although the horse may appear for a considerable time to be capable of ordinary work, he will occasionally fail even in that, and a few days' hard work will always lame him.*

THE EYES.—That inflammation of the eye of the horse which usually terminates in blindness of one or both eyes, has the peculiar character of receding or disappearing for a time, once or twice, or thrice, before it fully runs its course. The eye, after an attack of inflammation, regains so nearly its former natural brilliancy that a person even well acquainted with horses will not always recognize the traces of former disease. After a time, however, the inflammation returns, and the result is inevitable. A horse that has had one attack of this complaint, is long afterwards unsound, however perfect the eye may seem to be, because he carries about with him a disease that will probably again break out, and eventually destroy the sight. Whether, therefore, he may be rejected or not, depends on the possibility of proving an attack of inflammation of the eye, prior to the purchase. Next to direct evidence of this are appearances about the eye, of which the veterinary surgeon at least ought not to be ignorant. Allusion has been made to them in page 64. They consist chiefly of a puckering of the lids towards the inner corner of one or both eyes—a difference in the size of the eyes, although perhaps only a slight one, and not discovered except it be looked for—a gloominess of the eye—a dullness of the iris—a little dullness of the

---

* *Note by Mr. Spooner.*—The greater number of these cases, arising as they most frequently do from strains, we should consider as unsoundness, even although the probability may be that the horse will stand work without lameness. There is weakness of the part, and a possibility of lameness. There are, however, other cases in which the enlargement may be in the skin, or immediately under it, or on the outside of the bone, such cases being often produced by kicks or blows, or other external injuries. There are many such cases that we should regard as blemishes, but not as unsoundness

transparent part of the eye generally—a minute, faint, dusky spot deep in the eye, and generally with little radiations of white lines proceeding from it. If these symptoms, or the majority of them, existed at the time of purchase, the animal had assuredly been diseased before, and was unsound. Starting has been considered as unequivocal proof. It is usually an indication of defective sight, but it is occasionally a trick. Connected, however, with the appearances just described, it is a very strong corroborative proof.*

LAMENESS, from whatever cause arising, is unsoundness. However temporary it may be, or however obscure, there must be disease which lessens the utility of the horse, and renders him unsound for the time. So says common sense, but there are contradictory decisions on the case. "A horse laboring under a temporary injury or hurt, which is capable of being speedily cured or removed, is not, according to Chief Justice Eyre, an unsound horse; and where a warranty is made that such a horse is sound, it is made without any view to such an injury; nor is a horse so circumstanced within the meaning of the warranty. To vitiate the warranty, the injury the horse had sustained, or the malady

---

* *Note by Mr. Spooner.*—All internal diseases of the eye, or the remains of such diseases, constitute unsoundness; and even although no mischief can be discovered at the time of sale, yet, if inflammation can be proved to have existed previously, and such inflammation subsequently recurs, the horse is returnable. As, however, it is extremely difficult to obtain such proof, the most particular care should be taken with regard to an examination of the eyes. Distinction, however, must be made between those streaks or opaque spots often seen on the cornea alone, and without the axis of vision, and which invariably arises from blows or other external injuries, and which, although amounting to a blemish, does not constitute unsoundness. There are also occasional specks deeper in the eye, about the size of a pin's head, evidently on the surface of the crystalline lens, and not in its body. These false cataracts, as they may be called in contradistinction to true cataracts, are very frequently absorbed, and do not increase or injure vision. When, therefore, the examiner can satisfy himself that such is the nature of the specks in question, he will be justified, whilst pointing out their existence, in deciding in favor of soundness of the animal.

We cannot by any means agree with the doctrine implied in the text, that a blind horse is not returnable. If the horse is warranted sound, and proves to be blind, the warranty is broken, and the horse is returnable. Many purchasers of horses know no more about a horse than a horse does about them, and cannot be supposed to be capable of discovering the animal's defects, and they have a right to consider the warranty as their protection. The writer himself remembers, many years since, riding a horse twenty miles on a turnpike road, without knowing that the animal was blind. It was a case of amaurosis; the eye was clear and apparently free from disease, the animal went safe, straight and well, and he could scarcely believe it, the next morning, when he found that the animal was stone blind.

If, however, the horse is bought without a warranty, the defect being apparent, the horse is then not returnable on the ground of fraud.

under which he labored, ought to be of a permanent nature, and not such as may arise from a temporary injury or accident."

On the contrary, Lord Ellenborough says: "I have always held, and now hold, that a warranty of soundness is broken, if the animal at the time of sale has any infirmity upon him which renders him less fit for present service. It is not necessary that the disorder should be permanent or incurable. While a horse has a cough he is unsound, although it may either be temporary or may prove mortal. The horse in question having been lame at the time of sale, when he was warranted to be sound, his condition subsequently is no defence to the action.* The decision of Mr. Baron Parke, already referred to, confirms this doctrine.

NEUROTOMY.—A question has arisen how far a horse that has undergone the operation of the division of the nerve of the leg (see p. 86), and has recovered from the lameness with which he was before affected, and stands his work well, may be considered to be sound. Chief Justice Best held such a horse to be unsound, and in our opinion there cannot be a doubt about the matter. The operation of neurotomy does not remove the disease causing the lameness, but only the sensation of pain. A horse on whom this operation has been performed may be improved by it—may cease to be lame—may go well for many years; but there is no certainty of this, and he is unsound, within our definition, unless nature gave the nerve for no useful purpose.

OSSIFICATION OF THE LATERAL CARTILAGES constitutes unsoundness, as interfering with the natural expansion of the foot, and, in horses of quick work, almost universally producing lameness.

PUMICED-FOOT.—When the union between the horny and sensible laminæ, or little plates of the foot (see p. 305), is weakened, and the coffin-bone is let down, and presses upon the sole, and the sole yields to this unnatural weight, and becomes rounded, and is brought in contact with the ground, and is bruised and injured, that horse must be unsound, and unsound forever, because there are no means by which we can raise the coffin-bone again into its place.

QUIDDING.—If the mastication of the food gives pain to the animal, in consequence of soreness of the mouth or throat, he will drop it before it is perfectly chewed. This, as an indication of disease, constitutes unsoundness. Quidding sometimes arises from irregularity in the teeth, which wound the cheek with their sharp edges; or a protruding tooth renders it impossible for the horse to close his jaws so as to chew his food thoroughly. Quidding is unsoundness for the time; but the unsoundness will cease when

* 4 Campbell, 251, *Elton vs. Brogden.*

the teeth are properly filed, or the soreness or other cause of this imperfect chewing removed.

QUITTOR is manifestly unsoundness.

RING-BONE.—Although when the bony tumor is small, and on one side only, there is little or no lameness—and there are a few instances in which a horse with ring-bone has worked for many years without its return—yet from the action of the foot, and the stress upon the part, the inflammation and the formation of bone may acquire a tendency to spread so rapidly, that we must pronounce the slightest enlargement of the pasterns, or around the coronet, to be a cause of unsoundness.

SAND-CRACK is manifestly unsoundness. It may, however, occur without the slightest warning, and no horse can be rejected on account of a sand-crack that has sprung after purchase. Its usual cause is too great brittleness of the crust of the hoof; but there is no infallible method of detecting this, or the degree in which it must exist in order to constitute unsoundness. When the horn round the bottom of the foot has chipped off so much that only a skilful smith can fasten the shoe without pricking the horse, or even when there is a tendency in the horn to chip and break in a much less degree than this, the horse is unsound, for the brittleness of the crust is a disease of the part, or it is such an altered structure of it as to interfere materially with the usefulness of the animal.

SPAVIN.—Bone spavin, comprehending in its largest sense every bony tumor on the hock, is not necessarily unsoundness. If the tumor affects in the slightest degree the action of the horse, it is unsoundness;—even if it does not, it is seldom safe to pronounce it otherwise than unsoundness. But it may possibly be (like splint in the fore-leg) so situated as to have no tendency to affect the action. A veterinary surgeon consulted on the purchase will not always reject a horse because of such a tumor. His evidence on a question of soundness will depend on the facts. The situation and history of the tumor may be such as to enable him to give a decisive opinion in a horse going sound, but not often.

BOG or BLOOD SPAVIN is unsoundness, because, although it may not be productive of lameness at slow work, the rapid and powerful action of the hock in quicker motion will produce permanent, yet perhaps not considerable lameness, which can scarcely ever be with certainty removed.*

SPLINT.—It depends entirely on the situation of the bony tumor on the shank-bone, whether it is to be considered as unsoundness. If it is not in the neighborhood of any joint, so as to interfere with

---

* *Note by Mr. Spooner.—Blood-Spavin* is certainly unsoundness, unless extremely slight, although, in the majority of cases, it does not cause lameness.

its action, and if it does not press upon any ligament or tendon, it may be no cause of unsoundness, although it is often very unsightly. In many cases, it may not lessen the capability and value of the animal. This has been treated on at considerable length in page 256.*

STRINGHALT.—This singular and very unpleasant action of the hind-leg is decidedly an unsoundness. It is an irregular communication of nervous energy to some muscle of the thigh, observable when the horse first comes from the stable, and gradually ceasing on exercise. It has usually been accompanied by a more than common degree of strength and endurance. It must, however, be traced to some morbid alteration of structure or function; and it rarely or never fails to deteriorate and gradually wear out the animal.

THICKENING OF THE BACK SINEWS.—Sufficient attention is not always paid to the fineness of the legs of the horse. If the flexor tendons have been sprained, so as to produce considerable thickening of the cellular substance in which their sheaths are enveloped, they will long afterwards, or perhaps always, be liable to sprain, from causes by which they would otherwise be scarcely affected. The continuance of any considerable thickness around the sheaths of the tendons indicates previous violent sprain. This very thickening will fetter the action of the tendons, and, after much quick work, will occasionally renew the inflammation and the lameness; therefore, such a horse cannot be sound. It requires, however, a little discrimination to distinguish this from the *gumminess*, or roundness of leg, peculiar to some breeds. There should be an evident difference between the injured leg and the other.†

THOROUGHPIN, except it is of great size, is rarely productive of lameness, and therefore cannot be termed unsoundness; but as it is the consequence of hard work, and now and then does produce

---

* *Note by Mr. Spooner.*—We do not think the situation of this tumor has as much to do with the existence of lameness as is generally imagined. The lameness is occasioned by the tension of the periosteum, or covering of the bone, which has not had time to accommodate itself to the bony swelling beneath it. All splints, therefore, which evince tenderness on being pressed should be considered as unsoundness, and, indeed, all splints on horses under six years of age should be guarded against by a sufficient warranty though no lameness or tenderness may exist. In older horses, this precaution is unnecessary.

† *Note by Mr. Spooner.*—All enlargements of the sinews or ligaments, unless evidently produced by blows, constitute unsoundness. It is an old but mistaken idea, that the enlargement of sprung sinews, as it is termed, exists in the cellular membrane. It is the substance of the sinews themselves that becomes thickened.

lameness, the hock should be most carefully examined, and there should be a special warranty against it.*

THRUSH.—There are various cases on record of actions on account of thrushes in horses and the decisions have been much at variance, or perfectly contradictory Thrush has not been always considered by legal men as unsoundness. We, however, decidedly so consider it; as being a disease interfering and likely to interfere with the usefulness of the horse. Thrush is inflammation of the lower surface of the inner or sensible frog—and the secretion or throwing out of pus—almost invariably accompanied by a slight degree of tenderness of the frog itself, or of the heel a little above it, and, if neglected, leading to diminution of the substance of the frog, and separation of the horn from parts beneath, and underrunning, and the production of fungus and canker, and, ultimately, a diseased state of the foot, destructive of the present, and dangerous to the future usefulness of the horse.†

WINDGALLS.—There are few horses perfectly free from windgalls, but they do not interfere with the action of the fetlock, or cause lameness, except when they are numerous or large. They constitute unsoundness only when they cause lameness, or are so large and numerous as to render it likely that they will cause it.

In the purchase of a horse the buyer usually receives, embodied in the receipt, what is termed a WARRANTY. It should be thus expressed:—

"Received of A. B. forty pounds for a gray mare, warranted only five years old, sound, free from vice, and quiet to ride or drive.
"£40.   "C. D."

A receipt, including merely the word "warranted," extends only to soundness,—"warranted sound" goes no farther; the age, freedom from vice, and quietness to ride and drive, should be especially named. This warranty comprises every cause of unsoundness that can be detected, or that lurks in the constitution at the time of sale, and to every vicious habit that the animal has hitherto shown. To establish a breach of warranty, and to be enabled to tender a return of the horse and recover the difference of price, the purchaser must prove that it was unsound or viciously disposed at the time of sale. In case of cough, the horse must nave been heard to cough immediately after the purchase, or as

---

* *Note by Mr. Spooner.*—*Thoroughpins*, unless they are very slight, ought to be considered in the same light as *Bog Spavin*, which they resemble in their nature though not in situation. They indicate weakness of one of the most important points in the body, though lameness rarely attends it.

† *Note by Mr. Spooner.*—We cannot consider thrush as invariably unsoundness, as it may often be cured. In bad cases, of long standing, we are justified in considering it as unsoundness.

he was led home, or as soon as he had entered the stable of the purchaser. Coughing, even on the following morning, will not be sufficient; for it is possible that he might have caught cold by change of stabling. If he is lame, it must be proved to arise from a cause that existed before the animal was in the purchaser's possession. No price will imply a warranty, or be equivalent to one; there must be an express warranty. A fraud must be proved in the seller, in order that the buyer may be enabled to return the horse or maintain an action for the price. The warranty should be given at the time of sale. A warranty, or a promise to warrant the horse given at any period antecedent to the sale, is invalid; for horse-flesh is a very perishable commodity, and the constitution and usefulness of the animal may undergo a considerable change in the space of a few days. A warranty after the sale is invalid, for it is is given without any legal consideration. In order to complete the purchase, there must be a transfer of the animal, or a memorandum of agreement, or the payment of the earnest-money. The least sum will suffice for earnest. No verbal promise to buy or to sell is binding without one of these. The moment either of these is effected, the legal transfer of property or delivery is made, and whatever may happen to the horse, the seller retains, or is entitled to the money. If the purchaser exercises any act of ownership, by using the animal without leave of the vender, or by having any operation performed, or any medicine given to him, he makes him his own. The warranty of a servant is considered to be binding on the master.*

If the horse should be afterwards discovered to have been unsound at the time of warranty, the buyer may tender a return of it, and, if it be not taken back, may bring his action for the price; but the seller is not bound to rescind the contract, unless he has agreed so to do.

Although there is no legal compulsion to give immediate notice to the seller of the discovered unsoundness, it will be better for it to be done. The animal should then be tendered at the house or stable of the vender. If he refuses to receive him, the animal may be sent to a livery stable and sold; and an action for the difference in price may be brought. The keep, however, can be recovered only for the time that necessarily intervened between the tender and the determination of the action. It is not legally necessary to tender a return of the horse as soon as the unsoundness is discovered. The animal may be kept for a reasonable time afterwards, and even proper medical means used to re-

---

* The weight of authority decides that the master is bound by the act of the servant. Lord Kenyon, however, had some doubt on the subject.

move the unsoundness; but courtesy, and indeed justice, will require that the notice should be given as soon as possible. Although it is stated, on the authority of Lord Loughborough, that "no length of time elapsed after the sale will alter the nature of a contract originally false," yet it seems to have been once thought it was necessary to the action to give notice of the unsoundness in a reasonable time. The cause of action is certainly complete on breach of the warranty.

It used to be supposed that the buyer had no right to have the horse medically treated, and that he would waive the warranty by doing so. The question, however, would be, has he injured or diminished the value of the horse by this treatment? It will generally be prudent for him to refrain from all medical treatment, because the means adopted, however skilfully employed, may have an unfortunate effect, or may be misrepresented by ignorant or interested observers.

The purchaser possibly may like the horse, notwithstanding his discovered defect, and he may retain, and bring his action for the depreciation in value on account of the unsoundness. Few, however, will do this, because his retaining the horse will cause a suspicion that the defect was of no great consequence, and will give rise to much cavil about the quantum of damages, and after all, very slight damages will probably be obtained. "I take it to be clear law," says Lord Eldon, "that if a person purchases a horse that is warranted, and it afterwards turns out that the horse was unsound at the time of warranty, the buyer may, if he pleases, keep the horse, and bring an action on the warranty; in which he will have a right to recover the difference between the value of a sound horse, and one with such defects as existed at the time of warranty; or he may return the horse, and bring an action to recover the full money; but in the latter case, the seller has a right to expect that the horse shall be returned to him in the same state he was when sold, and not by any means diminished in value; for if a person keep a warranted article for any length of time after discovering its defects, and when he returns it, it is in a worse state than it would have been if returned immediately after such discovery, I think the party can have no defence to an action for the price of the article on the ground of non-compliance with the warranty, but must be left to his action on the warranty to recover the difference in the value of the article warranted, and its value when sold.*

Where there is no warranty, an action may be brought on the ground of fraud; but this is very difficult to be maintained, and not often hazarded. It will be necessary to prove that the dealer knew the defect, and that the purchaser was imposed upon by his

* *Curtis* v. *Hannay*, 3 Esp. 83.

false representation, or other fraudulent means. If the defect was evident to every eye, the purchaser has no remedy—he should have taken more care; but if a warranty was given, that extends to all unsoundness, palpable or concealed. Although a person should ignorantly or carelessly buy a blind horse, warranted sound, he may reject it—the warranty is his guard, and prevents him from so closely examining the horse as he otherwise would have done; but if he buys a blind horse, thinking him to be sound, and without a warranty, he has no remedy. Every one ought to exercise common circumspection and common sense.

A man should have a more perfect knowledge of horses than falls to the lot of most, and a perfect knowledge of the vender too, who ventures to buy a horse without a warranty.

If a person buys a horse warranted sound, and discovering no defect in him, and, relying on the warranty, re-sells him, and the unsoundness is discovered by the second purchaser, and the horse returned to the first purchaser, or an action commenced against him, he has his claim on the first seller, and may demand of him not only the price of the horse, or the difference in value, but every expense that may have been incurred.

Absolute exchanges, of one horse for another, or a sum of money being paid in addition by one of the parties, stand on the same ground as simple sales. If there is a warranty on either side, and that is broken, an action may be maintained: if there be no warranty, deceit must be proved.

The trial of horses on sale often leads to disputes. The law is perfectly clear, but the application of it, as in other matters connected with horse-flesh, attended with glorious uncertainty. The intended purchaser is only liable for damage done to the horse through his own misconduct. The seller may put what restriction he chooses on the trial, and takes the risks of all accidents in the fair use of the horse within such restrictions.

If a horse from a dealer's stable is galloped far and fast, it is probable that he will soon show distress; and if he is pushed farther, inflammation and death may ensue. The dealer rarely gets recompensed for this; nor ought he, as he knows the unfitness of his horse, and may thank himself for permitting such a trial; and if it should occur soon after the sale, he runs the risk of having the horse returned, or of an action for its price.

In this, too, he is not much to be pitied. The mischievous and fraudulent practice of dealers, especially in London, of giving their horses, by overfeeding, a false appearance of muscular substance, leads to the ruin of many a valuable animal. It would be a useful lesson to have to contest in an action or two the question whether a horse overloaded with fat can be otherwise than in a state of disease, and consequently unsound.

It is proper, however, to put a limit to what has been too frequently asserted from the bench, that a horse warranted sound must be taken as fit for immediate use, and capable of being immediately put to any fair work the owner chooses. A hunter honestly warranted sound is certainly warranted to be in immediate condition to follow the hounds. The mysteries of condition, as has been shown in a former part of the work, are not sufficiently unravelled.

In London, and in most great towns, there are repositories for the periodical sale of horses by auction. They are of great convenience to the seller who can at once get rid of a horse with which he wishes to part, without waiting month after month before he obtains a purchaser, and he is relieved from the nuisance or fear of having the animal returned on account of breach of the warranty, because in these places only two days are allowed for the trial, and if the horse is not returned within that period he cannot be afterwards returned. They are also convenient to the purchaser, who can thus in a large town soon find a horse that will suit him, and which, from this restriction as to returning the animal, he will obtain twenty or thirty per cent. below the dealers' prices. Although an auction may seem to offer a fair and open competition, there is no place at which it is more necessary for a person not much accustomed to horses to take with him an experienced friend, and, when there, to depend on his own judgment, or that of his friend. heedless of the observations or manœuvres of the bystanders, the exaggerated commendation of some horses, and the thousand faults found with others. There are always numerous groups of low dealers, copers, and chaunters, whose business it is to delude and deceive.

One of the regulations of the Bazaar in King Street was exceedingly fair, both with regard to the previous owner and the purchaser, viz.—

"When a horse, having been warranted sound, shall be returned within the prescribed period, on account of unsoundness, a certificate from a veterinary surgeon, particularly describing the unsoundness, must accompany the horse so returned; when, if it be agreed to by the veterinary surgeon of the establishment, the amount received for the horse shall be immediately paid back; but if the veterinary surgeon of the establishment should not confirm the certificate, then, in order to avoid further dispute, one of the veterinary surgeons of the college shall be called in, and his decision shall be final, and the expense of such umpire shall be borne by the party in error."

CHAPTER XXIII.

A LIST OF THE MEDICINES USED IN THE TREATMENT OF
THE DISEASES OF THE HORSE.

HE will rarely consult his own interest, who, not having had the advantage of a veterinary education, undertakes the treatment of any of the serious diseases of his horses. Many of the maladies of the horse nearly resemble each other. They are continually varying their character, and require, in their different stages, a very different treatment, and in the plainest case not only the characteristic symptoms of disease are obscure, but even the indications of returning health, or increasing danger, are often scarcely ascertainable, conseqently the sick horse, as well as the human being, needs the care of one whom study and experience have qualified for the task. A list of the drugs generally employed, with a slight account of their history, adulterations, and medicinal effects, will be interesting to the horse-proprietor as well as to the veterinary surgeon; and may occasionally be useful when professional aid cannot be obtained.*

Frequent reference will be made to Professor Morton's most valuable Manual of Pharmacy. This work will be found to be a treasure to every veterinary surgeon. Mr. W. C. Spooner's Materia Medica, in his recent compendium of White's account of the horse, will occasionally be laid under contribution.

ACACIA GUMMI, GUM ARABIC.—Many varieties of *gum arabic* are procured from Egypt, Arabia, and the East Indies. It is employed in the form of a mucilage, made by dissolving it in water, in the proportion of one part of the gum to three or four of water. Various insoluble powders may be thus suspended, or oils rendered miscible, or emulsions formed. Emulsions composed of gum arabic are supposed to be useful in urinary affections.

ACIDUM ACETICUM, ACETIC ACID, VINEGAR.—Vinegar is a very

---

* *Note by Mr. Spooner.*—We have little to add under this division of the work. The Pharmacopœia in the text was cautiously written, and is for the most part correct.

useful application for sprains and bruises. Equal parts of boiling water and cold vinegar will form a good fomentation. Extract of lead, or bay salt, may be added with some advantage. As an internal remedy, vinegar is rarely given, nor has it, except in large doses, any considerable medicinal power. The veterinarian and the horse-owner should manufacture their own vinegar. That which they buy frequently contains sulphuric acid and pungent spices, and irritates the inflamed part to which it is applied.

ACIDUM ARSENIOSUM, ARSENIC ACID.—Were it not that some practitioners continue to use it as a tonic, in doses of from ten to twenty grains daily, and others employ it to core out old ulcers, we should not include it in our list, for we have little faith in it. There are better and safer tonics, and far better and safer caustics.

ACIDUM MURIATICUM, OR HYDROCHLORIC ACID : SPIRIT OF SALT.—This acid is formed by distilling corrosive sublimate with antimony. The butter-like matter which is produced (whence the common name, *Butyr of Antimony*), has a strong affinity for water, which it attracts from the atmosphere, and thus becomes converted into a fluid. The less water it is suffered to attract to itself the more powerful it remains, and therefore it should be kept in stoppered bottles. The proof of its goodness is its weight. It is decidedly the best liquid caustic we have. It is most manageable, and its effect can most readily be ascertained. As soon as it touches any muscular or living part, a change of color is perceived, and the effect of the caustic can be fairly judged of by the degree of change. For corns, canker, indisposition in the sole to secrete good horn, wounds in the foot not attended by healthy action, and for every case where the superficial application of a caustic is needed, this acid is unrivalled.

ACIDUM NITRICUM : NITRIC ACID, AQUAFORTIS.—This is a valuable external application. It is both a caustic and an antiseptic. It destroys fungous excrescences. A pledget of tar should be dipped in the acid, and then firmly pressed on the cankerous surface. Every part with which the acid has come into contact will be deadened and slough off, and healthy granulations will spring up.

ACIDUM HYDROCIANICUM : PRUSSIC ACID.—This, in a concentrated state, is truly a deadly poison ; a few drops of it will kill a large animal. In a diluted form, it is a powerful sedative. In doses of six drops, largely diluted, it abates both pulmonary and gastric irritation. It may be worth trying in the form of injections in cases of tetanus. It may also be given by the mouth in the same disease. Nothing is more likely to tranquillize the general excitement of the nervous system. The author of this work was the first person who applied the hydrocyanic acid for the purpose of allaying irritation of the skin in dogs. It seldom fails of producing the desired effect, and it has had a similar good effect in subduing itchiness and mange in the horse.

ACIDUM SULPHURICUM, SULPHURIC ACID, OIL OF VITRIOL.—When mixed with tar in the proportion of an ounce to the pound, it is a good application for thrush and canker: a smaller quantity, mixed with olive oil, makes a good stimulating liniment. If too much sulphuric acid is added, either by mistake or wilfully, it inflames and corrodes the stomach and bowels. The proper antidotes in this case are magnesia, or the carbonate of soda or potash, with soft soap. The acid might possibly be neutralized by this combination.

ACTUAL CAUTERY.—See Caustics.

ADEPS, HOG'S LARD, very properly forms the basis of most of our ointments. It is tasteless, inodorous, and free from every stimulating quality. That cannot be said of all the ingredients used in the composition of our unguents.

ALCOHOL, RECTIFIED SPIRIT.—This is necessarily used in many of our tinctures and other preparations, and is sometimes given to the horse in almost a pure state. Some horses that are compelled to travel far and quickly, show evident fatigue before they arrive at the end of their journey. A cordial or carminative tincture, to the extent of three or four ounces, largely diluted, may occasionally be given, and they rally, and cheerfully pursue their journey to the end. The groom or the stableman gives the gin or whiskey of the country, in preference to any other stimulant. In cases of thorough fatigue, the Daffy's Elixir may be administered, and probably rendered more stimulant by the addition of pepper. Mr. Bracy Clark recommends four ounces of the tincture of allspice in cases of gripes. On the other hand, some veterinary surgeons have preferred simple hot water, or the infusion of several of our medicinal herbs, as peppermint, rosemary, &c. We should be loth, except on extraordinary occasions, to advocate the use of any spirituous drink.

ALOES.—There are two kinds used in horse practice, the Barbadoes and the Cape. The Socotorine, preferred by the human surgeon, are very uncertain in their effect on the horse, and are seldom to be met with pure. Of the Barbadoes and the Cape, the first are much to be preferred.

The Barbadoes are black, with a shade of brown, of an unctuous feeling, with a stronger smell, broken with difficulty, and the fracture dull. The Cape are darker colored, stronger smelling, very brittle, and the fracture perfectly glossy. Every veterinary surgeon who uses much aloes should buy them in the mass, and powder them at home, and then, by attending to this account of the difference of the two, he can scarcely be imposed upon. It is, however, the fact, that these are mostly adulterated, by their being melted together. Aloes purchased in powder are too often sadly adulterated.

The Cape aloes may be powdered at all times, and the Barbadoes in frosty weather, when enough should be prepared, to be kept in closed bottles, for the year's consumption. They may also be powdered when they have been taken from the gourd, and exposed to a gentle heat for two or three hours before they are put into the mortar. In the proportion of fifteen ounces of the powder mixed with one ounce of powdered ginger, and beaten up with eight ounces of palm oil, and afterwards divided into the proper doses, it will form a purging mass more effectual, and much less likely to gripe, than any that can be procured by melting the drug. If the physic is given in the shape of a ball, it more readily dissolves in the stomach, and more certainly and safely acts on the bowels when mingled with some oily matter, like that just recommended, than when combined with syrup or honey, which are apt to ferment, and be themselves the cause of gripes. It is also worse than useless to add any diuretic to the mass, as soap or carbonate of soda. The action of these on one set of organs will weaken that of the aloes on another. A physic mass should never be kept more than two or three months, for, after that time, it rapidly loses its purgative property.

Directions for physicking will be found at page 224. We will only add that, as a promoter of condition, the dose should always be mild. A few fluid stools will be sufficient for every good purpose. Violent disease will alone justify violent purging.

The Barbadoes aloes have a greater purgative power than the Cape exclusive of griping less and being safer. In addition to this, the action of the bowels is kept up longer by the Barbadoes aloes than by the Cape. If the horse is well mashed, and carefully exercised, and will drink plenty of warm water, the Cape may be ventured on, or at least mixed with equal quanties of the Barbadoes; but if there is any neglect of preparation for physic, or during the usual operation of the physic, the Cape are not always to be depended upon. The combination of alkaline compounds with aloes alters the results of the medicine. The action is quickened, but their purgative properties are impaired, and they cease to operate specifically on the larger intestines. Such is the opinion of Professor Morton, and undoubtedly the latter would be an advantage gained. The activity of the aloes may be occasionally increased by a few drops of the croton oil. Mashes are useful helps when physic is administered.

Some persons are fond of what are called half-doses of physic. Three or four drachms are given on one day, and three or four on the following: and perhaps, if the medicine has not operated, as in this divided state it will not always, two or three additional drachms are given on the third day. The consequence is, that the bowels having been rendered irritable by the former doses, the horse is over-purged, and inflammation and death occasionally ensue. In physicking a horse, whatever is to be done should be done at once. Whatever quantity is intended to be given should be given in one dose.

The system of giving small doses of aloes as alteratives is no good. These repeated minute doses lodging in some of the folds of the intestines, and at length uniting, often produce more effect than is desirable. It is never safe to ride a horse far or fast, with even a small dose of aloes within him.

Most of all objectionable is the custom of giving small doses of aloes as a nauseant, in inflammation of the lungs. There is so much sympathy between the contents of the chest and the belly in the horse, and inflammation of one part is so likely to be transferred to another, that it is treading on very dangerous ground, when, with much inflammation of the lungs, that is given which will stimulate and may inflame the intestines.

Aloes are most commonly, because most easily, administered in the form of ball, but in a state of solution their effect is more speedy, effectual and safe.*

Aloes are useful in the form of tincture. Eight ounces of powdered aloes, and one ounce of powdered myrrh, may be put into two quarts of alcohol, diluted with an equal quantity of water. The mixture should be daily well shaken for a fortnight, and then suffered to stand, in order that the undissolved portion may fall to the bottom. This will constitute a very excellent application for wounds, whether recent or of long-standing and indisposed to heal. It is not only a gentle stimulant, but it forms a thin crust over the wound, and shields it from the action of the air.

The principal adulteration of aloes is by means of resin, and the alteration of color is concealed by the addition of charcoal or lamp-black. This adulteration is easily enough detected by dissolving the aloes in hot water. All aloes contain some resinous matter, which the water will not dissolve and which has very slight purgative effect. The excess of this resin at the bottom of the solution will mark the degree of adulteration.

ALTERATIVES,—are a class of medicines the nature and effect of which are often much misunderstood, and liable to considerable abuse. It is a very convenient name in order to excuse that propensity to dose the horse with medicines, which is the disgrace of the groom, and the bane of the stable.

* See note by Mr. Spooner, on page 225

By alteratives we understand those drugs which effect some slow change in the diseased action of certain parts without interfering with the food or work; but by common consent the term seems to be confined to medicines for the diseases of the circulation, or of the digestive organs, or of the skin. If a horse is heavy and incapable of work from too good keep, or if he is off his food from some temporary indigestion—or if he has mange or grease, or cracked heels, or swelled legs, a few alteratives are prescribed, and the complaint is expected to be gradually and imperceptibly removed. For all skin affections there is no better alterative than that so often recommended in this treatise, consisting of black antimony, nitre, and sulphur. If there is any tendency to grease, some resin may be added to each ball. If the complaint is accompanied by weakness, a little gentian and ginger may be farther added, but we enter our protest against the ignorant use of mercury in any form, or any of the mineral acids, or mineral tonics, or heating spices, as alteratives. We indeed should be pleased if we could banish the term alterative from common usage. The mode of proceeding which reason and science would dictate is to ascertain the nature and the degree of the disease, and then the medicine which is calculated to restore the healthy action of the part, or of the frame generally.

ALUM,—is occasionally used internally in cases of over-purging in the form of alum-whey, two drachms of the powder being added to a pint of hot milk; but there are much better astringents, although this may sometimes succeed when others fail. If alum is added to a vegetable astringent, as oak-bark, the power of both is diminished. Its principal use is external. A solution of two drachms to a pint of water forms alone, or with the addition of a small quantity of white vitriol, a very useful wash for cracked heels, and for grease generally; and also for those forms of swelled legs attended with exudation of moisture through the skin. Some add the Goulard lotion, forgetting the chemical decomposition that takes place; the result of which is, that the alumine, possessing little astringency, is detached, and two salts with no astringency at all, the sulphate of lead and the sulphate of potash, are formed.

The BURNT ALUM is inferior to the common alum for the purposes mentioned, and we have better stimulants, or caustics, to apply to wounds.

ANISE SEED,—see ANISI SEMINA.

AMMONIA, HARTSHORN,—is, to the annoyance of the horse, and the injury of his eyes and his lungs, plentifully extricated from the putrefying dung and urine of the stable; but, when combined with water in the common form of hartshorn, it is seldom used in veterinary practice It has been given, and with decided benefit and when other things have failed, in flatulent colic; and is best administered in the form of the aromatic spirit of ammonia, and in doses of one or two ounces, in warm water.

CHLORIDE OF AMMONIA,—or SAL AMMONIAC, is scarcely deserving of a place in our list. It is not now used internally; and as an astringent embrocation, it must yield to several that are more effectual, and less likely to blemish.

ANISI SEMINA, ANISE SEED.—This seed is here mentioned principally as a record of old times, when it was one of the sheet-anchors of the farrier. It is not yet quite discarded from his shop as a stimulant, a carminative, and a cordial.

ANODYNES.—Of these there is but one in horse practice: Opium is the only drug that will lull pain. It may be given as an anodyne, but it will also be an astringent in doses of one, two, or three drachms.

ANTIMONY.—There are several valuable preparations of this metal.

The BLACK SESQUI-SULPHURET OF ANTIMONY, a compound of sulphur and antimony, is a good alterative. It is given with more sulphur and with nitre, in varying doses, according to the disease, and the slow or rapid effect intended to be produced. It should never be bought in powder whatever trouble there may be in pulverizing it, for it is often grossly adulterated with lead, manganese, forge-dust, and arsenic. The adulteration may be detected by placing a little of the powder on a red-hot iron plate. The pure sulphuret will evaporate without the slightest residue—so will the arsenic: but there will be an evident smell of garlic. A portion of the lead and the manganese will be left behind.

ANTIMONII POTASSIO TARTRAS, EMETIC TARTAR.—The tartrate of potash and antimony, or a combination of super-tartrate of potash and oxide of antimony, is a very useful nauseant, and has considerable effect on the skin. It is particularly valuable in inflammation of the lungs, and in every catarrhal affection. It is given in doses of from one drachm to a drachm and a half, and combined with nitre and digitalis. It is also beneficial in the expulsion of worms. It should be given in doses of two drachms, and with some mechanical vermifuge, as tin filings, or ground glass, and administered on an empty stomach, and for several successive days. Although it may sometimes fail to expel the worms, it will materially improve the condition of the horse, and produce sleekness of the coat. To a slight degree the emetic tartar is decomposed by the action of light, and should be kept in a jar, or green bottle. It is sometimes adulterated with arsenic, which is detected by the garlic smell when it is placed on hot iron, and also by its not giving a beautiful gold-colored precipitate when sulphuret of ammonia is added to a solution of it. It has also been externally applied in chest affections, in combination with lard, and in quantities of from one drachm to two drachms of the antimony, to an ounce of the lard; but, except in extreme cases, recourse should not be had to it, on account of the extensive sloughing which it sometimes produces.

AQUA FORTIS,—see ACIDUM NITRICUM.

ARABIC GUM,—see ACACIA GUMMI.

PULVIS ANTIMONII COMPOSITUS, THE COMPOUND POWDER OF ANTIMONY, JAMES' POWDER.—It is employed as a sudorific in fever, either alone or in combination with mercurials. The dose is from one to two drachms. The late Mr. Bloxam used to trust to it alone in the treatment of Epidemic Catarrh in the horse. It is, however, decidedly inferior to Emetic Tartar. It is often adulterated with chalk and burnt bones, and other white powders, and that to so shameful a degree, that little dependence can be placed on the antimonial powder usually sold by druggists. The muriatic or sulphuric acids will detect most of these adulterations.

ANTI-SPASMODICS.—Of these our list is scanty, for the horse is subject only to a few spasmodic diseases, and there are fewer medicines which have an anti-spasmodic effect. Opium stands first for its general power, and that exerted particularly in locked-jaw. Oil of turpentine is almost a specific for spasm of the bowels. Camphor, assafœtida, and various other medicines, used on the human subject, have a very doubtful effect on the horse, or may be considered as almost inert.

ARGENTUM, SILVER, LUNAR CAUSTIC.—One combination only of this metal is used, and that as a manageable and excellent caustic, viz., the *Lunar Caustic*. It is far preferable to the hot iron, or to any acid, for the destruction of the part if a horse should have been bitten by a rabid dog; and it stands next to the butyr of antimony for the removal of fungus generally. It has not yet been administered internally to the horse.

ARSENIC.—This drug used to be employed as a tonic, in order to core out old ulcers; but it is now seldom employed, for there are better and safer tonics, and far better and safer caustics.

BALLS.—The usual and the most convenient mode of administering veterinary medicines is in the form of balls, compounded with oil, and not with honey or syrup, on account of their longer keeping soft and more easily dissolving in the stomach. Balls should never weigh more than an ounce and a half, otherwise they will be so large as not to pass without difficulty down the gullet. They should not be more than an inch in diameter and three inches in length. The mode of delivering balls is not difficult to acquire; but the balling-iron, while it often wounds and permanently injures the bars, occasions the horse to struggle more than he otherwise would against the administration of the medicine. The horse should be backed in the stall;—the tongue should be drawn gently out with the left hand on the off side of the mouth, and there fixed, not by continuing to pull at it, but by pressing the fingers against the side of the lower jaw. The ball, being now taken between the tips of the fingers of the right hand, is passed rapidly up the mouth, as near to the palate as possible, until it reaches the root of the tongue. It is then delivered with a slight jerk, and the hand being immediately withdrawn and the tongue liberated, the ball is forced through the pharynx into the œsophagus. Its passage should be watched down the left side of the throat; and if the passage of it is not seen going down, a slight tap or blow under the chin will generally cause the horse to swallow it, or a few gulps of water will convey it into the stomach. Very few balls should be kept ready made, for they become so hard as to be incapable of passing down the gullet, or dissolving in the stomach, and the life of the horse may be endangered or lost. This is peculiarly liable to be the case if the ball is too large, or wrapped in thick paper.

BALSAM OF CAPIVI,—see COPAIBA.

BARK, PERUVIAN.—A concentrated preparation of this is entitled the SULPHATE OF QUININE. The simple bark is now seldom used If it has any good effect, it is in diabetes. The quinine, however, is strongly recommended by Professor Morton as singularly efficacious in the prostration of strength which is often the consequence of influenza.

BASILICON OINTMENT,—is a valuable digestive ointment, composed of resin, bees-wax, and olive-oil. If it is needed as a stimulant, a little turpentine and verdigris may be added.

BELLADONNÆ EXTRACTUM, EXTRACT OF DEADLY NIGHTSHADE.—
The inspissated juice is principally used as a narcotic and sedative, and indicated where there is undue action of the nervous and vascular systems, as in tetanus, carditis, and nervous affections generally. Externally, it is beneficially applied to the eye.

BLISTERS,—are applications to the skin which separate the cuticle in the form of vesicles containing a serous fluid. They excite increased action in the vessels of the skin, by means of which this fluid is thrown out. The part, or neighboring parts, are somewhat relieved by the discharge, but more by the inflammation and pain that are produced, and lessen that previously existing in some contiguous part. On this principle we account for the decided relief often obtained by blisters in inflammation of the lungs, and their efficacy in abating deeply-seated disease, as that of the tendons, ligaments, or joints; and also the necessity of previously removing, in these latter cases, the superficial inflammation caused by them, in order that one of a different kind may be excited, and to which the deeply-seated inflammation of the part will be more likely to yield. The blisters used in horse-practice are composed of cantharides or the oil of turpentine, to which some have added a tincture of the croton-nut.

The art of blistering consists in cutting, or rather shaving, the hair perfectly close; then well rubbing in the ointment, for at least ten minutes; and, afterwards, and what is of the greatest consequence of all, plastering a little more of the ointment lightly over the part and leaving it. As soon as the vesicles have perfectly risen, which will be in twenty or twenty-four hours, the torture of the animal may be somewhat relieved by the application of olive or neat's-foot oil, or any emollient ointment.

When too extensive a blister has been employed, or, from the intensity of the original inflammation, the blister has not risen (for no two intense inflammations can exist in neighboring parts at the same time), strangury—great difficulty in passing urine, and even suppression of it—has occurred. The careful washing off of the blister, and the administration of plenty of warm water, with opium, and bleeding if the symptoms run high, will generally remove this unpleasant effect.

For some important remarks on the composition, application, and management of the blister, see page 362.

BOLE ARMENIAN,—is an argillaceous earth combined with iron, and is supposed to possess some astringent property. The propriety of its being administered inwardly is doubtful; for it may remain in the intestinal canal, and become the nucleus of a calculus. On account of its supposed astringency, it is employed externally to give consistence to ointments for grease. Even the bole Armenian has not escaped the process of adulteration, and is largely mixed with inferior earths. The fraud may be suspected, but not satisfactorily detected, by the color of the powder, which should be a bright red.

CALAMINE POWDER.—See ZINC.

CALOMEL.—See HYDRARGYRUM.

CAMPHOR,—is the produce of one of the laurus species, a native of Japan, and too often imitated by passing a stream of chlorine through oil of turpentine. According to Professor Morton, it is a narcotic. It diminishes the frequency of the pulse, and softens its tone. When long exhibited, it acts on the kidneys. Externally applied, it is said to be a discutient and an anodyne for chronic sprains, bruises, and tumors. The camphor ball is a favorite one with the groom, and occasionally administered by the veterinary surgeon. Mr. W. C. Spooner uses it, mixed with opium, in cases of locked-jaw, and in doses of from one to two drachms. In the form of camphorated oil, it promotes the absorption of fluids thrown out beneath the skin, the removal of old callus, and the suppling of joints stiff from labor. Combined with oil of turpentine it is more effective, but in this combination it occasionally blemishes.*

CANTHARIDES, SPANISH FLIES,—are the basis of the most approved and useful veterinary blisters. The cantharis is a fly, the native of Italy and the south of France. It is destroyed by sulphur, dried and powdered, and mixed with palm-oil and resin. Its action is intense, and yet superficial; it plentifully raises the cuticle, yet rarely injures the true skin, and therefore seldom blemishes. The application of other acrid substances is occasionally followed by deeply-seated ulcerations; but a blister composed of the Spanish fly alone, while it does its duty, leaves, after a few weeks have passed, scarcely a trace behind.

An infusion of two ounces of the flies in a pint of oil of turpentine, for several days, is occasionally used as a liquid blister; and, when sufficiently lowered with common oil, it is called a *sweating* oil, for it maintains a certain degree of irritation and inflammation on the skin, yet not sufficient to blister, and thus gradually abates or removes some old or deep inflammation, or cause of lameness.

Of late cantharides have come into more general use. They were recommended by Mr. Vines, in combination with vegetable bitters, as a stimulating tonic, in cases of debility. He next applied them for the cure of glanders, and with considerable success. The veterinary public is much indebted to Mr. Vines for the steadiness with which he has followed up the employment of the Spanish fly. The dose is from five to eight grains given daily, but withheld for a day or two when diuresis supervenes.

CAPSICI BACCÆ, CAPSICUM BERRIES. GUINEA PEPPER.—They are valuable as stimulants affecting the system generally, yet not too much accelerating the pulse. Their beneficial effect in cases of cold has seldom been properly estimated. The dose is from a scruple to half a drachm.

CARAWAY SEEDS.—These and ginger, alone or combined, are the best stimulants used in horse-practice.

CARBONATE OF IRON.—See under FERRUM.

CASCARILLA BARK.—Tonic as well as aromatic. It must not, however, be used with the sulphates of iron or zinc.

CASTOR OIL, OLIUM RICINI.—An expensive medicine. It must be given in large doses, and even then it is uncertain in its effects.

* *Note by Mr. Spooner.*—Camphor is a sedative and slight narcotic, and as such, may be exhibited in fever balls with advantage. It has also been found useful, combined with opium, in relieving the spasms of locked-jaw.

Mild as is its operation in most animals, it sometimes gripes, and even endangers the horse.

CATECHU, JAPAN EARTH,—yet, no earth, but extracted from the wood of one of the acacia trees, is a very useful astringent. It is given in over purging, in doses of one or two drachms, with opium, as a yet more powerful astringent; chalk, to neutralize any acid in the stomach or bowels; and powdered gum, to sheath the over-irritated mucous coat of the intestines. It is not often adulterated in our country, but grossly so abroad—fine sand and aluminous earth being mixed with the extract. It is seldom given with any alkali, yet the prescription just recommended contains chalk: but, although the chalk, as an alkan, may weaken the astringency of the catechu, it probably neutralizes some acid in the stomach or bowels, that would have diminished the power of the catechu to a greater degree. It must not be given in conjunction with any metallic salt, for the tannin or gallic acid, on which its power chiefly or entirely depends, has an affinity for all metals, and will unite with them, and form a gallate of them, possessing little astringent energy Common ink is the union of this tannin principle with iron.

A tincture of catechu is sometimes made by macerating three ounces of the powder in a quart of spirit for a fortnight. It is an excellent application for wounds; and, with the aloes, constitutes all that we want of a balsamic nature for the purpose of hastening the healing process of wounds.

CAUSTICS,—are substances that burn or destroy the parts to which they are applied. First among them stands the red-hot iron, or actual cautery, and then pure alkalies, potash, and soda, and the sulphuric and nitrous acids. Milder caustics are found in the sulphate of copper, red precipitate, burnt alum, and verdigris. They are principally used to destroy fungous excrescences. or stimulate indolent tumors, or remove portions of cellular substance, or muscle infected by any poison.

CHALK,—see CRETA PREPARATA.

CHAMOMILE, ANTHEMIS.—The powder of the flower is a useful vegetable tonic, and the mildest in our list. It is given in doses of one or two drachms, and is exhibited in the early stage of convalescence in order to ascertain whether the febrile stage of the disease is passed, and to prepare the way for a more powerful tonic, the gentian. If no acceleration of pulse, or heat of mouth, or indication of return of fever, accompanies the cautious use of chamomile, the gentian, with carbonate of iron, may be safely ventured upon; but if the gentian had been first used, and a little too soon, there might have been considerable, and perhaps dangerous return of fever.

CHARCOAL,—is occasionally used as an antiseptic, being made

into a poultice with linseed meal, and applied to foul and offensive ulcers, and to cracked heels. It removes the fœtid and unwholesome smell that occasionally proceeds from them.

CHARGES,—are thick, adhesive plasters spread over parts that have been strained or weakened, and, being applied to the skin, adhere for a considerable time. The following mixture makes good charge—Burgundy or common pitch, five ounces; tar, six ounces; yellow wax, one ounce, melted together, and when they are becoming cool, half a drachm of powdered cantharides well stirred in. This must be partially melted afresh when applied, and spread on the part with a large spatula, as hot as can be done without giving the animal too much pain. Flocks of tow should be scattered over it while it is warm, and thus a thick and adhesive covering will be formed that cannot be separated from the skin for many months. It is used for old sprains of the loins, and also strains of the back sinews. The charge acts in three ways—by the slight stimulant power which it possesses it gradually removes all deep-seated inflammation—by its stimulus and its pressure it promotes the absorption of any callus or thickening beneath; and, acting as a constant bandage it gives tone and strength to the part.

CHLORIDE OF LIME,—see under LIME.

CHLOROFORM,—see note.*

CLYSTERS.—These are useful and too often neglected means of hastening the evacuation of the bowels when the disease requires their speedy action. The old ox-bladder and wooden pipe may still be employed, and a considerable quantity of fluid thrown into the intestine: but the patent stomach and clyster pump of Mr. Reid is far preferable, as enabling the practitioner to inject a greater quantity of fluid, and in a less time.

Two ounces of soft or yellow soap, dissolved in a gallon of warm water, will form a useful aperient clyster. It will detach or dissolve many irritating substances that may have adhered to the mucous coat of the bowels. For a more active aperient. half a pound of Epsom salts, or even of common salt, may be dissolved in the same quantity of water. A stronger injection, but not to be used if much purgative medicine has been previously given, may be composed of an ounce of Barbadoes aloes dissolved in two or three quarts of warm water. If nothing else can be procured, warm water may be employed; it will

---

* *Note by Mr. Spooner.*—Chloroform, or the perchloride of formyle, has been found to be a better anæsthetic agent than sulphuric ether, and has also been used internally for spasms of the bowels. The objection to its use as a destroyer of sensation is the quantity required to be taken, amounting, indeed, to several ounces. The writer has employed it successfully in many operations.

act as a fomentation to the inflamed and irritable surface of the bowels, and will have no inconsiderable effect even as an aperient.

In cases of over-purging or inflammation of the bowels, the injection must be of a soothing nature. It may consist of gruel alone, or, if the purging is considerable, and difficult to stop, the ruel must be thicker, and four ounces of prepared or powdered chalk well mixed with or suspended in it, with two scruples or a drachm of powdered opium.

No oil should enter into the composition of a clyster, except that linseed oil may be used for the expulsion of the ascarides, or needle-worms.

In epidemic catarrh, when the horse sometimes obstinately refuses to eat or to drink, his strength may be supported by nourishing clysters; but they should consist of thick gruel only, and not more than a quart should be administered at once. A greater quantity would be ejected soon after the pipe is withdrawn. Strong broths, and more particularly ale and wine, are dangerous ingredients. They may rapidly aggravate the fever, and should never be administered, except under the superintendence, or by the direction, of a veterinary surgeon.

The principal art of administering a clyster consists in not frightening the horse. The pipe, well oiled, should be very gently introduced, and the fluid not too hastily thrown into the intestine; its heat being as nearly as possible that of the intestine, or about 96° of Fahrenheit's thermometer.

COLLYRIA, LOTIONS FOR THE EYE.—These have been sufficiently described when inflammation of the eyes was treated of.

COPAIBA, BALSAM OF CAPIVI.—The resin is obtained from a tree growing in South America and the West India Islands. It is expensive, much adulterated, and seldom used; for its properties differ but little from those of common diuretics.

COPPER.—There are two combinations of this metal used in veterinary practice: the verdigris or subacetate, and the blue vitriol or sulphate.

VERDIGRIS, or *Subacetate of Copper* is the common rust of that metal produced by subjecting it to the action of acetic acid. It is given internally by some practitioners, in doses of two or three drachms daily, as a tonic, and particularly for the cure of farcy. It is, however, an uncertain and dangerous medicine. The corrosive sublimate, with vegetable tonics, as recommended at page 117, is preferable. Verdigris is, however, usefully applied externally as a mild caustic. Either alone, in the form of fine powder, or mixed with an equal quantity of the sugar (superacetate) of lead, it eats down proud flesh, or stimulates old ulcers to healthy action. When boiled with honey and vinegar, it constitutes the farriers' Egyptiacum, certainly of benefit in cankered or ulcerated mouth, and no bad application for thrushes; but yielding, as it regards both, to better remedies, that are mentioned under the proper heads. Some practitioners use alum and oil of vitriol in making their Egyptiacum, forgetting the strange decomposition which is produced.

BLUE VITRIOL or *Sulphate of Copper* is the union of sulphuric acid and copper. It is a favorite tonic with many practitioners, and has been vaunted as a specific for glanders; while others, and we think properly, have no very good opinion of it in either respect. As a cure for glanders, its reputation has nearly passed away. As a tonic, when the horse is slowly recovering from severe illness, it is dangerous, and its internal use should be confined to cases of long-continued discharge from the nostril, when catarrh or fever has ceased. It may then be given with benefit in doses of from one to two drachms twice in the day, and always combined with gentian and ginger. It is principally valuable as an external application, dissolved in water in the proportion of two drachms to a pint, and acting as a gentle stimulant. If an ounce is dissolved in the same quantity of water, it becomes a mild caustic. In the former proportion, it rouses old ulcers to a healthy action, and disposes even recent wounds to heal more quickly than they otherwise would do; and in the latter it removes fungous granulations or proud flesh. The blue vitriol is sometimes reduced to powder and sprinkled upon the wound for this purpose: it is also a good application for canker in the foot.

COPPERAS,—See under FERRUM.

CORDIALS,—are useful or injurious according to the judgment with which they are given. When a horse comes home thoroughly exhausted, and refuses his food, a cordial may be beneficial. It may rouse the stomach and the system generally, and may prevent cold and fever; but it is poison to the animal when administered after the cold is actually caught and fever begins to appear. More to be reprobated is the practice of giving *frequent* cordials, that by their stimulus on the stomach, (the skin sympathising so much with that viscus,) a fine coat may be produced. The artificial excitement of the cordial soon becomes as necessary to enable the horse to do even common work, as is the excitement of the dram to sustain the animal spirits of the drunkard.

In order to recall the appetite of the horse slowly recovering from illness, a cordial may sometimes be allowed; or to old horses that have been worked hard and used to these excitements when young; or to draught horses, that have exhibited slight symptoms of staggers when their labor has been unusually protracted and their stomachs left too long empty; or mixed with diuretic medicine, to fine the legs of the over-worked and debilitated animal, but in no other case should they obtain a place in the **stable, or** be used at the discretion of the carter or the groom.

CORROSIVE SUBLIMATE.—See under HYDRARGYRUM.

CREAM OF TARTAR.—See under POTASH.

CREASOTE,—has very lately been introduced into veterinary practice, and is much valued on account of its antiseptic properties. It is obtained by the destructive distillation of various subtances, as pyroligneous acid, tar, wood, smoke, &c. Pure creasote is colorless and transparent; its odor is that of smoked meat, and its taste is caustic and burning. It coagulates the albumen of the blood, and hence has been lately employed in stopping hæmorrhages. It acts very powerfully on the general system, and quickly destroys small animals. Professor Morton gives a very interesting and faithful account of it. It is, according to him, both a stimulant and a tonic. In an undiluted state it acts as a caustic. When diluted it is a general excitant and an antiseptic. In the form of a lotion, a liniment, or an ointment, it has been useful in farcy and glanders, also in foot-rot, canker, and thrush,—mange, carries excessive suppuration, and the oppression of fungous granulations. As a caustic it acts as a powerful stimulant, and is an antiseptic.

CRETA PREPARATA,—is principally used in combination with catechu and opium in cases of super-purgation. All adventitious matters are removed by washing, and the prepared or pulverized chalk remains in the form of an impalpable powder. It is usually administered in doses of two or three ounces. It is externally applied over ulcers that discharge a thin and ichorous matter.

CROTON SEEDS.—The croton-nut has not been long introduced into veterinary practice, although it has been used from time immemorial by the inhabitants of India as a powerful purgative. An oil has been extracted from it, and used by the surgeon; the meal is adopted by the veterinarian. It is given in doses from a scruple to half a drachm, and from its acrid nature, in the form of a ball, with an ounce of linseed meal. When it does operate the effect is generally observed in six or eight hours, the stools being profuse and watery, and the patient frequently griped. On account of its speedy operation, it may be given in locked-jaw and staggers: and also in dropsy of the chest or belly, from the watery and profuse stools which it produces; but it is often uncertain in its operation, and its griping, and the debility which it occasions, are serious objections to it as common physic. When placed on the tongue of the horse in quantities varying from twenty to forty drops, it produces purging, but the membrane of the mouth frequently becomes violently inflamed. This likewise happens, but not to so great a degree, when it is given in the form of a drink, or in a mash.

DEADLY NIGHTSHADE,—extract of, see BELLADONNÆ EXTRACTUM.

DEMULCENTS,—are substances that have the power of diminishing the effect of acrimonious or stimulating substances. The first, by some oily or mucilaginous substance, sheaths the sensible parts. The other dilutes the stimulus, and diminishes its power. It will rarely be difficult to determine which effect should be produced, and the means by which it is to be effected.

DIAPHORETICS,—are medicines that increase the sensible and insensible perspiration of the animal. As it regards the horse, they are neither many nor powerful. Antimony in its various forms, and sulphur, have some effect in opening the pores of the skin, and exciting its vessels to action, and especially when assisted by warmth of stable or clothing, and therefore is useful in those diseases in which it is desirable that some portion of the blood should be diverted from the overloaded, and inflamed, and vital organs of the chest, to the skin or the extremities. The only diaphoretics, however, on which much confidence can be placed, and especially to produce condition, are warm clothing and good grooming.

DIGESTIVES,—are applications to recent or old wounds, as mild stimulants, in order to produce a healthy appearance and action in them, and to cause them more speedily to heal. A weak solution of blue vitriol is an excellent digestive; so is the tincture of aloes, and the tincture of myrrh. The best digestive ointment is one composed of three parts of calamine ointment (Turner's cerate) and one of common turpentine.

DIGITALIS—FOX-GLOVE.—The leaves of the common fox-glove, gathered about the flowering time, dried carefully in a dark place, and powdered, and kept in a close black bottle, form one of the most valuable medicines in veterinary practice. It is a direct and powerful sedative, diminishing the frequency of the pulse, and the general irritability of the system, and acting also as a mild diuretic: it is therefore useful in every inflammatory and febrile complaint, and particularly in inflammation of the chest. It is usually given in combination with emetic tartar and nitre The average dose is one drachm of digitalis, one and a half of emetic tartar, and three of nitre, repeated twice or thrice in a day.

Digitalis seems to have an immediate effect on the heart, lessening the number of its pulsations; but effecting this in a singular manner—not by causing the heart to beat more slowly, but producing certain intermissions or pauses in its action. When these become marked—when at every sixth or seventh beat, the pulsations are suspended while two or three can be slowly counted, this is precisely the effect that is intended to be produced, and, however ill the horse may appear to be, or however alarming this intermittent pulse may seem to the standers-by, from that moment the animal will frequently begin to amend. The dose must then be diminished one-half, and in a few days it may be omitted altogether: but the emetic tartar and the nitre should be continued during some days after the practitioner has deemed it prudent to try the effect of mild vegetable tonics.

There is no danger in the intermittent pulse thus produced; but there is much when the digitalis fails to produce any effect on the circulation. The disease is then too powerful to be arrested by medicine. Digitalis requires watching; but the only consequence to be apprehended from an over-dose is, that the patient may be reduced a little too low, and his convalescence retarded for a day or two.

In the form of infusion or tincture, digitalis is very useful in inflammation of the eyes. It is almost equal in its sedative influence to opium, and it may with great advantage be alternated with it, when opium begins to lose its power. The infusion is made by pouring a quart of boiling water on an ounce of the powder. When it is become cold, a portion of the liquid may be introduced into the eye. One or two drops of the tincture may be introduced with good effect. This may be obtained by macerating three ounces of digitalis in a quart of spirit.

The infusion has been serviceable in mange; but there are better applications.

DIURETICS,—constitute a useful but much abused class of medicines. They stimulate the kidneys to secrete more than the usual quantity of urine, or to separate a greater than ordinary proportion of the watery parts of the blood. The deficiency of water in the blood thus occasioned, must be speedily supplied, or the healthy circulation cannot be carried on; and it is generally supplied by the absorbents taking up the watery fluid in some part of the frame, and carrying it into the circulation. Hence the evident use of diuretics in dropsical affections, in swelled legs, and also in inflammation and fever, by lessening the quantity of the circulating fluid, and, consequently, that which is sent to the inflamed parts.

All this is effected by the kidneys being stimulated to increased action; but if this stimulus is too often or too violently applied, the energy of the kidney may be impaired, or inflammation may be produced. That inflammation may be of an acute character, and destroy the patient; or, although not intense in its nature, it may by frequent repetition assume a chronic form, and more slowly, but as surely, do irreparable mischief. Hence the necessity of attention to that portion of the food which may have a diuretic power. Mow-burnt hay and foxy oats are the unsuspected causes of many a disease in the horse, at first obscure, but ultimately referable to injury or inflammation of the urinary organs. Hence, too, the impropriety of suffering medicines of a diuretic nature to be at the command of the ignorant carter or groom. In swelled legs, cracks, grease, or accumulation of fluid in any part, and in those superficial eruptions and inflammations which are said to be produced by humors floating in the blood, diuretics are evidently beneficial; but they should be as mild as possible, and not oftener given or continued longer than the case requires. For some cautions as to the administration of diuretics, and a list of the safest and best, the reader is referred to page 231. The expensive Castile soap, and camphor, so often resorted to, are not needed, for the common liquid turpentine is quite sufficient in all ordinary cases, and nitre and digitalis may be added if fever is suspected.

DRINKS.—Many practitioners and horse-proprietors have a great objection to the administration of medicines in the form of drinks. A drink is not so portable as a ball, it is more troublesome to give, and a portion of it is usually wasted. If the drink contains any acid substance, it is apt to excoriate the mouth, or to irritate the throat, already sore from disease, or the unpleasant taste of the drug, may unnecessarily nauseate the horse. There are some medicines, however, which must be given in the form of drink, as in colic; and the time, perhaps, in not distant when purgatives will be thus administered, as more speedy, and safer in their operation. In cases of much debility and entire loss of appetite, all medicine should be given in solution, for the stomach may not have sufficient power to dissolve the paper in which the ball is wrapped, or the substance of the ball.*

An ox's horn, the larger end being cut slantingly, is the usual and best instrument for administering drinks. The noose of a halter is introduced into the mouth, and then, by means of a stable-fork, the head is elevated by an assistant considerably higher than for the delivery of a ball. The surgeon stands on a pail or stable-basket on the off-side of the horse, and draws out the tongue with the left hand; he then, with the right hand, introduces the horn gently into the mouth, and over the tongue, and by a dexterous turn of the horn empties the whole of the drink —not more than about six ounces—into the back part of the mouth. The horn is now quickly withdrawn, and the tongue loosened, and the greater portion of the fluid will be swallowed. A portion of it, however, will often be obstinately held in the mouth for a long time, and the head must be kept up until the whole is got rid of, which a quick, but not violent slap on the muzzle will generally compel the horse to do. The art of giving

* See note on p. 225.

a drink consists in not putting too much into the horn at once, introducing the horn far enough into the mouth, and quickly turning and withdrawing it, without bruising or wounding the mouth, the tongue being loosened at the same moment. A bottle is a disgraceful and dangerous instrument to use, except it be a flat pint bottle, with a long and thick neck.

EMETIC TARTAR.—See ANTIMONIO POTASSIO TARTRAS.
EPSOM SALTS.—See under MAGNESIA.
ERGOT OF RYE.—See SECALE CORNUTUM.
ETHIOPS MINERAL.—See under HYDRARGYRUM.
EYE LOTIONS or WASHES.—See COLLYRIA.
FERRUM, IRON.—Of this metal there are two preparations adopted by veterinarians. The rust, or *Carbonate*, is a mild and useful tonic, in doses of from two to four drachms. The *Sulphate* (*green vitriol or copperas*) is more powerful. It should never be given in the early stages of recovery, and always with caution. The dose should be the same as that of the carbonate. The sulphate has lately been recommended for the cure of that deceitful stage or form of glanders, in which there is nothing to characterize the disease but a very slight discharge from the nostrils. It is to be dissolved in the common drink of the horse. It is worth a trial, but too sanguine expectations must not be encouraged of the power of any drug over this intractable malady. The iron should be given in combination with gentian and ginger, but never with any alkali or nitre or soap, or catechu, or astringent vegetable.

FEVER.—For the nature and treatment of the fever, both pure and symptomatic, reference may be made to page 163.

FORGE WATER,—used to be a favorite tonic with farriers, and also a lotion for canker and ulcers in the mouth. It owes its power, if there be any, to the iron with which it is impregnated.

FLAX SEED.—See LINSEED.

FOMENTATIONS,—open the pores of the skin and promote perspiration in the part, and so abate the local swelling, and relieve pain and lessen inflammation. They are often used, and with more benefit when the inflammation is somewhat deeply seated, than when it is superficial. The effect depends upon the warmth of the water, and not on any herb that may have been boiled in it. They are best applied by means of flannel, frequently dipped in the hot water, or on which the water is poured, and the heat should be as great as the hand will bear. The benefit that might be derived from them is much impaired by the absurd method in which the fomentations are conducted. They are rarely continued long enough, and when they are removed, the part is left wet and uncovered, and the coldness of evaporation succeeds to the heat of fomentation. The perspiration is thus suddenly checked, the animal suffers considerable pain, and more harm is done by the extreme change of temperature than if the fomentation had not been attempted.

Fox-Glove.—See Digitalis.

Gentian,—stands at the head of the vegetable tonics, and is a stomachic as well as a tonic. It is equally useful in chronic debility, and in that which is consequent on severe and protracted illness. It is generally united with chamomile, ginger, and, when the patient will bear it, carbonate of iron. Four drachms of gentian, two of chamomile, one of carbonate of iron, and one of ginger, will make an excellent tonic ball. An infusion of gentian is one of the best applications to putrid ulcers.

Ginger,—is as valuable as a cordial, as gentian is as a tonic. It is the basis of the cordial ball, and it is indispensable in the tonic ball. Although it is difficult to powder, the veterinary practitioner should always purchase it in its solid form. If the root is large, heavy, and not worm-eaten, the black ginger is as good as the white, and considerably cheaper. The powder is adulterated with bean-meal and the sawdust of boxwood, and rendered warm and pungent by means of capsicum.

Goulard's Extract.—See under Lead.

Glauber's Salt.—See Sodæ Sulphur.

Hartshorn.—See Ammonia.

Healing Ointment.—See under Zinc.

Hellebore, *white*,—This is a drastic cathartic, and should be used with great caution. It is a powerful nauseant, and lowers both the force and frequency of the pulse, and is therefore given with good effect in various inflammations, and particularly that of the lungs. In the hospital of the veterinary surgeon, or in the stable of the gentleman who will superintend the giving and the operation of every medicine, it may be used with safety; but with him who has to trust to others, and who does not see the horse more than once in twelve or twenty-four hours, it is a dangerous drug. If it is pushed a little too far, trembling and giddiness, and purging follow, and the horse is sometimes lost. The hanging of the head, and the frothing of the mouth, and, more particularly, the sinking of the pulse, will give warning of danger; but the medical attendant may not have the opportunity of observing this, and when he does observe it, it may be too late. Its dose varies from a scruple to half a drachm. In doses of a drachm, it could not be given with safety; and yet, such is the different effect of medicines given in different doses, that in the quantity of an ounce it is said to be a diuretic and a tonic, and exhibited with advantage in chronic and obstinate grease.

Hellebore, *black*,—This is used mostly as a local application, and as such it is a very powerful stimulant. Mr. E. Stanley, of

Banbury, frequently resorts to it in fistulous affections of the poll and withers, and with considerable success. The abscess having formed, and exit being given to the imprisoned fluid, it is allowed to discharge itself, for two or three days, being dressed with an ordinary digestive ointment. When the pus assumes a laudable character, he introduces a few portions of the fibrous part of the root, passing them down to the bottom of the sinus, and letting them remain for a fortnight or more; in the mean time, merely keeping the surrounding parts clean. On examination, it will be found that the healing process has commenced.

Professor Morton adds, that an ointment, formed of the powder of either the black or white Hellebore, in the proportion of one part of the powder to eight of lard, will be found exceedingly active for the dressing of rowels and setons.

HEMLOCK,—is used by some practitioners, instead of digitalis or hellebore, in affections of the chest, whether acute or chronic; but it is inferior to both. The dose of the powder of the dried leaves is about a drachm.

HOG'S LARD.—See ADEPS.

HYDRARGYRUM, MERCURY.—This metal is found native in many countries in the form of minute globules. It also occurs in masses, and in different varieties of crystallization. It has the singular property of being liquid in the natural temperature of our earth. It freezes, or assumes a singular species of crystallization, at $39°$ below 0 of Fah., and at $660°$ above 0 of Fah. it boils, and rapidly evaporates. In its metallic state it appears to have no action on the animal system, but its compounds are mostly powerful excitants, and some of them are active caustics.

The *Common Mercurial Ointment* may be used for ringworm, and that species of acarus which seems to be the source, or the precursor of, mange. The compound mercurial ointment is also useful in the destruction of the same insect. For most eruptions connecting with or simulating mange, the author of this work has been accustomed to apply the following ointment with considerable success:—

Sublimed sulphur	1 pound.
Common turpentine	4 oz.
Mercurial ointment	2 oz.
Linseed oil	1 pint.

The *Mercurial Ointment* is prepared by rubbing quicksilver with lard, in the proportion of one part of mercury to three of lard, until no globules appear. The practitioner should, if possible, prepare it himself, for he can seldom get it pure or of the proper strength from the druggist. It is employed with considerable advantage in preparing splints, spavins, or other bony or callous tu mors, for blistering or firing. One or two drachms, according to the nature and size of the swelling, may be daily well rubbed in; but it should be watched, for it sometimes salivates the horse very speedily. The tumors more readily disperse, at the application of a stronger stimulant,' when they have been thus prepared. Mercurial ointment in a weaker state is sometimes necessary for th cure of mallenders and sallenders; and in very obstinate cases of mange, one-eighth part of mercurial ointment may be added to the ointment recommended at page 409.

Calomel, the submuriate or protochloride of mercury, may be given, combined with aloes, in mange, surfeit, or worms. It is also useful in some cases of chronic cough, in farcy and in jaundice. Alone it has little purgative effect on the horse, but it assists the action of other aperients. It is given in doses from a scruple to a drachm. As soon as the gums become red, or the animal begins to quid or drop his hay, it must be discontinued. Calomel has lately gained much repute in arresting the progress of epidemic catarrh in the horse. Mr. Percival has succeeded in this attempt to a very considerable extent. In fact, the influence of calomel in veterinary practice seems to have been far too much undervalued.

Corrosive Sublimate, the oxymuriate or bichloride of mercury, combined with chlorine in a double proportion, is a useful tonic in farcy. It should be given in doses of ten grains daily, and gradually increased to a scruple, until the horse is purged, or the mouth becomes sore, when it may be omitted for a few days, and resumed. Some have recommended it as a diuretic, but it is too dangerous a medicine for this purpose. It is used externally in solution; in substance in quittor, as a stimulant to foul ulcers; and in the proportion of five grains to an ounce of rectified spirit n obstinate mange, or to destroy vermin on the skin. It is, however, too uncertain and too dangerous a medicine for the horse-proprietor to venture on its use.

Æthiop's Mineral, the black sulphuret of mercury, is not often used in horse-practice, but it is a good alterative for obstinate surfeit or foulness of the skin, in doses of three drachms daily. Four drachms of cream of tartar may be advantageously added to each dose.

INFUSIONS.—The active matter of some vegetable substances is partly or entirely extracted by water. Dried vegetables yield their properties more readily and perfectly than when in their green state. Boiling water is poured on the substance to be infused, and which should have been previously pounded or powdered, and the vessel then covered and placed near a fire. In five or six hours the transparent part may be poured off, and is ready for use. In a few days, however, all infusions become thick.

and lose their virtue, from the decomposition of the vegetable matter.

The infusion of chamomile is advantageously used instead of water in compounding a mild tonic drench. The infusion of catechu is useful in astringent mixtures; that of linseed is used instead of common water in catarrh and cold; and the infusion of tobacco in some injections.

INJECTIONS.—See CLYSTERS.

IODINE.—This substance has not been long introduced into veterinary practice. The first object which it seemed to accomplish, was the reduction of the enlarged glands that frequently remain after catarrh, but it soon appeared that it could reduce almost every species of tumor. Much concerned in the first introduction of iodine into veterinary practice, the writer of the present work bears willing testimony to the zeal and success of others, in establishing the claims of this most valuable medicine. Professor Morton has devoted much time and labor to the different combinations of iodine, and they are described at length in the useful "Manual of Pharmacy." He gives the formulæ of the composition of a liniment, an ointment, and a tincture of iodine, adapted to different species and stages of disease. He next describes the preparation of the iodide of potassium—the combination of iodine and potash—and then the improvement on that under the name of the diniodide of copper—the union of two parts of the iodide of potassium with four of the sulphate of copper.

The action of this compound is an admirable tonic and a stimulant to the absorbent system, if combined with vegetable tonics, and, occasionally, small doses of cantharides. Professor Spooner and Mr. Daws applied this compound, and with marked success, to the alleviation of farcy, nasal gleet, and glanders. It is pleasing to witness these triumphs over disease, a little while ago so unexpected, and now so assured.*

IODINE OINTMENT.—See under IODINE.

IRON.—See FERRUM.

JAMES'S POWDER.—See PULVIS ANTIMONII COMPOSITUS.

JAPAN EARTH.—See CATECHU.

JUNIPER, OIL OF.—This essential oil is retained because it has some diruetic property, as well as being a pleasant aromatic. It frequently enters into the composition of the diuretic ball.

---

* *Note by Mr. Spooner.*—Iodine is employed in various forms. In that of iodide of potassium it is best administered internally, as a promoter of absorption. Combined with the sulphate of copper it forms a powerful and useful tonic; whilst in the form of iodide of mercury, and combined with lard or palm oil, it becomes a powerful blister, and a useful promoter of absorption.

LEAD, PLUMBUM.—The *Carbonate of Lead* had a deleterious effect on the biped and the quadruped in the neighborhood of lead works. They are subject to violent griping pains, and to constipation that can with great difficulty, or not at all, be overcome. Something of the same kind is occasionally observed in the cider counties, and the "painter's colic" is a circumstance of too frequent occurrence—the occasional dreadful pains, and the ravenous appetite extending to everything that comes in the way of the animal. Active purgatives followed by opium are the most effectual remedies.

The *Acetate of Lead, Plumbi Acetas*.—Sugar of lead is seldom given externally to the horse, but is used as a collyrium for inflammation of the eyes.

The *Liquor Plumbi Subacetatis*, or *Goulard's Extract*, or, as it used to be termed at the Veterinary College, the *Aqua Vegeto*, is a better eye wash, and advantageously used in external and superficial inflammation, and particularly the inflammation that remains after the application of a blister.

LIME,—was formerly sprinkled over cankered feet and greasy heels, but there are less painful caustics, and more effectual absorbents of moisture. Lime-water is rarely used, but the *Chloride of Lime* is exceedingly valuable. Diluted with twenty times its quantity of water, it helps to form the poultice applied to every part from which there is the slightest offensive discharge. The fœtid smell of fistulous withers, poll-evil, canker, and ill-conditioned wounds, is immediately removed, and the ulcers are more disposed to heal. When mangy horses are dismissed as cured, a washing with the diluted chloride will remove any infection that may lurk about them, or which they may carry from the place in which they have been confined. One pint of the chloride mixed with three gallons of water, and brushed over the walls and manger and rack of the foulest stable, will completely remove all infection. Professor Morton, very properly, says tha the common practice of merely white-washing the walls serves only to cover the infectious matter, and perhaps to preserve it for an indefinite length of time, so that when the lime scales off, disease may be again engendered by the exposed virus. The horse furniture worn by a glandered or mangy animal will be effectually purified by the chloride. Internally administered, it seems to have little or no power.

LINIMENTS,—are oily applications of the consistence of a thick fluid, and designed either to soothe an inflamed surface, or, by gently stimulating the skin, to remove deeper-seated pain or inflammation. As an emollient, one composed of half an ounce of extract of lead and four ounces of olive oil will be useful. For sprains, old swellings, or rheumatism, two ounces of hartshorn, the same quantity of camphorated spirit, an ounce of oil of turpentine, and half an ounce of laudanum, may be mixed together; or an ounce of camphor may be dissolved in four ounces of sweet oil, to which an ounce of oil of turpentine may be afterwards added. A little powdered cantharides, or tincture of cantharides, or mustard powder, will render either of these more powerful, or convert it into a liquid blister.

LINSEED.—An infusion of linseed is often used instead of water, for the drink of the horse with sore-throat or catarrh, or disease of the urinary organs or of the bowels. A pail containing it should be slung in the stable or loose box. Thus gruel, however, is preferable; it is as bland and soothing, and it is more nutritious. Linseed meal forms the best poultice for almost every purpose.

LUNAR CAUSTIC.—See under ARGENTIUM.

MAGNESIA.—The sulphate of magnesia, or EPSOM SALTS, should be used only in promoting the purgative effect of clysters, or, in repeated doses of six or eight ounces, gently to open the bowels at the commencement of fever. Some doubt, however, attends the latter practice; for the dose must occasionally be thrice repeated before it will act, and then, although safer than aloes, it may produce too much irritation in the intestinal canal, especially if the fever is the precursor of inflammation of the lungs.

MASHES,—constitute a very important part of horse-provender, whether in sickness or health. A mash given occasionally to a horse that is otherwise fed on dry meat prevents him from becoming dangerously costive. To the over-worked and tired horse, nothing is so refreshing as a warm mash with his usual allowance of corn in it. The art of getting a horse into apparent condition for sale, or giving him a round and plump appearance, consists principally in the frequent repetition of mashes, and, from their easiness of digestion and the mild nutriment which they afford, as well as their laxative effect, they form the principal diet of the sick horse.

They are made by pouring boiling water or bran, and stirring it well, and then covering it over until it is sufficiently cool for the horse to eat. If in the heat of summer a cold mash is preferred, it should, nevertheless, be made with hot water, and then suffered to remain until it is cold. This is not always sufficiently attended to by the groom, who is not aware that the efficacy of the mash depends principally on the change which is effected in the bran and the other ingredients by boiling water rendering them more easy of digestion, as well as more aperient. If the horse refuses the mash, a few oats may be sprinkled over it, in order to tempt him to eat it; but if it is previously designed that corn should be given in the mash, it should be scalded with the bran, in order to soften it and render it more digestible. Bran mashes are very useful preparatives for physic, and they are necessary during the operation of the physic. They very soon become sour. and the manger of the horse, of whose diet they form a principal part, should be daily and carefully cleaned out.

When horses are weakly and much reduced, malt mashes will often be very palatable to them and very nutritive: but the water that is poured on a malt mash should be considerably below the boiling heat, otherwise the malt will be set, or clogged together. If the owner was aware of the value of a malt mash, it would be oftener given when the horse is rapidly getting weaker from protracted disease, or when he is beginning to recover from a disease by which he has been much reduced. The only exception to their use is in cases of chest affection, in which they must not be given too early. In grease, and in mange accompanied by much emaciation, malt mashes will be peculiarly useful, especially if they constitute a principal portion of the food.

MERCURY,—see HYDRARGYRUM.

MERCURIAL OINTMENT,—see under HYDRARGYRUM.

MURIATIC ACID,—see ACIDUM MURIATICUM.

MUSTARD, SINAPIS.—This will be found occasionally useful, if, in inflammation of the chest or bowels, it is well rubbed on the chest or the abdomen. The external swelling and irritation which it excites may, to a greater or less degree, abate the inflammation within.

MYRRH,—may be used in the form of tincture, or it may be united to the tincture of aloes as a stimulating and digestive application to wounds Diluted with an equal quantity of water, it is a good application for canker in the mouth, but as an internal medicine it seems to be inert, although some practitioners advocate its use, combined with opium, in cases of chronic cough.

NITRE,—see under Potash.

NITROUS ÆTHER, SPIRIT OF,—is a very useful medicine in the advanced stages of fever, for while it, to a certain degree, rouses the exhausted powers of the animal, and may be denominated a stimulant, it never brings back the dangerous febrile action which was subsiding. It is given in doses of three or four drachms.

OLIVE OIL,—is an emollient and demulcent. Its laxative effect is very inconsiderable and uncertain in the horse.

OPIUM.—However underrated by some, there is not a more valuable drug on our list. It does not often act as a narcotic, except in considerable doses; but it is a powerful antispasmodic, sedative, and astringent. As an antispasmodic, it enters into the cholic drink, and it is the sheet-anchor of the veterinarian in the treatment of tetanus or locked-jaw. As a sedative it relaxes that universal spasm of the muscular system which is the character-

:stic of tetanus; and, perhaps, it is only as a sedative that it has such admirable effect as an astringent, for when the irritation around the mouths of the vessels of the intestines and kidneys is allayed by the opium, the undue purging and profuse staling wil" necessarily be arrested.

Opium should, however, be given with caution. It is its secondary effect that is sedative, and, if given in cases of fever, its primary effect in increasing the excitation of the frame may be very considerable and highly injurious. In the early and acute stage of fever, it would be bad practice to give it in the smallest quantity; but when the fever has passed, or is passing, there is nothing which so rapidly subdues the irritability that accompanies extreme weakness. It becomes an excellent tonic, because it is a sedative.

If the blue or green vitriol, or cantharides, have been pushed too far, opium, sooner than any other drug, quiets the disorder they have occasioned. It is given in doses of one or two drachms, in the form of ball. Other medicines are usually combined with it, according to the circumstances of the case.

Externally, it is useful in ophthalmia. In the form of decoction of the poppy-head, it may constitute the basis of an anodyne poultice; but it must not be given in union with any alkali, with the exception of chalk, in over-purging; nor with the superacetate of lead, by which its powers are materially impaired; nor with sulphate of zinc, or copper, or iron.

From its high price it is much adulterated, and it is not always met with in a state of purity. The best tests are its smell, its taste, its toughness and pliancy, its fawn or brown color, and its weight, for it is the heaviest of all the vegetable extracts except gum arabic; yet its weight is often fraudulently increased by stones and bits of lead dexterously concealed in it. The English opium is almost as good as the Turkish, and frequently sold for it; but is distinguishable by its blackness and softness.

PALM OIL,—when genuine, is the very best substance that can be used for making masses and balls. It has a pleasant smell, and it never becomes rancid.

PEPPER,—see CAPSICI BACCÆ.

PITCH,—is used to give adhesiveness and firmness to charges and plasters. The common pitch is quite as good as the more expensive Burgundy pitch. The best plaster for sand-crack consists of one pound of pitch and an ounce of yellow beeswax melted together.

PHYSIC.—The cases which require physic, the composition of the most effectual and safest physic-ball, and the mode of treatment under physic, have been already described.

POTASH.—Two compounds of potash are used in veterinary

practice   The Nitrate of Potash (*Nitre*) is a valuable cooling medicine and a mild diuretic, and, therefore, it should enter into the composition of every fever-ball. Its dose is from two to four drachms. Grooms often dissolve it in the water. There are two objections to this : either the horse is nauseated and will not drink so much water as he ought ; or the salt taste of the water causes considerable thirst, and disinclination to solid food. Nitre, whilst dissolving, materially lowers the temperature of water, and furnishes a very cold and useful lotion for sprain of the back-sinews, and other local inflammations. The lotion should be used as soon as the salt is dissolved, for it quickly becomes as warm as the surrounding air. The Bitartrate of Potash (*Cream of Tartar*) is a mild diuretic, and, combined with Æthiop's mineral, is used as an alterative in obstinate mange or grease. The objection, however, to its use in such an animal as the horse, is the little power which it seems to exercise.

POULTICES.—Few horsemen are aware of the value of these simple applications in abating inflammation, relieving pain, cleansing wounds, and disposing them to heal. They are applications of the best kind continued much longer than a simple fomentation can be. In all inflammations of the foot they are very beneficial, by softening the horn hardened by the heat of the foot and contracted and pressing on the internal and highly sensible parts. The moisture and warmth are the useful qualities of the poultice ; and that poultice is the best for general purposes in which moisture and warmth are longest retained. Perspiration is most abundantly promoted in the part, the pores are opened, swellings are relieved and discharges of a healthy nature procured from wounds.

Linseed meal forms the best general poultice, because it longest retains the moisture. Bran, although frequently used for poultices, is objectionable, because it so soon becomes dry   To abate considerable inflammation, and especially in a wounded part, Goulard may be added, or the linseed meal may be made into a paste with a decoction of poppy-heads. To promote a healthy discharge from an old or foul ulcer ; or separation of the dead from the living parts, in the process of what is called coring out ; or to hasten the ripening of a tumor that must be opened ; or to cleanse it when it is opened,—two ounces of common turpentine may be added to a pound of linseed meal : but nothing can be so absurd, or is so injurious, as the addition of turpentine to a poultice that is designed to be an emollient. The drawing poultices and stoppings of farriers are often highly injurious, instead of abating inflammation.

If the ulcer smells offensively, two ounces of powdered charcoal may be added to the linseed meal, or the poultice may be made of water, to which a solution of the chloride of lime has been added in the proportion of half an ounce to a pound. As an emollient poultice for grease and cracked heels, and especially if accompanied by much unpleasant smell, there is nothing preferable to a poultice of mashed carrots with charcoal. For old grease some slight stimulant must be added, as a little yeast or the grounds of table beer.

There are two errors in the application of a poultice, and particularly as it regards the legs. It is often put on too tight, by means of which the return of the blood from the foot is prevented, and the disease is increased instead of lessened; or it is too hot, and unnecessary pain is given, and the inflammation aggravated.

POWDERS.—Some horses are very difficult to ball or drench, and the violent struggle that would accompany the attempt to conquer them may heighten the fever or inflammation. To such horses powders must be given in mashes. Emetic tartar and digitalis may be generally used in cases of inflammation or fever; or emetic tartar for worms; or calomel or even the farina of the croton-nut for physic: but powders are too often an excuse for the laziness or awkwardness of the carter or groom. The horse frequently refuses them, especially if his appetite has otherwise begun to fail; the powder and the mash are wasted, and the animal is unnecessarily nauseated. All medicine should be given in the form of a ball or drink.

PRUSSIC ACID.—See ACIDUM HYDROCIANICUM.

QUININE.—See under BARK, PERUVIAN.

RAKING.—This consists in introducing the hand into the rectum of the horse, and drawing out any hardened dung that may be there. It may be necessary in costiveness or fever, if a clyster pipe cannot be obtained; but an injection will better effect the purpose, and with less inconvenience to the animal. The introduction of the hand into the rectum is, however, useful to ascertain the existence of stone in the bladder, or the degree of distension of the bladder in suppression of the urine, for the bladder will be easily felt below the intestine, and, at the same time by the heat of the intestine, the degree of inflammation in it or in the bladder may be detected.

RESIN.—The yellow resin is that which remains after the distillation of oil of turpentine. It is used externally to give consistence to ointments, and to render them slightly stimulant. Internally it is a useful diuretic, and is given in doses of five or six drachms made into a ball with soft soap. The common liquid turpentine is, however, preferable.

ROWELS.—The manner of rowelling has been already described. As exciting inflammation on the surface, and so lessening that which had previously existed in a neighboring but deeper-seated part, they are decidedly inferior to blisters, for they do not act so quickly or so extensively; therefore they should not be used in acute inflammation of the lungs or bowels, or any vital part. When the inflammation, however, although not intense, has long continued, rowels will be serviceable by producing an irritation and discharge that can be better kept up than by a blister. As promoting a permanent, although not very considerable discharge, and some inflammation, rowels in the thighs are useful in swelled legs and obstinate grease. If fluid is thrown out under the skin in any other part, the rowel acts as a permanent drain. When the sprain of the joint or the muscles of the shoulders is suspected, a rowel in the chest will be serviceable. The wound caused by a rowel will readily heal, and with little blemish, unless the useless leather of the farrier has been inserted.

SAL AMMONIAC,—See CHLORIDE OF AMMONIA.

SALT, common, see SODII CHLORIDUM.

SECALE CORNUTUM, ERGOT OF RYE.—This is well known to be an excitant in assisting parturition in cattle, sheep, and dogs. It has been used with success in the mare by Mr. Richardson, of Lincoln. It should only be applied in difficult cases, and the dose should be two drachms, combined with some carminative, and given every hour.

SEDATIVES,—are medicines that subdue irritation, repress spasmodic action, or deaden pain. We will not inquire whether they act first as stimulants: if they do, their effect is exceedingly transient, and is quickly followed by depression and diminished action. Digitalis, hellebore, opium, turpentine, are medicines of this kind. Their effect in different diseases or stages of disease, and the circumstances which indicate the use of any one of them in preference to the rest, are considered under their respective titles.*

SODA.—The *Carbonate of Soda* is a useful antacid, and probably a diuretic, but it is not much used in veterinary practice. The *Chloride of Soda* is not so efficacious for the removal of unpleasant smells and all infection as the chloride of lime; but it is exceedingly useful in changing malignant and corroding and destructive sores into the state of simple ulcers, and, in ulcers that are not malignant, it much hastens the cure. Poll-evil and fistulous withers are much benefited by it, and all farcy ulcers. It is used in the proportion of one part of the solution to twenty-four of water.

SODII CHLORIDUM, *Common Salt*,—is very extensively employed in veterinary practice. It forms an efficacious aperient

---

* *Note by Mr. Spooner.—Sedatives.*—To the list enumerated in the text may be added the extract of belladonna, or the deadly nightshade, which is given in doses of two drachms.

clyster, and a solution of it has been given as an aperient drink. Sprinkled over the hay, or in a mash, it is very palatable to sick horses; and in that languor and disinclination to food which remain after severe illness, few things will so soon recall the appetite as a drink composed of six or eight ounces of salt in solution. To horses in health it is more useful than is generally imagined, as promoting the digestion of the food, and, consequently, condition. Externally applied, there are few better lotions for inflamed eyes than a solution of half a drachm of salt in four ounces of water. In the proportion of an ounce of salt to the same quantity of water, it is a good embrocation for sore shoulders and backs; and if it does not always disperse warbles and tumors, it takes away much of the tenderness of the skin.

SODÆ SULPHAS,—*Sulphate of Soda.*—Glauber's Salt.—This medicine is seldom used in the treatment of the horse. It appears to have some diuretic property.

SOAP,—is supposed to possess a diuretic quality, and therefore enters into the composition of some diuretic masses. See RESIN. By many practitioners it is made an ingredient in the physic-ball, but uselessly or injuriously so; for if the shoes are finely powdered and mixed with palm oil, they will dissolve readily enough in the bowels without the aid of the soap, while the action of the soap on the kidneys will impair the purgative effect of the aloes.

SPANISH FLY,—See CANTHARIDES.

STARCH,—may be substituted with advantage for gruel in obstinate cases of purging, both as a clyster, and to support the strength of the animal.

STOPPINGS,—constitute an important, but too often neglected part of stable management. If a horse is irregularly or seldom worked, his feet are deprived of moisture; they become hard and unyielding and brittle, and disposed to corn and contraction and founder. The very dung of a neglected and filthy stable would be preferable to habitual standing on the cleanest litter without stopping. In wounds, and bruises, and corns, moisture is even more necessary, in order to supple the horn, and relieve its pressure on the tender parts beneath. As a common stopping, nothing is better than cow-dung with a fourth part of clay well beaten into it, and confined with splents from the binding or larger twigs of the broom. In cases of wounds, a little tar may be added; but tar, as a common stopping, is too stimulating and drying. Pads made of thick felt have lately been contrived, which are fitted to the sole, and, swelling on being wetted, are sufficiently confined by the shoe. Having been well saturated with water, they will continue moist during the night. They are very useful in gentlemen's stables; but the cow-dung and clay are sufficient for the farmer.

STRYCHNIA.—This drug has frequently been employed with decided advantage in cases of paralysis in the dog; and lately, and with decided advantage, it has been administered to the horse. The dose is from one to three grains, given twice in the day.

SUGAR OF LEAD,—see under LEAD.

SULPHUR,—is the basis of the most effectual applications for mange. It is an excellent alterative, combined usually with antimony and nitre, and particularly for mange, surfeit, grease, hidebound, or want of condition; and it is a useful ingredient in the cough and fever ball. When given alone, it seems to have little effect, except as a laxative in doses of six or eight ounces; but there are much better aperients. The black sulphur consists principally of the dross after the pure sulphur has been separated.

TAR,—melted with an equal quantity of grease forms the usual stopping of the farrier. It is a warm, or slightly stimulant, and therefore useful, dressing for bruised or wounded feet; but its principal virtue seems to consist in preventing the penetration of dirt and water to the wounded part. As a common stopping it has been considered objectionable. From its warm and drying properties it is the usual and proper basis for thrush ointments; and from its adhesiveness, and slightly stimulating power, it often forms an ingredient in application for mange. Some practitioners give it, and advantageously, with the usual cough medicine, and in doses of two or three drachms for chronic cough. The common tar is as effectual as the Barbadoes for every veterinary purpose. The oil, or spirit (rectified oil) of tar is sometimes used alone for the cure of mange, but it is not to be depended upon. The spirit of tar, mixed with double the quantity of fish-oil, is, from its peculiar penetrating property, one of the best applications for hard and brittle feet. It should be well rubbed with a brush, every night, both on the crust and sole.

TINCTURES.—The medicinal properties of many substances are extracted by spirit of wine, but in such small quantities as to be scarcely available for internal use in veterinary practice. So much aloes or opium must be given in order to produce effect on the horse, that the quantity of spirit necessary to dissolve it would be injurious or might be fatal. As applications to wounds or inflamed surfaces, the tinctures of aloes, digitalis, myrrh, and opium, are highly useful.

TOBACCO,—in the hands of the skilful veterinarian, may be advantageously employed in cases of extreme costiveness, or dangerous cholic; but should never be permitted to be used as an external application for the cure of mange, or an internal medicine to promote a fine coat.

TONICS —are valuable medicines when judiciously employed;

but, like cordials, they have been fatally abused. Many a horse recovering from severe disease has been destroyed by their too early, or too free use. The veterinary surgeon occasionally administers them injuriously, in his anxiety to gratify the impatience of his employer. The mild vegetable tonics, chamomile, gentian, and ginger, and, perhaps, the carbonate of iron, may sometimes be given with benefit, and may hasten the perfect recovery of the patient; but there are few principles more truly founded on reason and experience, than, that disease once removed, the powers of nature are sufficient to re-establish health. Against the more powerful mineral tonics, except for the particular purposes that have been pointed out under the proper heads, the horse proprietor and the veterinarian should be on his guard.

TURNER'S CERATE,—see under DIGESTIVES, and also under ZINC.

TURPENTINE.—The common liquid turpentine has been described as one of the best diuretics, in doses of half an ounce, and made into a ball with linseed meal and powdered ginger. It is added to the calamine or any other mild ointment in order to render it stimulating and digestive, and, from its adhesiveness and slight stimulating power it is an ingredient in mange ointments. The oil of turpentine is an excellent antispasmodic. For the removal of colic it stands unrivalled. Forming a tincture with cantharides, it is the basis of the sweating blister for old strains and swellings. As a blister it is far inferior to the common ointment. As a stimulant frequently applied it must be sufficiently lowered, or it may blemish.—See RESIN.

VERDIGRIS,—see under COPPER.
VINEGAR,—see ACIDUM ACETICUM.
VITRIOL,—*blue*,—see under COPPER.
VITRIOL,—*green*,—see under FERRUM.
VITRIOL,—*white*,—see under ZINC.
VITRIOL,—*Oil of*,—see ACIDUM SULPHURICUM.

WAX.—The yellow wax is used in charges and some plasters to render them less brittle.

ZINC.—The impure carbonate of zinc, under the name of *Calamine Powder*, is used in the preparation of a valuable healing ointment, called Turner's Cerate. Five parts of lard and one of resin are melted together, and when these begin to get cool two parts of the calamine, reduced to an impalpable powder, are stirred in. If the wound is not healthy, a small quantity of common turpentine may be added. This salve justly deserves the name which it has gained, "The Healing Ointment." The calamine is sometimes sprinkled with advantage on cracked heels and superficial sores.

The sulphate of zinc, *White Vitriol*, in the proportion of three grains to an ounce of water, is an excellent application in opthalmia, when the inflammatory stage is passing over; and quittor is most successfully treated by a saturated solution of white vitriol being injected into the sinuses. A solution of white vitriol of less strength forms a wash for grease that is occasionally useful, when the alum or blue vitriol does not appear to succeed.

ZINGIBERIS RADIX.—*Ginger Root.*—This is an admirable stimulant and carminative. It is useful in loss of appetite and flatulent colic, while it rouses the intestinal canal to its propei action. The cordial mass resorted to by the best surgeons consists of equal parts of ginger and gentian beaten into a mass with treacle.

INDEX.

ACETABULUM, description of the, 272.
Acini, description of, 213.
Acetic acid, its properties, 436.
Adeps, properties of, 437.
Æthiop's mineral, an alterative, 411.
Age, natural, of the horse, 130; of the horse as indicated by the teeth, 122; other indications of, 129.
Air, a supply of pure, necessary for the health of the horse, 385.
Alcohol, its medicinal properties, 437.
Aloes, Barbadoes, far preferable to Cape, 437; description of the different kinds of, 438; principal adulterations of, 439; tincture of, its composition and use, ib.
Alteratives, the best, 439; nature and effect of, 440.
Alum, the use of, in restraining purging, 440; solution of, a good wash for grease, ib; burnt, a stimulant and caustic for wounds, ib.
Ammonia, given in flatulent colic, 440; vapor of, plentifully extricated from dung and urine, most injurious to the eyes and lungs, ib.
Anchylosis of bones, what, 149.
Animals, zoological divisions of, 44.
Anise-seed, its properties, 441.
Anodyne, opium the only one to be depended on, 441.
Antea-spinatus muscle, description of the, 251.
Antimonial powder, a good febrifuge, 441.
Antimony, black sulphuret of, method of detecting its adulterations, 441; used as an alterative, ib.; tartarized, used as a nauseant, diaphoretic and worm medicine, ib.
Antispasmodics, nature of, 442.
Apoplexy, nature and treatment of, 70.
Aqueous fluid, an, why placed in the labyrinth of the ear, 58; humor of the eye, description of the, 64.
Arabian Horses, different varieties of, 25, 26; character of, 26, 27; fondness of the Arabs for, 27; prices of, 28; unequal to the English race-horse, 29.
Arabian, 25; Darley, 19; Godolphin, 21.

Arched form of the skull, advantage of, 55.
Arm, description of the, 252; action of explained on the principle of the lever, 249, 252; extensor muscles of the, 252, 253; flexor muscles of the, 253, full and swelling, advantage of, ib.; should be muscular and long, 252; fracture of the, 338.
Arsenic, medical use of, 442.
Arteries, description of the, 140; of the arm, 252: of the face, 101; neck, 140 shoulder, 246.
Ascaris, account of the, 227.
Astragalus, account of the, 278.
Atlas, anatomy of the, 136.
Auscultation, the importance of, 171.

BACK, general description of the, 149; proper form of the, ib.; long and short, comparative advantages of, ib.; anatomy of the, ib.; muscles of the, 151.
Backing, of the colt, 371; a bad habit of the horse, usual origin of it, ib.
Back-sinews, sprain of the, 258; thickening of the, constituting unsoundness 429.
Balls, the manner of giving, 442; the manner of making, ib.
Barbary horse, description of, 21.
Barbs or paps, treatment of, 133.
Bark, Peruvian, the properties of it, 443.
Barley, considered as food for the horse, 396.
Barnacles, use of the, as a mode of restraint, 360.
Bar-shoe, description and use of, 352.
Bars, description and office of the, 296; proper paring of, for shoeing, 297 folly of cutting them away, ib.; removal of, a cause of contraction, ib.; corns, ib.
Basilicon ointment, 443.
Bay horses, description of, 413.
Beans, good for hardly-worked horses, and that have a tendency to purge, 397, 402; should always be crushed 398.
Bearing-rein, the use and abuse of, 118.
Beet, the nutritive matter in, 401.
Belladonna, extract of, 443.

Biceps femoris, account of the, 274.
Bile, account of the, 213.
Bishoping the teeth, description of, 128.
Biting, a bad habit, and how usually acquired, 372.
Bit, the, often too sharp, 118; sometimes got into the mouth, 372.
Biting of the colt, 242.
Black horses, description and character of, 414.
Blaze, 19.
Bladder, description of the, 234; inflammation of, symptoms and treatment, *ib.*; neck of, *ib.*; stone in the, 235.
Bleeding, best place for general, 166, 361; directions for, 140, 166; from veins rather than arteries, 140; finger should be on the pulse during, 360; importance of, in inflammation. *ib.*; at the toe described, 168; comparison between the fleam and lancet, 166, 167.
Blindness, usual method of discovering, 64; discovered by the pupil not dilating or contracting, *ib.*; of one eye, *ib.*
Blistering all round at once, barbarity and danger of, 363, 445; after firing, absurdity and cruelty of, 362.
Blisters, best composition of, 362; the different kinds and uses of, *ib.*; best mode of applying, *ib.*; caution with regard to their application, *ib.*; the principle of their action, 443; use of, in inflammation, 362; comparison between them and rowels and setons, 366, 367.
Blood, change in after bleeding, 167; changes in during respiration, 156; coagulation of, 189; horses, very subject to contraction, 309; spavin, nature and treatment of, 164.
Bloody urine, 233.
Bog spavin, nature and treatment of, 164, 281, 282, 287.
Bole-Armenian, medical use of, 444.
Bones, strength does not depend on the size of, 28.
Bone-spavin, nature and treatment of, 283.
Bots in the stomach, natural history of, 208, 209; not usually injurious, 209.
Bowels, inflammation of the, 220.
Brain, description of the, 55; its cortical and cineritious composition, 56; the office of each, *ib.*; compression of the, 56, 69; pressure on the, 69; inflammation of the, 74.
Bran, as food for the horse, 397.
Breaking in should commence in the second winter, 240; description of its various stages, 240, 241; necessity of gentleness and patience in. *ib.*; of the farmer's horse, *ib.*; of the hunter or hackney, *ib.*
Breast, muscles of the, 152.

Breathing, the mechanism of, 154.
Breeding, qualities of the mare of as much importance as those of the horse, 237; the peculiarity of form and constitution inherited, *ib.*; in-and-in, observations on, 26, 238.
Breeds, good effects of crossing them. 29; bad effects of ditto, *ib.*
Broken down, what, 259.
Broken knees, treatment of, 254; method of judging of the danger of, *ib.*; when healed, not unsoundness, but the form and action of the horse should be carefully examined, 421.
Broken-wind, nature and treatment of, 196; influenced much, and often caused by the manner of feeding, 198; how distinguished from thickwind, *ib.*
Bronchial tubes, description of the, 144
Bronchitis, nature and treatment of, 184
Bronchocele, account of, 174.
Bronchotomy, the operation of, 165.
Brood mare, description of the, 237 should not be too old, *ib.*; treatment of, after covering, 238; after foaling, 239.
Brown horses, description of, 387.
Buccinator muscle, description of the, 103.

CÆCUM, description of the, 211.
Calamine powder, account of, 417.
Calculi in the intestines, 226.
Calkins, advantages and disadvantages of, 346; should be placed on both heels, *ib.*
Camphor, the medical use of, 444.
Canadian horse, character of, 29; cross with American horse, 29.
Canker of the foot, nature and treatment of, 330.
Cannon, or shank-bone, description of the 256.
Cantharides, from the best blister, 445, given for the cure of glanders, *ib.*
Capillary vessels, the, 159.
Capivi, balsam of, 448.
Capped hock, nature and treatment of, 270, 285, 286; although not always unsoundness there should be a special warranty against it, 421.
Capsicum Berries, their stimulating effect, 445.
Carbonate of blood got rid of in respiration.
Carbonate of iron, a mild tonic, 454.
Carraways, a good aromatic, 445.
Carrots, excellent effects of in disease, 401.
Cartilages of the foot, description and action of the, 299; ossification of the 331, 427; a cause of unsoundness, 427
Caruncula lacrymalis, the, 93.
Cascarilla Bark, a tonic and aromatic. 445

Castor oil, not a purgative for the horse, 445.
Castration, method of, 245; proper period for, 244, 245; the operation by torsion, 245.
Cataract in the eye, nature of, 65; cannot be operated on in the horse, ib.; method of examination for, ib.; the occasional appearance and disappearance of, 96.
Catarrh, description and treatment of, 169, 170; distinguished from glanders, 170; distinguished from inflammation of the lungs, 169; epidemic, 175.
Catarrhal fever, nature and treatment of, 170.
Catechu, a good astringent, method of giving, and adulterations of, 446.
Catheter, description of one, 235, 236.
Caustic, an account of the best, 446.
Cawl, description of the, 214.
Cerebellum, description of the, 56.
Cerebrum, description of the, 56.
Chalk, its medicinal use in the horse, 446.
Chaff, attention should be paid to the goodness of the ingredients, 393; best composition of, ib.; when given to the hard-worked horse, much time is saved for repose, 394; quantity necessary for different kinds of horses, 393.
Chamomile, a mild tonic, 446.
Channel of the jaws, what, 121.
Charcoal, useful in a poultice, and as an antiseptic, 447.
Charges, composition and use of, 447.
Chest, anatomy of the. 145; proper form of the, 146; cut of the, 145; the importance of depth of, 146; narrow and rounded, comparison between, ib.; the broad chest, 147; founder, description of, 152.
Chestnut horses, varieties of, 412.
Chinked in the chine, what, 149.
Childers, Flying, cut of, 18; Bartletts, 19; their get, ib.
Chloride of lime, an excellent disinfectant, 412; of soda, useful in unhealthy ulcers, 415.
Chorea, 83.
Choroid coat of the eye, description and use of the, 63.
Chyle, the formation of, 211.
Ciliary processes of the eye, description of the, 64.
Cineritous matter of the brain, nature and function of the, 56
Cleveland Bay, character of, 39; imported into United States, ib.
Clicking, cause and remedy of, 380.
Clipping, recommendation of, 407.
Clips, when necessary, 346.
Clover, considered as an article of food, 400.
Clysters, the composition and great usefulness of, 447; directions as to the administration of, ib.
Coat, fine, persons much too solicitous to procure it, 390.
Cocktail horse, mode of nicking, 368
Coffin-bone, description of the, 299; the lamellæ, or leaves of, ib.; fracture of, 342.
Coffin-joint, sprain of, 368.
Cold, common, description and treatment of, 169.
Colic, flatulent, account of, 218; spasmodic, description and treatment of, 215.
Colon, description of the, 211, 212.
Color, remarks on, 411.
Colt, early treatment of the. 240.
Complexus major, description of the, 139; minor, description of the, ib.
Concave-seated shoe, the, described and recommended, 348.
Conjunctiva, description of the, 61; appearance of, how far a test of inflammation, ib.
Consternation, cut of, *frontispiece*; pedigree of, 22; character of, 23, 24.
Consumption, account of, 199.
Contraction of the foot, nature of, 307, 391; the peculiarity of the lameness produced by, 309; how far connected with the navicular disease, 312; is not the necessary consequence of shoeing 307; produced by neglect of paring, 308; wearing the shoes too long, ib.. want of natural moisture, 309; the removal of the bars, ib.; not so much produced by litter as imagined, 309 the cause rather than the consequence of thrush, 307; best mode of treating 310, 311; rarely permanently cured 311; does not necessarily imply un soundness, 421; although not necessarily unsoundness, should have a special warranty against it, 422; blood horses very subject to, 309.
Convexity of the eye, the proper, not sufficiently attended to, 62.
Copaiba, account of the resin, 448.
Copper, the combination of, used in veterinary practice, 448.
Corded veins, what, 114.
Cordials, the use and abuse of, in the horse, 449.
Cornea, description of the, 62; mode of examining the, ib.; its prominence or flatness, ib.; should be perfectly transparent, ib.
Corns, the nature and treatment of, 326; produced by cutting away the bars, ib.; not paring out the foot between the crust and bars, ib.; pressure, ib.; very difficult to cure, 329 constitute unsoundness, 422.
Coronary ligament, description of the 296; the crust principally produced from, ib.; ring, description of the, ib.

Coronet, description of the, 296.
Corrosive sublimate, a good tonic for farcy, 411.
Cortical substance of the brain, description and fraction of, 56.
Cough, the nature and treatment of, 190, 191; constitutes unsoundness, 421; the occasional difficulty with regard to this, 430.
Cow hocks, description of, 286.
Cradle, a safe restraint upon the horse when blistered, 363.
Cramp, the nature and treatment of, 82.
Cream coloured horses, account of, 412; peculiarity in their eyes, 63.
Cream of tartar, a mild diuretic, 414.
Creasote, its use in veterinary practice, 450.
Crib-biting, description of, 378; causes and cure, ib.; injurious to the horse, 378; constitutes unsoundness, 378, 379.
Cricoid cartilage of the windpipe, the, 143.
Cropping of the ear, absurdity of, 59.
Crossing the breeds, good effect of, 29; bad effects of ditto. ib.
Croton, the farina of, used in physic, 450.
Crust of the foot, description of the, 293; composition of the, 294; consisting within of numerous horny plates, ib.; proper degree of it, slanting. 295; proper thickness of the, ib.; brittleness of, remedy for, 297; the cause of sand-crack, 317.
Crystalline lens, description of the, 65.
Cuboid bones, description of the, 279.
Cuneiform bones, description of the, 55, 279.
Curbs, nature and treatment of, 280; constitute unsoundness, 424.
Cuticle, description of the, 405.
Cutis, or true skin, account of the, 405.
Cutting, cause and cure of, 266, 380; constitutes unsoundness, 424; away the foot, unfounded prejudice against, 308.

DANDRIFF, the nature of, 405.
Darley Arabian, 19.
Deafness, 98.
Depressor labii inferioris muscle, description of the, 103.
Diabetes, the nature and treatment of, 233.
Diaphoretics, their nature and effects, 451.
Diaphragm. description of the, 153; rupture of, 207; its connection with respiration, 154.
Digestion, the process of it described, 451.
Digestives. their nature and use, 451.

Digitalis, highly recommended in colds and all inflammatory complaints, 451.
Dilator magnus lateralis muscle, description of the, 274; naris lateralis muscle, description of, ib.
Distance, 42.
Diuretic medicines, the use and abuse of, 452.
Docking, method of performing, 367.
Dogs, danger of encouraging them about the stable, 76.
Dray horse, character of. 40.
Drinks, how to administer, 453; comparison between them and balls, ib.
Dropsy of the chest, 203; of the heart, 157.
Drum of the ear, description and use of the. 58, 59.
Dun horse, account of the, 412.
Duodenum, description of the, 211, diseases of the, ib.
Dura mater, description of the, 55.

EAR, description of the external parts, 58; internal parts, ib.; bones of the, description and use of. 58, 59; labyrinth of the, 58; indicative of the temper, ib.; clipping and singeing, cruelty of, 59; treatment of wounds or bruises of, 98; cruel operations on the, ib.
Eclipse, pedigree of, 20; form of, 20, history and performances of, 20, 21 thickwinded, 20.
Elasticity of the ligament of the neck, 54.
Elbow, the proper form and inclination of, 253; capped, 252; fracture of, 338; punctured, 253.
Emetic tartar, used as a nauseant, diaphoretic, and worm medicine, 441.
Enamel of the teeth, account of the, 122
English Eclipse, 20.
Ensiform cartilage, the, 146.
Entanglement of the intestines, description of, 226.
Enteritis, account of, 220.
Epidemic catarrh, nature and treatment of, 175; malignant, nature and treatment of, 181.
Epiglottis, description of the, 142.
Epilepsy, nature and treatment of, 84.
Epsom salts, used as a purgative, 460
Ergot of rye, the action of, 405.
Ethmoid bone, description of the, 55.
Ewe-neck, unsightliness and inconvenience of, 139.
Exchanges of horses stand on the same ground as sales, 433.
Exercise, directions for, 391; the necessity of regular, 392; want of, producing grease, 290; more injury done by the want of it than by the hardest work, 391.
Expansion shoe, description and use of the 353

Extensor pedis muscle. description of the, 267.
Eye, description of the, 89; cut of the, 62; fracture of the orbit of the, 68; healthy appearance of the, 61; diseases of the, 91; inflammation of, common, 93; ditto, specific, 94; ditto, causes, 95; ditto, medical treatment of, 94, 95; ditto, untractable nature of, 95, 96; ditto, consequences of, 95; ditto, marks of recent, 425; ditto, constitutes unsoundness, *ib.*; ditto, hereditary, 95; method and importance of examining it, 62, 64; indicative of the temper, 59; the pit above, indicative of the age, 48; muscles of the, 66.
Eyebrows, substitute for, 60.
Eyelashes, description of, 60; folly of singeing them, *ib.*
Eyelid, description of, 60.
Eyelids, diseases of the, 91.
Exostosis on the orbit of the eye, 68.

FACE, description of the, 99; cut of the muscles, nerves, and blood-vessels of, 102.
Falling in of the foot, what, 306.
False quarter, nature and treatment of, 320, 321.
Farcy, a disease of the absorbents of the skin, 114, 115; connected with glanders, 114; both general and infectious, 116; symptoms of, 115; treatment of, 116; buds, what, 115; the effect of cantharides in, 117; diniodide of copper, *ib.*
Feeding, high, connected with grease, 291; regular periods of, necessity of attending to, 402; manner of, has much influence on broken wind, 197.
Feet, the general management of, 403; attention to, and stopping at night, recommended, *ib.*
Felt soles, description and use of, 353.
Femur, fracture of the, 339.
Fetlock, description of the, 267.
Fever, idiopathic or pure, 163; symptoms of, *ib.*; symptomatic, 164.
Fibula, description of the, 276.
Firing, the principle on which resorted to, 364; mode of applying, 365; should not penetrate the skin, *ib.*; absurdity and cruelty of blistering after, *ib.*; horse should not be used for some months after, *ib.*
Fistula lacrymalis, 60; in the poll, 136.
Fits, symptoms, causes, and treatment of, 84.
Fleam and lancet, comparison between them, 166.
Flexor of the arm, description of the, 253; metatarsi muscle, description of the. 276; pedis perforatus, the perforated muscle, description of the, 253, 276; pedis perforans, the perforating muscle, description of the, 253, 258 276.
Flying Childers, the *ne plus ultra* of success reached in his days, 29.
Foal, early treatment of, 239; early handling of, important, 240; importance of liberal feeding of, *ib.*; time for weaning, *ib.*
Fomentations, theory and use of, 454.
Food of the horse, observations on, 392; a list of the usual articles of, 393, *et seq.* should be apportioned to the work, 393.
Foot, description of the, 293; diseases of the, 302; canker, 330; corns, 326, contraction, 307; false quarter, 320; founder, acute, 302; chronic laminitis, 305; inflammation, 304; navicular joint disease, 311; overreach, 319, prick, 324; pumiced, 305; quittor, 321; sandcrack, 317; thrush, 329; tread, 319; weakness, 331; wounds, 324.
Forceps, arterial, the use of, 168.
Forehead, the different form of, in the ox and horse, 56.
Fore-legs, description of, 246; diseases of them, 254; proper position of them, 270.
Forge-water occasionally used, 454.
Form, on the improvement of, 25.
Founder, acute, symptoms, causes, and treatment of, 302; chronic, nature and treatment of, 305.
Foxglove, strongly recommended in colds, and all fevers, 451.
Fracture of the skull, treatment of, 68; general observations on fractures, 333; of the skull, 335; orbit of the eye, *ib.*, nasal bones, *ib.*; superior maxillary or upper jaw-bone, *ib.*; inferior ditto, 336; spine, *ib.*; ribs, *ib.*; pelvis, 337; tail, *ib.*; limbs, *ib.*; shoulder, 338; arm *ib.*; elbow, *ib.*; femur, 339; patella, *ib.*; tibia, *ib.*; hock, *ib.*; leg, 340; sessamoid bones, *ib.*; pastern, *ib.*; lower pastern, 341; coffin-bone, 342; navicular bone, *ib.*
Frog, horny, description of the, 298; sensible, description of the, 298, 300; ditto, action and use of the, 298; pressure, question of the, 299; proper paring of, for shoeing, *ib.*; diseases of the, *ib.*
Frontal bones, description of the, 47; sinuses, description of the, 48; ditto, perforated to detect glanders, *ib.*
Furze, considered as an article of food, 401.

GALL, account of the, 213; bladder, the horse has none, *ib.*
Gall-stones, 229.
Gentian, the best tonic for the horse. 455

Gibbing, a bad habit, cause of, and means of lessening, 370.
Gigs, formation of, 133.
Ginger, an excellent aromatic and tonic, 455, 468.
Glanders, nature of, 107, 109; symptoms, 51, 107, 112; slow progress of, 107, 109; appearance of the nose in, 51, 107, 110; detected by injecting the frontal sinuses, 48; how distinguished from catarrh, 109; ditto from strangles, ib.; connected with farcy, 108, 110; treatment of, 113; causes, 111; both generated and contagious, 111, 112 429; oftenest produced by improper stable management, 112; mode of communication, ib.; prevention of, 113; account of its speedy appearance, 111, 112.
Glands, enlarged, it depends on many circumstances whether they constitute unsoundness, 424.
Glass-eye, nature and treatment of, 97.
Glauber's salt, its effect, 466.
Glutæi muscles, description of the, 274.
Goulard's extract, the use of it much overvalued, 460.
Gracilis muscle, description of the, 273.
Grains, occasionally used for horses of slow work, 396.
Grapes on the heels, treatment of, 291.
Grasses, neglect of the farmer as to the proper mixture of, 399.
Gray horses, account of the different shades of, 411, 412.
Grease, nature and treatment of, 288; cause of, 289; farmer's horse not so subject to it as others, 290; generally a mere local complaint, 289.
Grinders, construction of the, 122.
Grinding, of the food, accomplished by the mechanism of the joint of the lower jaw, 120; swallowing without, 377.
Grogginess, account of, 265.
Grooming, as important as exercise to the horse, 399; opens the pores of the skin, and gives a fine coat, 390; directions for, ib.
Grunter, the, description of, 198; is unsound, 423.
Gullet, description of the, 206; foreign bodies in, 208.
Gum-arabic, for what purposes used, 435.
Gutta serena, nature and treatment of, 97.

HABITS, vicious or dangerous, 370.
Hæmaturia, 233.
Hair, account of the, 405; question of cutting it from the heels, 291.
Haunch, description of the, 271; wide, advantage of, 272; injuries of the, ib.; joint, singular strength of it, 271; also of the thigh bones, advantage of the oblique direction of, ib.
Haw, curious mechanism of the, 60 diseases of, 92; absurdity and cruelty of destroying it, 61.
Hay, considered as food, 394; mow-burnt, injurious, 399; old preferable to new, 398.
Head, anatomy of the, 47; the numerous bones composing it the reason of this, 47, 48; section of the, 49; beautiful provision for its support, 53.
Healing ointment, account of the, 468.
Hearing of the horse, the very acute, 58.
Heart, description of the, 155; its action described, 156; inflammation of the, 157; dropsy of the, ib.
Heels, question of cutting the hair from them, 291; low, disadvantage of, 332, proper paring of, for shoeing, 343; washing of the, producing grease, 291.
Hellebore, white, used in inflammation of the lungs and fevers, 455; black, its use, ib.
Hemlock, given in inflammation of the chest, 456.
Hepatic duct, the, 213.
Hernia, the nature and treatment of, 227.
Hide-bound, the nature and treatment of, 383.
High-blower, or roarer, a description of the 193; is unsound, 423.
Hind legs, description of the, 271.
Hip-joint, the great strength of the, 272
Hips, ragged, what, 272.
Hobbles, description of the best, 359.
Hock, capped, 285, 286; description of the, 278; enlargement of the, nature of and how affecting soundness, 279, 425; inflammation of the small bones of, a frequent cause of lameness, 279; the principal seat of lameness behind, ib.; lameness of it, without apparent cause, 285; fracture of, 339.
Hogs' lard, properties of, 437.
Hoof, cut of the, 293; description of the, 294.
Horn of the crust, secreted principally by the coronary ligament, 297; once separated from the sensible part within, will never again unite with it, ib.
Horse, the race horse, 17; Arabian, 25; the Canadian, 29; the Cleveland bay, 38; the Norman, 29; the Morgan, 35; the dray, 39; the trotter, 40; superiority of American over English, 41, 42.
Humerus, description of the, 252.
Hydrocyanic acid, its occasional good service, 436.
Hydrothorax, symptoms and treatment of, 202.

INDEX. 477

Ileum, description of the, 211
Inflammation, nature of, 160; treatment of, 160, 161; hot or cold applications to, guide in the choice of, *ib.*; importance of bleeding in, 160, 361; when proper to physic in, 161; of the bowels, 220; ditto, distinction between it and colic, *ib.*; brain, 74; eye, 93; foot, 302; kidneys, 231; larynx, 171; lungs, 186; stomach, 207; trachea, 172; veins, 141.
Influenza, nature and treatment of, 175.
Infusions, manner of making them, 457.
Insanity, 90.
Intercostal muscles, description of the, 146.
Intestines, description of the, 210.
Introsusception of the intestines, treatment of, 226.
Invertebrated animals, what, 44.
Iodine, usefulness of, in reducing enlarged glands, 458.
Iris, description of the, 64.
Iron, the carbonate of, a mild and useful tonic, 454; sulphate of, a stronger tonic, *ib.*; ditto, recommended for the cure of glanders, *ib.*
Itchiness of the skin should always be regarded with suspicion, 458.

James's powder, 442.
Jaundice, symptoms and treatment of, 229, 230.
Jaw, the lower, admirable mechanism of, 120; upper, description of, 121.
Jejunum, description of the, 211.
Jointed shoe, the description and use of, 353.
Jugular vein, bleeding from the, 167.
Juniper, oil of, use of, 458.

Kicking, a bad and inveterate habit. 373.
Kidneys, description of the, 230; inflammation of, symptoms and treatment of, 231.
Knee, an anatomical description of the, 253; tied in below, 258; broken, treatment of, 254, 421.
Knowledge of the horse, how acquired, 46.

Labyrinth of the ear, description and use of the, 58.
Lachrymal duct, description of the, 60; gland, description and use of the, *ib.*
Lamellæ, or laminæ, horny, account of the, 297; fleshy, account of the, *ib.*; weight of the horse, supported by the, *ib.*
Lameness, shoulder, method of ascertaining, 246; from whatever cause, unsoundness, 426.
Lampas, nature and treatment of, 119; cruelty of burning the bars for, 120.
Laminæ of the foot. See Lamellæ.

Lancet and fleam, comparison between them, 166.
Laryngitis, chronic and acute, 172.
Larynx, description of the, 143; inflammation of the, 171.
Laudanum, the use of in veterinary practice, 461, 462.
Lead, the compounds of, used in veterinary practice, 459; extract of, its power much over-valued, *ib.*; sugar of, use of, *ib.*; white, use of, *ib.*
Leather, soles, description and use of, 353.
Leg, cut of the, 87; description of the, 256; fracture of the, 342.
Legs, fore, the situation of, 246; hind, anatomical description of the, 271; swelled, 287.
Levator humeri muscle, description of the, 250.
Lever, muscular action explained on the principle of it, 248.
Ligament of the neck, description and elasticity of the, 53, 54.
Light, the degree of, in the stable, 389.
Limbs, fracture of the, 337.
Lime, the chloride of, exceedingly useful for bad smelling wounds, &c., 459; the chloride of, valuable in cleansing stables from infection, *ib.*
Liniments, the composition and use of, 459.
Linseed, an infusion of, used in catarrh, 398, 460; meal forms the best poultice, 460, 463.
Lips, anatomy and uses of the, 117 lips the hands of the horse, *ib.*
Litter, the, cannot be too frequently removed, 387; proper substances for 388; contraction not so much produced by it as some imagine, 309.
Liver, the anatomy and use of it, 213; diseases of the, 228.
Locked jaw, symptoms, cause, and treatment of, 79.
Loins, description of the, 150.
Lucern, considered as an article of food, 400.
Lumbricus teres, or long white worm, the, 227.
Lunar caustic, a very excellent application, 442.
Lungs, description of the, 155; symptoms of inflammation of the, 186, causes of, *ib.*; how distinguished from catarrh and distemper, 186, 187; treatment of, 188, 189; importance of early bleeding in, 190; blisters preferable to rowels or setons in, 191.

Madness, the symptoms and treatment of, 76.
Magnesia, the sulphate of, 460.
Mallenders, the situation of, 270; the nature and treatment of, 286.

Mammalia, the, an important class of animals, 45.
Manchester, account of the course at, 42.
Mane, description and use of the, 139.
Mange, description and treatment of, 416; causes of, 416, 417; ointment, recipes for, 417; highly infectious, 418; method of purifying the stable after, *ib.*
Manger-feeding, the advantage of, 393.
Mare, put to the horse too early, 237, 238; deterioration in, 238; her proper form, *ib.*; breeding in-and-in, *ib.*; time of being at heat, 239; time of going with foal, *ib.*; best time for covering, *ib.*; management of, when with foal, *ib.*; management of, after foaling, *ib.*
Mark of the teeth, what, 122.
Mashes, importance of their use, 460; best method of making them, *ib.*
Masseter muscle, description of the. 103.
Maxillary bones, anatomy of the, 118; fractures of, 335, 336.
Medicines, a list of the most useful, 435
Medullary substance of the brain, its nature and function, 50, 56.
Megrims, cause, 69; symptoms, 70; treatment, *ib.*; apt to return, *ib.*
Melt, description of the, 213.
Mercurial ointment, the use of, in veterinary practice, 456.
Mercury, various preparations of, 456.
Mesentery, description of the, 211.
Metacarpals, description of the, 253.
Midriff, description of the, 153.
Moisture, want of, a cause of contraction, 309.
Moon-blindness, the nature of, 94.
Morgan horse, cut of, 35; origin of, 36, 37; character of, 37, 38.
Moulting, the process of, 410; the horse usually languid at the time of, *ib.*; no stimulant or spices should be given, *ib.*; mode of treatment under, *ib.*
Mounting the colt, 243.
Mouth of the horse, description of the bones of, 118; should be always felt lightly in riding, *ib.*; importance of its sensibility, *ib.*
Mowburnt hay injurious, 399.
Muriatic acid, its properties, 436.
Muscles of the back, description of the, 150; breast, ditto, 150; eye, ditto, 67; face, ditto, 102; neck, ditto, 138; ribs, ditto, 146; shoulder-blade, 250; lower bone of the shoulder, *ib.*; the advantageous direction of, more important than their bulk, 247—249.
Muscular action, the principle of, 252.
Mustard, the use of, 461.
Myrrh, the use of, for canker and wounds, 461.

NASALIS labii superioris muscle, description of the, 103.
Nasal bones, fracture of, 335; description of, 49.
—— gleet, 104.
—— polypus, 104.
Navicular bone, description of the, 300; the action and use of it, 301.
Navicular joint, disease, nature and treatment of the, 311; how far connected with contraction, 312; the cure very uncertain, *ib.*; fracture of, 342.
Neck, anatomy and muscles of the, 138, 139; description of the arteries of the, 140; description of the veins of the, *ib.*; bones of the, 138; proper conformation of the, *ib.*; comparison between long and short, 139; loose, what, *ib.*
Nerves, the construction and theory of, 46; spinal, the compound nature of, 57; of the face, 102.
Neurotomy, or nerve operation, object and effect of it, 86; manner of performing it, *ib.*; cases in which it should or should not be performed 87, 88; a vestige of the performance of it, constitutes unsoundness, 427.
Nicking, the method of performing, 368; useless cruelty often resorted to, 369.
Nitre, a valuable cooling medicine, and mild diuretic, 463.
Nitric acid, for what employed. 436.
Nitrous æther, spirit of, a mild stimulant and diuretic, 461.
Norman horse, cut of, 30; imported into United States, *ib.*; character of, 31.
Nose, description of the bones of the, 99, 100; spontaneous bleeding from, *ib.*; the importance of its lining membrane, 101, 169; the nose of the horse slit to increase his wind, 102.
Nosebag, importance of the, 401.
Nostrils, description of the, 99; peculiar inflammation of the membrane of the, 50; the membrane of, important in ascertaining disease, 103, 169; importance of an expanded one, 101, slit by some nations to increase the wind of the horse, 102.
Nutriment, contained in the different articles of food, 392, *et seq.*

OATS, the usual food of the horse, 395; should be old, heavy, dry, and sweet *ib.*; kiln-dried, injurious to the horse *ib.*; proper quantity of, for a horse *ib*
Oatmeal, excellent for gruel, and sometimes used as a poultice, 396.
Occipital bone, description of the, 5
Œsophagus, description of the, 206
Olfactory nerves, the importance of them, 102.
Olive oil, an emollient, 461.
Omentum, description of the, 214

Opacity of the eye, the nature and treatment of, 94.
Operations, description of the most important, 359.
Ophthalmia, 94.
Opium, its great value in veterinary practice, 461; adulterations of it, 462.
Orbicularis muscle of the eye, description of it, 67.
Orbit of the eye. fracture of, 68.
Os femoris, account of, 275.
Ossification of the cartilages, cause and treatment of, 332.
Over-reach, the nature and treatment of, 319, 380; often producing sandcrack or quittor, 380.
Ozena, account of, 105.

PACHYDERMATA, an order of animals, 44.
Pack-wax, or ligamentum colli, description of the, 53, 136.
Palate, description of the, 143.
Palm-oil, the best substance for making up balls, 462.
Palsy, the causes and treatment of, 84.
Pancreas, description of the, 230.
Paps or barbs, 133.
Parietal bones, description of the, 51.
Paring out of the foot for shoeing, directions for, 343; neglect of, a cause of contraction, 309.
Parotid gland, description of the, and its diseases, 103, 133.
Pastern, upper, fracture of, 340; lower, fracture of, 341; description of the, 263, 267; bones of the, *ib.*; cut of the, *ib.*; proper obliquity of the, 264.
Putella or stifle bone, description of the, 275; fracture of, 339.
Pawing, remedy for, 381.
Payment of the smallest sum completes the purchase of a horse, 431.
Peas, sometimes used as food, but should be crushed, 398.
Pectineus muscle, the, 273.
Pectorales muscles, description of the, 251.
Pedigrees of American trotters, 40.
Pelvis, fracture of the, 337.
Pericardium, description of the, 155.
Perspiration, insensible, no medicines will certainly increase it, 410.
Pharynx, anatomy of the, 135.
Phrenitis, 74.
Phthisis pulmonalis, description of, 199.
Physic balls, method of compounding the best, 442; should never be given in inflammation of the lungs, 154.
Physicking, rules for, 224.
Pia mater, description of the, 56.
Pied horse, account of the, 412.
Pigmentum nigrum, account of the, 63.
Piper, description of the, 198.

Pit of the eye, the, indicative of the age, 48
Pitch, its use for charges and plasters, 462.
Pleura, description of the, 154.
Pleurisy, the nature and treatment of, 154, 200.
Pneumonia, the nature and treatment of, 186.
Poll-evil, the cause and treatment of, 136 importance of the free escape of the matter, 137.
Postea spinatus muscle, description of the, 251.
Potash, the compound of, 462.
Potatoes, considered as an article of food, 401.
Poultices, their various compositions, manner of acting, and great use, 463.
Powders, comparison between them and balls, 464.
Pressure on the brain, effect of, 69.
Prick, in the foot, treatment of, 324; injurious method of removing the horn in searching for, 326.
Pulse, the natural standard of the, 158; varieties of the, *ib.*; importance of attention to the, *ib.*; the most convenient place to feel it, *ib.*; the finger on the pulse during the bleeding, 159.
Pumiced feet, description and treatment of, 305; do not admit of cure, 306; constitute unsoundness, 427.
Pupil of the eye, description of the, 64, the mode of discovering blindness in it, *ib.*
Purchase, to complete the, there must be a memorandum, or payment of some sum, however small, 431.
Purging, violent, treatment of, 222, 223.

QUARTERS of the horse, description of the, 272; importance of their muscularity and depth, *ib.*; foot, description of, 293; the inner, crust thinner and weaker at, 295; folly of lowering the crust, *ib.*
Quidding the food, cause of, 381; unsoundness while it lasts, 427.
Quinine, the sulphate of, 443.
Quittor, the nature and treatment of, 321; the treatment often long and difficult, exercising the patience both of the practitioner and owner, 322, 323; is unsoundness, 428.

RABIES, symptoms of, 76.
Race-horse, English, pedigree of, 17; excels the Arabian, 18; form of, 19; examples of, 19, 20, 21.
Racers may beget trotters, 40.
Racks, no openings should be allowed above them, 386.
Radius, description of the, 252.
Ragged-hipped, what, 272; no impediment to action, *ib*

Raking, the operation of, 465.
Rearing, a dangerous and inveterate habit, 375.
Recruit, beat the best Arabian in India, 18.
Recti muscles, of the neck, description of, 138; of the thigh, 273.
Rectum, description of the, 211, 212.
Reins, description of the proper, 118.
esin, its use in veterinary practice, 464.
Respiratory nerves, the, 57.
Restiveness, a bad habit, and never cured, 370.
Retina, description of the, 66.
Retractor muscle of the eye, description of it, 67.
Rheumatism, 85.
Ribbed-home, advantage of being, 148.
Ribs, anatomy of the, 146.
Ring-bone, the nature and treatment of, 268, 269; constitutes unsoundness, 428.
Roach-backed, what, 150.
Roan horses, account of, 412.
Roaring, the nature of, 172, 198; curious history of, 173; constitutes unsoundness, 423; from tight reining, 173; from buckling in crib-biting, *ib.*; treatment of, 174.
Rolling, danger of, and remedy for, 381.
Roman nose in the horse, what, 99.
Round-bone, the, can scarcely be dislocated, 275.
Rowels, manner of inserting, and their operation, 464; comparison between them, blisters, and setons, 366.
Running away, method of restraining, 375.
Rupture, treatment of, 227; of the suspensory ligament, 265.
Rye-grass, considered as an article of food, 400.

SADDLES, the proper construction of, 151; points of, *ib.*
Saddle-backed, what, 150; galls, treatment of, 152.
Saddling of the colt, 243.
Saintfoin used as an article of food, 400.
Sal ammoniac, the medical use of, 441.
Saliva, its nature and use, 132.
Salivary glands, description of the, 132.
Sallenders, nature and treatment of, 286.
Salt, use of in veterinary practice, 465; value of, mingled in the food of animals, 399.
Sampson, 18.
Sandal, Mr. Percivall's, 356.
Sandcrack, the situation of, 270; the nature and treatment of, 317, 318; most dangerous when proceeding from tread, 318; liable to return, unless the brittleness of the hoof is remedied, *ib.*; constitutes unsoundness, 428.
Sartorius muscle, description of the, 273.
Scapula, description of the, 246.
Sclerotica, description of the, 62.
Scouring, general treatment of, 218, 219
Secale cornutum, the effect of, 465.
Sedatives, a list of them, and their mode of action, 465.
Serratus major muscle, description of the, 250.
Sessamoid bones, admirable use of in obviating concussion, 366; fracture of, 264, 340.
Setons, mode of introducing, 366; cases in which they are indicated, *ib.*; comparison between them and rowels and blisters, *ib.*
Shank-bone, the, 256.
Shoe, the concave-seated, cut of, 342 described and recommended, *ib.*; the manner in which the old one should be taken off, 343; the putting on of the shoe, 345; it should be fitted to the foot, and not the foot to the shoe, *ib.*; description of the hinder, 347; the unilateral, or one side nailed shoe, 350; the bar shoe, 352; the tip, *ib.*: the hunting, 351; the jointed, or expansion, 353.
Shoeing not necessarily productive of contraction, 309; preparation of the foot for, 343; the principles of, 344.
Shoulder, anatomical description of the, 246; slanting direction of the, advantageous, 247, 248; when it should be oblique, and when upright, 249; sprain of the, 246; lameness, method of ascertaining, *ib.*; fracture of the, 338.
Shoulder-blade, muscles of the, 246; lower bone of the, description of, 252; muscles of the, 252, 253.
Shying, the probable cause of, 66, 381; treatment of, 382; on coming out of the stable, description of, 383.
Side-line, description of the, 359.
Sight, the acute sense of, in the horse, 59.
Silver, the nitrate of, an excellent caustic, 442.
Singeing, recommendation of, 407.
Sinuses in the foot, necessity of following them as far as they reach, 328 frontal, of the head, 49.
Sitfasts, treatment of, 151.
Skeleton of the horse, description of the, 45.
Skin, anatomical description of the, 405; functions and uses of it, 405, 406; pores of it, 409; when the animal is in health, is soft and elastic, 405
Skull, anatomical description of the, 47 arched form of the roof, 55; **fracture** of the, 68, 335.

Slipping the halter, remedy for, 383.
Smell, the sense and seat of, 101; very acute in the horse, ib.
Snap, 2.
Soap, its use in veterinary practice, 466.
Soda, chloride of, its use in ulcers, 465; sulphate of. ib.
Sole, the horny, description of, 297; descent of, 298; proper form of, ib.; management of, in shoeing, ib.; the sensible, 298; felt or leather, their use. 353.
Sore-throat, symptoms and treatment of, 171.
Soundness, consists in there being no disease or alteration of structure that does or is likely to impair the usefulness of the horse, 420; considered with reference to the principal causes of unsoundness, 421.
Spasmodic colic, nature and treatment of, 215.
Spavin, blood, the nature and treatment of, 165; is unsoundness, 428; bog, cause, nature and treatment of, 164, 165, 281; bone, 283; why not always accompanied by lameness, ib.; is unsoundness, 428.
Spavined horses, the kind of work they are capable of, 284.
Speedy-cut, account of, 257.
Sphenoid bone, description of the, 55.
Spine, description of the, 145, 146; fracture of, 336.
Spleen, description of the, 213, 230.
Splenius muscle, description of the, 138.
Splint, nature and treatment of, 256, 270; when constituting unsoundness, 429; bones, description of the, 256.
Sprain of the back sinews, treatment of, 258, 270; sometimes requires firing, 260; any remaining thickening constitutes unsoundness, 429; sprain of the shoulder, 246.
Stables, dark, an occasional cause of inflammation of the eye, 95; hot and foul, a frequent one of inflammation of the eye, ib.; ditto, lungs, 385; ditto, glanders, 112, 113; should be large, compared with the number of horses, ib.; the management of, too much neglected by the owner of the horse, ib.; the ceiling of, should be plastered, if there is a loft above, ib.; should be so contrived that the urine will run off, 388; the stalls should not have too much declivity, ib.; should be sufficiently light, yet without any glaring color, 388, 389.
Staggers, stomach, symptoms, cause, and treatment of, 70, 71, 401; generally fatal, 71; producing blindness, 73; sometimes epidemic, ib.; mad, symptoms and treatment, 74.

Staling, profuse, cause and treatment of, 233.
Stallion, description of the proper, for breeding, 237.
Starch, useful in superpurgation, 466.
Stargazer, the, 139.
Sternum, or breast-bone, description of the, 147, 251.
Stifle, description of the, 275; accidents and diseases of the, ib.
Stomach, description of the, 206, 207; very small in the horse, 207; inflammation of the, 207, 208; pump recommended in apoplexy, 72.
Stone in the bladder, symptoms and treatment of, 235; kidney, ib.
Stoppings, the best composition of, and their great use, 466.
Strangles, symptoms and treatment of, 133; distinguished from glanders, 109; the importance of blistering early in, 134.
Strangury, produced by blistering, 363; treatment of, 364.
Strawberry horse, account of the, 412
Stringhalt, nature of, 83; is decidedly unsoundness, 83, 429.
Structure of the horse, importance of a knowledge of, 46.
Strychnia, account of, 467.
Stylo-maxillaris muscle, description of the, 103.
Sublingual gland, description of the, 133.
Submaxillary glands, description of the, 133; artery, description of the, 103.
Sub-scapulo hyoideus muscle, description of the, 103.
Sugar of lead, use of, 459.
Sulphate of copper, use of in veterinary practice, 449; iron, 454; magnesia, 460; zinc, 468.
Sulphur, an excellent alterative and ingredient in all applications for mange, 467.
Surfeit, description and treatment of, 415; importance of bleeding in, 416.
Suspensory ligament, beautiful mechanism of the, 265; rupture of the, ib.; suspensory muscle of the eye, description of the, 67.
Swallowing without grinding, 377.
Swelled legs, cause and treatment of, 287; most frequently connected with debility, ib.
Sweetbread, description of the, 213.
Sympathetic nerves, description of the, 58.

Tail, anatomy of the, 145; fracture of the, 337; docking, 367; nicking, 368.
Tar, its use in veterinary practice, 467.
Tares, a nutritive and healthy food, 399.
Tartar, cream of, 463.

INDEX.

Tears, the secretion and nature of the, 60.
Teeth, description of the, as connected with age, 121; at birth, *ib.*; 2 months, *ib.*; 12 months, 122; 18 months, 123; the front sometimes pushed out, that the next pair may sooner appear, and the horse seem to be older than he is, 124; 3 years, *ib.*; 3½ years, 125; 4 years, *ib.*; 4½ years. 126; 5 years, *ib.*; 6 years, 127; 7 years, 128; 8 years, *ib.*; change of .ne, 123; enamel of the, 122; irregular, inconvenience and danger of, 131; mark of the, 122; frauds practised with regard to the, 124, 125; diseases of the, 130.
Temper denoted by the eye, 59; by the ear, 58.
Temperature, sudden change of, injurious in its effect, 385.
Temporal bones, description of the, 51.
Tendons of the leg, 256.
Tetanus, symptoms, causes and treatment of, 79.
Thick wind, nature and treatment of, 194, 198; often found in round-chested horses, 193.
Thigh and haunch bones, description of, 271, 272; form of, 272; should be long and muscular, *ib.*; description of the muscles of the inside of the upper bone of, 272, 273; do. of the outside, *ib.*; mechanical calculation of their power, 273, 274.
Thorough-pin, the nature and treatment of, 277; is not unsoundness, 429.
Thrush, nature and treatment of, 328; the consequences, rather than the cause of contraction, *ib.*; its serious nature and consequences not sufficiently considered, 329; constitutes unsoundness, 430.
Thymus gland, the, 153.
Thyroid cartilage of the windpipe, description of the, 143.
Tibia, account of the, 276, 279; fracture of, 339.
Tied in below the knee, nature and disadvantage of, 258.
Tinctures, account of the best, 467.
Tips, description and use of, 352.
Tobacco, when used, 467.
Toe, bleeding at the, described, 168.
Tongue, anatomy of the, 131; diseases of, 132; bladders along the under part of, *ib.*
Tonics, an account of the best, 467; their use and danger in veterinary practice, 468.
Torsion, the mode of castration by, 245; forceps, description of, *ib.*
Trachea, or windpipe, description of, 144; inflammation of, 172.
Tracheotomy, 143; operation of, 143, 144.

Trapezius muscle, description of the 250.
Trapezium bone, description of the, 253
Tread, nature and treatment of, 319 often producing sandcrack or quittor *ib.*
Tripping, an annoying and inveterate habit, 384.
Trochanter of the thigh, description of the, 272.
Trochlearis muscle, the, 67.
Trotter, American, cut of, 41; pedigrees of, 40, 41; superiority to the English, 41, 42; reasons for, 42, 43.
Turbinated bones, description of the, 101.
Turpentine, the best diuretic, 468; a useful ingredient in many ointments, *ib.*
Tushes, description of the, 125—127.
Twitch, description of the, 360.

ULCERS in the mouth, treatment of, 131.
Ulna, description of the, 252.
Ungulata, a tribe of animals, 44.
Unilateral shoe, 349.
Unsoundness, contraction does not always cause it, 307; being discovered, the animal should be tendered, 431; ditto, but the tender or return not legally necessary, *ib.*; the horse may be returned and action brought for depreciation in value, but this not advisable, 432; medical means may be adopted to cure the horse, they are, however, better declined, lest in an unfortunate issue of the case they should be misrepresented, 431.
Unsteadiness whilst mounting, remedy for, 374.
Urine, albuminous, 234; bloody, 233.

VASTUS muscle, description of the, 273.
Veins, description of the, 164; of the arm, description, &c., 250; of the neck, ditto, 140; of the face, ditto, 102; of the shoulder, ditto, 250; inflammation of the, treatment of, 141.
Vena portarum, the, 213.
Verdigris, an uncertain medicine, when given internally, 449; a mild caustic, *ib.*
Vermin, account of, 419.
Vertebræ, the dorsal and lumbar, 145.
Vertebrated animal, the horse a, 44.
Vices of horses, account of the, 370.
Vicious to clean, a bad habit that should be conquered, 375; to shoe, a bad habit that may also be conquered, 376.
Vinegar, its use in veterinary practice, 436.
Vines, Mr., his use of the Spanish fly in glanders, 445.
Vision, theory of, 63.

Vitreous humor of the eye, account of the, 65.
Vitriol, blue, use of, in veterinary practice, 449.

Wall-eyed horses, what, 64; whether they become blind, ib.
Warbles, treatment of, 152.
Warranty, the form of a, 430; breach of, how established, ib.; no price will imply it, 431; when there is none, the action must be brought on the ground of fraud, ib.
Warts, method of getting rid of, 419.
Washing of the heels, productive of grease, 291.
Washy horses, description and treatment of, 223.
Water, generally given too sparingly, 402; management of on a journey, 403; the difference in effect, between hard and soft, 402; spring, principally injurious on account of its coldness, ib.; stomach of the horse, the, 212.
Water farcy, nature and treatment of, 116.
Wax used in charges and plasters, 468.
Weakness of the foot, what, 331.
Weaving indicating an irritable temper, and no cure for it, 384.
Wheat, considered as food for the horse, 397; inconvenience and danger of it, 398.

Wheezer, description of the, 198; is unsound, 423.
Whistler, description of the, 398; is unsound, 423.
White lead, use of, 459; vitriol, its use in veterinary practice, 469.
Wind, broken, nature and treatment of 196; galls, description and treatment of, 261, 268; ditto, unsoundness when they cause lameness, or are likely to do so, 430; thick, nature and treatment of, 194.
Windpipe, description of the, 143, should be prominent and loose, ib.
Wind-sucking, nature of, and remedy for, 380.
Withers, description of the, 150; high, advantage of, ib.; fistulous, treatment of, 151.
Worms, different kinds, and treatment of, 227.
Wounds in the feet, treatment of, 324.

Yellows, symptoms and treatment of the, 229.

Zinc, its use in medicine, 468.
Zoological classification of the horse 44.
Zygomatic arch, reason of the strong construction of the, 52.
Zygomaticus muscle, description of the 103.

THE END.

www.ingramcontent.com/pod-product-compliance
Lightning Source LLC
Chambersburg PA
CBHW051848300426
44117CB00006B/310